Honor and Profit

ATHENIAN TRADE POLICY AND THE ECONOMY AND SOCIETY OF GREECE, 415–307 B.C.E.

Darel Tai Engen

THE UNIVERSITY OF MICHIGAN PRESS   *Ann Arbor*

Copyright © by the University of Michigan 2010
All rights reserved
Published in the United States of America by
The University of Michigan Press
Manufactured in the United States of America
⊚ Printed on acid-free paper

2013   2012   2011   2010   4   3   2   1

A CIP catalog record for this book is available from the British Library.

Library of Congress Cataloging-in-Publication Data

Engen, Darel Tai, 1963–
    Honor and profit : Athenian trade policy and the economy and
society of Greece, 415–307 B.C.E. / Darel Tai Engen.
        p.   cm.
    Includes bibliographical references and index.
    ISBN 978-0-472-11634-8 (cloth : alk. paper)
    1. Athens (Greece)—Commerce.   2. Decorations of honor—Greece—
History.   3. Greece—Economic conditions—To 146 B.C.   4. Athens
(Greece)—Social life and customs.   5. Athens (Greece)—History.   I. Title.
HF376.A7E54   2010
330.938′506—dc22   2009050350

Acknowledgments

It is a pleasure to acknowledge the help I have received from teachers, institutions, colleagues, friends, and family, without whom I could never have completed this book. I must thank again all those who helped me with this project in its earlier phases, including Ronald Mellor, Steven Lattimore, Robert Gurval, and especially Mortimer Chambers, who read numerous early drafts of the manuscript and to whom I owe a great debt for his expert advice and fatherly encouragement. David Tandy read several more recent versions of the manuscript and provided thorough critiques and suggestions, while the advice of Michael Lovano, Brian Rutishauser, and David Phillips helped me to keep this book from being even longer than it is. I am also thankful to Shaun Hargreaves Heap, David Whitehead, Vincent Gabrielsen, Peter Garnsey, and Stephen Lambert for taking the time to respond to my e-mail inquiries about their research. Whatever deficiencies and errors remain in this book are, of course, nobody's fault but mine.

I would also like to thank my colleagues in the Department of History at California State University San Marcos for their patience and support. In addition, the CSUSM College of Arts and Sciences allowed me reduced teaching loads for two semesters, and the university granted me a sabbatical, which were crucial for my completing the manuscript.

I am grateful as well to the publication committee at the University of Michigan Press for its decision to publish my book, as well as to the anonymous reviewers, whose candid and constructive criticisms have made this book far better than it might have been. I also thank my editors, including Christopher Collins, Chris Hebert, and Ellen Bauerle, for their confidence in me and my project. In particular I am thankful to Ellen for her efforts to allow me to keep the texts of the ancient Greek inscriptions in the book, despite the length and cost that they have added to it.

Many friends also deserve note here for their support, assistance, and encouragement along the way. They include the late Walter Ellis, Ralph Gallucci, Julie Laskaris, Sarolta Takacs, Gregory Dundas, Geoffrey Nathan, Michael Seaman, Stephen Chappell, Jason Moralee, John McDonough, Glorian Sipman, Kathleen Stribley, and especially Jessamyn Lewis.

I owe the greatest debt, though, to my family, beginning with my mother, Mabel, without whose support I could not have completed my education. I wish my father, Robert, were alive to see the completion of this book, since I owe him my love of learning and affinity for writing, and I know he would be very proud of me. My brother, Mark, inspired my interest in history long ago and would have written many books on history himself had circumstances beyond his control not kept him from doing so. My sisters Keri and Dee Dee have also been consistent sources of support, especially the latter, an ancient historian herself and a genius with computers, who always received late-night calls from me for assistance without complaint. My mother-in-law, Lan, has been an incredibly hardworking and loving caretaker for my wife's and my two children, Tai and Kenji, serving as a virtual daycare center while my wife and I have pursued our research projects and fulfilled our teaching duties. My wife's aunt Linh has also helped greatly with child care.

Without a doubt, my wife, Susie, deserves my greatest thanks. More than anyone else, she has encouraged me to complete this book, during which time she has also done the lion's share of child rearing; endured my late-night work sessions, lack of sleep, moodiness, and stress; and exhibited patience worthy of a saint year after year as I worked on this seemingly interminable project. I do not know if I will ever be able to repay her for all she has done for me, but I begin by making the small gesture of dedicating this book to her.

Darel Tai Engen
California State University San Marcos

Contents

Abbreviations

Abbreviations used in this book for journals follow those used in *L'année philologique*. Abbreviations for books and articles are as follows.

Agora 16   Woodhead, A. G., ed., *The Athenian Agora*. Vol. 16, *Inscriptions: The Decrees*. Princeton, NJ: Princeton University Press, 1997. Citations are to numbered inscriptions.

APF   Davies, John K. *Athenian Propertied Families, 600–300 B.C.* Oxford: Oxford University Press, 1971.

CAH²   *The Cambridge Ancient History*. 2nd ed.

Edmonds   Edmonds, John M. 1957–61. *Fragments of Attic Comedy*. Vols. 1–3. Leiden: Brill.

EM   The Epigraphic Museum in Athens.

FGrHist   Jacoby, Felix. *Die Fragmente der griechischen Historiker*. Vols. 1–15. Berlin and Leiden: Weidmann and Brill, 1923–58.

Fornara   Fornara, Charles W. *Archaic Times to the End of the Peloponnesian War*. 2nd ed. Cambridge: Cambridge University Press, 1983.

Harding   Harding, Phillip. *From the End of the Peloponnesian War to the Battle of Ipsus*. Cambridge: Cambridge University Press, 1985.

IG   *Inscriptiones Graecae*.

Lambert 1   Lambert, Stephen D. "Athenian State Laws and Decrees, 352/1–322/2: I. Decrees Honouring Athenians." *ZPE* 150 (2004): 85–120. Part 1 of a series of articles intended as prolegomena to fascicle 2 of *IG* ii³ (forthcoming). Citations are to numbered inscriptions.

Lambert 3   Lambert, Stephen D. "Athenian State Laws and Decrees, 352/1–322/2: III. Decrees Honouring Foreigners." *ZPE* 158 (2006): 115–58; 159 (2007): 101–54. Part 3, A ("Citizenship, Proxeny, and Euergesy") and B ("Other Awards"), in a series of articles by Stephen Lambert intended as prolegomena to fascicle 2 of *IG* ii³ (forthcoming). Citations are to numbered inscriptions.

LSJ⁹   Liddell, Henry G., and Robert Scott. *A Greek-English Lexicon*. 9th ed. Rev. Henry Stuart Jones. Oxford: Clarendon, 1989.

M-L   Meiggs, Russell, and David M. Lewis. *A Selection of Greek Histor-ical Inscriptions to the End of the Fifth Century B.C.* Rev. ed. Ox-ford: Oxford University Press, 1988.

Osborne Osborne, M. J. *Naturalization in Athens.* Vols. 1–3. Brussels: AWLSK, 1981–83.

PA   Kirchner, Johannes. *Prosopographia Attica.* Vols. 1–2 [1901–3]. Chicago: Ares, 1981.

RE   Pauly, August F. von, and Georg Wissowa. *Paulys Real-Ency-clopädie der classischen Altertumswissenschaft.* Vols. 1–83. Stuttgart: J. B. Metzler, 1894–1980.

RE Suppl. Pauly, August F. von, and Georg Wissowa. *Paulys Real-Ency-clopädie der classischen Altertumswissenschaft, Supplement.* Vols. 1–15. Stuttgart: J. B. Metzler, 1903–78.

R-O   Rhodes, Peter J., and Robin Osborne, eds. *Greek Historical In-scriptions, 404–323 BC.* Oxford: Oxford University Press, 2003.

Schäfer iii² Schäfer, Arnold D. *Demosthenes und Seine Zeit.* 1st ed. Vol. 3, pt. 2. Leipzig: Teubner, 1885.

Schwenk Schwenk, Cynthia J. *Athens in the Age of Alexander: The Dated Laws and Decrees of "the Lykourgan Era," 338–322 B.C.* Chicago: Ares, 1985.

SEG   *Supplementum Epigraphicum Graecum.*

SIG³   Dittenberger, Wihelm. *Sylloge inscriptionum Graecarum.* 3rd ed. Vols. 1–4. Leipzig: S. Hirzelium, 1915–24.

Tod   Tod, Marcus N. *Greek Historical Inscriptions from the Sixth Cen-tury B.C. to the Death of Alexander the Great in 323 B.C.* Vols. 1–2, [1933–48]. Reprint, Chicago: Ares, 1985.

V-T   Veligianni-Terzi, Chryssoula. *Wertbegriffe in den attischen Ehren-dekreten der Klassischen Zeit.* Stuttgart: Franz Steiner Verlag, 1997.

Walbank Walbank, Michael B. *Athenian Proxenies of the Fifth Century B.C.* Toronto and Sarasota, FL: S. Stevens, 1978.

PART ONE *Preliminaries*

CHAPTER ONE

Introduction

So after coinage was invented as a consequence of necessary exchange, another form of acquisition arose, trade, which at first was fairly simple but now has become more systematic through experience; for example, people learned from where and how one engages in exchange, one will make the most profit.

—ARISTOTLE

For receiving honors as these, they would hasten here as to friends on account of not only the profit but also the honor.

—XENOPHON

The preceding words of Aristotle and Xenophon illustrate the dynamic and complex nature of the economy and society of Greece in the late Classical period. Writing the *Politics* ca. 336–322, Aristotle believed that changes had been occurring in both the means and the goals of economic activity, whereby the use of coinage and the growing sophistication of exchange were leading to a greater desire and more opportunities for profit (*kerdos*).[1] By *profit*, Aristotle meant the monetary gain from an exchange that accrues to the seller of a good that is the difference between its sale price and all costs associated with bringing it to market, just as we generally define the word today. This is clear from the context of the passage (1256a1–1257a40) in which Aristotle describes "necessary exchange" as the earliest, "natural" form of exchange whose goal was only the acquisition of goods "necessary for life and useful for one's community of city or household" (1256b29–30). In such exchanges, one does not seek monetary gain. One seeks to obtain only goods that one needs but does not already have, in exchange for goods that one already has but does not need. Coinage, in Aristotle's view, was invented to facilitate such necessary exchanges as their scale and distance increased with the growth of house-holds into villages and of villages into *poleis*. But Aristotle contrasts nec-essary exchange with another form of "acquisition" (*chrematistike*) called "trade" (*kapelikon*),[2] which is roughly equivalent to the concept of "capi-talism" in its general sense.[3] Here, goods are not acquired for consump-tion but serve as capital: they are used in subsequent exchanges with the goal of receiving a greater sum of money than one spent to obtain them. It is this form of acquisition, according to Aristotle, that, although "unnat-ural," "is productive of wealth and money," that is, profit (1257b7–8).

It is clear that Xenophon uses the term *profit* (*kerdos* again) in the same "modern" sense as Aristotle. In his *Poroi* (Revenues), written ca. 355/4, Xenophon sets forth his proposals to increase Athenian revenues primar-ily by expanding taxable commerce and the number of foreign traders resident in Athens who could also be taxed.[4] Xenophon argues that Athens has many advantages that attract traders to its port (3.2). In par-ticular, it has excellent silver coinage that traders are happy to accept in exchange for their cargoes because they know it is in demand even out-side Athens, where they can use it in further exchanges and "everywhere obtain more than the principal cost." In other words, traders come to Athens because they know they can make a profit from exchanges there.

Like Aristotle, however, Xenophon contrasts the profit motive with another, more traditional goal of exchange. In this case the alternative goal is not necessary consumption but rather "honor" (*timé*). In 3.4–5 Xenophon urges Athens not to rely solely on the profit incentive to attract traders but to make itself even more attractive by providing traders with honors, such as reserved seats in the theater and public banquets, when the quality of their ships and cargoes entitles them to be considered bene-factors of the state. Considering such honors to be a fitting reward for benefactions to the *polis*, Xenophon must understand "honor" as his con-temporaries typically did in Classical Athens. Honor was the esteem of one's peers, the good reputation that one earns through deeds that further the good of the community.[5] Although theater seats and public banquets have a monetary value, their principal attraction for traders was not fi-nancial. Rather, these honors proclaimed the worthiness of their recipi-ents to be held in high esteem for their benefactions by the citizens of Athens. Xenophon emphasizes the nonprofit nature of such a transaction by noting that the prospect of obtaining honors will attract traders to Athens "as to friends," rather than just cash-carrying customers.

Judging from Aristotle and Xenophon, the Greeks of the fourth cen-tury B.C.E. appear to have employed diverse methods and to have had various goals when they engaged in economic activity. Some of these methods and goals were similar to those that are typical of our own day, such as exchanges involving money for profit, while others, such as exchanges undertaken in the pursuit of honor, are uncommon enough today to be deemed "irrational" in modern economic theory. In addition to this complexity, it is apparent from Aristotle that the prevailing methods and goals of economic activity were also dynamic; that is, they (or perceptions of them at least) changed over time.

It was the failure to acknowledge such complexity and dynamism that confounded attempts by scholars across several disciplines—including economics, sociology, and anthropology, in addition to history and classical studies—to resolve a century-long debate about the nature of the ancient Greek economy. As I will discuss at greater length in chapter 2, this debate began with the so-called Bücher-Meyer controversy between "primitivists" and "modernists" in the late nineteenth and early twentieth centuries; morphed into the opposing camps of "substantivists" and "formalists" thanks to the work of Karl Polanyi in the 1940s and 1950s; reached what might have been a conclusion with the wide acceptance of the primitivist-substantivist "model" proposed by Moses Finley in 1973; but, in the last decade of the twentieth century and first decade of the twenty-first, has now been reinvigorated with a plethora of studies that have called Finley's model into question and offer the hope of the creation of a new model.[6] Although the details of such a model have yet to be established, it will have to acknowledge an economy that was much more complex and dynamic than previously realized.[7]

The chief purpose of this book is to join this recent trend by offering a new perspective on the ancient Greek economy in the late Classical period that illustrates its complexity and dynamism through a focused analysis of a relatively well-documented practice of Athenian trade policy, namely, the granting of honors and privileges to those who had performed trade-related services for the city. To date, no book has focused on Athenian trade policy or any particular aspect of it, despite the fact that evidence for the practice of honoring men for trade-related services has long been known by modern scholars.[8] Such a practice shows that Xenophon and Aristotle were not alone in their understanding of the economy but must have been joined by a great many Athenian citizens, each of whom had the right to participate in formulating and implementing the trade policy of the city's democratic government. In granting honors and privileges for trade-related services, Athens adapted and manipulated traditional institutions to formulate a practice that was flexible enough to acknowledge and exploit the dual desires for honor and profit that existed in the Greek economy, thereby fulfilling its trade policy, which was aimed mainly (though not solely) at obtaining imports of needed goods and revenue from taxes on trade.[9]

Moreover, to the extent that honor was a common goal of economic activity and gift exchange was a common means of exchanging goods, it will be apparent that the economy was influenced by traditional social values and institutions. At the same time, however, it will also be seen that profit seeking through impersonal exchanges was also widespread in spite of the traditional social stigma attached to it. Thus, although it will be possible to conclude that social values influenced the ancient Greek economy greatly, they did not wholly dominate it. Groups and individuals could and did ignore social constraints on economic activity for reasons ranging from necessity to greed. Furthermore, the Athenian practice of granting honors and privileges for trade-related services shows that ancient Greek social values themselves were not static but subject to change over time under the influence of a variety of forces. The Athenian state could and did begin to acknowledge, or at least to represent, as worthy of honor trade for profit as well as trade in the form of gift exchange.

Because the politics, economy, and society of Greece during the fourth century B.C.E. were interconnected in this way, economic trends reflected as well as inspired trends in politics and society that contributed to the transformation of Greece as it made its way from the Classical to the Hellenistic period. The ideal of the closed, homogeneous, and largely self-sufficient *polis* of the Classical age was giving way to that of the more open, heterogeneous, and commercially interconnected city of the Hellenistic era.[10] These changes are commonly attributed to the military and political actions of the Macedonians Philip II and Alexander the Great and their successors, who brought together large areas of the Greek and Near Eastern worlds as never before. Although the impact of these men should not be minimized, focus on them has resulted in a failure to appreciate the significant role that concurrent and even preceding social, political, and economic developments of the late Classical period played in this transformation.

Scholarly Context

The conclusions of this book are not wholly consistent with Moses Finley's still widely accepted model of the ancient Greek economy (Finley

1985; see also chap. 2). The basic premise of Finley's substantivist model is that the economy of ancient Greece was embedded in social relations that were structured in accordance with concerns for status rather than wealth. Such a social structure prohibited the economy from ever becoming like our own market system, in which maximizing profit for its own sake and creating wealth are the acknowledged and esteemed goals of economic activity. Consequently, governments, even the democracies, which were disproportionately influenced by the elite, had little interest in the economy per se and no real economic or trade policies to speak of. The state's only interests in the economy were consumptive and political, namely, to obtain revenue through taxes and to acquire necessary goods through trade.

True, the ancient Greek economy was not just like our own, but neither was it completely different. It may seem as though the economy is a distinct sphere of activity in the modern Western world, "disembedded" from social and political relations, but social values and politics have always influenced economics, past and present, here and there (see, most recently, Morley 2007: xiii, 9). The question is how much, in what way, and to what effect. Similarly, since in reality the "economic policies" of modern Western states ultimately serve political goals, one should not conclude that ancient Greek states had no economic policies simply because they had political ends. Again, the question is how much, in what way, and to what effect. A policy that fulfills political goals through economic means may be called an "economic policy" to distinguish it from policies that employ other means. Similarly, a policy that fulfills political goals by means of trade may be called a "trade policy." Still, the goals of Athenian trade policy appear not to have been primarily concerned with economic growth, and profit was neither the exclusive nor the normally esteemed goal of the economic activity of individuals.[11] Honor, which was a key component of ancient Greek society's concern for status, was also an important goal of economic activity, and the trade policy of Athens took this into account even when, as we shall see, it was compelled to promote more purely profit-seeking behavior. Thus, the assumption of Classical economic theory that it is human nature to maximize profit or that the trade policies of states must seek growth does not hold in ancient Greece any more than does Finley's model of an economy predominantly and permanently constrained by social concerns for status and by minimal state interests in trade.

By fully embracing both honor and profit as goals of economic activity and not seeking to minimize either (as has often been done), this book will not so much take sides as occupy a "middle ground" in the long-running debate about the nature of the ancient Greek economy, a major theme of which has been whether the economy was a particular, socially constructed, historical phenomenon or simply another example of an economy governed by timeless and universal laws of human nature.[12] It will support the basic assumption of Finley's model that the prevailing organization of an economy is socially constructed, while at the same time acknowledging the validity of that model's critics who argue that it ignores (1) significant and increasingly numerous exceptions apparent in the empirical evidence, which indicate both extensive profit seeking for its own sake among individuals and changes in social values concerning the economy over time; and (2) the difficulty of interpreting evidence that may be a culturally specific representation rather than an objective testimonial.

Although such a middle ground may seem paradoxical and perhaps even intellectually cowardly, the soundness of this approach will become apparent throughout the course of this book. There are good reasons why the debate about the ancient Greek economy has lasted so long. The various sides in the debate have all been "right" to some extent, depending on the perspective from which one views the subject. One could choose to see the peculiarities of the ancient Greek economy as merely an obscuring veil beneath which lay the "real" economy of Greece, reducing the means and ends of economic activity in Greece to the timeless and universal laws of human nature assumed by Classical economic theory. Just as easily, however, one could choose to see those same peculiarities as the features that truly define the ancient Greek economy and distinguish it from the economies of other civilizations. Both perspectives are valid and useful for our understanding of history and of human behavior in general—one may obtain truth and understanding through an examination of either the forest or the trees.[13]

I view the subject as a historian. Although my undergraduate education was in economics, my graduate training in history confirmed my skepticism with regard to neat theoretical systems in which the complexities of human behavior are reduced to a universal set of simple assumptions and plotted quantitatively on a graph. Thus, I am more sympathetic to the sociologist's efforts to understand human behavior within the context of particular societies. Unlike the sociologist, however, I am, as a historian, less concerned with creating a model that will synchronically describe the general characteristics of a society and more interested not only in accounting for the details of a given society (which may deviate from the general model) but also in explaining either the continuity or change that occurs in a society's institutions over time. It is possible and also desirable to consider both the forest and the trees. There is no objective basis for privileging either the evidence for economic activity that appears to be common among people of all civilizations or the evidence for culturally specific economic activities. The choice to emphasize one or the other is subjective and depends on the perspective and goals of the observer.

In order to achieve a historical understanding of the ancient Greek economy, I will employ a balanced approach that gives equal weight to theory and empirical evidence. Yet another reason for the intractability of the debate about the ancient Greek economy is that those who have stressed the social embeddedness of the economy have emphasized theory and model building over empirical evidence, whereas their counterparts who have argued for an economy based on the supposedly natural human desire for material gain have tended to focus on empirical evidence without adequately explaining the theoretical assumptions of their analysis. Such is the general impression one gets when comparing Finley's *The Ancient Economy* to Cohen's *The Economy and Society of Athens: A Banking Perspective*. Most recently, Takeshi Amemiya, a Stanford economist who specializes in econometrics, has attempted to construct a "model" of the ancient Greek (Athenian, actually) economy with "minimal behavioral and institutional assumptions," substituting for them "a set of simple accounting identities alone" (Amemiya 2007: xii). The result of his attempt is disappointing, however, and amounts to little more than a balance sheet of income and expenses based on scattered quantitative data that in fact require countless assumptions and simplifications for analysis. Clearly, neither extreme is satisfactory, and it should come as no surprise that by balancing these two perspectives, this book will arrive at a conclusion that occupies a more inclusive, middle ground.

Organization and Scope

Part 1 of this book lays out the modern economic theory and the ancient Greek historical context that are the bases for the analysis of the empirical evidence in part 2. I begin, in chapter 2, with a survey of Finley's model and its progenitors. For all its strengths, Finley's model does not account fully for the complexity and dynamism of the ancient Greek economy, a shortcoming due in part to baggage it retained from its predecessors in the long-running debate about the ancient Greek economy. Recent work in the field of "economic sociology" and the concept of "expressive rationality," on the other hand, provides a theoretical basis that acknowledges the powerful influence of social norms on economic structures while also allowing for the expression of preferences and actions of individuals, networks, and small groups within a given society. Thus, I take a primarily "substantivist" approach to the ancient Greek economy, which holds that economic systems are not the product of a fixed human nature but are, in fact, constructed according to a given society's values and customs. At the same time, however, I also acknowledge that groups and individuals can and often do disregard social constraints, which, in any event, are not static but subject to change over time.

Given that social values are a benchmark against which we can evaluate economic preferences and actions and that political events necessarily shape state policy, chapter 3 contains an overview of the social and political context within which the Athenian practice of granting honors and privileges for trade-related services took place. The overview begins with a description of the traditional values and institutions of the elite that privileged honor over self-esteem, status over wealth, landownership over commerce, friendship over profit, and the individual over the community. Drawing on the work of Josiah Ober (1989), I then trace the democratization of those values and institutions with the triumph of the masses over the elite in Classical Athens. Although elite values and institutions were retained in form, they were altered in substance to serve the needs of the community as a whole, a process that allowed commerce and profit seeking a measure of honor and a place in state policy, which they had been previously denied. Politics also influenced the policies with which Athens could secure its interests in trade. The two main policy alternatives were war (imperialism) and peace, the former of which could obtain revenue and grain from abroad through coercion, the latter through voluntary commerce. The desirability and effectiveness of either course depended largely on Athens' military strength vis-à-vis its rivals. It is no mere coincidence that the Athenian practice of granting honors and privileges for trade-related services underwent its most dynamic periods of development after Athenian defeats in the Peloponnesian War (431–401), the Social War (357–355), and the Battle of Chaironeia (338). The consequent crises for Athenian revenues and imports forced Athens to turn increasingly toward peaceful means of obtaining them. Moreover, the interplay of trade and politics appears to have resonated in the Hellenistic period, during which Athenian trade policy continued to adapt to Athens' shifting internal and external political fortunes.

These trends are consistent with the empirical evidence for Athenian trade policy provided by the honorary decrees for trade-related services, a close analysis of which comprises part 2 of this book (the evidence itself is collected in the three appendixes). Chapters 4 and 5 identify and explain the significance of what and who were honored by Athens. The former chapter examines the types of trade-related services and goods that merited grants of honors and privileges from Athens, thus revealing the state's interests in trade, which will be seen largely to support Finley's model. Athens' main goal was to secure the import of vital goods, which it sought to accomplish by entering into a gift exchange with importers that bound them together in ritualized friendships (*xenia*). But although such relationships served to embed the exchanges in traditional social and political relations, some of the exchanges were in fact impersonal market ones, thus indicating further complexity in the ancient Greek economy than is apparent from Finley's model. Chapter 5 presents additional questions for Finley's model, this time concerning those who were responsible for trade. It identifies a diverse range of ethnicities and legal and socioeconomic statuses among those who received Athenian honors and privileges for their trade-related services, which runs counter to the notion that trade was left solely to poor noncitizen professionals of low status. The diverse group of men honored by Athens for trade-related services had equally diverse interests for engaging in trade, each of which Athens had to address in its attempt to encourage imports.

The types of honors and privileges granted by Athens for trade-related services are the subjects of chapters 6–8. Chapter 6 focuses on the laudatory language used in the decrees to characterize the honorands and their services, while chapters 7 and 8 respectively analyze the honors and privileges granted to them. Athenian honorary decrees for services relating to trade characterized their recipients with loaded, well-known terms of honor, describing them as "useful" (*chresimoi*) and as "good men" (*andres agathoi*) who have "goodwill" (*eunoia*), "excellence" (*arete*), and a "love of honor" (*philotimia*) concerning the citizens of Athens. The honors granted to such men included official commendations, gold crowns, bronze statues, stelai inscribed with their honorary decrees and set up for public viewing, seats in the theater, banquets at public expense in the Prytaneion, and the titles and functions of state friends (*proxenoi*) and benefactors (*euergetai*). The honorands also received concrete privileges, such as protection from seizure (*asylia*), exemption from obligations (*ateleia*), the right to own land in Attika (*enktesis*) and to pay emergency taxes (*eisphorai*) and serve in the military on par with citizens (these were indeed privileges), and even citizenship itself.

Such praise, honors, and privileges had both honorific and practical value, since they signified the People's debt of gratitude (*charis*), which had to be repaid not only through its esteem and the elevated status that came with it but also through more tangible benefits, including the monetary value of some honors, the use value of most of the privileges, and, perhaps most important of all, the implicit promise of the People to provide aid (*boetheia*) if and when the honorands should ever ask for it. The exchange of such items in return for trade-related services is consistent with a model that posits both honor and profit as coexisting goals of economic activity in ancient Greece. Moreover, by bestowing praise, honors, and privileges normally associated with elite citizens who performed traditionally esteemed civic, political, and military services on foreigners who had performed trade-related services, the Athenian state contributed to the transformation of traditional Greek values and institutions as it elevated the status of foreigners and those who engaged in nonlanded economic activity ever higher, all the way up to the level of even the noblest of citizens.[14]

Final conclusions appear in chapter 9 and are followed by three appendixes that present the empirical evidence for the Athenian practice of granting honors and privileges for trade-related services. Appendix 1 is a master chart that sets out in summary form essential information from the thirty-four known occasions on which Athens granted honors and privileges for trade-related services between 415 and 307 B.C.E. These occasions, to which I have assigned catalog numbers ranging from 1 to 34 in chronological order, are attested primarily by twenty-five extant inscriptions of honorary decrees passed in the Council and Assembly by "the People" of Athens, the adult male citizen population who had the right to vote in Athenian democratic government. The testimonia for the remaining nine occasions consist of references in the inscriptions and literary sources to other such official grants. Appendix 2 contains the texts of the extant inscriptions and literary testimonia both in their original ancient Greek and translated into English by me. Since the surviving inscriptions are often fragmentary and sometimes obscure in meaning, appendix 3 offers a commentary that explains my rationale for (1) accepting or rejecting proposed readings and restorations of various editions of the inscriptions and (2) assigning the evidence from the texts to categories that form the basis of my analysis in part 2 of this book.

All the inscriptions have been published previously but are currently scattered in numerous editions among various corpora, books, and articles, thus hindering them from being considered together as a whole, a perspective that is essential for understanding their significance for Athenian trade policy and the economy and society of ancient Greece. They will appear together in new editions in the forthcoming publication of *IG* ii–iii³, the third edition of volumes 2 and 3 of *Inscriptiones Graecae*, but even when this publication becomes available, they will still be interspersed among hundreds of other inscriptions and not conveniently at hand for verification of the analysis presented in this book. I have chosen, however, not to set forth new editions of the inscriptions here (despite having examined the stones of many of them myself), since such a task would greatly lengthen this book and detract from its chief goal, which is to illuminate Athenian trade policy and the economy and society of ancient Greece. Nevertheless, the editions presented in this book are the product of what I have determined to be the most accurate texts and reasonable restorations, based on the arguments of their various editors, including Stephen Lambert, who was kind enough to provide me with a preview of the new corpus (of which he is an editor) that appears in a series of recent articles in *Zeitschrift für Papyrologie und Epigraphik*. Hence, even though the texts presented in this book take into account the most current scholarship in the field of epigraphy, they will not necessarily duplicate those that will eventually appear in *IG* ii–iii³.

I have limited the evidence for this study geographically to Athens both because of the quantity of available evidence and because of the importance of trade for the city. As is well known, much of our evidence about Greek history in the Classical period concerns Athens, and such is also the case with regard to grants of honors and privileges for trade-related services. Besides Athens' predilection for inscribing government documents, the abundance of evidence surviving from Athens can also be attributed to the city's extensive use of such a practice. Athens was a center of commerce in the eastern Mediterranean, and its need for public revenue and imported goods compelled it to formulate practices that would encourage commerce, one of which was to grant honors and privileges for trade-related services. Athens was not alone in this practice among ancient Greek *poleis*, but it appears to have pioneered it and to have employed it more extensively than any other city. Thus, Athens was certainly exceptional, but its great economic influence in the eastern Mediterranean justifies it as a focal point for investigation into the ancient Greek economy as a whole.

The quantity of the evidence, as well as the nature of Athenian government from 415 to 307 B.C.E. and certain other practical considerations, has also influenced the chronological scope of this book. The evidence for the Athenian practice of granting honors and privileges for trade-related services first appears during the time of the Sicilian Expedition and continues through the fourth century with uneven frequency. I will argue that the frequency of grants coincided with Athens' trading needs. When the Athenian navy was not powerful enough to coerce tribute or goods from other cities or during times of great need, such as a shortage of grain, the state had to turn to other, less violent and more creative methods of acquiring goods and revenue from abroad. Granting honors and privileges for services relating to trade was one such method.

Moreover, the fact that Athens was a democracy for all but about ten years of this period means that these official honorary decrees reflect the attitudes of a large cross section of the Athenian citizenry toward trade, as opposed to other forms of documentary evidence that reveal the thoughts of only one person or a small elite group. Although democratic government in Athens was severely restricted after 321, the Assembly continued to grant honors and privileges for services relating to trade down to at least 317. During the rule of Demetrios of Phaleron (317–307), however, evidence exists for only a handful of decrees of any kind passed by the Assembly. Still, this study will continue down to 307, at which time the capture of Athens by Demetrios Poliorketes signals another major turning point in Athenian history, in order to include the grant of honors and privileges in around 309 to Eumelos, king of the Bosporos, for his services relating to trade. Eumelos' honors are part of a continuous tradition of Athenian grants to rulers of the Bosporos, which should be traced at least through the end of the fourth century.[15]

Practical considerations dissuade me from continuing my study in depth beyond 307. One such consideration is that to do so would double the size of this book. Another is that Graham Oliver has already examined the Athenian state's policy on grain supply in the early Hellenistic period in his Oxford PhD dissertation, now revised and available as a book published by Oxford University Press in 2007 (see n. 8). Although his focus is not specifically on Athenian trade policy but rather on the domestic grain supply and the degree to which political and military disruptions caused Athens to seek external sources through trade, he does examine Athenian grants of honors and privileges for trade-related services after 307 (considering this date, as I do, to be a seminal one), and I see no need for me to duplicate his treatment here. Instead, my book will address developments in the Athenian practice of granting honors and privileges for trade-related services after 307 only briefly, insofar as they appear either to continue or to break from the trends of the fourth century.

Methods, Approaches, and Evidence

The theoretical approach, choice of evidence, and organization of this book are necessitated by its subject matter. Classical or "formalist" economic analysis is not possible without sufficient evidence for quantification, a situation that prevails concerning most aspects of the ancient Greek economy. The many works that have attempted to estimate the human population and the annual production of grain in Athens as a means of determining the city's import needs have differed so much in their assumptions, methods, and conclusions that their usefulness in the study of Athenian trade policy is limited.[16] Although archaeological evidence concerning trade is extensive and can bear limited quantitative analysis in some sectors, it cannot by itself answer many of the questions posed in this book. Archaeological evidence can tell us what was traded, when it was traded, and where it was traded, but it is virtually silent concerning the organizational structure of trade, the goals and institutions of state trade policies, and the statuses, interests, and methods of those responsible for trade.[17] Besides, any calculation or archaeological data that might imply a limited need for an Athenian trade policy must still account for the numerous Athenian public institutions that were concerned with the grain trade and for the countless number of references to it in both the literary and epigraphic sources.[18]

A more fruitful approach to answering the questions posed in this book about the ancient Greek economy, therefore, is through institutions,[19] and this requires an analysis of documentary evidence informed by an interpretive framework whose assumptions are consistent with the prevailing values of the society in question. Unlike the archaeological evidence, the literary and epigraphic evidence is not "mute" and can provide insights into the thoughts, goals, and motivations of the historical actors responsible for creating and maintaining such institutions.

Unfortunately, although the literary evidence for Athenian overseas trade has been examined extensively, it does not present a balanced picture of Athenian trade and, by itself, can be interpreted in a variety of ways. Since almost all literature surviving from Classical Athens was written by the elite, it does not necessarily reflect the attitudes of the majority of the Athenian citizenry or even the "prevailing ideology," despite Finley's argument that the function of ideology is to cut across class lines so that the masses embrace the values of the elite.[20] In addition, although the literary evidence has been used by several studies to identify those who were responsible for trade as primarily poor foreigners who relied on borrowed capital to finance their ventures, other studies have examined the same evidence to conclude that many traders possessed sufficient capital to finance their ventures and that some of them were citizens.[21] Finally, since much of the literary evidence concerning trade is in the form of forensic speeches, it tells us about only one form of trade: that involving professional traders and maritime loans, which could lead to disputes that required resolution through trials.

Inscriptions of decrees granting honors and privileges to those who had performed trade-related services, however, provide a broader range of information about Athenian trade policy and the ancient Greek economy. As noted above, they speak for the majority of the Athenian citizenry and not just one specific group or individual. They also show that the Athenian state involved itself in forms of trade that did not require maritime loans or even the instigation of those who could be called "professional traders."

Nevertheless, the broad significance of this epigraphic evidence for our understanding of the ancient Greek economy has not been fully appreciated. Some scholarship has touched on this practice primarily in terms of its impact on the public finances of Athens.[22] Other studies have focused on it chiefly as a means of determining Athens' need for grain.[23] Others have used it for the study of epigraphic formulae or to investigate various types of honors and privileges.[24] Still others have used it for the narrow purpose of supporting the "primitivist" view of the ancient Greek economy. For example, concerning Athenian grants of honors and privileges for trade-related services, Hasebroek (1933: 114–17) concludes only that they did not constitute a "commercial treaty" between Athens and its benefactors and prove that Athens was only interested in obtaining imports, not in aiding foreign traders. Finley refers to the practice only twice in his many works on the ancient economy (1985: 162, 164) and does little more than to echo Hasebroek's conclusions. Only recently have the works of Burke and Morris begun to point to the significance of this practice for our understanding of the ancient Greek economy (see pp. 33–34).

It is true, though, that these honorary decrees, like the literary evidence, also present a somewhat one-sided view of trade, since they inform us only about those people and those trade-related services that merited honors from Athens. But as we shall see, there is an astonishing diversity among the honorands and their services (see chaps. 4–5), so much so, in fact, that we can be confident that they reflect more than just, as Davies puts it in his critique of the literary sources emphasized by cultural historians, "a tiny and untypical portion of the [economic] landscape" (Davies 2001a: 46). Moreover, since the chief subject of this book is Athenian state policy concerning trade, it is necessary to examine state documents. After all, those aspects of trade that appear in these decrees must have been concerns for Athenian trade policy. Whether they represent the entirety of Athenian trade is not all that relevant for the purposes of this study.

Cultural historians would also question the use of Athenian honorary decrees as evidence for Athenian trade policy, arguing that they are culturally specific "representations" that were not intended to provide objective information about them.[25] Even more problematic, they would continue, these decrees are carefully worded, official statements, loaded with what we would today call "government spin" in their highly subjective, agenda-driven descriptions of the honorands and their services for Athens. But democratically approved government spin concerning trade is among the chief aspects of Athenian trade policy that we wish to understand. In addition, so long as one analyzes the decrees with careful consideration of their authors, genre, and audience, such documents can also provide useful evidence about the realities of both Athenian trade policy and the economy and society of Greece as a whole in the late Classical period.

Before concluding this survey of the methods and parameters of this book, I should also say a few words about quantitative analysis. Since we cannot be absolutely certain that the surviving Athenian honorary decrees for trade-related services (thirty-four known grants between 415 and 307 B.C.E.) constitute a representative sample of all such decrees that once existed (though I argue that they do; see pp. 51, 77, and 97), quantitative analysis is useful only when it is directed at answering broad questions for which precision is unnecessary and when it is supported by other evidence. For example, in the surviving evidence, almost half (about 44 percent) of the occasions on which Athens granted honors and privileges for trade-related services concern men who were not professional traders of modest means but rather either wealthy professional traders or nonprofessional foreign potentates who either gave Athens gifts of imported goods or sold them at a price reduced from the going rate.[26] It is true that this number is unlikely to be a precise reflection of the actual proportion of such men involved in Athenian trade. It does raise the suspicion, however, that wealthy professionals and nonprofessionals who initiated trade without the goal of monetary profit played an important role in Athenian trade and trade policy. As such, they constitute more than just exceptions to Finley's model of the ancient Greek economy, in which trade is conducted solely by poor professionals who seek profit.

This suspicion is strengthened by other evidence, including the famous Kyrene distribution of grain to Athens that occurred at some point between ca. 333 and 324, which amounted to 100,000 *medimnoi* and was surely a gift from a potentate (see app. 3, no. 22). Estimates of Athens' total annual import of grain range from 800,000 to 240,363 *medimnoi*, based on a statement in Demosthenes 20.33 and the calculations of Garnsey (1988: 89–106), respectively (see pp. 82–83). Therefore, the amount of grain from the Kyrene gift alone constitutes anywhere from 12.5 to 41.6 percent of Athens' total annual grain imports. Even less-outstanding gifts, such as the one from Leukon, king of the Bosporos, in 357, amount to anywhere from 3.2 to 10.7 percent of total annual Athenian grain imports (Dem. 20.33; see also pp. 82–83). Such calculations, though rough, support the suspicion that arises from the number of foreign potentates and wealthy professional traders honored by Athens for their trade-related services, namely, that these men played a significant role in Athenian trade and trade policy. Thus, it seems reasonable to make broad inferences from the quantitative data concerning Athenian grants of honors and privileges for trade-related services so long as there is other independent evidence to support them.

The evidence for Athenian grants of honors and privileges for services relating to trade exists and should not be ignored simply because it has not survived in great abundance. Historians must do what they can with the evidence they have. As Finley himself stated in regard to the question of the interdependency of markets in trading networks, it "will never be resolved statistically," and "the only alternative is to analyse the factors involved in the trade and to draw whatever inferences seem legitimate" (Finley 1985: 178). Moreover, as more evidence is discovered, our picture of ancient Greece must constantly be revised. This book is not intended to provide the definitive statement about Athenian trade policy and the ancient Greek economy. It is intended to offer another perspective, to raise questions, to attempt answers, and to stimulate further debate. For these purposes, the evidence is sufficient.

CHAPTER TWO

Approaches to the Ancient Greek Economy

The most influential scholar of the ancient Greek economy is Moses Finley. With the publication of the first edition of *The Ancient Economy* in 1973, Finley created a model that is said to have constituted a "paradigm shift" in our understanding of the subject. By 1983 this model had become so widely accepted that Keith Hopkins could call it the "new orthodoxy." Even as recently as 1999, Ian Morris stated that "a quarter of a century after it was published, *The Ancient Economy* is still squarely at the center of the debate" and that "any informed discussion of these phenomena has to start with Finley's model."[1] My purpose in this chapter, therefore, is to lay down the theoretical basis of this book, acknowledging my debt to Finley's model while also highlighting my departures from it, thereby situating my analysis within the larger scholarly trends of the field, which appear to be on the verge of creating a new model of the ancient Greek economy.

Economics or Sociology?

Finley formulated his model within the context of a long-running debate that began eighty years earlier about the nature of the ancient Greek economy.[2] Although Finley's model constituted a "paradigm shift" in this debate, its weaknesses are largely the result of the oversimplification and polarization that characterized the debate itself. Initially the debate revolved around the question of whether the ancient Greek economy was "primitive" or "modern" in accordance with a notion that economies follow a universal path of development from primitive ones based on self-sufficient households to more complex ones that culminate in the capitalistic market economy that predominates in the modern world. Thus, the "primitivists," beginning with Bücher in 1893, argued that the ancient Greek economy was in an early stage of this development and like that of a tribal society, small in scale and centered on households that produced for themselves, allowing only limited specialization and personal exchanges between them. By contrast, the "modernists," led by Meyer in 1924 and Rostovtzeff in 1941, held that the ancient Greek economy was, by the Classical period, large in scale and qualitatively similar in organization to a market economy characterized by specialization and impersonal exchanges at prices determined by the aggregate supply and demand for goods among interconnected markets. Most scholars now agree that the primitivist-modernist debate was oversimplified and normative in its perspective. Both sides tried to characterize the ancient Greek economy as a whole, without consideration for variation among, for example, specific geographic regions or economic sectors, such as agriculture, labor, trade, and manufacturing. Moreover, the debate revolved around the degree to which the ancient Greek economy resembled our modern market economy, which was assumed to be the norm. Such flaws steered the primitivist-modernist debate toward a conceptual dead end, unable to yield a satisfactory model to explain the ancient Greek economy.

The sociologist Max Weber provided a more enlightening avenue to approach the ancient Greek economy by examining it within the context of its contemporary social values and institutions.[3] Although Weber acknowledged that a profit-seeking market mentality has existed to some degree among individuals throughout history, including in ancient Greece, he argued that it could not be the characteristic organizing feature of the ancient Greek economy, because it was dominated by concerns for status rather than class (Weber [1921] 1978: 302–7). Such status concerns were determined not necessarily through wealth, as class is, but rather by other marks of honor, such as birth, citizenship, education, and lifestyle, thereby stifling the development of a free market (ibid., 932, 937). These values made the ancient Greek a *homo politicus*, concerned first and foremost with the politics of his community, and not a *homo economicus* who devoted his life to accumulating wealth (ibid., 1354, 1359). Thus, the key to understanding the ancient Greek economy was not its quantity but rather its quality, which was the product of a society that was very different from our own (ibid., 928, 937).

Until Finley, however, the only ancient historian to apply Weber's approach was Johannes Hasebroek. Hasebroek's *Staat und Handel im alten Griechenland,* which first appeared in 1928 and was translated into English as *Trade and Politics in Ancient Greece* in 1933, argued that since trade and other nonagricultural (*banausic*) economic pursuits were not esteemed in ancient Greek *poleis,* they were left largely to poor foreigners (Hasebroek 1933: 8–10). On the other hand, citizens—particularly members of the elite, whose wealth came primarily from the land—had little interest or involvement in trade in their private lives (ibid., 9–10, 100–101). Since it was this latter group who had the most influence on government policy, ancient Greek states in turn also had little official interest or involvement in trade (ibid., 22). Their only interest in trade was political and consumptive, namely, to ensure the import of necessary goods for the citizenry and to obtain revenue from taxes on trade, neither of which served the productive interests of traders (ibid., 103). Hasebroek even went so far as to assert that the state "had *no reason* to promote the economic interests of producers or merchants" (ibid., 102; my emphasis). Thus, the trade policy of ancient Greek *poleis* was in no way like those of most modern states, which seek growth for both the private enterprises of their citizens and the economy of the state as a whole.

Though brilliant in many respects, Hasebroek's work did little to advance the debate among his contemporaries. The chief reason for this is that Hasebroek was conceptually too tightly bound to the framework of the primitivist-modernist debate. Although he was able to show that the ancient Greek *polis* had a consumptive interest in trade rather than a productive one, he chose not to explore the complexities of such an interest but concluded only that such an interest differed from those of modern states. In doing so, Hasebroek unwittingly fell into the same trap as the modernists before him. He could conceive of "trade" only in its market form: "a clearly defined and distinct form of economic activity, carried on by a class of whole-time professional traders."[4] Essentially, this definition of "trade" was a "formalist" one, involving impersonal exchanges of goods over long distances, at prices determined by the market forces of supply and demand, with a little haggling thrown in (see below). Overlooking other forms of trade and implying, therefore, that the trade policies of modern states are the only true measure of "trade policies" per se, Hasebroek left his readers with the impression that ancient Greek states had no trade policies at all (see Hasebroek 1933: 43 and the reaction in Gomme 1937b: 43).

Real progress in the debate had to wait until the work of Karl Polanyi. Like Weber, Polanyi saw the economy as a social construct. This notion is not obvious, because the economy we are most familiar with in the modern Western world, a market economy, *seems* to be governed by universal laws of individual human behavior that are totally divorced from social constraints. But markets are only one of several mechanisms by which an economy may be organized. With regard to trade, Polanyi identified three distinct types of organization: market trade, administered trade, and gift trade.[5] Gift trade links the parties in an exchange by relationships of reciprocity, such as those between guest-friends (*xenoi*) or allied states. Administered trade is controlled by governments so that exchanges take place through channels administered by treaties in which equivalencies and quantities are fixed by formal agreement. Market trade is that which takes place according to the impersonal laws (e.g., supply and demand) of price-making markets. Given that market trade is impersonal, profit is its goal. Administered and gift trade, on the other hand, may have goals other than profit, such as the welfare of the state, the bond of a relationship, or the status and honor of an individual.

Seeing the economy as a social construct, Polanyi held that Classical economic theory, which he called "formalist" economics, with its quantitative analysis of supply and demand, cost minimization, and profit maximization, applies only to a market economy. A broader, qualitative form of analysis, which Polanyi dubbed "substantivist," must be used in order to understand nonmarket economies. It follows that the substantivist definition of trade is inclusive ("a relatively peaceful method of acquiring goods which are not available on the spot"), whereas the formalist definition of trade specifically applies to a market economy alone (a "movement of goods on their way through the market") (Polanyi 1957b: 257–58). Substantivism allows us to recognize as "trade" not only exchanges carried out according to market principles but also exchanges carried out according to other principles, such as reciprocity, which is the essence of gift trade.

The substantivist view of economics makes the limitations of terms such as *primitive* and *modern* all too apparent. Polanyi suggested as an alternative that we examine economies and forms of trade in terms of the degree to which they are "embedded" in or "disembedded" from other social and political relations (Polanyi 1957a: 68). An economy is embedded when it is governed by mechanisms that are intertwined with other social and political relations. Such is the case, for example, in an economy in which prices are arbitrarily fixed by governmental decree. In contrast, an economy is disembedded when it is governed by mechanisms that function independently of other social and political relations. Such is the case in an economy in which prices are determined by the impersonal forces of supply and demand.[6]

In the same way, it is possible to conceptualize different forms of trade according to the degree to which they are embedded in or disembedded from other social and political relations. Administered and gift trade are bound by such social and political relations as blood ties, status, religious obligations, and legal restrictions. Market trade, however, is regulated by price-making markets that are governed by the impersonal laws of supply and demand. Thus, in Polanyi's view, only market trade can be said to be "disembedded" from other social and political relations. Polanyi's conceptual tools allow us to acknowledge and understand trade and other economic activities in ancient Greece even when they were not organized according to market principles and even if many ancient Greeks themselves failed to perceive the "economy" as a discrete sphere of activity, separate from other social and political relations.

The influence of Weber, Hasebroek, and Polanyi on Finley's model is readily apparent. Finley's basic argument is that the ancient Greek economy was qualitatively little like the market economies of today. It was, as Polanyi believed, thoroughly embedded in a society in which, as Weber had shown, social status was more important than economic class, and this served to inhibit the development of a market economy (Finley 1985: 17–62, especially 21, 26, 60). All economic activities outside of traditionally esteemed agricultural pursuits, so-called *banausic* occupations, such as manufacturing and trade, were disesteemed and left to poor citizens and noncitizens who could not afford or were barred from owning land (ibid., 60). Moreover, although Finley acknowledged that profit seeking existed in ancient Greece, he believed that it was esteemed only in traditional landed occupations and when it served social and political goals deemed worthy of honor (see Morris 1999: xii–xiii, xv, xxii). Seeking profit in *banausic* occupations, at the expense of others, for its own sake, or to be used as capital in the pursuit of even greater profit was disesteemed, and therefore it, too, was undertaken only by poor citizens or outsiders who had no hope of obtaining honor and high status in the close-knit communities of the ancient Greek *poleis*.[7] In fact, Finley states explicitly that there was "a tendency on the part of money-holding citizens to turn to the land from considerations of status, not of maximization of profit"; thus, "what we call the economy was properly the exclusive business of outsiders" (Finley 1970: 22–23). Under such conditions, according to Finley (here again following Hasebroek), the state, which was run by the landholding

elite or citizens who had slaves and thus did not have to engage in disesteemed economic activity, had little interest or involvement in the economy per se and nothing that we could call economic or trade policies. The
state's only interests in the economy were consumptive and political: the
"satisfaction of material wants," namely, to obtain revenue through taxes
and necessary goods through trade (Finley 1985: 62–94, especially 76, 79;
150–76, especially 160–64). Finally, since Finley, like the sociologist Weber, was interested in general models and characteristic features of societies, he argued that there was a single economy with the aforementioned
attributes that predominated not only throughout ancient Greek history
from 1000 B.C.E. onward but also throughout the entire Roman Mediterranean down to 500 C.E. (ibid., 27–34, especially 29, 33–34; see also 183).

Despite the fact that Finley's model did indeed create a paradigm
shift in the debate and has remained the orthodox view and starting point
for studies of the ancient Greek economy up to the present, it has not been
without its critics, who have been growing in number over the last
decade. Ian Morris has identified three basic categories of such criticism
(Morris 1999: xxvi–xxxi; see also Morris 2005: 144–49). Under the category
of "empiricists," Morris places those who have criticized the oversimpli-
fying tendencies of Finley's model, which focuses on what he argues are
the dominant attributes of a single economy that supposedly prevailed
for fifteen hundred years throughout the Greco-Roman Mediterranean.
These critics have attempted to illustrate the complexity and dynamism
of the ancient Greek economy with empirical studies of particular sectors
of economic behavior (e.g., labor, money, banking, agriculture, manufacturing, and trade), rather than attempting to characterize the economy as
a whole through theoretical approaches.[8] In general, their studies have
tended to emphasize the existence of disembedded profit-seeking behavior and market institutions in the ancient Greek economy.

Morris' second category includes scholars who have taken Finley's
model to task for being "oversocialized," a term codified by the economic
sociologist Mark Granovetter to describe the notion that economic behavior is determined by social values (Granovetter 1985: 483, after Wrong
1961: 183–93). Finley's model is based on the premise that the concerns for
status that prevailed in Greco-Roman society prevented the rise of the
homo economicus among the elite and therefore kept the economy from becoming disembedded from society. Some critics would argue, however,
that it is "human nature" for individuals to seek profit and ultimately to
formulate market relationships. Thus, regardless of social pressures,

profit seeking and market economics will exist in all societies, if not overtly, then at least under the surface. The concern for status that is expressed in the ancient literary sources cited by Finley reflects the ideology of the elite while masking the realities of everyday economics carried out by the masses. Like the studies of the empiricists, therefore, those who criticize the Finley model for being oversocialized tend to emphasize examples of disembedded profit seeking and market institutions in the ancient Greek economy.[9]

The third category of Finley critics identified by Morris includes proponents of the "new cultural history" who hold that Finley's conception of the ancient economy fails to account for the representational nature of the evidence (see p. 329). Such scholars have criticized Finley for not adequately addressing the culturally constructed, representational nature of references to the economy in the literary sources, which were created and contested within specific contexts of public discourse, such as legal trials or philosophical treatises. Thus, they do not provide objective evidence about the reality of economic behavior, only evidence for how individuals wanted to represent it to further their particular interests. Moreover, it was the discourse that created social values, not vice versa. Thus, a failure to account for this discursive context fails to account for the social influences on what we see represented as the economy in the literary sources. Ultimately, the analysis of the new cultural historians questions whether we can make any definitive characterizations of the ancient Greek economy based on the documentary evidence.

These criticisms of the Finley model are all valid, to a point. Finley tended to make overly broad generalizations, discounting what he called "exceptional" evidence, and did not adequately account for variation among the numerous sectors of the Greco-Roman economy or for changes in the economy over time (Finley 1985: 37–38, 52). He also took the literary evidence too much at face value, assuming that the elite values it reflects are also those of the masses, who accepted the values of their betters hook, line, and sinker (ibid., 37–38, 51–52). Finally, Finley did overemphasize the power of society to control individual economic behavior, thereby minimizing the impact of actions by individuals, networks, and groups that might contradict prevailing social values (ibid., 35– 61, especially 60).

In addition, the polarized character of the debate led Finley to present a picture of the ancient Greek economy that almost undermines the substantivist basis of his work. As a substantivist, Finley rejected the notion that ancient Greece had to have a "capitalist" or market economy and acknowledged that there are other types of economies. But in his zeal to argue against the modernists and to prove that the ancient Greek economy was not like our own, reminiscent of Hasebroek before him, he gave the impression that it had no economy at all (Finley 1985: 21–23). As Lin Foxhall puts it, much of Finley's *The Ancient Economy* "is a treatise on what the ancient economy was not" (Foxhall 1990: 22–23). For example, Finley dismissed the trade policies of ancient Greek *poleis* as merely the "satisfaction of material wants," which is "not synonymous with the needs of the economy, or trade as such."[10] The implication is that "the needs of the economy, or trade as such," must be those of a market economy, which are productive and not simply a consumptive interest in the "satisfaction of material wants."

Because of the profound influence of his model on subsequent scholarship, Finley's blurring of substantivism continues to taint even the most recent works, such as C. M. Reed's otherwise quite useful book *Maritime Traders in the Ancient Greek World*. Despite referring to his conclusions as "'substantivist' to the core," Reed focuses solely on professionals who engaged in market-oriented trade (Reed 2003: 4). Thus, he concurs with Finley (and Hasebroek before him) that trade was carried out by poor noncitizen foreigners (Reed 2003: 26, 35– 36). But such a focus ignores the evidence in the honorary decrees for nonprofessionals who initiated nonmarket trading exchanges. At one point Reed dismisses the famous Kyrene distribution of grain as "a *gift* of grain, not trade therein."[11] But according to the substantivist definition of trade, a long-distance exchange of gifts is, in fact, trade; it is just not "market trade." Neville Morley, in his otherwise excellent recent survey *Trade in Classical Antiquity*, perpetuates this confusion concerning the definition of "trade," stating that Polanyi "distinguished between reciprocity [gift], redistribution [administered], and *market exchange (trade)* as different modes for the distribution of goods within a society" (Morley 2007: 10; my emphasis). The implication is that only market exchange is "trade," whereas reciprocal and redistributive forms of "distribution" are not. But I must stress again that whether in the form of reciprocal (gift), redistributive (administered), or market exchange, any exchange that constitutes "a relatively peaceful method of acquiring goods which are not available on the spot" (Polanyi 1957b: 257–58) is "trade." This is not a trivial semantic distinction: it requires us to understand ancient Greek trade for what it was rather than what it was not.

An Interdisciplinary Approach

Despite its shortcomings, however, we should not rush to discard Finley's model, at least not entirely. First of all, it is debatable whether the empirical evidence has provided a sufficient number of exceptions to the model for it to be jettisoned. Second, even the "empiricists" would have to acknowledge that it is impossible to analyze empirical evidence without at least some theoretical assumptions. More often than not, those who advocate that we must simply let the evidence "speak for itself" take for granted the assumptions of Classical economic theory, which holds that rational entrepreneurs seek to maximize profit in their economic activities. As a result, wherever possible, the empirical evidence will be interpreted in such a way that vindicates the theory. Where it is not possible, the evidence will be labeled as "exceptional" or merely the result of the elite's obfuscation of its true, underlying desire for profit. Obviously, such conclusions would not necessarily be any more valid than those of Finley, at least not on the grounds that they are based more on the "facts" than was his more explicitly theoretical analysis. Finally, although Finley's somewhat polemical rhetoric gave the impression that ancient Greece had no economy at all because (in his view) it did not have price-making markets, he certainly knew that it did have some kind of economy (Finley 1985: 23), and we should not let his one-sided presentation completely nullify the good sense of much of his analysis.

When stripped of such peripheral issues, the real impasse between Finley and his critics boils down to two fundamental questions. The first is whether the ancient Greek economy was like our market economy, comprised of individuals acting independently to fulfill their seemingly natural desire for profit for its own sake, or was socially constructed in such a way as to promote reciprocal exchanges while suppressing profit-seeking activities unless they furthered traditional, honorable, social and political goals. The second question is whether the documentary evidence can really tell us anything at all about the ancient Greek economy as opposed to a particular group's (the elite's or the masses') representation of economic activity. I have already addressed the second question in chapter 1 and will only emphasize again here that the documentary evidence can indeed be used, albeit carefully, to understand the ancient Greek economy. The first question, however, will require a much more extensive response here, since I argue in this book that the ancient Greek economy was complex and dynamic, socially constructed in accordance with "noneconomic" values on the one hand while simultaneously allowing and even promoting profit-seeking ventures by individuals on the other.

The core theoretical basis of this book is substantivist economic theory. Although the term *substantivism* was first coined by Polanyi, the substantivist view is central, either explicitly or implicitly, in the work of Weber, Hasebroek, and Finley as well as the cultural anthropologist, Marshall Sahlins and proponents of "economic sociology," such as Neil Smelser, Richard Swedberg, and Mark Granovetter. It holds that the economy is a cultural construction and that individual economic choices and actions are largely shaped by social constraints particular to a given culture. In fact, even a market economy is not divorced from social norms but is as socially constructed and endorsed as any other form of economy (see Morley 2007: xiii, 9). In essence, there is neither a universal form of economic organization nor a universal economic man whose economic means and ends are consistent across all cultures at all times.

Yet this book will not be purely substantivist in its approach but incorporates essential refinements posited by economic sociologists, particularly Granovetter, that allow for individuals and groups to make choices that may not coincide with the particular norms of their society. Although economic structures generally reflect the cultural norms of a given society and though individuals and groups generally adhere to such norms, they are not all automatons who must adhere to these norms at all times. This accounts not only for the variety of ends and means that we see in the choices and actions of those who were honored by Athens for their trade-related services but also for the change we see in social norms with regard to the economy in fourth-century Athens. If individuals and groups can never contradict prevailing social norms, then there is no engine for change, and social norms become completely static.

The static nature of Finley's substantivist model of the ancient economy, which has been described above, can also be seen in Sahlins' substantivist critique of the formalist assumption that practical need determines economic structures. Sahlins argues that the universal need for scarce material resources, which is so central to Classical or "formalist" economic theory, does not determine the shape and character of social structures, including relations, values, and institutions. Rather, social structures are created by culture through the meaning it assigns to material needs. Since cultures may determine meaning in a variety of ways, social structures may take on a variety of forms. In other words, there is always more than one way of doing things, no matter how necessary or unnecessary such things may be for human survival. As Sahlins puts it, "men do not merely 'survive.' They survive in a definite way." It is "true that in so producing a cultural existence, society must remain within the limits of physical-natural necessity," but "within these limits, any group has the possibility of great range of 'rational' economic intentions" (Sahlins 1976: 168; see also 206). The *homo economicus* who selfishly seeks to satisfy material wants and maximize profits through economic activity is not universal but a product of a cultural construction that Sahlins believes is particular to the modern Western world (Sahlins 1976: 167, 210–11).

In a similar fashion, economic sociology assumes that "1. economic action is a form of social action; 2. economic action is socially situated; 3. economic institutions are social constructions" (Granovetter and Swedberg 1992a: 6). As Smelser puts it, the core concerns of the field are "the place in economic phenomena of personal interaction, the actions of groups and institutions, and norms and values" (Smelser 1963: 27–28). According to the basic tenets of economic sociology, then, the economy is not a function of universal laws of human nature, as formalist economics would have it, but a social construction, shaped by the prevailing values and relations that are particular to a given society in a given historical context. In reality "economic action cannot . . . be separated from the quest for approval, status, sociability, and power," and individuals are not fully independent, "atomized" actors who can be assumed to strive to maximize their own preferences without regard to their social or historical context (Granovetter and Swedberg 1992a: 7). Rather, the choices of individuals are shaped and influenced to a great extent by the particular societies in which they live. Consequently, economic sociology is descriptive rather than prescriptive and is more appropriate for investigations of economic history than is formalist economics, particularly investigations of ancient economic history, the evidence for which is rarely sufficient for the quantitative analyses that are typical of formalist economics.[12]

A "Middle Ground"

At the same time, however, "society" is not a monolithic, all-determining force on the choices of individuals, as substantivism would have it. The smaller social groups or "networks" in which individuals interact on a day-to-day basis often have more coercive power in influencing the choices of individuals than does society as a whole (Granovetter and

Swedberg 1992a: 9–13). Moreover, individuals can and routinely do act independently of the constraints imposed by their networks and societies. Finally, social constraints are subject to change over time. As important as society is in shaping individual economic action, it is mistaken to believe, as Sahlins does (1976: 55– 56), that there is no conceptual middle ground in which one can acknowledge the often nonpragmatic cultural basis of social structures while allowing that small groups or individuals may act contrary to such structures, sometimes for practical need, and thus have an impact in shaping culture in accordance with these practical needs.

In contrast to Sahlins' either-or view, Granovetter has pointed out the contradictions that arise from such an "oversocialized" conception of social constraints on economic activity.[13] Among other things, such a view leaves no room for individuals to exercise their own initiative, prohibiting any deviation from society's dictates. But then how do social values and institutions ever change, as we know they do? In reality, there is a give and take between society as a whole and the individuals who comprise it. Culture is an ongoing process: society shapes individuals even as individuals, through their unique choices and actions, shape society.

Herbert Simon tries to account for the complexity of economic thought and action in the real world with his notion of "bounded rationality" (Simon 1957: 196–202). Rejecting Classical economic theory's simple psychology of the rational person who as a consumer seeks to maximize his or her preferences and as an entrepreneur seeks to maximize profit, Simon notes that such a psychology takes no account for uncertainty. Since people are not omniscient about the future, they must create a simplified model of expected outcomes that are necessarily largely subjective. In order to understand the choices and actions of such a "rational" person, therefore, we must understand the way in which his or her simplified model of the world is constructed. According to Simon, the construction of such a model is influenced both by the individual's psychology and by the society in which he or she lives. Society provides the "givens" or premises on which the individual, depending on his or her role in society, makes rational choices (Simon 1957: 198, 201).

Simon is right in seeing that rational economic action among individuals can exist within an economy that is largely socially constructed. Nevertheless, his concept of "bounded rationality" still assumes that entrepreneurs naturally seek the individual goal of profit. Society influences them only insofar as they must rely (because of their individual cognitive limitations) on premises set by society as shortcuts for their individual decision-making processes.

A more refined view of the role of rational choice and action and the influence of society on economics, which will be adopted in this book, is the notion of "expressive rationality," originally put forth by Shaun Hargreaves Heap and adapted to the ancient Greek economy in the sector of mining in fourth-century Attika by Paul Christesen.[14] Christesen rightly points out that every concept of economic rationalism rests not only on a notion of an individual's decision-making process but also on a value system. Thus, "different definitions of economic rationalism contain different assumptions, either implicit or explicit, about values" (Christesen 2003: 31). Even the rational economic man of Classical economic theory is based on assumptions about values that are socially constructed.

Hargreaves Heap accounts for such assumptions about values by distinguishing between three basic types of economic rationalism: instrumental, procedural, and expressive rationality. According to Christesen's simplified definition, expressive rationality "assumes that individual agents are self-consciously reflexive about their preferences *and* that they are sensitive to societal norms" (Christesen 2003: 32). Thus, expressive rationality coincides with Granovetter's "middle ground" between "oversocialized" and "undersocialized" conceptions of economic action. Individual preferences may exist independently of social norms and even contradict them. It is possible, too, that prevailing social norms may be used to express or justify individual preferences when the two coincide.

Application to the Ancient Greek Economy

Expressive rationality accounts for the coexisting goals of honor and profit we see in Athenian grants of honors and privileges for trade-related services. Some honorands were wealthy, politically powerful men who were not professional traders but who arranged to ship Athens large quantities of timber and grain as a gift, free of charge. Others were wealthy professional traders who gave Athens grain, gave money to buy grain, or sold grain to Athens at discounted prices. Still others were professional traders of modest means who shipped grain to Athens themselves and sold it at the going rate during a time of shortage (see chaps. 4 and 5). Yet the People of Athens encouraged and rewarded these men similarly for their diverse actions, with honors and privileges that had both honorific and practical value, while at the same time representing the varied interests of these honorands as being simply for the "love of honor" (*philotimia*) (see chaps. 6–8).

All this makes sense within a complex economy in which profit-motivated market exchanges coexisted with reciprocal ones. Sally Humphreys (1969: 165–212; 1970: 1–26) was the first to begin to appreciate the complexity and dynamism of the ancient Greek economy, particularly with regard to Athenian trade. Since the economy was comprised of many different sectors (e.g., agriculture, local trade, overseas trade, slavery), each with potentially different economic structures and all undergoing significant change during the late Classical period, conceptual categorizations can be applied only with regard to particular sectors at particular times. Categorizing the entire ancient Greek economy in the late Classical period with one static and overgeneralizing term, whether it be *embedded* or *disembedded*, simply cannot account for the evidence satisfactorily.[15]

Edmund Burke has taken an important step in the right direction, therefore, by arguing for economic change in the sector of overseas trade in late fourth-century Athens.[16] He has shown that Athens granted those involved in maritime trade several honors and privileges (e.g., *proxenia*, *enktesis*, and citizenship) with greater frequency in the late fourth century than before. Although Burke's schematization of the evidence is somewhat oversimplified, his argument that many Athenian citizens were coming to the realization that their interests coincided with those of the men who engaged in maritime trade is certainly on the mark. In Burke's view, such a trend indicates the onset of a disembedding of at least some sectors of the economy from other social relations.

But Burke's analysis tells only part of the story, since it neither addresses in detail the nature of the honorands' involvement in trade, which encompasses a complex variety of trading activities, nor considers the representational nature of the evidence from honorary decrees, which calls the very notion of a disembedding of the economy into question. Ian Morris has taken up this latter issue, using the approach of the new cultural historians and focusing on the representational nature of the evidence, which includes not only the Athenian honorary decrees cited by Burke but also the writings of Aristotle.[17] Morris argues that what we see after 350 is not the partial disembedding of the market identified by Burke but a redefinition of "equality," so that it gradually became more legitimate for citizens to engage in economic transactions in which one party profited from the other (Morris 1994b: 68). The "equality" to which

Morris refers is the ideal of equality between citizens that prevailed in many Classical Greek *poleis,* particularly Athens. Economic activity involving market exchanges that allowed one person to profit at another's expense upset that ideal and was, therefore, traditionally frowned upon among citizens and instead relegated to outsiders, such as *metics* and other foreigners. But, according to Morris, economic growth and the prominence in government of wealthy citizens and officials concerned chiefly with finances, such as Euboulos and Lykourgos, were necessary to meet the growing financial needs of Athens in the fifth and fourth centuries. These changes, in turn, eroded the ideal of citizen equality and, consequently, led to a lessening of the traditional disdain for profit seeking for its own sake in market exchanges. It is these sociopolitical changes that are represented in the evidence, not any disembedding of the economy, according to Morris.

Resolution of the divergent views of Burke and Morris can again be found in a middle ground. Contrary to Burke's view, changes in the economy, the society, or even the political landscape of Athens do not account for all that we read in the written evidence. Some of the apparent changes are distorted, enhanced, or diminished by the manner in which they are represented. Profit-seeking, capitalistic behavior was present throughout ancient Greek history, going back to Homeric times, as even Weber ([1921] 1978: 164–65) acknowledged, but only in the late Classical period was such behavior beginning to sneak out from under the obscuring representations that had been imposed by prevailing traditional values against it. So, as Morris argues, perhaps what we see in the sources tells us less about the economy than it does about how the Greeks wanted to represent it.

But the changes in representations cannot be the entire story either, because one must then explain why the representations changed in the first place. The novel representations that we see in Athenian honorary decrees for trade-related services and in the writings of Aristotle were an expression of both a new perspective on trade for profit and the increasing scale of such trade (see Arist. *Pol.* 1256a41–1257b5 and pp. 3–5). My analysis later in this book of the language used in Athenian honorary decrees will show that the state tried to mask traditionally disesteemed economic activities by representing them in traditional terms of esteem as, for example, having been motivated by *philotimia,* or a "love of honor." Athens was at a crossroads, leaving behind a time when profit-seeking capitalism was wholly disesteemed, for a time when it was needed, and thus legitimized, by the state. One means by which the People of Athens smoothed over this transition to legitimacy was to embed traditionally disesteemed economic behavior within traditional social values by representing it with traditional terms of honor in official public decrees. By granting honors and privileges for trade-related services as part of their trade policy, the Athenians broadened not only the range of economic activities that were to be esteemed but also the range of people who could become honored and privileged members of their community. The importance of this for Greek economic and social history cannot be overestimated.[18]

Conclusion

The Athenian state and its trading benefactors had interests and involvements in trade that were particular to their cultural milieu. When the state sought to obtain imported grain instead of economic growth through its trade policy, and when professional traders or foreign potentates performed benefactions in order to obtain honor instead of profit, they were acting just as rationally as any state or individual that seeks economic growth or profit today, but within the cultural norms of ancient Greek society. Conferring and seeking honor were not necessarily just veils intended to obscure the underlying truth of material gain; they were often what truly mattered to the state and to those who provided it with trading services.

Moreover, those who did seek practical benefits or even pure monetary profit were not necessarily succumbing to a universal "natural" instinct of human beings; they were simply choosing one of many possible goals of economic activity in accordance with their particular needs and desires. Although such a goal traditionally was not esteemed by the elite in Greek society, it was probably often a necessity among the lower classes, who could not so easily eschew monetary gain. It is significant, therefore, that the Athenian state would grant honors and privileges not only to foreign potentates for large gifts of timber or grain but also to professional traders for sales of imported grain at the going price. Such a practice by the Athenian state indicates both a cultural shift in prevailing social norms concerning the means and ends of economic activity and a willingness on the part of the People of Athens to adapt their practices and policies to such changing circumstances.

Thus, we cannot go so far as to say, as Polanyi did, that the preindustrial ancient Greek economy was socially constructed and embedded in such a way as to suppress profit seeking, whereas modern capitalist market economies have broken free of social constraints and are disembedded to the extent that a rational person necessarily seeks profit through economic action (Polanyi 1957a: passim, especially 68; see also Granovetter and Swedberg 1992a: 10). There are too many exceptions in both societies to support such a rule. Profit seeking existed in ancient Greece as it exists now. Seeking honor through economic action exists now as it did in ancient Greece. In both places, the *prevailing* organization of the economy is the product of collective culture. But the collective culture itself is a *generalization* of the tendencies of the individuals who comprise society, the more powerful individuals (i.e., the elite) naturally having an influence that is disproportionately high in comparison with their numbers. This process resulted in an ancient Greek economy tilted toward the pursuit of honor and status and a modern American economy tilted toward the pursuit of profit for its own sake.

The ancient Greek economy, like all economies throughout history, was therefore in part socially constructed and in part not. To the extent that it was not socially constructed, the economy was subject instead to the whims and desires of individuals that gave rise to a wide variety of goals and practices at any given time. To the extent that it was socially constructed, the economy was nevertheless subject to change as well, since the social values and relations on which it was based were not static but changed over time. Thus, one is bound to see different possible behaviors, such as striving for honor or striving for profit, characterize economic action in different sectors of the ancient Greek economy at the same time or, conversely, in the same sector at different times.

CHAPTER THREE

Historical Context

The preceding chapter stressed that cultural norms shape the general structure of an economy but that the economic preferences of individuals, networks, and groups are not so constrained by such norms that they can never act independently of them. In fact, it is in the interests of some individuals and groups to disregard or to change the cultural status quo, just as it is in the interest of others to maintain it. The preferences and actions of these subsets of society contrary to established cultural norms are in fact essential for structural change ever to occur in an economy. Therefore, in order to understand the ancient Greek economy and its structural changes over time, we must be cognizant of both the cultural norms of ancient Greece and the social, political, and economic factors that influenced individuals, networks, and groups to disregard or even to change those norms. Only within this context will it be possible to appreciate honor and profit as coexisting goals of economic activity and as essential components of Athenian trade policy. The following, then, is a survey of the social and political context within which Athenian trade policy took shape.[1]

Elite Values and Institutions

A survey of ancient Greek social values must necessarily emphasize the values of the elite, since their dominance in early Greek history secured them an influential place at the core of Greek life even in Classical, democratic Athens. There were a variety of elite groups that experienced significant changes over the course of Greece's history. In the discussion that follows, the term *elite* will refer to that small minority of the population who possessed the greatest wealth and status, both of which were inherited by birth into a privileged landowning family (Ober 1989: 11–17). Their wealth and status allowed them leisure from work, high levels of education, and political prominence. The common people or masses (the *demos,* in a limited sense) constituted the rest of the male citizenry who were born into undistinguished families, had to work for a living, and possessed mediocre educations at best.

From Homeric times through the Classical period, honor (*timé*) was the central and overriding value in Greek culture. Honor was the good reputation, esteem, and respect a man held among his peers. Because of the importance of honor, historians have characterized Greek civilization as a "shame culture," in which the sanction for a person's behavior was not his or her own conscience but rather public opinion. *Philotimia,* the "love of honor," was therefore among the most powerful and esteemed motivations of action. There was such a "fundamental link between *philotimia* and the achievement of social status and power" that it has even been said that "no word, understood to its depths, goes farther to explain the Greco-Roman achievement."[2] But since the value of honor would be diminished if it were shared equally by all, the pursuit of honor and the fulfillment of one's *philotimia* had to take the form of "a contest of good men" (Dem. 20.107). Hence, a competitive or "agonistic" spirit permeated the aristocratic ethos and filtered down throughout Greek life. Moreover, since honor was a man's good reputation among his peers, it was necessary for one to advertise his victories in competition through visible symbols, such as trophies, monuments, and victor lists, so that his peers could not fail to be aware of his achievements.

Given the unstable political and economic context of the origins of these values in Homeric times, competition was most intense in three major areas on which survival and prosperity depended: the status of one's family, the amount of one's landed wealth, and the quality of one's skills in war. Throughout ancient Greek history, even in democratic Athens, birth into an old family of good repute, wealth, and political influence immediately qualified a man as *agathos* (good) or, better yet, a member of the *aristoi* (best men), who had *arete* (excellence). Land was the chief form of the aristocratic family's wealth, and the vast majority of production in the economy for the duration of ancient Greek history was directly tied to the land. Ideally, the family unit (*oikos*) was supposed to adhere to the principle of self-sufficiency (*autarkeia*), producing for itself everything that it needed for subsistence. Since the wealth and status of the *oikos* depended on landownership, the ability to protect one's land through excellence in war was also essential.

In the world of Homer, nonagricultural (*banausic*) occupations, particularly trade in the form of commercial exchanges among strangers, were small in scale, unspecialized, and for the most part left to commoners or outsiders who were looked upon with distrust and contempt. The disdain for *banausic* occupations as a means of livelihood would continue, at least among the elite, through the Classical period. But since such occupations were not esteemed among the elite, warfare was a major means, besides inheritance and landownership, of augmenting one's wealth and, even more important, status, through raiding and plundering the dominions of others. Although plunder constituted wealth and had functional uses, it also had symbolic value. Having been won by the spear rather than obtained through home production or peaceful trade, it served as physical proof of one's *arete* and status as an *aner agathos* (good man). Finley and others have gone so far as to conclude that the motives for acquiring wealth in the Homeric age had more to do with honor and the social status it entailed than with material gain.[3]

Wealth also served status interests by enabling the elite to form a network of guest or, to be more accurate, ritualized friendships (*xeniai*; see Herman 1987: 10). This network of ritualized friendships was the means by which the elite were able to engage in foreign relations and diplomacy with their elite counterparts abroad in the absence of well-developed state-organized institutions or international law, a situation that persisted from Homeric times at least until the Classical period. *Xenoi* abroad were somewhat "more than 'friends' yet somewhat less than 'kin,'" but like kinsmen, they would serve as protectors, representatives, and allies in foreign lands (Herman 1987: 16).

Given that the Greeks of Homer's epics were completely illiterate and that the majority of Greeks still could not read and write even in Classical Athens (Harris 1989: 114), a ceremonial exchange of gifts served as a symbolic act both to proclaim and to memorialize the establishment of a formal relationship.[4] Moreover, the exchange of valuable gifts and services also testified to the shared elite status, wealth, and mutual interests of the *xenoi*. Anything could be exchanged, but often the gifts consisted of objects that had even greater symbolic than functional value, and the more ostentatious the gift was, the more honorable the giver was deemed to be. Reciprocation among *xenoi* was expected—whether in the form of countergifts or future services, such as the all-purpose promise of aid (*boetheia*) when needed—since the recipient of a gift was supposed to feel gratitude (*charis*) and respond accordingly.

Some historians, such as Finley and Herman, stress that these gift exchanges were less about obtaining needed goods or creating wealth and more about forming relationships and signifying a shared elite status.[5] The exchanges were supposed to be carried out in a spirit of altruism, putting friendship and mutual aid ahead of material need or profit—at least this is how they are always portrayed in our elite sources, even though it is clear that the exchanged goods and services were often needed and that self-interest was ever present in *xenia*.[6] But regardless of whether reality lived up to the ideal, such gift exchanges should be distinguished from market trade. They obviously lacked a market pricing mechanism. In addition, when the exchanges involved needed goods or services, the need was for interests of status (the loan of soldiers for a raid, bronze crafts for future gifts to retainers, etc.), not for subsistence or profit. The goods and services always had symbolic value for the maintenance of the relationship in addition to their use value. Both parties to the exchange were supposed to benefit equally, with neither party profiting at the expense of the other. Lastly, the relationship between the parties to the exchange was a personal one maintained and/or renewed by repeated gift exchanges. In short, these gift exchanges were not onetime transactions for subsistence or profit between strangers, as is the case in market exchanges. In the gift exchanges associated with *xenia*, the creation and maintenance of the relationship took precedence as a goal over the acquisition of goods and wealth.

Nevertheless, gift exchanges did result in the transfer of goods, sometimes over long distances. Therefore, they do constitute "trade" according to Polanyi's "substantivist" definition. Trade was carried out in a variety of ways, and we shall see that the Athenian state included gift exchange in its trade policy in the late Classical period.

The Democratization of Values and Institutions

Given that warfare and agriculture continued to hold a central place in Greek life from the late Dark Age through the Hellenistic period, it is not surprising that the values of Homer's landed warrior elite continued to occupy a central place in the Greek system of values throughout its long history. Nevertheless, Greek civilization was not static but underwent significant social, political, and economic changes during the Archaic and Classical periods, ranging from the rise of the *polis* to the expansion of nonlanded occupations to the invention of democracy, all of which went hand in hand with the increasing status, wealth, and power of the common people. Thus, in order for the values of Homer's elite to remain relevant, it was necessary for them to undergo some reinterpretation and alteration. Essentially, a democratization of Greek values took place in which the masses expanded the criteria for *arete*, the *aner agathos*, and *timé* (as well as *philotimia*) to include their concern to emphasize the good of the community over the good of the individual (and his *oikos, philoi,* and *xenoi*) and to allow for other means of accomplishing this goal in addition to those exalted by Homer's landed warrior elite.

The *polis* created a new political unit that gradually superceded the *oikos* as the chief focus of one's sustenance and security, loyalty and responsibilities. By uniting the territories and families of many *oikoi*, both rich and poor, under one political organization, the *polis* came to represent a larger and more diverse group of individuals with shared loyalties and goals than had existed in Homer's world. The net result was a diminution of the status of the elite and an elevation of the status of commoners, since all were now citizens of a greater entity. Although the old elite continued to hold more rights and privileges than the masses in the Archaic *polis*, even the lowest of citizens from undistinguished and poor families had rights and privileges that far outstripped those of noncitizens, to whom they could feel superior.

The increased status and influence of the common man as a citizen of the *polis* went hand in hand with the growing scale and significance of nonagricultural occupations in manufacturing and trade during the Archaic period, which not only allowed the masses an avenue toward obtaining wealth without land but also called into question the old values of Homer's warrior elite. Tandy (1997) argues that the increasing opportunities for wealth through nonlanded pursuits were paradoxically a major factor in the retention of Homeric values during the Archaic period. The expansion of trade offered new opportunities for wealth, which were seized by the elite as well as by the masses, transforming the former from warriors into traders. The basis of the elite's power in the Archaic period therefore shifted from military prowess and landed wealth to wealth drawn from trade. In order to disguise this transformation and legitimize their claim to inherit the high status and political dominance of their warrior ancestors, they had to represent themselves as upholding Homeric values. Whether or not one accepts Tandy's thesis, it cannot be denied that the values of the Homeric age persisted to a great extent during the Archaic period even as changes were taking place in Greek life that called these values into question.

The democratization of Greek values reached its zenith when the masses gained the upper hand over the elite, first in Athens in 508/7 and then in other *poleis* during the Classical period. In democratic Athens, the masses had almost complete constitutional equality with the elite in politics and legal matters, which essentially gave them the final say in both arenas by virtue of their sheer numbers in the Assembly and on the juries of the law courts. Yet members of the elite could still wield much influence owing to the advantages of their birth, wealth, and education as well as the persistence of the values (by now traditional) that exalted their old way of life. Nevertheless, despite the tension and potential for strife that existed between these two groups, they for the most part did a remarkably good job of resolving their differences, reaching a *modus vivendi,* and allowing Athenian democracy to remain stable for the better part of two hundred years.

One key to resolving the contest between the masses and the elite was the "subversion and appropriation" of elite values to serve democratic ends (Ober 1989: 339; see also 291). Ober's analysis of this struggle and its resolution focuses on the use of rhetoric to reconcile the gap between the reality of social and economic inequality and the democratic political ideal of equality (Ober 1989: xiii–xiv, 38–49, 308). In his study of the trierarchy, on the other hand, Gabrielsen stresses the interdependence of the masses and the elite through reciprocity concerning tangible economic benefits (Gabrielsen 1994: 231 n. 28). The views of Ober and Gabrielsen are not mutually exclusive, however, but rather complementary. The *demos* was willing to grant the honor appropriate to the elite's claim to high status so long as the elite's *philotimia* put the broad interests of the *polis* ahead of the narrow interests of the *oikos* or the even narrower interests of the individual and proved its loyalty and goodwill to the community as a whole. The greatest proof of such loyalty and goodwill was the redistribution of tangible wealth from the elite to the masses, who expanded the criteria for such key rhetorical terms of value as *philotimia, arete,* and *aner agathos* from excellence in military pursuits to include other activities, most notably the expenditure of private wealth for the public good.[7] Those who failed to make their wealth available to the *demos* were denied both practical and symbolic honor and the high social status and political influence that accompanied it. By adapting the criteria for rhetorical terms of value to its own needs while continuing to use honor as an incentive for action, the *demos* was able to turn the elite values to its own advantage. At the same time, however, the elite was able to retain most of its wealth, its influence in politics, its high status, and, just as important, its honor. Thus, both the masses and the elite got what they wanted, thereby preserving stability in Athens.

It is generally held that the contest between the masses and the elite in democratic Athens was limited to the citizenry,[8] but we shall see that this is not entirely the case. It is true that the distinction between citizen and noncitizen that developed in concert with the rise of the *polis* became even sharper in democratic Athens, thereby obviating any solidarity between common citizens and their foreign counterparts.[9] Resident foreigners (*metics*) and nonresident foreigners (*xenoi*, the same word for "guest" or "ritualized" friends) did not have the full legal, political, and economic rights of citizens. In the competition for status, wealth, and power between common and elite citizens, therefore, it would appear that noncitizens were out of the status loop and had no opportunity to obtain honor. But we shall see that the persistence of ritualized friendships between elite citizens and foreigners, as well as Athens' need for nonlanded occupations, particularly overseas trade in grain and timber, would provide noncitizens with an opportunity to compete for honor with both common and elite citizens.

The Liturgic System of Athens

Among citizens, since the "democratic revolution" in Athens had taken place gradually over the better part of a century (from the time of Solon through the reforms of Cleisthenes in 508/7), the institutions whereby wealth was redistributed from the elite to the masses likewise developed gradually, as an adaptation of aristocratic traditions involving honor, reciprocal gift exchanges, and competition, hijacked, so to speak, for the benefit of the *demos*. The best example of such institutions is the liturgic system[10] of Athens, which instituted a relationship between the masses and the elite in which a benefaction (*euergesia*) from the elite, motivated by *philotimia* and displaying the *arete* of an *aner agathos*, would inspire the gratitude (*charis*) of the *demos*, which in turn would lead to reciprocation through grants of practical and symbolic honors by the *demos* to the elite benefactor.[11] The values, structures, and goals of the liturgic system served in turn as a model for the Athenian practice of granting honors and privileges for trade-related services, which itself spawned the Hellenistic institution of voluntary euergetism.

Liturgies (*leitourgiai*) were literally public "services" required by the Athenian state from its wealthiest citizens. Examples of such services include the trierarchy and *choregia*, for which a wealthy citizen had to pay the expenses of commanding and maintaining one of the city's warships or of preparing a dramatic or dithyrambic chorus for the festival of the City Dionysia. Liturgies had their origins in early Greece when aristocratic families occasionally and voluntarily offered some of their private wealth as largesse to their local community in the form of feasts or buildings for public use. At some point not long after the creation of democracy in Athens in 508/7, however, such services were institutionalized so that they would benefit the entire city and be performed on a regular and compulsory basis.

Although liturgies in Classical Athens mandated a redistribution of wealth and could be considered a form of taxation, they differed from taxes in that they were organized as competitions, thus providing an opportunity for honor that the payment of taxes under compulsion could not. Elite *choregoi* competed against each other, and a panel of judges, who were selected by lottery from the entire citizenry, determined whose productions were the best. Such competition introduced an element of volunteerism, since it tapped into the agonistic spirit and *philotimia* of the aristocratic ethos and gave liturgists an incentive to exceed their obligatory expenses in order to obtain the honor that came with victory. Thus, although technically an obligation, liturgies took on the appearance of a voluntary gift from the elite to the masses, which was represented by the elite as having been motivated by a "love of honor" (*philotimia*).[12]

As a show of *charis* from the *demos*, liturgists who spent enough to win the first prize earned honor that was manifested through symbolic tokens and practical benefits. Symbolic tokens included bronze tripods and crowns of ivy and gold, whose bestowal in public ceremonies enhanced their honorific value.[13] The so-called *Fasti*, the extant portions of which run from 472 to 328, were public inscriptions that recorded the names, tribes, and deeds of victorious liturgists for all the contests in the City Dionysia.[14] Liturgists themselves also personally took great pains to publicize their victories. Victorious *choregoi* in the dithyrambic contests often displayed their tripods atop ostentatious, inscribed monuments, many of which they dedicated along a road called simply "the Tripods." They could then point to these monuments with pride as proof of their *philo-timia* as well as a reminder to the *demos* of their monetary expenditures for the good of the community.[15] Victorious liturgists sought to put the honor in which they were held by the *demos* into practical use in the political and legal arenas.[16] Members of the elite frequently cited their public services in their legal speeches with the specific intention of proving their loyalty and goodwill to the members of the *demos* who sat on juries, implying that the latter must show their *charis* by reciprocating with a favorable verdict. Thus, honor had practical benefits in Classical Athens to go along with its symbolic ones, providing a compelling incentive for members of the elite to be lavish in spending their private wealth for public good.

Since Athens limited the performance of most liturgies to citizens, however, both the practical and symbolic honors that could be won through liturgies were available only to a small handful of foreigners. Although *metics* were obliged to participate in some festival processions and could serve as *choregoi* for the Lenaia, their inferior status and opportunity for honor were manifested in both types of service, since the Lenaia was less prestigious than the Dionysia and since *metic* participants in the processions were given only subordinate roles to perform.[17] In a similar fashion, although *metics* were obligated to pay the *eisphora* (an irregular tax imposed on the wealthy in extraordinary circumstances), they did not pay at the same rate as citizens. It is uncertain whether they paid more or less than citizens, but it is clear that the distinction between *metic* and citizen obligations was a mark of the inferior status of *metics*, since Athens considered it an honor for *metics* to pay "together with Athenians" (Whitehead 1977: 78–80). *Metics* were completely excluded from performing trierarchies.[18] Athenian citizens, on the other hand, could volunteer to perform any liturgy they wished, and the twelve hundred to two thousand citizens whose property exceeded the value of around one talent were obligated to pay the *eisphora,* while those (numbering around three hundred) whose property exceeded three to four talents were liable to serve as trierarchs and *choregoi.*[19] It is fair to say, therefore, that of the ninety-seven liturgies that occurred each year (118 in Panathenaic years) and the variable number of trierarchies that arose from time to time, wealthy Athenian citizens performed the vast majority and had a virtual monopoly on the honor to be obtained from them.[20] Poor citizens and foreigners of all classes were for the most part excluded.

By encouraging the *philotimia* of the elite in order to obtain public services from them, however, the *demos* was playing with fire. It was *philotimia*, after all, that had driven the elite to win distinction from the masses, a situation that had previously manifested itself in aristocratic rule (see Wilson 2000: 187–93). There was an inherent tension in the concept of *philotimia*: one's quest for personal honor could have either positive or negative consequences for the community (see Whitehead 1983: 55–60). This is evident from Aristotle's analysis of *arete* and his famous Doctrine of the Mean. According to Aristotle, *arete* (excellence or virtue) is a mean between two extremes. Courage, a form of *arete*, for example, is a mean between the extremes of rashness and cowardice (*NE* 1107b1–4). The philosopher is at a loss, however, to find a word that characterizes the mean between the *philotimos* man and the *aphilotimos* man (*NE* 1107b29–1108a2). The former is too ambitious, while the latter is not ambitious enough. The lack of a precise term for a socially appropriate level of *philotimia* reveals "a kind of battleground in which the realm of ideal practice is a no-man's land contested by the adversaries of excess and deficiency" (Wilson 2000: 190). Thus, while the *demos* of Classical Athens wished to encourage the *philotimia* of the elite in order to induce it to spend lavishly on public services, it was careful not to encourage it *too much*, especially in light of the elite's two attempts to replace democratic with oligarchic government in 411 and 404.

Such a concern on the part of the *demos* may be reflected in the epigraphic record. Beyond the immediate recognition that they received in the form of an ivy crown and/or bronze tripod and the inclusion of their name on inscribed lists of victors, victorious *choregoi* never received official honorary decrees from the Council or Assembly as other benefactors did. They received such official decrees only at the tribal or deme level (Wilson 2000: 171, 192, 198–99). This is true also of trierarchs who were the first to equip their ships. They received immediate recognition by the award of a gold crown and are listed on the inscribed naval records (*IG* ii^2 1629.196–204), but there is no evidence to suggest that they ever received official honorary decrees dedicated exclusively to them from the state. The Council and Assembly did not ascribe *philotimia* to resident native citizens in honorary decrees for public benefactions until the 340s, and even then they did so only when the benefactors served the *demos* as public officials.[21] Only after the mid-fourth century were circumstances such that the *demos* had to put aside its suspicion of elite *philotimia* in favor of other concerns (see pp. 59–64).

It is apparent that the liturgic system involved the *demos* and the elite citizens of Athens in a reciprocal relationship in which the former repaid the (often expensive) public services of the latter with tokens of honor. At the same time, however, the *demos* was careful to limit the amount of honor it conferred on its elite liturgists, for fear of disrupting the egalitarian ethos of democracy. Such fears, however, did not apply to foreign benefactors, since they could not officially participate in Athenian politics. Paradoxically, therefore, the *demos* could be more aggressive in using honor to induce nonliturgical services from foreigners. In fact, it *had to be* more aggressive to induce benefactions from nonresident foreigners, since they, unlike Athenian citizens and *melics*, could not be obligated to perform services for Athens. Such a situation illustrates the fact that the social values of ancient Greece were influenced by particular historical circumstances and the interests of particular groups, both of which were subject to change over time.

Ritualized Friendship and the Foreign Benefactor

Although they played a fairly insignificant role in the liturgic system, noncitizens did have the opportunity to strive for honor in Athens in two other areas in which the *demos* adapted aristocratic values and institutions to its own purposes, namely, *xenia* and trade. We have seen above that *xenia*, or "ritualized friendship," was "a bond of solidarity manifesting itself in an exchange of goods and services between individuals originating from separate social units," which arose in the late Dark Age among the elite who had the means to make such contacts abroad (Herman 1987: 10, 34–35). These relationships continued to flourish during the Archaic and Classical periods even as *poleis* took shape and as the *demos* became dominant in cities such as Athens. As a result, the ties of ritualized friendships crossed political boundaries and often conflicted with the intra-*polis* loyalties of citizens. Thus, the masses viewed elite *xeniai* with great suspicion, and there existed what could be described as a "cold" class war within *poleis* between the *demoi* and the elite who engaged in *xeniai*.[22] Once again, in order for democratic Athens to maintain stability, a means of resolving this tension had to be found, and once again the solution lay in an adaptation of elite values and institutions for democratic purposes.

The distrust with which the *demos* of Classical Athens viewed elite *xeniai* is apparent from the texts of the Attic orators. In sharp contrast to their boasts about their liturgies, the elite citizens of Athens throughout the Classical period rarely mentioned their own *xeniai* in speeches in the Assembly or the law courts, even when they benefited the city.[23] On the other hand, there are numerous passages in which elite speakers attack their political rivals by accusing them of "the receiving of bribes" (*dorodokia*) from their foreign *xenoi* for political favors in Athens.[24] For example, although he argued in favor of continuing exemptions from liturgies for the Bosporan kings (Dem. 20.29–33, 36) and even proposed erecting honorary bronze statues for them at state expense, Demosthenes never mentions his *xenia* with them, even though, as we shall see, it provided Athens with many important benefits. We have explicit evidence for this relationship only because Deinarchos (1.41–47) accuses Demosthenes of being "open to bribes" (*dorodokos*) and of accepting "bribes" (*dora*, technically meaning "gifts") from the Bosporan kings.

As a result of the suspicion with which the *demos* viewed elite *xeniai*, elite citizens were deprived of the honor that they might well have felt entitled to in return for the benefits that their *xeniai* sometimes provided for Athens. Herman believes that *every* foreign benefactor of a *polis* had private ties of *xenia* with elite citizens who served as intermediaries to procure benefactions from them for the city (Herman 1987: 84–88, 137–42). If this is true, had it not been for the ritualized friendships of the elite, *poleis* like Athens might not have received essential goods and services from foreign benefactors. Regardless of their value, however, no living, resident, Athenian citizens from the masses or the elite (with the possible exception of Konon in 394/3) received official state honors in Classical, democratic Athens for their role in procuring such services from their foreign *xenoi*.[25] Official honors for such men for such services do not appear with certainty until the 280s, by which time the Classical period was over and the power of the *demos* had diminished in Athens.[26]

In fact, with few exceptions, Athens as a rule honored its own living, resident, native citizens only when they themselves performed outstanding political, military, or religious services as public officials in Athens' democratic government, thus posing no threat to the dominance of the *demos*. Epigraphic evidence shows that Athens fairly routinely honored members of the Council and public priests.[27] Literary evidence attests to several generals who received honors for victorious military campaigns.[28] Others were honored for special embassies or financial contributions they made while holding public office.[29] The only possible exceptions are Konon (see n. 25) and Diphilos (Dein. 1.43), though we know next to nothing about the latter (see *APF*, pp. 168–69). In fact, there is not a single known case in which a native citizen benefactor ever earned the status of "benefactor" (*euergetes*) from Athens before the third century (Gauthier 1985: 10, 13–14, 16, 27). In the Classical period, the *demos* was in control: it could grant as much or as little honor to native citizens as it saw fit.

But while the *demos* was suppressing elite *philotimia* and *xenia* in this way during the Classical period, it was also democratizing them by involving itself in *xeniai* with foreign benefactors. Herman overstates the frequency with which the relationship between cities and their foreign benefactors were facilitated by elite citizen intermediaries and their private *xeniai*, since there is evidence that Athens also involved itself in *xeniai* without the aid of elite citizen intermediaries, particularly in the case of nonelite benefactors (see p. 155). But regardless of how Athens became involved in *xeniai*, by doing so it was democratizing the formerly private and elite institution. The collective citizenry of the democratic state now acted as a *xenos*, establishing ritualized friendships with foreigners, becoming part of the network of *xeniai*, and enjoying the benefits therein, including the exchange of goods and services in the form of gifts.

The Athenian state's *xeniai* with foreign benefactors are attested by numerous honorary decrees, which provide a sharp contrast to the manner in which the *demos* treated elite citizens involved in private *xeniai* and which also illustrate a further adaptation of elite values concerning honor for democratic purposes.[30] For noncitizen benefactors, Athens granted official and highly conspicuous honors, which had both honorific and practical value. In a typical honorary decree, the *demos* commended the honorand for his services; praised him as a useful (*chresimos*) and/or good man (*aner agathos*) for his *arête, philotimia,* and/or goodwill (*eunoia*) toward the *demos* of Athens; assigned him the status of a *euergetes* and/or *proxenos;* and awarded him symbolic honors (including a gold crown, a public banquet, and a seat in the theater) and/or privileges, among which were the right to own land in Attika (*enktesis*), the right to serve in the military and pay *eisphorai* on equal footing with Athenian citizens, and even Athenian citizenship itself. Furthermore, so that everyone would see that such beneficence toward the *demos* was rewarded, hence encouraging more benefactions from others, Athens inscribed the honorary decree on a stone stele, which it displayed in a public place.

The honorific value of such honors and privileges was surely a strong inducement for foreigners to provide benefactions for Athens. The centrality and power of the concept of honor in Greece's "shame culture" has been described above. Many of the noncitizens honored by Athens for their benefactions were Greeks from other cities who valued honor as much as any Athenian citizen. In fact, other Greek *poleis*, perhaps following Athens' lead, granted similar honors to their foreign benefactors (see Gauthier 1985: 130). Since elements of Greek culture were adopted by peoples throughout the Mediterranean from Archaic times onward, it is not surprising that non-Greeks also coveted official honors from Greek cities, particularly the internationally minded and culturally vibrant city of Athens, as a "badge of Hellenism" (Gauthier 1985: 156–57).

In addition to the honorific value of such honors and privileges, the foreign benefactor could also avail himself of their practical benefits either by exercising the privileges (e.g., *enktesis*) awarded to him or by pointing to his official honors and reminding the *demos* of its obligation to show *charis* (as in a ritualized friendship) and reciprocate. Should the honored benefactor ever need *boetheia* of any sort—if he were ever exiled from his homeland, for example, and needed a place of refuge; or if he should ever be involved in a lawsuit in an Athenian court (which was not uncommon for foreigners who did business with Athenian citizens); or if he should ever need military aid from Athens (which was not uncommon for foreign potentates)—he could expect the *demos* to look favorably on him and provide aid. It is common for Athenian honorary decrees to state that their honorands "shall not fail to obtain anything" from the People (*IG* ii^2 141.7–9). Two such requests from honorands that were fulfilled by Athens can be seen in case nos. 12 and 24 of this study. In the former case, Athens provided the ships' crews (*hyperesiai*) requested by the Bosporan kings; and in the latter, Athens sent an embassy to Herakleia on behalf of the *emporos* Herakleides to ask for the return of his ship's sails, which had been confiscated by the Herakleotes.

Enhanced opportunities for private ritualized friendships were another practical benefit of receiving honors from Athens. Athenian honors elevated the status and reputation of a man, signifying that he was good (*agathos*) and useful (*chresimos*) and performed benefactions not out of self-interest but rather because he had a love of honor (*philotimia*). Such a man was naturally a very desirable *xenos*, who could be assumed to have influence and be trusted to live up to the obligations of *xenia*. Because of this, those who received honors from Athens could expect to expand their network of friends and be able to count on their *boetheia* whenever needed. Moreover, ritualized friendship was not particular to the Greeks. Greeks were frequently involved in *xeniai* with non-Greeks, including Persians, Lydians, Egyptians, Phoenicians, and Romans. In fact, ritualized friendships akin to Greek *xenia* predate the latter by many centuries in Egypt.[31] Thus, non-Greeks as well as Greeks likely also desired Athenian honors for their practical use in expanding networks of *xeniai* and obtaining all the benefits that came with them.

It would seem to be a paradox that Athens honored foreign benefactors but not its own citizens who used their *xeniai* to procure benefactions from their foreign *xenoi* for Athens. After all, since the advent of the *polis* and the concept of citizenship, noncitizens were considered to be even lower in status than the lowest citizen. Lambert suggests that the absence of a regular practice of inscribing honorary decrees for citizens before the 340s might simply be the product of Athens' "epigraphic habit" (Lambert 2004: 86–87). In Lambert's view the regularization of such a practice was simply the result of an increasingly literate, bureaucratic, and epigraphic administrative culture in fourth-century Athens. But this explanation does not account for the fact that Athens commonly inscribed honorary decrees for foreigners well before the 340s.

Another explanation for the paradox (which is not mutually exclusive with Lambert's) concerns the tension between the masses and the elite among the Athenian citizenry. As noted above, the *demos* was reluctant to promote the private elite institution of *xenia*, even when it benefited the community, since it might encourage the *philotimia* of elite citizens too much, widen distinctions among the citizenry, and undermine the egalitarian ethos of democracy. Foreign benefactors, on the other hand, even if wellborn and wealthy and powerful in their own homelands, were no threat to the *demos'* control over politics in Athens. The *demos* could encourage unlimited *philotimia* among foreign benefactors without any negative repercussions. Moreover, when the Athenian state engaged in *xenia* with a foreign benefactor directly, with no elite citizen intermediary, the *demos* could feel confident that the foreign benefactor was its *xenos* alone, had no competing loyalties, and deserved a display of *charis* from Athens in the form of official honors.

For its part, the Athenian *demos* expected to receive further benefactions from its noncitizen *xenos* now that the two parties had completed the first cycle of gift exchanges. In return for honor and any *boetheia* he may have received, the *xenos* now had to show his *charis* to the *demos* of

Athens should it ever need his *boetheia*, whether it be an alliance, military aid, intercession on behalf of Athens with a foreign government, or other service. This explains why so many of Athens' foreign benefactors were awarded *proxenia*.[32] As the etymology of the word suggests, the institution of *proxenia* probably had its origins in *xenia*. It is simply an official, public form of *xenia* in which the community of the *polis*, rather than a specific citizen, bound itself in ritualized friendship with a foreign *xenos*. The *proxenos* was expected to act as a friend of Athens (as if he were kin to the Athenian citizenry) in his own land among his own people. Thus, if any Athenian should visit the *proxenos'* land, the *proxenos* was supposed to provide him with hospitality and see to his needs, whether he was visiting as a private citizen or as a representative of Athens on official business. Here again, therefore, we see an adaptation of a traditional elite institution, in this case *xenia*, so that it could now serve the needs of the broader community of the *polis* in the form of *proxenia*.

The majority of Athenian decrees honoring foreigners (primarily nonresident ones) for their benefactions involve, when we can identify their services, political, military, or financial ones.[33] This is not surprising, since, as we have seen above, *philotimia, timé, arete,* and the *aner agathos* had traditionally been associated with wealth, politics, and warfare, all of which were closely tied to the aristocratic ethos that continued to be influential in democratic Athens. After all, Classical democratic Athens needed political, military, and financial aid as much as Archaic aristocratic Athens had.

On the other hand, one would not expect to find foreigners being honored for services relating to *trade*. Despite the continuing growth of nonlanded occupations in manufacturing and trade in maritime Classical Athens, elite biases against *banausia* still persisted. Moreover, even though the *philotimia* of noncitizens was less threatening to the egalitarian ethos of democratic Athens than that of the citizen elite, it was one thing for the *demos* to honor an elite noncitizen for services relating to politics, military matters, or finances; it was quite another to honor him for services relating to trade.

So how can we explain the fact (as subsequent chapters will show) that Athens did honor noncitizens, elite and nonelite, for trade-related services? The basic answer should be clear from the preceding discussion and that of chapter 2: culture is not set in stone, unchanging, and fixed for eternity but is, in fact, subject to change. Although there were powerful social and political forces for maintaining values that had originated among the elite, groups and individuals among the masses of citizens and noncitizens and even among the elite themselves had contrary interests. Through their actions, they were able to "appropriate and subvert" elite values, adapting them to their own needs and/or what they saw to be the needs of Athens regarding trade. Thus, just as values were adapted to reduce the tension between the masses and the elite among the citizenry in political, military, and financial matters, so, too, were they adapted with regard to both elite and common noncitizens for similar activities and even those concerning trade. The role of trade in this adaptation of values has not received the attention it deserves in studies of the tension between the masses and the elite of Athens.

Of course, long-held social values do not change overnight, and the old and new can coexist indefinitely or not, depending on specific historical circumstances. The elite values that had their origins in the Homeric age were deeply entrenched throughout ancient Greek history. Greeks, whether citizens of Athens or other *poleis,* continued to value honor highly and considered it along with practical interests, including the desire for profit, when making decisions concerning the expenditure of money and/or the exchange of goods. Thus, wealthy Athenians were often willing to spend well beyond their legal obligations in the performance of liturgies, knowing that the *charis* it inspired in the *demos* would yield both honorific and practical benefits. These dual benefits also motivated those involved in gift exchanges among networks of ritualized friends, whether private *xenoi* or the citizenry of whole states, such as Athens.

Expressive rationality (see p. 32), which accounts both for cultural norms and for individual preferences in economic action, best explains the behavior of groups and individuals operating in specific historical contexts and the process by which cultural norms took shape over time in ancient Greece. All economies are indeed embedded in social relations, but since there is much variety in the structure of those relations and since those structures are subject to change over time, we generalize at the risk of oversimplification. As we shall see below, such changes occurred not only through the influence of the contest between the masses and the elite within Athens but also as a result of external political forces, the responses to which shaped the Athenian state's trade policy.

War, Peace, and Trade

According to Socrates, the chief concerns of the government of Athens in his day were (1) to protect the city from outside attack, (2) to obtain adequate revenues for the expenses of government, and (3) to make sure the citizenry had a sufficient supply of affordable food.[34] One can narrow down the policy debates on these issues to two basic positions: whether war or peace could best fulfill Athens' goals. The degree to which either policy was desirable or even feasible depended on a variety of internal and external factors, including one's socioeconomic status, ideology, and personal and political alliances; the abundance of domestic supplies of needed goods; the strength of the Athenian navy; and the actions of foreign powers. Since each of these factors was dynamic and shifted with particular circumstances over time, individuals and groups rarely remained wedded to one policy for extended periods. One consistent factor, however, which served as a "given" in all considerations of policy, was that from the mid-fifth century onward, Athens could not produce enough grain domestically to feed its population, a situation exacerbated from time to time by shortfalls in domestic production (see below). Whichever policy prevailed, it had to ensure the supply of grain from overseas sources.

Internal and external political factors influenced the means by which Athens could satisfy its needs for imported goods, particularly grain. Peter Garnsey classifies such means as force, diplomacy, incentive, and regulation (Garnsey 1988: 137–44). Athens employed all these methods to varying degrees during the fourth century, and the degree to which it emphasized one or the other was largely a function of internal and external politics. Force obviously coincided with a belligerent policy and required a strong navy and the absence of formidable enemies so that Athens could compel traders to ship their goods to Athens rather than elsewhere. Alternatives to force were diplomacy and incentive, both of which were elements of the Athenian practice of granting honors and privileges for trade-related services. Through diplomacy, Athens established agreements with foreign states not to harass merchants bound for Athens, to grant privileges in their ports for traders bound for Athens, or even to provide Athens with gifts of grain. Foreign states naturally required something in return, which they often received in the form of grants of honors and privileges from Athens, which had both honorific and practical benefits. Such grants also provided an incentive for individual traders as well as the leaders of foreign states and other wealthy men to provide Athens with imported goods. Besides their effectiveness as an alternative to force, grants of honors and privileges for trade-related services were also influenced by the politics concerning the tension between the masses and the elite and the decision whether to honor citizens, foreigners, or both. Regulation, which took the form of laws that required traders to bring grain to Athens, was the least influenced by politics, since such laws could be enforced at home regardless of the extent of Athens' power abroad and since both the masses and the elite agreed on their desirability.

The complex and dynamic interplay between politics and economics in Athenian grants of honors and privileges for trade-related services during the late Classical period contributed to the development of key characteristics of the Hellenistic period, including euergetism and the countless honorary decrees it inspired, the diminution of the power of the *demos* and the reassertion of aristocratic political dominance, and the breakdown of the Classical ideal of the exclusive *polis*. The impetus for the development of each of these characteristics was Athens' ever growing needs for revenue and imported food and its tradition of trying to meet such needs through the contributions of private individuals. With each new war, the needs became greater, and Athens had to adapt its practice of honoring trade-related services to meet them.

During the period of the Athenian Empire in the fifth century, the Athenian navy controlled the Aegean Sea and ensured that Athens was well supplied from external sources with vital goods, such as grain and timber, as well as revenue. There has been much debate on the subject, but even in the conservative view of Garnsey, Athens had to augment its domestic production of grain with supplies obtained from abroad in order to feed its population from as early as the mid-fifth century.[35] It is clear also that from at least 482, when Athens first built up its naval fleet, Athens could not supply itself with adequate ships' timber from domestic sources (Meiggs 1982: 121–23, 193). Hence, from around 480 to around 413, Athens' policy to ensure the supply of grain and timber while also bringing in revenue was quite simple: war. Athens used its powerful navy to control the sea, which enabled it (1) to colonize areas, such as the grain-producing islands of Lemnos, Imbros, and Skyros; (2) to force subject cities to pay tribute under the pretext of alliance and mutual protection; (3) to intimidate states to allow Athens to have access to their natural resources; and (4) to ensure that private traders were not prevented from bringing goods (most importantly grain) to Athens, which they were likely to do of their own accord for business reasons, since Athens was centrally located, possessed a good port, represented the single largest consumer market in the Aegean, and had desirable return cargo in the form of manufactured products and a widely circulating silver coinage. With few exceptions, Athens was able to carry out this policy. From the Battle of the Eurymedon River in the early 460s, when it destroyed the Persian fleet, until the loss of almost its entire navy as a result of the Sicilian Expedition (415–413), Athens dominated the Aegean Sea and the Hellespont, the vital sea route through which merchant ships brought grain to the Aegean from the fertile Black Sea region. It was so powerful that it could ensure its own supply of grain and timber while also determining who did and did not get such goods.[36] Thus, it appears that Athens felt no need to offer additional incentives to attract imports of grain and timber in the form of either sales from professional traders or gifts from foreign potentates. In contrast with its practice after 413, for example, although the Egyptian king Psammetichos gave Athens thirty thousand to forty thousand *medimnoi* of grain as a gift in 445/4 and although King Perdikkas of Macedon agreed at some time before 414 not to export timber to any other city besides Athens, there is no evidence that Athens honored these men or any other persons for a trade-related service during this time (see app. 3, R3 and R7).

In 413, however, the Spartan fortification of Dekeleia in Attika and the impending destruction of the Athenian fleet in Sicily severely strained Athens' revenues and threatened its supply of grain and timber. The fortification of Dekeleia virtually halted production at the lucrative silver mines of Laureion (Thuc. 7.27.5). In order to boost its revenues, Athens responded by replacing the tribute system with a 5 percent tax on all of its subjects' imports and exports carried by sea (Thuc. 7.28.4). The Spartan fortification of Dekeleia also hindered the production of grain in Attika as well as its import over land from Euboia (Thuc. 7.28.1). Even before the final destruction of the Athenian fleet in Sicily, the Syrakusans had destroyed ships laden with supplies from Athenian allies in Italy and burned ships' timber in Kaulonia that was also intended for the Athenians (Thuc. 7.25.). Moreover, with the destruction of Athenian fleet, many of its subjects, including Euboia, took the opportunity to revolt. This not only deprived Athens of revenue but also left it unable to keep merchants from shipping grain elsewhere or to protect them from piracy. Imports of other vital goods, particularly timber, which was needed to rebuild the fleet, were also further threatened, and Athens desperately sought them wherever it could (Thuc. 8.1.3). Not surprisingly, the earliest evidence of Athenian honorary decrees for trade-related services, two of which concern timber (nos. 4 and 6), date to this last phase of the war, beginning what was to become a trend in Athenian trade policy: when Athens was not powerful enough to control trade through force, it had to turn to peaceful means of fulfilling its trading needs, such as granting honors and privileges for trade-related services.

Athens' final defeat in the Peloponnesian War in 404 reduced its navy to a mere twelve ships and deprived it of its empire. Over the next ten years, the city could find no alternative source of revenue to offset the loss of tribute and taxes from its former subjects, and the slow recovery of silver-mining operations at Laureion only exacerbated the situation.[37] The grain supply suffered not only as a result of the now-tiny Athenian navy's inability to direct maritime trade but also on account of Athens' loss of control over the grain-producing islands of Lemnos, Imbros, and Skyros.[38] Moreover, having been scared off by the confiscations of the Thirty Tyrants and the civil war of 403, merchants were probably slow to return to Athens.

Athens' fortunes improved with the Corinthian War (395–386), which temporarily checked Spartan power and inspired a revival of Athenian imperial ambitions that would compete with peaceful means of obtaining food and revenue throughout much of the fourth century. The victory of a Persian fleet led by the Athenian exile Konon over the Spartans at Knidos in 394/3 and the subsequent rebuilding of the Long Walls of Athens with Persian aid gave Athens the strength to recover the grain-producing islands of Lemnos, Imbros, and Skyros in 392; to reject a Spartan peace offer in the same year; and even to capture Byzantion and restore its toll station on the Hellespont in 390. The reemergence of Athenian silver coinage in the late 390s shows that the mines at Laureion were beginning to be worked again, but there was no sense of urgency to exploit them to their full capacity.[39]

The grain supply was jeopardized again, however, when a Spartan fleet seized grain ships bound for Athens in the Hellespont in 387/6, while so-called pirates from Aigina harassed shipping in the Peiraieus. According to modern estimates, Athens' navy consisted of fifty to seventy triremes, which was not adequate to quell these threats (Gabrielsen 1994: 127 and n. 2). Lysias' speech *Against the Grain Dealers* adds that grain retailers (*sitopolai*) in Athens took advantage of the situation by raising their prices beyond the legal limit. More than any other concerns, it was these difficulties with its grain supply that compelled Athens to accept the King's Peace of 387/6 and to renew its efforts to employ peaceful means of obtaining imported grain (Xen. *Hell.* 5.1.28–29). Moreover, Lysias makes it clear that such efforts required Athens to promote the interests of the *emporoi* who provided it with grain (see also Seager 1966: 172–84). At around this time or shortly before, Athens also used diplomacy to establish with the ruling dynasty of the kingdom of the Bosporos in the grain-rich Crimea of the Black Sea a relationship that was to last for over a century, during which time the Bosporan kings provided numerous trade-related services for Athens (see the commentary on nos. 7 and 9 in appendix 3). An honorary decree for a Megarian who had performed trade-related services (no. 8) might date to this time as well.

Discontent among the cities of Greece with Spartan hegemony allowed Athens another military resurgence with the formation of the Second Athenian League of 378/7. Athens gathered together over sixty Greek cities to form an alliance that once again allowed Athens to have arguably the strongest navy in the eastern Mediterranean. For several years, Athens respected the alliance's safeguards against Athenian domination and prospered as a result. In fact, according to the first surviving naval lists of the Athenian dockyard superintendents, the fleet had increased in numbers from its level in 387, up to around one hundred triremes in 378/7.[40]

Nevertheless, another threat to Athens' revenues and trade occurred in 376/5, when the presence of a Spartan fleet off the southern tip of Euboia prevented merchant ships carrying grain from sailing to Athens (Xen. *Hell.* 5.4.60–61). Although at this time the Athenians were strong enough to send out a fleet and defeat the Spartans off the island of Naxos, according to Xenophon, piratical raids from Aigina and *eisphorai* to pay for military operations were wearing down the Athenians (ibid., 6.2.1). Athenian concerns for its financial and commercial well-being may be seen in a law of 375/4, proposed by Nikophon and instituting *dokimastai* (approvers) to monitor the quality of Athenian silver coins in the Agora and the Peiraieus. The law was designed to maintain the good reputation of Athenian silver coinage for quality and weight among foreign traders in order to avert a crisis in confidence that would have undermined demand for Athens' chief export (silver in the form of its coinage) and diminished the attractiveness of the Peiraieus as a destination for traders (Stroud 1974; Engen 2005). It might also have been in response to these difficulties of 376/5 that Athens passed a law in 374/3, proposed by

Agyrrhios (the uncle of Kallistratos), instituting an 8⅓ percent tax in kind on the grain produced by the cleruchs on Lemnos, Imbros, and Skyros, which would be collected by private merchants contracted by the state.[41] The grain would be sold to the citizenry of Athens, and the proceeds would go to the military treasury. Thus, by this law, Athens was able to supply its citizenry with grain while obtaining revenue at the same time.[42]

According to most accounts, the prosperity of Athens eventually gave rise to hubris, and Athens once again sought, as it had in the fifth century, to turn an alliance into an empire. By the end of the 360s, Athens had begun collecting "contributions" (*syntaxeis*, a euphemism for *phoros*, or "tribute") from the allies, had set up cleruchies in some recently acquired territories, and apparently had stationed garrisons and governors in some places.[43] It was also strong enough that simply by the threat of sending one hundred warships to the area, it could end an attempt by some Hellespontine states to seize grain ships in 362/1 ([Dem.] 50.17).

The hubris of Athens' renewed imperialism was struck down by a nemesis in the form of the Social War of 357–355, whose costs and adverse effects on trade inspired a new policy of peace abroad and exploitation of resources at home in order to fulfill Athens' needs for revenue and food. The Athenian naval records indicate a healthy fleet of 283 ships in the year 357/6, yet in the Social War, the allies of the Second Athenian League were able, with Persian aid, to revolt successfully from Athenian control, thus ending any realistic hope of Athens' ever restoring its fifth-century empire again, even if many in Athens never quite got this through their heads.[44] Athens' collection of *syntaxeis* from what was left of its league was severely reduced, and total annual revenue was down to 130 talents (Dem. 10.37). Although Athens retained its grain-producing cleruchies on Lemnos, Imbros, and Skyros, their security was always in doubt, since Athens no longer controlled the sea.

To these particular political crises may be added the possibility of prolonged drought coupled with overpopulation in Athens. John Camp has argued for the existence of an extended drought in Athens not only on the basis of periodic food shortages but also from apparent innovations in the design of private wells and from public efforts to construct more fountains in the third quarter of the fourth century (Camp 1982: 9–17). In fact, during this time, two overseers of fountains, important elected (rather than allotted) government officials, received public honors from Athens, the only two ever to have been so distinguished in Athenian history (*IG* ii² 215 and 338=Lambert 1.18 and 1.15, respectively). Also, Athenian cleruchies may be an indication not only of attempts at extending political domination but also of the need to reduce population pressures in Attika.[45] It is certain, however, that from the mid-fourth century onward, "Athens' food supply system was chronically insecure" (Garnsey 1988: 148). As Claude Mossé has pointed out, Athenians were unanimous in their concern to secure the grain supply. The debate was over how to accomplish this while at the same time securing enough revenue to pay for a navy strong enough to protect it (Mossé 1973: 54). The humbling of Athens in the Social War allowed those in the city who were opposed to attempts at resurrecting the empire to gain the ascendancy in politics and focus the city's efforts on finding peaceful ways of obtaining revenue and food.

Euboulos, who was the leading man on the board that administered the Theoric Fund between 355 and 344, is generally seen as the leader of this group, but its most vocal and articulate spokesmen were Isokrates and Xenophon.[46] The former's speech *On the Peace* details the adverse effect of war on revenues and trade, while the latter's *Poroi* offers concrete proposals for stimulating the production of the silver mines and encouraging trade, both of which would generate increased revenue for Athens. As quoted at the outset of this book, Xenophon's *Poroi* urged Athens to honor *emporoi* and *naukleroi* so that, "receiving honors as these, they would hasten here as to friends on account of not only the profit, but also the honor" (3.4). Xenophon explained that the consequent "rise in the number of residents and visitors would of course lead to a corresponding expansion of our imports and exports, of sales, rents, and customs" (3.5). Implicit in Xenophon's proposal is an understanding that in order for Athens to fulfill its interests in trade, it had to see to the interests of those who were responsible for trade, from foreign potentates all the way down the status hierarchy to common professional traders. Contrary to the view of Finley, such men would not simply benefit as an unintended by-product of Athenian policy; the satisfaction of their interests was integral to the success of Athenian trade policy.[47]

Though not often seen as an ideological bedfellow of Isokrates and Xenophon, Demosthenes seems to have shared many of their views on state trade policy in 355/4, as is apparent from his speech *Against Leptines*.[48] Demosthenes pleads with his fellow citizens not to rescind honors and privileges, including tax exemptions, granted to Athens' benefactors, on the grounds that they induce further benefactions that generate a net gain in both revenue and essential imported goods. As an example,

Demosthenes cites Leukon, king of the Bosporos, and his sons (20.30–40; see also nos. 9 and 12 in the present study). According to Demosthenes, the services of Leukon concern "things which our city especially needs," namely, imported grain. Leukon, who controlled trade in a region that provided Athens with much of its imported grain, granted an exemption from dues to the merchants who conveyed the grain to Athens and also allowed them priority in loading from his ports. Reckoning the total amount of grain that Athens imported from the Black Sea and the tax reduction granted by Leukon, Demosthenes concludes that Leukon's beneficence amounted to a gift of roughly thirteen thousand *medimnoi* of grain for Athens annually. In addition, during a severe grain shortage that occurred two years before the speech (357), Leukon had also sent a gift of so much grain to Athens that not only was the shortage alleviated but Athens was also able to obtain fifteen talents from the sale of either all or part of the grain.[49] If, Demosthenes continues, Athens were to revoke the honors and privileges granted to Leukon, it would at the same time be revoking honors and privileges enjoyed by "those of you who import grain from that man." Leukon would stop being a benefactor of Athens and would revoke the privileges he had granted to the merchants who conveyed grain to Athens from his ports. Athens as a whole would suffer by being deprived of much of its imported grain. Like Xenophon, then, Demosthenes believed Athens had to help fulfill the interests of those responsible for trade in order to fulfill its own interests in trade.

Xenophon and Demosthenes were not alone in their views on trade policy. Athenian honorary decrees themselves are explicit in describing the state's motivation for inscribing the text of decrees on stone stelai to be set up in public places for all to see. Although there are several formulae for the "hortatory intention," as the phrase that describes the motivation for inscribing the decree has come to be called, Alan Henry has categorized them into three basic types:

(A) in which future potential benefactors are encouraged by their *knowledge* that the Athenian People knows how to express its gratitude for services performed,

(B) in which stress is laid on *publicising* the evident fact of the Athenian People's gratitude

(C) in which the intention is to provide a *reminder* either of the service which led to the honour or privilege bestowed or of the People's gratitude.[50]

A good example of type A comes from *IG* ii^2 360 (nos. 24 and 27), which contains decrees passed by the People of Athens in the 320s in honor of Herakleides of Cyprian Salamis for his trade-related services. Lines 63–65 (closely echoed in lines 75–77) state that Herakleides' honorary decree shall be inscribed on a stone stele "in order that others also seek after honor, knowing that the Council honors and crowns those who seek after honor." The intent of Athens' practice of granting honors and privileges was not only to reward those who had performed trade-related services but also to encourage others to perform similar services. As Demosthenes 20.64 states, publicly displayed stone stelai bearing honorary decrees "stand as examples for those who wish to do good for you, that as far as they have done well for the city, the city had done well for them in return." This was not a passive practice in which Athens just hoped that benefactors would come along to help it with its import needs; rather, it was an active practice to induce trade-related services.[51]

That Euboulos effected policies along the lines suggested by Isokrates, Xenophon, and Demosthenes is indicated by the full revival of the mining industry and the expansion of institutions designed to encourage trade. The records of the *poletai* indicate a greater number of mining leases, and archaeological investigation shows increased exploration of silver veins at Laureion during this time (Crosby 1950: 205–25). Concerning trade, a clause in the Peace of Philokrates of 346 sought to protect traders from piracy, and Philip II of Macedon even acknowledged that the Athenian fleet was the police force of the Aegean ([Dem.] 58.53, 12.2, 7.14–15). Athens also improved the docks and provided hostels in the Peiraieus to make the port more accommodating to traders (Dein. 1.96; Cawkwell 1963: 64). Even more important, sometime between 355/4 and 343/2 Athens instituted the *dikai emporikai,* special law courts open to both citizens and noncitizens (which was unique among Athenian law courts) for the purpose of expediting disputes involving maritime loans for trading ventures during the winter months that were not preferred for sailing.[52]

In addition, if we can extrapolate on the basis of the surviving evidence, Athens seems to have invoked the practice of granting honors and privileges for trade-related services more frequently after 355/4 than beforehand. Whereas nine such decrees are extant that date from 413/12 to 356/5, there are twenty-five that date from 355/4 to 307/6 (see app. 1). Of course, it is possible that the apparent distribution is merely the result of the chance survival of the evidence or the so-called epigraphic habit of Athens (its increasing predilection for inscribing decrees on stone as the fourth century progressed). On the other hand, when one considers the advocacy of Isokrates, Xenophon, and Demosthenes for granting honors and privileges for trade-related services, it seems more likely that the greater number of surviving honorary decrees for trade-related services from the period after 355/4 is the product of a deliberate policy to promote trade (see below). Note, however, that there is evidence for only one certain honorary decree for trade-related services (no. 12) and four possible ones (nos. 10, 11, 13, and 14) that date between 355/4 and 338/7. It is difficult to explain why the number is not greater. Although there is no evidence for a major grain shortage in Athens and only one immediate threat to Athens' grain supply from after the Social War had ended down to 338/7 (Philip's siege of Byzantion in 340; see below), the grain supply was a chronic problem, and Athens did establish cleruchies in 353/2 and 344/3 in the Thracian Chersonese. Perhaps Athens' attention was focused more on its need for revenue than on its need for grain at this time, given Demosthenes' references to the depleted state of the treasury in the years immediately following the Social War (Dem. 10.37, 23.209).

In general, it appears that the period of Euboulos' prominence was a prosperous one for Athens, since there is no evidence for severe grain shortages, while annual revenues increased from 130 talents in 355 to 400 talents in 346 (Dem. 10.37–38; Theopompos *FGrHist* 115 F 166). Moreover, these revenues allowed the Athenian navy to continue to be strong enough so that even though it could not coerce revenue and goods from others, it could at least do much to minimize piracy against merchant ships. According to Demosthenes (14.13), Athens had 300 triremes in 354, and the naval records indicate the fleet consisted of 349 vessels in 353/2 (*IG* ii^2 1613.284–92).

The pacifist policies of Euboulos came under question as a result of the growing threat from Philip II of Macedon in the late 350s and 340s. Although Isokrates continued to advocate peace (at least within Greece) and actually looked to Philip to unite Greece and lead a land-grabbing crusade against Persia (Isokr. 5), Demosthenes appealed to his fellow Athenians' pride in their history as leader of the Greek world during the Empire of the fifth century and argued for strong action against Philip (Dem. 1–4, 6, 9–10). Looking back on these events in his speech *On the Crown* (18.301–2), Demosthenes explains that his main concerns were to protect Athens, maintain its alliances, and secure the sea routes for its grain imports. But Athens' response to Philip was slow, allowing him to take cities in the northern Aegean that were vital for securing the trade route from the Hellespont. Athens at least managed to prevent Philip's capture of Byzantion in 340, taking action only because Philip had seized merchant vessels carrying grain (variously reported as 230 or 180 ships), which was a direct threat to Athens' grain supply.[53]

All this was to no avail, as Philip decisively defeated Athens and its allies in 338 in a land battle at Chaironeia, thereby taking control of most of the Greek mainland and placing Athens' food supply, both from external sources through overseas trade and now also from domestic sources from the Attic countryside, in jeopardy (see Oliver 1995: 281–84). The city's immediate, panicked response reveals its deepest concerns at the time. Hypereides proposed citizenship for *metics* and freedom for slaves who volunteered for military service (Hyp. frag. 27–28 Jensen; Lyk. *Leokr.* 41). Although the proposal was rejected, it shows that even the hard line between citizens and noncitizens was negotiable, if the need were great enough. In response to a blockade of the Peiraieus and the seizure of grain ships bound for Athens by the Rhodians (Lyk. *Leokr.* 18; [Plut.] *Ten Orat.* 851a), Demosthenes was appointed to the position of grain commissioner (*sitones*), whose job was to obtain grain for the city—he himself contributed a talent of his own money to the fund set up for this purpose (Dem. 18.248; [Plut.] *Ten Orat.* 851b).

Philip turned out to be a lenient conqueror: he took Thrace and the Chersonese but did not invade Attika, and he allowed Athens to retain its cleruchies on Lemnos, Imbros, and Skyros as well as Delos and Samos. But from 338, Athens had to give up its imperial ambitions permanently and devote itself wholly to other means of obtaining revenue and grain. Athens created a new magistracy to administer the finances of the city (*ho epi ten dioikesin*). For a twelve-year period from either 338 or 336, this office was run either directly or indirectly by Lykourgos, whose implementation of policies that expanded on those of Euboulos resulted in the growth of Athenian revenues to almost unprecedented heights, some 1,200 talents per year (18,900 talents in all during his service), whereas they had been as low as 60 talents previously.[54] The peacetime sources of this newfound revenue varied, but most significant for this book are those that accrued as a result of Lykourgos' encouragement of voluntary financial contributions and promotion of trade, which could be taxed directly through import taxes and indirectly through taxes on the numerous *metics* who were active in commerce. Several wealthy citizens received public honors—some on the proposal of Lykourgos himself—for their voluntary financial contributions, often in conjunction with their performance of public offices.[55] The enhanced power and status accorded to these wealthy citizens for their largesse was a symptom of the erosion of egalitarian democracy and a precursor to a return to the "regime of the notables" that characterized the Hellenistic age (see below).

The large number of lawsuits involving commerce in our surviving literary evidence is a testament to the high volume of trade in Athens at this time, as are the cluster of at least nine honorary decrees for trade-related services (nos. 15–17, 21–24, 26, and 27)—with perhaps an additional five (nos. 14, 18–20, and 25)—issued between 338/7 and 325/4, including one proposed by Lykourgos himself (no. 17).[56] In addition, despite a lack of imperial ambitions, Lykourgos built up the Athenian navy to perhaps its strongest level ever, with warships numbering over four hundred, no doubt in part to contribute to the expansion of trade by protecting merchant vessels from piracy. The healthy treasury also allowed Lykourgos to initiate an extensive public works program that was reminiscent of the Age of Perikles.[57] Unlike that bygone era, however, Athens did not have an empire and did not extort its revenue from subject states; moreover, Lykourgos was an administrator and not a general. Clearly, the historical circumstances were different in the late fourth century from what they had been in the fifth, and Athens had to adapt to these circumstances by focusing on peaceful means of obtaining revenue and food in order to survive and prosper.

Though the city had built up a strong navy under Lykourgos, Athens' inability under Macedonian hegemony to use the fleet to control, rather than simply protect, trade, or coerce goods from subject states, as well as the threat that Macedon posed for Athens' domestic production, meant that the grain supply continued to be insecure. In fact, along with the destruction of most of its fleet in the Sicilian Expedition in 413 and the loss of its allies in the Social War in 355, Athens' defeat in the Battle of Chaironeia in 338 would prove to be another seminal event in the history of its trade policy, driving the state to expand its efforts to bring in revenue and food through trade.[58] In addition to a prolonged drought (see above), specific political emergencies contributed to at least five serious grain shortages (in 338/7, 335/4, 330/29, 328/7, and 323/2) and possibly eight (add 332/1, 329/8, and 325/4) in Athens between 338/7 and 323/2 (Garnsey 1988: 154–62). Besides the grain shortage brought on by Athens' defeat at Chaironeia in 338/7, another shortage occurred in 335/4 as a result of Thebes' ill-fated attempt to foment rebellion against Alexander and then of the latter's subsequent invasion of Greece.[59] The revolt of King

Agis III of Sparta in 331/0 and the campaign of Antipater to suppress it may have contributed to the grain shortage of 330/29, while the Lamian War and an associated naval battle in the Hellespont in 323/2 likely played a part in the shortage of that year.[60] Besides the honorary decrees for trade-related services passed during the Lykourgan period, Athens sought to cope with these difficulties by instituting the first *epidosis* (a call for voluntary financial contributions) for a purchase of grain in 328/7 and the establishment of a colony in the Adriatic to protect against pirates in 325/4.[61]

After the death of Alexander in June 323/2, the Hellenistic period began inauspiciously for Athens, as its attempt to shake off Macedonian control was crushed during the Lamian War. The Greek navy under the Athenian general Euetion was defeated in the Hellespont, and the land forces, having failed to capture the Macedonian army under Antipater at Lamia, eventually succumbed to the Macedonians in the Battle of Krannon. The naval defeat in the Hellespont naturally put the Athenian grain supply in jeopardy, and it is no wonder that there is surviving evidence for six honorary decrees for trade-related services that can be dated with some certainty between 323/2 and 319/18 (nos. 28–33) and another four that might date to this period as well (nos. 18–20 and 25). Antipater forced Athens to accept an oligarchic government, led principally by Phokion and Demades and supported by a Macedonian garrison in the Peiraieus that lasted from 322/1 to 318/7. Only citizens whose assets were worth two thousand drachmas or more had political rights, thereby reducing the franchise from twenty-one thousand to nine thousand citizens.

Over the course of the next few decades down to 301, Athens alternated between various degrees of democracy and independence, but almost always under the watchful eye of one or another of Alexander's Successors, on whom the city depended for its prosperity. Between 317 and 307, Athens was run by Demetrios of Phaleron, who, backed by Antipater's son Kassander and a Macedonian garrison in the Peiraieus, reigned as a benevolent tyrant.[62] Among the many blows to the power of the *demos* instituted by Demetrios of Phaleron was his abolition of the most visible of the liturgies, the *choregia*, replacing the elite competitors with one elected *agonothetes*, who oversaw the festivals and whose expenses were supposed to be reimbursed with public funds, though he often voluntarily provided many of his own (Wilson 2000: 270–76). Thus, the *demos* could no longer coerce the redistribution of wealth from the elite through liturgies but, in a throwback to Archaic, aristocratic euergetism, had instead to accept whatever contributions the elite chose to give to the community of its own accord.

Despite the appearance of a restoration of democracy in 307 by Demetrios Poliorketes, the reality was quite different. The liturgic system was not restored to its Classical form, and the dependence of the *demos* on the good graces of Demetrios Poliorketes was made manifest in a number of ways. Most significant for this study is that Demetrios Poliorketes, having ejected Kassander's garrison in the Peiraieus and in an effort to ingratiate himself on the population of Athens, supplied the city with gifts of 150,000 *medimnoi* of grain and enough timber for one hundred ships. The ploy worked: the *demos* not only accepted the authority of Demetrios Poliorketes and his father, Alexander's general Antigonos the One-Eyed, but also honored them as "kings" (*basileis*) and "savior gods" (*soteroi theoi*).[63] The *demos* was no longer in command but now had to cede authority back to the elite in order to obtain the security and resources it could not provide for itself.

It is clear, then, that during the Classical and into the beginning of the Hellenistic period, Athens' trade policy, whose aim was primarily to secure revenue and vital goods, such as timber and grain, was closely tied to political events, principally the shifting debate between those who wished to fulfill that trade policy through the use of military force and those who advocated a more pacifist policy that relied on diplomacy, legal regulation, and incentives to traders. When Athens had a dominating military power during the period of its empire in the fifth century, it was able to coerce others to supply it with the revenue and imported goods it required. After the loss of the empire and throughout the fourth century, however, the varying strength of Athens' navy and the shifting tides of external events limited Athens' ability to implement this policy to brief periods. For the most part and in the end, Athens had to employ more peaceful and more creative means of obtaining revenue and goods through trade, even if it ultimately meant a diminution of the power of the *demos* and a renewed ascendancy of the elite.

Conclusion: Into the Hellenistic Period

The Athenian state had an interest and involvement in trade that was closely intertwined with the political, social, and economic circumstances in which it found itself in the late Classical period. It sought to encourage trade largely in order to obtain needed imports, especially grain. It achieved this goal by acknowledging and appealing to the desire for both honor and profit among those who were responsible for trade, which included not only common professional traders but also foreign potentates, who engaged in market-oriented trade for profit as well as in gift exchange for honor. None of the men whom Athens honored for trade-related services before 290 were Athenian citizens by birth. Suspicious of the ambitions of the elite citizens of Athens, the *demos* could feel secure that honoring foreign benefactors posed no threat to democratic government. At the same time, however, the *demos* was further democratizing traditional elite values by extending honor and offering some or even all the privileges of citizenship to outsiders, some of whom were engaging in traditionally despised forms of trade. But these trends were to continue in the Hellenistic period only in part. By 290, circumstances had changed, and although Athens maintained its practice of honoring men for trade-related services, it stopped honoring professional traders for relatively small-scale benefactions. Instead, Athens began to honor elite native citizens along with foreign potentates who provided large-scale trade-related services, thus indicating a decline in the power of the *demos* and a reassertion of aristocratic power in Athenian government, which was to be a hallmark of the Hellenistic period.

Such conclusions add another perspective to the long-running debate about the ancient Greek economy and call key features of Finley's model into question. Although Finley's model of an unchanging, status-bound economy unable to develop market structures holds true in many ways, it oversimplifies the complexity of the ancient economy and does not account for the ways in which it responded and contributed to changing social values and political circumstances. The economy was indeed embedded in social relations that were highly influenced by concerns for status, but those social relations were fluid, allowing for individuals and groups to challenge social norms and instigate social change. The population of many Greek cities, particularly Athens, was involved in a long-standing struggle between the masses and the elite. During one phase of this struggle in the Classical period, elite values were democratized so that actions were deemed honorable only insofar as they served the *demos.*

Rather than a limitation, however, this new conception of honor expanded the range of honorable activities and men, since the *demos'* needs went well beyond the traditional parameters of elite concerns. Given the diminishing military power of Athens vis-à-vis its rivals, which became particularly acute as a result of the Sicilian Expedition (415–413) and its ultimate defeat in the Peloponnesian War in 404, again after the loss of the Second Athenian League in 355, and once more with its defeat in the Battle of Chaironeia in 338, it was imperative that the city find peaceful means of acquiring revenue and essential goods through trade. Yet Athens was either unable or unwilling to create entirely new government institutions and practices to achieve this end. Instead, it simply adapted preexisting institutions and practices, continuing to leave trade in the hands of private individuals, but now representing it as a praiseworthy activity in official honorary decrees whether the trade was carried out as a gift or a market exchange and whether those who were responsible for the trade were foreign potentates or common professionals of little wealth and low birth.

The complexity of historical change, however, is such that it does not necessarily follow a simple linear path toward an inevitable goal, and it turns out that while the trend toward extending honor to people of low status for such disesteemed activities as market trade did not continue far into the Hellenistic period, the trend toward extending honor to native citizen benefactors in addition to foreign potentates did.[64] There is only one likely example to show that Athens continued to honor professional traders for services relating to their profession after 319 (*IG* ii² 499).[65] In contrast to the one likely professional trader, numerous decrees show that Athens continued to honor foreign potentates (principally Alexander's Successors) for gifts of grain or money to purchase grain, and in the 280s, the city extended its practice to honor elite, native Athenian citizens for trade-related services as well.[66] A tentative explanation for this reversal is that by the beginning of the third century, increased needs for revenue and grain, coupled with its own diminishing power, compelled the *demos* not only to consider the services of professional traders to be insufficient but also to set aside its concern to maintain its own political supremacy in favor of obtaining the large-scale gifts that its elite citizens could provide. Preferring now to honor elite citizens and foreigners for large-scale gifts, Athens could return to the old elite values of disdaining market trade and professional traders, even though these traders were still probably responsible for the bulk of the aggregate movement of goods overseas and certainly did the dirty work of actually transporting the goods for which elite benefactors and public officials received all the honor.

Concomitant with the increasing reliance on and honor granted to both elite citizen and foreign benefactors for trade-related and other services is the declining power of the Athenian *demos* during the Hellenistic period. Paul Veyne has argued that the Hellenistic period should be characterized as a return to the pre-Classical "regime of the notables," to whom the masses conceded not only social status but also political power in return for their voluntary benefactions. Veyne characterizes these benefactions as "euergetism," a type of economic exchange in the substantivist sense that entails the "giving by an individual to the community" without the expectation of something material in return but with the result that the giver benefits in nonmaterial ways, most commonly through elevated social status and political influence.[67] Veyne traces back to the mid-fourth century the process whereby the elite in cities like Athens began to reestablish their preeminence after a period of egalitarian democracy (Veyne 1990: 85–94). Whereas the liturgic system was a tool with which the masses could compel members of the elite to redistribute their wealth, after 350 the *demos* increasingly allowed the elite to perform voluntary acts of euergetism that had the effect of legitimizing their claim to an elevated political as well as social and economic status.

Although Veyne's analysis holds true in general, it tends to oversimplify its picture of elite domination in the Hellenistic period and does not consider or acknowledge the role played by foreign benefactors who performed services relating to trade as a precursor to Hellenistic euergetism. Veyne presents the "regime of the notables" as a natural outcome of sociopolitical systems, given the ease with which the wealthy can shoulder the burdens of governing and the contrasting difficulty of the *demos* to do so (Veyne 1990: 83–85). But in the third century, the *demos* of Athens tenaciously exercised whatever political say it could maintain. Even in the most restricted periods, a large proportion of the traditional citizen population continued to have the right to participate in the institutions of democratic government and exercised its rights to the extent that it could.[68] It is true that honorary decrees for foreign benefactors in the late Classical period were "the model of the honorary decrees granted to citizens" that are so common in the Hellenistic period.[69] However, as Gauthier is careful to point out in his study of benefactors in the Hellenistic period, the Athenian *demos* maintained some control over the extent to which it would honor citizens (Gauthier 1985: 10, 16, 27, 68). Whereas foreign benefactors continued to receive the official status of *euergetai,* a practice that went back to the late fifth century, the *demos* never granted that status to a native citizen. Athens honored citizens for performing benefactions (*euergesia*) but would not grant them the status of *euergetai.* This seemingly small and often overlooked act shows that the *demos* was still fighting to promote its status in the political hierarchy of Athens and sometimes succeeded. Veyne failed to see how distinctions between the manner in which the *demos* honored citizens and foreigners made the triumph of the elite in its contest with the masses far from inevitable and still uncertain in the opening half century of the Hellenistic period.

Finally, although the line between citizen and noncitizen and between one *polis* and another never completely went away, it certainly became more blurred in the Hellenistic period, continuing the trend that can be seen in Athenian honorary decrees to foreigners for trade-related services, in which the ideal of the exclusive *polis* that had so characterized the Classical period was beginning to break down.[70] Some *poleis* were absorbed into the spheres of larger and more powerful kingdoms, while others that retained their independence sometimes granted the right of citizenship to the inhabitants of another city en masse (*isopoliteia*), thus diluting the citizen body and diminishing the prestige of citizenship (F. Walbank 1981: 150–52). Some philosophers went so far as to conjure up the notion of a *kosmopolis*, a "world city," unrestricted by the traditional bounds of the *polis* (Green 1990: 63–64). The Greeks who comprised the ruling class in the Hellenistic east came from a variety of cities, family backgrounds, classes, and statuses (F. Walbank 1981: 65–66). McKechnie argues that the increasingly mobile Greek population of the fourth century, whose members included traders and mercenaries, provided the politically unfettered manpower that allowed the Hellenistic kings to control large geographical areas with diverse populations (McKechnie 1989: 3–5, 10, 178–91). In addition, private institutions arose, such as the informal clubs known as *eranoi* or *thiasoi*, that were centered on social and religious activities and whose memberships did not discriminate between Greeks and non-Greeks or citizens and foreigners.[71] Such a breakdown of the Classical *polis* ideal of an exclusive and homogeneous citizen group was inadvertently encouraged by Athenian grants of honors and privileges to foreigners who had performed trade-related services.

Several aspects of this Athenian practice during the late Classical period, therefore, served as precursors to key developments of the Hellenistic period. As an illustration of the importance of fulfilling its trading needs, Athens granted foreigners who had performed services relating to trade a range of privileges that raised them up ever closer to the status of citizens and sometimes even to be citizens themselves. As this became more commonplace, traditional values concerning citizenship were eroded, and it was not, therefore, unprecedented for citizenship in the *polis* to lose some of its prestige and for the exclusivity of the *polis* to break down as it did in the Hellenistic period. Moreover, the increasing need for trade-related and other services that provided food and revenue for Athens also compelled the *demos* to honor its own elite citizen benefactors as it had foreign ones, thus officially elevating the status of elite citizens above that of their fellow citizens and acknowledging their claim to greater political authority, ushering in the "regime of the notables" of the Hellenistic era, even in the face of fierce resistance by the *demos*.

PART TWO   *Analysis*

CHAPTER FOUR

Goods and Services
WHAT DID ATHENS HONOR?

The general picture provided by Finley's model of an ancient Greek economy embedded in traditional social and political relations is that trade was disesteemed and, therefore, left to be carried out by small-time professional traders with little encouragement on the part of the state (pp. 6–7, 22, 24–25). The state formulated trade policy only to obtain revenue from taxes on trade and to ensure the import of essential goods for the citizenry. The state's interests in trade, therefore, were political and consumptive in nature (Finley 1985: 60, 160–62). The Athenian practice of granting honors and privileges for trade-related services provides an empirical basis with which to evaluate these tenets of Finley's model and their implications.

The present chapter examines the goods and trade-related services that merited honors from Athens. The goods in question seem to support Finley's model. It also appears, however, that the state's need for goods outweighed its desire for revenue and that the organization of trade in the fourth century was more complex than Finley realized. Finley, like Hasebroek, considered as "trade" only "a clearly defined and distinct form of economic activity, carried on by a class of whole-time professional traders."[1] Essentially, this definition of trade was a formalist one, involving impersonal exchanges of goods over long distances at prices determined through haggling for the purpose of making a profit. If one adopts the substantivist definition of trade, however, it is clear that trade was actually carried out by a variety of means, which ranged from gift exchange without the mediation of money to exchanges of goods at prices set by the market. Yet Athens was willing to grant honors and privileges to men who fulfilled Athenian trade interests no matter what their methods. Thus, although the Athenian practice of granting honors and privileges for trade-related services is very much in the spirit of an economy that is embedded in traditional social and political relations, the services that were honored are indicative of an economy that is embedded in those traditional relations in some ways but not in others.

This chapter also includes an examination of the frequency and chronological distribution of Athenian honorary decrees for each category of trade-related service and offers conclusions about the relative significance of each form of trade as well as changing attitudes toward them. It will be apparent that gifts of imported goods and sales of goods at prices reduced from the going rate accounted for more than a negligible percentage of Athenian trade, thereby calling into question Finley's failure to account for them. Moreover, the chronological distribution of honorary decrees for each category of trade-related service suggests that Athenian trade policy did not develop according to a preconceived plan or follow a gradual linear progression. It developed rather by fits and starts, in which Athens adapted its trade policy to meet unexpected and sporadic crises on an ad hoc basis.

Goods

In the twenty-five known cases of Athenian honorary decrees for trade-related services in which the trade goods can be identified, the goods are either foodstuffs (twenty-three cases) or ships' timber (two cases).[2] In all but possibly two cases, the food is grain. One exception concerns the import of fish, for which Athens honored Chairephilos and his sons (no. 16). No. 15 may also concern fish, but Lambert's new reading of the inscription makes that unlikely (see app. 3, no. 15). Whatever the case, it is clear that a primary goal of Athenian trade policy was to secure imported timber and food, particularly grain, and such a conclusion is confirmed by literary sources. For example, Demosthenes argues that the services of the Bosporan king Leukon were especially worthy of honor because they involved the import of grain (20.30–32). While also attesting to Athens' need for imported grain, Andokides' speech *On His Return* (2.11–12, 20–21) makes it clear that providing Athens with imported timber for the hulls and oars of warships should also be considered a service worthy of honor. Thus, the existing evidence for Athens' practice of honoring men for trade-related services supports Finley's model, which holds that the state's trade policy was motivated by a consumptive interest in acquiring necessary goods through imports (Finley 1985: 160).

The frequency with which Athens granted honors and privileges for services concerning trade in particular goods over the course of the fourth century is also significant. Most occasions involving foodstuffs, eighteen of twenty-three, occurred after 338, when Athens was beset with a series of grain shortages (nos. 15–27, 29–31, and 33–34). Garnsey identifies between five major grain shortages (in 338/7, 335/4, 330/29, 328/7, 323/2) and eight (add 332/1, 329/8, 325/4) in Athens between 338/7 and 323/2 (Garnsey 1988: 154–62). The two occasions on which Athens granted honors for services involving trade in ships' timber (nos. 4 and 6) occurred during the period between 410 and 407, when Athens, having lost most of its fleet in the Sicilian Expedition in 413, was trying to build up its navy again. Andokides says that his procurement of timber for oar spars from King Archelaos of Macedon in 411 was essential for the Athenian fleet at Samos to defeat the Spartans and save Athens (2.11–12). The coincidence of the greater frequency of Athenian honorary decrees for trade-related services with particular historical circumstances that heightened the need for imports argues for the value of the evidence as representative of actual practice, despite its small quantity. It is likely that the existing evidence has not been distorted either by the chance survival of some inscriptions and literary references or developments in the "epigraphic habit" of Athens.

The evidence also diminishes the emphasis that Gernet, Hasebroek, and Burke have placed on the acquisition of revenue as a motive for the trade policies of Greek states.[3] Gernet in particular argued that obtaining revenue was Athens' chief interest in trade until the late fourth century, when shortages of grain made Athens prioritize its acquisition (Gernet [1909] 1979: 347–85). But the decrees show that Athens honored men for providing it with imported goods, both grain and timber, even before the middle of the fourth century (nos. 4, 6, 7, and 9). Moreover, Gernet does not account for the variety of trading services or legal and socioeconomic statuses of the honorands, both of which indicate a complex distributional scheme and a varied set of motivations over time, which prohibited the practice of honoring men for trade-related services from following a simple linear scheme of development (see below and chap. 5).

More recently Burke has offered another argument in favor of Athenian trade policy's emphasis on obtaining revenue.[4] He cites Xenophon's *Poroi* 2.1–7 and 3.3–5, which advocates honoring trade-related services in order to increase the state's revenues. According to Xenophon, honors would attract more traders, thereby increasing tax revenue from trade. Although we should not ignore revenue as a goal of Athenian trade policy, the honorary decrees themselves are virtually silent about it. The only references to the monetary contributions of the honorands concern a gift of money and possibly also a loan of money that are used to buy grain (nos. 27 and 14, respectively). There is no mention of tax revenues to be obtained as a result of the activities of the honorands.

On the other hand, in seventeen of the twenty-five extant honorary decrees for trade-related services, Athens explicitly stated the types of goods involved in the services (nos. 4, 6, 11, 12, 15, 17–21, 24, 25, 27, 29– 31, and 33). Of the eight other extant decrees in which the types of goods are not explicitly mentioned, six contain lacunae that allow for the possibility that the types of goods were mentioned in the full decree (nos. 1, 3, 10, 13, 14, and 23). In only two of the twenty-five extant decrees (nos. 8 and 28) is it certain that Athens did not identify the specific types of goods involved in the trade-related services.

Naturally, Athens would probably not wish to proclaim a desire to exploit its benefactors for tax revenue in its honorary decrees, but the frequent mention of the types of goods begs for an explanation. Athens most likely had a need for those goods and used its honorary decrees in order to fulfill this need. The decrees, which were inscribed on stone stelai and placed in public venues, made potential benefactors aware of the goods that the city needed. In addition, the decrees also informed the People of Athens that the government was doing everything in its power to secure the imported goods that they desired. Thus, Athenian grants of honors and privileges for trade-related services point to a greater emphasis of Athenian trade policy on obtaining imported goods rather than revenue.

Services

Among the wide variety of trade-related services that were honored by Athens, it is possible to distinguish five broad categories:

- the gift of imported goods free of charge
- securing shipments of goods
- the sale of imported goods at a reduced price from the going rate
- the simple importation of goods
- miscellaneous trade-related services

Among these services, only the simple importation of goods meets the formalist definition of trade as an impersonal exchange of goods at market prices. According to the broader substantivist definition, however, all the services relate to trade, since they contribute to "a relatively peaceful method of acquiring goods which are not available on the spot" (Polanyi 1957b: 257–58).

Gifts of Imported Goods

On five of the thirty-four occasions on which Athens honored trade-related services, the honorands had given the city a gift of imported goods (or the money to buy them) free of charge (nos. 6, 9, 22, 23, and 27). This service constituted the most traditional and esteemed manner in which to trade goods that we see in Athenian honorary decrees. Goods were exchanged not impersonally and for immediate monetary profit but for an array of other interests particular to personal ties of ritualized friendship (see pp. 47–53). Thus, the gift of imported goods is most indicative of an economy embedded in traditional social and political relations and is most consistent with Finley's model.

When the honorary decrees are explicit, they refer to gifts of imported goods or the money to buy them with the following words and phrases: "he had given to them timber and oar spars" (no. 6; *IG* i^3 117.30); "he offered to the People to give" them grain (no. 23; *IG* ii^2 363.9–10); and "when there were *epidoseis*, he gave 3,000 drachmas for a purchase of grain" (no. 27; *IG* ii^2 360.11–12). Contrary to the view of Bresson (Bresson 2000: 136), we can be confident that even though these decrees employ the verb *didomi* without an explicit mention of a "gift," they are in fact referring to gifts of goods free of charge, since there is no explicit mention of the price of the goods, as is the case in other decrees that employ the word (nos. 21 and 24). On the two other occasions on which Athens granted honors to men for gifts of imported goods (nos. 9 and 22), both the epigraphic and literary sources are less explicit, and one must infer that imported goods were given free of charge (see pp. 286–87, 301).

On three of the five occasions on which Athens honored men for gifts of imported goods, the honorands were not professional traders and surely did not sail with their goods to Athens (nos. 6, 9, and 20). The significance of the status of these honorands, whom I have categorized as "foreign potentates" in this study, will be examined in chapter 5. For now, I will simply note that they or Athens probably hired professional traders to ship the goods. According to a law of 374/3, the Athenian state hired private traders to transport grain that was collected as a tax in kind for Athens from the islands of Lemnos, Imbros, and Skyros (Stroud 1998). In such cases, the traders were not acting as true entrepreneurs in shipping the goods of others to Athens. They neither initiated the enterprise nor risked any capital to purchase the goods in the hopes of making a profit on them after transport and resale. They were merely hired labor, and they were not recognized by Athenian honorary decrees.

The gifts of imported goods certainly went to the state, which in turn redistributed them to the citizenry. In his speech against Leptines (20.33), Demosthenes tells a panel of lawmakers that once during a shortage of grain, King Leukon of the Bosporos "not only sent enough grain to us, but so much that fifteen talents of silver, which Kallisthenes administered, accrued in addition." Although Demosthenes' language is not precise, his statement is sufficient to show that Leukon's gift was managed by the Athenian government, which either distributed the grain free of charge to its citizenry and then sold the surplus for a profit or, more likely, sold all the grain to the citizenry at a fixed price, thus obtaining the stated profit (see p. 333, n. 49).

Although three of the five Athenian honorary decrees for gifts of imported goods occurred during the grain shortages of the 330s and 320s, the other two grants occurred long before, in 407/6 and 389/8.[5] Thus, Athens recognized this particular service almost from the inception of its practice of honoring trade-related services. The case of no. 6 was motivated by immediate need, since Athens was desperate for the oar spars provided by King Archelaos of Macedon during the Peloponnesian War in 407/6. Occasion no. 9, however, was not for any immediate service but rather a renewal of honors and privileges for continuing services (including gifts of imported goods) by the kings of the Bosporos on the accession of Leukon to sole rule in 389/8. It is not surprising, however, that Athens would honor the gift of imported goods at an early date, since gift exchange was a traditional and esteemed institution in Greek life going back to Homeric times. Also consistent with traditional values was the fact that both honorands held high status as foreign potentates (see pp. 114–17).

Those who gave Athens gifts of imported goods, whether they were professional traders or men of high status who did not normally engage in trade, could not have been motivated by an entrepreneurial interest in making profits. Their service yielded no direct monetary profit for themselves and actually resulted in the loss of substantial wealth. Herakleides of Cyprian Salamis, a professional trader and the honorand of no. 27, gave

Athens three thousand drachmas, or half a talent, to purchase grain. Dionysios, another professional trader, is said to have given Athens three thousand *medimnoi* of grain (no. 23). If the grain was wheat, his gift amounted to fifteen thousand drachmas, or two and a half talents, at the normal price of five drachmas per *medimnos* (see pp. 86–88, concerning grain prices). Even if the grain was barley, for which the normal price was three drachmas per *medimnos*, his gift was still substantial, amounting to nine thousand drachmas, or one and a half talents. If Harpalos' gift of grain (no. 22) is identical with the grain listed on the famous Kyrene grain distribution list, it amounted to one hundred thousand *medimnoi* of grain. If the grain was wheat, then Harpalos' gift was five hundred thousand drachmas, or eighty-three and one-third talents. If the grain was barley, then his gift was three hundred thousand drachmas, or 50 talents. The fact that these men clearly did not desire monetary profits from their exchanges with Athens is consistent with Finley's model of an embedded economy. It should be noted, however, that the honors and privileges they received from Athens in return for their gifts had both honorific and practical benefits, as we shall see in chapters 6–8, and one could see the practical benefits as simply a nonmonetary form of profit.

The existence of Athenian honorary decrees for gifts of imported goods should be sufficient to prove that this type of exchange was an important aspect of Athenian trade in the late Classical period; nevertheless, it may also be possible to determine the significance of these exchanges by measuring them against estimates of the amount of grain consumed by individuals and of annual Athenian grain imports. Herodotus 7.187 indicates that the typical daily ration of wheat for a soldier while on campaign was one *choinix*, which is the equivalent of 0.02 *medimnos*. Of course, this does not necessarily tell us how much grain was normally consumed by an Athenian civilian, who would not have been as austere as a soldier on campaign and surely would not have been limited to an all-wheat diet. In his speech *Against Leptines*, Demosthenes states that the four hundred thousand *medimnoi* of grain that arrived in Athens from the Bosporan kingdom accounted for half of all Athenian grain imports (20.33). If we take this statement at face value, then it follows that total Athenian grain imports amounted to eight hundred thousand *medimnoi*. Unfortunately, Demosthenes does not say whether this sum was an annual figure or relative to some other period of time. Moreover, although the figure of four hundred thousand is probably accurate, since Demosthenes says that it can be verified by the records of the *sitophylakes,* the context and purpose of the speech are such that Demosthenes likely exaggerated the percentage of total Athenian grain imports that this sum represents.

The best we can do in terms of quantitative analysis, therefore, is to create a range of possible numbers for individual grain consumption and annual grain imports based both on the ancient evidence and on modern estimates, even though modern estimates are even more problematic than the ancient evidence (see pp. 15, 328 n. 16). I will use Garnsey's estimates, since he is well known for minimizing Athenian needs for grain imports and downplaying the significance of trade in ancient Greece (Garnsey 1988: 89–106). Using the ancient evidence, if we assume that the figure of eight hundred thousand *medimnoi* of grain from Demosthenes 20.33 represents the total *annual* imports of Athens, Dionysios' gift of three thousand *medimnoi* of grain (no. 21) would amount to 0.375 percent of the total. At the other end of the scale, the gift of one hundred thousand *medimnoi* of grain from Kyrene, which may have occurred at the instigation of Harpalos (no. 20), accounted for a sizable 12.5 percent of Athens' total annual grain imports.

If, on the other hand, we follow Garnsey's estimates, then we arrive at much different numbers. Garnsey believes that Athens produced enough grain domestically to feed up to 150,000 of its total population of between 120,000 and 200,000 people in the fourth century (Garnsey 1988: 90, 104). Thus, according to Garnsey, "Attica was capable of feeding . . . under normal conditions" almost all of its resident population in the fourth century (ibid., 104–5). At the height of its population in the fourth century, at 200,000 people, Athens would then have needed to import only enough grain to feed 50,000 of them. If, as Garnsey assumes, a person "likely" consumed 175 kilograms of grain per year (ibid., 91 and n. 6, 102), then 50,000 people would have needed 8,750,000 kilograms of grain a year. If we assume that this sum consisted of equal proportions of wheat and barley (4,375,000 kg each), then using Garnsey's estimates of 40 kilograms per *medimnos* for wheat and 33.4 kilograms per *medimnos* for barley (ibid., 98), Athens would have needed to import 240,363 *medimnoi* of grain per year to supplement its domestic production and feed its entire resident population. Under these assumptions, Dionysios' gift would amount to approximately 1.3 percent and the Kyrene gift to approximately 42 percent of Athens' total annual imports of grain.

There is no way of knowing for certain how much grain the Bosporan kings gave to Athens as a gift in 357 (see no. 11), but it is possible to make a rough estimate. As commonly (though not necessarily rightly) interpreted, Demosthenes 20.33 indicates that this gift not only sufficed to alleviate a grain shortage at Athens but also resulted in a surplus that was sold for fifteen talents (see p. 333, n. 49). There are six thousand drachmas in a talent, so the total sale of the surplus amounted to ninety thousand drachmas. If we assume that this surplus grain consisted of equal proportions of wheat and barley, then we can also assume that the grain was sold for an average of 4.25 drachmas per *medimnos*, which is the mean between the normal price of wheat, 5.5 drachmas per *medimnos*, and that of barley, 3 drachmas per *medimnos* (see pp. 87–88 concerning the normal price of grain). The total surplus of grain (wheat and barley combined), then, was 21,177 *medimnoi*.

To arrive at the total amount of the gift of the Bosporan kings, it is necessary to add the foregoing sum, which represents only the surplus from the gift, to the portion of the gift that was distributed to Athenians free of charge. Garnsey's estimate for the "likely" consumption of grain (wheat and barley) by an individual in Classical Athens is 175 kilograms of grain per year, which equals 0.013 *medimnos* of grain per day (see above). The gift was probably distributed free of charge only to the adult male citizen population, since such a practice is attested in the case of the gift of the Egyptian king Psammetichos in 445 (Plut. *Per.* 37; Philoch. *FGrHist* 328 F 90). If we assume that the adult male citizen population of Athens was twenty-five thousand in 357 (see above), then it would have taken 325 *medimnoi* of grain to feed them all for one day. If the gift of grain was sufficient to feed all of them for two weeks (in order to alleviate the immediate shortage), then we arrive at a sum of 4,550 *medimnoi* of grain for the amount of the Bosporan gift that was distributed to Athenian citizens. When combined with the surplus amount of 21,177 *medimnoi*, the total amount of the gift is 25,727 *medimnoi* of grain, or 3.2 percent of Athens' total annual grain imports set at 800,000 *medimnoi* of grain. If we follow Garnsey's figure of 240,363 *medimnoi* for total annual Athenian grain imports (see above), then the gift of the Bosporan kings amounts to 10.7 percent of the total.

Although we should not put too much weight on such rough estimates, it is clear that the nonmarket, gift trade of both foreign potentates and professional traders was significant enough to show that the Hasebroek/Finley model suffers from a kind of tunnel vision in considering as trade only exchanges that were both initiated and carried out by professional traders in the pursuit of profit. Hasebroek's statement that trade in ancient Greece "was a clearly defined and distinct form of economic activity, carried on by a class of whole-time professional traders," is a misleading overgeneralization (Hasebroek 1933: 4). Not only do the known cases in which Athens granted honors and privileges for those who had provided gifts of goods free of charge comprise a significant percentage of total annual Athenian grain imports, but if one considers the possibility that there may have been other cases for which the evidence no longer survives or other gifts that were not recognized with honors, then the significance of gift trade in Athenian trade policy and the ancient Greek economy in general becomes even more pronounced.

Securing Shipments of Goods

On three occasions, Athens honored those who had secured shipments of goods (nos. 13, 20, and 31). In performing such a service, the honorands were not acting as entrepreneurs seeking profits. Instead, since this service was carried out free of charge and facilitated the import of goods, it differed little in spirit from the gift of imported goods described above.

On one of the three occasions, the honorand provided an escort (*pompe*) for merchant ships (no. 31), guiding their shipments of goods safely to their destination. This act may have entailed protecting merchant ships from attacks by pirates or hostile navies; navigation to avoid hostile ships, areas of natural dangers, or getting lost; or a combination of both protection and navigation. On the two other occasions, the honorands provided protection to secure shipments of goods, but the form that such protection took is uncertain. The fragmentary nature of no. 13 does not reveal how the honorands secured shipments of goods, but it is likely that they did so in some way, since they appear to have been recognized for enforcing the decree of Moirokles, which forbade anyone from harming traders. *IG* ii^2 416b.6–12 states that the honorand of no. 20 "takes care of both the *emporoi* and the *naukleroi* in order that grain sails in as plentifully as possible for the People of Athens and no one of the Athenians either is hindered by anyone unjustly or forced into port." In both cases, the honorands provided some form of protection for shipments of goods, but whether such protection was military, legal, or diplomatic in nature is uncertain.

There is no indication that the honorands of nos. 13 and 20 were themselves directly involved in trading exchanges. Rather, they facilitated the exchanges between merchants and Athens by providing protection for the shipments of goods. On the other hand, the honorand of no. 31 was a professional trader who himself shipped goods in addition to providing guidance or protection for the shipments of others (see app. 3). There is no way of knowing whether one or the other of his services, the simple importation of goods or securing shipments of goods, was more decisive in Athens' decision to honor him. In the cases of the honorands of nos. 13 and 20, however, it is clear that Athens honored them not for engaging in trade themselves but for helping others to do so. Since providing protection and guidance was a more traditionally esteemed activity than trade, Athens was staying well within the confines of an economy embedded in traditional social and political relations when it honored this service.

Even though the honorands who secured shipments of goods were not exchanging goods themselves, they could still have profited monetarily from the performance of their service. Services and time, like goods, have value that can be quantified by price. But since there is no indication that the honorands charged either Athens or the traders whose goods they helped to secure, it is likely that the honorands undertook all the costs of the services without the prospect of making a monetary profit. Like those who gave imported goods to Athens as gifts, those who received honors and privileges for securing shipments of goods had no entrepreneurial interests.

All known Athenian honorary decrees for those who had secured shipments of goods occurred in the second half of the fourth century.[6] It is surprising that evidence for such a traditional service does not appear earlier. Given the random survival of the evidence, we can never be certain that Athens did not honor this service earlier, but if the surviving evidence reflects the actual chronological distribution of such grants, perhaps there simply was no one who had performed this service for Athens until the second half of the fourth century. It is hard to believe, at any rate, that Athens would not have felt the need to honor those who secured shipments of goods before that time. Although Athens was able to maintain a fairly powerful navy down to its loss in the Social War in 355/4, there were periods of weakness, including the years 413–407 and 404–394. In addition, Athens was compelled to accept the King's Peace of 387/6 because the Spartans had seized grain ships in the Hellespont and because the Aiginetan "pirates" were harassing ships in the Peiraieus (see pp. 57–58). So there definitely were occasions on which Athens would have been grateful to receive the help of others to secure shipments of goods before the mid-fourth century.

After the mid-fourth century, however, things got much worse for Athens as Philip of Macedon encouraged and even joined with pirates to hinder merchants who provided goods for the city.[7] To meet this increasing threat, Athens not only intensified its efforts to use its navy to protect merchants who shipped goods to Athenians at home and abroad, but also began to encourage this service from private individuals.[8] During the grain shortages of 337–320, Athens could not afford to allow pirates to hinder any merchants who shipped goods to Athenians. Perhaps it is no coincidence, then, that we find that Athens continued to send out naval expeditions to deal with pirates and to honor those who had helped to secure shipments of goods during this time.[9]

Sales of Imported Goods at Reduced Prices

On four of the thirty-four occasions on which Athens honored those who had performed trade-related services for the city, the honorands had brought goods to Athens and sold them at a reduced price from the going rate (nos. 15, 21, 24, and 33). Athens obviously benefited from such a service, which made more grain available at a lower price than would otherwise have been the case. For their part, the honorands gave up potential profit, but they still made sure to retain some money from the sale of goods for themselves. Thus, this service stands at a midpoint between gifts of imported goods free of charge and simple importations of goods for sale at market prices (see below), complicating our picture of the ancient Greek economy and the degree to which it was embedded in social and political relations.

Athenian honorary decrees indicate that traders sold their goods at a reduced price in a variety of ways. In the case of no. 15, *IG* ii² 283.3–4 states that the honorand had "brought grain . . . at a reduced price" ([ἐσιτ]ήγησεν . . . εὐωνοτέρων). For occasion no. 24, *IG* ii² 360.8, 29, 55, and 67 simply states that the honorand "gave" (ἐπέδωκεν) grain (identified as wheat in line 8) at five drachmas per *medimnos*. We know that this price was less than the going rate in Athens, because other sources inform us that wheat was selling at between sixteen and thirty-two drachmas per *medimnos* at that time.[10] *IG* ii² 400.6–8 states that the honorand of no. 33 promises to "give over" (παραδ[ώ]σ[ειν]) grain at "the established price" ([τῆς καθισταμ] ένης τιμ[ῆ]ς), which must refer to a price reduced from the going rate (see app. 3, no. 33). It is likely that the honorands of no. 21 also sold their grain at a reduced price, since *IG* ii² 408.13 states that they "gave" ([παραδεδω]κέναι) their grain at nine and five drachmas per *medimnos* of wheat and barley, respectively. Had these prices been the going rate, the decree would not have made explicit mention of them (see below).

It is possible to appreciate how much this service benefited Athens and how much sacrifice it entailed for those who performed it by considering the honorands' selling price in relation to the normal price of grain in the late fourth century and the much higher price of grain during specific shortages. Based on Athenian sales of public grain in the last half of the fourth century, it seems that the normal market price of wheat and barley at that time in Athens was five to six drachmas per *medimnos* and three drachmas per *medimnos,* respectively. On one occasion during the series of grain crises in the early 320s, the Athenian Assembly voted to sell public wheat among citizens at six drachmas per *medimnos* and barley at three (*IG* ii² 1672.283, 287). When the price of wheat skyrocketed to sixteen drachmas at another time during that period, Athens sold public wheat to its citizens at five drachmas per *medimnos* ([Dem.] 34.39). It is likely that the Athenians set the price of public grain at a level that approximated the market price under normal circumstances.[11]

During the grain crisis of 330/29, Herakleides of Cyprian Salamis, the honorand of *IG* ii² 360 (no. 24), sold his grain to Athens at five drachmas per *medimnos.* At this time, wheat sold for sixteen to thirty-two drachmas per *medimnos* and barley for as many as eighteen (see above and n. 10). It is likely that Herakleides purchased his cargo of grain for a price that was closer to the equivalent of the normal, noncrisis market price in Athens, since he probably obtained his grain in Egypt, which was a major source of grain for Greece at this time via a commonly used trade route that included stops in the Levant and Rhodes and skirted his homeland of Cyprus.[12] The grain crisis of the 320s apparently affected the whole of Greece and perhaps other areas of the eastern Mediterranean. Although Egypt was also adversely affected, it seems that it avoided the worst of whatever conditions gave rise to this crisis, most likely a drought, since the Nile River provided Egyptian crops with an almost unfailingly secure source of water ([Arist.] *Oik.* 1352a16). It was during this time that Cleomenes, Alexander's governor of Egypt, was able to capitalize on Greece's shortage of grain by buying up Egyptian supplies and shipping them to wherever in Greece he could obtain the highest price ([Dem.]

56.8; [Arist.] *Oik.* 1352a16). For Cleomenes to have profited from this scheme, the price of grain in Egypt had to have been lower than it was in Greece. Therefore, it is safe to assume that the going price of wheat in Egypt was somewhere in between the normal, noncrisis market price in Athens of five to six drachmas per *medimnos* and the inflated price of sixteen to thirty-two, perhaps around ten drachmas per *medimnos*.

IG ii² 360 records several honorary decrees for Herakleides that mention the same sale of grain at a reduced price. In some of the decrees, the type of grain is not specified; in one (line 9), however, it is referred to as wheat. If the grain in question was wheat, Herakleides sold it at a big discount off the going price, at five drachmas per *medimnos* instead of sixteen to thirty-two. Herakleides saved Athenians at least eleven drachmas per *medimnos* on three thousand *medimnoi* of wheat, for a total of thirty-three thousand drachmas, or five and a half talents (Garnsey 1988: 154). At the same time, however, he did not give the wheat to Athens as a gift, free of charge. He lost potential profits and probably some of his original investment as well, but he made sure to recover at least a portion, if not all, of his original investment.

The sale of imported goods at a reduced price was a service whose motivations lay somewhere between the nonentrepreneurial interests behind the outright gift of imported goods and the entrepreneurial interest in maximizing profits that we see in the simple importation of goods (absent the incentive of receiving Athenian honors, of course; see below). By honoring Herakleides' sale of imported goods at a reduced price, Athens was implicitly condoning an economic activity that was not entirely embedded in traditional social and political relations. The honorands were not as magnanimous in their generosity as they might have been, and their concern not to give up too much of their own money rivals their desire for the honors and privileges that Athens had to offer. Forging and maintaining social and political relations, therefore, was apparently not the sole principle that governed the economy of Greece at this time. Perhaps it is because their service betrayed a concern for money and departed from the traditional standards of gift exchange that there is no extant evidence to suggest that Athens granted honors and privileges to those who had sold imported goods at a reduced price until after the Battle of Chaironeia in 338.[13] It may have been that Athens was reluctant to honor professional traders who had performed trade-related services that were closely tied to the traditionally disesteemed activities of the market until it was compelled to do so by the frequent grain shortages of that period.

Another issue of interest concerning the sale of imported goods at reduced prices is the question, to whom did the honorands sell their goods? It is possible that they sold their goods wholesale to retailers, from whom the People of Athens then bought the grain in smaller amounts. Since the official "grain guardians" (*sitophylakes*) of Athens kept records of the prices at which retailers purchased grain from overseas traders, the state could conceivably have noticed those traders who had sold their grain for less than the going rate, or it at least could have had evidence supporting requests for their honors (Arist. *AP* 51.3).

Another possibility, which seems more likely, is that the state itself purchased imported goods at a reduced price directly from traders. During the grain shortage of 330/29, grain imported by private traders, who claimed to have sold the grain at a reduced price, was distributed to Athenian citizens by being "measured out in the Pompeion," which is a public building in Athens ([Dem.] 34.39). Athens also had public officials known as *sitonai* whose job was to secure grain for public distribution (Dem. 18.248). The *sitonai* no doubt obtained funds to purchase grain from *epidoseis*, monetary contributions from private individuals to the state, such as the one in 328/7, which was used for the public purchase of grain (Garnsey 1988: 82).

If Athens did indeed use public funds for purchasing grain at reduced prices from professional traders for distribution to its citizenry, then the Athenian state involved itself directly in trade. Athens' involvement would have taken the form of providing both money and honors to professional traders in return for their imported grain. If Athens had offered money alone, it would undoubtedly have had to pay the going, rather than a reduced, price. The honors made up for the monetary difference between these two prices. Even if Athens did not use public funds to purchase the grain, its honors and other benefits associated with them were still a factor in inducing the honorands to forgo profit and sell their grain to the Athenians at a reduced price (see chaps. 6–8). In either case, the Athenian state's involvement in the sales of goods at a reduced price cannot be easily categorized as characteristic of market or gift exchange. It has some of the characteristics of both and points to the dynamic and complex nature of the Athenian economy in the late Classical period.

Finally, as in the case of gifts of imported goods free of charge, it is possible to create a rough quantitative illustration of the significance of sales of imported goods at reduced prices by comparing them to individual grain consumption and annual Athenian grain imports based both on the ancient evidence and on modern estimates. Given Herodotus' statement (7.187) that a soldier's daily ration was a *choinix*, or 0.02 *medimnos*, of wheat and Garnsey's view that the adult male citizen population of Athens in the fourth century was around twenty-five thousand (Garnsey 1988: 89–90), then five hundred *medimnoi* (25,000 × 0.02) of wheat would be necessary to feed the adult male citizen population of Athens every day. According to these estimates, Herakleides' sale of three thousand *medimnoi* of wheat at a reduced price (no. 24) could have fed the adult male citizen population of Athens for almost six days (3,000 *med* ÷ 500 *med*/day). If we adopt Garnsey's assumptions for the average annual consumption of grain (wheat and barley combined) for an individual (see above; 175 kg grain = 4.8 *med* = 2.2 *med* wheat + 2.6 *med* barley = 87.5 kg ÷ 40 kg/*med* wheat + 87.5 kg ÷ 33.4 kg/*med* barley), then it would take 120,000 *medimnoi* of grain to feed the entire adult male population of Athens for a year (4.8 *med*/person × 25,000 persons) and 329 *medimnoi* of grain to feed the entire adult male population of Athens for a single day (120,000 *med*/yr ÷ 365 days). According to these estimates, Eucharistos' sale of eight thousand *medimnoi* of grain at a reduced price (no. 33) and promise to sell another four thousand *medimnoi* on the same terms could have fed the adult male citizen population of Athens for almost thirty-seven days (12,000 *med* ÷ 329 *med*/day).

Alternatively, we can measure the significance of Eucharistos' sale of imported grain (wheat and barley combined) at a reduced price as a percentage of total Athenian imports. On the basis of Demosthenes 20.33, which might indicate that annual Athenian grain imports (wheat and barley combined) amounted to eight hundred thousand *medimnoi*, Eucharistos' sale of twelve thousand *medimnoi* of grain at a reduced price comprised 1.5 percent of the total. If we adopt Garnsey's assumptions concerning the population of Athens and the amount of grain it could produce domestically, then Athens would have needed to import 240,363 *medimnoi* of grain per year to supplement its domestic production and feed its entire resident population (see above). Eucharistos' sale of twelve thousand *medimnoi* of grain at a reduced price represents close to 5 percent of this sum.

Such estimates, though again rough, tend to support the notion that sales of imported grain at reduced prices were an important aspect of

Athenian trade. Each estimate above considered only one case in isolation. It is possible that in any given year (especially when there were shortages of grain), additional cases occurred (for which there is no surviving evidence) in which Athens honored someone for the sale of imported goods at a reduced price. There may have been even further cases that Athens chose not to honor. This is likely, given the evidence provided by [Dem.] 34.38–39, in which the trader Chrysippos claims that he and his brother sold grain to Athens at a reduced price on several occasions, for one of which the amount of grain was ten thousand *medimnoi*. Chrysippos does not mention that Athens granted him and his brother honors for their services, nor do we have any other evidence that it did so. One wonders how many other such benefactions went unrecorded. By any measure, therefore, it is safe to say that sales of imported goods at reduced prices were an important part of Athenian trade and that the Hasebroek/Finley model suffers from their omission.

Simple Importations of Goods

On six of the thirty-four occasions on which Athens honored trade-related services, the honorands were responsible for a simple importation of goods to Athens (nos. 16–19, 25, and 31). I have chosen the term *simple importations* to refer to exchanges in which imported goods were sold at the going price set by the market. Such a service typically involved impersonal exchanges of goods initiated by men of low legal and socioeconomic status for the sole purpose of making a profit. By honoring these men and their services, Athens pushed the envelope on traditional Greek values concerning economic activity and the exclusiveness of the *polis.*

The reasons for believing that the goods in these six cases were sold at the going price are as follows. The epigraphic and literary sources refer to the trade-related services with words that have roots in ἄγω (bring, carry) or κομίζω (convey, bring), indicating that the honorands personally brought their goods into Athens, which in turn makes it likely that they were professional traders. By the fourth century, many of those who sailed the seas with cargoes for trade were not simply amateurs looking to unload some of their surplus agricultural produce in a nearby port (like Hesiod ca. 700) but rather professionals, referred to in the ancient sources as *emporoi* (traders) and *naukleroi* (shipowners), who routinely undertook long-distance, multiple-destination trading ventures (often financed at least in part by maritime loans) that were their primary means of making a livelihood (see pp. 109–13, and Reed 2003: 6–14). The honorands in the six cases in question were likely to have been such professional traders. It would be hard to believe, for example, that the Herakleote of no. 18 was an amateur who sailed directly from his home on the Crimean Peninsula on the Black Sea all the way to Athens simply to unload some of his surplus agricultural produce. It is much more likely that he had engaged in numerous trading ventures throughout the Black and Aegean seas, but happened to be honored for one that took him from an intermediate port to Athens.

In addition, unlike other cases in which the decrees employ words derived from ἄγω or κομίζω (nos. 6, 15, 21, 24, 27, and 33), in these six cases there is no indication of the price at which the honorands sold their goods or that they either sold their goods at a reduced rate from the going price or gave their goods to Athens free of charge. It is reasonable to assume, therefore, that the honorands sold their goods at the going price, which was typical of professional traders described in the literary sources. By the late fourth century in Athens, the going wholesale price for at least some imports, particularly grain, was determined by market mechanisms. Since there has been much debate on price formation in ancient Greece, it is necessary to justify this statement.[14]

Finley emphasized that the ancient Greco-Roman world did not have a market economy. By this he meant that the economy was not a conglomeration of interconnected price-making markets in which "there was a direct link between production and prices in *both* producing and consuming centres" (Finley 1985: 177). He is right, in general. But as is often the case with Finley's model, it is too general and obscures the fact that there were some sectors of the economy in which such a link did exist between suppliers (either those who traded or those who produced goods) and consumers, whose aggregate interaction resulted in the formulation of prices.

For example, in [Dem.] 56.7–9, the speaker describes the schemes of Cleomenes, Alexander the Great's governor of Egypt. Cleomenes bought up Egyptian grain for resale. If his agents informed him that grain was expensive (*timios*) in Athens, he would ship his grain there. But if prices fell in Athens, he would ship his grain elsewhere. The speaker says that this was the chief reason why the price of grain rose in Athens, which indicates his awareness that a decrease in the supply of grain in Athens caused the price of grain there to rise. A few lines later, the speaker places together the arrival of ships from Sicily (that they were loaded with grain is implied) with a decrease in the price of grain.[15]

Xenophon corroborates that Greeks understood the market relationship between supply and price, at least for some goods. In *Poroi* 4.7–10, Xenophon states that the demand for silver alone of all commodities is not diminished when supply increases. Although his view is obviously in error, he does understand (*Poroi* 4.6) that with regard to other goods (he specifically names grain and wine), when supply increases, prices decrease, and so do profits for the producers of such goods. We can be sure, therefore, that supply was one of the factors that determined prices in the overseas trade in grain and probably in wine and timber as well.

Finley acknowledges that "prices fluctuated considerably and rapidly, with an almost instantaneous response to changes in supply" (Finley 1985: 178). Yet Finley dismisses such price fluctuations as only "a temporary imbalance between supply and demand," which "of themselves . . . had no structural effect on grain production and not necessarily even on the profits of the producers" (ibid.). But whether a market determines a price that stands for one day or for a year is irrelevant; either way, the market still determines the price. If the relative levels of supply and demand never change, then prices would never change either. Moreover, is it necessary that a link exists between the *producers* of a good and its consumers in order for the market to formulate prices? Supply is not simply a matter of production. If middlemen exist through whose control goods must pass between producers and consumers, then they will determine the supply. It was middlemen in the form of foreign potentates and professional traders who determined the supply of imported grain in Athens, not primarily the producers themselves. Therefore, Finley's dismissal of price fluctuations in response to changes in supply sounds like special pleading simply to make his point that, *in general,* ancient Greece did not have a market economy.

But "exceptions" to the general rules of Finley's model are significant and should not be ignored. To be sure, there does not seem to have been a vast array of interconnected markets that determined the prices of all goods in ancient Greece. Moreover, many individual sectors of the economy, such as manufacturing, do not exhibit the kind of connection between supply and prices that are characteristic of a market system. But some sectors, such as the overseas trade in grain, do exhibit characteristics of a market economy, at least in the late Classical period.[16] The ancient Greek economy was not a monolithic, static entity. In the absence of a dominating governmental control of the economy, each sector developed freely and independently of others in accordance with the particular circumstances that prevailed in each.

The simple importations of goods honored by Athens likely resembled the trading ventures described in the private orations attributed to Demosthenes.[17] Professional traders in the fourth century typically raised a sum of capital (often with the contribution of investors), used the capital to cover the costs of acquiring a cargo from an overseas port (which included the cost of the cargo itself; the cost of transportation; and the cost of harbor, import/export, and/or transit taxes), transported it to Athens, and then sold it at the going price, which was hoped to be sufficient to cover the initial investment (including interest due to outside investors, if any) and leave them with a profit. Not only did traders (and any investors) take the risk that the sale price of the cargo might be less than the purchase price, but they also risked the loss of cargo in transport, owing to the dangers of traveling by sea, including bad weather and piracy.[18] In fact, it is because overseas trading ventures were so financially risky (especially for the investors) that the interest charged by investors ranged from 12.5 to 30 percent, which was much higher than the 3 percent typically charged for loans on landed security.[19]

Although Finley's brief suggestion (1985: 141, 252 n. 82) that maritime loans for trading ventures should be considered "as an insurance policy rather than as a form of credit" has been accepted with little argument, it is true only in part and greatly overstated. If traders purchased their cargoes entirely with their own funds, then they would also have to bear the loss of those cargoes entirely on their own. By Finley's logic, using investors' money to buy a portion of their cargoes would shift some of the risk of losing cargoes from the traders onto their investors. This is true but only to an extent. Millett, though very much a proponent of Finley's model, has been one of the few scholars to challenge his teacher's notion of maritime loans as insurance policies (Millett 1983: 44). For one thing, the insurance would cover only a portion of their cargoes. One can assume that traders would be able to sell the cargoes purchased with borrowed funds for an amount that would cover the interest they would have to pay to their investors, while still leaving some profit for themselves. It is only this profit that traders insured by taking on investors. The portion of the cargo purchased with borrowed funds is not insured for the traders, since it is not their cargo to begin with, and they are not held responsible should it be lost. Whatever portion of the cargoes that the traders purchased with their own money is also still "uninsured," since the traders would still bear the full financial responsibility for that portion of their cargoes should it be lost. Also, the assertion that traders took out loans for insurance contradicts a fundamental tenet of Finley's own model, which is that traders borrowed money for their ventures because they were poor and could not otherwise afford to trade. Finally, since professional traders sailed with their cargoes, what good would it do to insure them if the traders were also likely to go down with their cargoes in the event of a shipwreck?

Unless one is wedded to Finley's a priori rejection of entrepreneurship and productive investment in the ancient Greek economy, there is no reason to doubt that at least part of the motivation for traders to invest their own funds and borrow additional capital through maritime loans and for investors to provide these loans was to make a profit from their trading ventures. Despite his critique of Finley's insurance policy idea, for example, Millett (1983: 44–45) goes to desperate, but ultimately ineffective, lengths to maintain the notion that maritime loans did not constitute productive credit. Millett's argument "depends on Hasebroek's theory that traders were for the most part poor men who were forced to borrow to earn their living." Thus, traders sought loans "from necessity, not from choice," Millett argues, adding, "and that is one of the key distinctions between consumption and productive credit." This argument is circular, however, since the whole point of Millett's argument is to show that "on the role of maritime loans in the financing of trade—Hasebroek got it right" (Millett 1983: 39). It is unsound logic to make Hasebroek's argument (that traders must have been poor because they took out maritime loans) the assumption for another argument (that since traders took out loans from necessity, they do not constitute productive credit), which is then used as the basis for the general argument that "Hasebroek got it right" on the role of maritime loans in financing trade. A much simpler conclusion is that traders and investors participated in maritime loans in order to profit from their ventures in a sphere of the economy that was organized according to market principles.

One should be justified, then, in considering professional traders in Classical Greece to be "entrepreneurs" or "capitalists," but since Finley argued that these terms are inappropriate for the ancient world, further examination is necessary.[20] Much confusion arises simply because scholars do not agree on the definitions of these terms. Weber, whose works influenced Finley greatly, struggled to define the term *capitalism* precisely.[21] In one work, Weber writes simply that the pursuit of profit constituted capitalism (Weber [1909] 1976: 51). In another work, Weber holds that capitalists not only pursue profit but also renew profit by continually reinvesting their profits in order to make more (Weber [1904–5] 1958: 17). Yet Weber believed that capitalists thus defined have also existed throughout the history of civilization, including in ancient Greece (ibid., 19–20). What distinguishes capitalists of Classical times (whom he sometimes refers to as "precapitalists") and "modern capitalists" (whom he sometimes calls simply "capitalists") is that only in the modern Western world has the "spirit of capitalism" become a socially esteemed end in itself, so that capitalists attain satisfaction not from increased wealth but from their success at being capitalists, of which profits are merely the measure. In ancient Greece, Weber argues, traditional values prevented such behavior from ever becoming socially esteemed (ibid., 21–22, 51–78). In a later work, Weber distinguishes between six different types of capitalism (Weber [1921] 1978: 164–65). Although Weber states that his first type, "orientation to the profit possibilities in continuous buying and selling on the market ('trade') with free exchange—that is, absence of formal and at least relative absence of substantive compulsion to effect any given exchange," is peculiar to the modern Western world (ibid.), it, too, applies to the activities of the professional traders of Classical Greece as described by the Attic orators.

Weber's shifting definitions of "capitalism" have confused subsequent scholars to the point that even his admirers have mistakenly contradicted him by denying the existence of capitalism in ancient Greece. Both Finley and Millett, for example, do not distinguish between Weber's notion of ancient Greece as a "precapitalist" society and a "noncapitalist" society in which capitalism does not exist at all.[22] But the major distinguishing feature between a "precapitalist" and a "capitalist" society in Weber's view is whether a "spirit of capitalism" predominates, not whether capitalism exists. Indeed, Aristotle's famous condemnation of unnatural acquisition (chrematistike), the endless desire to acquire wealth solely for the sake of further acquisition, is another proof that such behavior existed and was prevalent enough to alarm the philosopher (Pol. 1256b40–1258a14).

There is no reason, therefore, to doubt that professional traders in ancient Greece were indeed "entrepreneurs" and "capitalists" (even if on a small scale) and that all six cases in which Athens honored those who had performed simple importations of goods are likely to have been such men. Although the desire for Athenian honors may have been a factor that induced them to bring their goods to Athens instead of another port where they might have obtained greater monetary profit for their cargoes (see chaps. 6–8), they still prioritized profit to the extent that they would not give their goods away as a gift or even sell them for anything less than the going rate.

It is difficult even to make a rough estimate of what percentage of Athenian trade was carried out according to the type of transactions that typified simple importations of goods. Unlike its practice concerning gifts of imported goods and sales of imported goods at reduced prices, Athens did not explicitly state the amount of goods exchanged when it honored men for simple importations of goods. It is reasonable to assume, however, that the market exchanges that comprised such a service accounted for whatever trade was not carried out either through gifts free of charge or sales at reduced prices. Although these latter two types of trade were significant, they typically constituted a minority of Athens' total annual imports (see above). Therefore, it is probably the case that the majority of Athenian trade consisted of market exchanges carried out by professional traders, which is the type of trade emphasized in the Hasebroek/Finley model (see pp. 21–22, 24–25).

The model underemphasizes, however, that the existence of such market trade is evidence that at least some sectors of the ancient Greek economy were not embedded in traditional social and political relations but organized according to impersonal market mechanisms. Yet Athens encouraged such market activities by honoring the men who carried them out as if they were performing traditional gift exchanges. The reasons for Athens' actions will be examined in further detail in chapter 5. Suffice it to say for now that the chronological distribution of honorary decrees for simple importations of goods might help to explain this phenomenon. All six grants occurred after the Battle of Chaironeia in 338/7.[23] Given the chance survival of ancient Greek inscriptions, one cannot be certain that there were no such grants before that time. But it would not be surprising, owing to the traditional disdain for professional traders and impersonal market exchanges, if Athenians had been reluctant to honor simple importations of goods before the late fourth century.

After 338/7, however, several grain shortages occurred in Athens, following its defeat at Chaironeia, when Alexander invaded Greece and destroyed Thebes in 335/4, and during the period of 330–323/2, from other political disruptions quite possibly coupled with an extended drought.[24] Thus, as the fourth century progressed, Athens needed more imported goods than it could obtain either by gift exchanges or by allowing the market to determine the quantity of imports on its own. In response to this need, Athens may have adapted its practice of honoring gifts of imported goods to include sales of imported goods at reduced prices and even simple importations of goods as well. Stretching the venerable institution of gift exchange to include the market activity of simple importations of goods may have been preferable to creating radically new ways of obtaining imports, even if it warped the traditional values embodied in the personal relationships fostered by gift exchange.

Miscellaneous Trade-Related Services

I have categorized as "miscellaneous trade-related services" those that do not correspond to any of the above four categories (nos. 7, 9, 11, 12, 14, 26, 29, 30, and 34). On the occasions of both nos. 29 and 30 Athens honored men for "sending" (*apostello*) grain to the city. Unfortunately, the extant portions of the honorary decrees do not provide further information about the service. There is no indication whether the honorands gave the grain as a gift to Athens, sold it at a price reduced from the going rate, or sold it at the going rate.

Kirchner restored *IG* ii^2 423, our only source of evidence for no. 14, to read in lines 13–15 that Athens honored Philomelos for lending money to the state during a grain shortage (ἐν τ[ῆ ι σιτοδείαι προεδάνεισ?]ε χρή-ματα [. . . 6 . . . χρήσιμον ἑαυτὸν παρα]σχόμε[νος . . .]). Assuming that this highly speculative restoration is right, one would also assume that Athens used the borrowed money for a purchase of imported grain. There is good evidence that Athens accepted outright gifts of money for such a purpose (no. 27). In this case, however, the honorand merely loaned ([προεδάνεισ?]ε) money to Athens. There is no indication in the decree that Philomelos expected interest on his loan. But whether the loan was at or free of interest, it was clearly not a gift. The honorand either profited from the transaction or at least broke even (excluding present value). This service, therefore, would be akin to the sale of goods at a reduced price. In both cases, honorands gave up potential profit but did not give away wealth that they already possessed. Thus, concerns both for material need and for social and political relations are present in the service performed by the honorand and the honors offered by Athens on the occasion of no. 16.

The only source of evidence for no. 11 (*IG* ii^2 207) is beset with numerous epigraphic problems that obscure the precise nature of the services for which Athens granted honors and privileges to Orontes, the Persian satrap of Mysia. It appears, however, that Orontes received honors for providing grain to the Athenian army while it was on campaign (see app. 3, no. 11). Orontes' service for Athens involves elements of both gift and market trade. Although there is no indication of the price that Orontes charged for the grain, he clearly did not give the grain free of charge. But whether he charged the market price, a higher one, or a reduced one, he certainly was not acting simply as an entrepreneur. This was not an impersonal exchange organized by the market and carried out to make a profit. Rather, as a Persian satrap, Orontes surely had political considerations in this transaction with Athens that counterbalanced any concerns for profit. Yet, as much as this transaction linked Orontes and Athens in a political relationship, since Orontes did charge Athens for the grain, it cannot be considered a pure gift exchange either.

Athens' trading relationship with the kings of the Bosporos also mixed political and trading interests but was maintained over a much longer period of time and is much better documented than that between Athens and Orontes.[25] From almost the outset of the fourth century and well into the third, Athens and the Bosporan kings were involved in a ritualized friendship sealed, reaffirmed, and renewed by periodic gift exchanges, in which Athens provided honors, privileges, and other benefits while the Bosporan kings provided various trade-related services, such as gifts of grain, exemption from export taxes, and priority in loading in Bosporan ports to those who shipped grain to Athens. Satyros was the first Bosporan king to provide Athens with these trade-related services on a permanent basis and to have been officially honored by Athens in return. The inception of Satyros' policy and Athens' honors for him took place sometime between ca. 395 and 389/8. Leukon continued to provide the trade-related services for Athens initiated by his father. In turn, Athens granted Leukon the same honors and privileges it had granted Satyros, probably in 389/8. On their accession to the corule over the Bosporos in 347/6, Spartokos II and Pairisades I continued to provide such trade-related services to Athens, which in turn honored them much as it had honored Leukon previously. After the death of Spartokos II in 344/3, Pairisades I took over as sole ruler of the Bosporos until his death in 311/10. It seems that there was a reorganization of both the trading and the political relationships between Athens and the Bosporos during

Pairisades I's reign as sole monarch, resulting in his obtaining further grants of honors from Athens. It is likely that Eumelos (r. 310/09–304/3) continued to provide Athens with the trade-related services reinstated by Pairisades I and received honors in return, since the relationship continued at least down to 285/4, when Athens honored Spartokos III for his continued services to Athens.

Finley (echoing Hasebroek) was not far off in characterizing the trading relationship between the Bosporan kings and Athens as an example of gift exchange rather than a "commercial agreement" in the modern sense.[26] Not only did the Bosporan kings give Athens an outright gift of grain on at least one occasion, but by exempting traders who brought grain to Athens from export taxes and by giving them priority in loading from their ports, the Bosporan kings were reducing traders' costs. Therefore, traders could sell their imported grain in Athens for a lower price than their competitors and still make a profit. Athenian citizens who purchased this imported grain in Athens would naturally benefit from these lower prices. In fact, based on the total amount of grain that Athens imported from the Black Sea and the tax reduction granted by the Bosporan kings, Demosthenes reckoned that their services amounted to the equivalent of a gift of thirteen thousand *medimnoi* of grain for Athens (Dem. 20.31–32). Note, however, that Athenians typically still had to purchase grain from traders who shipped it from the kingdom of the Bosporos. The thirteen thousand *medimnoi* of grain identified by Demosthenes was more like a price reduction than an outright gift, representing the additional amount of grain Athenians could afford as a result of the lower prices created by tax reductions. Note also that the Bosporan kings did not eliminate taxes on ships bound for Athens entirely. Thus, like the sales of imported goods at reduced prices, although the trade between Athens and the Bosporan kingdom certainly is not indicative of an unfettered market economy, neither is it an example of pure gift exchange in an economy embedded in traditional social and political relations. The perspective of the Bosporan kings in providing their trade-related services for Athens will be examined in chapter 5.

Conclusion

The picture presented by Athenian grants of honors and privileges for trade-related services conforms in many respects to Finley's model of the ancient Greek economy. Judging from the honorary decrees alone, one would have to say that the state's interest in trade was almost purely consumptive.[27] Moreover, the means by which Athens sought to fulfill its interests in trade are indicative of an economy that is largely embedded in traditional social and political relations. But such a picture is painted on a rather broad canvas. On closer inspection, one sees that the ancient Greek economy was more complex and dynamic than Finley's model would have us believe.

Athenian honorary decrees indicate that although the state had primarily a traditional, consumptive interest in trade, the trade itself was carried out in a variety of ways that were sometimes very untraditional. To fulfill its primary interest in obtaining essential imported goods Athens drew on the institution of ritualized friendship to create social and political ties that required gift exchanges that would supply the city with imported goods in return for Athenian honors and privileges. But the trade-related services that constituted such "gifts" on the part of the honorands varied considerably. Some involved actual gift giving, in which honorands had given Athens imported goods as a gift, free of charge. Others involved activities and motivations on the part of the honorands that were completely antithetical to gift exchange and characteristic of market exchanges, such as the sale of imported goods at the going price. Still other honored services occupied a gray area between gift and market exchange, such as the sale of imported goods at a reduced price, which contained elements of both types of exchange. The existence of such a variety of trade-related services honored by Athens indicates that overseas trade was carried out in diverse ways that call into question any notion that the economy of Greece in the late fifth and fourth centuries can be characterized according to a single organizing principle.

The chronological distribution of known Athenian honorary decrees for the various types of trade-related services might suggest that the complexity of overseas trade was also a function of changing trends over time in the manner in which trade was both carried out and esteemed. Whereas Athens honored the gift of imported goods as early as 407/6, less traditional trade-related services, such as the sale of imported goods at a reduced price or the simple importation of goods, do not appear in Athenian honorary decrees until after the Battle of Chaironeia in 338/7. At the same time, perceptions of trade also seem to have been changing. Athens began to represent traditionally disesteemed methods of trade, such as market exchange, as if they were just as worthy of honor as more traditional methods of trade, such as gift exchange. A plausible reason for this is that historical circumstances—such as Macedonian hegemony and the constant challenge to the Athenian navy to safeguard seaborne trade against increasing threats from private and state-sanctioned piracy, as well as frequent and sometimes severe shortages of grain due to droughts and other threats to domestic and foreign production—drove the People of Athens to take increasingly extreme measures to ensure the import of grain during the latter half of the fourth century.

Consequently, Athens broadened the criteria for acceptable "gifts," to establish ritualized friendships that would better ensure the import of goods as the threats to its supply increased. It would not have stretched the traditions of ritualized friendship too much to grant honors and privileges in return for gifts of imported goods. But granting honors and privileges for the market exchanges that constituted simple importations of goods turned tradition on its head. Yet Athens represented the service of simple importations of goods in much the same way as it did gifts of imported goods, because it needed whatever imported grain it could get, even at the market price, during a shortage. By representing the actions of those who performed traditionally disdained forms of trade as being worthy of honor after 338/7, Athens encouraged such activity and inadvertently contributed to whatever circumstances were already disembedding the economy from traditional social and political relations.

CHAPTER FIVE

Honorands

WHOM DID ATHENS HONOR?

Finley's model of the ancient economy considers as "trade" only impersonal exchanges of goods transported over long distances at prices determined through haggling in local markets. Such a nonlanded activity that served to break down traditional social relations was disesteemed and left to men of low status or outsiders who, because they could not own land on account of legal restrictions or poverty, were professionals who depended on trade for their livelihood (Finley 1985: 35–61, especially 60). Hasebroek, to whose work Finley's model is clearly indebted, summarizes the situation thus: trade "was a clearly defined and distinct form of economic activity, carried on by a class of whole-time professional traders," who were "entirely . . . metics" and "largely, if not predominantly, of non-Greek extraction."[1] Moreover, "if we may judge from those of them who appear in the private speeches of the Athenian orators," Hasebroek continues, they "were invariably without any capital worth mentioning of their own" and, therefore, "had to depend entirely upon borrowed funds for carrying on their business" (Hasebroek 1933: 4, 7, 10, 22).

   Over the last thirty years, several scholars have used the literary evidence to argue either in support of or against the Hasebroek/Finley model, but they have failed to reach a consensus, which is a testament to the inadequacy of the literary evidence by itself and an argument for supplementing such evidence with epigraphic sources.[2] Hence, it is refreshing that C. M. Reed, in his recent book *Maritime Traders in the Ancient Greek World* (2003), uses epigraphic evidence, including Athenian honorary decrees for trade-related services, to formulate a typology of those responsible for trade. Unfortunately, on the assumption that only market trade constitutes "trade," he ignores other forms, such as gift trade and the nonprofessionals who were responsible for it (see chap. 2, Economics or Sociology?, and Reed 2003: 17 n. 8). Consequently, Reed ultimately supports the view of the Hasebroek/Finley model concerning those who were responsible for trade in fourth-century Athens: they were professionals who were mostly poor non-Athenians (Reed 2003: 3, 27–28, 35–36). Although professional traders and market trade were certainly important in the ancient Greek economy and carried out the majority of trade (see chap. 4, Simple Importations of Goods), we cannot obtain a complete picture of the ancient Greek economy without accounting for the nonprofessionals who engaged in other forms of trade.

This chapter will examine those who were honored by Athens for their trade-related services and conclude that professional traders and their activities were indeed only a part, although a major part, of ancient Greek trade in the Classical period. Those who were responsible for trade—that is, the "relatively peaceful method of acquiring goods which are not available on the spot" (Polanyi 1957b: 257–58)—included both professionals and nonprofessionals, a motley crew of men of varying ethnicities and legal and socioeconomic statuses who had an equally diverse set of interests for engaging in trade. Thus, it will again be apparent that trade was more complex in Classical Greece than it is held to be by Finley's model of the ancient economy.

Legal Status

On none of the thirty-four occasions on which Athens honored trade-related services is there evidence that the principal honorands were native citizens of Athens. In the case of no. 26, the honorand was the Bosporan king Pairisades I, who was an Athenian citizen only because he had been naturalized by Athens when honored on a previous occasion for trade-related services. In another case (no. 11), Athenian citizen ambassadors who had facilitated a trading agreement with a noncitizen who was the principal honorand received commendations and crowns of olive from Athens. Concerning three of the thirty-four occasions (nos. 14, 19, and 31), it is impossible to be certain of the legal status of the honorands on account of lacunae in the inscriptions, but there is little reason to believe that Athens honored native citizens for trade-related services—the focus was clearly on foreigners.

There are several possible explanations for this phenomenon. It may be, as the Hasebroek/Finley model holds, that citizens did not engage in trade. It is also possible, however, that Athens simply deemed it inappropriate to honor its own citizens for such services, since trade was not a traditionally esteemed occupation (see chap. 3). The *demos* also seems to have been concerned not to confer too much honor on citizens for private benefactions (trade-related or otherwise), for fear of encouraging the *philotimia* of elite citizens so much that they might threaten the egalitarian ethos of democracy (see chap. 3).

Even if Athenian citizens did not engage in trade in significant numbers, most of the honorands were probably citizens of other *poleis*. There simply cannot have been sufficient numbers of men who were not citizens of any state to account for all the goods that were traded throughout the Aegean.[3] Ample evidence indicates that traders, even some who were *metics* in Athens, could retain citizenship in their home states despite long absences (Whitehead 1977: 9–10, 18, 71–72). If significant numbers of citizens did engage in trade, whether Athenian citizens or not, then perhaps trade was not as disesteemed throughout Greece as is held by the Hasebroek/Finley model. Moreover, despite the lower status of foreigners relative to Athenian citizens that is implied by Athens' conferral of honors only to foreigners for trade-related services, such honors elevated the status of these foreigners above that of their peers who had not received honors, thus bringing them closer, though in most cases not equal, to the status of Athenian citizens. Legal equality with Athenian citizens could be obtained only through naturalization, which was the highest and rarest of all honors.

It is difficult to determine whether the honorands were *metics* or simply *xenoi*. No honorary decree for trade-related services and very few other Athenian honorary decrees explicitly state whether the honorands were *metics*. Perhaps omitting to mention an honorand's status as a *metic* was itself a sort of honor (Whitehead 1977: 30). The common practice of referring instead to an honorand's ethnicity might have dignified him by mentioning only his highest legal status as a citizen of another city.

In the absence of explicit statements regarding residence status, one must examine the nature of the honors and the services of the honorands in order to determine their status as *metics* or *xenoi*. One might assume, for example, that if an honorand received citizenship or *enktesis*, he must be a *metic*, since only a resident of Athens could make any practical use of such privileges. But this was not always the case. Athens granted citizenship to Orontes for services relating to trade, but being a satrap of the Persian Empire, although he may have desired such privileges as insurance should he ever be forced into exile, he had no immediate intention of residing in Athens and was surely not a *metic* there (see no. 11). By the same token, one might assume that a grant of *proxenia* means that the honorand could not have been resident in Athens, since the duty of *proxenoi* was to represent Athenian interests in their home cities. But here again there are problems. First of all, it is uncertain whether *proxenoi* were required to reside in their home city in order to fulfill a fixed function as a state's guest-friend (see chap. 7, *Proxenia* and *Euergesia,* for a fuller discussion on *proxenia*). Second, it is certain that Athens granted *proxenia* to political exiles who were *metics* in Athens at the time, perhaps in the expectation that the exiles might someday return to their homelands and then be able to perform the functions of *proxenoi*.[4]

The services of honorands present similar problems. One might assume that if an honorand performed his services away from Athens, he was not resident in Athens. But there is no telling whether he was a resident of Athens before or after performing the service. One might assume that an honorand who performed services for Athens on several occasions was a *metic*. But it is still possible he performed all his services for Athens while living elsewhere. Lacunae in the inscriptions, as usual, provide a further complication.

My procedure in this study, therefore, has been to make conclusions on the basis of a preponderance of evidence. If, for example, an honorand performed repeated services for Athens and was granted *enktesis* but was also granted *proxenia,* I conclude that the honorand was a *metic* of Athens (see nos. 24 and 27). On this basis, of the thirty-four occasions on which Athens honored men for trade-related services, six honorands were *metics,* twelve were *xenoi,* and sixteen cannot be determined either way.[5]

Although there are a large number of cases in which it is impossible to determine the residence status of honorands, it is clear that Athens did not favor *metics* over *xenoi* in its honorary decrees for trade-related services. In twelve of the thirty-four cases, the honorands were not *metics,* and of the six that are identified as *metics* here, in no case is the identification absolutely certain. Thus, there is no reason to believe that Athens held *metics* to be superior in any way to *xenoi.*

One might be tempted to conclude that fewer *metics* were involved in overseas trade than *xenoi*. But it is important to note that, given the "substantivist" definition of trade, several of the honorands were not *emporoi* or *naukleroi* and did not actually sail the seas as entrepreneurs with goods for trade. If one considers only honorands who were professional traders, none of them can be identified with certainty as *xenoi,* whereas three of them appear to be *metics* (nos. 24, 25, and 27). Although it must again be cautioned that the identification of several honorands as *metics* is open to question and that the surviving evidence may not be representative of actual practice, here the evidence supports the Hasebroek/Finley model and calls into question Reed's conclusion that most professional traders were *xenoi* (Reed 2003: 56–61). If, however, one considers trade substantively and wishes to account for all forms of trade in ancient Greece, then one must not ignore the nonprofessionals who were honored for trade-related services. That none of these nonprofessionals were *metics* calls the broader implications of the Hasebroek/Finley model into question.

Finally, it is unlikely that Athens deliberately favored *xenoi* over *metics* for honorary decrees in an effort to encourage them to take up residence in Athens. As Xenophon advised in his *Poroi,* Athens could collect the *metoikion* (a tax imposed on *metics* simply for the privilege of living in Athens) as well as benefit from the trade-related services of *xenoi* who became *metics.* In reality, however, most of the *xenoi* who received honors from Athens for trade-related services were foreign potentates who probably never would take up residence in the city.

Ethnicity

Of the thirty-four occasions on which Athens honored men for trade-related services, seventeen involve Greek honorands, eight involve non-Greeks, and twelve involve men who cannot be identified as either Greek or non-Greek.[6] Of the eight occasions involving non-Greeks, five involve members of the Bosporan royal family (nos. 7, 9, 12, 26, and 34).

It is possible that Athens preferred to honor Greek over non-Greek honorands for reasons of racial bigotry or because Greeks involved in trade valued these honors and the ritualized friendships they created more than non-Greeks did and, therefore, came forth in greater numbers to perform trade-related services for Athens, but neither of these explanations is likely. We have already seen in chapter 3 that ritualized friendship was not a uniquely Greek institution and that honor was valued by non-Greeks as well as by Greeks (see pp. 50 and 332, n. 31). Subsequent analysis will show that racial bigotry was also not likely a factor in Athenian honorary decrees for trade-related services (see pp. 205 and 350–51, n. 38).

One other possible explanation for the greater proportion of Greek to non-Greek honorands is that it reflects the actual ethnic composition of those who engaged in trade with Athens in the late fifth and fourth centuries. This is probably the case, since it coincides with Reed's study of all known professional traders, which shows that the vast majority of those whose ethnicities can be determined were Greeks (Reed 2003: 96–132). This fact contradicts Hasebroek's assertion that trade was left to *metics* who were "largely, if not predominantly, of non-Greek extraction."[7] Hasebroek cites only Xenophon's *Poroi* 2.3 and Demosthenes 35.2 in support of his assertion. Xenophon, however, says merely that "so many" and not necessarily a majority of *metics* were non-Greeks. His reference to Lydians, Phrygians, and Syrians indicates that he is thinking primarily of freedmen *metics*, since a large proportion of Athenian slaves were of these ethnicities.[8] Concerning freeborn *metics*, however, the situation is different. Grave stelai show that the majority of freeborn *metics* in Athens, some of whom probably engaged in trade, were Greek (Isager and Hansen 1975: 69, 217–19, 223). In addition, Demosthenes 35.2 clearly states that both Greeks and "barbarians" frequented the *emporion* of Athens.

The ethnicities of the honorands might also provide some information about the geographic origins of Athenian imports. One problem, however, is that it is impossible to know whether those who were honored for trade-related services obtained their goods from their homelands or from elsewhere. It is probably no simple coincidence, however, that the homelands of many of the honorands, both Greek and non-Greek, lie along well-known trade routes.[9] A major source of grain for Athens was the region of the Black Sea, and there are several honorands from the kingdom of the Bosporos and Herakleia and one from Kyzikos. Another source of grain was Egypt, and there are honorands from Sidon, Tyre, Rhodes, and Salamis on Cyprus, all of which lie along a commonly used route from Egypt to the Greek mainland. Grain also came to Athens from Italy and Sicily, and there is one honorand from Akragas. But again, it is unwise to make too much of the correlations between the ethnicities of honorands and the sources of Athenian imports. *IG* ii² 408 (no. 21) is a cautionary example: although the honorands of this decree are Herakleotes, their cargo is explicitly described as Sicilian wheat and barley.

Socioeconomic Status

The socioeconomic status of those honored by Athens for trade-related services can be divided into the following categories:

- common professional traders
- moderately wealthy professional traders
- wealthy professional traders
- foreign potentates

"Common professional traders" comprise men who made their living primarily from trade and for whom there is no evidence to indicate that they were particularly wealthy. The assumption here, which is in accordance with Finley's model of the ancient economy, is that people who made their living primarily through trade usually did not have enough wealth to own their own ship. These men, known simply as *emporoi* (traders) were, therefore, of modest means. In several cases, however, the evidence indicates that an honorand who was a professional trader also owned a ship. I categorize such men, known as *naukleroi* (shipowners), as "moderately wealthy professional traders," unless there is evidence that they possessed even greater wealth. When there is such evidence, I categorize them as "wealthy professional traders." In addition, several of the honorands were not professional traders but rather men of wealth and power who sent others to Athens with goods on their behalf. I place such men in the category of "foreign potentates."[10]

Although the foregoing categories are not very precise, they are the best we can do, given the nature of the evidence.[11] Besides the few well-known potentates, we know very little about most of the honorands except what the decrees tell us about them, which typically does not include explicit information concerning their socioeconomic statuses. We must infer their statuses from, for example, references to their ownership of a trading vessel or the quantity or value of the goods involved in their trading ventures. Such inferences can yield no greater precision in determining the socioeconomic statuses of the honorands than the categories listed above.

Nevertheless, it is necessary that we make the attempt to determine the socioeconomic statuses of the honorands, even if only through broad categories, given the historiography of the ancient Greek economy. A pri-

mary emphasis of Weber's, Hasebroek's, and Finley's works on the ancient
Greek economy is the status of those who were involved in trade. In fact,
their sociologically based theses that the economy was limited in scale and
prohibited from taking on market structures relies on the assertion that
those who were involved in trade and other nonlanded economic activities
were held in low esteem in the ancient Greek system of social values. Thus,
in order to reconsider their theses through an examination of Athenian
honorary decrees for trade-related services, it is necessary that we try to
determine the socioeconomic statuses of the honorands.

Of the thirty-four occasions on which Athens granted honors and
privileges for trade-related services, eighteen concerned professional
traders. On seven of these occasions, the honorands were the typical,
common professional traders who are assumed to have been poor; on
three occasions, they were moderately wealthy; and on eight occasions,
they were more than moderately wealthy.[12] On nine occasions, the honorands were not professional traders but foreign potentates.[13] It is not
possible to determine the socioeconomic statuses of the honorands of the
remaining seven occasions.[14] Although we cannot be certain that the surviving evidence reflects actual practice, it suggests that the socioeconomic
statuses of those responsible for trade were much more diverse than the
Hasebroek/Finley model asserts.

The primary interest of common professional traders in bringing
their goods to Athens was to make a profit, and Athens did take some
steps to enhance profits for traders in order to increase imports. I argued
in chapter 4 (Simple Importation of Goods) that it is appropriate to identify professional traders in Classical Greece as "entrepreneurs" and "capitalists" who needed to profit from their ventures because their livelihood
depended on it (see also Thompson 1982: 64–67). As long as the market
made it profitable, common professional traders had an incentive to bring
their cargoes to Athens. However, the Athenian state did not rely on the
market alone to attract traders but enacted measures that would enhance
their profits if they brought their goods to Athens (see Reed 2003: 43–53).
One such measure was the well-known institution of the *dikai emporikai*,
special law courts designed to expedite suits involving nonresident
traders in order that they not be kept from profiting from their profession
by lengthy legal procedures.[15] Laws and decrees were also passed to enhance the profitability of traders by punishing those who harmed traders
in any way ([Dem.] 58.53) and who falsely brought lawsuits against *emporoi* and *naukleroi* ([Dem.] 58.10–13, 53–54). In addition, Lysias' speech

Against the Grain Retailers attests to regulations imposed on the retail sell-
ers of grain (*sitopolai*) so that they could not collude to drive down the
wholesale price of grain (which would reduce the profits of *emporoi* and
naukleroi) and then sell the grain at the retail level at inflated prices. Although it is clear from the speech that the chief goal of the regulations was
to protect Athenian citizen consumers from inflated retail prices of grain,
Lysias emphasizes that Athens also wished to "gratify and make more eager" the *emporoi* who supplied it with imported grain (Lys. 22.21). Lastly,
Athens sometimes protected traders and their cargoes from seizures by
pirates or enemy states by providing them with an escort of warships (see
Reed 2003: 48 n. 40 for the evidence). Each of these measures helped professional traders to carry out their trading ventures, thereby enhancing
their ability to make profits should they choose to bring their goods to
Athens.

Monetary profit was not the only interest of professional traders,
however, and their choice of destinations could be influenced by a variety
of factors to which Athens could appeal. As discussed in chapter 3, the acquisition of honor was a chief goal among ancient Greeks, and in chapters
6 and 7, I will examine the various means by which Athens conferred
honor as an inducement for traders to bring their goods to Athens. At the
same time, however, some of the honors that Athens conferred on men for
trade-related services had monetary as well as honorific value, thereby
appealing to traders' interests in both honor and profit. Moreover, in
chapter 8, we will see that Athens also granted privileges for trade-related
services that had a functional as well as honorific and monetary value. In
the real world of Classical Athens, common professional traders were not
one-dimensional automatons who sought either profit or honor alone.
They sought both, and their consideration for them in their decision to
bring goods to Athens was exploited by the city in its practice of granting
honors and privileges for trade-related services.

In addition to the seven occasions concerning common professional
traders, Athens also granted honors and privileges on eleven occasions to
professional traders who were moderately to extremely wealthy, a fact
that runs counter to the image of the impoverished, small-time professional trader emphasized by the Hasebroek/Finley model. The professional traders honored by Athens on three occasions must at least have
been moderately wealthy, since they appear to have been shipowners
(*naukleroi*). Even wealthier were those who received honors on the eight
occasions when professional traders were recognized for selling their

goods at a discount or giving away large amounts of goods free of charge. It should be noted, however, that the greater number of occasions on which moderately wealthy and wealthy professional traders received honors probably does not accurately reflect the proportions among all who engaged in trade with Athens. One can imagine that Athens was more inclined to honor the extraordinary trade-related services that only wealthier traders could afford to carry out rather than the trading exchanges made at market prices that were typical of common professional traders. Athens honored the latter only in times of severe shortages, when its need for imports was high (see chap. 3, War, Peace, and Trade, and chap. 4, Simple Importations of Goods). Nevertheless, the services of the wealthy professional traders that are attested by the honorary decrees indicate that they made important contributions to Athenian imports. Dionysios gave Athens three thousand *medimnoi* of grain free of charge at some time between 335/4 and 326/5 (no. 23). Herakleides sold three thousand *medimnoi* of wheat at a reduced price in 330/29 (no. 24) and then gave three thousand drachmas for the purchase of more grain in 328/7 (no. 27). Mnemon and his partner from Herakleia sold four thousand *medimnoi* of wheat and an additional (unspecified) amount of barley at a reduced price in 333/2 (no. 21). Eucharistos sold eight thousand *medimnoi* of grain at a reduced price in 320/19 and offered to sell another four thousand at a reduced price in the future (nos. 32 and 33).

As a rough quantitative measure of the significance of wealthy professional traders in Athenian trade during the late Classical period, I refer again to the estimates presented in chapter 4 that compare the amounts of grain from the gifts and sales at reduced prices of imported grain provided by wealthy professional traders to the amount of grain consumed by individuals and of annual Athenian grain imports. Based on Herodotus' statement that a soldier's daily ration was 0.02 *medimnos* of wheat and on Garnsey's view that the adult male citizen population of Athens in the fourth century was around twenty-five thousand, Herakleides' sale of three thousand *medimnoi* of wheat at a reduced price could have fed the entire adult male citizen population of Athens for almost six days. If we adopt Garnsey's "likely" estimate for the average annual consumption of grain (wheat and barley combined) by an individual (175 kg grain=4.8 *med* grain), then Dionysios' gift of three thousand *medimnoi* of grain could have fed the entire adult male citizen population of Athens for over nine days. Eucharistos' sale of twelve thousand *medimnoi* of grain could have fed the entire adult male citizen population of Athens for almost thirty-seven days.

We can also measure the significance of Dionysios' gift and Eucharistos' sale at a reduced price of imported grain as a percentage of total Athenian imports. If such imports amounted to eight hundred thousand *medimnoi* of grain (wheat and barley combined), as possibly indicated by Demosthenes 20.33 (see p. 82), then Dionysios' gift of three thousand *medimnoi* of grain comprised 0.375 percent of the total, and Eucharistos' sale of twelve thousand *medimnoi* of grain at a reduced price was 1.5 percent of the total. If we follow Garnsey's calculation, however, Athens would have needed to import 240,363 *medimnoi* of grain per year to supplement its domestic production and feed its entire resident population (see p. 82). By this estimate, Dionysios' gift of three thousand *medimnoi* of grain amounted to 1.3 percent of the total annual Athenian import of grain, and Eucharistos' sale of twelve thousand *medimnoi* of grain at a reduced price represents close to 5 percent of the total. These rough estimates support the notion that the wealthy professional traders who sold imported grain at reduced prices were an important aspect of Athenian trade, thus making their absence from the Hasebroek/Finley model one of its notable weaknesses.

Although the primary interest of both moderately wealthy and wealthy professional traders in their choice of destinations was surely profit (since they made their living from trade), moderately wealthy and wealthy professional traders, even more so than common professionals, could forgo some of their potential profits in order to fulfill other interests, such as their interest in obtaining honor. A good example is Herakleides, who voluntarily gave up sizable potential profits by selling grain to Athens at a price that was greatly reduced from the going, shortage-inflated rate (nos. 24 and 27). In return for this and other benefactions, Herakleides received honors and privileges from Athens that appear to have been as important to him as profit in his decision to bring his cargo of grain to Athens. Like common professional traders, therefore, moderately wealthy and wealthy professional traders sought both honor and profit from their trading ventures, just perhaps in slightly different proportions.

Since the interests of wealthy and common professional traders differed only slightly, the failure of Hasebroek and Finley to recognize the importance of wealthy professional traders is perhaps understandable; however, less understandable is their model's neglect of the role played by nonprofessionals in Athenian trade, since their interests differed greatly from those of professional traders. On nine of the twenty-seven occasions on which the socioeconomic status of those who received honors from Athens for trade-related services can be determined, the honorands were not professional traders but rather foreign potentates. They received honors because they were responsible for initiating or facilitating overseas exchanges of goods with Athens that others, probably professional traders, carried out.[16] For example, the Bosporan kings granted exemptions from port taxes to traders bound for Athens and gave Athens gifts of imported goods, benefactions that had a direct impact on some four hundred thousand *medimnoi* of grain bound for Athens each year (see nos. 7, 9, 12, 26, and 34). The Persian satrap Orontes participated in some sort of trading deal with Athens, in which he would supply an Athenian military expedition with grain (no. 11). The gift of grain provided to Athens by Harpalos, Alexander the Great's treasurer, may have been identical to the one attested by the famous inscription from Kyrene that amounted to one hundred thousand *medimnoi* (no. 22). The honorand of *IG* ii² 401 is said to have "dispatched" (ἀ[ποστολὴν]), but not personally to have brought, grain from Asia to Athens (no. 30).

The relatively high number of foreign potentates honored by Athens in proportion to men of lesser status (over one-third of the total) cannot by itself prove that they were responsible for a correspondingly equally high percentage of Athenian imports. Since the services of these foreign potentates were extraordinary, Athens may simply have chosen to honor them in greater numbers than perhaps the countless other men of lesser status who also performed lesser trade-related services but who collectively may have accounted for a much greater percentage of Athenian imports. That the relatively high numbers of foreign potentates who received honors from Athens for trade-related services does correspond to their relative significance for Athenian trade is supported, though, by comparisons of the amounts of their gifts of grain with estimates for individual grain consumption and total annual Athenian grain imports (see pp. 81–83). If, according to one interpretation of Demosthenes 20.33, total annual Athenian imports of grain were eight hundred thousand *medimnoi*, and if the gift of grain from the Bosporan kings in 357 indeed totaled 25,727 *medimnoi* (see pp. 82–83), then the gift amounted to 3.2 percent of Athens' total annual imports. At the other end of the scale, the gift of grain from Kyrene, which may have occurred at the instigation of Harpalos, would account for a sizable 12.5 percent of Athens' total annual grain imports. If, on the other hand, we follow Garnsey and assume that Athens had to import at most 240,363 *medimnoi* of grain in the fourth century (see p. 82), then the gift of the Bosporan kings in 357 would amount to 10.7 percent and the Kyrene gift approximately 42 percent of Athens' total annual imports of grain.

If such estimates are reliable, they strongly support the notion that foreign potentates played an important role in Athenian trade through their gift exchanges. In this light, it is difficult to maintain the Hasebroek/Finley model, which focuses only on trade that was both initiated and carried out by professional traders in the pursuit of profit. Hasebroek's statement that trade in ancient Greece "was a clearly defined and distinct form of economic activity, carried on by a class of whole-time professional traders" is an overgeneralization not adequately qualified by his few caveats (Hasebroek 1933: 4). For example, he acknowledged that some grain was transported from place to place by producers who wished to unload surpluses or by travelers who used it to help pay for their trips as a sort of "sideline" trade (Hasebroek 1933: 12–15). But this does not account for the large quantities traded by foreign potentates. Although Hasebroek did address *IG* ii^2 212, the honorary decree for the Bosporan kings, he (and Finley as well) saw it as evidence only that no "commercial agreements," in which two states attempted to develop their citizen industry or capture markets, existed in Classical Greece.[17] But given that a significant amount of Athenian grain imports was obtained through the initiative of foreign potentates who were not professional traders, it is apparent that trade was organized in a variety of ways and that Athens fulfilled its trading interests through correspondingly diverse means.

Generally, the interests of foreign potentates in trade were much different from those of professional traders, both rich and poor. Potentates had much less personal need to make monetary profits from trade, since their wealth and power allowed them to live comfortably without having to work. Honor, on the other hand, was clearly very important to men of high status, wealth, and power, whether they were Greeks or non-Greeks. Not only did Greek culture in particular hold honor up as one of its most important social values, but one's high reputation for providing aid (*boetheia*) in any form, including trade, to one's friends and allies insured that one would receive reciprocal benefits whenever they might be needed. For potentates who engaged in the unpredictable, high-stakes game of international politics, therefore, honor was priceless. Athenian honors and privileges made such honor manifest to the public and served to assure foreign potentates who had performed trade-related services for Athens that the city would reciprocate such benefactions with future *boetheia*.

The importance of honor for potentates does not, however, mean that they had absolutely no desire or need to make monetary profits from their involvement in trade. Even without the prospect of receiving official honors from Athens, foreign potentates doubtless would still have had at least some interest in trade for the sake of obtaining revenue. The desire of potentates for self-aggrandizement, for example, required large sums of money for its fulfillment. Self-aggrandizement in the ancient world included material comforts as well as the financial means of providing *boetheia* to friends, allies, and subjects. Moreover, those potentates who were the heads of states needed revenue in order to provide for the well-being of their realms and their citizens. Without money, it would have been impossible for leaders to carry out military campaigns, fortify their cities, and complete public works projects, all of which were necessary for them to stay in power.

A possible example of the ways in which foreign potentates may have profited from trade while performing trade-related services for Athens concerns the kings of the Bosporos. Among the services for which Athens honored the Bosporan kings was their granting priority of loading and exemption from taxes to traders in their ports who were bound for Athens with cargoes of grain. Although the Bosporan kings lost tax revenue, they may have recouped the loss and even come out ahead in the end. It is uncertain whether there was a royal monopoly on the production and/or export of grain, but if there were either of these (as was the case in Macedon with timber; see p. 353, n. 12), the Bosporan kings could have profited from their trade-related services for Athens in several ways. The tax exemption would lead to an increase in demand for their grain, both among professional traders, whose own profits would be enhanced, and in Athens (probably the biggest single consumer of Bosporan grain, accounting for perhaps a third of all Bosporan grain exports), whose citizens naturally desired grain at the lowest possible prices (Hagemajer Allen 2003: 236 n. 77). The increased demand for Bosporan grain would expand the quantity of grain exports, thereby increasing revenue from grain sales. The Bosporan kings could also raise the price of grain, both because their monopoly would not allow traders to obtain cheaper grain without having to incur transportation costs to seek it elsewhere and because it would be natural for market forces to offset a tax reduction with a rise in prices anyway. Thus, whether through an increased quantity of grain exports or through increased prices on grain, the tax exemption provided by the Bosporan kings for traders in their ports who were bound for Athens with grain could have generated increased profits for the Bosporan kings. In this way, the Bosporan kings may have had an interest in performing a trade-related service for Athens even without the prospect of earning Athenian honors. But given the importance of honor and its attendant benefits, Athenian honors surely would have been at least an additional, if not a primary, reason for potentates to aid Athens in fulfilling its interests in trade (see pp. 38–40).

One other issue is whether the evidence indicates any shift in the proportions of honorands from the various socioeconomic groups over time, which in turn might indicate whether socioeconomic status was considered by Athens in a development of its trade policy during the fourth century. Unfortunately, the evidence is insufficient to yield any firm conclusions. It is true that only one common professional trader is known to have received honors for services relating to trade before 350 (no. 8), whereas there are six occasions on which they were honored after 350 (nos. 10, 17, 18, 19, 25, and 31), which makes it tempting to think that Athens was reluctant to honor such men until greater threats to its grain imports put pressure on it to do so. However, moderately wealthy professional traders received honors from as early as 414 (nos. 1–3). Since the difference in status between common and moderately wealthy professional traders was not large, it is hard to believe that Athens would make such a distinction between them when it came to granting honors and privileges for their services. The more important distinction seems to be in the types of trade-related services they provided, since there is no evidence that simple importations of goods by men of any status were honored before 338/7 (see pp. 97–98).

What is certain, however, is that during the fourth century, Athens honored men of a variety of socioeconomic statuses, from foreign potentates down to common professional traders. Despite traditional social values that had been created by the elite and that reserved honor for the elite and its preferred activities, Athens' trade needs compelled it to consider even men of very low status worthy of honor so long as they performed the trade-related services that the city needed. But this is not to say that all distinctions on the basis of status disappeared. As we shall see in chapters

6–8, Athens held on to some of the bigotry inherent in traditional elite values in the manner in which it honored each socioeconomic group.

Conclusion

Athenian honorary decrees for trade-related services show that the organization of trade in Athens in the late fifth century and the fourth century was much more complex than it appears to be in Finley's model. Although these decrees tend to support Finley's view that those who were responsible for trade in Athens were not Athenian citizens, many were surely citizens of other Greek cities. Athens' reluctance to honor its own citizens was less a matter of the degree to which trade was esteemed, as Finley believed, and more a matter of political concerns, particularly the *demos'* desire to preserve the egalitarian ethos of democracy, which honoring fellow citizens for benefactions performed in private, rather than official, capacities might threaten.

Further complexity in Athenian trade is apparent from the variety of people who received honors from Athens for their trade-related services. Their services involved exchanging goods in accordance with the principles of market economics as well as through such substantivist economic activities as reciprocal gift giving. Most of those responsible for these various forms of trade were Greeks or Hellenized non-Greeks, but they also included both *metics* and *xenoi*, as well as people of diverse socioeconomic statuses, ranging from common and wealthy professional traders to nonprofessional foreign potentates. Moreover, the significant contributions of wealthy professional traders and foreign potentates to total Athenian imports of grain call into question the notion of the Hasebroek/Finley model that trade was carried out by poor, disesteemed professional traders.

Each socioeconomic group naturally had different interests motivating it to engage in trade with Athens. Despite their differences, however, Athenian honors and privileges were able to appeal to each group's particular interests. Exactly how Athens' interests in trade and those of its honorands came together will become apparent from an examination of the link that connected Athens with its honorands, namely, the honors and privileges themselves, which are the subjects of chapters 6–8.

CHAPTER SIX

Honorary Language

The language with which Athenian honorary decrees describe the city's benefactors and their trade-related services was itself an honor, since the praise of the People of Athens was inscribed on stone stelai and placed in public view to serve as a testimony to the high esteem in which the honorands were held. Moreover, the People of Athens drew on a rather exclusive set of laudatory epithets for use throughout the corpus of its honorary decrees (see Henry 1983 and V-T). For men who performed trade-related services, Athens commonly employed the following words:

- *aner agathos*
- *chresimos*
- *arete*
- *eunoia/eunous*
- *philotimia*

Although the repeated and seemingly formulaic use of these words in honorary decrees gives the superficial impression that the People of Athens were unconcerned with the language of the decrees, closer examination reveals that these terms express the precise manner in which the People wished to represent their esteem for the honorands and their services. Studies by Henry, Veligianni-Terzi (V-T), and Whitehead have shown that Athens made subtle distinctions between various types of services, situations, and honorands when employing laudatory language in honorary decrees and that this practice evolved over time.[1] For this reason, I will limit my analysis of such language to the extant decrees of the Council and Assembly of Athens that honor trade-related services, since the literary sources attesting to these decrees do not necessarily report their precise language. Another advantage of the extant decrees of the Council and Assembly is that they represent the voice of the People, the entire citizenry of Athens, who ratified them, whereas the literary sources required no such popular ratification and, therefore, tend to represent only the view of the educated and leisured elite who could compose them. For similar reasons, I will not consider inscriptions from Athenian tribes, demes, boards of officials, or private individuals, since they do not necessarily represent the attitude of the state as a whole or reflect the state's trade policy.

Three major trends in the use of honorary language in Athenian decrees are particularly relevant to the attitude of the state toward trade and the men who were responsible for it (see table 6.1). First, the state was

TABLE 6.1. Earliest Uses of Honorary Terms for Various Categories of Honorands and Services

Honorary Term	Native Athenian Citizens	Foreigners	Trade-Related Services
Aner agathos	**339/8** (*IG* ii² 1155=Lambert 1.27) c. 340–325 (*SEG* 28.52; V-T B10; Lambert 1.4)	**451/0 or 418/7** (*IG* i³ 17) c. 450 (*IG* i³ 29)	**407/6** (no. 6) c. 390–378/7 (no. 8)
Chresimos	**336/5 or 335/4** (*IG* ii² 330+445=Lambert 1.3) 328/7 (*IG* ii² 354+SEG 18.14=Lambert 1.11)	**364/3 or 359/8** (*IG* ii² 145=*Agora* 16.52) 363/2 (*SIG* 158) 337/6 (*IG* ii² 240=Lambert 3.33)	**c. 340–300** (no. 14) c. 337 (no. 15)
Arete[a]	**343/2** (*IG* ii² 223A=Lambert 1.1) 336/5 or 335/4 (*IG* ii² 330+445= Lambert 1.3)	**368/7** (*IG* ii² 107) 365–335? (*SEG* 3.83)	**347/6** (no. 12) After c. 330 (no. 25)
Eunoia	**307/6** (*IG* ii² 457+513) 304/3 (*IG* ii² 487)	**c. 410** (*IG* i³ 113) 405/4 (*IG* i³ 125) 359/8? (*SEG* 21.246)	**347/6** (no. 12) c. 337 (no. 15)
Eunous	**305/4** (*Hesp.* 5 [1934] 201–5)	**378/7** (*IG* ii² 42) 356/5 (*IG* ii² 127)	**c. 340–300** (no. 14) c. 337–320 (no. 18)
Philotimia[b]	**343/2** (*IG* ii² 223A=Lambert 1.1) 339/8 (*IG* ii² 1155=Lambert 1.27)	**c. 352/1–337/6** (*IG* ii² 273) c. 352/1–337/6 (*IG* ii² 277+428)	**c. 340** (no. 13) c. 340–300 (no. 14)

[a]The restoration of the word *arete* in *IG* i³ 127 (decree 3, 403/2) is rejected by V-T 45 (A46), since it results in awkward formulae that are unparalleled elsewhere. See also p. 38, n. 12.

[b]*Philotimia* in a verbal form is restored in *IG* i³ 113 (c. 410) and in *IG* ii² 183 (before 353/2, V-T A102). In both decrees, the *philotimia* word is heavily and implausibly restored (V-T A34 and Whitehead 1983: 72 n. 25, respectively). See also p. 38, n.12 below. Note that *IG* ii² 517 is a doublet of 183 (Peppas-Delmousou, 1965: 151–53).

willing to apply the language of praise to foreigners much earlier than it was to native Athenian citizens, which was probably because the *demos* did not fear the *philotimia* of foreigners as it did that of its elite native citizens (see chap. 3). Second, although Athens initially honored only traditional political and military services with such terms of praise, increasing needs for trade between 415 and 307 compelled the People to praise those who had performed trade-related services in a similar fashion. Finally, the language of praise was fairly general down to the mid-fourth century, the term *aner agathos* being the preferred term, but then Athens began to use a wider variety of honorary terms, such as *chresimos, arete, eunoia,* and *philotimia,* which to a great extent displaced *aner agathos* in honorary decrees. Once again, historical circumstances compelled Athens to become more aggressive in courting benefactors to help fulfill its increasing needs for security, revenue, and imported grain. The use of the word *philotimia* was a key element in this effort: it made it clear to Athens' prospective benefactors that the state would show gratitude (*charis*) for their services and reciprocate by granting honors and privileges.

Aner Agathos

Athens referred to honorands as *andres agathoi* (good men) in six of the twenty-five extant honorary decrees for trade-related services (nos. 6, 8, 11, 12, 14, and 28). Athens did not discriminate between the types of trade-related services, the ethnicities, or the legal and socioeconomic statuses of the honorands in these six decrees, except that all the honorands were foreigners, some of whom became naturalized. The first honorary decree for trade-related services that refers to the honorand as an *aner agathos* is no. 6 (D4), which honors Archelaos, king of Macedon, and dates to 407/6. There are at least thirty-one extant decrees that date from as early as 451 down to 407 in which Athens used the words *andres agathoi* to characterize honorands, and all of them are for political or military services (when they can be identified with any certainty).[2] On the other hand, none of these decrees honored native Athenian citizens. In fact, there is evidence for only two honorary decrees that may refer to native Athenian citizens as *andres agathoi* at any time during the fifth and fourth centuries, and the words *aner agathos* are heavily restored in both cases.[3] Yet there are at least sixty-six honorary decrees that refer to foreigners as *andres agathoi* from 405/4 down to the latest example in 314/3, including the five during this period for services relating to trade (nos. 8, 11, 12, 14, and 28).[4] Based on the surviving evidence, therefore, it appears that Athens deliberately refrained from describing native Athenian citizens as *andres agathoi* but was willing to apply the epithet to foreigners.

The surviving evidence is consistent with the notion that the *demos* was reluctant to grant too much honor to living, resident, native Athenian citizens and, through a gradual process, reshaped aristocratic values and terms of approbation for its own purposes. As discussed in chapter 3, *agathos* was second only to *arete* among the key value terms of ancient Greek society and was associated, from early times, with the aristocracy, who were referred to as the *kaloi k'agathoi*, "the beautiful and the good."[5] It is understandable, then, that the *demos* did not wish to honor resident, native Athenian citizens with a term that was so clearly identified with the elite, nondemocratic cause.

The *demos* was more flexible, however, when it came to the types of services for which it would honor men as *andres agathoi*. At first, from ca. 450 to 407, Athens honored only those who had performed political or military services as *agathoi*. This seems natural, since *agathos* had a long history of being associated with the political and military interests of the elite (see pp. 38–39). In fact, when used to refer to a specific deed with the formula ἀνὴρ ἀγαθὸς ἐγένετο , the epithet concerns military services exclusively throughout the fifth and fourth centuries (V-T 265–67, 270). In its general sense, as expressed in the formula ἀνὴρ ἀγαθός ἐστι, however, *aner agathos* came to be applied from 407/6 down to 314/3 to men who had performed any kind of service that indicated political friendship with Athens (V-T 247–54, 276–77). Thus, those who Athens considered *andres agathoi* included allies in the Second Athenian League, kings who maintained diplomatic ties and alliances with Athens, foreign ambassadors who helped negotiate treaties with Athens, and *proxenoi* who acted as friends of Athenians in their home cities (ibid.).

After 407, along with those who performed political and military services, Athens recognized as *andres agathoi* those who performed trade-related services. The impetus for this development was likely Athens' increasing need for revenue and imported goods, especially ships' timber, during the latter stages of the Peloponnesian War, particularly after the disastrous defeat of the Sicilian Expedition in 413. Athens honored King Archelaos of Macedon and referred to him as an *aner agathos* for providing a gift of oar spars and ships' timber in 407. Archelaos' service was not only vital to Athenian trading interests but also tied to political and military concerns, namely, the rebuilding of the fleet at a crucial point during the Peloponnesian War. Furthermore, Archelaos, being the king of Macedon, was in a position to provide further services for Athens, trade-related as well as political and military ones. Such a person and such circumstances provided a worthy occasion for Athens to break with tradition and refer to a man who had performed trade-related services as an *aner agathos*. A few decades later, however, even a professional trader who performed strictly trade-related services was deemed worthy of being called an *aner agathos* (no. 8).

Chresimos

The word *chresimos* appears in five of the twenty-five extant Athenian honorary decrees for trade-related services and characterizes the honorands as having been "useful" to the People of Athens.[6] Throughout the second half of the fourth century, Athens used the word *chresimos* to describe honorands without discriminating between their specific types of trade-related services, socioeconomic statuses, or ethnicities. The state's only distinction concerned the legal status of the honorands, who were all foreigners, including one who was also naturalized by virtue of the same decree that recognized his trade-related services (no. 29).

The word *chresimos* first appears in an honorary decree for trade-related services right around the time of the Battle of Chaironeia in 338/7. *IG* ii² 423 (no. 14), which dates ca. 340–300, contains the word *chresimos*, but it is completely restored by modern editors. The first certain appearance of the word in an honorary decree for trade-related services occurs in *IG* ii² 283 (no. 15), which dates to ca. 337. Only one other honorary decree containing the word *chresimos* for any kind of service is likely to predate it. The decree concerns a noncitizen who served Athens as herald of the Council and the People and dates to the mid-360s at the earliest.[7] After that time, Athens considered men who performed political, military, and trading services all to be worthy of the epithet *chresimos*, without preferring one type of service over another, at least when it came to foreign honorands.[8] In regard to native Athenian citizens, however, although Athens also honored them as *chresimoi* from at least 336 onward, it did so only for services performed as public officials, particularly as priests and ambassadors, down to the 280s.[9] The first native Athenian citizen who was called *chresimos* in an honorary decree for services performed not as a public official was Philippides the poet in 283/2 (*IG* ii² 657), who performed a wide array of services in capacities both public (as an *agonothetes*) and private (he procured grain for Athens from the Diadoch Lysimachos).

Two factors may explain why Athens did not apply the word *chresimos* to honorands until the mid-fourth century. One concerns the antidemocratic associations of its cognate *chrestos* (good). The word *chrestos* typically referred to the "good men" of Athens, that is, the elite. For example, writing at some time during the third quarter of the fifth century, the "Old Oligarch" begins his diatribe against Athenian democracy by stating that he does not approve of the constitution because it allows "the bad men to do better than the good men (*chrestoi*)."[10] It is reasonable to think that the *demos* deliberately avoided employing a word so closely associated with the elite in its honorary decrees, the purpose of which was to praise individuals for their services for the entire community of Athens, not to promote them to the ranks of the aristocracy.

Whitehead (1983 and 1993) has argued further that Athens' use of honorary language underwent a significant change in the mid-fourth century as part of a process whereby the *demos* created a new vocabulary to express the "cardinal virtues" of Athenian democracy. Athens replaced adjectives associated with elite values, such as *agathos*, with "abstract attributes" exhibited toward "the People of Athens," such as *andragathia, arete, eunoia,* and *philotimia.* In Whitehead's view, these abstract attributes were sufficiently distinct from the adjectives representing the traditional values of the elite that they did not threaten democratic values but rather promoted them. Consequently, Athens could then apply these attributes to native Athenian citizens as well as to foreigners without fear of undermining the democracy. According to Whitehead, Athens never abstracted *chresimos* into a cardinal virtue of democracy because it was unable to overlook its close association with the aristocratic *chrestos* (Whitehead 1993: 64).

Although Whitehead is right to note a change in Athens' use of language in its honorary decrees in the mid-fourth century, his explanation for this phenomenon is not entirely consistent and does not account for the appearance of *chresimos* in the mid-fourth century. The words *aner agathos* were every bit as aristocratic as the word *chresimos,* and yet only the former was abstracted into one of Whitehead's democratic cardinal virtues. Moreover, according to Whitehead's theory, one would not expect the word *chresimos* to come into use in the mid-fourth century at the same time that Athens was replacing adjectives that had aristocratic connotations, such as *agathos*, with democratic abstract attributes. In addition, as Whitehead acknowledges, Athens employed *andragathia* in several honorary decrees of the late fifth century and then continued to use it sporadically over the course of the fourth century. *Eunoia* also appears in two honorary decrees from the end of the fifth century and then again in 378/7 before becoming more common in the second half of the fourth century.[11] In contrast, the word *arete* does not appear in any extant honorary decrees before 368, and *philotimia* first appears only after ca. 350.[12] Thus, although the *demos* was concerned about the ambitions of elite Athenian citizens and does appear to have desired to create a vocabulary of democratic virtues, these were neither the only nor the chief motivations for changes in the language of Athenian honorary decrees in the mid-fourth century.

Hakkarainen (1997) has suggested an alternative explanation for change in Athens' use of honorary language in the mid-fourth century. In his view, the change was not specific to the use of abstract attributes or primarily for the purpose of controlling elite Athenian citizens. Instead, Athens was attempting to expand all aspects of the practice of granting honors and privileges for services to Athens, including the range of words used to praise Athenian benefactors. General terms, such as *aner agathos*, were supplemented and eventually replaced by more specific and numerous honorary terms, including both additional adjectives (*chresimos, eunous*) and abstract attributes (*arete, philotimia*) that could offer a richer variety of prizes for prospective benefactors. According to Hakkarainen, the purpose of the change was to strengthen and diversify the inducements for benefactors to supply the city with needed revenue.[13] Warfare and imperialism, Athens' traditional and preferred sources of revenue, were proving to be untenable in the mid-fourth century, as the city's attempts to re-create its fifth-century empire in the late 360s cost more money than it brought in and culminated in Athens' defeat in the Social War in 355 (see chap. 3). Thus, Hakkarainen argues, Athens, to make up for this shortfall, had to focus and improve on its other methods of obtaining revenue, including its practice of honoring benefactors who assisted the city financially.

Hakkarainen's analysis explains the evidence more finely than does Whitehead's; however, it, too, contains some oversimplifications. For one thing, it focuses solely on Athens' need for revenue as the motivating factor for change in Athens' use of honorary language. But equally important to Athens was securing its food supply, which required a significant quantity of imports of grain at this time and especially after 338. Thus, it is likely that the change in Athens' use of honorary language in the decades around the mid-fourth century was motivated as much by its interest in importing grain as it was by its desire to obtain revenue (see p. 59). In addition, like Whitehead, Hakkarainen would like to pinpoint a change in Athens' practice with regard to honorary decrees to the mid-fourth century. Although this certainly was a key transitional period for Athenian policy, it was not the only period in which Athens altered its practices. Rather, as we shall see below, Athens made numerous innovations in its practice of honoring benefactions on an ad hoc basis in response to specific circumstances and needs during the course of the late fifth and fourth centuries.

In this light, it is possible to sketch an outline of the development of Athens' use of the word *chresimos* in its honorary decrees. By the mid-fourth century, whatever fears the *demos* had concerning the ambitions of elite citizens had to take a backseat to its needs for security, revenue, and imported grain. Thus, as early as the 360s, Athens began to praise foreigners as *chresimoi* for political and military services in conjunction with its renewed imperialistic ambitions (see p. 59). Although its defeat in the Social War in 355 put a tremendous strain on Athenian revenues, it was not until Philip's siege of Byzantion in 340 and Athens' defeat in the Battle of Chaironeia in 338 that the threat to Athens' grain supply became so acute that the People put aside their disdain for *banausic* activities enough to praise as *chresimoi* those who performed trade-related services. In fact, it appears that the association between the word *chresimos* and trade-related services became so commonplace during the grain shortages of the 330s and 320s that the speaker of [Demosthenes] 34.38, which is dated to 327/6, proclaimed that he and his brother had proven themselves to be *chresimoi* to the People by selling imported grain to Athens at a reduced price.[14] During this time also, in 336, as the Classical period was nearing its end, the *demos* could even call native citizens *chresimoi* in honorary decrees so long as they were serving the community as public officials. But even that requirement fell by the wayside by the 280s, some forty years into the Hellenistic period, by which time Macedonian domination and the wars of the Diadochs had taken their toll, and the masses had lost much of their control over politics back to the elite.

Arete

Three of the twenty-five extant honorary decrees for trade-related services praise men for their *arete*, their "excellence" or "virtue" (nos. 12, 25, and 28). In these three cases, the services included simple importations of goods, miscellaneous, and unknown services. All the honorands were non-Greeks, though the honorands of no. 12 were naturalized Athenian citizens. The honorand of no. 25 was definitely a *metic*; the honorands of no. 12 were *xenoi* who were naturalized but not resident in Athens; it is uncertain whether the honorand of no. 28 was a *metic* or a *xenos*. One honorand was a common professional trader (no. 25), those of no. 12 were foreign potentates, and the socioeconomic status of the honorand of no. 28 is unknown.

Each of the three decrees dates to the years after 350, and as in the cases of the words *chresimos* and *aner agathos*, Athens seems to have been careful about when and for whom it used the word *arete* in its honorary decrees. There is no solid evidence for an honorary decree that employs the word *arete* until 368/7, when Athens honored the Mytilenaians, apparently for being loyal allies (*IG* ii² 107).[15] After that time, Athens ascribed *arete* to native citizens on seven occasions between 343/2 and the end of the fourth century and to foreigners on twenty occasions, including *IG* ii² 107, between 368/7 and the end of the fourth century.[16] All the native Athenian citizens whose services can be identified served in some official capacity on behalf of the People, for example, as members of the Council, overseers of public fountains, and priests. The honored foreigners whose services can be identified provided political, military, or trade-related services. Thus, it appears that Athens was reluctant to acknowledge *arete* officially until 368, when it honored foreigners for military services. After 350, it attributed *arete* to citizens as well as noncitizens, but the former were recognized exclusively for services they performed as public officials in the democratic government, whereas the latter earned such praise for political, military, and trade-related services.

Although the late appearance of the word *arete* in Athenian honorary decrees may have been in part a result of the *demos'* concerns over its aristocratic connotations, the driving force behind the inception of its use in honorary decrees was Athens' greater need to induce benefactions at that time, which prompted the city to add *arete* to the pool of terms with which it could praise its benefactors. It is true that *arete* had aristocratic connotations that may have made the *demos* reluctant to use it, for fear of encouraging the oligarchic ambitions of the elite citizens of Athens.[17] As we saw in chapter 3, *arete* was among the most powerful words of commendation and was used to describe those who were thought to possess all the qualities most highly valued at any time by Greek society. Early in Greek history, *arete* was most closely associated with military and political skills that could be obtained only by members of the elite. Such skills and their aristocratic connotations continued to be important even in democratic Athens.[18] For example, Isaios 5.46 praises the *arete* of the aristocrats Harmodios and Aristogeiton, who assassinated the tyrant Hipparchos in 514, while Aristotle associates *arete* with the "notables" (*gnorimoi*) and "wellborn" (*eugeneis*) who prefer oligarchy to democracy (*Pol.* 1291b14–30, 1301b1–4). Nowhere before the Classical period, however, do we find common people praised for their *arete* for performing *banausic* tasks.

But as reluctant as the *demos* was to attribute *arete* to native Athenian citizens in honorary decrees, one wonders why *arete* was not ascribed earlier, as *agathos* was, to foreign honorands who had performed political or military services. In fact, despite the protests of Whitehead, most scholars believe that *arete* is simply an abstraction of *aner agathos*. Although Whitehead has argued vigorously that *andragathia*, rather than *arete*, is the proper abstraction of *aner agathos*, Veligianni-Terzi has more recently shown that both *arete* and *andragathia* serve as abstractions of *aner agathos esti*, the formula that connotes a political friend of Athens in its honorary decrees (see above).[19] Thus, there must be another explanation for the belated use of *arete* to honor foreign benefactors.

As with the word *chresimos* (see above), the likely explanation is that Athens developed its practice of honoring benefactors on an ad hoc basis in response to specific needs. The renewed imperial ambitions of Athens in the 360s brought with it a greater need for military support; hence, it is perhaps not just a coincidence that the existing evidence attests to Athens' first use of *arete* to praise Mytilenaians for their loyalty to Athens during military campaigns in 368/7. By 347/6, not too long after its defeat in the Social War, Athens attributed *arete* to men who not only had performed trade-related services but also had provided financial assistance (no. 12). A native Athenian citizen is first praised for his *arete* in 343/2 for serving in the Council when it had performed well in overseeing the City Dionysia. Unfortunately, the decree does not provide enough information concerning the honorand's specific actions as a member of the Council, so it is impossible to tie his services to broader circumstances with any certainty. It would not be surprising, however, if this honorand and several other officeholders who were honored in the 340s and 330s had contributed some of their private funds to carry out the duties of their offices, as we know Demosthenes did as overseer of fortifications in 338.[20] Athens continued to attribute *arete* to both native citizens and foreign honorands into the third century, finally recognizing the *arete* of a native citizen who had performed benefactions for Athens as a private citizen as well as a public official in the 280s (*IG* ii[2] 657).

The growing importance of trade to the security and prosperity of Athens compelled the state to attribute *arete* to a new class of people who performed trade-related services for the city. One man so honored was clearly a professional trader of modest means (no. 25). Common professional traders were the antithesis of the wealthy, leisured aristocrat. They had neither the money nor the free time to hone political or military skills. Consequently, they had been barred from obtaining *arete* by traditional political and military means. It was not until trading needs became vital for Athens that it began to consider that even foreign, common, professional traders who had performed trade-related services could be capable of possessing *arete*.

Eunoia/eunous

The abstract noun *eunoia*, meaning "goodwill," and its adjectival form *eunous* (goodwilled) appear either extant or restored in sixteen of the twenty-five surviving Athenian honorary decrees for trade-related services.[21] The word characterizes the motivations of the honorands as altruistic (echoing Xen. *Poroi* 3.4), as if they performed their services in a spirit of friendship rather than for selfish gain. Veligianni-Terzi's analysis of honorary formulae concludes that the words *eunoia/eunous* carried a similar meaning to *aner agathos esti*, signifying that honorands had proven by their services that they were political friends of Athens. These services included general political and military ones, those that indicated democratic partisanship, and those that related to trade (V-T 254–62). The honorary decrees for trade-related services that employ *eunoia/eunous* include all the categories of services as well as honorands of a variety of ethnicities and legal and socioeconomic statuses, excluding native Athenian citizens. In addition, Athens does not appear to have made any distinction between the use of *eunoia* and *eunous* concerning those who had performed trade-related services. The application of both words to various types of services and honorands shows no discernable pattern.

But whereas Athens did not make distinctions between types of trade-related services and the legal and socioeconomic statuses of foreign honorands in its use of *eunoia/eunous*, it did distinguish between citizens and noncitizens and between political and military services, on the one hand, and services relating to trade, on the other. The earliest Athenian honorary decree known to attribute *eunoia* to a man who had performed trade-related services dates to 347/6 (no. 12). Although there are seven extant honorary decrees for trade-related services predating 347/6 and going back to ca. 414–412, none of them contain *eunoia* or *eunous* (nos. 1, 3, 4, 6, 8, 10, and 11). Yet Athens used *eunoia* or *eunous* to characterize those who had performed traditionally esteemed political or military services in at least seven honorary decrees also predating 347/6 and going back to 410.[22] All these honorands, however, were foreigners, including Euagoras, king of Cyprian Salamis, who was naturalized in the same honorary decree that praises his *eunoia*.

Honorary decrees that contain the words *eunoia* or *eunous* concerning native Athenian citizens are much rarer, appear much later, and are highly restricted compared to those for foreigners. The first known honorary decree that might attribute *eunoia* to a native Athenian citizen dates to 337/6 for a man who served as secretary of the Council, but *eunoia* is entirely restored.[23] The first honorary decree for a native Athenian citizen in which the word *eunoia* appears in the extant text is *IG* ii² 457+513 from 307, which praised (posthumously) the famous Lykourgos for his many services as administrator of Athenian finances. After these first two cases, the next five native Athenian citizens who are praised for their *eunoia* in honorary decrees down to 283/2 performed their services as officials of the Athenian government.[24] It is not until 283/2 that *eunoia* is attributed to a native citizen, Philippides the poet, who performed services in a private capacity, including the procurement of a gift of grain from the Diadoch Lysimachos, though he was also honored in part for his services as a public official (*agonothetes*) of Athens (*IG* ii² 657).[25]

Athens appears to have been careful about to whom and for what services it was willing to employ the words *eunoia* and *eunous* in its honorary decrees, and it seems to have changed its criteria for doing so over time. That Athens used the words *eunoia* and *eunous* in decrees from 410 down to 347 to honor foreigners solely for political or military services and did not use them to honor foreigners for trade-related services until after 347 is consistent with traditional Greek social values that disdained trade and other *banausic* activities. It is also consistent with the notion that the *demos*, despite the reality that many of its number had to work in *banausic* occupations themselves, accepted these values, which had originated among the elite, as its own. But the fact that the words *eunoia* and *eunous* were eventually used to honor men who performed trade-related services shows that social values were changing during the course of the fourth century. Two likely catalysts for this change were Athens' defeats in the Social War in 355 and the Battle of Chaironeia in 338, which compelled the People to intensify their efforts to obtain revenue and grain through trade.

Athens did not honor resident native citizens with the words *eunoia* and *eunous* until even later, because of the political concerns of the *demos* (Whitehead 1993: 52–54). Goodwill is not a civic virtue per se; one can have goodwill in private as well as in public life. In order for goodwill to have a civic connotation, it must be attached to the community. To say that one had goodwill "toward the Athenians" (i.e., toward the *polis*) and to say that one had goodwill "toward the *demos*," however, were not necessarily the same thing, given the tension between the masses and the elite in Athens, which was most volatile at the end of the fifth century, when there were two oligarchic revolutions (in 411 and 404). Using either phrase in honorary decrees for native Athenian citizens in the ensuing decades was too politically charged and could upset the fragile stability of the democracy. Since foreigners were barred from the political prizes that were at stake in the struggles between citizens in Athens, there was less reason to doubt that their goodwill was toward all Athenians. By the time the first living, native Athenian citizen received official recognition for his *eunoia* in an honorary decree, the 330s at the earliest, but probably not until the very end of the fourth century, the last oligarchic revolution was a distant memory, and loyalty to the *demos* and to the city had become identical. But some old habits die hard, so the *demos* still refrained from attributing *eunoia* to resident, native Athenian citizens unless they performed their services unequivocally on behalf of the *demos* as officials in the government. It was only in 283, well into the Hellenistic period, when the *demos* had to relent and praise a resident, native Athenian citizen for services performed as a private individual.

Philotimia

More than any other single concept, *philotimia* embodies the basic spirit of the Athenian state's practice of honoring those who had performed trade-related services for the city. As we saw in chapter 3, the "love of honor" was the most powerful driving force behind almost everything that the ancient Greeks did. In the contest for wealth, status, and political power, the elite had long held the upper hand and claimed a monopoly on *philotimia*, but with the political triumph of the *demos* in Classical Athens, the latter now had a say in what actions qualified as honorable and who could be said to have been inspired by a love of honor. Among these actions were trade-related services, and through the use of the word *philotimia* in its honorary decrees, Athens made an explicit promise to its prospective benefactors that the city would be grateful for their services and would reciprocate with the bestowal of honors and privileges.

Athens attributed *philotimia* to those who had performed trade-related services in six extant honorary decrees (nos. 13, 14, 18 [entirely restored], 24, 27, and 29). *Philotimia* appears as an abstract noun in six of these decrees and in its verbal form of *philotimeomai* in three of them (nos. 14, 24, and 27). In other honorary decrees, Athens used both of these forms as well as an adverbial form (*philotimos*). Since Athens' intent and meaning in referring to the concept of *philotimia* seem to have been consistent regardless of the grammatical form in which it appears in its honorary decrees, I will not distinguish between them in my analysis and will simply refer to *philotimia* in all cases.

There is no indication that Athens made any distinctions with regard to the various types of trade-related services in the use of the word *philotimia*, since it is employed for a gift of imported goods, a sale of imported goods at a reduced price, and other miscellaneous trade-related services. A similar lack of distinction in the use of the word *philotimia* concerns the socioeconomic statuses of the honorands. Two of the five were wealthy professional traders (nos. 24 and 27); one was probably a foreign potentate (no. 29); one was a common professional trader (no. 18); and the socioeconomic statuses of the honorands of nos. 13 and 14 are unknown. The only distinction is that none of the honorands were native Athenian citizens; the honorand of no. 29 was naturalized by the same decree that honored him for his trade-related services. Although each honorand whose ethnicity is known was Greek (nos. 13, 18, 24, and 27), the ethnicity of the two others is unknown, thus precluding any useful analysis.

All five surviving honorary decrees for trade-related services that contain the word *philotimia* or its cognates were passed in 340 or later. Of the four honorary decrees for trade-related services that might predate 340 and are sufficiently preserved to allow certainty, none employ the word *philotimia* or its cognates (nos. 3 [411/10], 6 [407/6], 8 [ca. 390–378], and 12 [347/6]). In fact, it appears that Athens did not use the word *philotimia* or its cognates in honorary decrees for any kind of service until the mid-fourth century[26] — interestingly enough in a decree that honors a native Athenian citizen who had served with distinction as a member of the Council. From that time onward, Athens attributed *philotimia* to both foreigners and native Athenian citizens, though in greater numbers for the former (twenty-nine to seventeen down to the end of the fourth century, with six indeterminate).[27] Since *philotimia* was such an important value in ancient Greece, Athens must have deliberately refrained from using it in honorary decrees before the mid-fourth century and must have just as consciously changed its practice thereafter.[28]

This phenomenon can be explained in a way that is consistent with the foregoing analysis concerning Athens' use of other laudatory language in its honorary decrees. Since the word *philotimia*, like most of Athens' honorary language, was closely tied to traditional Greek values that reflected the ethos of the elite, the *demos* was reluctant to praise the city's native citizens for their *philotimia*, lest they strive too much for honor and disrupt the egalitarian ethos of democracy. Although Athens did not employ the word *philotimia* for use in honorary decrees for foreigners as well until the mid-fourth century, the reason for this differs from that concerning native citizens, since Athens had little reason to fear encouraging the *philotimia* of foreigners. *Philotimia* was added to the pool of terms with which Athens could praise its foreign honorands, just as the other terms before it, in response to specific circumstances that compelled Athens to expand and improve its practice of inducing benefactions to the state through the bestowal of honors and privileges.

Athens introduced the word *philotimia* into its honorary decrees shortly after its defeat in the Social War in 355. This date signals a major turning point in Athens' use of honorary language. Up to this time, Athens had expanded its practice to cover not only a wider variety of services, including those relating to trade, but also a more diverse assortment of honorands, ranging from foreign potentates to common professional traders. The expansion had taken place by fits and starts as the city's needs for security, revenue, and imported goods had continued to increase from the late fifth century to the mid-fourth century. Things were so bad after 355, however, and the feasibility of warfare and empire was so discredited as a means of fulfilling its needs, that Athens further expanded its practice both to honor native citizens (but only for services performed as public officials) and to make what had been an implicit practice completely explicit. As discussed in chapter 3, a common phrase that appears in Athenian honorary decrees after the mid-fourth century, commonly referred to by scholars as the formula of "hortative intention," explicitly states that the decree shall be inscribed on a stone stele so that all may know that Athens honors those who have *philotimia*. Athens was issuing an advertisement for its prospective benefactors, proclaiming in no uncertain terms that it needed benefactions, that it knew its benefactors wanted honor and the symbolic and practical benefits that came with it, and that the city would gratefully give it to them in return for their benefactions.

Almost from the inception of democracy, Athens had encouraged its elite citizens to strive for honor, but only through the performance of public services on behalf of the entire community, as seen in the liturgic system. Though the *demos* was careful not to honor elite liturgists too much, the performance of liturgies provided members of the citizen elite with the opportunity to represent their *philotimia* publicly through victory monuments and other verbal and visual displays, from which they hoped to earn the *charis* of the *demos* (see pp. 43–47). Athens then adapted this practice to induce public services from foreign benefactors. Having little reason to be concerned about encouraging their *philotimia* too much, however, Athens did not simply leave it to them to advertise their own *philotimia* but took the initiative to represent its foreign benefactors as being motivated by *philotimia* in honorary decrees. The *demos* assumed that foreign benefactors desired the same honor as citizen benefactors and that appealing to the *philotimia* of foreigners would induce benefactions from them. Thus, foreigners who had been barred from the traditional avenues of obtaining honor and its benefits in Athens now had a means of doing so.

Since Athens had already offered honor to foreigners in return for benefactions, it simply took increasing needs brought on by changing social, political, and economic circumstances to motivate the city to extend this practice to native citizens after the mid-fourth century. Athens began to overlook distinctions between native citizen and foreign honorands and between the types of services that each group traditionally performed. Whitehead sums up the significance of such a trend as follows:

The introduction of φιλοτιμία into the laudatory stock-in-trade coincided with the beginning of the period during which virtually any citizen or alien, resident or non-resident, who offered himself as a benefactor of the state was apt to be welcomed with open arms and credited with any and all of the fashionable virtues of the day. The Athenians . . . seem to have realised . . . that the φιλοτιμία of others besides themselves was necessary to the survival of their πόλις in a changed and changing world . . . which glossed over the traditional gulf of legal status between citizen and foreigner; and φιλοτιμία πρὸς τὸν δ ῆμον τὸν Θηναίων was required of them both. (Whitehead 1983: 67–68)

Although the use of the word *philotimia* in connection with trade-related services was an innovation, the practice of using *philotimia* in honorary decrees for trade-related services was an aspect of Athenian trade policy that was still largely embedded in traditional social and political relations. With this practice, Athens fulfilled its trading interests in the same way it fulfilled its political and military interests: by inducing benefactors to perform public services with the promise that the city would express its *charis* for their *philotimia* by granting them the honor that they so desired. Thus, Athens represented the trading exchange as one of reciprocation, involving gratitude and honor, rather than an impersonal market exchange for profit. On the surface, this would appear appropriate when foreign potentates gave Athens gifts of imported goods, but it would seem somewhat of a sham when applied to common professional traders who had simply sold imported goods in Athens at the market price. Yet it is perhaps impossible to distinguish between representations and true feelings. Even in gift exchange, the parties to the transaction often have very practical needs that belie the seemingly social and noneconomic ideals of reciprocation, while market exchanges are not always totally impersonal and profit-centered (see chap. 3). Regardless of the true character of these honored exchanges, however, by attributing the motivations of its honorands to *philotimia*, Athens was legitimizing market-structured trade and those who engaged in it, elevating them to a status on par with traditionally esteemed gift trade and its practitioners.

Conclusion

Athens' use of language in its honorary decrees for those who had performed trade-related services illustrates the complex and dynamic economy of Greece in the late Classical period. It is not enough to say that because elite writers disdained trade and those who carried it out, states had little interest and involvement in trade other than to obtain revenue and imported goods. This argument fails to note how attitudes toward trade in Athens changed in response to shifting social, political, and economic circumstances during the fifth and fourth centuries. The changes may have been subtle, but a recognition of them provides us with a much more nuanced and, dare I say, accurate picture of the interplay between society, politics, and economics that necessarily occurs on account of the fact that all economies, even market economies, are embedded in social relations in some manner to some degree. What really distinguishes economies is the nature of the social relations that shapes them, not whether they are embedded in those relations.

The social, political, and economic circumstances that affected the use of laudatory language in Athenian honorary decrees were numerous and fluid. One was the long-standing rivalry between the masses and the elite citizens of Athens. When the *demos* triumphed over the elite in democratic Athens, rather than creating an entirely new vocabulary of praise, it simply appropriated elite honorary language and gave it new meaning in accordance with democratic ideals of egalitarianism and community service. But the *demos* was reluctant to praise benefactors among the Athenian citizenry (who were most likely to be from the elite) with words expressing traditional values, for fear of encouraging elite *philotimia* too much and undermining the egalitarian ethos of Athenian democracy. As a result, Athens was much more willing to praise foreign benefactors than native Athenian citizens in honorary decrees. Yet, although it readily praised foreigners who had performed traditionally esteemed political and military services, it resisted praising those who had performed trade-related services, on account of the residual aristocratic disdain for trade and other *banausic* occupations still embodied in the traditional honorary language.

The *demos* was compelled to make further adaptations in its use of honorary language, however, in response to a series of crises in the late fifth and fourth centuries. Athens' defeat in the Sicilian Expedition, the Peloponnesian War, the Social War, and the Battle of Chaironeia each severely damaged the city's ability to maintain its security, public revenues, and supply of necessary goods, particularly grain. In response, Athens expanded the types of services that it would praise in its honorary decrees to include those relating to trade. It also broadened the statuses of men deemed to be worthy of such praise to include not only foreigners of very low status, such as common professional traders, but also native Athenian citizens, so long as they were acting as public officials in the service of the *demos*. Lastly, Athens added to the vocabulary of praise both to match the increasing diversity in honored services and to clarify and make more explicit its *charis* to its benefactors.

Even thus democratized, Athens' application of such value-laden terms to those who had performed trade-related services characterized these men and their services in wholly traditional terms. Whether they were potentates or common professional traders, Athenian honorary decrees represented them as having little or no self-interest, as having been motivated by noble and traditionally noneconomic interests (in the formalist sense), such as a "love of honor" or at least "goodwill" toward Athens. Moreover, Athens acted as if it were the humble and grateful recipient of the benefactions of these exceptionally honorable men.

It is no wonder that many modern scholars have been led to believe that Athens had a very limited trade policy and passively waited for benefactors to come forth to fulfill its trading needs (see pp. 61–62). But Xenophon's *Poroi*, Demosthenes' speech *Against Leptines*, and the hortative clauses of such honorary decrees as *IG* ii² 360 (nos. 24 and 27) all indicate that Athens was deliberately putting a "spin" on its representation of its honorands. It did not simply wait for benefactions, humbly receive them, and then reward the benefactors with high praise, titles, and privileges. Athens fostered such an appearance as part of a conscious and deliberate attempt to encourage trade-related services by offering an elevated status to those who had performed them. Foreign potentates as well as wealthy and even common, professional traders were granted official recognition as useful, goodwilled, or honorable men in the city of Athens, which implied a status traditionally reserved implicitly for exceptional citizens and explicitly for foreigners performing traditionally esteemed, noneconomic services. Such praise offered an incentive in addition to profit for men to engage in trading exchanges with Athens.

Another tendency of modern scholarship has been to see such honorary language applied to trade-related services as evidence of a lack of differentiation between economic activities and social and political ones in the ancient Greek world. For example, Austin and Vidal-Naquet believe that the honorary language applied to trade-related services shows that Athenians considered such services to be "civic benefactions done to the people of Athens, and not just strictly economic services" (Austin and

Vidal-Naquet 1977: 118). For this to be true, however, Athens would have to have made no distinction between trade-related services and more traditional political or military services. But in the cases of every one of the honorary terms examined in this chapter, Athens applied them to political or military services first and to trade-related services only after a decade or more had elapsed and in trying circumstances. Thus, Athens clearly distinguished between trade-related services and political and military services.

Further evidence for such a distinction can be found in Whitehead's identification of the "cardinal virtues" of democratic Athens, ten abstract nouns repeatedly used in Athenian honorary decrees, mostly after the mid-fourth century (Whitehead 1993: 37–43, 65). Despite Whitehead's oversimplification of the motives behind the use of these "abstract attributes" in Athenian honorary decrees, he is right to point out that Athens distinguished between various types of services in the application of these words. Of the six words that Athens commonly used to praise those who had performed trade-related services, three (*arete, eunoia,* and *philotimia*) are among these so-called cardinal virtues. A fourth virtue, *andragathia,* is an abstraction of *aner agathos,* which was also commonly employed for trade-related services along with two other adjectives, *eunous,* whose abstraction is *eunoia,* and *chresimos.* The remaining six "cardinal virtues" identified by Whitehead are *dikaiosyne, epimeleia, eusebia, eutaxia, prothymia,* and *sophrosyne.* Whereas Athens applied five of these last six virtues (all except for *prothymia*) with respect to specific activities, those that it employed with regard to trade-related services were more general in nature (Whitehead 1993: 67–72). For example, the word *eusebeia* was used to praise services involving religious matters, such as the maintenance of a shrine, and the word *eutaxia* was used in military contexts, such as the training of ephebes. *Arete, eunoia, philotimia, andragathia,* and *prothymia,* on the other hand, were applied by Athens to a wide variety of services, including those relating to trade. Thus, the care with which Athens used its honorary language indicates that the city distinguished between different types of services, employing general, rather than specific, terms of praise for services, including trade-related ones, that did not fit conveniently into traditionally honored services.

Although honoring men for trade-related services was an aspect of Athenian trade policy that differed considerably from those of modern states, it often had the effect of encouraging more typically "modern" market-structured economic activities. Athens sought to increase imports

for consumption and used a traditional method of inducing public services by honoring those who provided them. In doing so, however,
Athens began including among the range of activities for which a person
could be described as *agathos, eunous,* and *chresimos* or as having *arete, eunoia,* and *philotimia* not only traditionally esteemed political and military
services but also trade-related services, including the sale of imported
goods at the market price. Moreover, the persons who were praised for
such a service were common professional traders who typically sought
only profit and traditionally had no opportunity for honor. But changing
social, political, and economic circumstances led to changes in values,
which Athenian praise for men who performed trade-related services
both reflected and contributed to.

CHAPTER SEVEN

Honors

In addition to praising those whom it honored for trade-related services with language that expressed the highest social values of ancient Greece, Athens also granted various honors as rewards and encouragements for their services. I classify as "honors" proclamations, titles, offices, gifts, and other items whose value as symbols of honor appears to outweigh the tangible rights or privileges that they also brought to their recipients. These honors include

- official commendation
- *proxenia* and *euergesia*[1]
- gold crowns
- bronze statues
- *xenia* in the Prytaneion
- seats in the theater for the Dionysia
- inscribed stelai

The classification of these items as "honors," as opposed to "privileges" (see chap. 8), is somewhat arbitrary, since all the honors and privileges granted by Athens had both honorific value and functional uses to varying degrees. For the purposes of analysis, however, it is necessary to make such a distinction, since it divides one large body of evidence into two smaller and, therefore, more manageable units, while also more clearly illustrating both honor and profit as components of Athenian trade policy.

Modern scholarship has not fully appreciated the significance of honorary decrees in Athenian trade policy, largely because it has failed to recognize both honor and profit as important goals of economic activity in Classical Greece. Some scholars have held, for example, that in granting honors in exchange for the services of its benefactors, Athens was getting the better end of the deal, since the monetary costs of its honors were minimal compared to the monetary value of its benefactors' services.[2] Others have pointed to the practical benefits of Athenian honors for their recipients and have concluded that the exchange was a commensurate one, just not one that was mediated through money.[3] As we shall see, the latter view is preferable to the former, since it acknowledges that honors had some kind of value for its recipients, but it still does not tell the whole story. Although honorands surely appreciated the practical benefits of Athenian honors, they also appreciated honor for its own sake, for the purely psychological satisfaction it brought in their "shame society."

It is true also that some honors, such as gold crowns and bronze statues, entailed monetary costs for Athens, but the more significant cost, of which Athens was certainly aware, lay in the corrosive effect that granting such honors for trade-related services had on traditional values. Although the monetary cost of some honors was significant enough to indicate Athens' greater interest in obtaining imported goods than in generating revenue from trade, most honorands, particularly the wealthier ones, were less interested in the monetary value of Athenian honors than they were in their honorific value and the practical benefits such honor entailed. Moreover, as in the case of using honorary language to induce trade-related services, granting honors such as gold crowns for trade-related as well as political and military services required an adjustment to long-held social values. This was especially true when the trade-related service was the simple importation of grain for sale at the going price, since in the absence of Athenian honors, such an act was motivated solely by profit seeking on the part of the honorand. Perhaps even worse for traditional Greek values, all the honorands who had performed trade-related services were foreigners, and some of them were common professional traders. For this latter group, the value of Athenian honors must have been very high, since such honors elevated their status considerably. Aware of the negative consequences that granting honors for trade-related services could have on its traditional values, Athens did not make such grants lightly, but only under the compulsion of necessity in specific circumstances.

On balance, both Athens and its honorands got what they wanted from the relationship created by the practice of granting honors for trade-related services. The relationship constituted a ritualized friendship in which Athens received necessary goods from abroad, while its honorands received both honor and profit, the latter in the form of the practical benefits that came with honor as well as any monetary profit they may have made, depending on the nature of their exchange with Athens. In addition, the ritualized friendship was intended to be a long-term relationship, in which each party could count on the other to provide *boetheia* whenever the need should arise. Thus, it is misleading to characterize the exchanges between Athens and those it honored for trade-related services as characteristically either reciprocal in nature, devoid of profit seeking and embedded in social and political relations, or market-structured, in which the relationship is unimportant while monetary or even just practical gain is the sole interest. They had elements of both.

Commendation

The most common means of honoring those who had performed trade-related services by official decree of the Council or Assembly was for Athens to commend (*epaineo*) them publicly.[4] Commendation was simply official Athenian recognition of services performed for the city, often as a preface to grants of more substantial honors and privileges. If one thinks in terms of a hierarchy of honors, with citizenship and bronze statues being the highest, then commendation was among the lowest (along with *proxenia* and *euergesia*), a baby step in a sort of *cursus honorum* of official Athenian honors. Commendations had neither a monetary value nor a practical use value; they were purely honorific. Not surprisingly, Athens officially commended many honorands for a variety of services for the city.

Commendation appears in seventeen of the twenty-five extant honorary decrees for trade-related services.[5] Seven of the remaining eight decrees in which commendation does not appear are too badly damaged to determine whether Athens commended the honorands.[6] This leaves only one (no. 8) of the twenty-five extant honorary decrees for trade-related services in which the honorands were definitely not commended. It is likely that a commendation is absent from no. 8 because, at the time of this decree (ca. 390–378/7), Athens was reluctant to commend a man of low status whose trade-related services did not also significantly further the city's political and military interests. All but one of the first six honorands down to 347/6 who received commendations from Athens for trade-related services were foreign potentates. The exception was Phanosthenes of Andros, the honorand of no. 4. Although he was directly engaged in trade and not a foreign potentate at the time he was honored by Athens, he certainly was not a typical professional trader. He seems to have been prominent in his home city of Andros before being exiled as a result of an oligarchic coup, and he later became a citizen and general of Athens (see app. 3, no. 4). Athens, therefore, probably considered him to be higher in status than a professional trader.

In addition, Phanosthenes and the other five honorands who were the first to receive commendations for trade-related services also benefited Athens politically and militarily. Phanosthenes and his associates had provided oar spars, while Archelaos (no. 6) had provided Athens with both oar spars and timber for constructing warships during a crucial stage of the Peloponnesian War. The next extant decree containing a commendation for trade-related services is no. 11, which dates to some forty-three years later. It commends Orontes, the Persian satrap of Mysia, for the service of providing grain for the soldiers on an Athenian military expedition. Next after that is no. 12, which commends Spartokos II and Pairisades I in 347/6 for such trade-related services as providing gifts of grain to Athens and trading privileges in Bosporan ports to traders bound for Athens. Although their honorary decrees are no longer extant, two earlier kings of the Bosporos, Satyros and Leukon, probably also received commendations from Athens as far back as ca. 395 (nos. 7 and 9). It appears, then, that Athens was initially reluctant to commend men of low status for services that related solely to trade, preferring instead to honor only men of high status in this way.

Athens also showed little reluctance in commending those who had performed political or military services.[7] At least eighteen such decrees predate 410/9, going back perhaps as early as 451/0.[8] Between 413 and 407, however, Athens was in a difficult situation and badly needed ships' timber to rebuild its fleet in the wake of the disastrous Sicilian Expedition (see p. 56). But since such timber was not available in Attika and since Athens was not at this time powerful enough to extort it from elsewhere, the state had to obtain timber through trade. In these circumstances, Athens granted commendations to Phanosthenes and his associates, who had conveyed oar spars to Athens sometime between 410 and 407/6 (no. 4), and to Archelaos, who gave Athens ships' timber and oar spars (no. 6) in 407/6.

It took extreme circumstances, the high status of Phanosthenes and Archelaos, and the political and military benefits of the honorands' services for Athens to grant commendations for trade-related services at this time. Perdikkas, Archelaos' predecessor on the Macedonian throne, had also provided oar spars to Athens as part of a military alliance at some time between ca. 432/1 and 414 (*IG* i³ 89; see app. 3, R7). Yet there is no evidence to suggest that Athens commended Perdikkas for his trade-related service, most likely because the circumstances surrounding his services were not as severe as those surrounding the services of Archelaos. Not only was the Athenian navy at full strength up until 413, but Athens could possibly obtain imports of ships' timber from southern Italy before that date.[9] Athens simply did not need to offer honor in return for the trade-related services from a Macedonian king before 413 to the degree that it needed to do so in 407/6.

The fact that Andokides, who performed similar trade-related services in similar circumstances in 409/8, did not receive an official commendation or any other honors or privileges from Athens was probably the result of exceptional political concerns and of his status as a native Athenian citizen, who, furthermore, had lost his rights and was currently living in exile.[10] During the oligarchy of the Four Hundred in 411, Andokides, who had been in exile since 415 for his part in profaning the Mysteries, used his connections with King Archelaos to supply the Athenian fleet at Samos with grain, bronze, and oar spars from Macedon at cost (And. 2.11–12). Yet Andokides (2.13–14) makes it clear that he was disappointed in his expectation of a commendation from Athens, which instead arrested him for aiding the enemy, since the Four Hundred were by that time in conflict with the fleet at Samos. In this case, therefore, political circumstances were clearly an important factor in Athens' decision not to commend Andokides for his trade-related service.

Athens' decision is also consistent with its reluctance to honor native Athenian citizens who performed any kind of services in private, rather than official, capacities, especially trade-related services. Andokides (2.17–18) says that Athens granted crowns and publicly proclaimed as "good men" those who added to the public revenues in the performance of public offices or who performed serviceable exploits as military commanders. Although there is no extant epigraphic evidence for official Athenian commendations for native citizens before 371, the evidence after that time is consistent with Andokides' remarks in that every native Athenian citizen who received commendations from Athens down to the late 280s was recognized for services performed as a public official (along with nonthreatening ephebes and some cleruchs and colonists living abroad).[11] As discussed previously, the *demos* of Classical Athens took care to limit official honors of any kind for native citizens, granting them almost exclusively to those who had proven their subservience to the *demos* by serving as officials in the democratic government (see pp. 48–49). Thus, Andokides was engaging in a bit of wishful thinking in hoping that he would be commended by Athens for his services, since he was an Athenian citizen by birth who performed his services in a private capacity and, even worse, while living in exile, having been stripped of his civic rights for sacrilegious acts.

In addition, the officeholders and generals whom Andokides cites as having received commendations and crowns from Athens had all performed political or military services for the city. This is also consistent with the epigraphic evidence cited above, which reveals that all official Athenian commendations down to 410/9 were for political or military services. After that time, Athens began to commend trade-related services, but only when performed by foreigners. Athens did not commend a native citizen for such services until the 280s (see above and pp. 341–42, n. 11). The reason Athens was especially reluctant to honor native citizens for trade-related services was most likely the disdain for such a *banausic* activity in traditional Greek social values (see p. 39). As a native citizen who had lost his civic rights and was now engaging in trade, Andokides was doubtless seen as being unworthy of a commendation by the Athenian People. But the difficult circumstances of the final stages of the Peloponnesian War after 410 did compel Athens to expand its practice of honoring foreigners for political and military services to include trade-related ones, so long as those who performed the latter were men like Phanosthenes and Archelaos, both of a higher status than professional traders and likely to be of political and military service to Athens as well.

The first commendation that can be dated with some precision (ca. 337) for a professional trader who performed trade-related services is no. 15. Besides selling grain (and possibly fish) to Athens at a reduced price (no doubt in the immediate aftermath of the Battle of Chaironeia), the honorand also performed the more traditionally esteemed services of both paying a ransom to release Athenian citizens held captive in Sicily and contributing to the defense of Athens leading up to the Battle of Chaironeia. Being a wealthy trader, the honorand of no. 15 was obviously higher in status than a common trader, and although not to the degree of a foreign potentate, he could be useful to Athens in spheres other than trade. Common professional traders might have received commendations for trade-related service as early as 337 as well (nos. 17–19), but it is uncertain, since we cannot date the decrees in question with precision.

Whatever the case, it is clear that Athens did not formally commend professional traders of any class until after the Battle of Chaironeia.

Regardless of their status, those who were in a position to perform trade-related services for Athens likely coveted commendations for their honorific value and for the practical benefits that came with such honor, since commendations had little immediate use or monetary value. Honor was, as we have seen, the most basic and powerful social value of ancient Greece, and one could also parlay it into such practical benefits as favor in the law courts, political alliances (for foreign potentates), and the all-purpose *boetheia* (see pp. 39–40). It is clear that Athens also took the granting of commendations seriously, since it appears that its relaxation of the qualifications for their conferral was made only grudgingly, over time and under duress.

Proxenia *and* Euergesia

Athens also granted *proxenia* and *euergesia* to those who had performed trade-related services. Although they were closely linked and almost always granted together, *euergesia* was primarily, though not purely, honorific, whereas *proxenia* entailed a complex and vaguely defined nexus of honorary and functional characteristics that went well beyond its intrinsic honorific value.[12] Because of the complexity of *proxenia*, it will be useful to discuss the nature of the institution and its possible connections with trade before examining the Athenian decrees granting *proxenia* and *euergesia* for trade-related services.

Proxenia had its origins in informal, private ties—commonly known as "hospitality" or "guest-friendship," but more broadly described as "ritualized friendship" by Herman—that were an integral feature of ancient Greek society from the time of Homer's epics through the Hellenistic period.[13] The word *proxenos* itself derives from the prefix *pro-*, which means "on behalf of" or "instead of," and from the word *xenos*, which means "guest-friend" or, more generally, "foreigner." Thus, a *proxenos* is one who acts "instead of a guest-friend" or "on behalf of a foreigner."[14] In the late sixth century and into the fifth, *poleis* adapted the private institution of *xenia* into the public institution of *proxenia* by assuming the role of *xenoi* and officially conferring the title of *proxenos* on an individual foreign counterpart with whom the city as a whole would be tied in ritualized friendship.[15] In some ways, *proxenia* resembled modern diplomatic institutions, such as a consulate or embassy, in which a diplomatic representative of one nation is stationed in another to look after the interests of his or her own country there. In Classical Greece, however, a state bestowed the title of *proxenos* on a citizen of another state, who represented the interests of the granting state in his own state.

The process by which *poleis* identified prospective *proxenoi* varied, but there are some features that are common to all cases. Herman argues that all *proxenoi* began as the private *xenoi* of individual citizens and continued to serve them first and their *poleis* second (Herman 1987: 137–38). The citizen *xenoi*, therefore, served as middlemen through whom states were able to identify and acquire new friends abroad. An alternative view, however, is that states and the foreigners who would become their *proxenoi* made direct contact without tapping the preexisting *xeniai* of private citizens (Marek 1984: 134). These two views are not mutually exclusive; it will be apparent from the analysis below that Athens identified *proxenoi* both through the private connections of their own citizens and through direct contacts between individual foreigners and state officials. In all cases, though, *poleis* granted *proxenia* only to those who had provided proof of their goodwill to the granting city through some sort of benefaction (*euergesia*). This is apparent from the fact that the vast majority of Athenian decrees coupled grants of *proxenia* with *euergesia*. Rarely did Athens grant either title without the other.[16]

Proxenia, therefore, had both honorary and functional characteristics, but there has been much disagreement about the degree to which either of these two characteristics may have predominated.[17] The evidence from Athenian grants of *proxenia* and *euergesia* tends to support those who believe that *proxenia* always had practical functions and was never strictly honorary. These functions, however, were not limited to that of a "state's guest-friend." The *polis* that granted *proxenia* expected the *proxenos* to continue to perform the same types of services for which he was honored in the first place. In short, *proxenia* entailed "an all-purpose reciprocal relationship" between the *proxenos* and the granting city.[18]

The Athenian state never granted either *proxenia* or *euergesia* to native citizens. This is not unexpected in the case of *proxenia*, given the origins of the institution in the private ritualized friendships between men of separate communities. It is less understandable, however, with regard to *euergesia*. On the face of it, there is no reason why Athens should honor only foreigners and not native citizens with the title *benefactor* for public services. The only plausible explanation for this phenomenon concerns the tension between the masses and the elite in Athens (see pp. 41–53). The *demos* expected Athenian citizens to perform benefactions for the city and did not wish to disrupt the egalitarian ethos of democracy by honoring some citizens above others for benefactions performed independently of official government institutions. Since foreigners were excluded from political power in Athens, the *demos* could reward their benefactions and encourage more such benefactions by honoring them with the title of *euergetai* without feeling any significant threat to its political supremacy in Athens.

It has been common for scholars to associate *proxenia* closely with intercity trade in both the private origins and the subsequent public functions of the institution.[19] They assume that just as individuals had relied on *xenoi* to facilitate their private intercity trade in pre-Classical times, *poleis* like Athens used *proxenoi* from the Classical period onward to create official intercity relations that facilitated their public trading interests.[20] Few of these scholars, however, specify either how *proxenoi* actually served intercity trading relations or what kind of trading interests such relations were supposed to fulfill: did *proxenoi* look after the interests of the appointing city's traders abroad, or did *proxenoi* somehow facilitate the import of necessary goods to the appointing city? Hasebroek, otherwise a staunch critic of those who advocate sophisticated intercity trading relations in ancient Greece, boldly states that the way a *proxenos* served the city that had appointed him was by acting as a middleman between citizens of the appointing city and local officials in his own city, particularly with regard to legal matters; in short, "he had to watch over all buying and selling and exchange of commodities between individuals from the one city and members of the other" (Hasebroek 1933: 129). Such a view implies that cities appointed *proxenoi* to aid the cities' own citizens who were involved in commerce in the home cities of their *proxenoi*.

Proxeny decrees are silent about the expected tasks of *proxenoi*, but several scholars have argued, on the basis of the geographical distribution of the home cities of *proxenoi*, that *proxenia* was a component of state trade policy. For example, Ziebarth believes that the geographical distribution of the *proxenoi* of Delos along a path leading directly to the Black Sea in the third century B.C.E. (distribution determined by their ethnics) makes it highly likely that Delos appointed *proxenoi* with an aim of securing imports of grain from the Black Sea.[21] More recently, Burke has written that *proxenia* in the Classical period "helped add to the nexus of interstate relations on which such [maritime] commerce depended" (Burke 1992: 207). A logical extension of this view is that the great number of known proxenies attests to the extensive trade interests of *poleis* in the ancient Greek world.

But such a connection between trade and *proxenia*, which involves state-organized intercity trade relations, is far from certain.[22] The geographic distribution of a city's *proxenoi* along known trade routes does not necessarily prove that trade interests motivated their appointment. First of all, one cannot assume that *proxenoi* remained "on call" in their home cities, since some *proxenoi* of Athens, for example, appear to have resided in Athens as *metics* (see below). Secondly, even if *proxenoi* always resided in their home cities, one would like to see evidence of actual trade taking place between the granting city and the home city of the *proxenos*. Thirdly, even when one can identify a *proxenos* as a professional trader, the relationship between Athens and the *proxenos* was one between the state and an individual, not between the Athenian state and the home state of the *proxenos* (Hasebroek 1933: 129).

Athenian grants of *proxenia* and *euergesia* to those who had performed trade-related services did serve the state's trade interests, just not as has been argued previously. Of the thirty-four occasions on which Athens honored men for trade-related services down to 307, eleven granted *proxenia*.[23] Of the remaining twenty-three occasions, ten are known from evidence that is too fragmentary for us to be certain whether *proxenia* and *euergesia* were among the honors.[24] Of the remaining thirteen occasions, there are twelve in which the honorands received honors such as citizenship or had already received *proxenia*, thus precluding grants of *proxenia* on those occasions.[25] This leaves one case (no. 24) in which it is certain that Athens did not grant *proxenia* and *euergesia* but for which we must seek other explanations for their absence.

In its criteria for granting *proxenia* and *euergesia*, Athens seems not to have distinguished between the types of trade-related services or the legal and socioeconomic statuses of those who had performed such services. Men who performed services in all the categories of trade-related services except for sales of imported goods at reduced prices and securing shipments of goods received these honors.[26] It is unlikely, however, that Athens considered either of these services unworthy of *proxenia* and *euergesia* per se, since Athens granted the honors to men who had performed the lesser trade-related service of simple importations of goods. Without discrimination, Athens granted *proxenia* and *euergesia* for trade-related services to Greeks and non-Greeks, *metics* and non-*metics*, common and wealthy professional traders, and foreign potentates.[27]

The presence of *metics* among the recipients of *proxenia* for trade-related services raises questions about the putative "function" and historical development of *proxenia*. Although most scholars now agree that "it is not axiomatic that only men living in their own city were appointed πϱόξενοι," they admit few exceptions to the old rule.[28] Yet on three of the eleven occasions on which Athens granted *proxenia* for trade-related services, the honorands were *metics*. Such men could not have acted as official guest-friends of Athenians in their home cities. Moreover, two of the occasions for these grants date to a period after 330 (nos. 25 and 27), whereas one dates to as early as 410 (no. 4), thereby contradicting any notion that *proxenia* originally signified a functional office but later became strictly honorific.[29] The evidence that Athens appointed *metics* as *proxenoi* shows that *proxenia* did not have a fixed function as an institution of official guest-friendship. Rather, the function of *proxenia* varied with each particular case. Such a view plausibly explains why Athens followed no strict rules that discriminated between the types of trade-related services or the ethnicities, residence statuses, and socioeconomic statuses of honorands when granting *proxenia*.

Although the chronological distribution of Athenian grants of *proxenia* and *euergesia* for trade-related services do not reveal that certain types of services or honorands were favored over others at any given time, the distribution does appear to show that Athens distinguished between political or military services and trade-related ones. Most Athenian grants of *proxenia* and *euergesia* in the fifth and fourth centuries were made in recognition of political or military services. Before 415, grants of these honors were made exclusively for political or military services (when the services can be identified).[30] The only possible case of an Athenian decree granting *proxenia* and *euergesia* for services other than political or military ones before 415 is Walbank no. 68 (416/5–410/9), in which the honorand may have been a doctor.[31] Walbank identifies trade-related services as the motive for seven decrees granting *proxenia* and *euergesia* before 415, but the decrees are not explicit, and Walbank's identifications are based on doubtful assumptions.[32]

The first certain example of an Athenian grant of *proxenia* and *euergesia* for a service that was not political or military in nature is *IG* i[3] 174 (no. 1), which was for a trade-related service. This decree is among the first of two groups of Athenian grants of these honors for trade-related services that are clustered in the years 414–407/6 and 330–319/8, respectively. From between 414 and 407/6, there exist four extant Athenian decrees that grant *proxenia* and *euergesia* for services other than political or military ones, and all concern trade.[33] During this same period, there are only two securely dated instances in which Athens granted *proxenia* and *euergesia* for purely political or military services.[34] With the difficulties and final destruction of the Sicilian Expedition, Athens obviously needed political or military services in order to maintain its hopes in the Peloponnesian War. In addition, it needed to encourage trade, particularly timber imports to rebuild and maintain a new fleet, which was the basis of its military strategy (see pp. 56–57). It would not be surprising if Athens began at this time to grant certain honors and privileges, such as *proxenia* and *euergesia,* not only to those who had performed political or military services but also to those who had performed trade-related services. In the two decrees of this latter kind, in which we know the specific nature of the trade-related services, both involve supplying Athens with oar spars for triremes (nos. 4 and 6).

From the end of the Peloponnesian War to 355, however, there is only one case (no. 8) in which Athens granted *proxenia* to a man who had performed a trade-related or any other service besides a political or military one, the latter of which we can identify in at least ten certain cases.[35] Although Athens did not suffer any crises as severe as those of the last fifteen years of the fifth century, there were times during the 390s and early 380s, for example, when it was certainly in need of services involving timber and grain imports (see pp. 57–58). Perhaps the small number of grants of *proxenia* and *euergesia* for trade-related services during this period can be explained by the fact that all except one person who received any kind of honors and privileges for such services at this time had already been granted citizenship, which precluded grants of *proxenia* and *euergesia* (nos. 7 and 9). The exception was the honorand of no. 8, and perhaps not coincidentally, he is the only one to have received *proxenia* for trade-related services during this time.

After 355 and the loss of the Second Athenian League, however, Athens once again experienced several periods in which it was severely lacking in revenue and grain. Its defeat in the Battle of Chaironeia in 338/7, the invasion of Greece by Alexander in 335/4, and the shortage of grain throughout Greece in the early 320s drove the state to take extreme measures in order to secure revenue and grain (see pp. 65–66). It is in such a historical context, between 355/4 and 307/6, that we find the second group (consisting of six decrees) of Athenian grants of *proxenia* and *euergesia* to those who had performed trade-related services (five of which can be dated with some confidence between 337 and 319), in which the grain supply of Athens was at the greatest risk.[36] In comparison, there are at least twelve extant decrees granting *proxenia* and *euergesia* that appear to be for political or military services between 355/4 and 307/6.[37] In addition to those for trade-related and political or military services, the only other decrees that grant *proxenia* and *euergesia* and in which the precise nature of the services can be identified are for services involving medicine, religion, and poetry/theater.[38] As a note of caution, it should be pointed out that there are also at least thirty-five other extant Athenian decrees from this period that grant *proxenia* and *euergesia* for which we cannot determine the nature of the honorands' services.[39]

Given that the motivations for so many proxeny decrees are unknown, it is unwise to try to draw any conclusions in regard to the relative proportions over time of such decrees for political and military services, on the one hand, and trade-related services, on the other. It is clear, though, that even as Athens continued to grant *proxenia* and *euergesia* for political and military services after the shocks of both 355 and 338, it increased the frequency of such grants for trade-related services, especially after 338, when the city's grain supply was at its most vulnerable. One could, of course, dismiss these numbers as simply the result of the chance survival of inscriptions or changes in the "epigraphic habit" of Athens, but support for the historical significance of the numbers comes from the evidence for other Athenian institutions, particularly legal ones, aimed at protecting the grain trade and from the concerns for obtaining revenue and imported goods expressed by such men as Isokrates, Xenophon, and Demosthenes.

The foregoing analysis points to a connection between Athenian trade policy and *proxenia;* the connection, however, is neither one in which Athens established a network of trade relations represented by *proxenoi* abroad nor one in which preexisting private trading contacts facilitated by *xenia* were appropriated by the state and transformed into official proxenies. Walbank is right to identify trade (in the substantivist sense) as being among the interests that bound men from various cities in private *xeniai* during the Archaic period (Walbank 1978: 2–3). As Herman and others have argued, however, such interests were not the primary

motivations for *xenia* and, if anything, were subordinate to social, political, and religious ones—which one would expect, since the bonds of *xenia*
were maintained among the landed elite in the Greek cities and did not
involve professional traders.[40] As members of the landed elite, *xenoi* were
more interested in maintaining their social status and long-term political
relationships through their gift exchanges than in obtaining needed
goods or making a profit.

Classical Athens clearly used *xenia* as its model for *proxenia* and may
very well have converted some preexisting private *xeniai* into public *prox-
eniai*. But those to whom Athens initially granted *proxenia* had performed
political or military services, not trade-related ones, down to 415. After
that time, however, Athens did expand its practice to grant *proxenia* to
those who had performed trade-related as well as political and military
services. But it did so not to set up an intercity trading network, since
proxenoi could not be expected to be "on call" in their home cities and
since *proxenia* established a relationship between Athens and a foreign individual, not a foreign state. Rather, Athens sought to reward them for
their trade-related services (which always involved providing Athens
with grain or timber from abroad) and to encourage more such services
from them and others in the future.

Marek is right to point out that such a practice is similar to Athens'
practice of granting *proxenia* and *euergesia* to those who had performed
other services, including political, military, medical, and financial ones.[41]
But he errs in reducing Athenian grants of *proxenia* and *euergesia* for each
type of service to one general practice without distinction. Although
Athens' modus operandi was the same when it granted *proxenia* and *euergesia* for political, medical, or trade-related services, its interest in each
case was different, even if, as in some cases, multiple, overlapping interests existed. Moreover, since it is clear that Athens initially granted *proxenia* and *euergesia* solely for political and military services and only included trade-related services later and in times of great need, the state
itself must have distinguished between these services and the interests
they served. Such a distinction in interests shows that despite its use of
traditional methods, Athens' trade policy was becoming differentiated
from its political and military policies.

Such a change had further ramifications for the social values of
Athens. The state now deemed those who had performed trade-related
services worthy of receiving *proxenia* and *euergesia*, titles whose roots

sprang from the most traditional of Greek institutions, ritualized friendship. In addition, such titles elevated foreign benefactors to a status somewhere above that of the mass of ordinary foreigners, though not quite to the level of Athenian citizens (Gauthier 1985: 129–30). Athens was now recognizing a middle status between the citizen and the foreigner, blurring the strict dichotomy that had long been a hallmark of the Greek *polis*. Moreover, although traditional *xenia* involved relationships between men of equal elite status (Herman 1987: 34–35), Athens' designation of nonelite men, such as professional traders, as *proxenoi* was a further alteration of traditional values and practices.

From the point of view of the honorands, *proxenia* and *euergesia* intrinsically had only an honorific value, but such honor could be parlayed into additional practical benefits. Scholars, however, have tended to overstate or overspecify such benefits. Walbank suggests that a *proxenos* "probably derived financial benefit from the commercial side of his duties as *proxenos*" (Walbank 1978: 3). But this view assumes that *proxenia* had a fixed set of duties related to trade, which is not the case (see above). Other scholars believe that the title of *proxenos* was an honor that in turn attracted other honors and practical privileges.[42] The vast majority of cases in which Athens granted *enktesis*, for example, also contain grants of *proxenia* and *euergesia* (see Pecirka 1966: 152–58). It is possible, however, that Athens granted other honors and privileges in conjunction with *proxenia* not because the honorand was now a *proxenos* but simply because the honorand's benefaction was considered worthy of them. Therefore, it seems prudent to distinguish between grants of *proxenia* and *euergesia* and other honors and privileges, even if the latter were as a rule granted in conjunction with these titles.

Herman's argument that all *proxenoi* began as private *xenoi* of individual citizens also implies practical benefits for *proxenoi* and their private connections in Athens that go beyond the honorific value of the title itself (Herman 1987: 137–38). In Herman's view, benefactions from the foreign elite were actually not intended for the benefit of the Athenian people per se but rather for the elite Athenian citizen who was bound to the foreign benefactor by *xenia*. This elite citizen benefited from his *xenos'* gift to the community of Athens (and may have requested the gift from his *xenos* for this specific purpose), since it served as proof of the citizen's usefulness and loyalty to the *demos*. By giving goods and services to Athens, the foreign *xenos* was giving his elite Athenian citizen counterpart the favor of the *demos* and the political clout it entailed. Thus, the foreign benefactor may have been less interested in being honored by the city with *proxenia* than he was in maintaining his relationship with a particular Athenian citizen who was his *xenos* and from whom he could expect *charis* and future *boetheia* (see pp. 47–53).

This may well have been true in some cases, but there were nonelite men, such as common professional traders, who were granted *proxenia* and who, therefore, probably did not have preexisting ritualized friendships with elite Athenian citizens. In these cases, the relationship between Athens and its *proxenoi* was a direct one without private elite citizens to serve as intermediaries. Such *proxenoi* could not use their position to benefit their private *xenoi* in Athens, since none existed. But all men who earned *proxenia* for their benefactions could expect *charis* and future *boetheia* from the Athenian state should they ever need it, whether they were elite men with private *xenoi* among the Athenian citizenry or men of lower status, such as common professional traders.

The elevation of an honorand's status as a result of the grant of *proxenia* and *euergesia* was surely also a sought-after benefit. Such an elevation of status is apparent from the fact that both honors were reserved for foreign benefactors during the Classical period (Gauthier 1985: 10, 16). Since Athens expected its own citizens to perform many public services as a duty, the willingness to perform public services was a defining characteristic of the citizen. A foreigner honored with *proxenia* and *euergesia* was recognized as having had the same willingness to perform public services as a citizen. Even if the recipient of these honors did not attain full citizen status, the titles placed him in a formal reciprocal relationship with Athens, whereby the city officially made public (often with an inscription of the decree that granted the titles) its debt of gratitude for the benefaction of the honorand (ibid., 21). Athens repaid this debt not only with the other practical privileges that it often granted along with these honors but also with the implicit understanding that it would treat the honorand as something more than the average foreigner to whom it had no obligations, either explicit or implicit. It is precisely because of such obligations that the *demos* of Athens did not grant *euergesia* (or *proxenia*, for that matter) to citizens during the Classical period. Had the *demos* acknowledged these obligations to individual citizens, it would have created a clear distinction between the statuses of it own citizens that would have threatened the egalitarian spirit of Athenian democracy (ibid., 21).

Gold Crowns

Crowns or wreathes of various materials were a traditional symbol of honor in the Greek world, best known as the prize for victors in athletic contests. Athens awarded crowns to victorious liturgists, including ones of ivy to winning *choregoi* and sometimes gold ones to trierarchs who outfitted their ships in a timely manner (see pp. 43–47). Although Athens granted gold crowns for a variety of services, it seems to have begun with political and military ones in the fifth century and then expanded this practice to honor men who performed trade-related services.[43] The latter men initially had to be foreign potentates, but then Athens further expanded its criteria for granting gold crowns for trade-related services to include men of a variety of statuses. The monetary costs for Athens in granting gold crowns were not exorbitant, but they were significant enough to argue against the notion that Athens geared its trade policy chiefly toward the acquisition of revenue. Perhaps more important than the monetary costs of granting gold crowns, however, were the costs for Athens' traditional social values, which were eroded by granting such traditional symbols of honor to foreign men, sometimes of very low status, who performed trade-related services. From the perspective of the honorands, gold crowns had both honorific and monetary value as well. Finley's words with regard to gift exchange in the late Dark Age Greece of Homer's poems are quite appropriate in summing up the relationship between Athens and those it honored with gold crowns for trade-related services.

> Because the concrete expressions of honour and friendship were always articles of intrinsic value, not cowrie shells, the prestige element was concealed under an overlay of treasure. In fact, both counted greatly, the wealth on the one hand, and the wealth as symbol on the other. That is why the giving and receiving were ceremonial acts, an added touch that would have been needless were possession sufficient unto itself. (Finley 1978: 123)

Although Finley stresses the relationship that was cemented by the honorific value of gifts such as gold crowns, it is clear that he well understood that such gifts also had value as wealth. This is especially true in the case of gold crowns, which were typically worth one thousand drachmas each, thus illustrating again the interplay of honor and profit as goals of economic activity in ancient Greece.

By the end of the fourth century, Athens granted gold crowns to those who had performed any of the five categories of trade-related services, without discriminating between Greeks and non-Greeks, between *metics* and *xenoi*, or between common professional traders, wealthy professional traders, and foreign potentates. But this appears not always to have been the case. Rather, Athens' practice of granting gold crowns to those who performed trade-related services seems to have undergone a gradual development during the Classical period. Athens awarded one or more gold crowns on at least thirteen of the thirty-four occasions on which it granted honors and privileges for trade-related services.[44] Lacunae in the extant decrees and incomplete literary accounts concerning sixteen of the twenty-one remaining occasions make it impossible to say whether gold crowns were among the honors.[45] Of the thirty-four occasions, this leaves five on which it is certain that Athens did not grant gold crowns to those honored for trade-related services.[46] An examination of why Athens chose not to grant gold crowns on these five occasions may illuminate the development of Athens' practice of granting gold crowns for trade-related services during the fifth and fourth centuries.

Pairisades I (of no. 26) did not receive a gold crown when honored by Athens in ca. 327 because he was still receiving new gold crowns every four years at the Great Panathenaia in accordance with Athenian honors granted to him in 347/6 by *IG* ii² 212. Sopatros of Akragas, the honorand of no. 17, received a commendation, *proxenia* and *euergesia, xenia* in the Prytaneion, a seat in the theater of Dionysos, and a stele inscribed with his honorary decree, but he did not receive a gold crown. The proposer of Sopatros' honorary decree was the famous financial administrator Lykourgos, who was equally stingy as the proposer of *IG* ii² 351+624, a decree in honor of Eudemos of Plataia, who was a resident of Athens. For the latter's offer of four thousand drachmas for Athens' military needs and the gift of one thousand oxen for the building of the Panathenaic stadium and theater, Lykourgos proposed that he receive only an olive crown and other honors that required no monetary expenditure from Athens. Lykourgos' interest in trade, therefore, may have been as much about preserving and expanding Athenian revenues (for which he was famous) as about obtaining imported grain for the city.

One other possible explanation for the absence of gold crowns among the honors specified for Sopatros is that Athens, for reasons unknown, tended to grant less expensive honors to citizens and *metics* than to *xenoi*. Henry cautiously suggests that Herakleides, the honorand of nos. 24 and

27, received gold crowns costing five hundred drachmas instead of the usual one thousand drachmas because he was a *metic* and not a *xenos* (Henry 1983: 24). But such an explanation is doubtful. Although Herakleides probably was a *metic*, the honorand of no. 31, who had brought grain into Athens himself and escorted grain being shipped by other men to Athens from Cyprus, was also probably a *metic*. Yet he received a gold crown of one thousand drachmas from Athens. It does not appear to be the case, therefore, that Athens was reluctant to grant gold crowns to *metics*. Lambert (2006: 133 n. 75) suggests that the Council, who conferred Herakleides' crowns of five hundred drachmas, may have been limited to granting crowns of this value, while only the Assembly could grant gold crowns of one thousand drachmas.

On the other hand, as is the case concerning honorary decrees in general, Athens was reluctant to grant gold crowns to native citizens for any kind of service until the mid-fourth century. The first such case is attested by Demosthenes' speech *On the Trierarchic Crown*, which indicates that Athens awarded a gold crown in 360/59 to the first trierarch to have his trireme ready to sail for an urgent expedition.[47] Epigraphic evidence attests to Athenian grants of gold crowns to native citizens for their services as public officials after 343/2.[48] The first certain case of a native citizen receiving a gold crown from Athens for services performed as a private citizen concerns Philippides the poet, who was honored in 283/2 (*IG* ii² 657).[49] Both before and after the mid-fourth century, Athens honored its native citizens with crowns or wreaths of less expensive materials, such as ivy, myrtle, or olive (Henry 1983: 38– 42). Athens honored victorious *choregoi* at the Great Dionysia with crowns of ivy and sometimes granted crowns of olive to its public officials.[50] The best explanation for Athens' discrimination against native citizens in granting gold crowns is that the *demos* did not wish for those of its citizens who were most capable of providing benefactions— namely, the elite—to receive so much honor that they might be in a position to threaten the egalitarian ethos of the democracy (see pp. 41–53).

Although Athens was not reluctant to honor foreign benefactors with gold crowns, it does appear to have been hesitant in granting them for trade-related services until the early fourth century. Before the first Athenian grant of a gold crown for trade-related services between ca. 395 and 389/8 (no. 7), it is probable that Athens had already granted gold crowns on at least four occasions going back to 410/09, all for political or military services.[51] By contrast, the honorands of the fairly well-preserved decrees of nos. 3, 4, and 6, whom Athens honored for trade-related services in 411, ca. 410, and 407/6, respectively, did not receive gold crowns. It is possible, therefore, that Athens reserved granting gold crowns in the late fifth century only to those who had performed traditional political or military services and began to award gold crowns for trade-related services only as a result of the food shortages of the 390s that followed the Peloponnesian War.[52]

Perhaps more certain is a development concerning the socioeconomic statuses of those who received gold crowns from Athens for trade-related services. The earliest grants of gold crowns for such services all went to foreign potentates. Whereas Athens granted gold crowns to Satyros, Leukon, Spartokos II, and Pairisades, all kings of the Bosporos, and to Orontes, a Persian satrap, for their trade-related services between the late ca. 395 and 347/6 (nos. 7, 9, 12, and 11, respectively), it did not do so for a common professional trader, who was the honorand of no. 8, which dates to ca. 390–378/7. Athens no doubt valued the foreign potentates for more than just their trade-related services. Not only were they of a more respectable social status than common professional traders, but they were also in a position to perform other important services for Athens outside the sphere of trade, such as lending the state money, as the Bosporan kings did (*IG* ii[2] 212.53–59).

Only in around 340, in a post-Social War context and possibly as the immediate result of Philip II's siege of Byzantion in that year and its threat to the Athenian grain supply, is there evidence that Athens granted gold crowns to people who were not potentates. The honorands appear to have been the citizens of an entire allied city of Athens who helped to enforce the law of Moirokles against those who harmed traders (no. 13). Soon thereafter, no doubt pushed by necessity after its defeat in the Battle of Chaironeia in 338/7 and the frequent grain shortages that followed, Athens freed itself from some of the traditional social values that may have previously restricted its decisions concerning grants of gold crowns in honorary decrees. For the next two decades, *metics*, *xenoi*, common professional traders, wealthy professional traders, and foreign potentates who performed any of the five categories of trade-related services received gold crowns from Athens.

The actual monetary cost of a gold crown was one thousand drachmas on all but two of the known occasions on which Athens granted gold crowns for trade-related services.[53] Both exceptions occur in *IG* ii[2] 360, in which Athens granted two gold crowns of five hundred drachmas on two different occasions (nos. 24 and 27) to the same honorand for his various trade-related services. For the Athenian state's overall budget, the impact of expenditures on honorary gold crowns for trade-related services varied depending on its annual revenues. In Demosthenes' *Fourth Philippic*, which dates to 341/0, the speaker asserts that there was a time not long ago in which annual revenues of Athens did not exceed 130 talents but that later revenues increased to 400 talents.[54] The lower figures probably correspond to the year 355, when Athens had lost control of its "allies" in the Social War, and the higher figure of 400 talents probably belongs to 346, after Euboulos had reorganized Athenian public finances.[55] During the time of Lykourgos (338–326 or 336–324), Athenian revenues were said to have expanded from 60 to an average of 1,200 talents per year ([Plut.] *Ten Orat.* 842f.). On the basis of these figures, a single gold crown of one thousand drachmas could cost Athens anywhere from 0.01 percent of total annual revenues (with revenues of 1,200 talents) to 0.30 percent of total annual revenues (with revenues of 60 talents).

Even if expenditure on the gold crowns that were granted for trade-related services never amounted to a large percentage of Athens' annual revenues, its financial significance should not be completely ignored. For purposes of comparison, the average cost of the hull of a trireme was probably in the range of five thousand to six thousand drachmas.[56] Therefore, a gold crown of one thousand drachmas was the equivalent of one-fifth to one-sixth the cost of a trireme hull, the backbone of Athenian military power and security. On one occasion (no. 12), several gold crowns were granted to the corulers of the Bosporos and their brother for their trade-related services. This amounts to an immediate expenditure of three thousand drachmas. The honorary decree also calls for the conferral of additional gold crowns of one thousand drachmas each for the two kings at every future Great Panathenaia, presumably for as long as the honorands shall live.[57] Therefore, the decree calls for the hefty expenditure of three thousand drachmas initially, or half a talent, and the additional sum of two thousand drachmas every four years for an indefinite period.[58]

In specifying the source of the funds for gold crowns, *IG* ii[2] 212 is unique among extant honorary decrees for trade-related services.[59] Lines 39–43 indicate that Athens would in the future use funds drawn by the Treasurer of the People from the Assembly's expense account to pay for the two gold crowns of one thousand drachmas that were to be presented to Spartokos and Pairisades every four years at the Great Panathenaia. But lines 42–44 indicate that on the present occasion of the decree, Spartokos, Pairisades, and Apollonios all would receive gold crowns of one thousand drachmas paid for by funds drawn by the *apodektai* from the Stratiotic (Military) Fund. In his comprehensive study of the formulae employed in Athenian honorary decrees, Henry argues that even in the present crowning, the Assembly's expense account had to bear the cost of the crowns (Henry 1983: 37). The money from the Stratiotic Fund was really only a temporary advance made for the year 347/6 to allow the *athlothetai* to proceed with the task of preparing the crowns for the Great Panathenaia of July–August 346. Presumably, money would be drawn from the Assembly's expense account to repay the amount in the year 346/5.

But the money from the Stratiotic Fund need not necessarily have been a temporary advance. Athens did on occasion use the Stratiotic Fund to fulfill its trade interests.[60] For example, in *IG* ii² 207b (see no. 11), Athens used money from the Stratiotic Fund to purchase grain from Orontes, the Persian satrap of Mysia, to supply its soldiers on a military expedition in 349/8. One could argue that this decree has nothing to do with trade, that it concerns merely a traditional interest of Greek states in military affairs; that is, although the money from the Stratiotic Fund purchased imported grain, its ultimate purpose was to support an Athenian military expedition. But Athens could fulfill its military interests only by also fulfilling its trade interests. The expedition required grain for the troops on campaign, and Athens' only means of obtaining this grain in a timely manner was to set up a trade deal with Orontes. By the same token, this decree was not concerned solely with trade. Instead, it is best to see Athens' military and trade interests as intertwined with each other. It is pointless to try to determine which was the foremost Athenian interest on this occasion. The money from the Stratiotic Fund served both military and trading interests.

A further example of the complexity of Athenian trade policy in regard to the Stratiotic Fund comes from a recently discovered inscription from 374/3, in which Athens made provisions for levying a tax of 8⅓ percent to be paid in grain on the islands of Lemnos, Imbros, and Skyros (Stroud 1998). Athens contracted private shipowners and traders to collect the grain and bring it back to Athens, where the state would sell the grain to its citizens. The proceeds from the sales were allocated to the Stratiotic Fund. It is true that the collection of this tax in grain does not constitute trade organized according to market principles. In fact, one would be hard pressed to categorize this as trade of any kind, since the people of the islands were forced to render their grain to Athens as a tax. Although one could argue that the taxpayers received government services in return for their taxes, payment and collection of taxes really lack the "two-sidedness" of voluntary exchange, which is necessary for trade (Polanyi 1957b: 258).

Nevertheless, this case confirms the connection between the Stratiotic Fund and Athenian trade policy. Instead of collecting taxes from the people of the islands in money and then putting that money into the Stratiotic Fund to be used strictly for military purposes or into a grain fund to be used strictly for the purposes of feeding its citizens, Athens did not distinguish between the various purposes for which this money would be used. It collected the tax in grain, sold the grain to the public to feed them, and then put the money from the sales into the Stratiotic Fund; that is, the law served a combination of trade and military purposes. Athenian interests and the methods used to achieve those interests often, though not always, overlapped various spheres of activity; in such cases, they were undifferentiated from each other.

With regard once again to the decree honoring the sons of Leukon, it is quite possible, therefore, that Athens used money from the Stratiotic Fund not simply as a temporary advance but as the ultimate source of funds to pay for the gold crowns. If this was indeed the case, then Athens spent money from the Stratiotic Fund for the purpose of ensuring the importation of grain. Since Athens' trade policy was closely tied to its military and foreign policy in this case, one can say that it was here largely embedded in political relations.

The monetary expense of granting gold crowns for trade-related services calls into question whether acquiring revenue was Athens' chief interest in promoting trade. In his *Poroi* (3.4), Xenophon was chiefly interested in increasing Athenian revenues by increasing the number of *metics* and the volume of trade in Athens, both of which were subject to taxation, by offering honors and privileges to foreigners who had good ships and cargoes. Yet gold crowns are notably absent from the various honors and privileges mentioned by Xenophon, perhaps because he realized that spending one thousand drachmas for them undermined his goal of increasing Athenian revenues. Moreover, in *Against Leptines* (20.30–32), Demosthenes states that Leukon, who had received honorary gold crowns from Athens, was worthy of Athenian honors and privileges primarily for services that benefited the city's grain supply. Therefore, Athens' chief interest in granting gold crowns for trade-related services was to increase its imports of grain and not to obtain revenue from increased commerce.[61]

In addition to a monetary cost, Athens had to pay a "social cost" in granting gold crowns for trade-related services. Gold crowns were among the highest symbols of honor in ancient Greece and a powerful incentive that Athens offered to its prospective benefactors for political and military services. Demosthenes (22.73–76, 24.181–83) eloquently describes these crowns as tokens of emulation (*zelos*) and love of honor (*philotimia*), symbols of excellence (*arete*) valued by Athens not as objects of material wealth but as mementos of honorable achievements. By granting gold crowns to foreigners who performed trade-related services, though, Athens had to acknowledge that it was not economically self-sufficient, that it could not provide for itself through the production of its own citizens' households but had to trade and depended on the activities of those responsible for trade for the city's sustenance.

From the point of view of the honorands, a gold crown had both monetary and honorific value. Aischines (3.47) tells us that in the 330s, recipients of gold crowns granted by the People of Athens were free to do with them as they saw fit. Thus, honorands could melt down their crowns and use the gold as money, or they could keep them intact, either in their own possession or as a dedication to serve as visible evidence of the Athenian People's esteem. For those who had performed trade-related services, receiving honorary gold crowns from Athens put them on par with those who had received such honors for political, military, or other, more traditionally esteemed activities.

For this reason, the relative value of an honorary gold crown for a given honorand would depend on his ethnicity, social status, and occupation as well as the amount of money he expended on his trade-related service for Athens. A skilled Athenian laborer working five days a week for fifty-two weeks a year in the fourth century earned around 520 drachmas per year.[62] Thus, a crown of one thousand drachmas was the equivalent of almost two years' earnings. For a common professional trader with little capital of his own who had to form a partnership with others and borrow around three thousand drachmas for his trading venture, receiving a gold crown costing one thousand drachmas in addition to whatever profit he made from his trading venture was a significant amount.[63] To a wealthy trader, however, the monetary value of a gold crown would probably have had less of an impact than its honorific value. If Herakleides of Cyprian Salamis could afford to give Athens three thousand drachmas for a purchase of grain (no. 27), the monetary value of receiving a gold crown of five hundred drachmas would have been welcome but not highly significant. Nor would it have adequately compensated him in a formal economic sense (i.e., monetarily) for his service. For foreign potentates, such as the kings of the Bosporos, the monetary value of gold crowns was so insignificant that they did not even bother to have the crowns sent to them; rather, they had them dedicated to Athena Polias in Athens. The public ceremony attached to the award at the Great Panathenaia, mentioned in *IG* ii^2 212.24–26, was probably worth more to the Bosporan kings than the monetary value of the gold crowns, since it not only brought them honor but also served as a visible symbol of the reciprocal relationship that existed between them and the Athenian citizenry.

The Athenian practice of granting gold crowns for trade-related services illustrates the goals of honor and profit for those who were responsible for overseas trade in Classical Greece and the nature, degree, and consequences of the Athenian state's interest and involvement in trade. Finley's analysis of gift exchange in early Greece explains this practice well in general, since the honorific value of gold crowns outweighed their monetary value for many honorands. Nevertheless, since it is hard to imagine that common or moderately wealthy professional traders would not consider the value of the crowns worth one thousand drachmas in their business calculations, it would be a mistake to assume that the monetary value was unimportant for honorands in all cases. At the same time, although the monetary costs for Athens in granting gold crowns were not exorbitant, they were significant enough to support the view that Athens' chief interest in trade was generally in obtaining imports of needed goods and not in the acquisition of revenue through taxes on trade. More important than the monetary costs of granting gold crowns, however, were the costs for Athens' traditional social and political values, which were eroded by granting such traditional symbols of honor to foreigners who performed trade-related services. Yet Athens was compelled to expand its criteria for such honor to include trade-related services along with political and military ones as a result of its increasing need for imported goods from the late fifth century onward.

Bronze Statues

Bronze statues in the likenesses of its benefactors were among the highest and rarest honors awarded by Athens.[64] Athens placed such statues, which were life-sized and in a few cases equestrian, in public places like the Agora, the Acropolis, and the Peiraieus to enhance the honor they brought to their recipients.[65] Although bronze statues were the most costly Athenian honor in monetary terms, they must have been coveted by honorands more for their honorific value, which was only enhanced by their material worth. Athens had long reserved this honor for those men, usually citizens, who had performed the most outstanding political and military services, but in around 327, its grant of bronze statues for display in the Agora and the Peiraieus to Pairisades I, king of the Bosporos, and his sons was primarily for the king's services relating to trade (no. 26). Thus, as with other honors, it appears that as the fourth century progressed, Athens felt the need to put aside its traditional disdain for trade and to expand its practice of granting bronze statues for political and military services to include those relating to trade.

Athens granted bronze statues rarely and only for the most vital services. Both Isokrates (9.57) and Demosthenes (23.143) believed that bronze statues, which were usually accompanied with grants of *sitesis* (or permanent maintenance in the Prytaneion) and a reserved seat (*proedria*) for public performances in the theater of Dionysos, were among "the highest honors" (*megistai timai*) Athens could bestow. Down to 307, the list of recipients was an exclusive one, consisting of only the tyrannicides Harmodios and Aristogeiton at the end of the sixth century; Konon in 393 (Dem. 20.70); Euagoras, the king of Cyprian Salamis who had aided Konon, in 393 (Isokr. 9.57; *IG* ii² 20+Stroud 1979); Chabrias in 376/5 (Dem. 20.75–86; Aischin. 3.243); Timotheos in 375 (Dem. 20.84; Aischin. 3.243); Iphikrates in 371 (Dem. 23.130, 136); Diphilos for unknown services at some time between 370 and 330 (Dein. 1.43); Demades in ca. 335 (Dein. 1.101); Pairisades I and his sons in ca. 327 (no. 28); an unknown honorand in 321/0 or 318/7 (*IG* ii² 379); Asandros of Macedon, who aided Athens militarily against Kassander in 314/3 (*IG* ii² 450b); and Lykourgos posthumously in 307 (*IG* ii² 457+513).[66] Each of the aforementioned honorands was a native Athenian citizen except Euagoras, Pairisades, and Asandros, who were naturalized citizens. Nevertheless, the potential threat to the egalitarian spirit of Athenian democracy of granting such high honors for native citizens was mitigated by the fact that all but Harmodios, Aristogeiton, and Konon were honored for services that they had performed while serving the *demos* of Athens in an official capacity. The three exceptions had proven their devotion to democracy by the very nature of their services, Harmodios and Aristogeiton by assassinating a tyrant and Konon by defeating the Spartans and rebuilding the Long Walls. Moreover, that the award of bronze statues to Harmodios and Aristogeiton was posthumous assured that it could not harm the democracy. Konon's award may likewise have been posthumous (see pp. 48 and 331, n. 5).

In each case in which the nature of the services of those honored with bronze statues can be identified, all but Pairisades were honored for performing political or military services. In fact, excluding Harmodios and Aristogeiton, whose service was unique both in nature and in time, all the recipients of honorary bronze statues down to 335 (Konon, Euagoras, Chabrias, Timotheos, and Iphikrates) had been responsible for crucial Athenian military victories. Beginning with Demades in 335, however, the recipients of honorary bronze statues from Athens increasingly included those who had performed services other than military ones. Demades carried out diplomacy that saved Athens from the wrath of Alexander. Pairisades provided Athens with trade-related services. Lykourgos was posthumously honored for his services as a financial administrator. Philippides the poet performed outstanding service as an *agonothetes* and engaged in diplomacy that procured a gift of grain from Lysimachos, which earned him an honorary bronze statue in 283/2 (*IG* ii^2 657). Kallias of Sphettos performed military services, leading troops into battle against Demetrios Poliorketes, but like Philippides, he also engaged in diplomacy to procure a gift of grain, this time from Ptolemy II of Egypt, and he was honored for these things with bronze statues in 270/69 (Shear 1978=*SEG* 28.60).

In his study of the relationship between Greek cities and their benefactors, Gauthier argues that the inclusion of diplomatic services among those considered worthy of the highest honors (bronze statues, *sitesis*, and *proedria*) reflects political changes in which the power and influence of Athens in international affairs diminished as the Classical period gave way to the Hellenistic (Gauthier 1985: 77–104). In these circumstances, the services of military commanders became less important, while those involving other skills became more essential for Athens' well-being. Gauthier stresses Athens' need for skilled speakers who could carry out diplomacy with the powerful Successors of Alexander and the large kingdoms of the Hellenistic age, entities against which Athens could not hope to compete militarily.

Although Gauthier is right to identify changing political circumstances among the causes of a shift in Athens' practice of granting bronze statues, he overlooks the role of trade in this process. It is true that Pairisades, Philippides, and Kallias all either performed or had the poten-

tial to perform vital political services for Athens, but trade-related services were prominent among the motivations for their honors and were
explicitly stated in the two extant decrees for Philippides and Kallias. Although such services blur the lines between politics and economics, we
should not ignore their economic significance. Goods were exchanged,
and Athens was fulfilling its need for imported grain, which became great
enough during a series of shortages in ca. 327 to compel Athens to grant
its highest honors to those who helped it to achieve this end.

In granting bronze statues to Pairisades, Philippides, and Kallias,
Athens was able for the most part to keep its monetary costs down and to
uphold traditional social values concerning trade. The only evidence concerning the monetary cost of honorary bronze statues comes from *IG* ii^2
555, dated between 307 and 304 in the corpus, in which Athens granted
Asklepiades of Byzantion a bronze statue costing three thousand drachmas. This is a significant sum for a single honor, but since Athens granted
so few bronze statues, the overall monetary costs for the state in granting
them for trade-related services were relatively minor. Nevertheless, in
granting its highest honor to those who had performed trade-related services, Athens was elevating trade to a higher status in the pecking order of
honorable activities, on par with the highest political and military services. However, the cost was mitigated by the fact that the trade-related
services of those who received bronze statues were traditional in nature,
either the gift of imported goods or, in the case of Pairisades, a tax exemption to traders that amounted to virtually the same thing. Moreover,
the honorands were invariably members of the elite, either wealthy citizens from prominent aristocratic families, like Philippides and Kallias, or
foreign potentates, such as Pairisades, whose services were political as
well as economic and whose status, wealth, and power made them valuable friends. There are no known cases of Athens' honoring professional
traders with bronze statues for trade-related services, such as the simple
importation of goods, that were clearly differentiated from social and political relations. Athenian trade policy had its limits.

By the same token, honorands did not seek to make monetary profit by
earning grants of honorary bronze statues in return for their trade-related
services. Pairisades' service was to reinstate the trading privileges for
Athens that his predecessors had instituted but that he had previously
halted. These privileges, which included allowing traders bound for
Athens with grain to have priority of loading and exemption from taxes in
Bosporan ports, actually had the immediate effect of decreasing tax rev-

enues for the Bosporan king. As we have seen, however, the Bosporan kings may have recouped this loss of revenue through the increased price of grain and the greater volume of commerce in Bosporan ports that would have resulted from such a tax cut (see pp. 116–17). Hence, Pairisades may have profited from these services independently of any honors he received from Athens. But did Athenian honors contribute to further profits for Pairisades that would have acted as an additional incentive for him to perform his services for Athens? With regard to an honorary bronze statue, although its monetary value certainly enhanced its honorific value, there is no evidence to suggest that Pairisades or any other recipient of this honor could take possession of his statue and convert it into cash by, say, melting it down and selling the metal. It is clear that for the honorands, the value of bronze statues was primarily honorific.

Such honorific value alone was a powerful incentive for the potential recipients of bronze statues to perform trade-related services. This is especially true for a foreign potentate like Pairisades, who had little need for the three thousand drachmas comprising the value of a bronze statue but who could use honor for a variety of purposes. Not only was honor highly sought after for its intrinsic value even among non-Greeks (see pp. 49–50), but it also brought practical benefits, particularly an honor as visible as a bronze statue in one's likeness displayed in a public place in Athens. It was a powerful way to remind Athenians that they were tied in a ritualized friendship with their benefactor and owed him *charis* both in the form of honors, such as bronze statues, and in the form of *boetheia* whenever he should need it. In fact, in addition to granting Pairisades bronze statues for himself and his sons, Athens also promised to provide him with military aid at any time upon his request (see app. 3, no. 26). The benefits of maintaining good relations with Athens for the Bosporan kings went beyond political and military needs and into the realm of economic profit as well, since Athens was most likely the single biggest market for Bosporan grain (see pp. 116–17). Thus, Pairisades no doubt valued his bronze statue in a complex variety of ways that spanned the extremes between honor and profit and everything in between.

Xenia *in the Prytaneion*

Athens also granted *xenia* to those who had performed trade-related services. *Xenia,* or hospitality, consisted of a formal reception and took place in the Prytaneion, a structure specifically devoted to the entertainment of visiting dignitaries as well as Athens' most honored citizens.[67] This honor was among the most traditional that Athens could offer its benefactors. *Xenia* was a ubiquitous practice among Homer's elite heroes, who customarily offered hospitality and feasts to guests both to win over friends and to bolster their status with a show of wealth (see pp. 38–40). In Classical Athens, the *demos* took up the role of host when it granted this honor to its benefactors, creating and maintaining ritualized friendships and solidifying its status as master of the state. Although the monetary costs for Athens in granting this honor to those who had performed trade-related services were not great, the costs in terms of traditional social values were potentially high, given the customary disdain for trade and traders. The *demos* was able to control these latter costs, however, by maintaining a distinction between native citizen and foreign benefactors, reserving a more prestigious form of hospitality, *deipnon,* for the former. The existence of Athenian grants of *xenia* for trade-related services mirrors Xenophon's recommendations in his *Poroi* and serves as a testament to the practical nature of this treatise.

That Athens granted *xenia* in the Prytaneion to those who had performed trade-related services is certain on two occasions (nos. 8 and 17). In both cases, Athens honored professional traders. The honorand of no. 8 had performed trade-related services, the exact nature of which is not specified in the extant portions of his honorary decree, at some time between 390 and 378/7. Sopatros of Akragas, the honorand of no. 17, enjoyed *xenia* in the Prytaneion for his simple importation of grain into Athens at some time between 337 and 325. Also of note is no. 12, in which envoys of those honored for trade-related services, rather than the principal honorands themselves, were invited for *xenia* in the Prytaneion. Sosis and Theodosios were two representatives of the Bosporan kings who had taken care of Athenian ambassadors when the latter visited their kingdom. The precise nature of the Athenian ambassadors' visit to the Bosporos is uncertain, but it most likely had at least something to do with the trade-related services for which the Bosporan kings received honors.

On three of the thirty-two other known occasions on which Athens granted honors and privileges for trade-related services, it is certain that Athens did not grant *xenia* in the Prytaneion (nos. 24, 27, and 28). These cases date after 330, when Athens seems to have ceased granting this honor (see Osborne 1981a: 157). In the twenty-nine remaining cases, lacunae in the inscriptions or possibly incomplete literary accounts prevent us from knowing for certain whether Athens granted hospitality in the Prytaneion. It is likely, however, that in at least four of these twenty-nine cases, Athens did not grant this honor, since they postdate 330 (nos. 29, 32, 33, and 34). Given the fragmentary nature of the evidence for the remaining twenty-five occasions when Athens honored men for trade-related services, it is uncertain whether Athens offered *xenia* in the Prytaneion.

The monetary cost of *xenia* in the Prytaneion was probably not a significant burden on Athenian public finances; however, the costs in terms of traditional social values were potentially significant.[68] The *demos* of Athens was apparently concerned about such "social costs," since it issued invitations to the Prytaneion not capriciously but rather according to a set of legally defined categories that distinguished between native citizens and foreigners as well as the types of actions considered worthy of the honor.[69] The law prescribed that all foreign ambassadors be invited to the Prytaneion, whereas the decision whether to invite foreign benefactors, including those who had performed trade-related services, was left to the discretion of the People.[70] All foreigners who were invited to the Prytaneion received *xenia*, which was a single reception. By contrast, citizens who performed services worthy of an invitation to the Prytaneion received *deipnon*, which was a single full-scale meal in the company of the state's most exalted benefactors, including the descendants of the tyrannicides Harmodios and Aristogeiton, who had received the higher honor of *sitesis*, which was permanent maintenance in the Prytaneion.[71] Unlike other honors and privileges (and even honorary language), the Athenian *demos* did not need to fear encouraging the *philotimia* of its native citizen benefactors too much in granting them *deipnon*, since the *demos* maintained its superior status by acting as the host of the hospitality, taking the place traditionally occupied by the elite. Thus, it could give priority to its disdain for foreigners over its concerns about threats to the egalitarian ethos of democracy in honoring native citizen benefactors through invitations to the Prytaneion.

The distinctions made by Athens between the types of services worthy of invitations to the Prytaneion reveal further concerns with regard to traditional social values. In his study of the Prytaneion, Stephen Miller collected some 102 references to Athenian invitations for *xenia* and *deipnon* in the Prytaneion down to the end of the fourth century B.C.E. (Miller 1978: 146–61). The motivations for approximately half the invitations are unknown, being either unstated or lost in lacunae. When the motivations

for the invitations are known, the overwhelming majority involve traditional political interests. Only 6 of the 102 references involve anything
that might be considered trade interests.[72] Even among the six cases in
which trade interests appear, these interests were closely intertwined
with political interests in no fewer than four.[73] Clearly, the chief purpose
of Athenian invitations for *xenia* in the Prytaneion was to fulfill the city's
political interests.

There is only one example of an Athenian invitation for *xenia* or *deipnon* in the Prytaneion before the end of the fourth century that was motivated solely by trade interests, namely, no. 17. The text of no. 8, which
dates between ca. 390 and 378/7, is not explicit enough for us to be certain
that trade interests alone motivated Athens to grant *xenia*. Although trade
interests were the primary motivation for Athenian honors in the case of
no. 12 in 347/6, Athens may also have had political interests in inviting the
Bosporan ambassadors for *xenia* in the Prytaneion. Only with regard to
no. 17 and the years between 337 and 325 in which it was passed is it certain that Athens differentiated between trade-related services and political ones in inviting people, in this case a common professional trader, for
xenia in the Prytaneion.

Although the existing evidence is inadequate for us to pinpoint the
circumstances that may have compelled Athens to expand the criteria for
granting *xenia* in the Prytaneion to include trade-related services, the 380s
and the 330s and early 320s provide plausible scenarios. When Persian
subsidies ceased, so, too, did Athens' brief resurgence in the late 390s. In
the 380s, the Athenian military was once again weak, and the city suffered
through shortages in public revenue and grain.[74] After its defeat at
Chaironeia in 338/7, Athens was militarily constrained, thus leaving it unable to aid rebellions against Macedonian control of Greece in 335/4 and
331/0, despite the fact that Lykourgos was eventually able to restore its finances and its military. Over the same period and into the 320s, a series of
grain shortages only compounded Athens' problems. In both the 380s and
the 330s/320s, Athens may have lacked the political and military power to
fulfill its now acute trade interests by continuing to consider them embedded in its political and military interests. Either of these periods, particularly the latter, were likely occasions when Athens began to differen-
tiate between trade-related and political or military services in its decision
to invite people for *xenia* in the Prytaneion.

Such a departure from its traditional outlook and practice constituted

a "social cost" for Athens, but one that the People again sought to miti-
gate. Austin and Vidal-Naquet go so far as to describe the invitation of a
trader to the Prytaneion as "deeply subversive" to traditional Greek social
and moral values, given that such an invitation was "an exceptional honour" (Austin and Vidal-Naquet 1977: 367 n. 14). But despite such an innovation, Athens did not legally require that foreign benefactors, including
those who had performed trade-related services, be granted *xenia* in the
Prytaneion as it did in the case of foreign ambassadors, who were performing a more traditional service (see above). Of course, Athenian citizens received the more prestigious invitation to *deipnon* in the Prytaneion,
and none of them earned it by performing trade-related services.

For the honorands, the monetary value of being invited for *xenia* in
the Prytaneion would be negligible, but the honorific value would be significant. As Miller points out, "to invite someone into the prytaneion for
entertainment at the expense of the city was one of the highest honors
paid by a Greek city to an individual" (Miller 1978: 4). The foreigner who
had performed trade-related services was put on a par with foreign ambassadors and benefactors who had performed more traditional political
or military services for Athens. As with other types of honors and privileges, recipients of *xenia* in the Prytaneion could parlay the honor and the
elevation of status that it entailed into practical benefits as well.

Xenophon was well aware that those who could perform trade-related
services for Athens would be encouraged to do so as much for the honor of
an invitation for *xenia* in the Prytaneion as for the monetary profit of trading with Athens. However, Xenophon's views on the subject, expressed in
Poroi 3.3–4, are usually interpreted to be hypothetical, fanciful, and even
downright naïve.[75] But one of the three decrees (no. 8) by which Athens invited those who had performed trade-related services for *xenia* in the Prytaneion was passed well before the 350s, thus calling for a reevaluation of
Xenophon's supposed naïveté. In *Poroi* 3.3–4, Xenophon states,

> [3] If one were to establish prizes for the magistrate of the *emporion* who
> should most justly and quickly decide disputes so that he who wishes to
> sail out is not hindered, on account of these things many more men
> would more gladly come to trade. [4] It *is* [my emphasis] also a good and
> fine thing to honor traders and shipowners who are reputed to benefit
> the city with worthy ships and merchandise, with front seats and even
> sometimes to invite them for *xenia*. For receiving honors as these, they
> would hasten here as to friends on account of not only the profit but also

the honor. (Translated by the author from the Oxford Classical Texts edition by E. C. Marchant)

The orthodox interpretation of this passage is that Xenophon's suggestions in both sections 3 and 4 are hypothetical. It holds that at the time of Xenophon's writing, Athens had neither offered prizes for magistrates of the *emporion* who had most justly and quickly decided disputes nor provided seats in the theater or invitations to *xenia* for worthy *emporoi* and *naukleroi*. Only subsequently did Athens, perhaps at the instigation of Euboulos, create some institutions, particularly the *dikai emporikai*, along these lines. Xenophon's use of the optative mood for the verbs in the first and last sentences of this passage clearly indicates the hypothetical nature of the suggestions contained in these two sentences. In the second sentence, however, Xenophon does not make the main verb, which should obviously be some form of "to be," explicit. Most translators supply the verb in the optative mood, so that Xenophon's suggestions in this sentence, which include *proedria* and invitations to *xenia* for worthy *emporoi* and *naukleroi*, can be understood as hypothetical, just as in sections 3 and 4: Marchant translates, "It would also be an excellent plan . . ."; Austin, "It would also be an excellent idea . . ."; and Schütrumpf, "Es wäre auch gut und ehrenvoll . . ."[76]

But no. 8 is evidence for an Athenian invitation to a trader who had performed trade-related services (even if possibly coupled with other political or military services) for *xenia* in the Prytaneion long before the 350s. Thus, it makes more sense for us to understand the verb implied by Xenophon in the second sentence of this passage to be in the indicative mood and to assume that he was aware that the state was already engaging in such a practice. His statement in this sentence might then have been intended to express his approval of the practice and to explain how it would complement his other, truly innovative and unprecedented schemes to increase Athenian revenues by increasing the number of merchants who visited Athens. Xenophon's *Poroi* should not be seen as the fanciful ramblings of a single man that in no way reflect an actual Athenian trade policy or lack thereof in the fourth century. The practice of encouraging trade-related services by inviting those who had performed them for *xenia* in the Prytaneion was not simply an absurd concoction of Xenophon but a real Athenian practice that was employed on at least one occasion (no. 8) well before he wrote the *Poroi*.

Seats in the Theater for the Dionysia

It is possible but unlikely, however, that Xenophon's *Poroi* was responsible for inciting Athens to grant a seat (*thea*, literally "a view") in the theater for the Dionysia festival to those who had performed trade-related services. Xenophon recommended that Athens grant *proedria*, the privilege of a permanent, reserved seat in the theater, in order to encourage *emporoi* and *naukleroi* to hasten to Athens with their cargoes (Xen. *Poroi* 3.4). In granting *thea*, Athens did something similar, the main distinction with *proedria*, besides the quality of the seat, being that *thea* was good for a seat at a single festival only, whereas *proedria* provided a seat for all festivals in perpetuity (Henry 1983: 292). In addition, *proedria* was one of the highest and rarest honors Athens ever bestowed, normally granting it along with *sitesis* (permanent maintenance in the Prytaneion) and bronze statues in the honorand's likeness (see above). Regardless of whether Athens was influenced by Xenophon's recommendations, it chose not to go so far as to grant *proedria* for trade-related services. Rather, it reserved that high honor for outstanding political and military services, while those relating to trade were considered to be worthy of only the lesser honor of *thea* (Henry 1983: 291). Nevertheless, *thea* still had much honorific value for its foreign recipient, who was invited to sit side by side with Athenian citizens at one of the city's most important festivals.

The only Athenian grant of *thea* for trade-related services postdates Xenophon's *Poroi* by some twenty years (no. 17, ca. 337–325), and it is unlikely that there were any earlier such grants. No. 17 is the earliest of only four extant grants of *thea* for any service, the other three of which all date to the very end of the fourth century.[77] Of the thirty-four occasions on which Athens granted honors for trade-related services, only no. 17 contains a grant of *thea* for the Dionysia. Although the evidence for twenty-seven of the remaining thirty-three occasions is too fragmentary for us to be certain that they did not contain grants of *thea*, there are six other occasions for which the evidence is sufficient to be sure that there was no such grant.[78] The honorand of no. 17 was a foreign, common professional trader whose residence status is unknown but who had performed the service of a simple importation of grain to Athens. There is nothing outstanding about him to suggest why he received *thea* for the Dionysia whereas the honorands of the six other sufficiently well-preserved decrees did not. These latter honorands range from common professional traders to foreign potentates; their services range from simple importations of goods to gifts of goods, and the dates of their honors range from ca. 410 to 323/2.

Since a typical seat in the theater for one day's performances of the Dionysia cost two obols, the monetary value of this honor was insignificant for both the state and the honorand.[79] Athens kept the "social costs" to a minimum as well, since it granted *thea* for trade-related services, rather than its more esteemed counterpart, *proedria*, which it reserved for the most outstanding services in the political and military realms. Moreover, even as early as the fifth century, Athens had allowed foreigners to attend the Dionysia, using the occasion as an opportunity to showcase the power, wealth, and sophistication of the city before the rest of the Greek world.[80]

On the other hand, by granting a seat for the Dionysia at state expense, Athens was at least providing the foreign honorand with a unique opportunity to receive the equivalent of the *theorikon,* a state subsidy originally intended to cover the cost of theater tickets, which was an otherwise exclusive privilege of Athenian citizens. Most of those who received *proedria* were citizens as well, though foreigners were not excluded (Henry 1983: 291). All four extant grants of *thea* from before the end of the fourth century, however, were to foreigners, three of whom were ambassadors and one of whom was a professional trader (see above). In order to ensure trade-related services from foreigners, Athens was willing to chip away, even if only a little, at the barriers between citizens and noncitizens, to include a foreign trader in some of the citizens' formerly exclusive rights. Thus, the social and monetary inexpensiveness of the honor for Athens did not diminish its honorific value for the recipients. Traditionally excluded from most of the privileges of citizens and community activities, those who were honored for trade-related services with seats in the theater for the Dionysia could enter into the exclusive domain of the citizen for their deeds. They could sit side by side with Athenian citizens and participate with the community in a religious and patriotic festival of Athens.

Inscribed Stelai

Among the less costly Athenian honors for trade-related services was to inscribe the text of an honorary decree on a stone stele. Despite its low monetary cost, such an honor entailed disproportionately high costs in terms of the traditional social values of Athens, since, like bronze statues, it provided highly visible evidence of the state's practice of honoring those who had performed trade-related services. Conversely, the recipients of stelai inscribed with their honorary decrees obtained great honorific value, which they could convert into more practical benefits, even if not necessarily direct monetary profit. It is most likely for this reason that Athens seems to have been reluctant to grant such an honor to those who had performed trade-related services until it was compelled to do so by the necessity of its trade needs.

Athens did not limit inscribing honorary decrees on stone stelai to specific types of trade-related services or honorands. It explicitly called for inscribed stelai on as many as twelve of the thirty-four occasions on which it granted honors and privileges for trade-related services.[81] Even though thirteen of the extant inscriptions bearing honorary decrees for trade-related services either do not mention or have lost the lines that record provisions for inscribing their decrees, their very existence attests to the fact that these decrees were also inscribed on stone stelai.[82] But although their quality and appearance are typical of state-inscribed decrees, it is impossible to be certain whether the state paid for their production or to know how much they cost or even whether the cost was covered by the state or by the honorands themselves. Nevertheless, the existing evidence shows that each of the five categories of trade-related services and both resident and nonresident honorands of a variety of ethnicities and socioeconomic statuses were eligible to have their honorary decrees inscribed on stone stelai.

The cost of inscribing an honorary decree for trade-related services on a stone stele was modest, never amounting to more than thirty drachmas (nos. 12, 17, and 24/27). In one of the earliest cases, no. 8, dated ca. 390–378/7, the cost is twenty drachmas. No. 28 contains a lacuna in line 21 before the word for "drachmas," exactly where the cost of the inscription was inscribed. Köhler (*IG* II) and Kirchner (*IG* ii²) believe that the lacuna consists of three letter spaces, which leaves room for ΔΔΔ, or thirty drachmas, after restoration. Pecirka, however, believes that, owing to irregularities in the stoichedon pattern at this point in the inscription, the lacuna consists of two letter spaces, which leaves room for only ΔΔ, or twenty drachmas (Pecirka 1966: 66). Since there are precedents for the inscribing of stone stelai costing twenty drachmas, either restoration is possible.

Prior to the mid-fourth century, honorands often had to provide for the cost of inscribing their own honorary decrees, but after that time, the

Assembly of Athens made sure to cover the cost of inscribing its decrees with money drawn from its expense account.[83] Honorary decrees commonly referred to this procedure with the formula "from the People's fund for expenditure on decrees" (nos. 12, 17, 24/27, and 28). Athens allocated ten talents annually for the Assembly's expenses, and *IG* ii² 43.66–69 (378/7) and 141.16–19 (ca. 364) both state that the inscription will be paid for by monies drawn "from the ten talents."[84] After ca. 364, there are no further references to "the ten talents" in regard to inscribing decrees of the Assembly, only references to the Assembly's expense account. It is likely that the two funds are identical and that "the ten talents" took on the more functional name of the Assembly's expense account after 364. From a treasury of ten talents, expenditures for inscribing honorary decrees for services relating to trade did not require a significant monetary outlay. Such expenditures were small in proportion to the rest of those paid for out of the treasury of the Assembly, which included inscribing the many nontrade related decrees, entertaining foreign envoys, and providing traveling expenses for Athenian envoys (Jones [1957a] 1986: 102, 154 n. 33).

Despite its minimal monetary cost, by inscribing honorary decrees for trade-related services on stone stelai, Athens contributed to an erosion of long-held social values that disdained trade and those who were responsible for it. Not every decree of the Athenian Assembly was inscribed on a stone stele. Usually, the mover of a decree had to call for its publication explicitly, and the People had to vote their approval.[85] Thus, Athenians had to weigh the consequences of inscribing an honorary decree for trade-related services. The people surely realized that an inscription on stone would magnify the importance of an honorary decree, serving as a permanent monument rather than the simple record of a government act on a papyrus text.[86] The symbolism was obvious: so long as the decree was "written in stone," it had force. Upon the revocation of a decree, law, or alliance, it was common, in fact, for Athens to destroy the stele on which it was inscribed. A famous example of this practice is the destruction of the stelai bearing democratic decrees and laws revoked by the Thirty Tyrants in 403, the latter of which were then reinscribed by the restored democracy to give them back their force.[87]

Moreover, inscribed honorary decrees were visible to a wide audience, since the stelai were usually placed in highly public and often sacred places in Athens (e.g., the Acropolis, the Agora, and the Peiraieus) and not simply stored behind closed doors in the Metröon, the public records office of Athens.[88] Such publicity would be the equivalent of a neon sign today, testifying to the honorand's *philotimia* and his *eunoia* toward Athens. At the same time, the stele, standing side by side with those bearing honorary decrees for political and military services, would make manifest the high degree of esteem in which the city of Athens officially held the honorand and his trade-related services. The intended audience of these advertisements would be not only Athenian citizens, who would be reminded of their debt of gratitude (*charis*) to their benefactors, but also foreign visitors, for whom the stelai served notice that Athens generously rewarded its foreign benefactors with the honor they so desired (Hagemajer Allen 2003: 227).

It is also important to note that the decision to inscribe an honorary decree on a stone stele was also a decision to grant not only a permanent monument but also a public space to the honorand—real, often sacred, property in Athens (Hagemajer Allen 2003: 226). The right to own property in Attika was coveted by Athenian citizens. By granting a space on the soil of Athens for an honorary stele, the city was extending a fundamental right of citizenship to its foreign benefactors, thereby elevating their status above that of other foreigners and closer to that of Athenian citizens. Such an elevation of status was even greater for the foreigner who had performed trade-related services and was only further magnified by the fact that the spaces granted for the display of honorary stelai were often sacred ones. Sanctified by the hallowed ground on which they stood, stone stelai bearing honorary decrees for Athens' benefactors assumed the attributes of a sacred oath to cement a bond of ritualized friendship between Athens and its benefactors. In fact, many honorary stelai contain not only the text of honorary decrees but also a decorative sculptural relief reminiscent of those adorning sacred places that depict a worshiper making a votive offering to the gods.[89] The stele of the decree for no. 12 includes such sculptural decoration, depicting Spartokos II, Pairisades I, and Apollonios, the sons of Leukon and royal dynasts of the Bosporos, who are distinguished by their foreign dress and hairstyles. By exalting those who performed trade-related services in this way, Athens was breaking down social values that had traditionally disdained them.

Given the serious consequences of its decision to inscribe honorary decrees, it would not be surprising to find that Athens was reluctant to pass such decrees for those who had performed trade-related services and to inscribe them on stone stelai for public viewing. It does appear likely, though not certain, that Athens initially inscribed honorary decrees on stone stelai for political and military services and only later extended the practice to include trade-related services. Most inscribed honorary decrees dating before 414 are reticent concerning the exact nature of the services of their honorands; however, several seem to have honored political and military services, while none appear to have honored trade-related ones.[90] The first inscribed honorary decree for trade-related services dates to 414–412 (no. 1), after which honorary decrees for political, military, and trade-related services are routinely inscribed. Trade now occupied an important place among Athenian interests, and those responsible for trade received recognition and honors formerly denied to them by traditional Greek social values. Thus, even though inscribing honorary decrees for trade-related services had insignificant monetary costs, it entailed a "social cost" for Athens.

From the honorands' point of view, the insignificant monetary value of stelai inscribed with their honorary decrees was offset by their honorific value and its consequent practical benefits. Unlike gold crowns, honorary stelai could not be melted down and converted into cash. But the stelai did have great honorific value, providing honorands with permanent, highly visible monuments on Athenian soil that publicized Athens' official esteem for them and their services. In this way, those who had performed trade-related services were elevated to a status on par with those who had performed more traditional political or military services. As Veyne notes, of all honors, "the one that was closest to the heart of the *euergetes* was not so much the honour itself as the engraving of the decree which awarded it and which posterity would be able to read" (Veyne 1990: 127). Of course, the more visible the honor, the more Athenians would be aware of the honorand's benefactions, and the more he could parlay his honor into practical benefits, such as favor in the law courts, political alliances, and the offer of refuge, should he ever need them.

Conclusion

The foregoing analysis of Athenian honors for trade-related services is consistent with the findings of earlier chapters that the relationship between Athens and its honorands was a complex and dynamic one whose exchanges cannot be reduced simply to gift or market trade. It is true that the exchange of grain and other imported goods for Athenian honors had the appearance of a gift exchange between two parties in a ritualized friendship, and to a significant extent, this was true in reality. There is no doubt that the creation or maintenance of a relationship was a major goal of the exchanges and that the honorands surely coveted Athenian honors for their intrinsic honorific value. At the same time, however, Athens did need the imported goods it received, and the honorands did profit by their honors, if not monetarily, at least through the practical benefits that honor engendered in Athens. Such practical benefits included the functional uses of some honors but primarily the all-purpose *boetheia* that one could expect from his counterparts in ritualized friendships. The bottom line, therefore, is that both Athens and its honorands got what they wanted from the relationship created by the Athenian practice of granting honors for trade-related services.

Although the monetary costs of granting honors for trade-related services were sizable enough to call into question the notion that Athens' chief interest in trade was revenue, they were not normally a major strain on the state's budget, so the real cost for Athens was to its traditional values rather than to its treasury. Athens at first granted several types of honors—namely, commendations, gold crowns, and inscribed stelai—only to foreigners who performed political and military services. In time, Athens expanded this practice to include foreigners who performed trade-related services. But its initial reluctance betrays Athens' desire to maintain the traditional values that disdained trade and those who were responsible for it. Only the compelling motivation of survival during the latter stages of the Peloponnesian War forced Athens to undermine these values and offer such honors for trade-related services. Athenian citizens did not receive these honors until even later, probably because of the *demos'* fear that such honors would promote the ambitions of the citizen elite and threaten the egalitarian ethos of Athenian democracy.

Although the line of development is more complex with regard to *proxenia* and *euergesia*, bronze statues, *xenia* in the Prytaneion, and seats in the theater for the Dionysia, Athens' practice with regard to these honors is consistent with the notion that only under duress did Athens honor foreigners who performed trade-related services. Athens never granted *proxenia* and *euergesia* to its own citizens, the former because of its origins in *xenia* and the latter because Athenian citizens were expected to be benefactors of the state per se. Otherwise, these honors followed the pattern outlined above, in which honors were first awarded to those who performed political or military services and were only later extended to include those who performed services relating to trade. Bronze statues were among the highest and most expensive honors awarded by Athens. Down to the late fourth century, Athens granted them almost exclusively for military services. From the 330s, however, Athens began to consider trade-related and other political services, including diplomacy and administration, to be worthy of the honor. Unlike most Athenian honors, though, bronze statues were more commonly awarded to Athenian citizens than to foreigners. In these cases, however, the honorands had performed outstanding services that proved their loyalty to the *demos* of Athens, most often great military victories. Although seats in the theater for the Dionysia appear to have been granted to visiting foreign ambassadors before being granted to anyone who had performed trade-related services, both this honor and *xenia* in the Prytaneion were clearly lesser than *proedria* and *deipnon* in the Prytaneion, similar honors that were not awarded for trade-related services. *Deipnon* was available only to Athenian citizens. Hence, it is a constant that Athens paid a social cost in granting honors for trade-related services; however, the magnitude of that cost varied with the specific type of honor and over time, attesting to the complex and dynamic nature of the ancient Greek economy.

CHAPTER EIGHT

Privileges

In addition to the honors discussed in chapter 7, Athens also granted various privileges to those who had performed services relating to trade. These privileges included the following:

- *asylia*
- *ateleia*
- *enktesis*
- military service and payment of the *eisphora* tax with citizens
- citizenship

I have categorized these items as "privileges" rather than "honors" because each of them conferred on foreign honorands distinct rights that were, with the exception of *ateleia*, normally the privilege of Athenian citizens. Hence, besides *ateleia*, none of these privileges was ever conferred by decree on Athenian citizens, and they were not an issue in the contest between the masses and the elite of Athens. For trade-related services, Athens also granted other favors that defy categorization, such as the ships' crews (*hyperesiai*) that it provided for the Bosporan kings. Although all these privileges brought honor to their recipients, they also entailed functional benefits far in excess of the honors that were discussed in chapter 7. Like those honors, however, grants of such privileges for trade-related services illustrate the complexity and dynamism of Athenian trade policy and its role within the shifting social, political, and economic circumstances of the late Classical period, while also further illuminating the diverse backgrounds and interests of those who were responsible for trade.

For such men, from common professional traders to foreign potentates, Athenian privileges could fulfill a variety of interests ranging from honor to profit. The profits of professional traders were enhanced by privileges, such as *asylia* and *ateleia*, which protected their cargoes from seizure and exempted them from taxes and other costly obligations. Professional traders also obtained great honor through privileges, such as *enktesis*, the right to own land in Attika, as well as the right to serve in the Athenian military and pay the *eisphora* tax together with Athenian citizens. Such rights elevated the status of honored traders above that of typical foreigners who had no share of the rights accorded to Athenian citizens. Despite their greater status in their homelands, foreign potentates would naturally also appreciate an enhanced status among the Athenian citizenry, if not for admiration of Athens' proud history and reputation, then certainly for the practical benefits that it would bring them in their political as well as commercial dealings with Athens.

As in the case of its grants of honors for trade-related services, in granting coveted privileges to foreigners for such services, Athens was reshaping its attitude toward trade and those who were responsible for it, despite making every effort not to do so. This had novel consequences. Athens not only further cheapened its formerly exclusive citizen rights but also encouraged what had been disesteemed market-structured economic activity.

Asylia

An Athenian privilege that was particularly useful for professional traders was *asylia*, which literally means "inviolability," a guarantee of protection for the honorand and his property from forcible seizure. Modern scholars are not in complete agreement about the details of *asylia*, however, and have offered various interpretations concerning to whom its protection applied (Athenian citizens or foreigners), where its protection was enforced (within Athenian territory or abroad), and against whose assaults the protection applied (Athenian citizens or foreigners).[1] Based on the Athenian grant of *asylia* (securely restored) to Phanosthenes for trade-related services (no. 3), it is clear that the privilege offered protection to a foreigner wherever Athens had the power to enforce it.

On five of the thirty-four occasions on which it honored men for trade-related services, Athens made provisions to insure unhindered sailing for traders and their cargoes (nos. 1, 3, 8, 10, and 24). On three of these five occasions (nos. 3, 8, and 10), Athens explicitly granted *asylia*, whose formula typically reads, "it was resolved . . . that there be *asylia* for him and his goods." In addition to these explicit grants of *asylia*, however, Athens implicitly took steps on two other occasions to insure that traders could sail the seas unhindered. In the case of no. 24, which dates between 330/29 and 328/7, Athens decreed the election of an envoy to request that Dionysios, tyrant of Herakleia, return the ship's sails of Herakleides of Cyprian Salamis, which had been confiscated by the Herakleotes, and to obtain assurances that the Herakleotes desist from hindering those sailing to Athens in the future. In another case, no. 1, which dates to ca. 414–412, the honorand received the right to sail freely and to carry his goods wherever Athens ruled. On twenty of the remaining twenty-nine occasions on which Athens granted honors and privileges for trade-related services, it is uncertain whether Athens granted *asylia* or any other protections, on account of lacunae in the extant decrees or incomplete literary accounts (nos. 2, 4–6, 11, 13, 14–16, 18–23, and 29–33). This leaves only nine occasions when Athens did not grant any form of *asylia*, but five of these concern honors for foreign potentates, who had little need for *asylia*, since they themselves did not sail the seas with cargoes for trade (nos. 7, 9, 12, 26, and 34). One of the remaining cases, no. 27, is exceptional, since the honorand, Herakleides of Cyprian Salamis, had already received *asylia* when he was honored on a previous occasion (no. 24). This leaves only three certain occasions on which Athenian honorary decrees for professional traders for trade-related services did not include *asylia* (nos. 17, 25, and 28). A possible explanation for the absence of grants of *asylia* in these three cases will be offered below.

Given the small number of attested occasions on which Athens granted *asylia* for trade-related services, it is difficult to observe many telling patterns. In the three explicit grants of *asylia*, the specific types of services are unknown on account of lacunae in the extant decrees. In the two implicit grants of *asylia*, the trade-related service of the honorand of no. 1 is also unknown, but the honorand of no. 24 sold imported goods at a reduced price. Both honorands who received *asylia* (one explicitly and the other implicitly) and whose ethnicity is known were Greek (nos. 8 and 24). It is impossible to know whether any of the honorands who received an explicit grant of *asylia* for trade-related services were *metics*, but it is almost certain that the honorand of no. 24, who received an implicit grant of *asylia*, was indeed a *metic*.

One pattern that is apparent in both explicit and implicit Athenian grants of *asylia* for trade-related services is that all the honorands were foreign professional traders. One of them was moderately wealthy, while another was clearly very wealthy, but it is not possible to determine the wealth of the other two. The fact that there is no evidence that Athenian citizens ever received *asylia* through a special grant is not surprising, since it was likely an implicit privilege of citizenship, extended to the masses as well as the elite, without distinction. It is also not surprising that Athens granted *asylia* only to professional traders and not to foreign potentates who had performed trade-related services. A grant of *asylia* from Athens brought important practical benefits to professional traders who sailed the seas as private persons with valuable cargoes. Foreign potentates naturally had much less personal need of Athenian protection from seizure on the high seas. In fact, they might even have found it an insult if Athens had presumed to offer such protection, which would have implied their subservience to Athens. The Aphytaians, for whom Athens granted *asylia* in ca. 426 when they sailed with their goods in Athenian controlled waters, were just the sort of loyal subjects of the fifth-century Empire for whom such a grant would be more appropriate (*IG* i^3 63; see app. 3, R6).

The grant of *asylia* to the Aphytaians for their political loyalty is the earliest known grant of this privilege, but at some point thereafter, Athens tailored grants of *asylia* specifically to professional traders who had performed trade-related services. From 411 onward, only benefactors who had performed trade-related services received grants of *asylia* from Athens, according to the extant evidence.[2] The turning point probably came after the destruction of the Sicilian Expedition in 413. It was in the period between 414/3 and 407/6 that Athens—its navy terribly weakened, its grain supply hindered by the Spartan occupation of Dekeleia, and unable to coerce others to supply it with timber and grain but still hoping to preserve the Empire—began to offer incentives to encourage others to import goods into the city (Thuc. 7.27–28, 8.1.3, 8.4). Given the limited number of grants of *asylia* over the course of the fourth century (nos. 10 and 24) and a lack of precision in our dating of one of those grants, it is impossible to draw any conclusions about the development of the practice during that time. It is also difficult to explain why the honorands of nos. 17 and 28, who were professional traders, did not receive *asylia* from Athens in return for their trade-related services.

One thing that does seem certain, however, is that Athenian grants of *asylia* were not made lightly and were not simply "empty gestures," even after the loss of the fifth-century Empire, as some have suggested.[3] Although Athens could not consistently protect traders on the high seas throughout the fourth century, it certainly made every effort to do so, and there were periods in which its navy was strong enough and political circumstances were such that it could succeed. During the era of Lykourgos, the Athenian navy was larger than it had ever been (see p. 65). Although international circumstances prohibited Athens from using its navy to coerce trade, it could at least protect it from the depredations of pirates. One example was a naval mission led by the general Diotimos in 334/3, which was apparently successful enough to earn him honors.[4] In 325/4, Athens sent out a fleet in conjunction with the founding of a colony in the Adriatic that also had the purpose of protecting traders against piracy (IG ii² 1629.163–232). Athens could even expect to receive some help from its allies in policing the seas on behalf of traders, as is attested by no. 13, in which Athens honored an allied city for helping it to enforce the law of Moirokles that prohibited anyone from harming traders. It is clear, then, that Athens took its grants of asylia seriously and made every effort to back them up with real action.

Since grants of asylia were never empty gestures, the "social cost" of such grants for trade-related services far outweighed any monetary cost to Athens. The city would have spent money to maintain the political and military power necessary to enforce grants of asylia even if it had had no trade interests and had never granted asylia to anyone. But in granting asylia, Athens guaranteed the same protection to foreign honorands as it had always implicitly guaranteed to its own citizens. Grants of asylia created an opening in the barrier that had traditionally separated citizens from foreigners in the polis. Furthermore, in granting an honor specifically tailored to professional traders who had performed trade-related services, Athens took another step toward treating trade as a distinct sphere of activity, disembedded and differentiated from traditional social and political relations. Yet it still remains that Athens' interest in trade was consumptive rather than productive and that the practice of granting privileges, such as asylia, was a traditional method of fulfilling that interest.

The professional traders who received grants of asylia from Athens for their trade-related services reaped important practical benefits from the grant. Asylia gave them an economic advantage over their competitors. Most significantly, they could reduce both the real and potential costs associated with the risk of sailing. Such a risk was the chief factor in the high yields due to investors in maritime trade ventures (see p. 94). These high yields were basically a cost associated with the business of overseas trade. Asylia reduced the risk of losing one's cargo (and ship, if the trader himself owned it) to the man-made threats presented by pirates and the navies of hostile Greek cities. Perhaps a trader who could prove himself a recipient of *asylia* from Athens could negotiate the payment of lower yields to his investors, thereby cutting down his costs and increasing his profits. A wealthy trader who employed solely his own capital could rest easier and expect greater long-term profits, knowing that the risks and costs of seizure were much reduced as a consequence of his *asylia* (see also Hopper 1979: 199).

Asylia also held an honorific value for traders. Just as it was a social cost for Athens to grant the same guarantee of protection to foreign traders as it had always implicitly done for Athenian citizens, it was also a great honor for traders. Traders thus honored received one of the traditional benefits that had previously been the exclusive possession of citizens. Although *asylia* did not entail all the rights of citizens, it nonetheless elevated the status of its foreign recipients above that of their peers who had not received such a privilege from Athens.

It is clear, therefore, that the Athenian motivation for granting *asylia* to professional traders who had performed trade-related services was not a desire to provide for "the welfare of its own merchants."[5] Whatever protections Athens provided for its own citizen merchants were achieved by other means. On the other hand, it would also be a mistake to conclude that grants of *asylia* were "empty gestures" that have no more significance than to illustrate again that Athens never swayed from its consumptive interest in trade (see Hasebroek 1933: 128, 130). Athenian grants of *asylia* to professional traders indicate an Athenian interest in trade as a distinct sphere of activity, disembedded and differentiated at least to some extent from traditional political and military concerns.

Ateleia

On six occasions, Athens granted *ateleia*—exemption from various public obligations, including the performance of liturgies and the payment of taxes—to those who had performed trade-related services (nos. 4, 7, 9, 10, 12, and 34).[6] *Ateleia* obviously enhanced the profitability of professional traders, but it also held a high honorific value that was especially coveted by the foreign potentates who comprised the majority of those who received this privilege for trade-related services. In fact, because *ateleia* was not a basic right of Athenian citizenship but was conferred only on a select few of the state's most outstanding benefactors, both citizen and foreign, it may have entailed even greater honor than citizenship itself. Granting *ateleia,* therefore, not only cost Athens monetarily in the form of forsaken revenue, but it also degraded traditional social values by honoring those who performed trade-related services on par with some of the most highly honored political and military benefactors in Athenian history.

Two kinds of *ateleia* appear in Athenian honorary decrees for services relating to trade. *Ateleia* could be limited to a specified obligation, such as the *metoikion,* the head tax levied on *metics* in Athens.[7] In the case of no. 4, Athens declared the honorands to be *ateles* (or *azemios,* depending on the restoration) from payment of the one-hundredth tax, which was probably a harbor tax for the privilege of using the Peiraieus.[8] Another type of *ateleia,* which Athens granted for the trade-related services of the Bosporan kings (nos. 7, 9, 12, and 34) and the honorand of no. 10, was an exemption from all obligations (*ateleia panton*), which included liturgies and taxes, except perhaps for the trierarchy and the *eisphora* tax.[9]

Four of the six honorands who received *ateleia* from Athens for trade-related services were foreign potentates, and it seems that Athens was reluctant to grant this prestigious privilege to men of low socioeconomic status. One of those who was not a foreign potentate, Phanosthenes of Andros, was the first person that we know of to have received *ateleia* for trade-related services (no. 4, ca. 410–407). It is likely, however, that Phanosthenes engaged in trade only because he was temporarily exiled from Andros and either needed the money or thought that he could ingratiate himself on Athens through a trade-related service (see app. 3, no. 4). Whatever the case, since Phanosthenes eventually became a naturalized citizen and general of Athens, Athenians must surely have regarded him as more than a professional trader. After Phanosthenes, the next three occasions on which Athens granted *ateleia* for trade-related services all concerned members of the ruling dynasty of the Bosporos. These grants occurred in ca. 395–389/8, 389/8, and 347/6, respectively. It was not until the third quarter of the fourth century that Athens granted *ateleia* to a professional trader for trade-related services (no. 10). *IG* ii[2] 141, which dates to 364, grants *ateleia* to Sidonian traders resident in Athens, but only as a rider to a decree that honors Straton, the king of Sidon, with *proxenia* for his political services to Athens (see app. 3, R8).

Not only was Athens reluctant to grant *ateleia* to men of low status for trade-related services, but it appears to have been reluctant to grant this privilege for such services at all, doing so only when it was compelled to by necessity. Athens granted *ateleia* or its equivalent some twenty times for political and military services, beginning with Harmodios and Aristogeiton at the end of the sixth century down to the end of the fourth century. Most commonly, Athens granted *ateleia* from the *metoikion* to political exiles who had aided Athens. In addition to these men, however, recipients of *ateleia* included some of the most prominent Athenian citizens who achieved Athens' greatest military victories of the fourth century, namely, Konon, Chabrias, Iphikrates, and Timotheos. All the Athenian citizens who received *ateleia* from Athens had proven their loyalty to the *demos* either by acting in an official capacity as generals or by such extraordinary services that their democratic sympathies could not have been doubted, thereby mitigating any fears that the *demos* might have about encouraging their *philotimia* too much.[10]

The first decree granting *ateleia* for trade-related services (no. 4) dates to ca. 410–407, when Athens was desperately trying to restore its naval supremacy after the disastrous Sicilian Expedition.[11] The decree honors Phanosthenes and his associates for having supplied the city with imported oar spars. It is not likely to be a mere coincidence that the first attested Athenian grant of *ateleia* for trade-related services occurred at the same time that Athens is first attested also to have granted *asylia* for trade-related services (no. 3). Lacking the power to coerce needed imports, such as ships' timber, from subject states, Athens had to shift its policy toward providing incentives to reward and encourage men like Phanosthenes to fulfill its interests in trade.

Although grants of *ateleia* might have encouraged traders and potentates alike to provide Athens with imported goods, such exemptions from financial obligations would at the same time have deprived Athens of revenue. Doubtless aware of this fact, Xenophon omits *ateleia* as well as costly gold crowns from the honors and privileges he advocates granting to worthy merchants in his *Poroi*. Although grants of *ateleia* to merchants would increase commerce in the Peiraieus, they would also reduce the revenues from taxes on that commerce. The evidence is inadequate for us to estimate just how much revenue Athens lost as a result of granting *ateleia*, but Demosthenes, who was interested in trade primarily to provide Athenians with affordable grain, downplays the loss of revenue (20.20–21) and focuses instead on the amount of grain that the Bosporan kings provided for Athens in return for their *ateleia*. In granting *ateleia* for trade-related services, the state, like Demosthenes, would seem to exhibit a greater interest in providing the city with vital imported goods, such as grain and timber, than in obtaining revenue.[12]

Since *ateleia* was such an exclusive privilege, however, even more than other honors and privileges discussed up to this point, its monetary cost for Athens paled in comparison to the deleterious effect that granting it to foreigners for trade-related services would have on traditional social values. Demosthenes estimated that there were no more than thirty men who had received Athenian grants of *ateleia* down to 355 (20.20–21). It is true that the orator had an interest in minimizing the number in order to downplay its negative effect on Athenian revenues, but the epigraphic record corroborates his estimates, attesting to no more than seventeen occasions on which Athens granted *ateleia* to individuals or small groups down to ca. 355 in addition to the seven occasions mentioned by Demosthenes (see p. 348, n. 10). Those privileged few whom Athens honored with *ateleia* were among the most honored benefactors of Athens who had performed crucial political and military services. Athens appears to have been conscious of the threat that granting *ateleia* for trade-related services presented to traditional social values and to have tried for several decades to limit such grants to high-status foreign potentates. Not counting Phanosthenes, who was a special case in ca. 410–407, it was not until the mid-fourth century that Athens granted *ateleia* to a professional trader for services relating to trade (no. 10). Yet Demosthenes, reflecting the reality of Athens' increasing need for imported grain in the fourth century, emphasizes the trade-related services of the Bosporan kings in his effort to preserve the practice of granting *ateleia* as a means of encouraging benefactions for the city.

Demosthenes also stresses that the chief benefit of *ateleia* for its recipients was honorific rather than monetary, and this appears to be true, at least among those who had performed trade-related services. Athenian citizens who received *ateleia*, most of whom were from the elite, saved more money than Demosthenes lets on as a result of their exemption from obligatory liturgies, such as the very expensive *choregia* (see pp. 44–46), even though they probably did not benefit much from the exemption from taxes, most of which were levied indirectly on activities, such as commerce, that elite citizens did not, as a rule, engage in directly. Foreign professional traders, on the other hand, would surely have profited greatly from tax exemptions on commerce and, if they were wealthy and resident in Athens, on liturgical obligations as well.

There is only one certainly attested foreign professional trader among the recipients of *ateleia* from Athens, however, and his residence is unknown (no. 10).

Most of those who received *ateleia* from Athens for trade-related services were foreign potentates who, since they did not themselves sail into the Peiraieus with goods to trade, would probably not profit monetarily from commercial tax exemptions. I say "probably" because it is possible that the *ateleia* of the Bosporan kings covered not only their persons but also products originating from their realm. If this was the case and if the kings controlled the production and export of grain from the Bosporos, then a tax exemption on the large quantities of Bosporan grain known to enter the Peiraieus each year would enhance the profits of the kings tremendously. However, as I argued elsewhere, it is unlikely that the *ateleia* of the Bosporan kings applied to their goods as well as their persons; therefore, they probably did not profit monetarily from such tax exemptions (see app. 3, no. 7).

As Demosthenes stressed, the primary benefit of a grant of *ateleia* for the Bosporan kings was honor, and although Demosthenes stresses the very real innate value of such honor (20.41, 44), one can also see underlying this argument a subtext that acknowledges the practical benefits of honor in the ancient Greek world. Demosthenes frequently refers to *ateleia* as a "gift" (*doreia*) of gratitude (*charis*) from Athens to those who have performed services for the city, which he also calls "gifts" (e.g., 20.35, 40–41, 45–46). Thus, he characterizes the relationship between Athens and its benefactors in terms of a classic reciprocal gift-giving, ritualized friendship (see chap. 3). Honor, one's good reputation, was essential for *xenoi* to be able to trust in each other's loyalty and mutual aid (*boetheia*) in times of need. Demosthenes makes this explicit in describing Athens' relationship with Epikerdes of Kyrene, who was honored with *ateleia* for multiple services, including aiding Athenian prisoners in Sicily and giving Athens a talent during difficult times late in the Peloponnesian War (20.42). The orator states flatly to his fellow citizens that Epikerdes "had *ateleia* in word and honor" but never used it, adding that should Athens rescind Epikerdes' exemption, "he will lose trust in you" (20.44). Thus, foreign potentates like Epikerdes and the Bosporan kings esteemed a grant of *ateleia* from Athens chiefly as a badge of honor, which was valuable both for its own sake and for the practical benefits it entailed. Recipients of *ateleia* could bask in the glow of a spotlight that shone on such heroes of Athens as Harmodios and Aristogeiton, Konon, and Chabrias. At the same time, they could enjoy a trusted friendship with Athens, a loyal ally in international politics that would provide aid whenever it should be needed.

Enktesis

The social values of ancient Greece esteemed landownership and agriculture, which stood in sharp contrast with the disgrace of landlessness and nonagricultural, *banausic* occupations, such as manufacturing and trade (see pp. 38–39). Citizens and foreigners were regarded similarly: the former were honorable, while the latter were something less. Perhaps not coincidently, the right to own land and a dwelling (*enktesis*) was one of the most basic privileges of citizenship in the *poleis* of the ancient Greek world.[13] The geographical extent of most *poleis* was small, and in even the larger ones, such as Athens, the amount of good farmland was relatively scarce. Athens restricted landownership to its own citizens and granted the privilege only to those few foreigners who had proven themselves worthy of the honor through the performance of extraordinary services for the city. It is a testament to the degree to which Athens was concerned about trade, therefore, that it granted *enktesis* to foreigners for trade-related services.

Athens granted *enktesis* on four of the thirty-four occasions on which it honored trade-related services and does not appear to have followed any strict guidelines for doing so (nos. 17, 25, 27, and 28).[14] In each case Athens granted *enktesis* in conjunction with *proxenia* and *euergesia,* but this was not required, since on at least two of the 30 remaining occasions, it is certain that Athens granted *proxenia* and/or *euergesia* without *enktesis* (nos. 1 and 8). Three of the *enktesis* grants specified "*enktesis* of land and a house" (nos. 25, 27, and 28), and one (no. 17) called for *enktesis* without qualification, perhaps the result of scribal or secretarial error (Henry 1983: 205 n. 9).

Athens granted *enktesis* for a variety of trade-related services and did not discriminate between Greeks and non-Greeks who performed them. In two of the four grants (nos. 17 and 27), the honorands were Greeks; in the remaining two (nos. 25 and 28), the honorands were non-Greeks. Altogether they performed three of the four specific categories of trade-related services, including the simple importation of goods (nos. 17 and 25), the gift of imported goods (more specifically, money to purchase imported goods; no. 27), and securing shipments of goods (no. 28, probably). The honorand of no. 27 had received other honors from Athens on a previous occasion for the sale of imported goods at a reduced price, another trade-related service that probably also influenced Athens' decision to grant him *enktesis*.

In regard to the residence status of those who received *enktesis* for trade-related services, what at first appears to be a pattern favoring *metic* honorands is not likely to be significant. On two occasions, the honorands were *metics* (nos. 25 and 27), while on the other two (nos. 17 and 28), it is impossible to tell. There is, however, evidence for Athenian grants of *enktesis* to foreigners who did not reside in the city for other services. In his study of thirty-nine decrees containing Athenian grants of *enktesis* down to 307/6, Pecirka identifies four honorands as *metics* and six as nonresident foreigners (*xenoi*), while the remaining thirty-one cases include five instances of political exiles temporarily residing in Athens and twenty-six cases in which the residence status of the honorands is unknown.[15] Although I identify eleven cases involving *metics* and six cases involving *xenoi* from the same group of thirty-nine inscriptions, the conclusion remains the same: Athens granted *enktesis* to both *metics* and *xenoi* without discrimination, and this is probably as true for trade-related as for other types of services.[16]

The absence of any foreign potentates among those who received *enktesis* for trade-related services also does not appear to have any special significance. In all four grants, the honorands were professional traders, three of whom were probably common (nos. 17, 25, and 28) and one of whom was wealthy (no. 27). Unlike the situation involving *metic* honorands, Pecirka's study of the thirty-nine decrees granting *enktesis* for all services confirms the pattern with regard to grants for trade-related services: no foreign potentate ever explicitly received *enktesis* through a specific grant from Athens. But the explanation for this is probably only that foreign potentates implicitly received the privilege of landownership in Athens through grants of full citizenship, which they received much more often than did professional traders and other men of lower status (see below). In fact, Demosthenes (20.40) states that Leukon, the king of the Bosporos and a naturalized citizen of Athens, held property (*chremata*) in Attika of some sort, possibly land. The lack of Athenian grants of *enktesis* to foreign potentates, therefore, is no indication of a desire to deny these men the privilege of owning land in Attika.

Since all four extant Athenian grants of *enktesis* for trade-related services down to 307/6 occurred during a brief period in the third quarter of the fourth century, it is impossible to detect any chronological development concerning the types of trade-related services, ethnicities, or residence or socioeconomic statuses that were deemed worthy of such grants. Once Athens began to grant *enktesis* for trade-related services after the Battle of Chaironeia in 338/7, it did so for all types of services and honorands, except foreign potentates, who received the privilege implicitly through grants of citizenship.

On the other hand, a pattern does emerge concerning Athenian grants of *enktesis* for trade-related services within the broader context of such grants for all services. The first known Athenian grant of *enktesis* goes back to the early 420s, and all six grants securely dated before 350 in which the honored services are known involve political or military ones.[17] Among the eight grants of *enktesis* that cannot be dated more securely than between 367 and 333, the only one in which the services can be identified was for political services.[18] Of the nineteen grants of *enktesis* that can be securely dated to between 350 and 307/6, three are for political and military services; seven are for other services; one is for political, military, and other services together; and eight are for unknown services.[19] Of the seven grants for services other than political or military ones, five are for trade-related services (nos. 17, 25, 27, and 28; *IG* ii[2] 337=R11), one is for medical services (*IG* ii[2] 242+373=Lambert 3.34), and one is for services involving the Dionysia (*IG* ii[2] 551=Lambert 3.101). In the one grant of *enktesis* for political, military, and other services together, the honorand had made monetary contributions for an Athenian war effort and had given Athens one thousand oxen for use in the construction of the Panathenaic stadium (*IG* ii[2] 351+624=Lambert 3.42).

Although we can never know for certain whether the existing evidence is truly representative of all grants of *enktesis* that were once passed by the Assembly, it does appear that Athens changed its policy concerning grants of *enktesis* after around 350. The state seems to have decided to grant *enktesis* for services other than political and military ones and even to favor the former over the latter.[20] One reason for such a change is likely to have been the limits put on Athenian military activity by Macedonian dominance after 338; there are no extant Athenian grants of *enktesis* for political or military services between 337 and 323. On the other hand, as we have seen, Athens had increasing needs for revenue and imported grain after 355. The situation was particularly bad after Athens' defeat in the Battle of Chaironeia, especially concerning the grain supply, so it is not surprising to find that the earliest grants of *enktesis* for services other than (or in addition to) political or military ones were for trade-related services and contributions for public works after that time (no. 17; *IG* ii² 337=R11 and 351+624=Lambert 3.42). Three other grants of *enktesis* for trade-related services involving the import of grain occurred during the grain shortages that fell between 330 and 322 (nos. 25, 27, and 28). Assuming that the surviving grants of *enktesis* reflect the actual chronological distribution of all grants that were originally passed (they are a random selection, after all), it appears that Athens adapted its practice of granting *enktesis* for political and military services to meet specific needs involving trade and the acquisition of revenue as they arose. Once Athens had opened the doors to grants of *enktesis* for services other than political and military ones, it had set a precedent for further adaptations, so that it was not long before the state was granting *enktesis* for medical services (*IG* ii² 242+373=Lambert 3.34) or even services for the Dionysia (*IG* ii² 551).

In what is likely to be more than a chance coincidence, Xenophon's *Poroi* advocates using grants of *enktesis* to stimulate commerce at just about the same time as the shift in Athenian policy that is apparent from the honorary decrees. In 2.6, he states,

> Next, since there are many building sites without houses within the walls, if the city were to grant the right to own land to those who wish to build a house and who, after petitioning, are deemed worthy to do so, I believe that through these measures as well, many more and much better men would seek to reside in Athens. (Translated by the author from the Oxford Classical Texts edition by E. C. Marchant)

Recall that Xenophon wrote the *Poroi* in ca. 355/4 to suggest ways in which Athens could raise revenues after its defeat in the Social War effectively ended the Second Athenian League (see pp. 4, 59–60). Many of his proposals sought to increase revenues by facilitating commerce and attracting to Athens greater numbers of the *metics* who engaged in such commerce, both of which were subject to peacetime taxes. It is clear that Xenophon believed that granting *enktesis* would attract more such *metics*. Most historians agree that Athens, under the leadership of Euboulos, did institute at least some of Xenophon's proposals, including faster trials for those engaged in commerce and improved lodgings for traders and other visitors in the Peiraieus.[21] Thus, there is no reason to doubt that Athens might also have instituted Xenophon's suggestion concerning *enktesis* (whether directly influenced by him or not), especially since it coincides so well with the surviving epigraphic evidence.[22]

In undertaking such a practice to fulfill its trade interests, Athens had to break with some long-cherished social and political values that revolved around landownership (see pp. 38–39). The ability to own land and a house in Attika was one of the exclusive rights that defined the constitutional status of Athenian citizens.[23] Even after Athens began to grant *enktesis* to foreigners in around 430, it did so only rarely over the next eighty years; there is evidence for no more than twenty-one grants down to about 350 (Pecirka 1966: 152–54). Xenophon himself proposed in *Poroi* 2.6 to allow only highly restricted grants of *enktesis* to foreigners: only *metics* who sought *enktesis* and who were deemed worthy would have been granted the privilege under his scheme, and then only to own a house within the city walls. No one in Athens ever went so far as to allow foreigners en masse to own land in Attika without restriction (Austin and Vidal-Naquet 1977: 96). To do so would have been to deprive citizens of the exclusive right to reap the practical and economic advantages of landownership that came from agriculture, buying and selling land, and using land as security for loans (Finley 1952: 77–78).

Just as dear to Athenian citizens as the practical advantages of citizenship was the honor that attached to it as well (Whitehead 1977: 70–71). The honor associated with the right of landownership sprang from the values of the elite, which dominated Greek life during the Archaic period (see chap. 3, Elite Values and Institutions). During that time, possession of civic rights in many *poleis*, including Athens, depended on the ownership of land (Austin and Vidal-Naquet 1977: 96–97). In the Classical period, when Athens had become a democracy, although one no longer had to own land in order to have full civic rights, the right to own land continued to distinguish the status of even the lowest of citizens as superior to that of the foreigner who could not own land in the *polis*.

Athenian grants of *enktesis* to foreigners for trade-related services diluted both the practical privileges and the honor of citizenship. It was serious enough to grant *enktesis* to foreigners who had performed traditionally esteemed political and military services, but to grant it for trade-related services was a radical break with the past. It is a telling indication of the kind of change that was occurring in Athens in the late fourth century that the city sought to fulfill its trade interests by granting a right that was formerly not only the exclusive prerogative of citizens but had even been essential in defining a citizen's status and economic activity (farming) to foreigners who performed services entailing economic activity (trade) that could not have been more antithetical to that of the traditional civic ideal (Burke 1992: 210).

From the point of view of the honorands, it is clear that *enktesis* had both an honorific value and a practical economic value. The person who received *enktesis* from Athens could now own land, which comprised the bulk of the city's economic base. He could farm the land and reap its wealth, buy and sell it, and even obtain loans on the security of his land. Thus, he could bridge the gap between land and money that was insurmountable to the mass of foreigners who were at a severe economic disadvantage because they could not own land in Athens.[24] But more important for honorands must have been the honorific value of *enktesis*. Few, if any, foreigners migrated to Athens in search of land to make their livelihood. Most came because Athens provided more opportunities for *banausoi* than any other city in the Greek world during the Classical period. But there was a connection between economic activity and social status in Classical Athens. If foreigners wished to rise to the status of elite citizens, wealth alone would be insufficient. They would have to earn the right to own land and live the traditional lifestyle of a landowner. Foreigners and even citizens without land had no choice but to make their livelihood through dishonorable *banausic* occupations.

Military Service and Payment of the Eisphora *together with Athenians*

Although modern observers may find it difficult to appreciate, serving in the Athenian army and paying the *eisphora* "together with Athenians" (*meta Athenaion*) was considered by foreigners as a privilege, which they could earn in return for performing trade-related services. Like its grants of *enktesis*, Athens' grants of military service and payment of the *eisphora* together with Athenians coincided with the spirit, if not the letter, of Xenophon's suggestions for increasing the state's revenues. In fact, Athens incurred no monetary cost in granting this privilege and even made money directly by requiring honorands to pay the *eisphora* on par with citizens. But also as with its grants of *enktesis* and other honors and privileges, Athens did suffer a "social cost" in the form of the corruption of long-held values concerning the exclusiveness of the *polis* that privileged citizens over foreigners and held trade and traders in low esteem.

Athens seems to have guarded the privileges of serving in the army and paying the *eisphora* "together with Athenians," since it did not grant them often and did so only twice for trade-related services (nos. 23 [335/4, 331/0, or 326/5] and 27 [325/4]). The honorands on both occasions were wealthy professional Greek traders who probably resided in Athens as *metics.* Dionysios of Pontic Herakleia, the honorand of no. 23, provided Athens with a gift of grain, while the honorand of no. 27, Herakleides of Cyprian Salamis, performed a similar service by giving Athens money for an *epidosis* to purchase grain. Note also that Herakleides had also sold imported goods at a reduced price on an earlier occasion, for which he had received other honors and privileges from Athens. Of the eleven total occasions on which Athens granted the privileges of serving in the Athenian army and paying the *eisphora* together with Athenians, four involved honorands who had performed traditionally esteemed political or military services, one was for political and military services and contributions for Athenian public works, two were for trade-related services, and four were for services that cannot be identified.[25] All known grants of these privileges fall between 352/1 and 302/1, so it is likely that Athens was reluctant to grant them until 355/4, when its defeat in the Social War severely damaged its ability to obtain revenue through military means. When it finally did grant such privileges, Athens first reserved them for political and military services, only stooping to confer them for trade-related ones after 335/4 at the earliest, during a period of severe grain shortages.

Other than the fact that Athens almost always granted these two privileges together, we know little of their precise nature and, therefore, exactly what Athens was giving up and what the honorands were receiving.[26] Ordinarily, all free adult male residents of Attika, both citizens and *metics,* had to serve in the Athenian army as hoplites, but most scholars believe that *metics* served in separate contingents from citizens, interpreting Xenophon's *Poroi* 2.5 (see below) as indicating that *metics* and citizens both served in the infantry but not necessarily in integrated contingents.[27] All adult males, whether citizens, *metics, xenoi,* or even slaves, could serve for pay as rowers in the navy, but only citizens could serve in the cavalry.[28] All free adult male residents of Attika also were subject to the *eisphora,* a tax that Athens levied on property in special circumstances, such as a military crisis (Thomsen 1964: 11). Each person's burden was assessed in proportion to his declared taxable capital. It seems that *metics* had their own *symmories,* each with its own treasurers, and that their contributions were assessed by an *epigrapheus.*[29] But there is still no consensus among scholars whether *metics* or citizens as a rule had a greater burden to pay (Whitehead 1977: 78–80). Any attempt, therefore, to identify the precise nature of the privileges of serving in the Athenian army and paying the *eisphora* together with Athenians inevitably involves much speculation.

The simplest hypothesis concerning military service, however, is that the privilege allowed *metics* to serve in the Athenian army as hoplites in citizen contingents "together with Athenians," as opposed to separate *metic* contingents. In his study of Athenian *metics*, though, Whitehead (1977: 128) does not mention this possibility, omitting it perhaps on account of his belief that Xenophon opposed the integration of *metics* and citizens in hoplite contingents. In *Poroi* 2.2, Xenophon advocates relieving *metics* of their obligation to serve in the army as hoplites for several reasons, including the risk to the *metics* and the economic inconvenience of having to leave their trades during active service.

> We also should relieve metics from the duty of serving in the army as hoplites with the citizens. For on the one hand the danger for them is great, and on the other it is a serious matter for them to leave their trades and homes. (Translated by the author from the Oxford Classical Texts edition by E. C. Marchant)

Xenophon's motivations in this passage are clearly economic and consistent with the overall purpose of the *Poroi*, which is to increase Athenian revenues by attracting more *metics* to the city, who, by their very presence and economic activity, provide a significant peacetime tax base for Athens. He proceeds, in 2.3–4, however, to point out that the state would also benefit by having an all-citizen infantry, which would bolster the citizens' pride and self-sufficiency. Such a motivation is traditional, political, and noneconomic and indicates a certain disdain on the part of Xenophon for the very *metics* whom he wishes to attract (and exploit) for the sake of Athenian revenues. Thus, this passage is consistent with Whitehead's view that Xenophon opposed the integration of *metics* and citizens in hoplite contingents.

But for Whitehead's view to hold, it is necessary to reconcile Xenophon's desire to relieve *metics* of hoplite service with his suggestion in both *Poroi* 2.5 and *Hipparchikos* 9.3–7 that Athens allow *metics* to serve in the Athenian cavalry. Whitehead argues that Xenophon wished to honor only a small minority of the *metics* who were deemed worthy on account of their services to Athens.[30] The vast majority of *metics*, however, were contemptible to Xenophon and useful only to increase Athenian revenues. Therefore, Xenophon would relieve *metics* from hoplite service so they could work and provide revenue for Athens while the infantry was comprised purely of citizens. On the other hand, Xenophon would also honor the few worthy *metics* by letting them serve in the cavalry so that they might be "more good-willed" (*eunousteroi*) to the city (*Poroi* 2.5). In *Hipparchikos* 9.6, Xenophon says,

> I think also that some of the *metics* would seek after honor if appointed to the cavalry: for I see that whenever the citizens give them other things that are good, some [*metics*] desire for honor's sake to accomplish what has been commanded. (Translated by the author from the Oxford Classical Texts edition by E. C. Marchant)

Whitehead is right to believe that Xenophon wished for Athens to provide exceptional honors and privileges only to worthy *metics*; however, such a view need not preclude Athens from having allowed *metics* to serve along with citizens in integrated hoplite contingents. If Xenophon was willing to suggest that Athens allow worthy *metics* to serve in the cavalry, there is no reason to believe that he would have been opposed to allowing worthy *metics* to serve in the infantry as well, even along with citizens in integrated contingents. Moreover, regardless of Xenophon's views, Athens could have instituted such a practice anyway.

If Athens did in fact allow worthy *metics* to serve along with citizens in integrated hoplite contingents, it would have been following the spirit, if not the letter, of Xenophon's proposals, just as it had done in granting *enktesis*. Whitehead (1977: 128) argues that Athens did not put Xenophon's suggestions concerning *metic* service in the infantry and cavalry into practice, since Athens neither abolished *metic* hoplite duty nor included *metics* in the cavalry. But by allowing *metics* to participate along with citizens in integrated hoplite contingents, the state would have provided foreigners with an incentive to settle in Athens, perform services, and contribute to the revenues of the city, a goal thoroughly in keeping with the overall purpose of Xenophon's *Poroi*. Unlike Xenophon, however, the Athenian *demos* was not ready to eliminate *metic* hoplite contingents altogether and to bear the city's military burdens alone at this time (see Dem. 4.20–21, 24). Nor did the *demos* let *metics* into the cavalry, which was a privilege for the Athenian citizen elite. In this way, the *demos* could satisfy its revenue and trade interests by providing exceptional *metics* with the incentive of serving along with citizens in integrated hoplite contingents, while at the same time keeping separate hoplite contingents for all other *metics* and a cavalry composed solely of citizens. It is impossible to know whether the state was actually influenced, even if only in spirit, by Xenophon's *Poroi* or *Hipparchikos* in granting *metics* the privilege of serving along with citizens in integrated hoplite contingents. It is certain, however, that none of the extant grants of the privilege of serving in the Athenian army together with Athenians predate either the *Hipparchikos* (ca. 365) or the *Poroi* (ca. 355), since the first such grant was in 346/5.

Xenophon made no proposals concerning payment of the *eisphora*, but here, too, the most plausible hypothesis is that the privilege of paying the *eisphora* together with Athenians provided its recipients with honor rather than any direct practical or monetary benefits (see Whitehead 1977: 78–79). For *metics* to benefit monetarily from paying the *eisphora* together with citizens, the burden of citizens would normally have had to have been lower than that of *metics*. But this is highly unlikely, because the law normally barred *metics* from owning land in Attica, making their property almost entirely movable and easy to hide and to underassess in order to evade taxation. Furthermore, Demosthenes 22.61 and *IG* ii^2 244.20 for 378/7 seem to indicate that *metics* contributed one-sixth of the total *eisphora*. Since *metics* comprised more than one-sixth of the free population of Athens, they must have been paying less in proportion to their population than citizens (Whitehead 1977: 79). It is likely, then, that citizens normally bore a greater burden of the *eisphora* than *metics*.

In this case, the privilege of paying the *eisphora* together with Athenians would require the honorand to pay a greater amount of the *eisphora* tax than he had previously. Hence, not only was there no monetary benefit from such a privilege, but there was an actual monetary loss for the honorand. The benefit of receiving the privilege of paying the *eisphora* together with Athenians must have been primarily honorific, as was the privilege of serving in the Athenian army together with Athenians. The honorary value of these two privileges lay in the elevation of the status of the honorands. Having to serve in separate *metic* hoplite contingents or to pay *eisphorai* along with their fellow *metics* marked out their inferior status, segregating them from Athenian citizens. Receiving this privilege, however, erased some of that distinction. The honorands, although still not citizens, would at least be closer to citizens than the mass of common *metics*. Strange as it may seem, the likelihood that honorands had to pay a higher *eisphora* would actually add to this honorific value. The burdens of citizenship, just as much as its practical benefits, distinguished citizens from noncitizens. In fact, such burdens were part of what brought *timé* to citizens in the first place. By taking on the increased burden of paying the *eisphora* together with Athenians, honorands could obtain some of the honor of citizens. Of course, such honor brought on by sacrifice for the state did entail further benefits of a practical nature: the *metics* who bragged in legal speeches that they paid the highest *eisphorai* believed that the *demos* should look favorably upon them (see Lys. 12.20; Isokr. 17.41; and pp. 49–51).

In granting such privileges, Athens incurred no monetary cost. In fact, it actually benefited financially by the increased *eisphora* burden shouldered by *metic* honorands. But the state did incur costs of other kinds. The obligations of military service and paying taxes were no doubt burdensome to Athenian citizens. But serving in citizen contingents and paying the *eisphora* distinguished them from noncitizens and were, thus, obligations in which they could take pride and receive honor. By allowing foreigners to serve in citizen hoplite contingents and pay citizen *eisphora*, the state was granting them an opportunity to obtain *timé* equal to that of citizens, who formerly held an exclusive monopoly on it. Moreover, the cost to social values was even greater when the foreign recipients of such privileges were professional traders who had performed traditionally disesteemed trade-related services.

It is no wonder that the reactionary Plato, even in regard to the "practical" state of the *Laws*, makes no mention of *metic eisphora* or of *metics* serving in the military.[31] In Plato's view, the *polis* must remain of the citizens, for the citizens, and by the citizens. But Athens had to deal with the reality of the late fourth century, not the timeless theoretical realm of philosophy. Thus, it granted the privileges of serving in the Athenian army and paying the *eisphora* together with Athenians to foreigners in order to encourage them to perform needed services for the city, including those related to trade.

Citizenship

Grants of *asylia, ateleia, enktesis,* and the privileges of serving in the Athenian army and paying the *eisphora* together with Athenians elevated honorands to a status above the mass of foreigners in Athens, but not quite up to the status of citizens. At best, the recipients of such privileges were "quasi citizens." In making these grants, Athens created a hierarchy of statuses among foreigners, while still maintaining the strict barrier that separated them from citizens. Beginning in the fifth century and continuing with increasing frequency during the course of the fourth, however, even this barrier did not escape the numerous changes besetting Athens and the rest of the Greek world. In order to fulfill its growing needs, Athens took the ultimate step of granting full citizenship to foreign benefactors, some of whom had performed trade-related services.[32]

Athens granted citizenship not for just any trade-related services but rather for those that required significant monetary expense from its honorands and benefited both the city's trade and political and military interests. Of the thirty-four occasions on which Athens granted honors and privileges for trade-related services, there are nine in which Athens granted citizenship to sixteen people (not counting reaffirmations) who had either performed such services or were their kin.[33] Because of incomplete evidence, it is uncertain whether Athens granted citizenship on twelve of the remaining twenty-five occasions (nos. 13–15, 18–21, 23, 26, 30, 31, and 33). On the remaining thirteen occasions, it is certain that Athens did not grant citizenship, since the inscriptions are either complete and do not mention such grants or contain grants of other honors and privileges, such as *proxenia*, that preclude grants of citizenship (nos. 1–4, 6, 8, 10, 17, 24, 25, 27, 28, and 32). On five of the nine occasions on which Athens granted citizenship for trade-related services, the honorands had provided gifts of imported goods or money to purchase imported goods, often in addition to other miscellaneous trade-related services (nos. 7, 9, 12, 22, and 34). Four of these occasions concern the Bosporan royal family (nos. 7, 9, 12, and 34), who not only gave grain to Athens in large quantities but also provided trading privileges in their ports to merchants who transported goods to Athens. The fifth occasion involves Harpalos, who gave what was undoubtedly a sizable gift of grain to Athens, which may have been identical to that mentioned in the famous inscription recording the Kyrene grain distribution (Tod 2.196).

The other four occasions on which Athens granted citizenship for trade-related services involved lesser services in terms of the costs to the honorands and the trading benefits to Athens (nos. 5, 11, 16, and 29). In three of these cases, however, it is apparent that trade interests were not the only factors motivating Athens to grant citizenship, since the trade-related services of the honorands served nontrade as well as trade interests and since many were performed at crucial times when Athens was particularly in need. Moreover, the honorands in these three cases also performed other services in addition to trade-related ones. Phanosthenes of Andros received citizenship from Athens at some time between 410 and 407 (no. 5; see app. 3). He had already received a commendation, *proxenia* and *euergesia*, and *ateleia* a short time beforehand for having imported ships' oars and for having provided some other services apparently in connection with an Athenian naval expedition. Orontes earned a grant of citizenship from Athens by selling grain to an Athenian military expedition (no. 11). Although Orontes' trade-related service was the equivalent of a simple importation of grain, it carried additional weight because it simultaneously helped to fulfill vital Athenian political and military interests. The honorand of no. 29 provided supplies to the Athenian fleet for a naval battle in the Hellespont, in addition to his dispatch of grain to Athens.

The last of the four cases, which concerns Chairephilos and his sons (no. 16), is problematic because the evidence is sketchy, coming as it does from some chance remarks by two orators and a comic poet (see app. 2 and app. 3). One certainty is that his importation of fish was a factor in Athens' decision to grant citizenship to him and his sons. Yet there is reason to doubt that such a service alone could have induced Athens to bestow one of its highest honors. It is possible that Chairephilos, who was a wealthy man, had also given large sums of money to Athens in addition to his simple importations of fish.[34] Such speculation seems to be borne out by an analysis of all known Athenian grants of citizenship down to 307/6. As a rule (in 107 of 113 cases), the honorands had performed services (or were expected to perform services in the future) that required either a sizable monetary outlay or a risk to the honorand's life and that almost always helped to fulfill vital political and military interests of Athens.[35]

Exceptions to the rule are rare. On five occasions, Athens granted citizenship to poets and artists, apparently considering the products of their talents to be as useful to the city as political or military services.[36] Athens granted citizenship to the son of Perikles by Aspasia, which was obviously a special grant in recognition of Perikles' outstanding contributions to the city and his misfortune at having lost his legitimate sons by an Athenian wife on account of the plague.[37] Chairephilos did not fall into either of these exceptional categories and would have been unique if he obtained citizenship just for simple importations of fish. It is possible, then, that Chairephilos either performed other services for Athens (probably monetary contributions for public use) in addition to his simple importations of fish or, as Deinarchos (1.43) suggests, made monetary contributions of another kind in the form of a bribe to Demosthenes for proposing the grant for him. Even if he did bribe Demosthenes (which is certainly plausible), the People of Athens still must have had reasons of their own for voting in favor of the proposal for naturalization. It is probably the case that Chairephilos did other services in addition to his sale of imported fish and that the Athenians' traditional disdain for trade and other *banausic* activities remained potent enough that Athens would not grant citizenship for trade-related services unless they were extraordinary ones or coupled with other vital and more traditional services.

Athens' high standards concerning the types of services worthy of naturalization took precedence over all other considerations, including the ethnicities and socioeconomic statuses of the honorands. The city appears not to have been especially concerned with the ethnicities of the honorands to whom it granted citizenship. Of the nine occasions on which Athens granted citizenship for trade-related services, two were for Greeks (nos. 5 and 22), five were for non-Greeks (nos. 7, 9, 11, 12, and 34 [Bosporans and a Persian]), and two cannot be identified (nos. 16 and 29). Although Osborne's study of naturalization in Athens for all services shows that a greater number of Greeks received Athenian citizenship than non-Greeks, the latter were not so uncommon as to indicate any kind of discrimination along ethnic lines.[38] As long as the services were worthy, Athens granted citizenship to benefactors regardless of their ethnicity.

Despite the fact that most of those who received citizenship from Athens for trade-related services were wealthy or powerful men, the socioeconomic statuses of the honorands were also not a deciding factor per se but rather a consequence of the types of services deemed worthy by Athens for such a privilege. In seven of the eight cases in which the socioeconomic statuses of those who received grants of citizenship from Athens for trade-related services are known, the honorands either possessed personal wealth or occupied powerful positions in their society, which enabled them to further the political and military interests of Athens as well as its trade interests.[39] The honorands of six of the eight cases were foreign potentates. These include the Bosporan kings (nos. 7, 9, 12, and 34); Orontes, the Persian satrap of Mysia (no. 11); and Harpalos, Alexander's treasurer (no. 22). Chairephilos (no. 16) was no potentate, but he was certainly very wealthy. After his naturalization, he and his sons became diligent performers of liturgies as citizens of Athens (*APF* 15187, pp. 566–67). The exception is Phanosthenes of Andros (no. 5), whose exact status is uncertain but who was undoubtedly considered to be more than just a professional trader, since he later became a general in Athens (see app. 3). Thus, the socioeconomic statuses of those who received citizenship from Athens was simply a factor of the types of services deemed worthy of such a privilege, which required exceptional wealth, power, or both, not because of any considerations of status per se.

There are at most only two occasions on which those who received Athenian citizenship for trade-related services were *metics*. One case, that of Phanosthenes of Andros, is certain. The other case concerns Chairephilos and his sons, whose status as *metics* is uncertain. Even if Chairephilos was a *metic*, the number of non-*metics* who received grants of citizenship from Athens for trade-related services would still far outnumber the number of *metics*. In fact, of the 140 Athenian grants of citizenship down to 307/6 for all types of services, only nine are certain to have concerned *metics* exclusively.[40] In seven of these nine cases, the honorands were bankers and their sons. One of the two cases, in which the honorand was not a banker or related to one, concerned the exceptional case of the son of Perikles by Aspasia (Osborne 1983: 211, Checklist no. 6). The other case involved Phanosthenes of Andros (no. 5 of the present study).

The evidence provides no certain explanations for the small number of *metic* honorands, but one possibility is that fewer *metics* than foreign potentates (who were, of course, not *metics*) were in a position to do the kind of outstanding political and military services that merited a grant of citizenship from Athens. For the most part, only those few *metics* who possessed a great deal of personal wealth, such as bankers, could perform such services. Absent explicit evidence, it is likely that most *metic* bankers who received grants of citizenship from Athens had given large sums of money to the state for political and military uses (Osborne 1983: Checklist nos. 55 [Phormion] and 78 [Epigenes and Konon]). The banker Pasion received his grant of citizenship on account of an expensive gift of one thousand shields and five triremes, which he also equipped and manned, all of which would have obviously benefited Athens' political and military interests.[41] The paucity of wealthy *metics* in general might explain the correspondingly low number of *metics* who received citizenship from Athens.

It is also possible, however, that Athens preferred to grant citizenship to those who would probably never reside in Athens and take up the practical privileges of citizenship but who would treat the grant as an honor alone. Perhaps Athens was reluctant to include outsiders as functioning (and benefiting) members of its citizen body. That the *metics* Herakleides of Salamis (nos. 24 and 27) and Eudemos of Plataia (*IG* ii^2 351+624=Lambert 3.42), who had both performed several noteworthy and expensive services for Athens, did not receive grants of citizenship from Athens might support such a view. Although Herakleides' services benefited only Athens' revenue and trading interests, Eudemos not only had contributed money and oxen for an Athenian public works project but had also contributed four thousand drachmas "for the war" (*IG* ii^2 351.13–15). The services of Eudemos in particular, which touched on Athenian political and military interests, measure up well in comparison to those of others who did receive grants of Athenian citizenship. Nevertheless, it is uncertain that his *metic* status was the decisive factor hindering him from being naturalized. After all, there were seven other *metics* who received grants of citizenship from Athens for similar services.

Although the chronological distribution of citizenship grants during the fifth and fourth centuries show that political and military services were always in great demand in Athens, it appears that after the destruction of the Sicilian Expedition in 413, Athens began to grant citizenship more frequently while also increasingly, albeit reluctantly, deeming other services, including trade-related ones, to be worthy of such a privilege. In the sixty-two years between ca. 476 and 414, there were a total of seven grants of citizenship in Athens, six of which were for political and military services and one of which was for the painter Polygnotos.[42] From 414 down to 355/4, a fifty-nine-year period, there were sixty-seven grants, including forty-nine for political and military services exclusively, two in which the services cannot be identified, one for a poet, and fifteen for other services.[43] In the forty-eight years between 355/4 and 307/6, there were a further sixty-six grants, including twenty-nine that were for political and military services exclusively, twenty-one for which the services cannot be identified, three that were for poets and an artist, and thirteen for other services.[44] It is apparent that the percentage of grants for which political or military services were the only motivations steadily declined from 86 percent in the first period, to 73 percent in the second, to 44 percent in the third. Nevertheless, such grants still comprised the single largest percentage in each period, attesting to Athens' continuing need for political and military services.

Beginning in the period after the destruction of the Sicilian Expedition and continuing down to 307/6, however, Athens also granted citizenship to those who were neither poets nor artists and who had performed services that were not exclusively political or military in nature. From 414 to 355/4, fifteen of the sixty-seven total grants, or 22.5 percent, were for services not exclusively political or military in nature and also having nothing to do with poetry or art. From 355/4 to 307/6, thirteen of sixty-six total grants, or 20 percent, fit this category. These other services, therefore, comprise a significant percentage of the grants from 414 to 307/6 and attest to a change in the Athenian practice of granting citizenship. But the change was not a radical one, since grants of citizenship for services not exclusively political and military in nature never supplanted the primacy of grants for those reasons. In the fifteen grants for services not exclusively political or military in nature and having nothing to do with poetry or art between 414 and 355/4, five were for bankers who probably gave monetary gifts to Athens, and ten were for trade-related services. In the period between 355/4 and 307/6, three grants of citizenship were for bankers or other men who gave gifts of money to Athens, and, again, ten were for trade-related services.[45] In each of these cases, except possibly that of Chairephilos, the honorands performed services that served or had the potential to serve Athenian political and military interests as well as revenue or trade interests. Thus, there was a change from its practice before 414, but one whose impact Athens minimized by restricting grants of citizenship to those who had performed services that could or did serve political and military interests as well as trade or other interests.[46]

One would expect such Athenian conservatism concerning grants of citizenship, given that the rights and privileges of citizens as well as the civic ideology that grew up around them lay at the heart of the Classical Greek ethos.[47] Only adult male Athenian citizens could participate in politics. Only citizens could own land or lease mining concessions in Attika without special decree. Only citizens could receive pay from the state for serving in government offices or on juries. Only citizens could receive financial assistance from the state in the form of the *theorika*, grain distributions, or assistance to orphans whose fathers died in battle for Athens.[48] Only citizens could be full members of the community and live according to the ideology and ethos that developed around such rights and privileges.[49] The ideal citizen was a landowner, who lived off the produce of the land and had leisure to participate in community life.[50]

Granting citizenship to too many outsiders would increase the number of citizens beyond that which was workable for the *polis*, since it would be impossible for all adult male citizens to hold office and to take part in public life.[51] The government would require ever more revenue to provide the disbursements customary for citizens, who, since they paid no direct regular taxes, would not offset increasing public expenditures with increasing tax revenues. There would not be enough land to go around. Furthermore, the honor of being a citizen would be diluted. The more people who were citizens, the less prestigious and exclusive such a status would be. The fourth-century orators believed that such a degradation of the honor of citizenship was in fact already occurring.[52]

It would be even more corrupting to grant citizenship to men engaged in trade. Professional traders lived lives completely antithetical to that of landed citizens. They sought to profit through buying and selling and lending and borrowing, activities that the elite considered to be unnatural and an impediment to the cultivation of virtue.[53] Traders were away from their homes for most of the summer months and, therefore, could not hold annual public offices at all or serve in the army or participate in community life during that time. Too many such citizens would undermine the *polis*. Thus, Aristotle (*Pol.* 1278a8–10) states it plainly and simply: "the best *polis* will not make a *banausos* a citizen."

Yet Athens' increasing need for imported goods during the late fifth and fourth centuries had to be addressed, and Athens accomplished this through a careful adaptation of existing institutions that attempted to preserve their integrity as much as possible even while inevitably resulting in their corruption. Granting citizenship for trade-related services was Athens' attempt to fulfill its interests in trade through an adaptation of the institution of ritualized friendship (*xenia*). This institution had already been undergoing numerous transformations, from its origins in private *xenia* during the Archaic period to its adoption by states for use in international diplomacy (see chap. 3, Ritualized Friendship and the Foreign Benefactor). Moreover, such a practice also existed outside of Greece among such peoples as the Bosporans and the Persians, who used marriage alliances and adoptions in the same way as Athens used grants of citizenship to cement foreign alliances (Hagemajer Allen 2003: 236–38 and n. 82). Athens simply took this process one step farther by using it to fulfill not only its political and military interests but also its interests in trade. A grant of citizenship was the highest expression of *charis* that Athens could offer to its foreign benefactors, thereby cementing between the two parties a tie of *xenia* through which they could expect mutual services in the future.

By granting citizenship to foreigners in the Classical period, Athens did perhaps cheapen the honor of citizenship and pave the way toward the greater blurring of citizen lines during the Hellenistic period (see Ste.

Croix 1981: 94–95). But down to the end of the fourth century, Athens was able to minimize the potential "social costs" of granting citizenship to those who had performed trade-related services. Almost without exception, only those who performed trade-related services coupled with traditional political or military services or who were in a position to serve the political and military interests of Athens were honored with citizenship.

As a result of both the central importance of citizenship in the Greek ethos and the precautions that Athens took to preserve its integrity, Athenian grants of citizenship for trade-related services were an aspect of Athenian trade policy that is only slightly distinguishable from its political and military policies; it remained embedded in traditional activities, values, and interests. Trading interests comprised only a portion of the motivations for a minority of Athenian grants of citizenship, and even when they did serve as a motivation, they were almost always coupled with traditional political and military interests. Nevertheless, the Athenian practice of granting citizenship for trade-related services exhibits a realization on the part of the Athenian People that the state had a need for trade and that it would have to fulfill that need even at the expense of some of its most cherished values.

Athenian conservatism with regard to granting citizenship down to the end of the fourth century did, however, manage to preserve much of the honor and practical value of Athenian citizenship for the honorands, thereby providing them with a strong incentive to perform services for Athens (Osborne 1981b: 5; 1983: 187). Certainly for Phanosthenes and Chairephilos and his sons, who resided in Athens after their naturalization, Athenian citizenship provided a host of valuable practical privileges, including landownership, full protection under Athenian law, and political participation. Though he never resided in Athens, King Leukon of the Bosporos appears to have owned property (*chremata*) there (Dem. 20.40). But even for the vast majority of those who received citizenship from Athens but had no intention of residing in the city or owning property there, citizenship still held practical value, since it cemented a ritualized friendship that entailed a variety of benefits. Foreign potentates who received a grant of Athenian citizenship could rest assured that they had a safe haven in Athens and could enjoy the rights of citizens if ever circumstances forced them to leave their homelands. Such was indeed the case for several political exiles.[54] Short of relocation, their *xenia* with Athens would also give them confidence that they could count on Athenian assistance of any kind (*boetheia*) should they need it in the future (see

Hagemajer Allen 2003: 237). *IG* ii² 207, which grants citizenship to the satrap Orontes for his services relating to trade (no. 11), also contains explicit arrangements for facilitating future diplomatic contact. In *IG* ii² 212, Spartokos II and Pairisades I, kings of the Bosporos who had received citizenship from Athens for their dynasty's trade-related services (no. 12), not only received assurances that they would obtain whatever they should need from Athens; they were actually given the services of Athenian *hyperesiai* (see below). Finally, Pairisades I was later able to obtain an alliance for mutual defense with Athens in ca. 327 (no. 26).

Although its value as a diplomatic tool in a tie of ritualized friendship was probably the chief lure of a grant of citizenship for most foreign potentates, such a grant also had a significant honorific value.[55] Athens had had a renowned history and remained the largest and one of the more powerful *poleis* in Greece down to the late fourth century. It was never supplanted as the cultural center of Greece during the Classical period. Thus, a grant of citizenship from Athens held more prestige than one from any other *polis*. Such prestige could provide a foreign potentate not only with legitimacy at home but with respect abroad as well.

For people like Chairephilos and his sons, however, receiving a grant of Athenian citizenship held the highest honorific value. He had been a professional trader and, though a very successful and wealthy one, was doubtless looked down on by even the lowliest of Athenians citizens on account of his noncitizen status in Athens. Although becoming a citizen would not instantly wipe away all such prejudices (as Apollodoros, the son of Pasion, often complained — rather hypocritically, it turns out), it went a long way toward legitimizing him and his family and elevating their status in Athens.[56] Chairephilos and his sons now had access to the avenues through which one could gain honor in Athens, through service to Athens in public life, holding offices, performing liturgies, and so forth. Thus, Chairephilos could parlay the honor of citizenship that he earned through his various services, including trade-related ones, to earn further honor through the traditional avenues of Athenian political life.

The Hyperesiai *of No. 12*

One final privilege granted by Athens for trade-related services concerns the *hyperesiai* mentioned in no. 12. In return for the trade-related services of the Bosporan kings, Athens "gave" the *hyperesiai* that the kings had requested. Exactly what these *hyperesiai* were and did has been the subject of some debate. Jordan argues that *hyperesiai* were publicly owned slaves who served as rowers on Athenian warships and that Athens literally gave an unspecified number of them to the Bosporan kings.[57] Since the complement of rowers on a trireme was normally some 170 men, the number of *hyperesiai* given to the Bosporan kings must have been in the several hundreds to have been useful. If Jordan's thesis about *hyperesiai* is right, the cost of Athens' gift of *hyperesiai* to the Bosporan kings would have been extremely high.

Most historians, however, now reject Jordan's thesis and believe that *hyperesia* is a collective term for the free-citizen, nonrowing crew members of a trireme, that is, the petty officers, such as the helmsman and bow officer and their assistants.[58] In Morrison's view, Athens was "giving" not men to the Bosporan kings but rather "the duty (presumably legal) for the ὑπηρεσίαι to serve in the Athenian fleet if required" (Morrison 1984: 54). The Athenian *hyperesiai* would then have served the Bosporan kings as mercenaries with no monetary expenditure from the Athenian state's treasuries.

But even though there was no monetary cost for Athens in providing citizen *hyperesiai* for the navy of the Bosporan kings, the practical and honorific value of the privilege was great, once again illustrating the dual goals of honor and profit in the ancient Greek economy. Hasebroek goes too far in stressing that "it is clearly impossible to regard a covenant of this kind [the transaction between Athens and the Bosporos] as a commercial treaty," implying that it had no economic function whatsoever.[59] By the same token, Hagemajer Allen (2003: 237) is also extreme in stating that "it was the normal practice in Athens to disguise a commercial and a political treaty as an honorary grant," as if honor was just a sham and had no real value in the economy of ancient Greece. The truth lies somewhere in between these extremes. Indeed, the transaction between Athens and the Bosporos was a manifestation of the ritualized friendship that existed between the two states. Ritualized friendship was a means of both maintaining and enhancing one's status as well as providing for one's economic and political needs through the exchange of goods and services as gifts (see chap. 3, Ritualized Friendship and the Foreign Benefactor). Hence, through the gift exchange of *hyperesiai* for trade-related services, Athens was able to fulfill its trade interests in a manner that was not entirely dishonorable, since it drew on traditional methods. At the same time, the Bosporan kings were able to fulfill their political interests, acquiring the use of experienced Athenian military men for their navy, while also enhancing their prestige both in Athens and internationally.

Conclusion

Athenian grants of *asylia, ateleia, enktesis,* the privilege of serving in the army and paying the *eisphora* together with Athenians, and citizenship to those who had performed trade-related services attest to the city's keen interest and active involvement in trade. Despite the fact that such privileges required little monetary expenditure or potential loss of revenue from Athens, they entailed "social costs" that had a more profound impact on Athens in the long run. By granting such privileges to those who had performed traditionally disesteemed trade-related services, Athens altered its social values and civic ideology. Yet Athens did not make such changes lightly but tenaciously resisted what might have been a cultural revolution. Only over time and in response to unexpected crises that intensified its trade interests did Athens grant such privileges to foreigners who had performed trade-related services. Moreover, the more esteemed the privilege, the more grudging was Athens in granting it.

For the honorands, such privileges had practical as well as honorific value. The economic activities of professional traders benefited greatly from grants of *asylia* and *ateleia,* and foreign potentates surely desired the practical value of citizenship, which cemented ties of *xenia* that could be employed for personal uses as well as interstate diplomacy and alliances. But such privileges also brought great honor to their recipients, elevating their status above that of other foreigners. High status and honor also served as capital that could generate further honor and practical benefits. Thus, the transaction by which Athens granted these privileges in return for the trade-related services of the honorands can be seen in both formalist and substantivist economic terms. Both honor and profit were at stake, and it seems fruitless, if not impossible, to try to draw a sharp line between these two goals of economic activity in Classical Athens. To the extent that the line between market trade and gift trade was blurred, one could say that the economy of ancient Greece was embedded in the broader nexus of social relations, but it is also apparent that the degree to which the economy was embedded was changing over the course of the fifth and fourth centuries. In short, the economy of ancient Greece was too complex and dynamic to be fit neatly into any general characterization.

CHAPTER NINE

Conclusion

Aristotle and Xenophon were right: the ancient Greek economy was complex and dynamic. It was not a uniform, monolithic entity but was comprised of many sectors, including agriculture, manufacturing, labor, finance, and trade, each of which was structured according to its own set of organizing principles that may or may not have characterized the others. In the sector of overseas trade, Aristotle and Xenophon realized that there was not a single goal of exchange but rather two, namely, honor and profit. Aristotle, at least, also recognized that due to the extent to which this sector of the economy was undergoing change, the scale of exchanges was expanding, and the quest for profit was becoming increasingly sophisticated. Such a view stands in opposition to the still widely accepted model of the ancient economy put forth by Moses Finley in 1973. Finley's model is certainly brilliant and still appears to hold true in many of its general outlines; however, it has become increasingly clear that the model is too general and suffers from an oversimplified and extremely static view of the ancient economy. Finley was right to stress the embedded nature of the ancient Greek economy in traditional "noneconomic" social and political relations, but he failed to appreciate the fact that all economies, including our own "modern" market economy, are to a great degree the product of larger social and political structures. Thus, the question really is not about whether the ancient Greek economy was embedded but about the nature of the social and political structures in which it was embedded and how they shaped that economy. In order to answer this question, one must take into account the particular historical circumstances that, in turn, shaped those social and political structures and necessarily caused them to change over time.

The foregoing examination of Athenian trade policy through its practice of granting honors and privileges to those who had performed trade-related services has attempted to merge theory with empirical historical evidence to illustrate the complexity and dynamism of the ancient Greek economy in the late Classical period. Part 1 both explored the long-running debate about the nature of the ancient Greek economy, identifying the theoretical assumptions and approaches that formed its basis, and provided an overview of the social and political context within which that economy existed. It is clear that the debate failed to reach a resolution largely because of oversimplification and polarization and because of a tendency to see the ancient Greek economy normatively in comparison to our own market economy. A way out of that conceptual quagmire is substantivism, which sees economies as socially constructed and, therefore, allows us to consider the economy in its broadest sense—as a means of producing, distributing, and consuming resources—as opposed to a narrow conception of "economy" as a market economy. Further developments in the field of economic sociology have provided greater sophistication and nuance to substantivism by acknowledging the role played by groups and individuals in shaping economies, sometimes in opposition to prevailing social norms. The notion of "expressive rationality" encapsulates the interplay between individuals and society that provides the mechanism for structural change in an economy over time in response to specific historical circumstances.

The historical circumstances that shaped the ancient Greek economy consisted of long-standing social values and the shifting tides of internal and external politics. Standing atop the ancient Greek system of values was honor (*timé*), the criteria for which were born of the elite preoccupation with warfare and landownership and privileged war over peace, self-sufficiency over dependence, and status over wealth, resulting in a disdain for profit seeking in nonlanded occupations, such as manufacturing, banking, and trade. By the Classical period in Athens, however, political changes, including the rise of the *polis* and the subsequent triumph of the masses over the elite, democratized these traditional values, directing them toward the good of the community over the good of the individual and imparting a measure of honor to all citizens simply by virtue of their insider's status as full members of the *polis*. A barrier was erected between citizens and foreigners, and members of the elite were required to demonstrate their allegiance to their fellow citizens over their private ties to their families and friends at home and their ritualized friendships (*xenia*) with members of the elite abroad. In such circumstances, the masses, or *demos*, carefully controlled the ambitions of the members of the elite, their "love of honor" (*philotimia*), while at the same time softening some of its society's disdain for the nonlanded occupations that preoccupied many members of the masses. Despite these changes, however, the core traditions of elite values always remained central in ancient Greek life.

In addition to the prevailing values toward trade, internal and external political developments also influenced the Athenian state's trade policy. Besides the security of its borders, public revenues and the food supply were the most important items on the government's list of concerns. The degree to which and the manner in which the government took measures to address these concerns was largely a matter of the strength of its military, the threat posed by its enemies, and the capacity of domestic production. If Athens had been wholly self-sufficient, the state would have had no interest in trade. But Athens did not tax its citizenry regularly and effectively, and from the mid-fifth century onward, it could not produce enough grain domestically to feed its entire resident population or enough timber to maintain its fleet of warships. This situation was further exacerbated from time to time by natural disruptions and man-made political crises. Chief among these was the Sicilian Expedition (415–413), the Social War (357–355), the Battle of Chaironeia (338), and what may have been a prolonged period of drought during the 330s and 320s. Such circumstances compelled Athens to seek grain and timber from external sources. Its first choice, completely in line with traditional Greek values, was to do so through warfare and imperialism, a method that had worked well during the Empire of the fifth century. With the aforementioned military defeats, a navy of inconsistent strength, and the growing power of rivals, such as Macedon, however, it became necessary for the state policy of Athens from 413 to 307 to turn increasingly toward trade.

Among the many practices employed to fulfill Athenian trade policy during this period was the granting of honors and privileges to those who had performed trade-related services for the city. Part 2 of this book presented an analysis of the evidence for this practice, which consists of thirty-four known occasions on which Athens made such grants (the textual evidence for which appears in app. 2). Prima facie the evidence makes manifest the fact that the Athenian state did have an interest and involvement in trade and, thus, a trade policy. Further analysis, informed by the preceding theoretical discussion, however, revealed the nature and historical significance of that interest and involvement. It is apparent that the Athenian state had a primarily consumptive interest in trade. One object of consumption was public revenue, to which the honorary decrees contributed by encouraging trade, the expansion of which provided, in turn, a larger tax base. Although obtaining revenue was one likely goal of this practice, the decrees are explicit concerning another, more pressing goal, which was obtaining imports of essential goods, particularly ships' timber and grain. In each case in which the evidence is complete and clear, the honorands somehow contributed to Athenian imports of these goods. This supports Finley's model in that the goal of Athenian trade policy appears to have been directed toward acquiring goods for consumption, not toward a productive interest in expanding markets for home production. Nor were the honorary decrees meant to aid traders who were Athenian citizens, since in all cases in which the legal status and ethnicity of the honorands can be identified, they are not native Athenian citizens.

The honorary decrees for trade-related services also illustrate the various ways in which trade was organized during the late Classical period. Athens provided honors and privileges in return for gifts of imported goods, thereby engaging in a gift exchange that established a ritualized friendship between Athens and its benefactors. Though traditional in nature, such gift exchanges not only fostered relationships but also served as a mechanism for the acquisition of needed goods that were not available on the spot, that is, trade, according to the substantivist definition. On the other end of the spectrum, Athens also honored men who had simply shipped goods to Athens and sold them at prices determined by the market, a type of trade that conforms to the narrower, formalist definition. Thus, trade in late Classical Greece was complex. It was neither "primitive" nor "modern" but was carried out in a variety of ways.

This variety in the organization of trade was matched by the diversity of those who were responsible for it. The stereotype of the poor, cityless, professional trader that features so prominently in the works of Hasebroek and Finley is much overstated. The absence of native Athenian citizens among the recipients of Athens' honorary decrees for trade-related services down to 307 might support the assertion that traders were outsiders and not citizens of Athens. Another explanation for this phenomenon, however, is that the *demos* of Athens restricted the amount of honor it would confer on its own citizens, especially elite ones, for fear of encouraging their *philotimia* (their "love of honor" or ambition) too much and undermining the egalitarian ethos of Athenian democracy. Foreign benefactors posed much less of a threat, since they were not citizens and had little chance of asserting dominance over the city. In fact, in the eyes of the Athenian *demos*, foreigners ranked below even the lowest Athenian citizen in the social hierarchy.

Although it is probably true that many of the men who actually shipped goods over long distances for exchange were poor, cityless, and professional traders, this is not the end of the story. Athenian honorary decrees for trade-related services reveal men of other statuses who were responsible for trade as well, some of whom also sailed the seas to exchange goods, but others of whom only initiated trading exchanges and directed others to carry them out. The former included professional traders who were wealthy enough to be able to give Athens large quantities of goods free of charge or to sell them at a price reduced from the going rate. The latter consisted of foreign potentates who were not professional traders at all but who arranged to ship sometimes very large quantities of goods to Athens as gifts free of charge. The diversity of those responsible for trade was matched by the variety of their interests in trade. Poor professional traders doubtless sought profit above all in their trading enterprises. Foreign potentates, on the other hand, had less need for profit and were more interested in the prospect of obtaining honor and the other practical benefits that came with establishing a ritualized friendship with the city of Athens. Wealthy professional traders had interests that probably lay somewhere in between these two extremes.

It is probably the case, however, that all those who were responsible for trade had interests in both honor and profit to varying degrees, and Athenian trade policy formulated practices and institutions that appealed to both these interests in order to encourage trade. Athens regulated its coinage, created special law courts, and improved port facilities in an effort to reduce the transaction costs and enhance the profits of professional traders. Grants of honors and privileges to those who had performed trade-related services aimed beyond the profit motive of professional traders to provide an additional incentive that appealed to the desire of all ancient Greeks—and, to a significant extent, to non-Greeks as well—for honor as well as the other practical benefits that Athenian honorary decrees provided.

The honor accorded to Athens' benefactors began with the language of the honorary decrees themselves. Athens described its trade benefactors with words, such as *aner agathos, chresimos,* and *eunous,* to characterize them as "good men" who were "goodwilled" and "useful" to the People of Athens. The benefactors were recognized for their *arete, eunoia,* and *philotimia,* attributes that attested to their "excellence," "goodwill," and "love of honor." Besides such laudatory language, Athens bestowed other honors, including formal commendations, *proxenia* and *euergesia,* gold crowns, bronze statues, hospitality in the Prytaneion, seats in the theater for the Dionysia, and stelai inscribed with their honorary decrees and set up for public display in Athens. Although these honors entailed practical benefits and, in some cases, monetary value as well, they were no doubt appreciated primarily for their honorific value. They symbolized honor normally unattainable for foreigners, thus elevating their status in the pecking order of Athenian society, a benefit that was particularly important not only to those honorands who were *metics* resident in Athens but also to any foreigner who wished to be in Athens' good graces, whether for favor from an Athenian jury in a lawsuit or for an interstate alliance with Athens.

Although the privileges granted by Athens for trade-related services also carried great honorific significance, more than the honors mentioned above, they also entailed functional, practical benefits for their recipients. Most of these privileges were normally the exclusive possessions of Athenian citizens and included *asylia* (protection from seizure), *enktesis* (the right to own land in Attika), the right to serve in the military and to pay the *eisphora* (an emergency property tax) together with Athenians, and Athenian citizenship itself. Another privilege, *ateleia* (exemption from taxes and liturgies), was so special that even citizens could obtain it only by special grant of the city in recognition of extraordinary services. Foreigners who received these privileges from Athens not only approached the status of Athenian citizens but could also make practical use of the privileges. The business of professional traders benefited greatly from a grant of *asylia,* while the right to own land in Attika provided both the opportunity to engage in agriculture and the ability to use land as security for loans. Even if an honorand had no immediate intention of making use of these privileges, he could rest assured that should he ever need to—if, for example, he was a foreign potentate who might someday be driven into exile—he could always take up residence in Athens with at least some of the privileges of a citizen or even citizenship itself. Finally, particular honors and privileges aside, the very relationship of a ritualized friendship, which the exchange of trade-related services for honorary decrees entailed, promised the all-purpose benefit of *boetheia,* aid of any kind from one another should either party ever need it.

The honorands' gain, however, was also in some ways Athens' loss. It is true that the Athenian practice of granting honors and privileges for trade-related services helped the state to obtain the revenue and goods it needed from trade at minimal monetary cost, but it also required the payment of what can be termed a "social cost." Honor was a traditional value, ritualized friendship was a traditional institution, and granting honors and privileges was a traditional way of encouraging benefactions for the city. But whereas this practice had long been employed to reward and encourage equally traditional political and military services, usually from men of high status, Athens adapted it to encourage trade-related services that were much less esteemed and the men of low status who sometimes performed them. Unable or unwilling to create radically new public institutions that would acknowledge the economic needs of the state and the benefits of traditionally disesteemed market-oriented, profit-seeking behavior from lowly outsiders, Athens adapted the traditional value of honor and institutions of ritualized friendship to include trade-related services and the men who provided them.

The honorary decrees represent the services and characters of the honorands in wholly traditional terms, as motivated by a love of honor and goodwill toward the People of Athens. This was not a big stretch when describing the gifts of goods by foreign potentates, but it must have appeared as somewhat of a sham in cases when common professional traders simply sold their imported goods in Athens at the market price. Because of this, Athens only grudgingly and under the compulsion of necessity adapted its traditional values and institutions in this way. Though the evidence is limited, it appears that Athens was careful about which kind of trade-related services and which statuses of men it honored. The general trend appears to be that with each shock that threatened the city's revenues and food supply—in particular, its defeats in Sicily, in the Social War, and at Chaironeia—Athens expanded the range of trade-related services and statuses of men that it would deem worthy of honor.

Over the course of the late Classical period, then, Athenian trade policy maintained a fair degree of continuity with the past, while it also underwent significant changes that would pave the way for further developments characteristic of the Hellenistic age. In an attempt to hold on to the past, Athenian trade policy sought to uphold traditional values, methods of exchange, and roles for the government in the economy. Compelled to live in the present and face the future, however, the Athenians granted honors and privileges for trade-related services, thereby stretching those values, legitimizing disesteemed forms of trade and the lowly outsiders who engaged in them, on the one hand, while acknowledging the *demos'* increasing dependence on the euergetism of the elite, on the other. Such changes served to break down the exclusiveness of the *polis,* contributing to a more vibrant and extensive overseas trade but also to a less homogeneous, cohesive, and democratic community at home, both hallmarks of the Hellenistic period.

The bottom line is that there was, as Aristotle and Xenophon realized, a complex and dynamic economy in Greece during the late Classical period. For all its merits, Finley's model failed to express these fundamental truths. All economies are indeed embedded in society, even our own market economy. But the manner in which they are embedded is contingent on particular historical circumstances, social values, political structures, and the course of events, only some of which are within the control of governments. These events and the actions of individuals and groups within society constitute forces that push and pull on prevailing economic structures, sometimes reinforcing them, sometimes compelling them to change. It is these things—the tug-of-war between continuity and change, the common experiences that bind us all together as human beings, and the cultural differences that make each civilization unique—that make the study of history so compelling. Every person and every civilization must find a way to live, but how they go about it is a product of their own particular culture, which is, in turn, a product of their own particular historical circumstances. When we examine Athenian trade policy and the ancient Greek economy, we inevitably find things that we share in common but also things that make each of us unique.

APPENDIXES

APPENDIX ONE *Master Chart*

Athenian Grants of Honors and Privileges for Trade-Related Services, 415–307 B.C.E.

Occasion	Extant Decree	Honorand	Testimonia	Date	Proposer	Services	Goods	Ethnicity	Legal Status	Socio-Economic Status	Laudatory Language	Honors and Privileges	Cost
1	D1	Lykon of Achaia	*IG* i³ 174	c. 414–412	Peisander	Unknown	Unknown	Greek (Achaian)	Noncitizen	Moderately wealthy professional trader	None	*Proxenia, euergesia,* inscribed stele, sailing privileges	Unknown
2	N.A.	Pythophanes (1)	*IG* i³ 98	before 411	Unknown	Unknown	Unknown	Unknown	Noncitizen	Moderately wealthy professional trader	N.A.	*Proxenia, euergesia*	None
3	D2	Pythophanes (2)	*IG* i³ 98	411/10	Hippomenes	Unknown	Unknown	Unknown	Noncitizen	Moderately wealthy professional trader	None	Inscribed stele, *asylia*	Unknown
4	D3	Phanosthenes of Andros (1) and Antiochides	*IG* i³ 182, Plato *Ion* 541c–d, Athenaios 506a, Xen. *Hell.* 1.5.18, And. 1.149	c. 410–407/6	Unknown	Unknown	Ships' timber, oar-spars	Greek (Andrian)	Noncitizen, *metic*	Unknown	None	*Ateleia* (or *azemia*), commendation, *proxenia, euergesia,* inscribed stele	Unknown
5	N.A.	Phanosthenes of Andros (2)	*IG* i³ 182	c. 410–407/6	Unknown	Unknown	Unknown	Greek (Andrian)	Noncitizen, *metic*	Unknown	N.A.	Citizenship	Unknown
6	D4	Archelaos of Macedon	*IG* i³ 117	407/6	Alkibiades	Gift of imported goods	Ships' timber, oar-spars	Greek (Macedonian)	Noncitizen, *xenos*	Foreign potentate	*Aner agathos*	Commendation, *proxenia, euergesia,* inscribed stele	Unknown
7	N.A.	Satyros I and sons of the Bosporos	Isokr. 17.57, Dem. 20.33, *IG* ii² 212	c. 395–389/8	Unknown	Misc.	Grain	Non-Greek (Bosporan)	Noncitizens *xenoi*	Foreign potentate	N.A.	Commendation, gold crown, *ateleia,* citizenship, inscribed stele	Unknown

Occa-sion	Extant Decree	Honorand	Testimonia	Date	Proposer	Services	Goods	Ethnicity	Legal Status	Socio-Economic Status	Laudatory Language	Honors and Privileges	Cost
8	D5	A Megarian	*IG* ii² 81, Walbank 1990: no. 5=*SEG* 40.57	c. 390–378/7	Unknown	Unknown	Unknown	Greek (Megarian)	Noncitizen	Common professional trader	*Aner agathos*	*Proxenia, asylia,* inscribed stele, *xenia* in the Prytaneion	20 drachmas
9	N.A.	Leukon and sons of the Bosporos	Dem. 20.29–41, *IG* ii² 212	389/8	Unknown	Gift of imported goods, misc.	Grain	Non-Greek (Bosporan)	Noncitizens, *xenoi*	Foreign potentate	N.A.	Commendation, gold crown, *ateleia,* citizenship, inscribed stele	Unknown
10	D6	Achaians	*IG* ii² 286+625, Walbank 1990: no. 11=*SEG* 40.72	c. 350–325?	Unknown	Unknown	Unknown	Greek (Achaians)	Noncitizen	Common professional trader	None	*Proxenia, euergesia, ateleia, asylia,* inscribed stele	Unknown
11	D7	Orontes satrap of Mysia	*IG* ii² 207, Osborne 1981b: 53–54 (his D12)=*SEG* 41.43, Lambert 3.2	349/8?	Polykrates, son of Polykrates	Misc.	Grain	Non-Greek (Persian)	Noncitizen, *xenos*	Foreign potentate	*Aner agathos*	Commendation, gold crown, citizenship, inscribed stele	1,000 drachmas
12	D8	Spartokos II, Pairisades I, and Apollonios of the Bosporos	*IG* ii² 212	347/6	Androtion, son of Andron	Misc.	Grain	Non-Greek (Bosporan)	Noncitizens, *xenoi*	Foreign potentate	*Aner agathos, arete, eunoia*	Commendation, citizenship, *ateleia,* gold crowns, inscribed stele, use of Athenian *hyperesiai*	3,000 drachmas, 30 drachmas, indefinite sum in the future
13	D9	Unknown	*IG* ii² 543, Lambert 3.73	c. 340	Unknown	Securing shipments of goods	Unknown	Greek	Noncitizens, *xenoi*	Unknown	*Philotimia*	Commendation, gold crown, inscribed stele	Unknown

						Misc					[Eunous], philotimia, aner agathos, [chresimos]		
14	D10	Philomelos	IG ii² 423	c. 340–300	Unknown		Grain	Unknown	Unknown	Unknown		Inscribed stele	Unknown
15	D11	Ph— of Cyprian Salamis	IG ii² 283	c. 337	Unknown	Sale of imported goods at a reduced price	Grain, possibly fish	Greek (Cyprian Salaminian)	Noncitizen, xenos	Wealthy professional trader	Chresimos, eunoia	Commendation, gold crown, inscribed stele	Unknown
16	N.A.	Chairephilos and sons	Din. 1.43, Hyperid. frags. 63–64 (Kenyon), Athenaios 3.119f–120a	c. 337–330	Demosthenes, son of Demosthenes	Simple importation of goods	Fish	Unknown	Noncitizens	Wealthy professional trader	N.A.	Citizenship	Unknown
17	D12	Sopatros of Akragas	Camp 1974: no. 3	c. 337–325	Lykourgos, son of Lykophron	Simple importation of goods	Grain	Greek (Akragan)	Noncitizen	Common professional trader	Eunoia	Commendation, proxenia, euergesia, inscribed stele, xenia in the Prytaneion, seat at the City Dionysia	30 drachmas
18	D13	Pandios of Herakleia	Schweigert 1940: no. 39	c. 337–320	Unknown	Simple importation of goods	Grain	Greek (Herakleote)	Noncitizen	Common professional trader	[Eunous], eunoia, [philotimia]	Commendation, inscribed stele	Unknown
19	D14	Potamon and unknown honorand	IG ii² 409, Lambert 3.82	c. 337–320?	Unknown	Simple importation of goods	Grain	Greek (Milesians)	Unknown	Common professional traders	None	Commendation, inscribed stele	Unknown
20	D15	—das from Kos	IG ii² 416(b)	334/3–321	Unknown	Securing shipments of goods	Grain	Greek (Koan)	Noncitizen, xenos	Unknown	Eunoia	Inscribed stele	Unknown
21	D16	Mnemon and —ias of Herakleia	IG ii² 408, Lambert 3.81	333/2	Unknown	Sale of imported goods at a reduced price	Grain	Greek (Herakleote)	Noncitizens	Wealthy professional trader	[Eunous], [eunoia]	Commendation, gold crowns, inscribed stele	Unknown

Occasion	Extant Decree	Honorand	Testimonia	Date	Proposer	Services	Goods	Ethnicity	Legal Status	Socio-Economic Status	Laudatory Language	Honors and Privileges	Cost
22	N.A.	Harpalos of Macedon	Atheniaos 13.586d and 13.596b	c. 333–324	Unknown	Gift of imported goods	Grain	Greek (Macedonian)	Noncitizen, *xenos*	Foreign potentate	N.A.	Citizenship	Unknown
23	D17	Dionysios of Herakleia	*IG* ii² 363; Malouchou: 2000–2003: no. 2, Lambert 3.84	335/4, 331/0, or 326/5	Polyeuktos, son of Sostratos	Gift of imported goods	Grain	Greek (Herakleote)	Noncitizen, *metic*	Wealthy professional trader	N.A.	Right to pay *eisphorai* and serve on campaigns together with Athenians, inscribed stele	30 drachmas
24	D18	Herakleides of Cyprian Salamis (1)	*IG* ii² 360	330/29–328/7	Telemachos, son of Theangelos, Kephisodotos, son of Eucharides	Sale of imported goods at a reduced price	Grain	Greek (Cyprian Salaminian)	Noncitizen, *metic*	Wealthy professional trader	*Philotimia*	Commendation, gold crown, embassy to Herakleia	505 drachmas
25	D19	Apses of Tyre and his father	*IG* ii² 342, Walbank 1985: 107–11=SEG 35.70	After c. 330	Unknown	Simple importation of goods	Grain	Non-Greek (Tyrian)	Noncitizens, *metics*	Common professional trader	*Arete, eunoia*	Commendation, gold crowns, *proxenia, euergesia, enktesis*, inscribed stele	Unknown
26	N.A.	Pairisades I and sons of the Bosporos	*IG* ii² 653, [Dem.] 34.36, Dein. 1.43	c. 327	Demosthenes, son of Demosthenes	Misc.	Grain	Non-Greek (Bosporan)	Naturalized citizen, noncitizens *xenoi*	Foreign potentates	N.A.	Bronze statues	Unknown
27	D20	Herakleides of Cyprian Salamis (2)	*IG* ii² 360	325/4	Phyleus, son of Pausanias, Demosthenes, son of Demokles	Gift of (money to purchase) imported goods	Grain	Greek (Cyprian Salaminian)	Noncitizen, *metic*	Wealthy professional trader	*Philotimia, eunoia*	Commendation, gold crown, *proxenia, euergesia, enktesis*, right to pay *eisphorai* and serve on campaigns together with Athenians, inscribed stele	530 drachmas

28	D21	Apollonides of Sidon	IG ii² 343, Schweigert 1940: 343, Schwenk no. 84	323/2	Unknown	Unknown	Unknown	Non-Greek (Sidonian)	Noncitizen	Unknown	*Aner agathos, [eunous], arete, eunoia*	Commendation, gold crown, *proxenia, euergesia, enktesis,* inscribed stele	1,000 drachmas
29	D22	—phanes	IG ii² 398(a)+438, Walbank 1987a: 10–11=SEG 40.78	c. 322/1 320/19	Demades, son of Demeas?	Misc.	Grain	Unknown	Noncitizen, *xenos*	Unknown	*[Eunoia], chresimos, philotimia*	Citizenship, inscribed stele	Unknown
30	D23	Son of Metrodoros of Kyzikos	IG ii² 401	c. 321–319	Unknown	Misc.	Grain	Greek (Kyzikene)	Noncitizen, *xenos*	Foreign potentate	*[Eunous], chresimos*	Commendation, gold crown, inscribed stele	1,000 drachmas
31	D24	Unknown	IG ii² 407+SEG 32.94, Walbank 1987b: 165–66	c. 321–318	Unknown	Simple importation of goods, securing shipments of goods	Grain	Unknown	Unknown	Common professional trader	*Eunous, [chresimos]*	Commendation, gold crown, inscribed stele	1,000 drachmas
32	N.A.	Eucharistos (1)	IG ii² 400	Before 320/19	Unknown	Unknown	Unknown	Unknown	Noncitizen	Wealthy professional trader	N.A.	*Proxenia, euergesia*	Unknown
33	D25	Eucharistos (2)	IG ii² 400	Before 320/19	Demades, son of Demeas	Sale of imported goods at a reduced price	Grain	Unknown	Noncitizen	Wealthy professional trader	Unknown	Commendation, inscribed stele	Unknown
34	N.A.	Eumelos of the Bosporos	IG ii² 653	310/09	Unknown	Misc.	Grain	Non-Greek (Bosporan)	Noncitizen, *xenos*	Foreign potentate	N.A.	Citizenship, *ateleia*	Unknown

Texts

A. Checklist of Grants

Although there are many ways in which the evidence for Athenian grants of honors and privileges for services relating to trade can be organized, I have chosen to do so in terms of the occasions on which such grants were decreed. I consider each occasion a discrete unit for analysis regardless of the number of honorands or honors and privileges and regardless of whether the occasion was a reaffirmation of an earlier grant. This procedure seems reasonable since each occasion represents a decision by the People (the *demos,* in the broadest sense the entire adult male citizen population) of Athens to honor those who had performed trade-related services. It will thus be possible to trace general trends in the frequency and development of the grants and to analyze the factors that led to each decision by the People of Athens to decree them.

In the checklist of grants that follows, numbers prefixed by the letter *D* indicate occasions for which there is an extant inscription of the actual decree that grants honors and privileges for trade-related services. For example, *IG* i[3] 98 is an inscription that provides evidence for two occasions on which Athens honored Pythophanes. The inscription contains the text of one of the decrees, which I designate as "Pythophanes (2)" and "D2." The text of *IG* i[3] 98, however, also makes reference to an earlier occasion on which the People passed another decree in honor of Pythophanes but for which there is no extant inscription. I designate this earlier and separate occasion simply as "Pythophanes (1)."

TABLE A2.1. Checklist of Athenian Grants of Honors and Privileges for Trade-Related Services, 415–307 B.C.E.

Occasion	Extant Decree	Honorand	Testimonia	Date
1	D1	Lykon of Achaia	IG i³ 174	c. 414–412
2	N.A.	Pythophanes (1)	IG i³ 98	before 411
3	D2	Pythophanes (2)	IG i³ 98	411/10
4	D3	Phanosthenes of Andros (1) and Antiochides	IG i³ 182	c. 410–407/6
5	N.A.	Phanosthenes of Andros (2)	IG i³ 182	c. 410–407/6
6	D4	Archelaos of Macedon	IG i³ 117	407/6
7	N.A.	Satyros I and sons of the Bosporos	Isokr. 17.57, Dem. 20.33, IG ii² 212	c. 395–389/8
8	D5	A Megarian	IG ii² 81, Walbank 1990: no. 5=SEG 40.57	c. 390–378/7
9	N.A.	Leukon and sons of the Bosporos	Dem. 20.29–41, IG ii² 212	389/8
10	D6	Achaians	IG ii² 286+625, Walbank 1990: no. 11=SEG 40.72	c. 350–325?
11	D7	Orontes satrap of Mysia	IG ii² 207, Osborne 1981b: 53–54 (his D12)=SEG 41.43, Lambert 3.2	349/8?
12	D8	Spartokos II, Pairisades I, and Apollonios of the Bosporos	IG ii² 212	347/6
13	D9	Unknown	IG ii² 543, Lambert 3.73	c. 340
14	D10	Philomelos	IG ii² 423	c. 340–300
15	D11	Ph—— of Cyprian Salamis	IG ii² 283	c. 337
16	N.A.	Chairephilos and sons	Dein. 1.43, Hyperid. frags. 63–64 (Kenyon), Athenaios 3.119f–20 a	c. 337–330
17	D12	Sopatros of Akragas	Camp 1974: no. 3	c. 337–325
18	D13	Pandios of Herakleia	Schweigert 1940: no. 39, V-T A149	c. 337–320

Occasion	Extant Decree	Honorand	Testimonia	Date
19	D14	Potamon and unknown honorand	*IG* ii² 409, Lambert 3.82	c. 337–320?
20	D15	——das from Kos	*IG* ii² 416(b), Tracy 1995: 123, 127–28	c. 334/3–321
21	D16	Mnemon and ——ias of Herakleia	*IG* ii² 408, Lambert 3.81	333/2
22	N.A.	Harpalos of Macedon	Atheniaos 13.586d and 13.596b	c. 333–324
23	D17	Dionysios of Herakleia	*IG* ii² 363, Malouchou 2000–2003: no. 2, Lambert 3.84	335/4, 331/0, or 326/5
24	D18	Herakleides of Cyprian Salamis (1)	*IG* ii² 360	330/29–328/7
25	D19	Apses of Tyre and his father	*IG* ii² 342+, Walbank 1985: 107–11	After c. 330
26	N.A.	Pairisades I and sons of the Bosporos	*IG* ii² 653, [Dem.] 34.36, Dein. 1.43	c. 327
27	D20	Herakleides of Cyprian Salamis (2)	*IG* ii² 360	325/4
28	D21	Apollonides of Sidon	*IG* ii² 343, Schweigert 1940: 343, Schwenk no. 84	323/2
29	D22	——phanes	*IG* ii² 398(a)+438, Walbank 1987a: 10–11= *SEG* 40.78	c. 322/1–320/19
30	D23	Son of Metrodoros of Kyzikos	*IG* ii² 401	c. 321–319
31	D24	Unknown	*IG* ii² 407+*SEG* 32.94, Walbank 1987b: 165–66	c. 321–318
32	N.A.	Eucharistos (1)	*IG* ii² 400	Before 320/19
33	D25	Eucharistos (2)	*IG* ii² 400	Before 320/19
34	N.A.	Eumelos of the Bosporos	*IG* ii² 653	310/09

B. Texts and Translations

What follows is a collection of all the known epigraphic and literary testimonia of Athenian decrees that granted honors and privileges for trade-related services between 415 and 307, both in their original ancient Greek and translated into English by me. Translating restored ancient Greek inscriptions necessarily entails some subjectivity, so I will state here my rationale for the manner in which I have translated and indicated restored passages.

I will omit brackets for editorial restorations in the translations when the restorations are pretty certain either because most of the word is intact, the lacuna is small and the context is such that the chances are very good that the restored word is the only possibility, or the lacuna is part of a formulaic phrase commonly used in Athenian decrees. When restorations are more speculative, I will include brackets.

In the case of partially restored words, as a rule, rather than bracket only the restored portion of the word, I will either bracket or not bracket the entire word, depending on the degree of certainity of the restoration, since there is not a one-to-one correspondence between ancient Greek and English with regard to either words or the spellings of words. I will make exceptions to this rule, however, when the word is either a proper name or particularly important with regard to the arguments put forth in this book, so that the Greekless reader can see that the word or name is partially restored, no matter how certain the restoration may be. This will result in some arbitrariness in my choice of which letters to bracket in the translated words, but my aim is simply to show that the word is partially restored.

When only a few isolated words or letters appear on the inscription and two cannot be restored into coherent ideas, I will not attempt a translation but will simply bracket the entire section as a series of dots or dashes. I will also either include or completely omit dotted letters, depending on how certain they are within the context of the inscription. I will try to preserve the word order of the inscriptions as much as possible but will alter it in the interest of producing readable translations that are not too convoluted or offensive for the English ear. Greek inscriptions divide words at the end of lines without respect to syllable breaks. I have avoided dividing words between lines, and when a word is thus divided in the Greek inscription, I put the entire word either at the end of the line or at the beginning of the next. Variations in readings and restorations will be noted in the commentaries of appendix 3 only when they concern issues that are essential for the arguments put forth in this book. Finally, since this book is not an epigraphic study per se, I have chosen to minimize the amount of information in the lemma for each entry, including citations only of those editions of the inscriptions that had a direct bearing on my choice of texts, of the sources of key restorations and other important discussions made outside the context of full editions, and of editions that are readily available to a wide audience in ancient Greek or in translation. The particular edition that served as the basis for each text is indicated in bold print.

1 (D1). *IG* i³ 174 (*IG* i² 93; Walbank no. 50; V-T A25) (ca. 414–412)

ΣΤΟΙΧ. 21

[ἔδοξεν τῆι βολῆι καὶ τῶι δ]-
[ήμωι· . . . . . ηὶς ἐπρυτάνευε, Θ]-
[ε]αῖος ἐγ[ρα]μ[μάτευε, Ἀρι]σ[τ]-
4 αίνετος ἐπεστάτε, Πείσαν-
δρος εἶπε· Λύκωνα τὸν Ἀχαι-
όν, ἐπειδὴ εὖ ποεῖ Ἀθηναίο-
[ς], ἀναγραψάτω πρόξενον κα-
8 ὶ εὐεργέτην Ἀθηναίων ἐν σ-
τήληι λιθίνει ἐμ πόλει ὁ γρ-
αμματεὺς ὁ τῆς βολῆς καὶ κ-
αταθέτω ἐμ πόλει. τὴν δὲ να-
12 ῦν ἧν δῆται ἐκκομίσασθαι
ἐξ Ἀχαΐας ἐκκομισάσθω κ-
αἰ ἐξῆναι αὐτῶι πλῆν καὶ χ-
ρήματα ἐσάγεν ὅσης Ἀθηνα-
16 ῖοι κρατῶσι, καὶ ἐς τὰ Ἀθην-
[α]ίων φρόρια· ἐς δὲ τὸν κόλπ-
[ον μ]ὴ ἐξῆ[ναι . . . .] αὐ | τῶι
- -

[It was resolved by the Council and the]
[People, ... held the *prytany*],
[The]aios was sec[retary; Ari]s[t]ainetos
4 was president; Peisandros
made the motion: whereas Lykon the
Achaian does well for the Athenian[s],
let the secretary of the Council
8 inscribe (him as) a *proxenos* and
a *euergetes* of the Athenians on a
stone stele on the Acropolis, and
let him set it up on the Acropolis: but let his
12 ship, which he needs to bring out
from Achaia, be brought out and
let him be allowed to sail and to bring
his goods as far as the Athenians
16 rule and to the garrisons
of the Athenians. But [let him not be allowed]
[. . . into the gulf . . . .]

2. See no. 3 (before 411)

3 (D2). *IG* i³ 98 (*IG* ii² 12; *SEG* 39.10, Walbank no. 75; V-T A28)
(411/10)

```
        [....8....]ην[..........20..........]              ΣΤΟΙΧ. 30
        [...6...]ῃι ην τε[..........18.........]
        [...6...]άτης Ἰκα[ριεὺς ἐγραμμάτευεν˙]
    4   [βολῆ]ς ἐπεστάτε [.........17........]
        [...κ]αὶ μετ' αὐτõ π[........16........]
        [. Ξυ]πεταιών, Διωπ[........16........]
        [..] Κεφαλῆθεν, Καλ[........16........]
    8   [.Ἱ]ππομένης εἶπε˙ [........16........]
        στίωι, ἐπειδὴ πρόξ[ενός ἐστι Ἀθηναίω]-
        ν καὶ εὐεργέτης κ[αὶ εὖ ποεῖ ὅ τι δύνατ]-
        αι τὴν πόλιν τὴν Ἀθ[ηναίων καὶ τὴν ...]
   12   στίων τὸ ψήφισμα τ[ὸ προψηφισμένον α]-
        ὐτῶι ἀναγράψαι ἐν σ[τήληι λιθίνηι τὸ]-
        ν γραμματέα τῆς βολ[ῆς τὸν νῦν γραμμα]-
        τεύοντα καὶ καταθε̃ν[αι ἐν πόλει. τὰ δὲ]
   16   χρήματα, ἅ ἐστιν Πυθοφά[νει Ἀθήνησιν]
        ἢ ἄλλοθί πο ὦν Ἀθηναῖοι κ[ρατõσιν, καὶ]
        περὶ τῆς νεὼς ἃ λέγει καὶ [περὶ τῶν χρη]-
        [μ]άτων, μὴ ἀδικε̃ν μηδένα κ[αί ἀσυλίαν ἔ]-
   20   ναι αὐτῶι καὶ τοῖς χρήμα[σι αὐτõ καὶ ἀ]-
        νιόντι καὶ ἀπιόντι. ταῦτ[α μὲν ἔστω ἐψ]-
        ηφισμένα ὅσης Ἀθηναῖοι [κρατõσι πᾶσ]-
        ι τοῖς Πυθυφάνος κατὰ τα[υτά˙ ὅπως δ' ἂν]
   24   ταῦτα γίγνηται, τοὺς στ[ρατηγὸς τὸς α]-
        [ἰ]εὶ στρατηγõντας ἐπιμ[έλεσθαι καὶ τ]-
        [ὴ]ν βολὴν τὴν αἰεὶ βολεύ[οσαν. προσανα]-
        [γ]ράψαι δὲ καὶ τόδε τὸ ψή[φισμα ἐς τὴν α]-
   28   [ὐ]τὴν στήλην τὸγ γραμμ[ατέα τῆς βολῆς]
        ˅˅ ἐπὶ Ἀριστοκράτος ἄ[ρχοντος ˅˅˅˅˅ ]
        [ἔδ]οξ[εν] τῆ[ι] β[ολ]ῆι, Κεκρ[οπὶς ἐπρυτάνε]-
        [υε, ....7... ἐγρα]μμάτε[υεν, Ἀριστοκρά]-
   32   [της ἦρχε ....7...]ς ἐπε[στάτε, - - - -]
```
- -

```
        [......]-ates of Ik[aria was secretary:]
    4   [of the Council] was the president [..........]
        [............................]
        [. of Xy]pete, Diop[...............]
        [..] Kephale, Kal[..............]
```

8   [. Hi]ppomenes moved: [. . . . .]

[. . . . .], whereas [he is] a *prox[enos* of the Athenian]s

and a *euergetes* [and does whatever good he can]

for the city of the Ath[enians and the . . .]

12   [. . . . .], the secretary of the Council [who is now secretary]

shall inscribe the decree [previously decreed]

for him on [a stone stele]

and set it up [on the Acropolis. The]

16   goods, which Pythopha[nes] has [at Athens]

or anywhere else over which the Athenians [rule, and]

the things which he says concerning his ship and [his goods],

no one shall harm, [and there shall be *asylia*]

20   for him and for [his] goods [both]

when he arrives and when he departs. [Let] these things [be]

decreed as far as the Athenians [rule for all]

the family of Pythophanes on the same [conditions].

24   The [generals who are]

in service [at the time and] the Council which

is deliberating at the time [are to take care in order that] these things happen.

The secretary [of the Council] shall inscribe this decree as an addition

28   [on the sa]me stele.

In the archonship of Aristokrates . . .

It was resolved by the Council, Kekr[opis held the prytany . . .]

---

4 (D3). *IG* i³ **182** (*IG* i² 122; *SEG* 33.11 and 39.308; Walbank no. 60; Osborne T9; V-T A41) (ca. 410–407/6)

```
- - - - - - - - - - - - - - - - - - - - - - - - - - - - - - - - - - - - -    ΤΟΙΧ. 42
```

b   [. . . . 7 . . . Ἀν]τιοχίδει κα[ὶ Φανοσθένει . . . . . . 12 . . . . . .]

[. . . . . 10 . . . . .]ς Ἀθεναίοις [. .]ι[. . . . . 19 . . . .]

[. . . . . 10 . . . . .]ορας καὶ τὰ ἄλλα hοτ[. . . . . . . 16 . . . .]

4   [. . . . . 9 . . . . τὸ]ν δêμον τὸν Ἀθεναί[ον . . . . 14 . . . .]

[. . . 6 . . . καθάπε]ρ καὶ νῦν αὐτός, καὶ ḥ[όπος ἂν φαίνεται]

[Ἀθεναίον ὁ δêμο]ς ḥος περὶ πολλô ποι[όμενος τὸς ἐσάγ]-

a   [οντας κο]πέας [κα]ὶ χάριν ἀποδόσον τὸ λ[οιπόν, ἀτελὲς τ]-

8   [όκο ἑκα]τοστô [τὸ]ς κοπέας ḥὸς ἔγαγον [ἀποδόντον τοῖς]

[τρι]εροποιοῖς, κ[αὶ] ḥοι τριεροποιοὶ/// [. . . . . . 12 . . . . . .]

[τιθ]έντον ἐς τὸ να[υπέ]γιον, καὶ ἐὰν δέ[ονται αὐτôν ḥοι]

[στ]ρατεγοὶ χρôσθο[ν φρ]άζοντες τêι β[ολêι καὶ ἀποδιδ]-

12   [όν]τες τὲν τεταγμέγ[εν] τιμέ[ν], καὶ ḥο[ι ναυπεγοὶ δόντο]-

[ν τοῖς τριεροποιο[ῖς τὰ τε]ταγμέν[α . . . 5 . .? Ἀντιοχίδε]-

[ς καὶ] Φανοσθένες το[. . . . . 26 . . . .]

[. . . 5 . .]το ḥο hελλενο[ταμίας . . . . 20 . . . .]

16 [. . . 6 . . .]ς χρε͂σθαι ἐς τ[. . . . . 25 . . . .]
    [. . . . αὐτ]οῖν ἀγαγόντ[οιν . . . . 22 . . . .]
    [. . . . 7 . . .]σοραι, ἐπαιν[έσαι Ἀντιοχίδεν καὶ Φανοσθέν]-
    [εν ὅτι ἐδια]κονεσάτε[ν . . . . 24 . . . .]
20 [. . . . 7 . . . καὶ] προσάγ[εν αὐτὸ τὸς πρυτάνες . . . . . 9 . . . .]
    [. . . . 8 . . . . ἐκ]κλεσί[α . . . . 26 . . . .]
    [. . . . . . 11 . . . . . ἄ]λλο -
         3–4 *vv.desunt*
c τι˙ ἐπα[ινέσαι τε αὐτὸς καὶ ἀναγράφσαι προχσένος κα]-
24 ὶ εὐεργέτας. ἐν[αι δὲ αὐτοῖς hευρέσθαι ἄλλο hον ἂν δέ]-
    ονται παρὰ Ἀθεν[αίον˙ ἀναγράφσαι δὲ . . . . 8 . . . . ἐν στέ]-
    λει εὐεργέτας Ἀθ[εναίον ἐμ πόλει τὸν γραμματέα τε͂ς]
    βολε͂ς   ✂   *vacat*
                  vacat 0,11
       fragmenta incerti loci ///
d 28 - | [. . . . . 10 . . . . .]
    [- τὲ]ν βολ[ὲν . . . 6 . . .]
    [- - - - - - - - - - - - - - - - - - - τό]δ<ε> φσέ[φισμα ἀνα]-
    [γραφσάτο hο γραμματεὺς hο τε͂ς βολ]ε͂ς ἐν στ[έλει λιθί]-
32 [νει -]ι δὲ τὸς [. . . . 8 . . . .]
    -

    [. . . . . . An]tiochides an[d Phanosthenes . . . .]
    [. . . . .] Athenians [. . . . .]
    [. . . . .] and the other [. . . . .]
4 [. . . . . the] People of Athe[ns . . . .]
    [. . . . . . just as] also now he, and [in order that the People]
    [of Athens appear to consider] important [those who]
    [import o]ars [and] to give favor in the [future, a tax exemption from]
8 [interest of the one hundredth to those] who brought oars, [let them
        give (the oars) to the]
    trieropoioi, and let the *trieropoioi* [. . . . .]
    [place] (the oars) in the shipyard, and if [the] generals [need (the oars),
        let them]
    use (the oars), making it known to the [Council and paying]
12 the established price, and [let the ship builders give]
    [to the] *trieropoioi* [the] established [things . . . Antiochides]
    [and] Phanosthenes [. . . . .]
    [. . . . .] the *Helleno[tamias* . . . .]
16 [. . . . . .] to use for [. . . . .]
    [. . . .the two] men who bri[ng . . . .]
    [. . . . . . .], to comme[nd Antiochides and Phanosthenes]
    [because they have] served [. . . . .]
    vacat vv. 20–22

[They shall be commended and inscribed as *proxenoi* and]
24   *euergetai*. [They] shall [be allowed to obtain whatever else]
[they may need] from the Athen[ians. The secretary] of the Council
[shall inscribe]
[on a stele] as *euergetai* of the Ath[enians on the Acropolis . . .]
28   -
[- the] Council [. . . . . .]
[- - - - - - - - - - - - - - - - - let the secretary of the Council]
[inscribe this decree] on a [stone] st[ele . . .]

5. See no. 4 (ca. 410–407/6)

6 (D4). IG i³ 117 (*IG* i² 105; Tod 1.91; M-L no. 91; Fornara no. 161; *SEG* 40.16; Walbank no. 90; V-T A37) (407/6)

[ἔδοχσεν τῆι βολῆι καὶ τõ]ι δέμοι· Ἀκα[μα]- a   ΣΤΟΙΧ. 31
[ντὶς ἐπρυτάνευε, Φελ]λεὺς [ἐγρ]αμ[μ]άτ[ευ]-
[ε, Ἀντιγένες ἔρχε, Σιβ]ύρτιο[ς ἐ]πεστά[τε],
4   [Ἀλκιβιάδες εἶπε· ἐς τ]ὲν πο[ίε]σιν τὸν [νε]-
[õν δανεῖσαι τὸς στρα]τεγὸς τ[ὸ]ς μετὰ Π[ε]-
[ρικλέος ἀργύριον παρ]ὰ τὸν {τ̣[õ]ν} ὄντον ἀ-
[ποδεκτõν τοῖς ναυπεγ]οῖς· hὸ δ' ἂν δανεί-
8   [σοσιν, ἀποδόντον αὐτο]ῖς πάλιν hοι τρι-
[εροποιοί· τὸς δὲ τεταγ]μένος πλῆν ἐπὶ τ-
[ὲν πλέροσιν τõν νεõν h]ος τάχιστα ἀποσ-
[τελάντον hοι στρατεγ]οί· εἰ δὲ μέ, ἐσαγό-
12   [σθον προδοσίας ἐς τὸ δ]ικαστέριον· ho[ι]
[δὲ στρατεγοὶ περὶ τõ μ]ὲ ἐθέλοντος ἀπι-
[έναι ἐσαγόντον· τὲς δ]ὲ κομιδὲς τõν νε[õ]-
[ν, hὰς ἂν hοι ναυπεγοὶ] ἐγ Μακεδονίας στ̣-
16   [έλλοσι, τὲν βολὲν ἐπι]μελεθῆναι, hόπος
[ἂν σταλõσιν hος τάχισ]τα Ἀθέναζε καὶ π-
[λεροθõσι καὶ ἐπὶ Ἰονί]αν κομίζεται hε
[στρατιὰ φυλάχσοσα φυ]λακὲν τὲν ἀρίστ-
20   [εν· ἐὰν δέ τις μὲ ποέσει] κατὰ ταῦτα, ὀφέλ-
[εν μυρίας δραχμὰς αὐτὸ]ν hιερὰς τῆι Ἀθ-
[εναίαι· τõι δὲ πρότοι ἐλθ]όντι καὶ κομ[ι]-
[σαμένοι ναῦν δõναι δορεὰν κ]αθάπ[ερ ἔδ]-
24   [οχσεν τõι δέμοι· ἐπειδὲ δὲ Ἀρχέλας καὶ]   b
[νῦν καὶ ἐν τõι πρόσθεν χρ]όγοι ἐσ[τὶν ἀν]-
[ὲρ ἀγαθὸς περὶ Ἀθεναίος τός τε ἐκπ[λεύ]-
[σαντας Ἀθεναίον ἀνέλ]αβεν καὶ ἐς τὸ [ἐπ]-
28   [ὶ Πύδνει στρατόπεδον] ἀ̣πέπεμφσεν κα[ὶ]
[εὖ ἐπόεσεν Ἀθεναίον τ]ὸ στρατόπεδον κ-
[αὶ ἔδοκεν αὐτοῖς χσύλ]α καὶ κοπέας καὶ

[ἄλλα hόσον ἐδέοντο παρ'] αὐτō ἀγαθά, ἐπα-
32 [ινέσαι Ἀρχέλαι hος ὄν]τι ἀνδρὶ ἀγαθōι
[καὶ προθύμοι ποιēν hό τ]ι δύναται ἀγαθ-
[όν, καὶ ἀνθ' ὅν εὐεργέτεκ]εν τέν τε πόλιν
[καὶ τὸν δēμον τὸν Ἀθεναί]ον ἀναγράφσα
36 [ι αὐτὸν καὶ παῖδας προχσένο]ς καὶ ε[ὐερ]-
[γέτας ἐμ πόλει ἐστέλεν λιθίνε]ν κ[αὶ ἐπι]-
[μέλεσθαι αὐτὸν - - - - - - - - - - - - - - - - - - -]

[It was resolved by the Council and the] People, Aka[mantis]
[held the *prytany*, Phel]leus was secretary,
[Antigenes was the archon, Sib]yrtio[s] was president,
4 [Alkibiades made the motion: for] the making of the [ships]
[the generals] with P[erikles shall loan]
[money from] the current
[*apodektai* to the ship builders]. But that which they (the generals)
8 [lend, let] the [*trieropoioi* give back to them] again.
Let the [gener]als dis[patch those who are appointed] to sail
[to man the ships as] quickly as possible.
But if not, let them bring
12 [charges of treason to the] *dikasterion*. [Let the]
[generals bring charges concerning him who] does [not] wish to de-
[part. The Council] shall take care of [the]
conveyance of the [ships, which the ship builders]
16 [send from] Macedonia, in order that
[they may be sent as quickly as possible] to Athens and
[manned and] the [army] may be conveyed [to Ionia]
[to keep guard] as well as possible.
20 [But if anyone shall not act] according to these things,
[he shall have to pay ten thousand drachmas] dedicated to Ath[ena].
[But to the first man who arrives] and
[conveys a ship, a gift shall be given just as]
24 [it was resolved by the People. Whereas Archelaos]
[now and previously has been a]
[good man concerning the Atheni]ans and [took in] the
[Athenians who sailed out] and sent (them) back to the
28 [fleet at Pydna] and
[did well for] the fleet [of the Athenians]
[and has given to them timbe]r and oar spars and
[as many other] good [things as they needed from] him,
32 [Archelaos shall be commended as being] a good man
[and eager to do wh]atever goo[d] he can,
[and in return for that which he has provided as a benefac]tion to
both the city

[and the People of Athe]ns, [he and his sons] shall be inscribed

36 [as *proxeno*]*i* and *e*[*uergetai*]

[on the Acropolis]

[on a stone stele, and they shall]

[take care of them . . .]

7. See also nos. 9 and 12, Isokrates *Trapezitikos* 17.57 (Loeb text by
L. R. van Hook; Osborne T21) (ca. 395–389/8)

Ἄξιον δὲ καὶ Σατύρου καὶ τοῦ πατρὸς ἐνθυμηθῆναι, οἵ πάντα τὸν
χρόνον περὶ πλείστου τῶν Ἑλλήνων ὑμᾶς ποιοῦνται, καὶ
πολλάκις ἤδη διὰ σπάνιν σίτου τὰς τῶν ἄλλων ἐμπόρων ναῦς
κενὰς ἐκπέμποντες ὑμῖν ἐξαγωγὴν ἔδοσαν . . .

It is right to think highly of Satyros and my father, who always
consider you most important of the Greeks, and often in the past on
account of a scarcity of grain, although they sent away the ships of
other *emporoi* empty, they gave the export to you.

8 (D5). *IG* ii² 81 (text by **Walbank 1990: no. 5**=*SEG* 40.57; V-T A64)
(ca. 390–378/7)

```
- - - - - - - - - - - - - - - - - - - - - - - - - - - - - - -        ΣΤΟΙΧ. 28
   . . δωρος ε[ἶ]π[εν· ἀναγράψαι . . . 6 . . .]
   [ον] Μεγαρέα [π]ρ[όξενον αὐτὸν καὶ τὸ]-
   [ς ἐ]γγόνος τõ δ[ήμο τõ Ἀθηναίων, ἐπει]-
4  [δ]ή ἐστιν ἀνὴρ ἀ[γαθὸς περὶ τὸν δῆμο]-
   [ν] τὸν Ἀθηναίων κα[ὶ νῦν καὶ ἐν τῶι πρ]-
   όσθεν χρόνωι. εἶν[αι δὲ ἀσυλίαν καὶ]
   αὐτοῖς καὶ χρήμα[σι τοῖς τούτων· τὸ]
8  δὲ ψήφισμα τόδε ἀ[ναγραψάτω ὁ γραμ]-
   [μ]ατεὺς ὁ τῆς βολῆ[ς ἐν στήληι λιθίν]-
   ηι καὶ καταθέτω ἐ[ν ἀκροπόλει· εἰς δ]-
   [ὲ] τὴν ἀναγραφὴν δ[οῦναι τοὺς ταμί?]-
12 [α]ς εἴκοσι δραχμ[άς. καλέσαι δὲ . . . .]
   . . ον ἐπὶ ξένια [εἰς τὸ πρυτανεῖον]
   [εἰς] αὔριον. *vacat*
                    *vacat*
```

. . . -doros [moved: shall inscribe . . . . . .]

[-os] the Megarian as a [*p*]*r*[*oxenos*, both him and his]

descendants, of the [People of Athens, since]

4 he is a g[ood] man [concerning the People]

of Athens [both now and previously]
There shall [be *asylia* both]
for them and [their] goo[ds: Let the secretary]
8   of the Council [inscribe] this decree
[on a stone stele]
and let him set (it) up [on the Acropolis. For]
the inscribing [the treasurers? shall give]
12   twenty drachm[as]. -os [shall be invited . . . .]
[. .] for hospitality [in the Prytaneion]
tomorrow.

9. See nos. 7 and 12 (389/8)

10 (D6). *IG* ii² **286+625** (Walbank 1990: no. 11–*SEG* 40.72)
(ca. 350–325?)

ΣΤΟΙΧ. 18

. . . . . . 11 . . . . . I Ο . . . 5 . .
[. . . 5 . . εὐ]εργέτα . . . 5 . .
[. . . 5 . . κ]αὶ προξε[. . . . ε]-
4   [ὑερ]γεσίαν. εἶνα[ι δὲ αὐ]-
[τοῖ]ς ἀτέλειαν πά[ντων]
[καὶ] ἀσυλίαν καὶ α[ὐτοῖ]-
[ς καὶ χ]ρήμασιν κα[ὶ πολ]-
8   [έμου ὄ]ντος καὶ εἰ[ρήνη]-
[ς . . . . . 9 . . . .]ους . . . 5 . .
. . . . . 10 . . . . . καὶ . . . 5 . .
. . . . . 10 . . . . 6 . . .

- - - - - - - - - - -

. N T A I T
. 'A X A I A
. . A N T Ω
. . . K A I

- - - - - - - - - -

[. . . . . *eu*]*ergeta* . . . . .
[. . . . . and] *proxe*[. . . .]
4   [bene]faction. [They] shall have
ateleia (tax exemption) from [all things]
[and] *asylia* (protection from seizure) both for [them]
[and their g]oods, both [when there is]
8   [war] and (when there is) pe[ace]

- - - - - - - - - - -

. Achaians

- - - - - - - - - -

11 (D7). *IG* ii² **207** (text of fragment [a] by **Osborne 1981b: 53–54 (his D12)**=*SEG* 41.43; archon's name in line 12 by Lambert 3.2; V-T A86) **(349/8?)**

a ἔδοξε τῶι δήμωι· Πανδιονὶς <ἐ>πρυτάνευ[ε· ΣΤΟΙΧ. (?)
   Φλυεὺς ἐπεστάτει· Πολυκράτης Πολυκράτους [- - - εἶπεν· περὶ ὧν
      ἀπαγγέλλουσιν οἱ]
   πρέσβεις οἵ τε Ἀθηναί<ω>ν καὶ οἱ παρὰ <Ὀ>ρόν[του ἥκοντες
      τῶι δήμωι καὶ τῆι βουλῆι]
4 τῆι Ἀθηναί<ω>ν· ΠΟΙΕΙΝ ΤΟΝ ΔΗΜΟΝ ΛΕΓΕΤΑΙ [- - - - - - - ..
      ἐπαινέσαι Ὀρόντην ὅτι ἐστὶν]
   ἀνὴρ ἀγαθὸς περὶ τὸν δῆμον [τὸν Ἀθηναίων καὶ πρόθυμος ποιεῖν
      ἀγαθὸν ὅτι ἂν δύναται καὶ νῦ]-
   ν καὶ ἐν τῶι ἔμπροσθεν χρόνωι <καὶ> εἶναι Ὀρό[ντην Ἀθηναῖον
      καὶ ἐκγόνους αὐτοῦ, καὶ γρά]-
   <ψασθαι αὐτὸν φυλῆς καὶ δήμου καὶ φρατρίας ἥστινος ἂν
      βούληται εἶναι· δοῦναι δὲ τὴν>
8 ψῆφον περὶ αὐτοῦ τοὺς πρυτάνεις ἐν τῆι <πρώτηι> ἐκκλησίαι
      [τῶι δήμωι· καὶ στεφανῶσι αὐ]-
   τὸν χρυσῶι στεφάνωι ἀπὸ χιλίων δραχμῶν· [- - - - - - - - - - - -]
   τοῦ στεφάνου· βουλεύσασθαι Π Ν Α - - - ὁπόθε[ν - - - - - - - - - - - -]
   πάντα Μ Ι Ν Η Ι Η Φ - - - Ὀρόντου πρὸς τὸ - - - ΟΠΟ. . .ΧΩΝ
      ΟΙ Φ - - [- -]
12 [τοὺς θε]σμοθέτας τοὺς ἐπὶ Κα<λλι>μάχου ἄρχοντος . . .
      Β Ο Υ Λ Ε Υ Ο Ν Α Χ Ο Δ Ι Ο - - [- - - τῶν]
   Ἀθηναίων ἢ τῶν συμμάχων μὴ Λ Ι Π Ο Μ ΕΝ - - - [Ὀρ]<ό>ντου
      ἀρχ [- -]
   δήμου τοὺς μὲν Ἀθηναίους δί[κα]ς δοῦναι ἐν τοῖς συμβόλ[οις
      - - - - - -]
   ΤΙΘ εἰσὶν ἐκ τῆς Ὀρόντου ἀρχῆς Ε Τ - - - - - συμμ<α>χ [- - - - - - - -]
16 ἐξεῖναι τῶι ἐγκ<λ>ήματι Ω Ι Λ Λ Ο Ε Π - - - Α Ν - - [- - - - - - - -]
   [- - - - -] υσιν· τὴν δὲ βουλὴν τὴν [- - - - - - - - - - - - - - - - - -]
   [- - - - - -] καὶ τῶι δήμωι [- - - - - - - - - - - - - - - - - - -]

b - - - - - - - - - - - - - - - - - - Ω < - - - - - - - - -
   - - - - - - - - - - - - - - - - - - // ΙΛΙ(. .ΟΥ - - - - -
   - - - - - - - - - - - - - - - - - α πλοίων - - - - - -
4 φίλοι καὶ σ[ύμμαχοι - - - - -]
   - - - - - - - - - - - - - - Ὀρό]ντης ὅπως [ἂν] παραλάβηι - - - - - - -
   - - - - - - - - - - - - - - σι καὶ τὰ σύμβολα δειχθῆι καὶ - - - - - -
c - - - - - - -σιτ - - - - - - \ ἑλέσθαι τὸν δῆμον αὐτίκα μ[άλα - - - -]

8   [- - - - τοὺς] δὲ αἱρε[θέντας τὸ ἀρ]γύριον λαβόντας ὁπόθεν
        ἂν ὁ δῆμος [ψηφίσηται? - -]
        - - Ο / Λ Ι Λ -. Δ Ε . . Α - - - ωι ἐν τῶι Θαργηλιῶνι μηνὶ καὶ
        ἀπάγ[ε]ιν - -
        [παρὰ] τὰ ἐν τῶιδε τῶι ψηφ[ίσματι] γεγραμμένα καὶ ἄλλο
        ἀγαθὸν ὅτι ἂν [δ]ύν[ηται - -]
        [τὸ δὲ ἀργ]ύριον εἶναι εἰς τὴ[ν πα]ράληψι[ν] τοῦ σίτου ἐκ
        τῶν στρ[α]τιωτικῶν - - - -
12   [- - - τ]ῶι στρατοπέδ[ωι - - παρ]ὰ Χάρητος καὶ Χαριδήμου
        καὶ [Φ]ωκίωνο[ς - - -]
        - - - - δὲ καὶ τ[- - - - - χρ]ήματα τῶν συντάξεων τῶν ἐλ Λέσβωι
        |καὶ - - -]
        - - - - οντ[- - - - - - - Χ]αριδήμου καὶ Φωκίωνος τά τε παρὰ
        τῆ[ς π]όλ[εως]
        - - - -ος - - - - - - - - ης λαβόντας παραλαβεῖν τὸν σῖτον π[α]ρὰ
        τῶ[ν - - -]
16   - - - ἐπισ[- - - - - - - ὡς τ]άχιστα καὶ γένηται μισθὸς τοῖς
        στρατι[ώτα]ις- -
        [- - - κο]μιδῆς [- - - - - -δε]ῖξα[ι τ]οὺς ταμίας καὶ τοὺς πρέσβεις
        τῶι δήμω[ι- - -]
        [- - ὅ]τι ἂν βούλη[ται - - - - τα]μίαι μὴ ποιῶσιν τὰ ἐν τ[ῶι]δε
        τῶι ψηφί[σματι - - -]
        [- - - - - - - - - - - - δι]ακωλύοντας τὸμ πόλεμον πολεμε[ῖσ]θα[ι
        - - - -]
20   [- - - - - - - - - - - - -ὅπ]ως κομίζηται ἐπιμε[λ]εῖσθαι τοὺς με - - - - - -
        [- - - - - - - - - - - τ]<u>οὺς συμμάχους</u> Χάρητα καὶ Χαρίδημον
        τοὺς σ[τρατηγούς ?- -]
        - - - - - - - - - - - - - - <u>ταμίαι καὶ</u> [τ]ὰ χρήματα ὡς Ὀρό[ν]την καὶ
        πλοῖα παρὰ - - -
        - - - - - - - - - - - - - - <u>Πρόξενον τ</u>[ὸν] στρατηγὸν μετὰ τῶν
        πρέσβεων - - - - -
24   [- - - - - - - - - - - τὸν τα]<u>μίαν τοῦ δήμ</u>[ου τὰ] ἐ[φ]όδια τῶν πρέσβεων
        [ἑκ]άστωι [δραχμάς - -]
        - - - - - - - - - - - ωι. <u>ἐπαινέσα</u>[ι δὲ κα]ὶ τοὺς πρέσβεις
        τοὺς πεμφθέ[ντας]
        [- - - - - - - - - τοὺς δ]ὲ <u>πρέσβεις</u> [- - - σ]τεφανῶσαι θαλλοῦ
        στεφά[νωι - -]
        - - - - - - - - - - - <u>Εὐωνυμέα,</u> - - ν Λυκόφρονος Ἀχ[α]ρνέα, Φ - - - - - -
28   [- - - - - - - - - ἐπαινέσαι] <u>δὲ καὶ τοὺ</u>[ς- -] νους με. οπα - - - - - - - - -

a   It was resolved by the People: Pandionis held the *prytany*:
       Phlyeus was president: Polykrates son of Polykrates
          [- - - made the motion: concerning the things which the]
       ambassadors of the Athenians and those [who have come]

from Oron[tes report to the People and the Council]

4   of the Athenians: the People say…to do [- - - - - - - - - - -, they shall commend Orontes because he is]

a good man concerning the People [of Athens and eager to do whatever good he can both now]

and previously <and> Oro[ntes] shall be [an Athenian, as shall his descendants, and he shall be]

[re]<gistered in a tribe and *a deme* and a *phratry,* to whichever he wishes to belong>. The *prytaneis* <shall render the>

8   vote concerning him [to the People] in the <first> assembly: [and they shall crown]

him with a gold crown of one thousand drachmas: [- - - - - - - - - -]

of the crown: …shall deliberate [-]

all - - - - - - - - - - - - - of Orontes to the -]

12   [the] *thesmothetai* in the archonship of Kallimachos

[- - - - - - - - - - - - - of the]

Athenians or of the allies not - - - - - - - - - - - [Or]<o>ntes [- - - - - - - -]

of the People, the Athenians shall give [justice] according to the *symbol*[a - - - -]

. . . are from the dominion of Orontes [- -]

16   it shall be possible for the comp<l>aint [- -]

[- - - - -]: …the Council…[- -]

[- - - - - -] and to the People [- -]

b   - - - - - - - - - - - - - - of ships -

4   friends and [allies - - - - -]

- - - - - - - - - - - - - Oro]ntes in order [that] he receive - - - - - - -

- - - - - - - - - - - - - and the *symbola* be displayed and - - - - - -

c   - - - - - - - - - - - - - the People shall choose immediately [- - - -]

8   [- - - - those] who have been [chosen] shall take [the money] from wherever the People [decree? - -]

- - - - - - - - - - - - - - - - - in the month of Thargelion and carry out - - - -

[according to] the things written in this decree and what other good [it can - -]

[the mon]ey shall be for th[e re]ceip[t] of the grain out of the Str[a]*tiotic* funds - -

12   [- - - to t]he arm[y - - from] Chares and Charidemos and [Ph]okio[n- - -]

- - - - - - - - - - - money] of the *syntaxes* in Lesbos [and - - -]

- - - - - - - - - - - - - of Ch]aridemos and Phokion…from [the city - -]

- - - - - - - - - - - - - - having received…shall take the grain [from the- - -]

16   - - - - - - - - -] as quickly as possible, and there shall be pay for the soldiers - - -

[- - - of the con]veyance [- - - - - - the] treasurers and the ambassadors [shall display] to the People [- - -]

[- - whatever he wishes - - - - (if) the treasurers] do not do the things in this [decree- - -]

[- - - - - - - - - - - - prevent] the war from being [fought - - - -]

20   [- - - - - - - - - - - -] they shall take care [in order that] it be conveyed - - - - - - -

[- - - - - - - - - - - the] allies...the [generals?] Chares and Charidemos [- - - -]

- - - - - - - - - - - - treasurers...the money to Oro[n]tes and ships from - - -

- - - - - - - - - - - - Proxenos [the general together with the ambassadors - - - - -

24   [- - - - - - - - - - - the treasurer] of the [People...the] traveling money of the ambassadors [...drachmas for each - -]

- - - - - - - - - - - - - -. They shall commen[d also] the ambassadors who were sent [out - - - -]

[- - - - - - - - - the] ambassadors [- - -] they shall crown with a cro[wn] of olive - -

- - - - - - - - - - - - of Euonymon, - - son of Lykophron of Ach[a]rnai, Ph - - - - - -

28   [- - - - - - - - - shall commend] also [the - -] -

12 (D8). See also nos. 7 and 9, _IG_ ii² 212 (_SIG_³ 106; R-O no. 64; Tod 2.167; Harding no. 82; _SEG_ 36.148; V-T A110) (347/6)

ΣΤΟΙΧ. 24

Σπαρτόκωι Παιρισάδηι
Ἀπολλωνίωι Λεύκωνος παισί
     vacat 0,275
Ἐπὶ Θεμιστοκλέους ἄρ[χ]οντο[ς]
4 ἐπὶ τῆς Αἰγηῖδος ὀγδό[η]ς πρυ[τ]-
ανείας ἧι Λυσίμα[χ]ος Σωσιδή[μ]-
[ο Ἀχα]ρ[ν]εὺς ἐγραμμάτευεν· Θε[ό]-
φιλος [Ἁλι]μούσιος ἐπεστάτε[ι]·
8 Ἀνδροτίων Ἄνδρωνος Γαργήττ[ι]ος [ε]ἶπεν· π[ε]-   ΣΤΟΙΧ. 34
ρὶ ὧν ἐπέστειλε Σπάρτοκος κ[αὶ] Παιρ[ισά]δ[η]-
ς καὶ οἱ πρέσβεις οἱ ἥκοντ[ε]ς π[α]ρ' αὐτῶν ἀπ[α]-
γγέλλουσιν, ἀποκρί[ν]ασθαι αὐ[τ]οῖ[ς], ὅτι ὁ [δῆ]-
12 μος ὁ Ἀθηναίων ἐπαινεῖ Σπάρτ[ο]κον καὶ Παι-
ρισάδην ὅτι εἰσὶν ἄνδρες [ἀ]γα[θ]οὶ καὶ ἐπ[αγ]-
γέλλονται τῶι δήμωι [τ]ῶι Ἀ[θ]ην[α]ίων ἐπιμε[λ]-
ήσεσθαι τῆς ἐκ[π]ομπῆς τοῦ [σ]ίτ[ο]υ καθάπερ ὁ
16 πατὴρ αὐτῶν ἐπεμελεῖτο καὶ ὑ[π]ηρετήσειν π-
ροθύμως ὅτου ἂν ὁ δῆμ[ος] δ[έη]ται καὶ ἀπαγγέ-

λλειν αὐτο[ῖ]ς τ[ο]ὺς π[ϱέσβ]εις ὅ[τι] ταῦτα ποι-
οῦντες οὐδενὸ[ς] ἀτυχήσ[ο]υσιν τοῦ δήμου το-

20 ῦ Ἀθηναίων· [ἐπ]ε[ι]δὴ δὲ [τὰ]ς δω[ϱει]ὰς διδόασι-
ν Ἀθηναίοι[ς ἅσ]πεϱ Σ[άτ]υ[ϱ]ος καὶ Λεύκων ἔδοσαν εἶναι [Σπαϱτ]ό[κ]ωι [κ]αὶ Παιϱισάδει τὰς δ-
ωϱειάς, ἃς [ὁ δῆμ]ος ἔδωκε Σατύϱωι καὶ Λεύκω-

24 νι καὶ στεφ[ανοῦν] χϱυσῶι στεφάνωι Παναθη-
ναίοις το[ῖς μεγ]άλοις ἀπὸ χιλίων δϱαχμῶν
ἑκάτεϱ[ο]ν· [ποιε]ῖσθαι δὲ τοὺς στεφάνους τοὺς ἀθλοθέ[τας] τῶι προτέϱωι ἔτει Παναθηνα-

28 ίων τῶν μεγ[άλ]ων κατὰ τὸ ψήφισμα τοῦ δήμου
τὸ πρότεϱον ἐψηφισμένον Λεύκωνι καὶ ἀνα-
γοϱεύειν ὅτι στεφανοῖ ὁ δῆμος ὁ Ἀθηναίων
Σπάϱτοκον καὶ Παιϱισάδην τοὺς Λεύκωνος

32 παῖδας ἀϱετῆς καὶ εὐνοίας ἕνεκα τῆς εἰς τ-
ὸν δῆμον τὸν Ἀθηναίων· ἐπειδὴ δὲ τοὺς στεφάνους ἀνατιθέασι τῆι Ἀθηνᾶι τῆι Πολιάδι
τοὺς ἀθλοθέτας εἰς τὸν νεὼ ἀνατιθέναι το-

36 ὺς στεφάνους ἐπιγϱάψαντας· Σπάϱτοκος vv
καὶ Παιϱισάδης Λεύκωνος παῖδες ἀνέθεσα-
ν τῆι Ἀθηναίαι στεφανωθέντες ὑπὸ τοῦ δήμου τοῦ Ἀθηνα[ί]ων. τὸ δὲ ἀϱγύϱιον διδόναι το-

40 ῖς ἀθλοθέταις εἰς τοὺς στεφάνους τὸν τοῦ
δήμου ταμίαν ἐκ τῶν εἰς τὰ κατὰ ψηφίσματα
τῶι δήμωι με[ϱι]ζομένων· τὸ δὲ νῦ[ν] εἶναι παϱ-
αδοῦναι τοὺς ἀποδέκτας τὸ εἰς [τ]οὺς στεφ[ά]-

44 νους ἐκ τῶν στ[ϱ]ατιωτικῶν χϱ[η]μάτων· ἀναγ[ϱ]-
άψαι δὲ τὸ ψήφισμα τόδε τὸγ γϱαμματέα τῆ[ς]
Βουλῆς ἐν στήλῃ λιθίνῃ καὶ στῆσαι πλη[σ]-
ίον τῆς Σατύϱου καὶ Λεύκωνος, ἐς δὲ τὴν ἀν[α]-

48 γϱαφὴν δοῦναι τὸν ταμίαν τοῦ δήμου τϱιά[κ]-
οντα δϱαχμάς. ἐπαινέσαι δὲ τοὺς πϱέσβει[ς]
Σῶσιν καὶ Θεοδόσιον ὅτι ἐπιμελοῦνται τ[ῶ]-
ν ἀφικ[ν]ουμένων Ἀθήνηθεν εἰς Βόσποϱον [κα]-

52 ὶ καλέσαι αὐτοὺς ἐπὶ ξένια εἰς τὸ πϱυτα[νε]-
ῖον εἰς αὔϱιον· πεϱὶ δὲ τῶν χϱημάτων τῶν [ὀφ]-
[ει]λ[ο]μένων τοῖς παισὶ τοῖς Λεύκωνος ὅπ[ως]
[ἃ]ν ἀπολάβωσιν, χϱηματίσαι τοὺς πϱοέδ[ϱος]

56 [οἳ] ἂν λάχωσι πϱοεδϱεύειν ἐν τῶι δήμωι [τῆι]
[ὀγ]δόῃ ἐπὶ δέκα πϱῶτον μετὰ τὰ ἱεϱά, ὅπ[ως ἂ]-
[ν] ἀπολα[β]όντες τὰ χϱήματα μὴ ἐγκαλῶσ[ι τῶι]
[δ]ήμωι τῶι Ἀθηναίων· δοῦναι δ[ὲ τὰ]ς ὑπη[ϱεσί]-

60 [α]ς, ἃς αἰτοῦσι Σπάϱτοκος καὶ Παιϱισ[άδης, τ]-
[οὺ]ς δὲ πϱ[έ]σβεις ἀπογϱάψαι τὰ ὀνόμα[τα τῶν

[ὑπ]ηρ[εσι]ῶν, ὧν ἂν λάβωσιν τῶι γραμμα[τεῖ τῆ]-
[ς β]ουλῆς· οὓς δ' ἂν ἀπογράψωσιν, εἶνα[ι ἐν τῶι]
64 τ[ε]ταγμένωι ποιοῦντας ἀγαθὸν ὅ τι [ἂν δύνω]-
νται τοὺς παῖδας τοὺς Λεύκωνος. Π[ολύευκτ]-
ος Τιμοκράτους Κριωεὺς εἶπε· τὰ [μὲν ἄλλα κ]-
[α]θάπερ Ἀνδροτίων, στεφανῶσα[ι δὲ καὶ Ἀπολ]-
68 λώνιον τὸν Λεύκωνος υὸν ἐκ τῶ[ν αὐτῶν].

             vacat

For Spartokos, Pairisades,
Apollonios, sons of Leukon.
             vacat
In the archonship of Themistokles,
4 in the eighth *prytany,* which was held by Aigeis,
Lysima[ch]os son of Soside[mos]
[of Archa]r[n]ai was secretary:
The[o]philos [of Hali]mous was president:
8 Androtion son of Andron of Gargettos made the motion:
concerning the things which Spartokos and Pair[isa]d[e]s
sent and the ambassadors who have come from them
report, a response shall be made to them that the People
12 of Athens commend Spart[o]kos and Pairisades
because they are good men and they promise
to the People of A[th]en[s] that they will take
care of the sen[di]ng out of the [g]ra[i]n just as their
16 father took care and that they will readily do whatever service
the People need, and the ambassadors shall report
back to them that, should they do these
things, they shall not fail to obtain anything from the People of
20 Athens. Whereas they give the gifts
to the Athenian[s, the same ones which] S[at]y[r]os and Leukon gave,
[Spart]o[k]os and Pairisades shall have the
gifts which the People gave to Satyros and Leukon,
24 and they shall be crow[ned] with a gold crown of one thousand
drachmas each at the Great Panathenaia.
The *athlothe[tai* are to m]ake the crowns
in the year preceding the Great Panathenaia
28 according to the decree of the People,
which they decreed previously for Leukon, and they are to
proclaim that the People of Athens crown
Spartokos and Pairisades the sons of Leukon
32 on account of their excellence and goodwill toward
the People of Athens. When they
dedicate the crowns to Athena Polias,

the *athlothetai* are to place the crowns in
36   the temple after they have inscribed (them): Spartokos
and Pairisades sons of Leukon dedicated (these)
to Athena, after they were crowned by the People
of Athen[s]. The treasurer of the People is to give
40   the money to the *athlothetai* for the crowns
from the People's allotment of funds for
decrees. But for now the *apodektai*
shall give out (money) for the cro[w]ns
44   from the St[r]*atiotic* mo[n]ies. The secretary
of the Council shall inscribe
this decree on a stone stele and place (it) near
that of Satyros and Leukon. For the
48   inscribing the treasurer of the People is to give thi[r]ty
drachmas. The ambassadors Sosis and Theodosios
shall be commended because they take care of those
who come from Athens to the Bosporos and
52   they shall be invited to hospitality in the Pryta[ne]ion
tomorrow. Concerning the monies which are
[owed] to the sons of Leukon, in order
that they receive payment, the *proedroi*
56   chosen by lot to be *proedroi* shall deliberate among the People on the
eighteenth day immediately after the sacrifices, in order that,
having received the money, they not claim a debt against the
People of Athens. T[he] *hype*[*resia*]*i,* for which
60   Spartokos and Pairis[aides] ask, shall be given
and the ambassadors shall register the names [of the]
[*hyp*]*er*[*esi*]*ai,* whom they take, for the secretary of the
Council. Those whom they shall register shall be [in the]
64   appointed position to do whatever good they can
for the sons of Leukon. P[olyeukt]os
son of Timokrates of Krioa made the motion: the [other things]
    (shall be)
just as Androtion (made the motion), [but Apol]onios
son of Leukon, their brother, shall be crowned accordance to the
    [same terms].

vacat

Demosthenes *Against Leptines* 20.29–33, 36 (OCT text by M. R. Dilts;
Osborne T32)

...ἀφαιρεῖται καὶ Λεύκωνα τὸν ἄρχοντα Βοσπόρου καὶ τοὺς
παῖδας αὐτοῦ τὴν δωρειὰν ἣν ὑμεῖς ἔδοτ' αὐτοῖς. ἔστι γὰρ γένει
μὲν δήπου ὁ Λεύκων ξένος, τῆι δὲ παρ' ὑμῶν ποιήσει πολίτης·

κατ' οὐδέτερον δ' αὐτῶι τὴν ἀτέλειαν ἔστιν ἔχειν ἐκ τούτου τοῦ
νόμου. καίτοι τῶν μὲν ἄλλων εὐεργετῶν χρόνον τινὰ ἕκαστος
ἡμῖν χρήσιμον αὑτὸν παρέσχεν, οὗτος δ', ἂν σκοπῆτε, φανήσεται
συνεχῶς ἡμᾶς εὖ ποιῶν, καὶ ταῦθ' ὧν μάλισθ' ἡμῶν ἡ πόλις
δεῖται. ἴστε γὰρ δήπου τοῦθ', ὅτι πλείστωι τῶν πάντων ἀνθρώπων
ἡμεῖς ἐπεισάκτωι σίτωι χρώμεθα. πρὸς τοίνυν ἅπαντα τὸν ἐκ τῶν
ἄλλων ἐμπορίων ἀφικνούμενον ὁ ἐκ τοῦ Πόντου σῖτος εἰσπλέων
ἐστίν. εἰκότως· οὐ γὰρ μόνον διὰ τὸ τὸν τόπον τοῦτον σῖτον ἔχειν
πλεῖστον τοῦτο γίγνεται, ἀλλὰ διὰ τὸ κύριον ὄντα τὸν Λεύκωνα
αὐτοῦ τοῖς ἄγουσιν Ἀθήναζε ἀτέλειαν δεδωκέναι, καὶ κηρύττειν
πρώτους γεμίζεσθαι τοὺς ὡς ὑμᾶς πλέοντας. ἔχων γὰρ ἐκεῖνος
ἑαυτῶι καὶ τοῖς παισὶ τὴν ἀτέλειαν ἅπασι δέδωκεν ὑμῖν. τοῦτο δ'
ἡλίκον ἐστὶ θεωρήσατε. ἐκεῖνος πράττεται τοὺς παρ' αὐτοῦ σῖτον
ἐξάγοντας τριακοστήν. αἱ τοίνυν παρ' ἐκείνου δεῦρ'
ἀφικνούμεναι σίτου μυριάδες περὶ τετταράκοντά εἰσί· καὶ τοῦτ' ἐκ
τῆς παρὰ τοῖς σιτοφύλαξιν ἀπογραφῆς ἄν τις ἴδοι. οὐκοῦν παρὰ
μὲν τὰς τριάκοντα μυριάδας μυρίους δίδωσι μεδίμνους ἡμῖν, παρὰ
δὲ τὰς δέκα ὡσπερανεὶ τρισχιλίους. τοσούτου τοίνυν δεῖ ταύτην
ἀποστερῆσαι τὴν δωρειὰν τὴν πόλιν, ὥστε προσκατασκευάσας
ἐμπόριον Θευδοσίαν, ὅ φασιν οἱ πλέοντες οὐδ' ὁτιοῦν χεῖρον εἶναι
τοῦ Βοσπόρου, κἀνταῦθ' ἔδωκε τὴν ἀτέλειαν ἡμῖν. καὶ τὰ μὲν
ἄλλα σιωπῶ, πόλλ' ἂν ἔχων εἰπεῖν, ὅσ' εὐεργέτηκεν ὑμᾶς οὗτος
ἀνὴρ καὶ αὐτὸς καὶ οἱ πρόγονοι· ἀλλὰ πρωπέρυσι σιτοδείας παρὰ
πᾶσιν ἀνθρώποις γενομένης οὐ μόνον ὑμῖν ἱκανόν σῖτον
ἀπέστειλεν, ἀλλὰ τοσοῦτον ὥστε πεντεκαίδεκα ἀργυρίου
τάλαντα, ἃ Καλλισθένης διώικησε, προσπεριγενέσθαι.
[36]Ὡς μὲν εἰκότως καὶ δικαίως τετύχηκεν τῆς ἀτελείας παρ'
ὑμῶν ὁ Λεύκων, ἀκηκόατ' ἐκ τῶν ψηφισμάτων, ὦ ἄνδρες
δικασταί. τούτων δ' ἁπάντων στήλας ἀντιγράφους ἐστήσαθ' ὑμεῖς
κἀκεῖνος, τὴν μὲν ἐν Βοσπόρωι, τὴν δ' ἐν Πειραιεῖ, τὴν δ' ἐφ'
Ἱερῶι.

Both Leukon, the ruler of the Bosporos, and his sons are deprived [by
Leptines' proposed law] of the gift which you gave to them. For
indeed although Leukon is a foreigner by birth, he is a citizen by
adoption from you: but according to neither may he have tax
exemption from this law. And yet, although each of our other
benefactors rendered himself useful to us at one time, if you think
about it, Leukon will be seen to do well for us continually, and
concerning these things which our city especially needs. For certainly
you know this, that we use imported grain most of all men.
Moreover, the grain imported from Pontos is equal to all that comes
from the other *emporia*. Naturally: for this happens not only because
this place has the most grain, but also because Leukon is the master

of it and has given tax exemption to those who bring it to Athens, and he proclaims that those who sail to you shall load (their cargo) first. For that man, having tax exemption for himself and his sons, has given it to all of you. Consider how important this is. He exacts a thirtieth from those who export grain from him. Moreover, there are around four hundred thousand (*medimnoi*) of grain that come here from him: and this anyone may know from the list kept by the *sitophylakes*. Therefore, from three hundred thousand (*medimnoi*) he gives ten thousand *medimnoi* to us, and from one hundred thousand (*medimnoi* he gives) around three thousand. Further, so far is he from depriving the city of this gift that he equipped in addition Theudosia as an *emporion*, which those who sail say is not inferior whatsoever to the Bosporos, and there he has given tax exemption to us. I will keep silent, though I could say many other things, like how great a benefactor this man and his ancestors have been for you: but two years ago, when there was a shortage of grain for all men, he not only sent enough grain to us, but so much that fifteen talents of silver, which Kallisthenes administered, accrued in addition. [36]That Leukon has obtained tax exemption from you reasonably and justly, you have heard from the decrees, men of the jury. You and he have set up identical stelai of all these things, one in the Bosporos, one in the Peiraieus, and one at Hieron.

13 (D9). *IG* ii² 543 (text by **Lambert 3.73**) (ca. 340)

```
- - - - - - - - - - - - - - - - - - - - - - - - - - - - - - - NON-ΣΤΟΙΧ.
[- c. 9 -]ωκρ[ατ- - - - - - - - - - - - - - - - - - - - - - - - - - - - -Ἐλευ]-

        σίνιος εἶπεν· ἐπ[ειδὴ- - - - - - - - - - - - - - - - - - - - - - - -τῶ]-
        ι δήμωι τῶι Ἀθη[ναίων- - - - - - - - - - - - - - - - - - - - - - - - -]
   4    τωι πρὸς τὸν δῆ[μον- - - - - - - - - - - - - - - - - - - - - - - -ἤγ]-
        αγον εἰς τὸ ἐνπ[όριον- - - - - - - - - - - - - - - - - - - - - -ἐψ]-
        ηφίσαντο [Μ]οιροκ[λ- - - - - - - - - - - - - - - - - - - - - - - - - ]
        υν καὶ ἀφείλοντο τὸ π[- - - - - - - - - - - - - - - - - - - - - - -]-
   8    ς τὸν Πειραεᾶ διατ[- - - - - - - - - - - - - - - - - - -δεδόχθαι τῶι δ]-
        ήμωι ἐπαινέσαι [- -καὶ στεφανῶσαι - χρυσῶι στεφάνωι ἀπὸ -]
        [δ]ραχμῶν φιλο[τιμίας ἕνεκα - - - - - - - - - - - πρὸς τὸν δῆμον -]
        [. .], ὅπως ἂν εἰδῶσ[ι πάντες - - - - - - - - - ὅτι ὁ δῆμος ὁ Ἀθηναί]-
  12    [ων] στεφανοῖ τ[οὺς - - - - - - - - - - - - - - - - - - - - - - - -]
        [- 2-3 -] πλεοντ[- - - - - - - - - - - - - - - - - - - - - - - - - -]
        [- 2-3 -]ΒΓΓ[- - - - - - - - - - - - - - - - - - - - - - - - - - -]
- - - - - - - - - - - - - - - - - - - - - - - - - - - - - - - - - - - - - - -
```

of Eleusis made the motion: whereas [- - - - - - - - - - - - - - - - - - -for the]

People of Athens [- -]

4   toward the People [- -br]-

ought to the *emp*[*orion*- -they de]-

creed Moirok[les- -]

and they took away the [- -]

8   the Peiraieus [- -it was resolved by the]

People to commend [and to crown with a gold crown of - - - - - - - - -]

drachmas [on account] of their love of honor [- - - -concerning
    the People]

[. .], in order that [everyone] know [- - - - - - - -that the People
    of Athens]

12   crown [those -]

[- - -] who sail [- -]

---

14 (D10). *IG* ii² 423 (V-T A170) (ca. 340–300)

```
- - - - - - - φ. . . 6 . . . λου κα[ὶ .]                    ΣΤΟΙΧ. 32
[. . . . . . .13 . . . . . .] ὅπως] ἂν [κ]αὶ οἱ ἄλλοι ὅσο-
[ι ἂν εὔνοι ὄντες φι]λοτιμῶνται περὶ τὸν
4  [δῆμον τὸν Ἀθηναίω]ν εἰδῶσιν ὅτι τιμήσε-
[ι αὐτοὺς ὁ δῆμος κα]τὰ τὴν ἀξίαν ἑκάστου
[ἐψηφίσθαι τῆι βο]υλῆι : τοὺς προέδρους ο
[ἳ ἂν λάχωσι προεδ]ρεύειν εἰς τὴν πρώτην
8  [ἐκκλησίαν προσα]γα[γ]εῖν Φιλόμηλον πρὸ-
[ς τὸν δῆμον καὶ χρ]ηματίσαι πρ[ώ]τωι μετὰ
[τὰ ἱερά, γνώμην δὲ] ξυμβάλλεσθαι τῆς βου-
[λῆς εἰς τὸν δῆμον] ὅτι δοκεῖ τῆι βουλῆι, [ἐ]-
12 [πειδὴ Φιλόμηλος] ἀνὴρ ἀγαθός ἐστι [περὶ]
[τὸν δῆμον τὸν Ἀθη]ναίων καὶ ἐν τ[ῆι σιτοδ]-
[είαι προεδάνεισ?]ε χρήματα [. . .6 . . . χρῆσ]-
[ιμον ἑαυτὸν παρα]σχόμε[νος . . . . .10 . . . . .]
16 . . . . . . . .15 . . . . . . .ομ - - - - - - -
```

[. . . . . in order also] that however many others
[who are goodwilled seek] after honor concerning the
4   [People of Athen]s, that they may know that [the People] will hono[r]
[them according] to the worth of each,
[it was decreed by the Council]: the *proedroi*
[chosen by lot to be *proedroi* shall introduce]
8   Philomelos [to the People] immediately after
[the sacrifices and] deliberate.
[But the decision] of the Council shall be contributed
[to the People] that it is resolved by the Council:
12   [whereas Philomelos] is a good man [concerning]

[the People of Athe]ns and in [the shortage]
[of grain he lent?] money [. . . . . . having]
[shown himself useful . . . .]

15 (D11). *IG* ii² 283 (V-T A135; Walbank 2002: 61–65, no. 5; Lambert 2002: 73–79) (ca. 337)

<pre>
. . . . 16 . . . . L. I - - - - - - -   ΣΤΟΙΧ. 34
[. . . . . 10 . . . . . ἐσιτ]ήγησεν ἐξ Αἰγύπτου τ . . .
. . . . 14 . . . . ΥΛΛΩΝ εὐωνοτέρων ὑπη Ι // .
4   . . . . 14 . . . . κ]αὶ προαιρούμενος τῶι δ-
        [ήμωι τῶι Ἀθηναίων κ]αὶ ἐν τοῖς ἄλλοις τοῖς
        [τῆς πόλεως ἀγῶσι χρ]ήσιμον ἑαυτὸν παρασ[κ]-
        [ευάζων διατετέλεκ]εν ἐμ παντὶ καιρῶι κα[ὶ]
8   [πολλοὺς τῶν πολιτῶν] λυτρωσάμενος ἐξ Σικ-
        [ελίας ἀπέστειλε Ἀθ]ήναζε τοῖς αὐτοῦ ἀναλ-
        [ώμασιν καὶ ἰδίαι κα]ὶ κοινῆι πρὸς τὸν δῆμο-
        [ν ἀποδέδεικται τ]ὴν εὔνοιαν ἣν ἔχων διατ-
12   [ελεῖ ἐκ προγόνων κ]αὶ νῦν εἰς τὴν φυλακὴν ʋ
        [ἐπέδωκε τάλαντον] ἀργυρίου· ἀγα[θῆι τ]ύχη[ι]
        [δεδόχθαι τῶι δήμ]ωι ἐπαινέσαι Φ . . . 5 . . Ο .
        [. . . . . . 13 . . . . . . Σ]αλαμίνιον καὶ [στεφανῶσ]-
16   [αι θαλλοῦ στεφάνωι] εὐν[οία]ς ἕ[νεκα . . . 6 . . .]
</pre>

[. . . . . 10 . . . . . he bro]ught grain from Egypt . . . .
. . . . 14 . . . . -*ullon* at a reduced price . . . . . .
4   . . . . 14 . . . . and] giving preference...for the
        [People of Athens and] in the other [contests of
        [the city, he has continued] to [make] himself
        [useful] on every occasion.
8   Having [also] ransomed [many of the citizens] from Sic[ily],
        [he sent them back to Ath]ens at his own
        [expense, and both in private and] in public [he has displayed]
        to the People the goodwill which he [continues] to have
12   [from his ancestors, and] now for the guarding
        [he has given in addition a *talent*] of silver. With [good fortune]
        [it has been resolved by the People] to commend Ph- . . . .
        [. . . . . . 13 . . . . . . of S]alamis and [to crown]
16   [(him) with a crown of olive on account of his] good[will . . . 6 . . .]

16. Deinarchos *Against Demosthenes* 1.43 (Loeb text by J. O. Burtt; Osborne T75) (ca. 337–330)

εἴπατέ μοι πρὸς Διός, ὦ ἄνδρες, προῖκα τοῦτον οἴεσθε γράψαι

Διφίλωι τὴν ἐν πρυτανείωι σίτησιν, καὶ τὴν εἰς τὴν ἀγορὰν
ἀνατεθησομένην εἰκόνα; ἢ τὸ ποιῆσαι πολίτας ὑμετέρους
Χαιρέφιλον καὶ Φείδωνα καὶ Πάμφιλον καὶ Φείδιππον, ἢ πάλιν
Ἐπιγένην καὶ Κόνωνα τοὺς τραπεζίτας; ἢ τὸ χαλκοῦς ἐν ἀγορᾶι
στῆσαι Βηρισάδην καὶ Σάτυρον καὶ Γόργιππον τοὺς ἐκ τοῦ
Πόντου τυράννους, παρ᾽ ὧν αὐτῶι χίλιοι μέδιμνοι τοῦ ἐνιαυτοῦ
πυρῶν ἀποστέλλονται τῶι οὐδ᾽ ὅποι καταφύγηι αὐτίκα φήσοντι
εἶναι;

Tell me, by Zeus, gentlemen, do you think that this man
(Demosthenes) proposed for Diphilos *sitesis* in the Prytaneion and
the statue to be set up in the Agora for free? Or that he made
Chairephilos and Pheidon and Pamphilos and Pheidippos your
fellow citizens, or again the bankers Epigenes and Konon? Or that he
placed in the Agora the bronze statues of Berisades and Satyros and
Gorgippos, the tyrants from Pontos, from whom a thousand
medimnoi per year of wheat are sent out to him, who now says that
there is nowhere he can flee?

Athenaios *Deipnosophistai* 3.119 f–20a (Loeb text by C. B. Gulick)

Τοσαύτην δ᾽ Ἀθηναῖοι σπουδὴν ἐποιοῦντο περὶ τὸ τάριχος ὡς καὶ
πολίτας ἀναγράψαι τοὺς Χαιρεφίλου τοῦ ταριχοπώλου υἱούς, ὥς
φησιν Ἄλεξις ἐν Ἐπιδαύρωι οὕτως·
     τοὺς Χαιρεφίλου δ᾽ υἱεῖς Ἀθηναίους, ὅτι
     εἰσήγαγεν τάριχος, οὓς καὶ Τιμοκλῆς
     ἰδὼν ἐπὶ τῶν ἵππων δύο σκόμβρους ἔφη
     ἐν τοῖς Σατύροις εἶναι.
μνημονεύει αὐτῶν καὶ Ὑπερείδης ὁ ῥήτωρ.

The Athenians made such a big deal about salted fish that they even
enrolled as citizens the sons of Chairephilos, the salted fish seller, as
Alexis says thus in *Epidauros*:
    the sons of Chairephilos are Athenians, because
    they imported salted fish; and Timokles,
    after seeing them on horses, said in his *Satires*
    that they were two mackerels.
The orator Hypereides also mentions these things.

17 (D12). Camp 1974: no. 3 (V-T A160) (ca. 337–325)

ἔδοξ[εν τῶι δήμωι· Λυκοῦργο]-   ΣΤΟΙΧ. 22
ς Λυκό[φρονος Βουτάδης εἶπ]-
εν· περ[ὶ ὧν ἡ βουλὴ προεβούλ]-

4 ευσεν ἐψ[ηφ]ίσθαι τ[ῶι δήμωι·]
ἐπειδὴ Σώπατρος Φιλιστ[ίω]-
νος Ἀκραγαντῖνος ἐνδεί[κν]-
υται τὴν εὔνοιαν ἣν ἔχει π[ρ]-

8 [ὸ]ς Ἀθην[αί]ους ἐπιμελούμε[ν]-
[ος], καὶ π[ρ]άττων ὅπως ἂν ὡς ἀ[φ]-
[θο]νώτα[τ]ος Ἀθήναζε κομίζηται σῖτ[ο]ς ἐπαινέσαι αὐτὸν

12 εὐνοίας ἕνεκα τῆς εἰς τὸν δ-
[ῆ]μον τ[ὸ]ν Ἀθηναίων εἶναι δ[ὲ]
[π]ρόξενον καὶ εὐεργέτην α[ὐ]-
[τ]ὸν καὶ ἐκγόνους τοῦ δήμο[υ]

16 [τ]οῦ Ἀ<θ>ηναίων καὶ εἶναι αὐ[τ]-
ῶι ἔνκτησιν · ἀναγράψαι δὲ [τ]-
όδε τὸ ψήφισμα ἐν στήληι λ[ι]-
θίνηι τὸγ γραμματέα τὸν κ[α]-

20 τὰ πρυτανείαν καὶ στῆσαι [ἐ]-
ν Ἀκροπόλει · εἰς δὲ τὴν ἀνα[γ]-
ρ<α>φὴν τῆς στήλης δοῦναι τὸ-
ν ταμίαν τοῦ δήμου : ΔΔΔ : δρ-

24 αχμὰς ἐκ τῶν εἰς τὰ κατὰ ψηφίσματα ἀναλισκομένον τῶι
δήμωι· καλέσαι δὲ καὶ ἐπὶ
ξε[ν]ία Σώπατρον εἰς τὸ πρυτα[ν]-

28 [ε]ῖον εἰς αὔριον καὶ καταν[ε]-
[ῖ]μαι θέαν αὐτῶι τὸν ἀρχιτέ-
κτονα εἰς τὰ Διονύσια ννν

It was resolved [by the People: Lykourgo]s
son of Lyko[phron of Boutadai made the motion]:
[concerning the things which the Council deliberated in advance]

4 it was decreed by [the People]:
whereas Sopatros son of Philist[io]n
of Akragas displays
the goodwill which he has toward

8 the Athenians by taking care
and acting so that
grain is conveyed as plentifully as possible to Athens,
he shall be commended

12 on account of his goodwill toward the
People of Athens, and he and his descendants shall be
[p]roxenoi and euergetai
of the People

16 of Athens, and he shall have

enktesis. The secretary during the *prytany*
shall inscribe this decree
on a stone stele

20   and place it
on the Acropolis. For the inscribing
of the stele, the treasurer of the People
shall give 30 drachmas

24   from the People's fund for
expenditure on decrees.
Sopatros shall be invited
to hospitality in the Prytaneion

28   tomorrow and the manager
shall assign a seat for him
in the Dionysia.

18 (D13). Schweigert 1940: no. 39 (line 17 by V-T A149 [pp. 89, 274])
(ca. 337–320)

[. . . . . 18. . . . .] μο[. . . .]   ΣΤΟΙΧ. 24
[. . . . 7 . . . εἶπεν · ἐπειδὴ] Πάνδιο-
[ς διατελεῖ εὔνους ὢν τ]ῶι δήμω-

4   [ι τῶι Ἀθηναίων καὶ πρά]ττων κα-
[ὶ λέγων ὅτι δύναται ἀ]γαθὸν τὸ-
[ν σῖτον ἀπῆγε τῶι δήμ]ωι, ὅ τε πα-
[τὴρ . . . . 7 . . . καὶ αὐτὸ]ς σιτηγῶ-

8   [ν εἰς τὸ ἐμπόριον τὸ Α]θηναίων
[καὶ τῆς τοῦ σίτου πομπ]ῆς καὶ [.]
[. . . . . 18. . . . .] καὶ τ[. .]
[. . . . . 18. . . . .] ενο [.]ιρ

12   [. . .5 . . παρὰ τῶν προγόν]ων αὐτο-
[ῦ διαφυλάττων τὴν εὔν]οιαν ἐμ
[πᾶσι καιροῖς τῶι δήμωι] τῶι Ἀθ-
[ηναίων· δεδόχθαι τῶι δή]μωι ἐπ-

16   [αινέσαι Πάνδιον . . .5 . . ο]υ Ἡρα-
[κλεώτην εὐνοίας ἕνεκα καὶ φ]ι-
[λοτιμίας - - - - - - - - - - - - -]

[. . . . . . . made the motion: whereas] Pandio[s]
[continues to be goodwilled] to the People

4   [of Athens by doing and]
[saying whatever] good [he can, (whereas) he]
[brought back grain to the People], and his
[father . . . . and when he] brought grai[n]

8   [to the *emporion* of A]thens

[and of the send]ing/[esco]rt [of the grain] and [.]
[. . . . .] and [. . .]
[. . . . .]
12 [. . . . . maintaining from his forefathers]
[at all times the good]will
[for the People of]
[Athens, it was resolved by the People to]
16 [commend Pandios son of . . . .] the Hera[kleote]
[on account of his goodwill and]
[love] of honor - - - - - - - - - - - - - - - -

19 (D14). *IG* ii² 409 (Wilhelm 1942: 150–152; V-T A151; **Lambert 3.82**)
(ca. 337–320?)

ΣΙ. [- -]   ΣΤΟΙΧ. 31
τὸ λ[οιπὸν - - - - - - - - - - - - - - - - - - -]
ιοις Ι//[- - - - - - - ἐμπόρων καὶ? ναυ]-
4 κλήρων[- - - - - - - - - - - - - δεδόχθ]-
αι τῶι δή[μωι ἐπαινέσαι? - - - - - κα]-
ὶ Ποτάμων[α - - - - - - - - - - - - - - -ἐν]
τῶι : πρόσ[θεν χρόνωι - - - - - - - ὄν?]-
8 τες καὶ εὐν[- - - - - - - - - - - - - - - - σῖ]-
τος ἐξάγετα[ι - - - - - - - - - - - - - - τῶι]
δήμωι · χειρο[τονῆσαι δὲ - - - - - - ἄν]-
δρας αὐτίκα μ[άλα - - - - - - - - - οἵτι]-
12 νες ἀφικόμεν[οι - - - - - - - - - - - - - - -]-
ιν τὸν δῆμον τ[ὸν - - - - - - - - - - - - - -]-
αι ὅπως ἂν σῖ[τος - - - - - - - - - Ἀθήν]-
αζε καὶ ὅτι [- - - - - - - - - - - - - - - - ο]-
16 υσιν ὄντε[ς - - - - - - - - - - - - - - - Μι]-
λήσιοι α. [- - - - - - - - - - - - - - - - - - - -]-
ων καὶ ου [- - - - - - - - - - τοῦ δήμου]
τοῦ Ἀθη[ναίων - - - - - - - - - - - - - - - -]
20 δῆμον τ[ὸν - - - - - - - - - - - - - - - - - φ]-
ίλοι ὄ[ντες -]-
ν ἐπε[- -]-
ΛΙΤΙ [- -]
24 Ἀθη[ν -]
ΟΤ [- - - - - - - - - - - -]
- -

the [remaining -]
[- - - - - - - - - - - - - - - - of the *emporoi* and?]
4 [*nau*]klero[i - - - - - - - - - - - it was resolved]

by the [People to commend - - - - - - - - and]
Potamo[n - in]
previously [- -]
8 and [- gr]ain
is brought [- - - - - - - - - - - - - - - - - - - the]
People [of Athens. Men shall be elected [- -],
at once [- who],
12 when they have arrived [- - - - - - - - - - - - -]-
that the People [- - - - - - - - - - - - - - - - - - -]-
in order that gr[ain - - - - - - - - - to Athens]
and that [- -]
16 that they are [- - - - - - - - - - - - - - - - - - -]
Milesians [- -]
and [- - - - - - - - - - - - - - - - - - of the People]
of the Athenians [- - - - - - - - - - - - - - - - -]
20 the People [- -]
they are friends [- - - - - - - - - - - - - - - - - -]
- -

20 (D15). *IG* ii² **416(b)** (Tracy 1995: 123, 127–128; *SEG* 26.78; V-T
A152) (334/3–321)

b   . . . . φ - - - - - - - - - - -   ΣΤΟΙΧ. 25
      [οἱ ἔ]μποροι ο[ἱ Ἀθηναίων καὶ ὁ δῆ]-
      [μος] ὁ ἐν Σάμωι καὶ ο[ἱ ἄλλοι οἱ πα]-
4   [ρ]ατυγχάνοντες Ἀθη[ναίων καὶ τ]-
      [ῶ]ν ἄλλων ἀποφαίνου[σιν . . . 6 . . .]-
      δαν τὸν Κῶιον τῶν τε [ἐμπόρων κα]-
      ὶ τῶν ναυκλήρων ἐπι[μελούμενο]-
8   ν ὅπως ἂν σῖτος ὡς ἀφ[θονωτάτως]
      εἰσπλεῖ τῶι δήμωι τ[ῶι Ἀθηναίω]-
      ν καὶ μηδεὶς μήτε κ[ωλύηται τῶν]
      Ἀθηναίων μηδ᾽ ὑφ᾽ ἑνὸ[ς ἀδίκως μη]-
12 δὲ κατάγηται καὶ τἆ[λλα ἐνδείκ]-
      νυται τῶι ἀεὶ παραγ[ιγνομένωι]
      [Ἀθ]ηναίων εὔνοιαν· ἐ[ψηφίσθαι τ]-
      [ῆι βουλῆ]ι τοὺς προέ[δρους οἳ ἂν]
16 [λάχωσιν π]ροεδρεύε[ιν εἰς τὴν π]-
      [ρώτην ἐκκλ]ησίαν χρ[ηματίσαι.]
      - - - - - - - - - - -

- -

[the e]*mporoi* [of the Athenians and the People]
on Samos and [the others who]

4 happen to be present of the Athe[nians and]
of the others display [. . . . . .]
-das the Koan takes [care]
of both the [*emporoi* and] the *naukleroi*
8 in order that grain sails in as pl[entifully as possible]
for the People of [Athens]
and no one [of the] Athenians
either [is hindered]
12 by [anyone unjustly or]
forced into port, and [in other respects he]
[shows] his goodwill to any [Ath]enian
who is always [present]. [It was decreed by]
16 [the Council] that the [*proedroi* chosen]
[by lot] to be *proedroi* shall conduct this busi[ness in the]
[first assembly.]

21 (D16). *IG* ii² **408** (lines 1–8 by Lambert 3.81; line 6 by Tracy 1995:
34 n. 20 [after Habicht]; line 12 by Wilhelm 1942: 152–53; *SEG*
40.1172; V-T A150) (333/2)

[ἐπὶ Νικοκράτους ἄρχοντος ἐπὶ τῆς Πανδιο]-   ΣΤΟΙΧ. 34
[νίδος δευτέρας πρυτανέας ἧι Ἀρχέλας Χαι]-
[ρίου Παλληνεὺς ἐγραμμάτευε· Μετα]γε[ιτνι]-
4   [ῶνος . . . . 22 . . . .]ι καὶ δεκ[ά]-
[τηι τῆς πρυτανείας· ἐκκλησία· τ]ῶν προέδρ[ω]-
[ν ἐπεψήφιζεν Φανόστρατος Φι]λαίδης· ἔδο[ξ]-
[εν τῶι δήμωι· . . . . 14 . . . .]λου Ἐρχιεὺ[ς]
8   [εἶπεν· περὶ ὧν Μνήμων καὶ . . . .]ιας οἱ Ἡρακλ-
[εῶται λέγουσιν καὶ ἀποφαίνο]υσιν Διότι[μ]-
[ός τε ὁ στρατηγὸς καὶ Διονυσ]όδωρος, ὃν κα[τ]-
έστη[σεν Διότιμος ἐπιμελε]ῖσθαι τῆς παρ[α]-
12   πομπῆς [τοῦ σίτου, εὔνοί τε ε]ῖναι τῶι δήμω[ι]
τῶι Ἀθην[αίων καὶ παραδεδω]κέναι τῶι δήμ[ω]-
ι πυρῶν Σ[ικελικῶν μεδίμνο]υς ΧΧΧΧ χιλίο[υ]-
ς ἐννεαδρ[άχμους, κριθὰς δ' ὁπό]σας ἦγεν ἀπά-
16   [σ]ας πεντε[δράχμους, δεδόχθαι] τῶι δήμωι, ἐ[π]-
ειδὴ Μνήμω[ν καὶ . . . . ιας οἱ Ἡ]ρακλεῶται [ἐν]-
δείκνυντα[ι εὔνοιαν τῶι δήμωι] καὶ ποι[οῦσ]-
[ι]ν ὅτι ἂν δύν[ωνται ἀγαθὸν τὸν δῆ]μον [τὸν Ἀθ]-
20   [η]ναίων, ἐπα[ινέσαι Μνήμονα καὶ . . . . ίαν το]-
[ὺ]ς Ἡρακλεώτας καὶ στεφανῶσαι αὐτῶν ἑκάτ]-
ερο[ν χρυσῶι στεφάνωι εὐνοίας ἕνεκεν τῆς]
π[ρ]ὸ[ς τὸν δῆμον τὸν Ἀθηναίων - - -]

[In the archonship of Nikokrates, in the second]
[*prytany*, that of Pandionis, in which Archelas son of]
[Chairios of Pallene was secretary: the month of Metageitnion]
4 [. . . . . 22 . . . .] and on the tenth
[(day) of the *prytany*: assembly: Phanostratos]
[of Phi]laidai [of the] *proedroi* [put (the motion) to the vote: it was]
[resolved by the People: . . . . 14 . . . . . .] of Erchi[a]
8 [made the motion: concerning the things which Mnemon
and . . . .]-ias the Herakl-
[eotes say and] Dioti[mos]
[the general and Dionys]odoros, whom [Diotimos]
[appointed to oversee] the con[v]oying
12 [of the grain, show,] they are [goodwilled] to the People
of Athe[ns and have so]ld to the People
4,000 thousa[n]d [*medimno*]i of S[icilian] wheat
at nine dr[achmas, but all the barley] he brought (he sold)
16 at five [drachmas, it has been resolved] by the People:
whereas Mnemo[n and . . . . -ias the Her]akleotes
[display goodwill to the People] and [do]
whatever [good they can for the People of Athe]ns,
20 [Mnemon and . . . . -ias the] He[rakleotes]
shall be com[mended and ea]c[h of them shall be crowned]
[with a gold crown because of their goodwill]
[toward the People of Athens - - -]

22. Athenaios *Deipnosophistai* 13.586d (Loeb text by C. B. Gulick; Osborne T82) (333–324)

ὁ δὲ γράψας τὸν Ἀγῆνα τὸ σατυρικὸν δραμάτιον, εἴτε Πύθων
ἐστὶν ὁ Καταναῖος ἢ αὐτὸς ὁ βασιλεὺς Ἀλέξανδρος, φησίν·
    καὶ μὴν ἀκούω μυριάδας τὸν Ἅρπαλον
    αὐτοῖσι τῶν Ἀγῆνος οὐκ ἐλάττονας
    σίτου παραπέμψαι καί πολίτην γεγονέναι.
    Β. Γλυκέρας ὁ σῖτος οὗτος ἦν· ἔσται δ' ἴσως
    αὐτοῖσιν ὀλέθρου κοὐχ ἑταίρας ἀρραβών.
13.596b
    Β. καὶ μὴν ἀκούω μυριάδας τὸν Ἅρπαλον
    αὐτοῖσι τῶν Ἀγῆνος οὐκ ἐλάσσονας
    σίτου διαπέμψαι καὶ πολίτην γεγονέναι.
    Α. Γλυκέρας ὁ σῖτος οὗτος ἦν· ἔσται δ' ἴσως
    αὐτοῖσιν ὀλέθρου κοὐχ ἑταίρας ἀρραβών.

The author of *Agen*, the satyric drama, whether he is Python of
Katana or King Alexander himself, says:

and yet I hear that Harpalos sent
to them no fewer myriads of grain
than Agen and became a citizen.

B. This was the grain of Glykera: but it will probably be
a deposit for them on ruin and not on a courtesan.

13.596b

B. And yet I hear that Harpalos sent
to them no fewer myriads of grain
than Agen and became a citizen.

A. This was the grain of Glykera: but it will probably be
a deposit for them on ruin and not on a courtesan.

23 (D17). *IG* ii² 363 (text by **Lambert 3.84;** Malouchou 2000–2003: no.
2; lines 1–4 by Schwenk no. 67; line 7 by Schweigert 1939: 33–34; line
12 by Wilhelm in *IG* ii²) (331/0)

- -

    [ἐπὶ τῆς . . . . . . 11 . . . . . ἑβδόμ]η[ς πρυταν]-   ΣΤΟΙΧ 29
    [είας ἧι . . . . 15 . . . .]ΑΓΟ[. . .5 . .]
    [. . . . 8 . . . . ἐγραμμάτευεν· Ἀ]νθε[στηρι]-
4   [ῶνος . . . . 15 . . . . τῆ]ς πρυ[τανε]-
    [ίας· ἐκκλησία κυρία· τῶν π]ροέδρω[ν ἐπ]-
    [εψήφιζεν . . .]Σ[. . . . 9 . . . .]εύς· vacat
a   [ἔδοξεν] τῶι δήμω[ι · Πολύευκ]τος Σωσ[τρ]-
8   [άτου Σφ]ήττιος ε[ἶπεν· ἐπει]δὴ Διον[ύσ]-
    [ιος πρό]τερόν τε [ἐπηγγείλ]ατο τῶι [δή]-
    [μωι ἐπι]δώσειν τ[ρισχιλίου]ς μεδίμν-
    [ους εἴ τ]ι δέοιτ[ο καὶ εὐεργέτ]ηκεν ἐν
12   [τῆι προ]τέρ[αι σπανοσιτίαι . . .]ΑΣΤΙ
    [. . .6 . . .]ΟΡΙ[. . . . . 17 . . . .]ΛΓ[.]
    [. . . . 7 . . .].[. . . . . .21 . . . .]
                      lacuna

    [. . . 5 . . καὶ σ]τρατ[εύεσθαι αὐτὸν τὰς σ]-
    [τρατιὰ]ς καὶ τὰς ε[ἰσφορὰς εἰσφέρει]-
    [ν μ]ετὰ Ἀθηναίων· ἀ[ναγράψαι δὲ τόδε τ]-
    [ὸ ψ]ήφισμα τὸν γραμ[ματέα τῆς βουλῆ]-
    ς ἐν στήληι λιθίνη[ι καὶ στῆσαι ἐν ἀκ]-
    ροπόλει· εἰς δὲ τὴν [ἀναγραφὴν τῆς στ]-
    ήλης δοῦναι τὸν τα[μίαν τοῦ δήμου : ᵛ]
    ΔΔΔ δραχμὰς ἐκ τῶν [εἰς τὰ κατὰ ψηφίσ]-
    ματα ἀναλισκομένω[ν τῶι δήμωι. vac.]

        in corona   [*in corona*]
          [ὁ δῆμος]   [ἡ βουλή]

[In the . . . . . . 11 . . . . . seventh prytany]
[in which . . . . 15 . . . .]
[. . . . 8 . . . . was secretary: in the month of Anthesteri]-
4   [on . . . . 15 . . . . of the *prytany*]:
[principal assembly: of the] *proedroi*
[put (the motion) to the vote . . . .]-eus.
[It was resolved] by the People: [Polyeuk]tos son of Sos[tratos]
8   [of Sph]ettos [made the motion: whereas] Dion[ysios]
[previously offered] to the [People]
[to g]ive th[ree thousa]nd *medimn[oi]*
[if there was any] need [and was a benefactor] in
12   [the ea]rli[er grain shortage - - - - - - - - - - - -]
[- -]
[- -]
        lacuna
[. . . 5 . . and he shall] serve [on]
[campaign] and [pay] *e[isphorai]*
[together] with Athenians: the sec[retary]
[of the Council shall inscribe this] decree
on a stone stele [and place it on the]
Acropolis: for the [inscribing of the]
stele the [the treasurer of the People] shall give:
30 drachmas from [the People's fund for]
expenditure on decrees.
        In a wreath   In a wreath
        The People   The Council

24 (D18). See also no. 27, *IG* ii² 360 (R-O no. 95; Schwenk no. 68; *SEG* 38.66; V-T A157) (330/29–328/7)

         Θ   ε   ο   ί
Ἐπ᾿ Ἀντικλέους ἄρχοντος ἐπὶ τῆς Αἰγεῖδος πέμπτ-   ΣΤΟΙΧ. 39
ης πρυτανείας, ἧι Ἀντιφῶν Κοροίβου Ἐλευσὶ ἐγρα-
μμάτευεν· ἐνδεκάτηι· τετάρτηι καὶ τριακοστῆι τῆς πρυταν-
4   είας· τῶμ προέδρων ἐπεψήφιζεν Φίλυλλος Ἐλευσί·
Δημοσθένης Δημοκλέους Λαμπτρεὺς εἶπεν· ἐπειδ-
ὴ Ἡρακλείδης Σαλαμίνιος διατελεῖ φιλοτιμούμ-
ενος πρὸς τὸν δῆμον τὸν Ἀθηναίων καὶ ποιῶν ὅτι δ-
8   ύναται ἀγαθόν, καὶ πρότερόν τε ἐπέδωκεν ἐν τῆι σ-
πανοσιτίαι : ΧΧΧ: μεδίμνους πυρῶν : Π: δράχμου-
ς πρῶτος τῶν καταπλευσάντων ἐνπόρων· καὶ πάλιν
ὅτε αἱ ἐπιδόσεις ἦσαν ἐπέδωκε : ΧΧΧ: δραχμὰς εἰ -
12   ς σιτωνίαν, καὶ τὰ ἄλλα διατελεῖ εὔνους ὢν καὶ φι-
λοτιμούμενος πρὸς τὸν δῆμον· δεδόχθαι τῶι δήμω-

ι ἐπαινέσαι Ἡρακλείδην Χαρικλείδου Σαλαμίνιον καὶ στεφανῶσαι χρυσῶι στεφάνωι εὐνοίας ἕνεκ-
16 α καὶ φιλοτιμίας τῆς πρὸς τὸν δῆμον τὸν Ἀθηναίων·
εἶναι δ᾿ αὐτὸν πρόξενον καὶ εὐεργέτην τοῦ δήμου
τοῦ Ἀθηναίων αὐτὸν καὶ ἐγγόνους, εἶναι δ᾿ αὐτοῖς
καὶ γῆς καὶ οἰκίας ἔγκτησιν κατὰ τὸν νόμον καὶ σ-
20 τρατεύεσθαι αὐτοὺς τὰς στρατείας καὶ εἰσφέρειν τὰς εἰσφορὰς μετὰ Ἀθηναίων. ἀναγράψαι δὲ τόδ-
ε τὸ ψήφισμα τὸν γραμματέα τὸν κατὰ πρυτανείαν
καὶ τοὺς ἄλλους ἐπαίνους τοὺς γεγενημένους αὐ-
24 τῶι ἐν στήληι λιθίνει καὶ στῆσαι ἐν ἀκροπόλει, ε-
ἰς δὲ τὴν ἀναγραφὴν τῆς στήλης δοῦναι τὸν ταμία-
ν Δ Δ Δ δραχμὰς ἐκ τῶν εἰς τὰ κατὰ ψηφίσματ᾿ ἀναλισκομένων τῶι δήμωι. vacat.
28 Τηλέμαχος Θεαγγέλου Ἀχαρνεὺς εἶπεν· ἐπειδὴ Ἡρακλείδης Σαλαμίνιος ἐπέδωκεν τὸν σῖτον τῶι δήμωι πεντέδραχμον πρῶτος τῶν καταπλευσάντων ἐ-
μπόρων ἐπ᾿ Ἀριστοφῶντος ἄρχοντος, ἐψηφίσθαι τῶ-
32 ι δήμωι ἐπαινέσαι Ἡρακλείδην Χαρικλείδου Σαλαμίνιον καὶ στεφανῶσαι αὐτὸν χρυσῶι στεφάνωι
φιλοτιμίας ἕνεκα τῆς εἰς τὸν δῆμον τὸν Ἀθηναίω-
ν· ἐπειδὴ δὲ καταχθεὶς ὑπὸ Ἡρακλεωτῶν πλέων Ἀθή-
36 ναζε παρειρέθη τὰ ἱστία ὑπ᾿ αὐτῶν ἑλέσθαι πρέσβ-
ευτὴν ἕνα ἄνδρα ἐξ Ἀθηναίων ἁπάντων, ὅστις ἀφικόμενος ε-
ἰς Ἡράκλειαν ὡς Διονύσιον ἀξιώσει ἀποδοῦναι τ-
ὰ ἱστία τὰ Ἡρακλείδου καὶ τὸ λοιπὸν μηδέν ἀδικε-
40 ῖν τῶν Ἀθήναζε πλεόντων· καὶ ταῦτα ποιῶν τά τε δί-
καια ποιήσει καὶ οὐθενὸς ἀτυχήσει τοῦ δήμου τ[ο]ῦ Ἀ-
[θηναίων] τῶν δικαίων· δοῦναι δὲ τῶι αἱρεθέντι πρεσβευ-
τεῖ εἰς ἐφόδια τὸν ταμίαν τοῦ δήμου :Π: δραχμὰς ἐκ τῶ-
44 ν κατὰ ψηφίσματ᾿ ἀναλισκομένων τῶι δήμωι. Εἱρέθ-
η πρεσβευτὴς Θηβαγένης Ἐλευσίνιος.   vacat
Τηλέμαχος Θεαγγέλου Ἀχαρ εἶπεν · ἐψηφίσθαι τῶι
δήμωι τὴν βουλὴν προβουλεύσασαν ἐξενεγκεῖν ε-
48 ἰς τὴν πρώτην ἐκκλησίαν περὶ Ἡρακλείδου καθότ-
ι εὑρήσεται ἂν τι δύνηται ἀγαθὸν παρὰ τοῦ δήμου
τοῦ Ἀθηναίων.   vacat
Κηφισόδοτος Εὐαρχίδου Ἀχαρνεὺς εἶπεν· περὶ ὧν ὁ
52 δῆμος προσέταξεν τῆι βουλῆι προβουλεῦσαι περ-
ὶ Ἡρακλείδου τοῦ Σαλαμινίου, δεδόχθαι τῆι Βουλῆι, ἐπειδὴ Ἡρακλείδης καταπλεύσας Ἀθήναζε σῖτον ἄγων ἐπέδωκεν τῶι δήμωι τρισχιλίους μεδίμν-
56 ους πέντε δραχμῶν ἕκαστον, τοὺς προέδρους οἳ ἂν λάχωσι-
ν προεδρεύειν εἰς τὴν πρώτην ἐκλησίαν προσαγα-

γεῖν Ἡρακλείδην πρὸς τὸν δῆμον καὶ χρηματίσαι,
γνώμην δὲ ξυμβάλλεσθαι τῆς βουλῆς εἰς τὸν δῆμο-
60 ν ὅτι δοκεῖ τῆι βουλεῖ ἐπαινέσαι Ἡρακλείδην Χαρικλείδου Σαλαμίνιον καὶ στεφανῶσαι χρυσῶι στεφάνωι ἀπὸ ΙΗ δραχμῶν· εἶναι δ᾽ αὐτῶι καὶ εὑρέσθαι παρὰ τοῦ δήμου ὅτι ἂν δύνηται ἀγαθόν, ὅπως ἂ-
64 ν καὶ οἱ ἄλλοι φιλοτιμῶνται εἰδότες, ὅτι τιμᾶι καὶ στεφανοῖ ἡ
βουλὴ τοὺς φ[ι]-
λοτιμουμένους. *vacat*
Φυλεὺς Παυσανίου Οἰναῖος εἶπεν· ἐπειδὴ Ἡρακλείδης Σαλαμίνιος
καταπλεύ-
σας Ἀθήναζε σῖτον ἄγων ἐπ᾽ Ἀριστοφῶντος ἄρχοντος ἐπέδωκεν
τῶι δήμωι XXX με-
68 δίμνους Π δράχμους καὶ διὰ ταῦτα ὁ δῆμος ἐψηφίσατο αὐτῶι τὴν
βουλὴν προβου-
λεύσασαν ἐξενεγκεῖν εἰς τὸν δῆμον καθ᾽ ὅτι εὑρήσεται ἄν τι
δύνηται ἀγαθὸν παρὰ
τοῦ δήμου τοῦ Ἀθηναίων, καὶ πάλιν ἐπ᾽ Εὐθυκρίτου ἄρχοντος
ἐπέδωκεν τῶι (δήμωι) εἰς σιτωνίαν XXX δ-
ραχμάς, δεδόχθαι τῆι βουλῆι τοὺς προέδρους οἳ ἂν λάχωσι
προεδρεύειν εἰς τὴν κυρίαν
72 ἐκκλησίαν προσαγαγεῖν Ἡρακλείδην πρὸς τὸν δῆμον καὶ
χρηματίσαι, γνώμην δὲ ξυ-
μβάλλεσθαι τῆς βουλῆς εἰς τὸν δῆμον ὅτι δοκει τηι βουλῆι
ἐπαινέσαι Ἡρακλείδην
Χαρικλείδου Σαλαμίνιον καὶ στεφανῶσαι χρυσῶι στεφάνωι ἀπὸ:
ΙΗ δραχμῶν·
εἶναι δ᾽ αὐτῶι καὶ εὑρέσθαι ἀγαθὸ[ν πα]ρὰ τοῦ δήμου ὅτου ἂν
δοκεῖ ἄξιος εἶναι, ὅπως
76 ἂν καὶ οἱ ἄλλοι ἐθέλωσι [ἑτοίμ]ω[ς εὐεργετεῖν τὴν βου]λὴν καὶ τὸν
δῆ[μ]ο[ν] ὁρῶντες
τοὺς φιλοτιμουμέ[νους - - - - - - - - - - - - - - - - - τὸν] δῆμον
- πάσ[α]ς
α - *vacat*

| *in corona* | *in corona* | *in corona* | *in corona* |
| Ὁ δῆμος | Ὁ δῆμος | Ἡ βουλή | Ἡ βουλή |

Gods.

In the archonship of Antikles in the fifth prytany, that
of Aigeis, in which Antiphon son of Koroibos of Eleusis was
secretary: on the eleventh: on the thirty-fourth day of the prytany:
4 Philyllos of Eleusis of the *proedroi* put (the motion) to the vote:
Demosthenes son of Demokles of Lamptrai made the motion: whereas

Herakleides of Salamis continues to seek after
honor concerning the People of Athens and to do whatever

8   good he can, and previously he has sold in the
grain shortage 3,000 *medimnoi* of wheat at 5 drachmas,
having been the first of the *emporoi* to sail in, and again
when there were *epidoseis,* he gave 3,000 drachmas for a

12   purchase of grain, and in other respects he continues to be goodwilled
       and to
seek after honor concerning the People, it was resolved by the People
to commend Herakleides son of Charikleides of Salamis
and to crown (him) with a gold crown on account of his goodwill

16   and love of honor concerning the People of Athens.
He shall be a *proxenos* and a *euergetes* of the People
of Athens, both he and his descendants, and they shall have
enktesis of both land and a house according to the law, and

20   they shall serve on campaign and pay
eisphorai together with the Athenians. The secretary
during the *prytany* shall inscribe this decree
and the other honors that have accrued to him

24   on a stone stele and place it on the Acropolis, and
for the inscribing of the stele the treasurer shall give
30 drachmas from the People's fund for expenditure
on decrees.

28   Telemachos son of Theangelos of Archarnai made the
      motion: whereas
Herakleides of Salamis has sold the grain to the
People at 5 drachmas and was first of the *emporoi* to
sail in during the archonship of Aristophon, it was decreed by the

32   People to commend Herakleides son of Charikleides of Salamis
and to crown him with a gold crown
on account of his love of honor concerning the People of Athens.
Whereas, when he was forced to shore by the Herakleotes while he
      was sailing

36   to Athens, he was stripped of his sails by them, an ambassador shall be
      selected,
one man from all the Athenians, who when he arrives
in Herakleia shall ask Dionysios to give back
the sails of Herakleides and in the future to harm nothing

40   of those who sail to Athens. In doing these things, he shall be
doing what is right and fail in obtaining no just things from the People
of Athens. The treasurer of the People shall give 5 drachmas
for traveling expenses to the chosen envoy from the

44   funds to be spent concerning the decrees of the People. Thebagenes

of Eleusis was chosen as envoy.

Telemachos son of Theangelos of Acharnai made the motion:
> it was decreed by

the People that the Council bring forth its preliminary deliberation

48   to the first assembly concerning how Herakleides
shall obtain whatever good he can from the People
of Athens.

Kephisodotos son of Euarchides of Acharnai made the motion:
> concerning

52   the things which the People instructed the Council to deliberate in
advance concerning Herakleides of Salamis, it was resolved by the
Council: whereas Herakleides, when he sailed in to Athens bringing
grain, sold to the People 3,000 *medimnoi*

56   at 5 drachmas each, the *proedroi* chosen by lot
to be *proedroi* shall introduce Herakleides to the People
in the first assembly and deliberate,
but the opinion of the Council shall be contributed to the People

60   that it is resolved by the Council to commend Herakleides son
of Charikleides of Salamis and to crown (him) with a
gold crown of 500 drachmas. But he shall also be allowed
to obtain from the People whatever good he can, in order that

64   others also seek after honor, knowing that the Council honors and
crowns those who seek after honor.

Phyleus son of Pausanias of Oinoi made the motion: whereas
Herakleides of Salamis, when he sailed
in to Athens bringing grain during the archonship of Aristophon, sold
to the People 3,000

68   *medimnoi* at 5 drachmas and because of these things the People
decreed for him that the Council bring forth
its preliminary deliberation to the People how he shall obtain
whatever good he can from
the People of Athens, and again during the archonship of Euthykritos
he gave to the People in a grain shortage 3,000
drachmas, it was resolved by the Council that the *proedroi* chosen by
lot to be *proedroi* introduce

72   Herakleides to the People in the principal assembly and deliberate,
but that the opinion
of the Council be contributed to the People that it is resolved by the
Council to commend Herakleides
son of Charikleides of Salamis and to crown (him) with a gold crown
of 500 drachmas.
But he shall also be allowed to obtain from the People whatever good
he seems to deserve, in order that

76   others also may wish [readily to benefit the Council] and the People

when they see

that those who seek after honor [- - - - - - - - - - - - - - - - - - - the] People

- -

- -

In a wreath   In a wreath   In a wreath   In a wreath
The People   The People   The Council   The Council

25 (D19). *IG* ii² 342+ (Stroud 1971: no. 29; *SEG* 24.104; Walbank 1985: 107–11=*SEG* 35.70; V-T A159 Lambert 3.44) (after ca. 330)

a   [. . . . 7 . . . Ἰτα]λίαι ? [. . . . . 15 . . . .]
         [. . . . . 9 . . . . ἐ]κ Καρχη[δόνος . . . . 8 . . . .]
         [. . . . 8 . . . . κ]εκόμικ[εν . . . . . . 12 . . . . . .]
b   4   [. . . . . 9 . . . .]ν ἢ ὃ ἐξ Ἰτ[α]λίας καθίστ[ησι]-
         [ν καὶ εἰς τ]ὸν λοιπὸν χρόνον ἐπαγ[γέλ]-
  c   [λετ]α[ι] σιτ[ηγήσει]ν Ἀθήναζε καὶ π[οήσ]-
         [ει]ν Ἀθηναίου[ς ἀγ]αθὸν ὅτι ἂν δύν[ητα]-
    8   [ι] καὶ αὐτὸς καὶ τ[ὸ]ν πατέρα τὸν αὑ[τοῦ],
         [ἐ]παινέσαι Ἄψην [Ἱέρω]νος Τύριον [καὶ]
         [Ἱ]έρωνα Ἄψου Τύρ[ιον ἀρετῆ]ς ἕνεκα κ[α]-
         [ὶ] εὐνοίας τῆς εἰ[ς τὸν δῆμον τ]ὸν Ἀθη[ν]-
   12   [αί]ων καὶ στεφανῶ[σαι ἑκάτερον αὐτῶ]-
         [ν] χρυσῶι στεφάνω[ι· εἶναι δὲ αὐτοὺς π]-
         [ρ]οξένους καὶ εὐερ[γέτας τοῦ δήμου τ]-
         [ο]ῦ Ἀθηναίων αὐτοὺ[ς καὶ ἐκγόνους αὐ]-
   16   [τῶ]ν καὶ γῆς καὶ οἰκ[ίας ἔγκτησιν εἶν]-
         [αι αὐτο]ῖς κατὰ τὸν [νόμον· ἀναγράψαι]
         [δὲ τόδε τὸ ψή]φισμα [. . . . . . . 14 . . . .]

         [. . . . . . Ita]ly ? [. . . . .]
         [. . . . . from] Cartha[ge . . . .]
         [. . . . . . . he]has convey[ed . . . .]
    4   [. . . . .] which he [has established] from It[a]ly
         [and in the] future he
         [offers] to bri[ng grai]n to Athens and [to]
         [do] for Athen[s] whatever [go]od he c[an],
    8   both he and his father,
         Apses [son of Hiero]n the Tyrian [and H]ieron son of Apses
         the Tyr[ian] shall be commended on account [of their excellenc]e
         [and] goodwill [toward the People of] Athe[n]s
   12   and [each of them] shall be crown[ed]
         with a gold crow[n. They shall be *pr*]oxenoi
         and *euer*[*getai* of the People of]
         Athens, both [they and their descendants],

16   and [they shall have *enktesis*] both of land and a hou[se]
      according to the [law. ...shall inscribe]
      [this decree . . . .]

26. See also nos. 16 and 34, [Demosthenes] *Against Phormio* 34.36
(Loeb text by A. T. Murray) (ca. 327)

κήρυγμα γὰρ ποιησαμένου Παιρισάδου ἐν Βοσπόρωι, ἐάν τις
βούληται Ἀθήναζε εἰς τὸ Ἀττικὸν ἐμπόριον σιτηγεῖν, ἀτελῆ τὸν
σῖτον ἐξάγειν, ἐπιδημῶν ἐν τῶι Βοσπόρωι ὁ Λάμπις ἔλαβε τὴν
ἐξαγωγὴν τοῦ σίτου καὶ ἀτέλειαν ἐπὶ τῶι τῆς πόλεως ὀνόματι...

For when Pairisades made a proclamation in Bosporos, if anyone
wishes to bear grain to Athens for the Attic emporion, he shall export
the grain tax free, Lampis, who was living abroad in the Bosporos,
received the right to export the grain also tax free in the name of the
city...

27 (D20). See no. 24 (325/4)

28 (D21). *IG* ii² 343 (lines 1–9 by Schweigert 1940: 343; lines 9–10 by
Schwenk no. 84; *SEG* 24.103; V-T A162 Lambert 3.50) (323/2)

[Ἐπὶ Κηφισοδώρου ἄρχοντος ἐπὶ τῆς Πανδιονί]-
[δος πέμπτης πρυτανείας ἧι Ἀρχίας Πυθοδώρο]-
[υ Ἀλωπεκῆθεν ἐγραμμάτευεν· Ποσιδεῶνος ἕκτ]-
4   ηι μετ᾽ εἰκάδας, μιᾶι καὶ εἰκοστῆι τῆς πρυταν]-
[είας· ἐκκλησία κυρία· τῶν προέδρων ἐπεψήφιζ]-
[ε]ν Ἐπαμεί[νων . . . . . . 11. . . . .] ΚΕΡΔΗ[Σ (?) . . . .8 . . . .]
Ἀναγυράσιο[ς εἶπ]ε[ν· ἐπειδὴ οἱ] ἔμπορο[ι καὶ να]-
8   ύκληροι ἀποφαίνουσ[ιν Ἀπ]ο[λλ]ωνίδην [Δημητρ]-
ίου Σιδώνιο[ν ε]ἶ[ναι] ἄ[νδρα ᵛ ἀγα]θὸν ᵛ κ[αὶ εὖνο]-
[υ]ν τῶι δήμωι τῶι Ἀθηναί[ων, δε]δόχθαι τῶ[ι δήμωι]
[ἐ]παινέσαι Ἀπολλωνίδην [Δημ]ητρίου Σι[δώνιον]
12   [κ]αὶ στεφανῶσαι αὐτὸν ᵛ χρυ[σ]ῶι στεφάνω[ι ἀπὸ]
[χ]ιλίων δραχμῶν ἀρετῆς ἕνεκα καὶ εὐνοία[ς τῆ]-
[ς] εἰς τὸν δῆμον τὸν Ἀθηναίω[ν]· καὶ εἶναι αὐ[τὸν]
[π]ρόξενον καὶ εὐεργέτην τοῦ δήμου τοῦ Ἀθ[ηναί]-
16   [ων] αὐτὸν καὶ ἐκγόνους· εἶναι δὲ αὐτῶι καὶ [γῆς]
[κ]αὶ οἰκίας ἔγκτησιν κατὰ τὸν νόμον. ἀναγ[ράψαι]
δὲ τόδε τὸ ψήφισμα τὸν γ[ρ]αμματέα τῆς βου[λῆς]
ἐν στήλει [λιθί]νει καὶ στῆσαι ἐν ἀκροπό[λει],
20   εἰς δὲ τὴ[ν ἀναγραφὴν] τῆς στήλης δοῦν[αι τὸν]
ταμίαν τ[οῦ δήμου . . .] δραχμὰ[ς ἐκ] τῶν [εἰς τὰ κα]-

[τ]ὰ ψηφίσμα[τα ἀναλισκ]ομένων τῶι [δήμωι].
    vacat 0,03

[In the archonship of Kephisodoros, in the fifth]
[*prytany*, that of Pandionis, in which Archias son of Pythodoros]
[of Alopeke was secretary: on the twenty-sixth day]
4   [of Posideon, on the twenty-first day of the *prytany*:]
[principal assembly]: Epameinon [of the *proedroi* put (the motion) to the]
[vote: . . . .]
of Anagyrous made the motion: whereas the *emporoi* and *naukleroi*
8   declare that Apollonides son of Demetrios
the Sidonian, [is] a [good] man [and goodwilled]
to the People of Athens, it was resolved by the People
to commend Apollonides son of Demetrios the Sidonian,
12 and to crown him with a gold crown of
one thousand drachmas on account of his excellence and goodwill
toward the People of Athens: and he and his descendants
shall be a *proxenos* and a *euergetes* of the People of Ath[ens]:
16 He shall also have *enktesis*
of both land and a house according to the law. The secretary
of the Council shall inscribe this decree
on a stone stele and place it on the Acropolis.
20 For the inscribing of the stone the treasurer
of the People shall give . . . drachmas from the People's fund
for expenditure on decrees.

29 (D22). *IG* ii² 398(a)+438 (text by **Walbank 1987a:** 10–11=*SEG* 40.78;
Osborne D40; V-T A167) (ca. 322/1 or 320/19)

[. . 3 .]φάν[η]ς πα[τρικὴν ἔχων εὔνοιαν]   ΣΤΟΙΧ. 27
[πρ]ὸς τὸν δῆμο[ν τὸν Ἀθηναίων διατ]-
[ε]λεῖ χρήσιμο[ς ὢν καὶ κοινεῖ καὶ ἰ]-
4   [δ]ίαι τοῖς ἀφ[ικνουμένοις Ἀθηναί]-
[ω]ν εἰς τὴν Ἀσί[αν καὶ τοῖς στρατευ]-
ομένοις Ἀθη[ναίων, τῆς δὲ ναυμαχί]-
[α]ς τῆς ἐν Ἑλλη[σπόντωι γενομένης]
8   [π]ολλοὺς διέσ[ωισεν καὶ ἐφόδια δο]-
[ὺ]ς ἀπέστειλε[ν καὶ αἴτιος ἐγένετ]-
[ο τ]οῦ σωθῆναι [καὶ κατελθεῖν αὐτο]-
[ὺς κ]αὶ σπάνεως [σίτου γενομένης τ]-
12 [ὸν σ]ῖτον τὸν ἐν [Ἑλλησπόντωι ἀπέσ]-
[τει]λεν πυρῶν μ[εδίμνους . . 3 . Ἀθήν]-
[αζε] φανερὰν πο[ιῶν τὴν πρὸς τὸν δῆ]-

. [μον] φιλοτιμ[ίαν . . . . . . .14 . . . .]
   lacuna
[. . . . . . .14 . . . . καὶ φυλάττων δι]-
[ατ]ελε[ῖ τὴν πρὸς Ἀθηναίους εὔνοι]-
αν· εἶναι [δὲ Ἀθηναῖον αὐτὸν καὶ το]-
4 ὺς ἐκγόνο[υς] α[ὐτοῦ· εἶναι δὲ καὶ αὐ]-
τῶι γραψάσθαι φ[υλῆς καὶ δήμου κα]-
ὶ φρατρίας ἧς ἂν [βούληται κατὰ τὸ]-
ν ν]όμον, [ὅπω]ς ἂν φαί[νηται ὁ δῆμος .]
8 . . . .8. . . .] Λ[.]Ν ἀξίω[ς . . . . .11. . . . . .
  . . . .9. . . . .]ονα[.]το[. . . . . .12. . . . . .
  . . . .8. . . .] τιμων[.]ω[. . . . . .12. . . . . .]

[...]-phan[e]s, [having fatherly goodwill]
toward the People [of Athens, continues]
[to be] useful [both publicly and]
4 [privately] to those [Athenians who come]
to Asi[a and to those Athenians on campaign],
[and when the naval battle]
[occurred] in the Helle[spont],
8 [he saved] many men, and after giving (them) supplies]
he sent (them) back [and was responsible]
for saving [and returning (them)],
and [when there was] a shortage [of grain],
12 [he sent] out grain in [the Hellespont],
[...] m[edimnoi] of wheat, [to Athens],
[making] clear his love of ho[nor]
[concerning the People . . . .]
   lacuna
[. . . . . and he continues]
[to maintain goodwill toward the Athenians]:
[He and his] descenda[nts] shall be
4 [Athenian. He shall also be allowed]
to register [in a tribe and a deme and]
a phratry which [he wishes according to the]
[law, in order that the People show]
8 -

30 (D23). *IG ii*² 401 (for alternative restorations of lines 1–5, see
Wilhelm 1906: 215–18; Scullion 2001: 116–17; Henry 2001: 106–8; and
Scullion 2002: 81–84) (ca. 321–319)

    [ἐπειδὴ - - - - - εὔνους ὢν διατε]-   ΣΤΟΙΧ. 22
    [λεῖ - - - - - - - - Ἀθηναί]-

οις κ[οινῆι τε ὅτι ἂν δύνητα]-
ι ἀγαθὸν π[οῶν τὸν δῆμον τὸν]
Ἀθηναίων κ[αὶ τ]ο[ὺς ἀφικνου]-
4   μένους Ἀθηναίων [πρὸς αὐτὸ]-
ν ἰδίαι, ἔν τ[ε τ]ῶι ἔμπροσθεν
χρόνωι καὶ νῦ[ν μ]ετ᾽ [Ἀρριδαί?]-
ου ὢν τοῦ καθ[εσ]τῶτο[ς σατρά]-
8   που ὑπὸ βασιλ[έω]ς καὶ [Ἀντιπ]-
άτρου καὶ τῶ[ν ἄ]λλων Μ[ακεδο]-
νων χρήσιμο[ν αὐ]τὸν [παρασκ]-
[ε]υάζει περί [τε τ]ὴν ἀ[ποστολ]-
12 [ὴν] τοῦ σίτου [ἐ]κ τῆς [Ἀσίας κα]-
[ὶ τ]ἄλλα πρά[ττε]ι τὰ [συμφέρο]-
[ντα] Ἀθηναί[οι]ς· δεδ[όχθαι τῶ]-
[ι δή]μω[ι] ἐπα[ιν]έσα[ι . . . . 7. . .]
16 [. . Μητ]ροδώρου Κυ[ζικηνὸν ? κ]-
[αὶ στεφα]νῶσαι χ[ρυσῶι στεφ]-
[άνωι ἀπὸ Χ δ]ρ[αχμῶν κτλ.]

[whereas - - - - - - continues to be goodwilled]
[- the Athenians]
[both publicly doing whatever] good
[he can for the People]
of Athens [and] privately [for those]
4   Athenians [who come to him],
both previously
and now, being [with Arrhidai]os?
who was appointed [satrap]
8   by the King and [Antip]ater
and the other [Macedo]nians,
he [makes] himself useful
concerning the s[ending out]
12 of the grain from [Asia and]
in [other respects] he does [useful things]
for Atheni[an]s, [it was resolved
by the People to] com[me]nd [. . . . . . .]
16 [. .] son of Met]rodoros the Ky[zikene?]
[and to cro]wn (him) with a g[old crown]
[of 1,000 d]r[achmas - - - - - - - - -]

31 (D24). *IG ii² 407+SEG 32.94* (Walbank 1982: no. 6; Walbank 1987b: 165–66) (ca. 321–318)

- - - - - - - - - - - Σ Υ . . . .   ΣΤΟΙΧ. 31

[- - - - - - - - Ἀθ]ηναίων κα[ὶ . . .]
[- - - - - - - τῆ]ς Ἀθηναίων . . . .

4   [. . . . . . 12. . . . . . αὐτ]ός τε σιτηγῶν εἰς τ[ὸ]
[ἐμπόριον τὸ Ἀθην]αίων διατελεῖ [κα]ὶ τῆ-
[ς τοῦ σίτου πομπ]ῆς ἐκ Κύπρου συνε[πι]με-
[λεῖται ὅπως ἂν σ]ῖτος ἀφι[κ]νῆτα[ι ὡς π]λε-
8   [ῖστος Ἀθήναζε] καὶ δ[ι]ατε[λ]εῖ εὔνους ὢν
[καὶ χρήσιμος κα]ὶ ἐνδει[κ]νύμενος τὴν ε-
[ὔνοιαν τῶι δήμωι τ]ῶι Ἀθηναίων, τύχει [ἀ]-
[γαθεῖ δεδόχθαι τῶι] δήμωι ἐπαινέσαι [.]
12 [. . . . . 12 . . . . . . Μιλή]σιον καὶ στεφα[νῶσ]-
[αι χρυσῶι στεφάνωι ἀπ]ὸ : Χ : δραχμῶ[ν . . 4 . .]
        lacuna
[. . . . . . 14 . . . .]ΩΙΣΤ[. . . . . . 13 . . . . .]
[. . 4 . . ὅπως] ἂν πάντες εἰ[δῶσιν ὅτι ὁ δῆμο]-
[ς τιμᾶι τ]οὺς εὐεργετο[ῦντας κατὰ τὴν ἀ]-
4   [ξίαν· ἀν]αγράψαι δὲ τόδε [τὸ ψήφισμα τὸν]
[ἀναγρα]φέα [ἐ]ν στήληι λ[ιθίνηι καὶ στῆσ]-
[αι ἐν Ἀκ]ρο[π]όλει· εἰς δὲ [τὴν ἀναγραφὴν τ]-
[ῆς στήλης] δοῦναι [τὸ]ν τ[αμίαν τοῦ δήμου]
8   [ΔΔΔ δρα]χμὰς ἐκ τῶν [κατὰ ψηφίσματα ἀνα]-
[λισκομ]ένων τῶι δήμωι   *vacat*   ]
     vacat

- -

[- - - - - - - - - - of the] Athenians and [. . . .]
[- - - - - - - of the]...of the Athenians . . . . .

4   [. . . . . he] both continues to bring grain to
[the *emporion* of Athe]ns [and]
helps [to take care of the send]ing [of the grain] from Cyprus
[in order that as much gr]ain [as possible] comes
8   [to Athens], and he continues to be goodwilled
[and useful and] to show his
g[oodwill to the People] of Athens. With [good]
fortune [it was resolved by the] People to commend
12 [. . . . . the Mile]sian and to cro[wn]
[him with a gold crown of] 1,000 drachmas.
        lacuna
[. . 4 . . in order that] everyone [knows that the People]
[honor] those who do bene[factions according to their]
[worth: the secre]tary shall inscribe this [decree]
4   on a [stone] stele [and place]
[it on the] Acropolis: for [the inscribing of]
[the stele the treasurer of the People] shall give

[30] drachmas from the People's fund for
8 [expenditure on decrees].

32. See no. 33 (before 320/19)

33 (D25). *IG* ii² 400 (before 320/19)

[...6... καὶ συμπρόεδρ]οι· ἔδοξε[ν τ]-   ΣΤΟΙΧ 27
[ῶι δήμωι· Δημάδης Δη]μέου Παιαν[ιε]-
[ὺς εἶπεν· ἐπειδὴ Εὐ]χάριστος Χει .
4 [......12......σῖτ]ον ἄγων Ἀθήνα[ζ]-
[ε χρείας παρέχετ]αι τῶι δήμωι τῶ[ι]
[Ἀθηναίων, φησὶν δ]ὲ αὐτῶι ἤδ[η] ὀ[κ]τα-
[κισχιλίους μεδί]μνους παραδ[ώ]σ[ε]-
8 [ιν τῆς καθισταμ]ένης τιμ[ῆ]ς καὶ τ[ὸ]
[λοιπὸν ἄλλους τ]ετρακισχιλίου[ς]
[μεδίμνους καὶ ἐν] τῶι πρόσθεν χρ[ό]-
[νωι καὶ νῦν πρόξενο]ς ὢν καὶ εὐεργ-
12 [έτης τοῦ δήμου τοῦ Ἀθ]ηνα[ί]ων ποι[ε]-
[ῖ ὅτι δύναται ἀγαθόν, δ]εδόχθαι τ[ῶ]-
[ι δήμωι ἐπαινέσαι Εὐχά]ριστον Χε-
[ι - - - - - - - -] του . . .

[......and the *symproedroi*]: it was resolved
[by the People: Demades son of De]meas of Paian[ia]
[moved: whereas Eu]charistos son of Chei...
4 [............], by bringing [gra]in to Athen[s],
[provides services] to the People of
[Athens, and whereas he says that he will sell] to them now
e[i]ght [thousand *medi*]*mnoi*
8 [at the establish]ed pri[c]e and [in the]
[future another f]our thousan[d]
[*medimnoi*, and (whereas) in] the past
[and now as [a *proxeno*]s and a *euerg*[*etes*]
12 [of the People] of Athens,
[he does whatever good he can], it was resolved by the
[People to commend Eucha]ristos son of Chei...

34. See no. 26, *IG* ii² 653 (285/4)

a [Ἐπὶ Δ]ιοτίμου ἄρχοντος ἐπὶ τῆς Ἀντι[γονίδος ἑ]-   ΣΤΟΙΧ. 36–38
[βδό]μης πρυτανείας, ἧι Λυσίστρατο[ς Ἀριστομά]-
[χου] Παιανιεὺς ἐγραμμάτευεν · Γα[μηλιῶνος ἕνει]
4 [καὶ] νέαι. ἐνάτηι καὶ εἰ[κο]στῆι τῆ[ς πρυτανείας·]

[ἐκκ]λησία· τῶν προέδρω[ν ἐπε]ψ[ήφιζεν . . . . 8. . . .]
[Αὐτ]οσθένου Ξυπετ[αιῶν καὶ συμπρόεδροι· ἔδο]-
[ξε]ν τῶι δήμωι· Ἀγύρ[ριος Καλλιμέδοντος Κολλυ]-
8   τεὺς εἶπεν· ἐπειδὴ [πρότερόν τε οἱ πρόγονοι οἱ]
Σπαρτόκου χρείας [παρέσχηνται τῶι δήμωι καὶ]
νῦν Σπάρτοκος πα[ραλαβὼν τὴν εἰς τὸν δῆμον οἰ]-
κειότητα κοινῆι [τε τῶι δήμωι χρείας παρέχε]-
12 ται καὶ ἰδίαι Ἀθη[ναίων τοῖς ἀφικνουμένοις]
πρὸς αὐτόν· ἀνθ᾿[ῶν καὶ ὁ δῆμος ὁ Ἀθηναίων αὐτοὺς]
b   πολίτας ἐποιή[σατο καὶ ἐτίμησ]εν [εἰκόσιν χαλ]-
καῖς ἔν τε τῆι [ἀγορᾶι καὶ] ἐν τῶι ἐμπορίωι [καὶ]
16 ἄλλαις δωρεα[ῖς αἷς προσῆ]κει τιμᾶσθαι τοὺ[ς]
ἀγαθοὺς ἄνδρ[ας καὶ διέθε]˙ιυ, ἐάν τις βαδίζε[ι]
ἐπὶ τὴν ἀρχὴν τ[ὴν τῶν προγόνω]ν αὐτοῦ καὶ τὴν Σπα[ρ]-
τόκου, βοηθε[ῖν παντὶ σθένε]ι κ[α]ὶ κατὰ γῆν καὶ
20 κατὰ θάλατ[ταν· ἔτι δὲ Σπάρτ]οκος ἀφικομένης
πρεσβείας [παρ᾿ Ἀθηναίων ἀκ]ούσας ὅτι ὁ δῆμος
κεκόμιστ[αι τὸ ἄστυ συνήσ]θη τοῖς εὐτυχήμασ[ι]
τοῦ δή[μ]ο[υ καὶ δέδωκεν σίτ]ου δωρεὰν μυρίου[ς]
24 καὶ πε[ντακισχιλίους με]δίμνους, ἐπαγγέλλε[τ]-
[αι δὲ καὶ εἰς τὸ λοιπὸν χρ]είαν παρέξεσθαι τῶ[ι]
[δήμωι τῶι Ἀθηναίων καθό]τι ἂν δύνηται, καὶ ταῦ-
[τα πράττει προαιρούμεν]ος διαφυλάττειν τὴν
28 [εὔνοιαν τὴν εἰς τὸν δῆμ]ον τὴν παραδεδομένην
[αὐτῶι παρὰ τῶν προγόνω]ν· ὅπως ἂν οὖν φαίνηται
[καὶ ὁ δῆμος φιλοτιμού]μενος πρὸς τοὺς εὔνους
[διὰ τοῦ ἔμπροσθεν χρ]όνου διαμεμενηκότας αὐ-
32 [τῶι, τύχηι ἀγαθῆι δε]δόχθαι τῶι δήμωι ἐπ[αινέ]-
[σαι μὲν τὸν βασιλέ]α Σπάρτοκον Εὐμήλου [Βοσπ]-
[όριον καὶ στεφανῶ]σαι χρυσῶι στεφάνωι [κατὰ]
[τὸν νόμον ἀρετῆς] ἕνεκα καὶ εὐνοίας ἣν ἔχω[ν δ]-
36 [ιατελεῖ πρὸς τὸν] δῆμον καὶ ἀνειπεῖν τὸν στέ[φα]-
[νον Διονυσίων] τῶν μεγάλων τραγωιδοῖς ἐν τῶι
[ἀγῶνι· τῆς δὲ π]οιήσεως τοῦ στεφάνου καὶ τῆς ἀ-
[ναγορεύσεω]ς ἐπιμεληθῆναι τοὺς ἐπὶ τῆι διοι[ι]-
40 [κήσει · στῆσαι] δ᾿ αὐτοῦ καὶ εἰκόνα χαλκῆν ἐν τῆ[ι]
[ἀγορᾶι παρὰ] τοὺς προγόνους καὶ ἑτέραν ἐ[ν ἀκρ-
[οπόλει· ὅπω]ς ἂν δὲ καὶ εἰδῆι ὁ βασιλεὺς Σπάρτ[ο]-
[κος τὰ ἐψηφ]ισμένα τῶι δήμωι, χειροτονῆσαι πρέ -
44 [σβεις τρεῖς ἄνδρας ἐξ Ἀθηναίων ἁπάντων, οἵτι[ν]-
[ες αἱρεθέ]ντες ἀπαροῦσιν καὶ τό τε ψήφισμα ἀ-
[ποδώσου]σιν καὶ ἀπαγγελοῦσι τὴν εὔνοιαν ἣν
[ἔχει πρὸ]ς αὐτὸν ὁ δῆμος καὶ παρακαλοῦσιν αὐ-
48 [τὸν βοηθ]εῖν τῶι δήμωι καθότι ἂν δύνηται· δοῦ-

[ναι δὲ ἐφό]δια τῶν πρέσβειων ἑκάστωι τὸ τετα –
[γμένον]· ὅπως ἂν δὲ καὶ ὑπόμνημα ἦι τῆς οἰκειό-
[τητος κ]αὶ τῶν δωρειῶν τῶν προστιθεμένων αὐ-
52 [τῶι πρ]ὸς ταῖς ὑπαρχούσαις, τὸν γραμματέα τὸν
[κατὰ π]ρυτανείαν ἀναγράψαι τόδε τὸ ψήφισμα
[ἐν στ]ήληι λιθίνηι καὶ στῆσαι ἐν ἀκροπόλει, τὸ
[δὲ ἀν]άλωμα τὸ γενόμενον μερίσαι τοὺς ἐπὶ τῆι
56 [διο]ικήσει.

in corona
Ὁ δῆμος

[In] the archonship of Diotimos in the seventh
prytany, that of Antigonis, in which Lysistrato[s son of
[Aristomachos] of Paiania was secretary, on the [old and]
4 new day of Ga[melion]. On the twenty-ninth day of the [*prytany*]:
assembly: of the *proedroi* [. . . . . . . son of Aut]osthenes of Xypet[e]
[and the *symproedroi* put (the motion) to the vote. It was]
[resolved] by the People: Agyr[rhios son of Kallimedon, of Kolly]tos
8 made the motion: whereas [previously the ancestors of]
Spartokos [provided] services [to the People and]
now Spartokos, [taking up the relationship]
[to the People, provides services both] publicly [to the People]
12 and privately [to those of the Athenians who come]
to him, in return for [which also the People of Athens]
made [them] citizens [and honored (them)] with statues of bronze]
in the [Agora and] in the *emporion* [and]
16 with other gifts [with which it is proper] to honor
good men, and [(the People) set forth], if anyone marches
against the kingdom of his [ancestors] and of Spa[r]tokos,
(the People) shall aid (him) [with all strength] both by land and
20 by sea. [In addition, Spartokos], when an embassy arrived
[from the Athenians] and he heard that the People
had recovered [the city, he rejoiced at the successes
of the People [and gave] a gift of 15,000
24 *medimnoi* of [gra]in, [and] he promises
[also in the future] to provide [service] to the
[People of Athens in whatever manner] he can, and
[he does these things, preferring] to maintain the
28 [goodwill toward the People] that has been handed over
[to him from his ancestors]. In order, therefore, that [the People]
are seen [also to seek after] honor concerning those who
[throughout the past] have remained goodwilled to
32 [them, with good fortune it was resolved] by the People to
co[mmend King] Spartokos son of Eumelos [the Bosporan],

[and to cro]wn (him) with a gold crown [according]
[to the law] on account of [his excellence] and goodwill which
　　[he continues]
36　to have [toward the] People and to proclaim the cr[own]
　　at the tragedies in the [contest] of the Greater
　　[Dionysia]. The managers of the [financial
　　administration] shall take care of [the] making of the crown and the
40　[proclamation]. A bronze statue of him [shall be placed] in the
　　[Agora beside] those of his ancestors and another [on the]
　　[Acropolis. In order that] King Spartokos
　　also know [what has been decreed] by the People,
44　[ambassadors] shall be elected, [three] men from all the Athenians,
　　who, [after they have been selected], shall depart and both [deliver]
　　the decree and report the goodwill which
　　the People [have toward] him and appeal to him
48　[to help] the People in what manner he can.
　　Each of the envoys [shall be given travel expenses]
　　[in the appointed amount]. Also, in order that there be a memorial
　　　of the
　　[relationship] and of the gifts which are given to
52　[him in addition to those which already exist, the secretary
　　[during] the *prytany* shall inscribe this decree
　　[on a] stone stele and place it on the Acropolis,
　　[but] the managers of the [financial administration] shall distribute
　　the [expense] that arises.
　　　　　The People

APPENDIX THREE

Textual and Historical Commentaries

This appendix consists of commentaries on the evidence for each occasion on which Athens granted honors and privileges for trade-related services. I have numbered each occasion and assign an additional number beginning with the letter *D* to occasions for which the actual honorary decree is extant in the form of an inscription. The commentaries explain the rationale for the dates assigned to these occasions as well as for textual restorations to lacunae in the inscriptions. They also describe the immediate historical context of the honorary decrees, when it is relevant, and assign the particulars of each decree to categories for analysis. The categories include the following:

- the proposers of the decrees
- the types of trade-related services
- the goods that were traded
- the honorands
- the laudatory language of the decrees
- the types of honors and privileges granted in the decrees

Full explanations for the use of these categories and their subcategories can be found in the preceding chapters. Here I simply remind the reader of the various subcategories and provide a brief description of them. The types of trade-related services are subdivided as follows:

- simple imports of goods
- sales of imported goods at reduced prices
- gifts of imported goods
- securing imports of goods
- miscellaneous services
- unknown services

"Simple imports of goods" encompass what seem to be typical acts of trade in which goods were brought into Athens from abroad and sold at the going price as determined by the market. Services are categorized as "sales of imported goods at reduced prices" when there is evidence that the honorand did not charge the going price as determined by the market for his imported goods but sold them at a discount. "Gifts of imported goods" comprise situations in which imported goods were not sold but given to the city of Athens free of charge. Services in which goods being traded to Athens were protected from pirates or other dangers fall under the category of "securing imports of goods." "Miscellaneous services" relating to trade are those that cannot be reasonably assigned to any of the aforementioned categories. Services that clearly have something to do with trade but for which there is no further distinguishing information are categorized simply as "unknown services."

The honorands are analyzed according to the following categories:

- ethnicity
- legal status
- socioeconomic status

"Legal status" encompasses the following categories:

- citizens or noncitizens of Athens
- *metics*
- *xenoi*

Metics were free noncitizens who resided in Athens for extended periods. *Xenoi* were free noncitizens who resided elsewhere than Athens and visited Athens for only short periods or not at all.

"Socioeconomic status" refers to categories based on Reed's study of maritime traders in the ancient Greek world,[1] as follows:

- common professional traders
- moderately wealthy professional traders
- wealthy professional traders
- foreign potentates

"Common professional traders" comprise men (commonly referred to as *emporoi*) who made their living primarily from trade and for whom there is no evidence to indicate that they were particularly wealthy. I classify professional traders who at least owned their own ships (commonly referred to as *naukleroi*) as "moderately wealthy professional traders." When there is evidence that professional traders had even greater wealth, I categorize them as "wealthy professional traders." I place in the category of "foreign potentates" honorands who were not professional traders but rather wealthy, powerful men who sent others to Athens with goods on their behalf.

Before proceeding with the commentaries, it is necessary to make a cautionary statement about the evidence. The evidence provided by the epigraphic and literary *testimonia* is often extremely fragmentary. Most of the inscriptions are severely damaged and riddled with lacunae, and the literary references are often vague and sometimes subjective and tendentious. Hence, the data are insufficient to prove, for example, that the activity of bringing grain to Athens during a shortage always prompted the award of a gold crown valued at one thousand drachmas from the Athenian People. Such precise and absolute conclusions are impossible. In addition, it seems that the Athenians themselves had no set guidelines for awarding honors for trade-related services. Often a single decree mentions more than one type of service for which one or more honors were granted, leaving us no way of knowing which particular honor was granted for which particular service.

Athens also was not consistent in its description of the various types of trade-related services. For example, forms of the word δίδωμι, which generally means "to give," are often used. In some decrees, however, δίδωμι is followed by an explicit statement of a price, which must indicate that the object "given" was actually sold for money. The practice followed in this study, therefore, will be to translate δίδωμι as "to sell" when followed by an explicit mention of a price but as "to give free of charge" when there is no mention of a price and no significant lacuna wherein such a mention may once have existed. It is also well known that honorary decrees from the fifth century are fairly reticent concerning the deeds of honorands and became more detailed in their information only progressively through the course of the fourth century. Arguments from silence concerning fifth-century decrees, therefore, can carry little weight. Likewise, rigorous systematization or statistical analysis of the evidence for the Athenian practice of granting honors and privileges for trade-related services is problematic and cannot yield definitive conclusions. But despite these difficulties, there is enough evidence to attempt some categorization and to suggest trends that will provide a basic picture concerning this practice, its development, and its place in Athenian trade policy.

Case Commentaries

1. (D1). Lykon, ca. 414–412 (*IG* i³ 174)
Proposer: Peisander
Services: unknown
Goods: unknown
Ethnicity: Greek (Achaian)
Legal status: noncitizen
Socioeconomic status: moderately wealthy professional trader
Laudatory language: none
Honors and privileges: *proxenia, euergesia,* inscribed stele, sailing
    privileges

Walbank has argued convincingly for the circumstances surrounding this grant, which he dates to ca. 414–412.[2] Although the extant portions of the decree do not state the honorand's services, he must have been a professional trader, since he owned his own ship (lines 11–12) and since Athens granted him the right to sail with his goods in waters under its control and to its garrisons (Reed 2003: no. 47). Since Lykon owned a ship, he was a *naukleros* rather than simply an *emporos* and must also have been wealthier than the typical professional trader.[3] At the same time, however, there is nothing in the evidence to suggest that he had a great degree of wealth, and he should thus be categorized as only moderately wealthy. Since he received the title of *proxenos* from Athens, Lykon could not have been an Athenian citizen.

The proposer of this decree is likely to have been the same Peisander who was influential in politics in Athens during the late fifth century and one of the leaders of the oligarchy of the Four Hundred in 411.

2. Pythophanes (1), before 411 (*IG* i³ 98)

Proposer: unknown
Services: unknown
Goods: unknown
Ethnicity: unknown
Legal status: noncitizen
Socioeconomic status: moderately wealthy professional trader
Laudatory language: N.A.
Honors and privileges: *proxenia, euergesia*

IG i³ 98 is an inscription from 399/8 of three separate decrees (lines 1–2, 3–28, and 29–32, respectively), the third of which provides the date with its extant archon formula. The second decree, however, must date to 411/10, during which time the normal *prytany* system was not in operation. This is clear from the presence of the names of five men of different tribes in the fragmentary preamble to the decree (lines 4–7). The first decree, therefore, must date to before 411.[4] Either the first decree or one even earlier provided the first occasion on which Pythophanes received honors from Athens, since the second decree states that he was already a *proxenos* and a *euergetes* at the time of its passage (lines 9–10). The decree by which Pythophanes initially received these titles must, therefore, have been passed before 411. His *proxenia* also attests to the fact that he was not a citizen of Athens. Pythophanes was surely a professional trader, since the second decree refers to his ship and his goods (lines 15–19; Reed 2003: no. 48). Without any further evidence, the fact that Pythophanes owned his own ship indicates that he was at least moderately wealthy.[5]

Since only two fragmentary lines of the decree granting Pythophanes *proxenia* and *euergesia* survive, it is impossible to know for what services he was honored. It is likely, however, that his services had something to do with trade, since the third decree of 399/8 reaffirms the honors granted to Pythophanes by the second decree of 411/10. This would not have happened had the services for which Pythophanes was honored in the second decree of 411/10 been political or military in nature, because such services would have benefited the oligarchic government that was in power at the time, a government totally opposed by the democratic government of 399/8. Thus, the services for which Pythophanes was honored by the second decree of 411/10 were almost certainly related to trade. Given that Pythophanes was a trader and was honored for services relating to trade by the second decree, it is very likely that the services for which he was honored by the first decree were trade-related as well (Walbank 391).

3. (D2). Pythophanes (2), 411/10 (*IG* i³ 98)
    Proposer: Hippomenes
    Goods: unknown
    Ethnicity: unknown
    Legal status: noncitizen
    Socioeconomic status: moderately wealthy professional trader
    Laudatory language: none
    Honors and privileges: inscribed stele, *asylia*

Concerning the date of the second of the three decrees of *IG* i³ 98, which constitutes the second occasion on which Pythophanes was honored by Athens, see no. 2 above. This second decree called for the inscribing of the earlier decree by which Pythophanes received *proxenia* and *euergesia* and granted him the additional privilege of *asylia* for further services relating to trade (see no. 2 above). The contents of the third decree of *IG* i³ 98 are completely lost and do not permit speculation.

4. (D3). Phanosthenes (1) and Antiochides, ca. 410–407/6 (*IG* i³ 182)
    Proposer: unknown
    Services: unknown
    Goods: wooden oar spars
    Ethnicity: Greek (Andrian)
    Legal status: noncitizens, one *metic*
    Socioeconomic status: unknown
    Laudatory language: none
    Honors and privileges: *ateleia* (or *azemia*), commendation, *proxenia* and
        euergesia, inscribed stele

The two honorands of this decree imported oar spars to Athens. It is uncertain, however, whether they sold them at the going price or gave them as a gift to Athens. The decree uses the words for "import" and "brought" ([ἐσάγοντας], ἔγαγον, lines 6–8) to describe the importation of the oar spars.

In line 8, however, Lewis, the editor of *IG* i³, restores a word derived from δίδωμι to describe the honorands' "giving" the oar spars to the *trieropoioi,* Athenian officials who oversaw the construction of warships. It could be that this simply refers to the traders' handing over the oar spars to these officials after the Athenian state has purchased them, but one cannot rule out that the oar spars were given to Athens as a gift, free of charge. The reference to "the established price" (τὲν τεταγμέν[εν] τιμέ[ν]) in line 12 seems to concern a transaction involving not the honorands but rather the Athenian generals and the *trieropoioi.*

That the oar spars were given as a gift becomes somewhat more likely in light of the fact that the honorand is almost certainly the same Phanosthenes who was exiled from Andros after an oligarchic coup in 411. He then took up residence in Athens, where he eventually became a citizen and even served as a general in 407/6.[6] At the time he was honored for providing oar spars for Athens, therefore, he was not an Athenian citizen but most likely a *metic.* Not so clear, however, is his socioeconomic status. Until he became a citizen of Athens, he was prohibited from owning land. It is possible, then, that he may have been making a living as a professional trader in the manner of Andokides (And. 1.144). But one suspects that he was a man of means, since he was able to become a general in Athens within only a few years. Chances are that he was neither a professional trader nor poor and that he used whatever wealth and connections he was able to retain after his exile to undertake the shipment of oar spars in order to ingratiate himself with Athens and become naturalized. Reasonable as this speculation may be, it is still speculation, and without more explicit evidence, Phanosthenes' trade-related service and socioeconomic status will both be categorized as "unknown." Even more uncertain is the legal and socioeconomic status of Antiochides. He may have been a high-status Andrian compatriot of Phanosthenes, or he may have been a professional trader hired by Phanosthenes to help him provide the oar spars to Athens.

The date of this decree has also been a matter of some dispute. The letter-forms are compatible with a date between 420 and 405. Several scholars have narrowed the dates to a period between 424 and 414, arguing that the 1 percent tax mentioned in line 8 was superceded by the general 5 percent tax that was instituted by Athens in 414.[7] More recently, however, MacDonald has shown that the 5 percent tax, which was an import-export tax, need not have superceded the 1 percent tax, which was likely to have been a harbor tax. Eschewing arguments based on the 1 percent tax, MacDonald dates the decree to between 410 and 407 instead, on historical grounds, since it was only after the destruction of the Sicilian Expedition that Athens was in desperate need of imported timber in order to rebuild its fleet. Strengthening this argument is the fact that Phanosthenes took up residence in Athens only after 411.[8]

Among the honors that Athens conferred on Phanosthenes and Antiochides was an exemption from payment of the 1 percent tax. Although editors have had to restore either ἀζήμιος or ἀτελής in their entirety in line 7 to signify such an exemption, the context of the decree makes it almost certain that Athens granted some sort of tax exemption. It is also certain that the honorands received commendations and *euergesia*. Whether they also received *proxenia*, however, has been disputed. Walbank believes that the honorands did not receive *proxenia*, and he in general holds that *metics* in Athens could not be *proxenoi*, on the grounds that the duties of a *proxenos* required that he be resident in his home city (Walbank 313–24, no. 60; 1985: 110 and n. 15). But there appear to be exceptions to Walbank's rule, and it seems that *proxenia*, like other privileges, such as *enktesis*, was sometimes granted for its honorary value without requiring its recipient to carry out duties that necessitated residence in his home city (see nos. 14, 27, and 29). Moreover, in the vast majority of cases in which Athens granted *euergesia*, it granted *proxenia* as well (there are only two certain exceptions).[9] Thus, it is reasonable to accept Lewis' restoration of προχσένος in line 23 and to believe that Phanosthenes and Antiochides were honored with *proxenia*.

5. Phanosthenes (2), ca. 410–407/6 (*IG* i³ 182; Plato *Ion* 541c–d; Athenaios 506a; Xen. *Hell.* 1.5.18; And. 1.149)

    Proposer: unknown
    Services: unknown
    Goods: unknown
    Ethnicity: Greek (Andrian)
    Legal status: noncitizen, *metic*
    Socioeconomic status: unknown
    Laudatory language: N.A.
    Honors and privileges: citizenship

At the time of *IG* i³ 182, Phanosthenes was clearly not a citizen of Athens. Since, however, he served as a general in Athens in 407/6, he must have received Athenian citizenship at some time between 410 and 407/6. Although it is not certain that Athens granted citizenship to Phanosthenes because of services relating to trade, it is highly likely that this was the case, since he was a *metic* at the time and had already performed such services in the recent past, services for which Athens continued to have a pressing need. Yet even if something other than a service relating to trade was the immediate motivation for the Athenian grant of citizenship, Phanosthenes' previous service relating to trade surely must have contributed to his receiving this honor.

6. (D4). Archelaos, 407/6 (*IG* i³ 117)

    Proposer: Alkibiades
    Services: gift of imported goods
    Goods: ships' timber and oar spars
    Ethnicity: Greek (Macedonian)

Legal status: noncitizen, *xenos*
Socioeconomic status: foreign potentate
Laudatory language: *aner agathos*
Honors and privileges: commendation, *proxenia, euergesia,* inscribed
    stele

Scholars are unanimous in accepting the restoration of "Archelaos" in lines 24 and 32 and "Antigenes" in line 3. The restoration of "Alkibiades" in line 4 as the proposer of the decree has been accepted by all except for Walbank, who is skeptical.[10] With no compelling reason to doubt the majority view concerning these restorations, I will assume that in 407/6, Archelaos, the king of Macedon, received honors from Athens on the proposal of Alkibiades, who is to be identified with the famous general who had been repatriated to Athens at this time. Line 30 indicates that Archelaos received his honors because he "gave . . . ships' timber and oar spars ([ἔδοκεν . . . χσύλ]α καὶ κοπέας) to Athens. Since there is neither explicit mention of a price for these goods (as is the case in other decrees; see nos. 18 and 27) nor a significant lacuna wherein such a mention may once have existed, one can assume that Archelaos gave them as a gift, free of charge.[11] After Athens lost most of its naval fleet in the Sicilian Expedition, its only source of ships' timber was Macedon. Archelaos, who controlled the timber trade in Macedon, not only gave Athens timber but also allowed Athenian shipbuilders to come to Macedon to build ships (lines 26–28), in order to spare Athens the risk of shipping timber at a time when its navy was not strong enough to secure overseas trade.[12] Although there was some dispute in ancient times (as there is today) concerning the ethnicity of the ancient Macedonians, I will assume that they were Greek.

7. Satyros I and sons, ca. 395–389/8 (Isokr. 17.57; Dem. 20.30–33; *IG* ii² 212)

Proposer: unknown
Services: miscellaneous
Goods: grain
Ethnicity: non-Greek (Bosporan)
Legal status: noncitizens, *xenoi*
Socioeconomic status: foreign potentate
Laudatory language: N.A.
Honors and privileges: commendation, gold crown, *ateleia,* citizenship,
    inscribed stele

The kingdom of the Bosporos in the northern Black Sea consisted primarily of the Kerch Peninsula on the eastern side of the Crimea and the Taman Peninsula farther to the east, across the Cimmerian Bosporos. Although the kingdom had a mixed population of Greeks, Sindi, Scythians, Cimmerians, and Maiotians, the ruling Spartokid dynasty (438–110 B.C.E.) was probably of the

Odrysian tribe of Thracians and considered barbarian by Athenians (Hind 1994: 476–511, especially 491, 495–96, 506). Thus, the Bosporans of the Athenian honorary decrees treated in this study will be considered non-Greeks.

IG ii^2 212.20–24 states that Athens granted "the gifts" to Spartokos II and Pairisades I that it had granted to Satyros and Leukon, two earlier kings of the Bosporos. Since Demosthenes 20.30 states that Leukon and his sons received grants of citizenship and *ateleia* from Athens, it is certain that Athens awarded Satyros the same two honors. Hasebroek (1933: 113–14) argues that the Bosporan kings received *ateleia* only with regard to the performance of liturgies, since this is the sole exemption explicitly mentioned by Demosthenes, who also states, at 20.40, that should this exemption be rescinded, the Bosporan kings would be subject to an *antidosis,* an exchange of property, which is a procedure that occurs when there is a dispute about liturgical obligations. Contrary to Hasebroek, Hagemajer Allen (2003: 236) assumes that the Bosporan kings were exempt from taxes as well as liturgies. She goes even further to assert that goods from the Bosporos were, therefore, also exempt from Athenian import and harbor taxes, thus allowing traders to bring goods from the Bosporos into the Peiraieus tax-free. If this is true, then traders would have had an even greater incentive to ship goods from the Bosporos to Athens (see below), thereby further expanding Bosporan exports. If the Bosporan kings controlled grain production and export, then they might have profited greatly from their relationship with Athens. I am inclined to assume that since Demosthenes explicitly limits the *ateleia* granted to the Bosporan kings only with regard to the trierarchy and *eisphora* (20.18, 30–41), Hagemajer Allen is right to hold that it included exemption from taxes as well as liturgies. At the same time, though, Hagemajer Allen cites no evidence or precedents that compel me to believe that both the Bosporan kings and goods shipped by private traders from their kingdom were covered by the Athenian grant of *ateleia* to the kings. The *ateleia* granted to the Bosporan kings, therefore, included taxes as well as liturgies, but only for the kings themselves, not for goods from the Bosporos shipped to Athens by private traders.

It is very likely that Satyros received other honors and privileges in addition to citizenship and *ateleia. IG* ii^2 212.44–47 calls for an inscription of the decree on a stone stele to be placed next to the one for Satyros and Leukon, which indicates that the honorary decree for Satyros was also inscribed on a commemorative stele. Satyros probably also received a commendation and a gold crown from Athens. Commendations were more or less de rigueur in Athenian honorary decrees, and Spartokos II and Pairisades I received them as well. They also received gold crowns (every four years at the Great Panathenaia), as did their father, Leukon (*IG* ii^2 212.26–33). Although there is no specific mention that Satyros received a gold crown, this omission may be explained if his crown was awarded only on a onetime basis, rather than every four years as would be the case for his descendants (Tuplin 1982: 126). Moreover, since Leukon's sons were included in his grant of honors and privileges, the same was probably true for Satyros' sons: Leukon, Gorgippos, and Metrodoros (Osborne 1983: 43, T21).

The nature of Satyros' services is fairly clear. Demosthenes 20.31–32 states that Leukon received honors from Athens for his many services and proceeds to describe only those that relate to trade, which include allowing Athens-bound merchants priority of loading and exemption from export taxes in his ports and giving gifts of grain to Athens (see no. 9).[13] Satyros was probably the first Bosporan king to institute such benefactions for Athens and to have received honors in return, since *IG* ii² 212 mentions honors for Satyros but not for any of his predecessors.

The inception of Satyros' policy and the subsequent grant of honors from Athens must have occurred at some time between the late 390s and 389/8.[14] Before that time, Satyros and possibly his predecessor, Spartokos I (r. 438–433), the founder of the Spartokid dynasty, provided only sporadic trade-related services for Athens and were not officially honored. In Isokrates' *Trapezitikos* (17.57), which dates to between 395 and 390, the speaker tells an Athenian jury that both Satyros and the speaker's father "always consider you most important of the Greeks, and often in the past on account of a scarcity of grain, although they sent away the ships of other *emporoi* empty, they gave the export to you." Had Athens already officially granted honors for Satyros in return for his services, surely the speaker would have mentioned it, but he does not. In all likelihood, then, Spartokos initiated fixed trade-related services and received honors in return for them from Athens only sometime after Isokrates' speech and before his death, which is generally agreed to have taken place in 389/8.[15]

8. (D5). A Megarian, ca. 390–378/7 (*IG* ii² 81; Walbank 1990: no. 5=*SEG* 40.57)

> Proposer: unknown
> Services: unknown
> Goods: unknown
> Ethnicity: Greek (Megarian)
> Legal status: noncitizen
> Socioeconomic status: common professional trader
> Laudatory language: *aner agathos*
> Honors and privileges: *proxenia, asylia,* inscribed stele, *xenia* in the Prytaneion

It is difficult to pinpoint the date of no. 8. In the corpus, Köhler dated *IG* ii² 81 to before 378/7 on the basis of its orthography. Dinsmoor dated the decree to a precise 386/5 on the basis of Johnson's restoration of δ [ôναι τὸς ἀποδέκτα]ς (the *apodektai* shall give) in lines 10–11 in place of Köhler's δ[οῦναι τούσς τα-μία]ς (the treasurers shall give) and on the basis of his contention that the *apodektai* were responsible for dispersing funds for stelai only in that year.[16] But Dinsmoor's contention about the activities of the *apodektai* is not without its doubters, including Johnson himself, who believes that these officials functioned thus between 387 and ca. 384.[17] Henry provides a more cautious date, between 390 and 378/7, on the basis of the usage of "Acropolis" in line 10 instead of simply "polis," which is too short a word for the number of letter spaces requiring restoration (Henry 1982: 101). To be safe, Henry's range of dates will be adopted here.

The Megarian honorand was clearly a professional trader (Reed 2003: no. 49). According to Köhler's restoration, he and his sons received *asylia* for both themselves and their goods. There is no indication that the honorand was wealthy, however, and so it is probable that he was of modest means, like most professional traders. As a professional trader, it is hard to imagine that the services for which he was honored by Athens were anything other than ones relating to trade.

As published in *IG* ii[2,] the honorand received the title of *euergetes* ([ε]ὐ[εϱγέτην], line 2) without the usual accompanying title of *proxenos*. But the reliability of Köhler's restoration is dependent on his reading of an extant letter on the stone as an upsilon. Walbank has challenged this reading and maintains that only the lower part of a vertical in the left portion of the *stoichos* remains. In this view, the letter is more likely to have been a rho than an upsilon, and Walbank has restored the line to read, [π]ϱ[όξενον] (Walbank 1990: 438–39, no. 5). Since there are only two certain examples of Athens' granting *euergesia* without *proxenia*, whereas decrees containing grants of *proxenia* without *euergesia* are more abundant (see n. 9 above), Walbank's restoration of a grant of *proxenia* will be accepted here. The honorand could not have been an Athenian citizen, since he received *proxenia*.

9. Leukon and sons, 389/8 (Dem. 20.29–41; *IG* ii² 212)

> Proposer: unknown
> Services: gift of imported goods, miscellaneous
> Goods: grain
> Ethnicity: non-Greek (Bosporan)
> Legal status: noncitizens, *xenoi*
> Socioeconomic status: foreign potentate
> Laudatory language: N.A.
> Honors and privileges: commendation, gold crowns, *ateleia*, citizenship, inscribed stelai

Demosthenes 20.31–32 is explicit in stating that Leukon continued to allow merchants bound for Athens priority in loading and exemption from taxes in Bosporan ports, thereby continuing the trade-related services for Athens that had been initiated by his predecessor, Satyros. In addition, Demosthenes also refers to an occasion in 357 when Leukon gave Athens a gift of grain. Whether one believes that Athens then distributed a portion of the grain free of charge to its people and then sold the remainder for fifteen talents (as translated by C. H. Vince in the Loeb edition) or sold the entire amount of grain to its people at a discounted price that yielded fifteen talents, it is clear that Leukon had given Athens the grain free of charge, and Demosthenes implies that Leukon had performed this service on other occasions as well (Bresson 2000: 209–10).[18]

Athens granted Leukon the same honors and privileges it had granted Satyros (Dem. 20.31, 33; *IG* ii² 212.20–24). Leukon received Athenian citizenship and *ateleia* along with Satyros in the late 390s or early 380s (see no. 7). In addition, Athens, hoping to encourage Leukon to maintain his father's policy of providing services relating to trade, almost certainly reaffirmed his citizenship and other honors and privileges while at the same time extending them to his sons—Spartokos II, Pairisades I, and Apollonios—when Leukon became sole ruler of the Bosporos in 389/8.[19]

It is true that *IG* ii² 212.44–49 states that the stele of Spartokos II and Pairisades I shall be placed close to that of Satyros and Leukon, which might imply that there was one decree honoring both Satyros and Leukon that was inscribed on a single stele. It is more likely, however, that there were two separate decrees honoring Satyros and Leukon and that Leukon's was inscribed at a later time, on the stele that already bore the decree for Satyros (Tuplin 1982: 123). *IG* ii² 212.26–33, which contains provisions for crowning Spartokos II and Pairisades I, states that the crowning will be done "according to the decree of the People, which they decreed earlier for Leukon." Note that this decree concerns Leukon alone; there is no mention of Satyros. Although it was argued above (see no. 7) that Satyros also received a crown from Athens, the particular provisions for making and presenting the crowns for Leukon and then later for Spartokos II and Pairisades I were in accordance with a decree that was separate from the one concerning Satyros. Furthermore, Demosthenes 20.35 calls for a reading of "the decree concerning Leukon" and makes no mention of Satyros.

10. (D6). Achaians, ca. 350–325? (*IG* ii² 286+625; Walbank 1990: no. 11)

> Proposer: unknown
> Services: unknown
> Goods: unknown
> Ethnicity: Greek (Achaians)
> Legal status: noncitizens
> Socioeconomic status: common professional traders
> Laudatory language: none
> Honors and privileges: *proxenia, euergesia, ateleia, asylia,* inscribed stele

Kirchner (*IG* ii²), Walbank (1990: 442, no. 11), and Lambert (3.53) all date this inscription to the third quarter of the fourth century on the basis of its letterforms. Walbank also associated *IG* ii^2 286 with *IG* ii^2 625, which is a small fragment that contains little information except that the honorands may have been Achaians, either Peloponnesian or Phthiotic (see Mattingly 1966: 214). Walbank suggests that they might even have been descendants of the honorands of *IG* i^3 174 (no. 1), who were also Achaians. Since the unknown honorands of *IG* ii^2 286 received *asylia* for both themselves and their goods (lines 6–7), it is certain that they were professional traders and likely that Athens honored them for services relating to trade. In the absence of any further evidence, I assume that they were of modest means, like most professional traders.

The decree specifies that the *ateleia* is "from [all things]," which is unprecedented and depends on restoration. But Henry, who has authored a study of the formulae used in Athenian honorary decrees, accepts the restoration (Henry 1983: 245–46). This *ateleia* probably applied not to taxes both on themselves and on their goods (as the *asylia* did) but rather to all those, such as import and export taxes, that could be levied on their goods (Lambert 2006: 136 n. 99). The explicit grant of *asylia* in an Athenian decree is also unusual (Henry 1983: 225 n. 40). It has been suggested that the decree is actually that of a foreign state in honor of an Athenian (see Lambert 2006: 136 n. 100), but the fact that the inscription was found on the Acropolis is reason enough to believe that this is an Athenian decree. Also problematic, however, is the possible restoration of a grant of *euergesia* and *proxenia* in lines 2–3, chiefly because of the word order, which is reversed from the usual practice. It is likely, nonetheless, that Athens would grant these titles along with *ateleia* and *asylia*, and so these restorations will be accepted here.[20] The grant of *proxenia* makes it certain that the honorands were not Athenian citizens. The existence of *IG* ii^2 286 is evidence that Athens also made provisions for the inscribing of the honorary decree on a stone stele.

11. (D7). Orontes, 349/8? (*IG* ii^2 207; Osborne 1981b: 53–54; *SEG* 41.43; Osborne D12; Lambert 3.2)

Proposer: Polykrates, son of Polykrates
Services: miscellaneous
Goods: grain
Ethnicity: non-Greek (Persian)
Legal status: noncitizen, *xenos*
Socioeconomic status: foreign potentate
Laudatory language: *aner agathos*
Honors and privileges: commendation, gold crown, citizenship, inscribed stele

IG ii^2 207 presents several difficulties to both epigraphers and historians. As published, the inscription consists of four fragments. Fragments (b), (c), and (d) are currently in the Epigraphic Museum in Athens and clearly belong to the same inscription. Fragment (a) has unfortunately disappeared, and its text is known only from facsimiles made by Pittakys, one published (Pittakys 1835: 500–501) and the other only recently discovered by Lambert (2006: 124 and 145, fig. 3). The texts of Osborne (1981b: 53–54, D12) and Lambert (3.2) are based directly on these facsimiles of Pittakys, who is the only editor to have seen the stone itself. All other editions are based on the text of Rangabe (1855: no. 397), who in turn based his text on the facsimiles of Pittakys. For this study, I have chosen to use Osborne's text rather than Lambert's, because although the differences between their readings are minor (with the exception of the archon's name; see below), Osborne includes restorations that I find to be compelling and useful for further analysis.

Fragment (a) contains an honorary decree for Orontes, most likely the Persian satrap of Mysia who is best known for his part in the Great Satrap Revolt of 362/1.[21] On the basis of a report by Athenian ambassadors, the People of Athens decreed a commendation, citizenship, and a gold crown of one thousand drachmas for Orontes. The fragment ends with mention of an alliance between Athens and Orontes, a *symbola* treaty taken by many to be concerned with matters of trade, and some judicial arrangements.[22] Fragments (b)+(c)+(d) are not entirely coherent in their damaged state. There are references to ships, friends and allies, Orontes, and a *symbola*, which is probably identical to the one referred to in fragment (a) (see Lambert 2006: 126). There is also a statement that "money for the receipt of the grain" is to come "from the *Stratiotic* funds." Some further references mention a military expedition, a receipt of grain, treasurers, and "the money to Orontes and ships." Finally, the People of Athens commend two groups of ambassadors and grant to them crowns of olive.

The orthodox view, originally put forth by Kirchner in *IG* ii², is to associate fragment (a) with (b)+(c)+(d) as parts of one decree from the year 349/8.[23] Osborne's attempt to challenge this orthodoxy with the argument that the fragments represent two decrees from 364/3 has lost much of its force on account of the recent treatment by Lambert, whose identification of the archon as Kallimachos on the basis of the second, newly discovered facsimile of Pittakys supports the orthodox view, which I, therefore, also adopt for this study.[24] On this view, the decree honors Orontes in fragment (a) for having agreed to sell grain to the Athenian army on campaign in Asia Minor, and the details of the agreement are outlined in fragments (b)+(c)+(d). It is clear that Orontes did not give the grain to the Athenian army as a gift, free of charge, and there is no indication that he sold it for a reduced price. At the same time, however, one cannot categorize his service as a simple importation of goods, since the grain was not shipped to Athens. Therefore, I will categorize Orontes' trade-related service as a miscellaneous one.

Concerning the honors and privileges that Athens granted to Orontes, the existence of *IG* ii² 207 is evidence that in addition to a commendation, gold crown, and citizenship, Orontes also received the honor of having his honorary decree inscribed on a stone stele. According to the texts of both Osborne and Lambert, who follow Pittakys' facsimiles of fragment (a), the proposer of the decree is the otherwise unknown Polykrates, son of Polykrates, and not the son of Polyeuktos (*PA* 12027) as in the corpus.

12. (D8). Spartokos II, Pairisades I, and Apollonios, 347/6 (*IG* ii² 212)

> Proposer: Androtion, son of Andron
> Services: miscellaneous
> Goods: grain
> Ethnicity: non-Greek (Bosporan)
> Legal status: noncitizens, *xenoi*
> Socioeconomic status: foreign potentates
> Laudatory language: *aner agathos, arete, eunoia*
> Honors and privileges: commendation, citizenship, *ateleia*, gold crowns
> > on the present occasion (Spartokos II, Pairisades I, and Apollonios),
> > gold crowns every four years henceforth (Spartokos II and
> > Pairisades I only), inscribed stele, use of Athenian *hyperesiai*

Spartokos II, Pairisades I, and Apollonios had acquired Athenian citizenship and *ateleia* along with their father, Leukon, in 389/8 (see no. 9). On their accession to joint rule of the Bosporos in 347/6, Athens reaffirmed the citizenship of Spartokos II and Pairisades I in *IG* ii² 212 (the extant archon formula of which dates it to the same year), granting to them the same "gifts" that it had granted Leukon and Satyros (lines 22–26). Like Leukon, they would receive gold crowns every four years at the Great Panathenaia (lines 26–33; note the present tense of the verb [ποιε]ῖσθαι, "make"). Athens granted Apollonios, who did not share rule with his brothers, just one gold crown on this occasion, by a rider to the decree (lines 655–68). Concerning the *hyperesiai*, see the discussion in chapter 8. The decree instructs that the inscribed stele be placed next to that of Satyros and Leukon. Demosthenes tells us that there were two stelai for Leukon, one in the Peiraieus and one at Hieron in the Bosporos (20.36). *IG* ii² 212 was found in the Peiraieus.

Since lines 20–22 state that the gifts of Spartokos II and Pairisades I were "the same ones which Satyros and Leukon gave," it is certain that they continued their predecessors' policy of allowing merchants bound for Athens priority of loading and exemption from export taxes in their ports. Note also that Spartokos II and Pairisades I also seem to have lent an unspecified sum of money to Athens (lines 53–59) for unknown purposes.

Two envoys of the Bosporan kings also received honors from Athens for their hospitality to Athenian ambassadors in the Bosporos, who were probably there to get assurances that the trading privileges provided by Satyros and Leukon would continue under Spartokos II and Pairisades I (lines 49–53).

Athens granted the Bosporan envoys commendations and invited them to hospitality in the Prytaneion.

13. (D9). Unknown honorands, ca. 340 (*IG* ii² 543; Lambert 3.73)

Proposer: unknown
Services: securing shipments of goods
Goods: unknown
Ethnicity: Greek
Legal status: noncitizens, *xenoi*
Socioeconomic status: unknown
Laudatory language: *philotimia*
Honors and privileges: commendation, gold crown, inscribed stele

Although *IG* ii² 543 is not well preserved, Lambert's new edition (3.73) provides sufficient evidence for us to be certain that it is an honorary decree for trade-related services. By this decree, Athens honored a group of men for bringing something into the *emporion* ([ἤγ]αγον εἰς τὸ ἐνπ [όριον]). The extant portions of this fragmentary decree also refer to men who had passed a decree that somehow concerned Moirokles (lines 5–6), men who had taken something away (line 7), and men who had sailed (line 13). That the decree concerns trade is indicated by the mention of the name *Moirokles*, which was uncommon in Athens (Lambert 2006: 112 n. 60) and probably, therefore, refers to the man by the same name who was responsible for a decree that made it illegal for anyone to harm traders, which was to be enforced by Athens and its allies ([Dem.] 58.53).

Lambert believes that the honorands were the citizens of an allied city that had performed the service of carrying out Moirokles' decree by protecting traders on their way to Athens from pirates. Athens certainly enforced Moirokles' decree by punishing those, such as the people of Melos, who aided pirates in harming traders ([Dem.] 58.56), so it is likely that it would also encourage and reward those who aided traders against pirates. Such men could be the citizens of an entire city (as the negative example of Melos attests), and Lambert believes that the men who had passed a decree, referred to in lines 5–6, are the honorands of this honorary decree, an entire city rather than a private individual or group.

Although Lambert's reconstruction is somewhat speculative, it is persuasive and will be adopted here. Thus, the honorands must be Greeks and noncitizen *xenoi*, since they are to be understood as citizens of an allied city of Athens, the remnants of its Second Athenian League. Their services fall under the category of "securing shipments of goods." I also accept Lambert's date of ca. 340 for the decree, since its reference to Moirokles makes sense in the immediate context of [Demosthenes] 58, which dates to that time as well (Hansen 1976: 137–38), and since honorary decrees for whole cities are otherwise unattested in Athens from the Battle of Chaironeia in 338 and the Lamian War in 323/2.

14. (D10). Philomelos, ca. 340–300 (*IG* ii² 423)

>   Proposer: unknown
>   Services: miscellaneous
>   Goods: grain
>   Ethnicity: unknown
>   Legal status: unknown
>   Socioeconomic status: unknown
>   Laudatory language: [*eunous*], *philotimia, aner agathos, chresimos*
>   Honors and privileges: inscribed stele

The decree that honors Philomelos is dated to ca. 340–300 on the basis of its orthography and the presence of the clause of "hortatory intention."[25] The precise nature of the honorand's services and even whether they had some relation to trade is uncertain, since the references to a shortage of grain were almost completely restored by Kirchner in *IG* ii² Although such a restoration is reasonable and is accepted here, the restoration of [προεδάνεισ?]ε in line 14 is more doubtful, since there are no other examples of anyone *lending* money to Athens to purchase grain.[26] Also uncertain is the legal status and ethnicity of the honorand, since no telling honors or ethnic are preserved on the stone. *Philomelos* is a Greek name, but there are many examples of non-Greeks who had Greek names at this time. It is certain, however, that Athens provided Philomelos with at least the honor of inscribing his honorary decree on a stone stele, as the existence of *IG* ii² 423 attests.

15. (D11). Ph—— of Cyprian Salamis, ca. 337 (*IG* ii² 283)

>   Proposer: unknown
>   Services: sale of imported goods at a reduced price
>   Goods: grain (possibly also fish)
>   Ethnicity: Greek (Cyprian Salaminian)
>   Legal status: noncitizen, *xenos*
>   Socioeconomic status: wealthy professional trader
>   Laudatory language: *chresimos, eunoia*
>   Honors and privileges: commendation, gold crown, inscribed stele

This decree certainly predates 336/5, as stated in *IG* ii² and it is possible to pinpoint the date further.[27] Walbank (2002: 63) argues for a date between 338/7 and 336/5 for two reasons. The decree states in lines 7–9 that the honorand paid a ransom at his own expense to release Athenian captives held in Sicily, which may be connected to the campaigns of Timoleon in the 340s. If that is the case, then his donation of a talent of silver to Athens for its defense (lines 9–10) is likely to be associated with Athenian preparations before the Battle of

Chaironeia in 338. Since the battle also disrupted the food supply of Athens, the honorand's trade-related services provide another reason to believe that this decree was passed in ca. 337 (see also Lambert 2002: 77–78).

The trade-related services of the honorand would certainly have helped to alleviate Athens' problems in food supply. They included importing grain ([ἐσιτ]ήγησεν, line 2) into Athens from Egypt and probably also selling it at a price arbitrarily reduced (εὐωνοτέρων) from the going rate. However, it is also possible that the honorand imported and sold fish at a reduced price. Line 3 contains a lacuna that is followed by the letters ΥΛΛΩΝ. The word may be either ὗλλος, which refers to a fish that was common to the waters of Egypt (*LSJ⁹*), or, more likely, μύλλος, a fish from the Black Sea commonly sold salted (*LSJ⁹*), since Walbank (2002: 63) has examined the stone and detected traces of a letter that he believes is a mu (M) before the upsilon. On the other hand, Lambert, who has also examined the stone, believes that the obliqueness of the right diagonal that remains of the letter requires it to be an alpha (A) rather than a mu (Lambert 2002: 47). On this basis, he suggests a restoration of [ν]αύλλων, meaning "freight charges" or "fares," and believes that the decree is pointing to the honorand's reduction in the price of transporting either goods (most likely grain) or people (possibly the ransomed Athenian captives). Given the conflicting reports of the two highly esteemed epigraphers, it is best simply to conclude no more than that the honorand imported grain into Athens and probably also sold it at a reduced price.

More certain, however, is that the honorand was a professional trader, since the word, [ἐσιτ]ήγησεν (brought), indicates that he personally sailed with his goods into Athens (Reed 2003: 126, no. 50). He was also quite wealthy, to judge from his sale of goods at a reduced price, payment of a ransom to release Athenians held captive in Sicily, and gift of a talent of silver for the defense of Athens (Reed 2003: 126, no. 50). In all likelihood, the honorand was Greek. The extant letters of the honorand's name, "Ph——," suggest a Greek name. Although Lambert (2002: 76) is right to point out that a Greek name is not necessarily an indication of a person's ethnicity, the fact that the honorand came from Salamis on Cyprus is good reason to believe that he was Greek, since the city was a Greek settlement (supposedly founded by the Greek hero Teucer) and, despite periods of Phoenician control, was ruled by Euagoras (possibly a member of the Teucrid royal family) and his descendants for much of the fourth century (Karageorghis 1969a: 65; 1969b: 20–21; 1982: 115, 163–64). Lambert's argument (2002: 76 and n. 8) that many tombstones in Attika for Cypriots from Kition are bilingual (Greek-Phoenician) is not relevant, since Kition was not a Greek foundation and continued to be dominated by Phoenicians in the Classical period (Karageorghis 1969: 65; Karageorghis 1982: 117, 162; *CAH²* 3.3.59). Lambert is on firmer ground, however, in his assertion that the honorand was probably not a *metic*, since line 4 seems to indicate that he was honored particularly for preferring to bring his goods to Athens rather than elsewhere (2002: 75–76 and n. 7). Had the honorand been a *metic* rather than simply a *xenos*, he would have been obligated by Athenian law not to ship grain anywhere else but Athens.[28]

The material from which the honorand's crown was to be made is uncertain. Although Köhler supplied the word θαλλοῦ (meaning "of olive") in the lacuna in line 16, it is equally possible that the word was χρυσοῦ (meaning "of gold") or, even more likely, χρυσῶι (meaning "gold," modifying στεφάνωι [crown]), the choice of Lambert (2002: 75). Athens commonly awarded olive crowns to citizens and to foreign ambassadors (Henry 1983: 38–40). Most noncitizens who performed such generous services as those of the honorand of *IG* ii[2] 283, however, received gold crowns, and this is likely to have been the case here as well (see, e.g., nos. 7, 9, 10, 11, 14, 18, 27, 29, 31, and 35). The honorand also received a commendation and a stone stele inscribed with his honorary decree, as the existence of *IG* ii[2] 283 attests.

16. Chairephilos and sons, ca. 337–330 (Dein. 1.43; Hyperid. frags. 63–64 [Kenyon]; Athenaios 3.119f– 120a)

Proposer: Demosthenes, son of Demosthenes, of Paiania
Services: simple importation of goods
Goods: fish
Ethnicity: unknown
Legal status: noncitizens
Socioeconomic status: wealthy professional trader
Laudatory language: N.A.
Honors and privileges: citizenship

The date of Chairephilos' naturalization is uncertain. It must, of course, have been no later than 323, the date of Deinarchos' speech *Against Demosthenes*, which attests to Chairephilos' naturalization on the proposal of the famous orator and statesman Demosthenes, supposedly in return for a bribe (1.43). Schäfer dated Chairephilos' naturalization to the early 320s on the assumption that Chairephilos must have made contributions that aided Athens during the grain shortages of those years (Schäfer iii[2] 296). Davies, however, places the date no later than 330 on two grounds.[29] First, Chairephilos' sons were liturgically active in the 320s, which means that Chairephilos was likely dead by that time and that his sons were then in control of their own property long enough to perform their numerous liturgies. Second, the comic poet Antiphanes, who died ca. 333–330, alludes to the relations that Chairephilos' sons had with the *hetaira* Pythionike. Worthington (2000: 297–98) has rightly dismissed Davies' second argument, since Chairephilos' sons need not have been citizens while they were involved with Pythionike. But Davies' argument concerning the liturgical activity of Chairephilos' sons is compelling, as is Schäfer's argument that Chairephilos' naturalization should be connected with a time of food shortage in Athens. Since food shortages are known to have occurred in Athens in 338/7, 335/4, and 330/29 (Garnsey 1988: 154–62), Chairephilos could have been naturalized in or shortly following any of these years down to 330.

The only explicit statement concerning the services for which Athens granted citizenship to Chairephilos comes from Athenaios (3.119f–120a). He refers to Chairephilos as a "salted fish seller"(τοῦ ταριχοπώλου) and quotes from the *Epidauros* by the comic poet Alexis (6.218 Edmonds), which states that Chairephilos became a citizen of Athens because he "imported salted fish" (εἰσήγαγεν τάριχος). Reed has raised questions regarding whether Chairephilos was a retail seller of salted fish in Athens or a trader who shipped salted fish to Athens (Reed 2003: 121–22, no. 39). But words rooted in the verb ἄγω are normally used in Athenian honorary decrees to denote the act of personally transporting goods for trade (see nos. 13, 14, 23, 25, 26, 27, and 33). Moreover, it is hard to believe that Athens would honor a retail seller at all, let alone with the highest honor of all, citizenship, since retailers did not increase the supply of goods available to Athenians but were merely middlemen between overseas traders and Athenian consumers. If Chairephilos had sold goods to Athens at a reduced price or given them as a gift, then he might have been able to obtain honors even as a retailer. But there is no indication that he did so. The only service relating to trade for which he could reasonably be honored was importing goods into Athens and selling them at the going rate. It should also be noted that it is the later source, Athenaios, who refers to Chairephilos as a *tarichopolos*, or "salted fish seller" (i.e., a retailer), while the earlier source, Alexis, says only that Chairephilos imported salted fish into Athens. Hence, the most likely conclusion is that Chairephilos was a professional trader who was honored by Athens at least in part for a simple importation of goods.

But although there are many other cases in which Athens honored men for importing goods, in only one other case did the goods possibly include fish (*IG* ii² 283), and in no case did Athens grant honors as great as citizenship. It is true that salted fish from the Black Sea region, which had abundant fisheries and deposits of salt, were in high demand in Athens (Michell 1957: 286–89). Nevertheless, the vast majority of those who were naturalized by Athens performed exceptional services that either required large expenditures of money or aided Athens in political or military crises (see Osborne). Thus, it is likely that importing salted fish was only one of the services for which Chairephilos received citizenship from Athens. Since his sons were said to have patronized an expensive *hetaira* and were members of the trierarchic class in Athens, Chairephilos was almost certainly wealthy and in a position to do a variety of services for Athens, including making direct monetary contributions for the city's needs.[30]

It is impossible to be certain about either Chairephilos' ethnicity or his legal status before his naturalization. His name is Greek, but that is not decisive evidence. Chairephilos certainly could not have been an Athenian citizen before his naturalization, but since Athenaios' reference to him as a retailer (which would require residence in Athens) was probably inaccurate, there is no telling whether he was a *metic* or a *xenos*.

17. (D12). Sopatros, ca. 337–325 (Camp 1974: 314–24, no. 3; V-T A160)

> Proposer: Lykourgos, son of Lykophron, of Boutadai
> Services: simple importation of goods
> Goods: grain
> Ethnicity: Greek (Akragan)
> Legal status: noncitizen
> Socioeconomic status: common professional trader
> Laudatory language: *eunoia*
> Honors and privileges: commendation, *proxenia, euergesia,* inscribed
> stele, *xenia* in the Prytaneion, seat at the Dionysia

Since the archon formula is lost from this otherwise well-preserved decree honoring Sopatros of Akragas, it is possible to provide only a range of dates for it on the basis of its letterforms and likely historical context. The inscription's letterforms conform to Tracy's category of "litterae volgares saec. IV," which characterize Athenian inscriptions between ca. 345 and 320 (Tracy 1995: 76–81; see also 33–34 and 107). As a rule, I will assume that all inscribed decrees without extant archon formulas but containing such letterforms and concerning the grain trade date to ca. 337–320, since the first known grain shortage in Athens after 345 took place in 338/7 as a result of the Battle of Chaironeia.[31] In the case of the decree honoring Sopatros, this *terminus post quem* is confirmed by its proposer, the famous statesman Lykourgos, son of Lykophron of Boutadai, who does not appear to have been active before 338/7. Camp narrows the date to ca. 331–324, years that encompass the period of the worst grain shortages in Athens, but since Athens also suffered shortages in 338/7 and as a result of Alexander's invasion of Greece in 335/4, it is best to date the occasion of Sopatros' honors no more narrowly than to between ca. 337 and 325, the date of Lykourgos' death.

Athens honored Sopatros for conveying grain to the city ('Αθήναζε κομί-ζηται σῖτ[ο]ς, lines 9–11). There is no mention of a gift or sale of the grain at a reduced price, and it is clear that Sopatros brought grain to Athens personally, since he is honored with *xenia* in the Prytaneion and a seat at the Great Dionysia, which would require his presence in Athens to enjoy.[32] Thus, it is likely that Sopatros was a common professional trader who simply imported grain into Athens and sold it at the going rate during a time of great need in Athens. Though Sopatros' honors required him to be in Athens in order to enjoy them, they did not require an extended residence there. Hence, it is uncertain whether Sopatros was a *metic* or a *xenos*. On the other hand, the grant of *proxenia* and the reference to his ethnic make it certain that he was not an Athenian citizen.

18. (D13). Pandios, ca. 337–320? (Schweigert 1940: 332–33, no. 39; V-T A149)

Proposer: unknown
Services: simple importation of goods
Goods: grain
Ethnicity: Greek (Herakleote)
Legal status: noncitizen
Socioeconomic status: common professional trader
Laudatory language: [*eunous*], *eunoia*, [*philotimia*]
Honors and privileges: commendation, inscribed stele

Schweigert's restoration of the words *eunous* and *philotimia* in this inscription are likely, but his restoration of *arete* is not (V-T A149, pp. 89, 274). The phrase διατελεῖ εὔνους ὢν is common before τῶι δήμωι and matches the number of letter spaces in the lacuna of line 3 (V-T p. 201). The word [εὔν]οιαν is, therefore, an obvious restoration in line 13, since the honorific language of the commendation/crowning formulae tends to reflect that of the motivation clause (V-T p. 274). On the other hand, Schweigert's restoration of *arete* in lines 17–18 ([ἀρετῆς ἕνεκεν καὶ φ]ι[λοτιμίας]) is unlikely for a couple reasons. First, the coupling of *arete* and *philotimia* has no parallel in honorary decrees for noncitizens (V-T p. 221). Second, the language of the commendation/crowning clause should reflect that of the motivation clause (V-T p. 274). Thus, a better restoration of lines 17–18 is [εὐνοίας ἕνεκα καὶ φ]ι[λοτιμίας].

Schweigert's date for this decree in ca. 330 is a bit too narrow, since its letterforms and probable connection to the grain shortages in Athens could place it at any time between ca. 337 and 320 (see commentary on no. 17 and Lambert 2007: 105 n. 34). It is almost certain that the honorand, Pandios of Herakleia (a Greek settlement on the Black Sea), was a professional trader, since lines 7–8 of the decree state that he "brought grai[n to the *emporion* of A]thens," employing a word derived from *ago* (σιτηγῶ[ν εἰς τὸ ἐμπόριον τὸ Ἀ]θηναίων, Reed 2003: 127, no. 56), which indicates that he transported the grain personally. But since there is no indication that he either gave the grain as a gift, free of charge, or sold it at a reduced price from the going rate, it is assumed here that one of the services for which he was honored was a simple importation of goods and that Pandios himself was of modest means, like most professional traders. As restored by Schweigert, the decree also makes a reference to "the sending/escort of grain" ([τῆς τοῦ σίτου πομπ]ῆς, l. 9). Since the passage is almost entirely restored and since there is a significant lacuna after it, it is best not to attempt to analyze the significance of this line.

Although such interpretation is dependent in part on Schweigert's restoration, it is likely that Pandios was a Herakleote, since there does seem to have been extensive trade between Athens and Herakleia in the fourth century (see nos. 18 and 21 above). Unfortunately, besides the commendation, there is little certainty concerning the honors that Pandios received or the laudatory language employed by Athens in the decree, since it has been largely restored by Schweigert. There is also no indication whether he was a *metic* or a *xenos*, but the likely mention of an ethnic rules out his being an Athenian citizen. The existence of the inscription also makes it certain that Athens made provisions for inscribing Pandios' honorary decree on a stone stele.

19. (D14). Potamon and unknown honorand, ca. 337–320? (*IG* ii² 409; Wilhelm 1942: 150–52; Lambert 3.82)

> Proposer: unknown
> Services: simple importation of goods
> Goods: grain
> Ethnicity: Greeks (Milesians)
> Legal status: unknown
> Socioeconomic status: common professional traders
> Laudatory language: None
> Honors and privileges: commendation (restored), inscribed stele

This fragmentary decree can be dated only by its letterforms and likely connection to the grain shortages of 337–320 (see commentary on no. 17 and Lambert 2007: 115). According to the decree, "grain [is] brought" (ὑπ᾽ αὐτῶν σῖ]τος ἐξάγετα[ι], lines 8–9) from abroad to Athens by two honorands, one of whom was named Potamon. The odds are that they were professional traders and also of modest means, since there is no indication that they gave their grain as a gift, free of charge, or sold it at a reduced price from the going rate (Reed 2003: 128, nos. 57 and 58). It is likely that the honorands were Milesians, but Wilhelm's restorations (1942: 150–52), which indicate that the source of their grain was Sinope and which contain provisions for a trade agreement between that city and Athens, are too speculative to serve as the basis for any analysis. Equally speculative are Wilhelm's restorations of the words *eunous* and *aner agathos*, which will not be included in this study, though they meet with the approval of Veligianni-Terzi (V-T A151). The only certain honor or privilege decreed by Athens for these honorands is an inscribed stele, attested by the existence of *IG* ii² 409. A commendation is highly likely but must be fully restored. Other than that, little is known about the honorands and their services.

20. (D15). ——das from Kos, ca. 334/3–321 (*IG* ii² 416[b]; Tracy 1995: 123, 127–28)

> Proposer: unknown
> Services: securing shipments of goods
> Goods: grain
> Ethnicity: Greek (Koan)
> Legal status: noncitizen, *xenos*
> Socioeconomic status: unknown

Laudatory language: *eunoia*
Honors and privileges: inscribed stele

IG ii² 416 is comprised of two nonjoining fragments. Tracy has shown, how-ever, that the two fragments cannot be from the same inscription.³³ Given the relevance of *IG* ii² 416(b) to the grain shortages of 337–320, the letterforms of the inscription (which Tracy identifies with a stonecutter who was active be-tween 334/3 and 314/3), and the mention of the Athenian cleruchy on Samos (which was ejected in 321), the decree must date to ca. 334/3–321. The honor-and secured shipments of grain to the Athenian cleruchs on Samos, but the manner in which this service was accomplished is not specified in the extant inscription. It simply states that he "takes [care] of both the [*emporoi* and] the *naukleroi* in order that grain sail in as pl[entifully as possible] for the People of [Athens] and no one [of the] Athenians either [is hindered] by [anyone un-justly or] forced into port" (τῶν τε [ἐμπόρων κα]ὶ τῶν ναυκλήρων ἐπι[με-λούμενο]ν ὅπως ἂν σῖτος ὡς ἀφ[θονωτάτως] εἰσπλεῖ τῶι δήμωι τ[ῶι Ἀθηναίω]ν καὶ μηδεὶς μήτε κ[ωλύηται τῶν] Ἀθηναίων μηδ' ὑφ' ἑνὸ[ς ἀδίκως μη]δὲ κατάγηται, lines 7–12).

Because there is no indication of how the honorand helped the *emporoi* and *naukleroi* to ship their grain, it is impossible to determine his socioeco-nomic status. Reed (2003: 94–95, no. 8) puts the honorand of *IG* ii² 416(b) in his category of "very unlikely candidates" to be either *emporoi* or *naukleroi*. Ac-cording to Reed, in the inscriptions concerning the men in this category, "it is either stated or implied that the recipients looked after Athenian interests or merchants from Athens in their own states." "If," he asks, "they thus were on hand in their cities to help merchants arriving in the sailing season, how could they themselves be at sea?" But Samos, where the honorand of *IG* ii² 416(b) performed his service, was clearly not his home city, since the decree states that he was from Kos. Because he was a Koan who performed his service at Samos, it is certain that the honorand was not an Athenian citizen, and it is also unlikely that he was a *metic* who resided in Athens. Although no honors are listed in the extant portions of the inscription, the existence of *IG* ii² 416(b) is evidence that Athens at least provided the honorand with a stone stele in-scribed with his honorary decree.

21. (D16). Mnemon and —ias, 333/2 (*IG* ii² 408; Lambert 3.81)

Proposer: unknown
Services: sale of imported goods at a reduced price
Goods: grain
Ethnicity: Greek (Herakleotes)
Legal status: noncitizens
Socioeconomic status: wealthy professional traders
Laudatory language: [*eunous*], [*eunoia*]
Honors and privileges: commendation, gold crowns, inscribed stele

The restorations of the words *eunous* and *eunoia* in this inscription are fairly secure (V-T A150, pp. 89–90). It is common for the word *eunoia* to follow the word [ἐν]δείκνυντα[ι]; thus, its restoration in line 16 is almost certain (V-T p. 201). The *eunoia* of the commendation/crowning clause of line 20 would be expected after the *eunoia* in the motivation clause of line 16 (V-T p. 274). Likewise, then, one would also expect [εὔνοι] in the lacuna in line 10, as suggested by Wilhelm (1942: 152–53).

The date of *IG* ii² 408 can be pinpointed to 333/2 on the basis of the name of the president of the *proedroi*, reasonably restored in line 4, which also appears in *IG* ii² 337, whose archon formula is well preserved (Tracy 1995: 34 n. 20). There are further epigraphic and historical reasons for a date around this time as well.[34] References to the type of Assembly, which appears in line 3, do not predate 335/4 in Athenian decrees. Diotimos, who is referred to in lines 7–10, was general in 335/4 and was honored in the following year for campaigning against pirates.[35] Kirchner restored the name of the proposer in *IG* ii² as that of Brachyllos, son of Bathyllos (the proposer of *IG* ii² 223C, a decree honoring the Council in 343/2). But since -*los* is a common ending for Greek names, I will not consider the restoration in this study (see also Lambert 2007: 114).

The year 335/4 was a difficult one for Athens in terms of its grain supply. Not only were pirates a problem, but Alexander's campaign in Greece and his destruction of Thebes also seem to have had negative consequences for Athens' grain imports.[36] The honorands of *IG* ii² 408 received honors and privileges for selling wheat and barley at nine and five drachmas per *medimnos*, respectively. Even though a form of the word δίδωμι ([παραδεδω]κέναι, "give") is used in line 11 to describe this act, the subsequent listing of prices indicates that the honorands did not "give" grain as a gift, free of charge, but sold it to the Athenians. The prices were above normal for both these grains and yet Athens still thought the deed worthy of honor. Thus, the honorands' sale prices must have been a reduction from currently inflated prices. It is likely that this deed took place in 335/4 but was officially honored by Athens only on the recommendation of Diotimos and his subordinate Dionysodoros in 333/2. The existence of *IG* ii² 408 is evidence that in addition to a commendation and gold crowns, Athens provided the honor of inscribing the honorary decree on a stone stele for its two benefactors.

The two honorands were certainly professional traders (Reed 2003: 127, nos. 53 and 54). The decree employs a form of the word ἄγω (ἦγεν) in line 13, indicating that one of the honorands personally "brought" grain into Athens. It is probable that they were wealthy, since they gave up potential profits by selling their grain at reduced prices. Being from Herakleia, which was a Greek settlement on the southern coast of the Black Sea, they were most likely Greek. The decree's mention of their ethnic makes it certain that the honorands were not Athenian citizens, but there is nothing to indicate whether they were *metics* or *xenoi*.

Graham Oliver has raised the intriguing possibility that ——ias (preceded by a lacuna of four letter spaces) of Herakleia is identical or related to the Pyr—— (followed by 8–15 letter spaces, which may include a patronymic, in a nonstoichedon inscription) of Herakleia of *IG* ii² 479.[37] The latter received the honor of a crown of olive from Athens for having somehow aided Demetrios Poliorketes with an operation involving Mounychia in the Peiraieus ca. 307/6 and for contributing from his private funds on two occasions (three talents and four thousand drachmas, respectively) for a *sitonia*, a public fund for the purchase of grain, probably in 305/4. Although possible, the identification seems unlikely, since there is no evidence that the honorand of *IG* ii² 479 was a professional trader, and he seems to have been much more highly placed than even the wealthiest of professional traders. More damaging to this hypothesis is the report by Lambert (2007: 114) that there are faint traces of an alpha and a lambda, thus yielding the very common name *Kallias,* as opposed to *Pyrrias.*

22. Harpalos, ca. 333–324 (Athenaios 13.586d and 13.596b; Diod. 17.108.6)

Proposer: unknown
Services: gift of imported goods
Goods: grain
Ethnicity: Greek (Macedonian)
Legal status: noncitizen, *xenos*
Socioeconomic status: foreign potentate
Laudatory language: N.A.
Honors and privileges: citizenship

A fragment from a satyr play, the *Agen,* written either by an obscure playwright named Python or by Alexander the Great himself and quoted by Athenaios (13.586d, 596b), states that "Harpalos sent to them [the Athenians] no fewer myriads of grain than Agen and became a citizen." Although the *Agen* was a satyr play, the context is such that the reference to Harpalos' sending grain to Athens and receiving citizenship in return surely describes historical events.[38] Unfortunately, Athenaios provides no details concerning how this grain transaction took place. The text says merely that Harpalos "sent" (παραπέμψαι) grain, and so it is uncertain whether the grain was sold at the going rate, sold at a reduced rate, or given as a gift. But since this Harpalos is surely the famous Harpalos who was Alexander the Great's treasurer and longtime friend, he was not a professional trader himself and probably hired professional traders to transport the grain. Moreover, being a powerful man with much wealth at his disposal, it would not be surprising if he, like several other foreign potentates, gave the grain to Athens as a gift, free of charge (see nos. 6, 9, and 21).

Kingsley's argument that Harpalos' service should be linked with the famous inscription that records the Kyrene grain distributions offers a possible explanation for the process by which Harpalos may have given grain to Athens free of charge (Tod 2.196; Kingsley 1986: 165–77). The distribution of grain from Kyrene has long been attributed to Alexander's initiative or influence, since his mother and sister both received unusually large amounts (Oliverio 1933: 87). But Kingsley argues that the so-called first flight of Harpalos to Greece (Arrian 3.6) was undertaken not because he and Alexander had a falling out, as most scholars believe, but on the orders of Alexander. In her reconstruction of events, Alexander instructed Harpalos to purchase grain from Kyrene and distribute it to various Greek cities at some time between 333 and 331. The purpose of the distribution was to maintain the loyalty of the Greeks to Alexander while he was campaigning in the east and while Memnon was operating a fleet in the Aegean on behalf of the Persian king. Therefore, Kingsley believes that we should identify Harpalos' gift of grain to Athens, for which he was honored with Athenian citizenship, with the one hundred thousand *medimnoi* of grain listed for Athens in the Kyrene inscription.

Kingsley's reconstruction is not without its detractors. Most date the grain distribution to between 330 and 324, arguing that it must be assigned to known years of food shortage throughout Greece.[39] Many also believe that Kyrene did not give the grain as a gift but sold it, either at the going rate or at a reduced price.[40] They argue that the inscription uses the word ἔδωκε (it gave) figuratively as part of the formal language of international relations. Bresson (2000: 136), in particular, thinks it unlikely that Kyrene would have purchased from producers no fewer than eight hundred thousand *medimnoi* of grain and then given it away free of charge. Brun (1993: 189–90) also wonders how the grain could have been distributed if, as Kingsley proposed, the Persian fleet was such a menace in the Aegean at the time. Finally, Isager and Hansen (1975: 204–5) believe that the Kyrene grain distribution must have occurred between 330 and 325, when both Olympias and Kleopatra were together in Epiros.

But none of these objections is decisive. One cannot rule out that the distribution took place between 333 and 331 just because there is no explicit evidence for a food shortage in Greece in those years. If such a date for the grain distribution is likely for other reasons, then the inscription itself might stand as evidence of a food shortage in those years. In Kingsley's reconstruction, Harpalos purchased the grain from Kyrene and then authorized Kyrene to distribute the gain among the Greek cities as a gift. Since Harpalos could easily afford to purchase the grain and then have it given away, Bresson's objection is nullified, and the inscription could literally mean that Kyrene "gave" the grain as a gift.[41] At any rate, it is highly unlikely that Kyrene sold the grain to the Greek cities at the going rate during a year of shortage, say in 330, when wheat reached a price of sixteen drachmas per *medimnos*. If that had been the case, then Athens would have had to pay 1,600,000 drachmas, or 266 talents, for its one hundred thousand *medimnoi* of wheat. This sum would have been a large portion of the state's annual budget even at its height under Lykourgos, when it averaged about twelve hundred talents per year ([Plut.] *Ten Orat.* 842f). In addition, it is certain that Alexander had at least some influence on the composition of the distribution.[42] Kyrene made the distribution to some cities either on his orders or simply just to please him, as clearly seems to be the case in the distributions to Alexander's sister and mother. It is unlikely, then, that Kyrene would have sold the grain directly to them at prices inflated by a shortage, and Alexander would have seen to it that at least his sister and mother, if not all the cities, received the grain as a gift. In response to Isager and Hansen, I can see no reason to suppose that the grain distribution required Olympias and Kleopatra to be together in Epiros. The inscription makes no reference to their location—they are not even listed on adjacent lines.

One other possibility suggested by Bresson (2000: 136–38) is that Kyrene did not distribute the grain itself but granted "export licenses" for particular amounts of grain to the cities listed on the inscription. However, although such an institution is not unprecedented, there is no evidence that it was in operation in the case of the Kyrene inscription. Finally, although Brun questions whether it was feasible for Kyrene to make such a large grain distribution at a time when the Persian fleet was menacing the Aegean, he does not rule out its possibility (Brun 1993: 190). Thus, Kingsley's reconstruction is reasonable, and there is a possibility that Harpalos' gift of grain to Athens was associated with distributions from Kyrene. Even if her reconstruction is rejected, however, it is still certain that Harpalos received citizenship from Athens for giving a gift of imported goods at some time between 333 and 324.

23. (D17). Dionysios, 335/4, 331/0, or 326/5 (*IG* ii² 363; Schweigert 1939: 33–34; Schwenk no. 67; Malouchou 2000–2003: no. 2; Lambert 3.84)

> Proposer: Polyeuktos, son of Sostratos, of Sphettos
> Services: gift of imported goods
> Goods: grain
> Ethnicity: Greek (Herakleote)
> Legal status: noncitizen, *metic*
> Socioeconomic status: wealthy professional trader
> Laudatory language: N.A.
> Honors and privileges: right to pay *eisphorai* and serve on campaigns together with the Athenians, inscribed stele

The date of *IG* ii² 363 depends entirely on the restoration of the prescript of the decree. Plausible restorations provide several possible dates, including 336/5, 335/4, 331/0, 326/5, and 324/3.[43] Schwenk points out the epigraphic and historical problems connected with all the proposed restorations, but she argues that the restoration that provides a date of 326/5 is the least problematic epigraphically and is the only one that explains the "earlier shortage" of grain mentioned in line 13, for which Schwenk provides a vague date of 330–326 (Schwenk pp. 326–27, 332). Lambert (2007: 119 and n. 88), however, points out a serious weakness for Schwenk's proposed date of 326/5: a principal Assembly on another day in the seventh prytany is already attested by *IG* ii² 359 (=Schwenk no. 63). In addition, there were also grain shortages in 338/7 and 335/4 that could account for the reference to the "earlier shortage" if the decree is dated to 335/4 or 331/0, respectively (Garnsey 1988: 154–62). However, there were no grain shortages in 331/0 or 326/5 (or in 324/3 for that matter, though this date is the least likely epigraphically anyway) that could account for the immediate service for which Dionysios was being honored, which is a blow to Lambert's preferred date of 331/0. But there was such a grain shortage in 335/4. Historically, then, a date of 335/4 for *IG* ii² 363 would be most preferable. Given, however, that there are epigraphic problems connected with all the proposed dates, it is perhaps wise to conclude only that the least objectionable dates for the honorary decree for Dionysios are 335/4, 331/0, and 326/5.

Meritt's suggestion that the honorand was the same Dionysios who was tyrant of Herakleia was accepted by many, but the new fragment makes this identification impossible.[44] The decree states that in an earlier shortage of grain, the honorand had promised to "give" ([ἐπι]δώσειν) Athens three thousand *medimnoi*. Unfortunately, a description of the immediate services for which Dionysios was presently being honored is lost. It is highly likely, however, that Athens honored Dionysios for fulfilling his promised service or carrying out a similar one, since the decree takes care to note his earlier promise. Thus, I will categorize Dionysios' service as a gift of grain. The ability to give away such a large gift of grain qualifies Dionysios as a wealthy man. Yet it is clear that he was not a potentate, the tyrant of Herakleia, because the new fragment indicates that Athens granted him the privilege of paying *eisphorai* and serving on campaigns together with the Athenians. Such a privilege was inappropriate for a foreign potentate and much more suited to a professional trader, particularly one who was a *metic*, resident in Athens (see no. 27 below). Besides the aforementioned privilege, the existence of *IG* ii² 363 attests to the fact that Athens also honored Dionysios by inscribing his honorary decree on a stone stele.

All subsequent editors have accepted Schweigert's restoration of the proposer of *IG* ii² 363 as Polyeuktos, son of Sostratos, of Sphettos.[45] This Polyeuktos was a close associate of Demosthenes and shared his policy of active Athenian resistance to Philip II of Macedon.[46]

24. (D18). Herakleides, 330/29–328/7 (*IG* ii² 360)

Proposer: Telemachos, son of Theangelos, of Acharnai (first request of
the People of Athens for a *probouleuma*, lines 46–50; decree of the

Assembly, lines 28–45); Kephisodotos, son of Euarchides, of Achar-
nai (first *probouleuma*, lines 51–65)
Services: sale of imported goods at a reduced price
Goods: grain
Ethnicity: Greek (Cyprian Salaminian)
Legal status: noncitizen, *metic*
Socioeconomic status: wealthy professional trader
Laudatory language: *philotimia*
Honors and privileges: commendation, gold crown of five hundred
drachmas, embassy to Herakleia on honorand's behalf

IG ii² 360 contains five decrees (all inscribed during the archonship of Antikles in 325/4) that attest to two separate occasions on which Athens granted
honors and privileges to Herakleides of Cyprian Salamis for his services relating to trade. Three decrees concern the first occasion, identified here as no.
24 in the catalog: lines 46–50 contain the Assembly's request for a *probouleuma*
from the Council, lines 51–65 contain the Council's *probouleuma*, and lines 28–
45 contain the Assembly's honorary decree. None of these three decrees include an archon formula. Line 31, however, states that Herakleides performed
his services during the archonship of Aristophon in 330/29, and so the first occasion on which Herakleides received honors and privileges from Athens for
services relating to trade must have occurred at some time between that year
and 328/7, when he performed further services for which he was honored
later (see no. 27) but that are not mentioned in this decree.

Athens honored Herakleides on this occasion because he was the first of
the *emporoi* to sail into Athens with grain (specified as wheat in line 9) during
the shortage of 330/29. He sold three thousand *medimnoi* of it at five drachmas
per *medimnos* (lines 29–31 and 54–56). The price must have been a reduction
from the going rate, since there is evidence for sales of wheat at sixteen and
even thirty-two drachmas per *medimnos* in 330/29.[47] The fact that Herakleides
sold his wheat at a price reduced from the going rate accounts for Athens' care
in explicitly stating the price of his sale.

Herakleides was from Salamis on Cyprus, which was a Greek settlement.
Given the description of him in *IG* ii² 360 as an *emporos* who sailed into Athens
bringing grain (καταπλεύσας Ἀθήναζε σῖτον ἄγων, lines 66–67), he clearly
made his living as a professional trader (Reed 2003: 128–29, no. 60). In order
to perform the services of selling goods at a reduced price in 330/29 and giving three thousand drachmas to Athens for a purchase of grain in 328/7 (lines
11–12 and 70–71), Herakleides must also have been quite wealthy. It also appears that Herakleides owned his own ship—despite the references to him as
an *emporos*, rather than a *naukleros*, in the decree (lines 10 and 30–31)—since
the decree calls for an embassy to be sent to Herakleia to demand the return
of Herakleides' sails, which had been seized there (line 39).

The mention of Herakleides' ethnic and the nature of his subsequent honors (see no. 27) make it certain that he was not an Athenian citizen. Most scholars believe that Herakleides was a *metic* who resided in Athens.[48] Reed (2003: 129) rejects this view on the basis that a grant of *enktesis* is not sufficient evidence that Herakleides was a *metic*. Although one had to live in Athens in order to make practical use of the right to own land and a house there, that right also had an honorary value independent of its practical value. There are, in fact, cases in which someone who clearly did not reside in Athens received *enktesis* (see no. 25 and n. 50). But Herakleides also received the right to pay *eisphorai* (emergency taxes) and serve on campaigns "together with the Athenians" (στρατεύεσθαι αὐτοὺς τὰς στρατείας καὶ εἰσφέρειν τὰς εἰσφορὰς μετὰ Ἀθηναίων, lines 20–21). Although it is possible that these rights were also intended to be merely honorific and not to be used for their practical value, the fact that Herakleides performed services for Athens on more than one occasion indicates that he had a closer connection to the city than that of the typical *xenos*. Thus, the preponderance of evidence seems to indicate that Herakleides was indeed a *metic*.

Despite the value of Herakleides' services relating to trade in 330/29, however, Athens bestowed rather mediocre honors on him. He received only a commendation and a gold crown of five hundred drachmas instead of the more common one thousand drachmas. Athens did not even bother to inscribe his honorary decrees on a stone stele until it honored him a second time, in 325/4. Perhaps the proposers of Herakleides' first honorary decree believed that sending an embassy to recover his sails from the Herakleotes was gratitude enough.

25. (D19). Apses and his father, after ca. 330 (*IG* ii² 342+; Stroud 1971: no. 29; *SEG* 24.104; Walbank 1985: 107–11=*SEG* 35.70; V-T A159)

Proposer: unknown
Services: simple importation of goods
Goods: grain
Ethnicity: non-Greeks (Tyrian)
Legal status: noncitizens, *metics*
Socioeconomic status: common professional traders
Laudatory language: *arete, eunoia*
Honors and privileges: commendation, gold crowns, *proxenia, euergesia, enktesis*, inscribed stele

The text used here concerning the honors for Apses and his father has been provided by Walbank (1985: 107–11), who connects *IG* ii² 342 with another fragment, EM 13412.[49]

In *IG* ii²· Kirchner dated the decree to before 332/1 on epigraphic and historical grounds. But the historical explanation does not hold up, since it is based on the assumption that the honorands were not *metics* and, therefore, would not have survived the destruction of their home city of Tyre by Alexander the Great in 332/1 as free men. Such an assumption is unfounded, however, since it assumes that *proxenoi* could not be *metics* and had to reside in their home cities (see Walbank 1985: 110 and n. 15). Likely exceptions to this rule make it possible that the honorands were *metics* (see nos. 4, 24, and 27). Indeed, *IG* ii² 342+ states (lines 4–8) not only that the honorands had performed trade-related services for Athens but that they promised to do more in the future, which may indicate that they frequented Athens to the point of being residents. Moreover, the honorands also received *enktesis*, the right to own land and a house in Athens, which was normally restricted to citizens. Although there were a few occasions on which Athens granted this privilege to honorands who clearly were not resident in Athens, *enktesis* would certainly have more usefulness if the honorands were resident in Athens.[50] Thus, it is likely that the honorands were *metics*.[51] The honorands were certainly not citizens, as the mention of their ethnic and the award of *proxenia* and *enktesis* make clear. A date after ca. 330 is called for, however, since the formula used in this decree for granting *enktesis*, "according to the law" (κατὰ τὸν νόμον line 17), was apparently not in effect in 330/29 (see *IG* ii² 351+624) but does appear by 325/4, in no. 27 (Lambert 2006: 133 n. 77). Further precision concerning the date is not possible.[52]

Of the honorands, Apses and his father, Hieron, the former was certainly a professional trader. The decree states (lines 3 and 6) that Apses "conveyed" ([κ]εκόμικ[εν]) something and also promised to "bring in grain" (σιτ[ηγήσει]ν). Since there is no indication that he sold his goods for anything but the going price, he was probably a typical professional trader of modest means. Although an attempt was made to associate *IG* ii² 342 with *IG* ii² 418 and to argue that Apses and Hieron received honors for conveying a Carthaginian embassy to Athens, the author of this theory has since retracted it.[53]

26. Pairisades I and sons, ca. 327 (*IG* ii² 653; [Dem.] 34.36; Dein. 1.43)

> Proposer: Demosthenes, son of Demosthenes, of Paiania
> Services: miscellaneous
> Goods: grain
> Ethnicity: non-Greek (Bosporan)
> Legal status: one naturalized citizen, two noncitizen *xenoi*
> Socioeconomic status: foreign potentates
> Laudatory language: N.A.
> Honors and privileges: bronze statues

After the death of Spartokos II in 344/3, Pairisades I took over as sole ruler of the Bosporos until his death in 311/10. It is apparent from *IG* ii² 653 and Deinarchos 1.43 that a reorganization of the relationship between Athens and the Bosporos during this time resulted in further honors and privileges for Pairisades I in return for his services relating to trade.[54] The Athenian Assembly passed the decree of *IG* ii² 653 in 285/4 to honor Spartokos III (r. 304/3–284/3). Lines 8–20, however, state that Athens had honored his forefathers with Athenian citizenship, bronze statues ([εἰκόσιν χαλ]καῖς) in both the Agora and *emporion*, and other gifts and had promised that "if anyone marches against the kingdom of his [ancestors] and of Spa[r]tokos, (the People) shall aid (him) [with all strength] both by land and by sea." The implication of the reference to "his ancestors" ([τῶν προγόνω]ν αὐτοῦ) is that the defensive alliance predates the accession of Spartokos III in 304/3. Moreover, since the bronze statues are referred to in the plural but only one king, Eumelos (r. 310/09–304/3), reigned between Spartokos III and Pairisades I, one of the statues must have been for Pairisades I. *IG* ii² 212 says that Pairisades I received citizenship and other gifts, such as gold crowns, in 347/6, but it makes no mention of either bronze statues or a defensive alliance between Athens and the Bosporos. Deinarchos 1.43, however, makes it clear that by 324, Demosthenes had persuaded the Athenians to set up bronze statues of Pairisades I and his two sons, Satyros and Gorgippos, in the Agora.[55] Although Athenian grants of bronze statues were often accompanied by grants of *sitesis* (permanent maintenance in the Prytaneion) and *proedria* (permanent seats of honor at contests), such was not always the case.[56] Therefore, it cannot be assumed that Pairisades I and his sons received *sitesis* and *proedria* from Athens along with bronze statues. In addition, there is no evidence that Pairisades I's sons, Satyros and Gorgippos, received citizenship from Athens as he had in 347/6 (no. 11).

A possible date for Athens' grant of bronze statues and a new defensive alliance with Pairisades I would be at his accession to sole rule in 344/3. There seems to have been a tradition in which Bosporan kings reaffirmed their trade-related services for Athens at the commencement of their reigns, while, at the same time, Athens renewed the honors that it had conferred on their predecessors, often with grants of additional honors. For example, Leukon received a new gold crown every four years, whereas his predecessor, Satyros, seems to have received only one gold crown (see no. 7). But Burstein offers a better date for Athens' grant of bronze statues and a new defensive alliance with the Bosporan kings. He points out that relations between Pairisades I and Athens were not on consistently good terms throughout his reign. According to [Demosthenes] 34.36, which dates to 327, Pairisades had declared during that year that grain exported to Athens was to be shipped duty-free.[57] The speech clearly implies that before this time, the privilege of exemption from export taxes afforded to traders bound for Athens from the Bosporos, which had been originally instituted by Satyros, was canceled or allowed to lapse. Between 347/6 and 327, the relationship between Athens and the Bosporos had deteriorated. Archaeological evidence points to a decline of Athenian imports to the Bosporos after the mid-fourth century (Brashinsky

1968: 107). In addition, Aischines 3.171–72, dated to 330, tries to prejudice an Athenian audience against Demosthenes by emphasizing the latter's ties with the Bosporan kings. Aischines' strategy depends on the assumption that his audience was not well disposed toward the Bosporan kings at that time, and unlike Deinarchos several years later, he makes no mention of bronze statues. It is likely, then, that Athens granted the statues to Pairisades I and his sons in around 327 in response to his resumption of its trading privileges.

The defensive alliance was probably also put in place in 327. *IG* ii^2 212 (from 347/6) says nothing about a defensive alliance. An explicit and binding defensive alliance between Athens and the Bosporan kings, therefore, represents a major departure from previous Athenian policy. The year 327 was an appropriate time for such a shift, since Athens had been suffering through a series of grain shortages at the time. In addition to granting Pairisades I and his sons bronze statues, Athens was compelled to go the extra mile to have its trading privileges with the Bosporos reinstated, and so it entered into a binding defensive alliance with Pairisades I as well. For his part, Pairisades sorely needed the defensive alliance, since, according to [Demosthenes] 34.8, he was at war with the Scythians by the summer of 327 (Isager and Hansen 1975: 169).

Although Deinarchos' assertion that Demosthenes proposed the bronze statues for Pairisades I and his sons in return for a bribe of one thousand *medimnoi* of grain per year may have been unfounded, it is not improbable, and there is no reason to doubt that it was indeed Demosthenes who proposed the honors. It is likely, then, that Demosthenes was also responsible for proposing the defensive alliance with Pairisades I.

27. (D20). Herakleides, 325/4 (*IG* ii^2 360)

> Proposer: Phyleus, son of Pausanias (first request of the People of Athens for a *probouleuma*); Demosthenes, son of Demokles, of Lamptrai (decree of the Assembly)
> Services: gift of (money to purchase) imported goods
> Goods: grain
> Ethnicity: Greek (Cyprian Salaminian)
> Legal status: noncitizen, *metic*
> Socioeconomic status: wealthy professional trader
> Laudatory language: *philotimia, eunoia*
> Honors and privileges: commendation, gold crown, *proxenia, euergesia, enktesis*, right to pay *eisphorai* and serve on campaign together with the Athenians, inscribed stele

Of the five decrees contained in *IG* ii^2 360, two date to 325/4 and comprise a single occasion (no. 27) on which Athens granted honors and privileges to Herakleides for services relating to trade that he performed in 328/7. Lines 66–69 contain the *probouleuma*, and lines 1–27 contain the Assembly's decree, which was proposed by Demosthenes, son of Demokles, of Lamptrai, who is not to be confused with the famous orator. Preserved archon formulae date the decrees to 325/4. The decrees explicitly state that Herakleides "gave" (ἐπέδωκε) three thousand drachmas in an *epidosis* for a purchase of grain in the archonship of Euthykritos in 328/7 (lines 11–12 and 70–71).[58] Herakleides' ethnicity and status as a *metic* and wealthy professional trader has already been discussed (see no. 24). For his gift of money to purchase grain, Athens granted Herakleides much more significant honors and privileges than it had for his previous services. On the present occasion, in addition to another commendation and gold crown of five hundred drachmas, he also received *enktesis, proxenia* and *euergesia,* the right to pay *eisphorai* and serve on campaign together with the Athenians, and the honor of having all his honorary decrees inscribed on a stele and placed on the Acropolis. The seemingly mutually exclusive honors of *proxenia* and *enktesis* and their relation to the honorand's status as a *metic* have already been discussed (see nos. 24 and 25).

28. (D21). Apollonides, 323/2 (*IG* ii² 343; Schweigert 1940: 343; Schwenk no. 84; V-T A162)

Proposer: —kerdes of Anagyrous
Services: unknown
Goods: unknown
Ethnicity: non-Greek (Sidonian)
Legal status: noncitizen
Socioeconomic status: unknown
Laudatory language: *aner agathos,* [*eunous*]*, arete, eunoia*
Honors and privileges: commendation, gold crown, *proxenia, euergesia, enktesis,* inscribed stele

Schweigert (1940: 342–43) has been able to restore the prescript of this decree, since it shares the same *epistates* of the *proedroi* as *IG* ii² 448, which also contains a preserved archon formula for the year 323/2. Although most scholars accept Schweigert's restoration, there is still the possibility that the *epistates* of the *proedroi* was not the same person in the two decrees, since his demotic is not extant in either one.[59] Thus, a date of 323/2 for *IG* ii² 343 will be accepted here, but with caution. Schweigert's restoration of lines 9–10 ([ε]ἰ[ς τὰ] ἅπα[ντα] ἀγαθὸν ἐκ [τῶν ἰδίω]ν), however, is unlikely because it does not provide the necessary infinitive or participle for the verb ἀποφαίνουσ[ιν] (V-T A162, p. 99). Schwenk (no. 84, pp. 418–20) provides a more compelling restoration, [ε]ἶ[ναι] ἄ[νδρα ἀγα]θὸν κ[αὶ εὔνου]ν, not only because it provides a necessary infinitive but also because *eunous* commonly precedes the dative τῶι δήμωι as it would here and because it is reflected by *eunoia* in the commendation/crowning clause of line 13 (V-T pp. 201, 274).

The honorand's services are unknown, but they must have been related to trade, since Athens honored him on the recommendation of *emporoi* and *naukleroi* (lines 7–8). Such a recommendation is reminiscent of no. 20 (attested mainly by *IG* ii^2 416[b]), in which the honorand secured shipments of goods. It may be that the honorand of *IG* ii^2 343 did likewise, but it is impossible to know for certain. Equally uncertain is the honorand's socioeconomic status. Several scholars have categorized Apollonides as a professional trader.[60] On the other hand, Reed (2003: 94– 95, no. 7) puts Apollonides in his category of "very unlikely candidates" to be either *emporoi* or *naukleroi*. According to Reed, men in this category performed services for traders near their homes and were, thus, not likely to have been traders themselves. Presumably, traders would be away from their homes during the sailing season. But there is no indication in *IG* ii^2 343 that Apollonides performed his services near his home city. On the other hand, *IG* ii^2 343 also provides no indication that Apollonides was a professional trader. Given the lack of evidence either way, Apollonides' socioeconomic status will simply be classified as "unknown" here. Although Apollonides is a Greek name, the decree is explicit in referring to him as a Sidonian (lines 9 and 11), which also makes it certain that he was not an Athenian citizen. It is uncertain, though, whether he was a *metic*, since neither his services nor his honors provide any definitive evidence concerning his residence.[61]

29. (D22). —phanes, ca. 322/1–320/19 (*IG* ii^2 398[a]+438; Walbank 1987a: 10–11=*SEG* 40.78)

    Proposer: Demades, son of Demeas?
    Services: miscellaneous
    Goods: grain
    Ethnicity: unknown
    Legal status: noncitizen, *xenos*
    Socioeconomic status: unknown
    Laudatory language: [*eunoia*], *chresimos, philotimia*
    Honors and privileges: citizenship, inscribed stele

IG ii^2 398 appears in the corpus as two fragments designated as (a) and (b). The former fragment recounts the services of an unknown honorand, while the latter contains procedures for enrolling the honorand as a citizen of Athens. It is clear, however, that fragments (a) and (b) are not parts of the same inscription and should not be associated with one another (Osborne 1971b: 323–25). On the other hand, Walbank has convincingly associated *IG* ii^2 398(a) with *IG* ii^2 438, which also contains a grant of citizenship.[62] The letter-forms of the inscription allow a date in the 320s (Osborne 1982: 111, D40). Moreover, several scholars have noted that the language of *IG* ii^2 398(a) is strikingly similar to that of *IG* ii^2 399, which was proposed by the famous orator and statesman Demades.[63] If Demades was also the proposer of *IG* ii^2 398(a)+438, as Brun (2000: 148 and n. 79) believes, then the decree probably dates to his most active years, between 322/1 and 320/19, the year in which he died (*APF* 3263, p. 101). The naval battle mentioned in lines 6–7 of *IG* ii^2 398(a) might then be the one that was fought under the command of the navarch Euetion in 323/2 during the Lamian War.[64]

The extant portions of the decree provide little information about the honorand. The grant of citizenship makes it obvious that he was not previously an Athenian citizen. He was also not likely a *metic*, since he aided Athenians in Asia (lines 3–5) and in a naval battle in the Hellespont (lines 6–11), which may have been connected to the Lamian War of 323/2 (Garnsey 1988: 157). Only the last few letters of his name, "——phanes," survive. Although such an ending indicates a Greek name, it is not decisive in determining his ethnicity. The honorand's socioeconomic status and the precise nature of his trade-related services are also uncertain. The decree states that he "sent" ([ἀπέστει]λεν) wheat to Athens. In other cases in which it is clear that a person personally brought his goods into Athens, the decrees employ words derived from ἄγω or κομίζω (see nos. 14, 22, 23, 25, 26, 27, 29, 32, and 33). Moreover, a reference in Demosthenes 56.8 indicates that words derived from ἀποστέλλω are used to signify when someone is responsible for sending goods through others but does not personally sail with the goods. The passage distinguishes between those who "sent" (ἀπέστελλον) grain to Athens and those who "sailed on board" (ἐπέπλεον; see *LSJ*[9,] s.v. ἐπιπλέω) with their cargoes. It is likely, therefore, that the honorand of *IG* ii² 398(a)+438 did not accompany his grain to Athens.

It is possible, then, that the honorand was a foreign potentate or a wealthy professional trader who could authorize others to ship grain to Athens. Unfortunately, there is no explicit evidence to substantiate either of these possibilities. Moreover, in the cases in which foreign potentates sent grain to Athens, they gave the grain as a gift, free of charge (nos. 9, 20, and 21). But in the case of *IG* ii² 398(a)+438, there is no indication that the honorand either gave his grain to Athens as a gift or sold it at a reduced price. Thus, the honorand's trade-related service can only be categorized as "miscellaneous," and his socioeconomic status must remain unknown. The existence of *IG* ii² 398(a)+438, however, is evidence that Athens made provisions for inscribing the honorary decree on a stone stele.

30. (D23). Metrodoros, ca. 321–319 (*IG* ii² 401)

    Proposer: unknown
    Services: miscellaneous
    Goods: grain
    Ethnicity: Greek (Kyzikene)
    Legal status: noncitizen, *xenos*
    Socioeconomic status: foreign potentate
    Laudatory language: [*eunoia*], *chresimos*
    Honors and privileges: commendation, gold crown, inscribed stele

This decree must date to 321–319, since Antipater is mentioned in connection with Philip III Arridaios.[65] Although there is some dispute about the restoration of lines 1–5, the proposed alternatives do not have a significant impact on matters relevant to this book.[66] The honorand was recognized by Athens for having helped with the "sending out" of grain ([τ]ὴν ἀ[ποστολὴν] τοῦ σίτου, lines 11–12). Exactly how he accomplished this is not stated in the decree, and so his trade-related service will be categorized simply as "miscellaneous." The fact that the honorand helped in sending out grain to Athens but did not personally bring grain to the city is reason to believe that he was not a common professional trader (see no. 29). In addition, it is clear from the decree that the honorand had some connection with the satrap of Asia, a man named Arridaios, who was appointed by his namesake King Philip III Arridaios of Macedon and his regent Antipater (lines 6–8). For these reasons, the honorand is categorized here as a foreign potentate. The honorand was a Kyzikene named Metrodoros. But although he was a Greek, the mention of his ethnic indicates that he was not an Athenian citizen, and it is unlikely that he was a *metic* of Athens as well, since he sent out grain from Asia and was associated with the satrap there. The existence of *IG* ii² 401 is evidence that Athens provided the honorand with the additional honor of inscribing his honorary decree on a stone stele.

31. (D24). Unknown honorand, ca. 321–318 (*IG* ii² 407+*SEG* 32.94; Walbank 1982: no. 6; Walbank 1987b: 165–66)

> Proposer: unknown
> Services: simple importation of goods, securing shipments of goods
> Goods: grain
> Ethnicity: unknown
> Legal status: unknown
> Socioeconomic status: common professional trader
> Laudatory language: *eunous*, [*chresimos*]
> Honors and privileges: commendation, gold crown, inscribed stele

The date of *IG* ii² 407 is uncertain. Kirchner assigned it in *IG* ii² to ca. 330–326 on account of its letterforms and relevance to the grain shortages of the early 320s. On the basis of an examination of squeezes and papier-mâché impressions, however, Walbank has associated *IG* ii² 407 with another fragment of a decree (*SEG* 32.94=Walbank 1982: no. 6).[67] This fragment, which contains provisions for inscribing the decree and placing it on the Acropolis, probably follows closely after the end of *IG* ii² 407, though it does not directly adjoin it. Walbank dates the entire decree to 321–318 on the basis of a reference in line 5 of the new fragment to the *anagrapheus*, an official that existed during that time when an oligarchy was in power in Athens (Walbank 1982: 47–48, no. 6). But since Walbank has not verified the association of *IG* ii² 407 and *SEG* 32.94 through inspection of the stones themselves, only the text of *IG* ii² 407 will be used in this study.

In *IG* ii² 407, it is clear that Athens honored a man for performing a simple importation of goods and helping to secure the shipment of goods as well. The honorand brought grain into Athens, but he did not give it as a gift, free of charge, or sell it at a reduced price from the going rate. He also joined in overseeing the escort of grain from Cyprus to Athens (τῆ[ς τοῦ σίτου πομπ]ῆς ἐκ Κύπρου συνε[πι]με[λεῖται ὅπως ἂν σ]ῖτος ἀφι[κ]νῆτα[ι ὡς π]λε[ῖστος Ἀθήναζε], lines 5–9). The exact manner in which such an escort was accomplished is uncertain. It is likely that the honorand brought his grain from Cyprus to Athens on the same voyage in which he escorted other merchant ships. He was also most likely a professional trader, as indicated by the decree's use of the word σιτηγῶν (bringing grain) in line 4 (Reed 2003: 128, no. 59). Since there is no indication that the honorand was wealthy, it is assumed that he was of modest means, like most other professional traders. Köhler's restoration of line 12 assumes that the honorand was a Milesian, but there is no way of confirming this identification. Likewise, there is inadequate evidence to determine the honorand's legal status.

32. Eucharistos (1), before 320/19 (*IG* ii² 400)
Proposer: unknown
Services: unknown
Goods: unknown
Ethnicity: unknown
Legal status: noncitizen
Socioeconomic status: wealthy professional trader
Laudatory language: N.A.
Honors and privileges: *proxenia, euergesia*

IG ii² 400 contains evidence for two separate occasions on which Athens granted honors and privileges for someone who had performed trade-related services. The decree itself must have been passed no later than 320/19, since its proposer, Demades, died in that year (*APF* 3263, p. 101). This decree primarily concerns the second of the two occasions on which the honorand received honors and privileges from Athens, which is designated as no. 33 in the catalog. The first occasion is attested by lines 10–11, which refer to the honorand as a *proxenos* and a *euergetes*, indicating that he had received honors and privileges in return for services at least once before. Naturally, this first occasion must also have taken place at some time before 320/19.

Although the precise nature of the services for which Athens granted *proxenia* and *euergesia* to the honorand cannot be known, it is almost certain that they had some relation to trade. Line 4 indicates that on the second occasion of his receiving honors, the honorand was recognized for bringing grain ([σῖτ]ον ἄγων) to Athens, which means that he must have been a professional trader. It is also likely that the honorand was wealthy, since he was honored on the second occasion for selling goods at a reduced price from the going rate.

Concerning the honorand's legal status, it is certain only that he was not an Athenian citizen, since he was granted *proxenia*. Some scholars, such as Walbank (1985: 110 and n. 15), would argue that his *proxenia* precluded him from being a *metic* as well. At the same time, though, the honorand performed at least two services for Athens, which may indicate that he resided there. But in the absence of any further evidence one way or another, whether the honorand was a *metic* or a *xenos* must remain uncertain. The honorand's ethnicity is also uncertain, since his Greek name, *Eucharistos*, is not adequate evidence that he was indeed Greek (see no. 28).

33. (D25). Eucharistos (2), before 320/19 (*IG* ii² 400)
Proposer: Demades, son of Demeas, of Paiania
Services: sale of imported goods at a reduced price
Goods: grain
Ethnicity: unknown
Legal status: noncitizen
Socioeconomic status: wealthy professional trader
Laudatory language: unknown
Honors and privileges: commendation, inscribed stele

Concerning Eucharistos' ethnicity and legal and socioeconomic status and the date of the decree (*IG* ii² 400) that constitutes the second occasion on which he received honors and privileges from Athens for services relating to trade, see no. 32. The proposer of this decree has been restored as the famous Athenian orator and statesman Demades on the firm basis of the surviving letters of his patronymic and demotic. *IG* ii² 400 states that Eucharistos provided a service for Athens by bringing grain ([σῖτ]ον ἄγων) to the city and by saying that he would "give" (παραδ[ώ]σ[ειν]) eight thousand *medimnoi* at present and another four thousand in the future at "the established price" ([τῆς καθι-σταμ]ένης τιμ[ῆ]ς, lines 7–8), a phrase partially restored by Wilhelm but supported by parallels from literary sources.[68]

Unfortunately, the literary sources are ambiguous with regard to the meaning of "established" (καθισταμένος) in connection with prices. *LSJ*⁹ (s.v. καθίστημι) allows for such translations as "the established price," "the prevailing price," or "at cost." Fränkel (in Böckh 1886: 2.26 n. 163), Gernet ([1909] 1979: 374), Jardé (1925: 178), and Figueira (1986: 165) have stated that the phrase referred to the market price as determined by the forces of supply and demand at any given moment. Böckh (1886: 1.118 n. c; 1857: 130 n. 1), Dittenberger (1903–5: 1.4 n. 12), Francotte (1910a: 296 n. 4), and Isager and Hansen (1975: 200 n. 3) thought that the phrase described the normal price over the long run as determined in the market by the forces of supply and demand, but excluding extreme short-term fluctuations. Reger (1993: 313) has stated that the phrase referred to a fixed price, set by the state in accordance with the normal price. Wilhelm (1889: 148–49) and Migeotte (1997: 38–39) have argued that the phrase indicated a fixed price, but one set by the state only for occasional public sales of grain. Finally, Bresson (2000: 183–206) believes that it is a price that the state suggested but did not mandate for private sales.

The lack of a consensus concerning the meaning of the "the established price" arises from the seemingly contradictory uses of the term in two fourth-century legal speeches from the Demosthenic corpus. Demosthenes 56.8 concerns the schemes of Cleomenes, Alexander the Great's governor of Egypt, who is said to have had agents in Athens who would send letters to him concerning the "established prices" (τὰς καθεστηκυίας τιμὰς).[69] If grain were "scarce" (τίμιος) in Athens, Cleomenes would ship his Egyptian grain there. But if the price of grain "fell" (εὐωνότερος γένηται) in Athens, he would ship his grain elsewhere. In this context, the "established price" seems to mean the "market" or "prevailing" price, that is, that which is "established" freely by the market and prevails in a given place at a given time.

On the other hand, in [Demosthenes] 34.39, the "established price" seems to mean the "normal" price, that is, that which is established by the market in normal circumstances, excluding extreme short-term fluctuations. One of the two plaintiffs in the case, Chrysippos, says that when the price of grain rose to sixteen drachmas per *medimnos*, he and his partner imported over ten thousand *medimnoi* of wheat and sold it to Athens at the "established price" (τῆς καθεστηκυίας τιμῆς) of five drachmas per *medimnos*. The latter price was clearly not the "market" or "prevailing" price, that is, the going rate established by the market in Athens at that time. Chrysippos is boasting that he and his partner did a service to Athens by selling their grain at a price below that which was prevailing at the time. "At cost" is almost just another way of saying "the normal price." If one excludes other costs, such as that for transportation, the cost at which Chrysippos and his partner had acquired their grain in the first place was the price established by the market in the place where they purchased the grain, that is, "the normal price of grain" *there*, which may have been unaffected by the factors that drove up the market price in Athens.[70] The few existing references to the price of wheat in Greece from the late fourth and early third century also indicate that it was normally somewhere between three and five drachmas per *medimnos*.[71]

Given these two seemingly conflicting uses of the phrase "established price," two courses of interpretation are possible. One can believe that the phrase was a generic term that could have more specific connotations depending on context. It could refer to a price established in accordance with the "market" price at the moment, as in Demosthenes (?) 56.8. Or, as in [Demosthenes] 34.39, it could refer to a price established in accordance with the "normal" price determined by the market over the long run, excluding extreme fluctuations of the short run. Or it could refer to a price established by any two parties, whether between the state and private traders, as in Ptolemaic Egypt, or an Athenian general and the people of an Attic deme.[72]

The other course would be to try to reconcile the uses of the phrase in Demosthenes 56.8 and [Demosthenes] 34.39 on the assumption that the term is a technical one that must somehow mean the same thing in both contexts. This is the course taken by Bresson (2000: 183–206, especially 205–6), who concludes that "established price" referred to a price suggested by the state for regular private sales and fixed in accordance with the market price so as to allow for traders to make a "just profit" while at the same time providing the citizens of Athens with grain at a price discounted from the inflated market prices of the moment. Thus, the "established price" as envisioned by Bresson fluctuated along with the market price enough to account for Cleomenes' actions in Demosthenes 56.8 and yet is reduced enough from that market price in order to explain the actions of Chrysippos in [Demosthenes] 34.39. According to Bresson, traders were willing to forgo some of their profits and sell grain in Athens at the "established price" because of the honors and privileges offered by Athens for such a service and the inherent advantages of trading in Athens, including its large market, excellent port facilities, and abundant variety of return cargoes and sound coinage, all of which positively offset to a significant extent their forgone profits.

Although I support the interpretation of "established price" as a generic term and reject Bresson's hypothesis as too elaborate and otherwise unattested, whatever the true meaning of the phrase, the honorand of *IG* ii[2] 400 must have sold grain at a reduced price in Athens in a manner analogous to that of Chrysippos and his partner in [Demosthenes] 34.39 or Herakleides in *IG* ii[2] 360. Since Athens took care to mention that the honorand had sold his grain at the "established price," he must have been performing a service that was more beneficial to Athens than simply importing goods and selling them at the prevailing price. In the case of the latter, Athens had no reason to make the prices of the sales explicit in their honorary decrees (see nos. 14, 22, 23, 25, and 26).

The precise date and historical circumstances of this decree are uncertain, but it is likely that the honorand's services took place during the Lamian War of 323/2 and its associated disruption of the Athenian grain supply from the Black Sea through the Hellespont (see no. 34 and Brun 2000: 148 and n. 80).

34. Eumelos, 310/09 (*IG* ii[2] 653)

Proposer: unknown
Services: miscellaneous
Goods: grain
Ethnicity: non-Greek (Bosporan)
Legal status: noncitizen, *xenos*
Socioeconomic status: foreign potentate
Laudatory language: N.A.
Honors and privileges: citizenship, *ateleia*

IG ii² 653, the decree that honors Spartokos III (r. 304/3–284/3) of the Bosporos in 285/4, states in lines 8–15 that Athens had earlier granted citizenship to him and his ancestors. It is reasonable to conclude, then, that Eumelos, who reigned as king of the Bosporos between 310/09 and 304/3, received a grant of citizenship from Athens.[73] It is also likely that Eumelos received this grant of citizenship along with *ateleia* at the time of his accession to the throne, just as his predecessors had, for continuing the trading privileges that the Bosporos had traditionally provided for Athens (see nos. 7, 9, 12, and 26).

IG ii² 653.15–16 also states that Athens had granted bronze statues to the ancestors of Spartokos III. In line 41, the decree grants a bronze statue to Spartokos III that is to be set up in the Agora "beside those of his ancestors" ([παρὰ] τοὺς προγόνους). It is possible that "ancestors" includes both Pairisades I and Eumelos, the immediate predecessors of Spartokos III. On the other hand, the "ancestors" in question may simply refer to Pairisades I and his two sons, Satyros and Gorgippos, who are known to have received bronze statues from Athens in ca. 327 (see no. 26). Unlike citizenship, which Athens seems to have granted to the Bosporan kings on a regular basis at the beginning of their reigns, bronze statues were granted only when the kings provided additional services for Athens above and beyond the ones traditionally handed down from reign to reign. Pairisades I and his sons received bronze statues in ca. 327 in return for resuming trading privileges for Athens that had previously been halted. Spartokos III received bronze statues from Athens when he had already been ruling for nine years in 285/4 in return for his gift of grain (*IG* ii² 653.23–25). Therefore, one cannot assume that Athens granted a bronze statue to Eumelos at the time of his accession to sole rule or that the bronze statues mentioned in *IG* ii² 653 (lines 15–16 and 40–41) included one for him.

Rejected Cases

The following decrees have some bearing on Athenian trade policy, but since they do not constitute occasions on which men were honored by Athens for services relating to trade, they have been rejected from inclusion in this study.

R1. Hdt. 8.136, 143

According to Herodotus, King Alexander of Macedon was a *proxenos* and *euergetes* of Athens at the time of the Second Persian War in 480. Wallace has suggested that Athens granted such honors to Alexander in return for a gift of ships' timber that was used to build the Themistoklean fleet (Wallace 1970: 199–200 and n. 13). Meiggs, however, rejected this suggestion on the grounds that Macedon was in no position to aid Athens at a time when it was being careful not to provoke the Persians (Meiggs 1982: 123–24). Given the lack of explicit evidence for Macedonian trade-related services at this time and the historical objections of Meiggs, this possible case will not be included in the present study.

R2. *IG* i³ 30 (Walbank no. 16)

This inscription, which is dated in the corpus to ca. 450, mentions a shortage of grain in line 6. Unfortunately, owing to the exceedingly fragmentary state of the decree, it is impossible to determine whether it is an honorary decree.

R3. Philoch. *FGrHist* 328 F 90; Plut. *Per.* 37

According to a fragment from the atthidographer Philochoros and Plutarch's *Life of Perikles*, a king (either of Libya or Egypt) named Psammetichos gave Athens a gift of either thirty thousand or forty thousand *medimnoi* of grain in 445/4. There is no evidence, however, that Athens granted him honors and privileges in return. Concerning the significance of a lack of honors for such a significant trade-related service, see below (R7) and p. 56.

R4. *IG* i³ 61

IG i³ 61, the so-called Methone Decree of the early 420s, is not an honorary decree and does not concern Athenian trading interests. Rather, it concerns the trading interests of Methone. The decree begins with a proposal for a vote concerning the assessment of tribute from the Methonaians (lines 1–17). Provisions are then made to guarantee that the Methonaians can trade freely on the seas and in the territory of Macedon (lines 17–29). After recording the vote concerning the assessment of tribute (which was favorable to Methone), the text continues with a rider stating that the Methonaians shall be permitted to import a certain amount of grain from Byzantion without hindrance from the Athenian "Guardians of the Hellespont" and with exemption from taxes. It is clear that Athens simply aimed to reward the people of Methone for their loyalty to the Empire, not for any trade-related services that they performed for Athens and not in order to fulfill its own trading interests.

R5. *IG* i³ 62

This decree shares similar concerns with *IG* i³ 61, except that it regards Aphytis rather than Methone. The corpus dates the decree to ca. 426. It begins, after a lacuna, with some fragmentary references to an amount of grain that the Aphytaians may have care of just as the Methonaians. The decree also stipulates that the Aphytaians make contributions just as the Methonaians (a command that the Aphytaians pay the *aparche* to the god appears later), and it records an oath of the Aphytaians to support both the colonists at Potidaia and the Athenians. The Aphytaians are then commended for being good men concerning the Athenians and are promised to obtain whatever they need from the Athenians. The text also describes provisions for inscribing the decree on a stone stele to be set up on the Acropolis. Thus, *IG* i³ 62 appears to regulate trade into Aphytis and the monetary contributions of the Aphytaians to Athens. It is not an honorary decree for Aphytaian services relating to trade for Athens.

R6. *IG* i³ 63

This decree, which also concerns the Aphytaians and is dated in the corpus to ca. 426, may have aimed in part at fulfilling Athenian trading interests. It provides guarantees that the Aphytaians be able to sail the seas and to Athens with their goods, including grain, without hindrance. The decree also calls for itself to be inscribed on a stone stele to be set up on the Acropolis. It is uncertain exactly what the Aphytaians had done to receive such privileges from Athens. The Aphytaians as a group may have provided trade-related services for Athens in the past, and *IG* i³ 63 may be an Athenian attempt to encourage the Aphytaians to continue to perform such services. The decree does explicitly state that the Aphytaians shall not be hindered from sailing to Athens or from "bringing goods to the Athenians," including grain (lines 13–15). Such an action by Athens would help to fulfill its own trading interests in acquiring more imports of grain.

It is more likely, however, that the Aphytaians had performed political or military services, probably by showing loyalty to the Empire (see the discussion concerning *IG* i³ 62 above), and that the decree rewards them for such services by providing them with trading privileges. In this case, even though Athens would be serving its own trading interests by making it easier for Aphytaian traders to bring their goods into Athens, the decree would not have honored the Aphytaians for trade-related services, and its main purpose would have been to serve the political interests of Athens. Such a scenario has a precedent in *IG* i³ 61 (see R4).

R7. *IG* i³ 89

This decree records a treaty between the Athenians and King Perdikkas of Macedon, in which Perdikkas provides a trade-related service for Athens but does not receive honors or privileges in return. Lines 22f. state that as part of the treaty, Perdikkas swore an oath not to export timber for oar spars to any other city besides Athens (and possibly its allies). Despite Perdikkas' valuable trade-related service, there is no indication in the decree or any other source that Athens ever granted him honors and privileges in return for his services. Because *IG* i³ 89 is not an honorary decree, it does not lie within the parameters of this book.

The decree is important, however, because it might help us to understand the development of Athenian trade policy. Unfortunately, the date of the decree is uncertain, and scholars have argued for dates ranging from "before 432" to 413, when Perdikkas died.[74] It is certain, however, that the decree dates to before the summer of 414, since Perdikkas was on good terms with Athens from that time, when he joined an Athenian expedition against Amphipolis (Thuc. 7.9), until his death. Therefore, the decree predates the final destruction of the Sicilian Expedition in 413 and even Nikias' letter (Thuc. 7.10ff.), when the Athenians were still confident of victory. Their confidence is also apparent in *IG* i³ 89, in which Athens not only failed to honor Perdikkas for his trade-related services but also appears to have forced him to provide these services (see Hammond and Griffith 1979: 139). The contrast between *IG* i³ 89 and *IG* i³ 117 (no. 6) — the honorary decree for Perdikkas' successor, Archelaos, for similar but lesser trade-related services — reveals how the defeat of Athens' Sicilian Expedition in 413 radically changed Athenian trade policy (see above and pp. 56–57).

R8. *IG* ii² 141

IG ii² 141 is an honorary decree but is not for services relating to trade. Athens honored Straton, the king of Sidon, for helping a group of Athenian ambassadors on their way to meet with the Persian king (lines 1–3). Moysey argues persuasively that this decree should be dated to 364 and associated with an Athenian embassy that secured Persian recognition of Athens' right to Amphipolis (Moysey 1976: 184–85 and n. 18). The Athenian ambassadors had to go through Sidon on their way to Persia on account of the revolt of the Persian satrap Ariobarzanes, which was in full swing in Asia Minor at that time.

In a rider to the decree, Athens granted exemption from the *metic* tax, the *choregia* liturgy, and *eisphorai* levies to all citizens of Sidon who resided in the *emporion* of Athens (lines 29–36). The motives for this rider are uncertain. It is possible that the proposer considered that granting privileges to Sidonian traders would provide a pleasing reward to Straton in return for his political services for Athens. This assumes, however, that Straton had an interest in promoting his exports and in increasing the economic opportunities of Sidonian traders, which is far from certain.

A more plausible scenario is that the proposer saw the occasion of honoring Straton for political services as a good opportunity to grant privileges to Sidonian traders in order to encourage them to continue to trade with Athens. Athens had good cause to be worried about its grain imports at this time, since Epaminondas of Thebes was preparing a naval fleet that would have threatened Athens' grain supply.[75] It is also interesting to note that Menexenos, who proposed the rider to *IG* ii² 141, may have been the same man referred to in Isokrates 17.9 who was involved in trading activities. If this is so, it is not surprising that he would be sufficiently interested in Athenian trade to propose the rider to this decree. He may even have sought to profit both himself and associates among the Sidonian traders by proposing privileges that would reduce their costs of trading with Athens.

Nevertheless, Athens granted privileges to Sidonian traders not for any trade-related services that they had performed but as a rider to a decree honoring their king, Straton, for political services. Thus, *IG* ii² 141 will not be included in the catalog.

R9. *IG* ii² 584+679+Add.

The precise nature of this heavily damaged inscription is uncertain, but it appears to be an honorary decree for a man named Xenokrates of Chios. Kirchner has restored line 4 of the inscription to read, . . . νεσθαι τ[ῶι δή]μωι τὴν σιτων[ίαν — — —. Although the decree has something to do with the purchase of grain, it also mentions that Xenokrates has apprehended and returned fugitive slaves. Given the fragmentary nature of the inscription, however, it is impossible to know exactly for what services Xenokrates is being honored. Regardless of this confusion, the decree lies outside the chronological parameters of this book. Kirchner dated *IG* ii² 584 to the end of the fourth century and *IG* ii² 679 to 275/4. But recent study has shown that the two inscriptions are part of one stele and form one decree dated to 247/6 or 246/5 (*SEG* 39.128 and 45.108).

R10. Woodward 1956: 1–2, no. IV; Lambert 3.63

Although this very fragmentary inscription certainly contains an honorary decree from some time after ca. 350, its connection with trade rests solely on many highly speculative and "unconvincing" restorations by Woodward (Lambert 2007: 102 n. 10).

R11. *IG* ii² 337

IG ii² 337 is a well-preserved inscription that provides important insights into Athenian trade policy; however, it is not an honorary decree. Rather, it is an official and favorable Athenian response proposed in the Assembly by the famous financial administrator Lykourgos to a request by Kitian *emporoi* for *enktesis*, the right to own land in Athens, so that they could construct a temple of Aphrodite. The People of Athens must have believed that the Kitian *emporoi* performed valuable services for the city, since *enktesis* was normally a privilege exclusively limited to Athenian citizens and granted only in recognition of noteworthy public services. Since *IG* ii² 337 explicitly refers to the Kitians as *emporoi*, their services were probably connected with trade. In this case, though, Athens did not single out any particular trade-related service for recognition but rather honored the Kitian *emporoi* simply because it valued their day-to-day trading activities and sought to provide them with an incentive to continue such activities into the future. In other ways, too, the decree does not contain the typical features of Athenian honorary decrees: there is no commendation; there is no motivation clause; there is no honorary language; there is not even a provision for the inscribing of the decree, which the Kitians may have had to accomplish at their own expense. Therefore, even though *IG* ii² 337 represents an important aspect of Athens' efforts to encourage traders, it is not an honorary decree and will not be included in this study.

R12. *IG* ii² 369+414(b)+(c); Schweigert 1940: 335–39, no. 42; Lambert 2001: 65–70; Lambert 3.92, 93, 106, and 142

Schweigert associated several fragments, including *IG* ii² 369 and 414(b)+(c), as parts of one inscription containing honorary decrees for two groups of honorands.[76] The first group (lines 6–13) received a commendation and gold crowns for somehow assisting those who came to the Bosporos. The second group (lines 14–33) consisted of one man, the son of Demetrios, who, if one accepts Schweigert's restorations, gave ([ἐπιδέδω]κεν, line 14) three thousand *medimnoi* of wheat to the People and then gave ([ἐπιδέδωκεν], line 15) something to the People "for the war" ([εἰς τὸν πόλεμον], lines 15–16). It is possible that the honorand gave grain to Athens during the shortages of 337–320 and then gave either money or grain again during the Lamian War of 323–322. Owing to the extremely fragmentary state of the inscription, though, it is impossible to be certain about the exact nature of the services of the honorand or the goods involved in those services. Schweigert (followed by others), however, was prompted to connect the honorary decree to trade because of its reference to the Bosporos in line 8 and the date of the decree (set by Schweigert at 323/2 on the basis of his restoration of the prescript), which lies within a period when Athens was suffering through frequent grain shortages.[77]

Unfortunately, there are problems with Schweigert's reconstruction, both epigraphically and historically. Lambert (2001: 65–70) rejects Schweigert's association of the various fragments on epigraphic grounds and sees them instead as three separate inscriptions plus some miscellaneous fragments. All three inscriptions contain honorary decrees, and two of them may have a connection to trade, but the connection is too tenuous for them to be included in this study. One (*Agora* 16.94, frags. [a]+[b]+[i]+[d]=Lambert 3.106) is an honorary decree for the son of Demetrios, but its putative connections with trade are wholly dependent on Schweigert's restored text, which states that the honorand was recognized for giving Athens three thousand *medimnoi* of wheat. Schweigert himself inserted a question mark after the restoration, and it has not been accepted by Lambert (2001: 66 and 69). The son of Demetrios might just as well have been honored for performing services of a political or military nature.

The other inscription (*Agora* 16.94, frags. [c]+[j]=Lambert 3.92) commends and grants gold crowns to two men, Astym— and Polysthenes, for doing good both publicly and privately for those who come to the Bosporos. In connecting this to the decree for the son of Demetrios, Schweigert conjectured that the honorands somehow helped the son of Demetrios to ship grain from the Bosporos to Athens. Despite the fact that he does not accept a connection between the two inscriptions, Lambert still believes that it is "sehr wahrscheinliche" (very probable) that Astym— and Polysthenes received honors for assisting Athens in the grain trade (Lambert 2001: 70). He conjectures that they were representatives of the Bosporan royal family whom Athens honored in the same way as the Bosporan ambassadors who had somehow facilitated the trade relations between their kings and Athens in *IG* ii² 212 (no. 12 of this study). Although this might be the case, it rests purely on speculation. As in the case of the son of Demetrios, Astym— and Polysthenes might have been honored for political or military services rather than trade-related ones. Because there is no way to tell for certain, I will not include this decree in this study.

R13. *IG* ii² 312; Lambert 3.80

Lambert (2007: 104 and n. 32) includes this decree among his collection of honorary decrees for foreigners and states that it honored two (probably) men "for the import of grain." Despite the fact that almost no text of the decree is extant, Lambert does provide some evidence for his assertion, in the form of a relief on the inscription that depicts the prow of a ship with projecting stalks of grain and two inscribed wreathes. Thus, it is quite possible that this inscription is an honorary decree for trade-related services. In the absence of any text, however, even if one could be certain of the purpose of the inscription, it provides no information for analysis, and I will, therefore, exclude this inscription from my study.

R14. *IG* ii² 427; Lambert 3.158

IG ii² 427 is included in Lambert's collection of honorary decrees for foreigners, and there he speculates that it might concern the grain trade (Lambert 2007: 127 and n. 145). Very little text is extant, however, and only the letters ΣΙΤΟ (followed by a T) provide any reason to believe that we have here an honorary decree for services relating to trade. This is not enough to include this decree in the present study.

R15. Walbank 1980: 251–55, no. 1

This inscription does contain an honorary decree for trade-related services, but it does not fall within the chronological limits of the present study. In the absence of an extant archon formula, Walbank dated the decree to 331–324, assuming that it was relevant to the period of severe grain shortages in Athens. He did note, however, that the letterforms seemed more compatible with a date in the third century (Walbank 1980: 253). Despite Henry's affirmation of Walbank's restoration of the inscription and conclusion that it is compatible with a date in the late fourth century, Tracy has confirmed Walbank's suspicions concerning the date by identifying the scribal hand of this inscription with that of a stonecutter who did not become active until 295.[78] Tracy narrows the range of dates down to ca. 287–284 on historical grounds, thus placing it outside the chronological limits of this study.

R16. Dubious identifications by Walbank and Burke

Walbank has identified trading interests as the motivation for several Athenian decrees that grant *proxenia*. These cases are designated by Walbank in his book *Athenian Proxenies of the Fifth Century B.C.* as nos. 1, 2, 3, 6, 9, 16, 55, and 91. To this list of *proxenia* grants to "men actively involved in maritime trade," Burke adds Walbank's nos. 17, 27, and 30 (Burke 1992: 207 and n. 34). Both scholars assume that if the ethnic of a *proxenos* corresponds to a place situated along a trade route, Athens must have made the grant of *proxenia* to fulfill its trading interests. Such an assumption, however, is not secure enough for these possible cases to be included in the present study.

Notes

Chapter One

1. Quotation from Aristotle from Arist. *Pol.* 1257a41–1257b5, translated by the author from the Oxford Classical Texts edition by W. D. Ross. Quotation from Xenophon from Xen. *Poroi* 3.4, translated by the author from the Oxford Classical Texts edition by E. C. Marchant. For the date 336–322, see the Loeb edition of Aristotle's *Politics*, edited by Hugh Rackham (Cambridge, MA: Harvard University Press, 1998).

2. See Finkelstein 1935: 320–36 for a detailed discussion of the meaning of *kapelike* and its derivatives. Although these words normally refer to "retail" trade, which involves strictly local exchanges of goods by nonproducers for profit, there was some flexibility in their usage, and it is clear that Aristotle is using *kapelikon* in the broad sense of "commercial exchange," which I have translated simply as "trade."

3. See pp. 95–96, for a more detailed discussion of the concept of capitalism and its existence in Classical Greece.

4. See Gauthier 1976: 1–7 for the date of Xenophon's *Poroi*.

5. See Dover 1974: 226–42; Ferguson 1989: 17–33; and chapter 3 of this book for a more thorough discussion of the ancient Greek concept of honor.

6. Among the many surveys of the debate are Will 1954: 7–22; Polanyi 1944: 43–55; Pearson 1957: 3–11; Polanyi 1957: 67–78; Humphreys 1969: 165–212; Humphreys 1970: 2–9; Austin and Vidal-Naquet 1977: 3–8; Lowry 1979: 65–86; Millett 1991: 9–18; Cartledge 1983: 1–15; Andreau and Etienne 1984: 55–69; Cartledge 1998: 4–7; Morris 1994a: 351–66; Tandy and Neale 1994: 9–10, 20–24; Silver 1995: xxii–xxiii, 97–177; Tandy 1997: 84–87; Davies 1998: 230–42; Morris 1999: ix–xxxvi; Horden and Purcell 2000: 105–8, 143–52; Engen 2001: 179–85; Morris and Manning 2005: 142–49; Hall 2007: 235–37; and Morley 2007: 2–12. Many of the recent studies that challenge the Finley model can be found in Parkins and Smith 1998; Archibald, Davies, Gabrielsen, and Oliver 2001; Mattingly and Salmon 2001; Meadows and Shipton 2001; Cartledge, Cohen, and Foxhall 2002; and Scheidel and von Reden 2002. See also Halstead 1987: 77–87; Cohen 1992a; Burke 1992: 199–226; Bresson 2000; Engen 2001: 179–202; Engen 2004: 150–65; and Engen 2005: 359–81.

7. See Davies 1998: 225–56; Davies 2001a: 12–14; and Davies 2006: 73, 90. The proposed "model" of Amemiya 2007 is really no model at all (see below).

8. Graham Oliver's 1995 Oxford PhD dissertation, "The Athenian State under Threat: Politics and Food Supply, 307 to 229 B.C.," which treats Athe-

nian trade policy in the early Hellenistic period, has just been published in revised form (Oliver 2007) but was unavailable to me as I wrote this book.

9. See chapters 4 and 8, *Ateleia*, of this book concerning the goals of Athenian trade policy. Recent studies, including Shipton 2001 and Engen 2005, show that there were important exceptions to the general rule of consumption-oriented state economic policy. In *Poroi* 3.5, Xenophon himself states that his proposals will lead to an expansion of both imports and exports.

10. Concerning these changes, see Veyne 1977; Veyne 1990; McKechnie 1989; Oliver 1995: 280–89; Davies 2001a: 18–19; Reger 2003: 342–51; and Davies 2006: 78–79, 83–86, 88–89. As Davies (2001a: 19) puts it, "we are looking at a period when many processes . . . were moving rather faster, or were affecting wider areas, or were moving (absolutely or relatively) more goods and services and people, than had been the case in (say) the sixth or fifth century in the same regions."

11. See Samuel 1983: 1–10 concerning the general absence of a growth mentality in the ancient Greek economy.

12. See Davies 1998: 230–32; Davies 2001a: 12; and Morley 2007: 82–89, especially 84–85.

13. See Engen 2004: 150–65.

14. Among these noble citizens were the men who proposed the honorary decrees for trade-related services. They include such famous Athenian statesmen as Alkibiades, Androtion, Demosthenes, Lykourgos, and Demades. In a forthcoming article, I will examine their backgrounds, political careers, and involvement with trade in order to identify their public and private interests in honoring those who performed trade-related services.

15. Concerning the organization of Athenian government and the numbers of Assembly decrees produced during this period, see Tracy 1995: 18, 36–37.

16. See, e.g., Gernet [1909] 1979; Jardé 1925; Isager and Hansen 1975: 11–27; Foxhall and Forbes 1982; Gallo 1984: 48–57; Garnsey 1985: 62–75; Garnsey 1988: 89–106; Sallares 1991; Gallant 1991; Oliver 1995; Whitby 1998: 102–28; and Amemiya 2007: 74–78. See also Garnsey 1998: 195–200 for a convenient summary of some of these estimates (with commentary) by Walter Scheidel. Note also Whitby's pessimistic assessment of the reliability of such estimates and their multitude of assumptions, which are often drawn from proxy data from modern Greek peasant agriculture. Morley (2007: 35–36) provides another critique of this method.

17. See Cartledge 1998: 7–8; Davies 2001a: 28; and Morley 2007: 5–6 on the limitations of archaeological evidence for studying the ancient Greek economy.

18. Whitby (1998: especially 117–27) also stresses the Athenian need to obtain more grain than was simply sufficient to feed its population, in order to keep prices reasonable and to provide a cushion against sudden shortfalls. Garnsey (1988: 139–45) provides a survey of the evidence for Athenian institutions and laws concerned with the grain trade in the fourth century. Tsetskhladze (1998: 52–74) believes that Athenian imports of grain from the Bosporos have been exaggerated on the basis of limited archaeological evidence for Athenian exports in the Black Sea region.

19. This approach is supported by Reger 2003: 339. See also North 1990.

20. Finley 1985: 35–61, especially 37–38 and 52. See also below and Osborne 2001. Osborne's review of Archibald et al. 2001 criticizes its studies for not being sensitive enough to the bias of their sources, which leads them to take too Finleyan a view.

21. For the former view, see Hasebroek 1933: 4, 7, 10, 22; Erxleben 1974; Millet 1983; and Millet 1991. For the latter, see Isager and Hansen 1975; Hansen 1984; and Cohen 1992a. Montgomery (1986: 43–61) accepts the view that Athenian citizens did not as a rule participate directly in trade, but he attributes this reluctance to practical impediments, such as the inability of citizens to gain expert knowledge of the profession and the foreign sources of grain, as opposed to a prevailing mentality against trade.

22. See, e.g., Böckh 1857: 342, 584, 689, 758–59 and Busolt 1920: 602–3, 1213.

23. See, e.g., Gernet [1909] 1979: 347–81, particularly 379; Isager and Hanson 1975: 20–27, 200–206; and Garnsey 1988: 137–44. Garnsey does, however, acknowledge that this practice was part of a trade policy designed to secure imports of grain.

24. For epigraphic studies, see Henry 1983 and Veligianni-Terzi 1997. For studies of honors and privileges, see Pecirka 1966 (*enktesis*); Marek 1984 (*proxenia*); and Osborne 1981b, 1982, and 1983 (citizenship).

25. Examples of the work of such cultural historians can be seen in Kurke 1991, 1999, and 2001 and von Reden 1995, 1997, and 2001. See also chap. 2, Economics or Sociology?; Morris 1994a: 355–60; and Morris and Manning 2005: 147–48.

26. Wealthy professional traders who gave gifts of imported goods or sold them at a reduced price appear in nos. 15, 21, 23, 24, 27, and 33 (throughout, numbers refer to the catalog in the appendixes). Foreign potentates who gave gifts of imported goods or performed other trade-related services that did not earn immediate and direct monetary profits appear in nos. 6, 7, 9, 11, 12, 22, 26, 30, and 34.

Chapter Two

1. The quotations are from Morris 1999: x–xi, xxiii–xxvi; Hopkins 1983: xi; and Morris 1999: xxxi–xxxii, respectively. For other affirmations of the continuing importance of Finley's model, see Archibald 2001: 2; Reger 2003: 352; and Hall 2007: 236, 253.

2. See p. 327, n. 6, for surveys of the debate.

3. Weber's focus on values and institutions in characterizing societies is pointed out by numerous modern observers, including R. I. Frank (in Weber [1909] 1976: 25) and Austin and Vidal-Naquet (1977: 6). For an example of his emphasis on institutions from Weber himself, see Weber [1909] 1976: 45–46.

4. Hasebroek 1933: 4. For a recent critique of this narrow view, see Morley 2007: xiii, 8.

5. Polanyi 1957b: 262. See also Tandy 1997: 94–127 for a more recent and extended discussion of the various types of exchange.

6. Parsons and Smelser (1956: 5–8, 39–51, and passim) originated the use of the terms *differentiated* and *undifferentiated* to refer to the degree to which the economy is conceived of as being distinct from other social institutions, but though more precise, these terms differ little in substance from Polanyi's use of the terms *disembedded* and *embedded*.

7. Finley 1970: 14–17, discussing Aristotle's analysis of a just exchange in *NE* 1096a5–6 and of acquisition (*chrematistike*) and trade (*kapelike*) in *Pol.* 1258b1–2.

8. See p. 327, n. 6.

9. Cohen 1992; Halstead 1987: 77–87; Hodkinson 1988: 35–74; Hodkinson 1992: 53–60; Jameson, Runnels, and Tjeerd 1994: 383–94; Hanson 1995.

10. Finley 1985: 160; see also 23 and 60 for Finley's assumption that the term *trade* refers to "market trade."

11. Reed 2003: 17 n. 8. For Kyrene's grain distribution see app. 3 (no. 22).

12. See Smelser and Swedberg 1994b: 3–8 and Smelser and Swedberg 2005b: 3–6 for an overview of economic sociology in comparison with mainstream "formalist" economics.

13. Granovetter 1985: 485–87. See also Granovetter and Swedberg 1992a: 12.

14. Hargreaves Heap 1989: 1–11; Christesen 2003: 31–56.

15. Recent scholarship has tended to acknowledge the coexistence of a variety of economic structures in Classical Greece; see Tandy 1997: 113–14 and Cartledge 1998: 4–24, the latter of which provides an overview of the bibliography.

16. Burke 1992, echoed from a banking perspective by Cohen 1992a: 87–88.

17. Morris 1994b. See also Morris 1994a: 354; Morris 1999: xxix–xxxi; and Morris 2005: 147–48. The relevant passages of Aristotle are *NE* 1096a5–6, 1157b35, 1158b11–1159a5, and 1171b32 and *Pol.* 1252b30–1253a1, 1256b30–34, 1278a6–8, and 1329a2–39.

18. Morris (1994b: 61) is too quick to dismiss Burke's emphasis on the significance of Xenophon's *Poroi*, insisting that the work does not indicate real change in the Athenian economy but is quite traditional in relegating commercial activity to *metics*. The *Poroi*, however, is in fact radical in its suggestion that the state should involve itself in this process and actually provide honors and privileges to such outsiders for traditionally disesteemed economic activities.

Chapter Three

1. For the following survey, see, in general, Knorringa 1926; Adkins 1960; Dover 1974; Austin and Vidal-Naquet 1977; Finley 1978; Herman 1987; Ober 1989; Murray 1993; Wilson 2000; and Hall 2007: 235–54.

2. Wilson 2000: 193; MacMullen 1974: 125.

3. Finley 1978: 121–22. See also Austin and Vidal-Naquet 1977: 40–44.

4. On gift exchange in "primitive" societies in general, see Mauss [1923–24] 1967.

5. Finley 1978: 66–67, 98; Herman 1987: 10, 61 and n. 62, 80, 121–22, 128–29.

6. Herman 1987: 78–80, 84, 121; Murray 1993: 48.

7. Adkins 1960: 156–57, 198, 205–8, 226, 238; Dover 1974: 165, 175, 230; Whitehead 1983: 59–60.

8. Austin and Vidal-Naquet 1977: 105; Finley 1985: 48; Ober 1989: 249.

9. Austin and Vidal-Naquet 1977: 94–95; Finley 1985: 48; Ober 1989: 5–7.

10. On liturgies in general, see Böckh 1857: 584–607, 689–755; Andreades 1933: 130–31, 291–92; Michell 1957: 375–81; Davies 1967: 33–40; Pickard-Cambridge 1968: 41, 71–73; Austin and Vidal-Naquet 1977: 121– 22; and Finley 1985: 150–52. See Wilson 2000 for a thorough study of the *choregia*.

11. This is the basic thesis of Wilson 2000 (see in particular p. 173). See also Davies 1971: xvii; Davis 1981: 92– 100; Finley 1985: 151–52; and Ober 1989: 226–47.

12. Whitehead 1983: 60–68; Finley 1985: 151–52; Ober 1989: 243; Wilson 2000: 54, 144–45, 172–73.

13. Pickard-Cambridge 1968: 77–78; Wilson 2000: 59, 102, 192, 207. See also Dem. 51 and *IG* ii^2 1629.176ff.

14. *IG* ii^2 2318.

15. Ober 1989: 243–44; Wilson 2000: 198, 202–3, 209, 214. See also Wilson 2001: 198–243 for a thorough examination of choregic monuments.

16. Ober 1989: 228–40; Gabrielsen 1994: 10–12; Wilson 2000: 113, 147, 179.

17. Whitehead 1977: 80–81 and n. 85; Pickard-Cambridge 1968: 41; Wilson 2000: 25–31, 318–19 nn. 70 and 88–89.

18. Whitehead 1977: 81–82; Gabrielsen 1994: 61, 240 n. 25.

19. Davies 1971: xxiv; Ober 1989: 14 n. 24; Gabrielsen 1994: 45, 58. The financial obligations of the trierarchy were further spread out among the top twelve hundred wealthiest Athenian citizens by the reforms of Periander in 358/7 and Demosthenes in 340/39; see Gabrielsen 1994: 182–99, 209–12.

20. Davies 1967: 33–40; Gabrielsen 1994: 213; Wilson 2000: 191.

21. Whitehead 1983: 66–68; Lambert 2004: 86–87.

22. Herman 1987: 6, 142–65, especially 149, 153, 155, 160–64.

23. One exception can be seen in And. 2.11, in which Andokides seeks favor from the *demos* by pointing to his *xenia* with King Archelaos of Macedon, which allowed him to procure much-needed oars for Athenian warships during a crisis.

24. See Davies 1971: 133–35; Ste. Croix 1981: 609 n. 58; Ober 1989: 236–38, 245–46; and Herman 1987: 7, 73–81.

25. Konon was honored by Athens for deeds that were largely financed by the Persians, which included leading a Persian fleet that defeated the Spartans off Knidos and rebuilding the Long Walls of Athens (Xen. *Hell.* 4.3.10–12, 4.8.9; Diod. 14.81.4–6, 83.4–7, 85.2–4). Whether Konon was honored during his lifetime or posthumously, however, is uncertain, since he died shortly after performing these two services.

26. *IG* ii^2 657; ^{2}=IG ii^2 682 (concerning the latter, see also Habicht 1997: 96–97, 127–28). Herman (1987: 85) believes that *IG* ii^2 655, which honors Timo— (name incomplete) in 285/4 is a case of an Athenian grant of honors to a citizen for procuring a benefaction from his *xenos*, but there is insufficient evidence to know whether Timo— was a citizen.

27. Lambert 2004.

28. These generals include Kleon (Ar. *Hipp.* 573–76), Chabrias (Dem. 20.75–86; Aischin. 3.243), Iphikrates (Dem. 20.84, 23.130 and 136; Aischin. 3.243), and Timotheos (Dem. 20.84; Aischin. 3.243).

29. For Demades' embassy to Alexander in 335/4, see Dein. 1.101; Diod. 17.15.3–5; and Plut. *Dem.* 23.6. For Demosthenes' financial contributions while holding public office, see Dem. 18.54–55, 118; Aischin. 3.24, 27–28, 31; Plut. *Dem.* 24.2–3; and [Plut.] *Ten Orat.* 845f–846a, 851a.

30. There are too many honorary decrees for noncitizens to cite them all. In addition to those that are the focus of this book, some well-preserved ones from the fourth century include *IG* ii² 8, 31, 82, 103, 106, 110, 133, 141, 149 (=Lambert 3.24), 174, 206 (=Lambert 3.23), 233, 238 (=Lambert 3.32), 284+Add. (=Lambert 3.19), 351+624+Add. (=Lambert 3.42), 448, and 466.

31. Herman 1987: 12, 31–34, 88–89 and n. 49, 98–103, 106–15, 162, 166–75.

32. Herman 1987: 132–42. On *proxenia* in general, see also Gschnitzer 1973; Walbank 1978; Marek 1984; and Gauthier 1985: 131–50. The dual nature of *proxenia* as both honor and duty will be examined in chapter 7.

33. There are too many honorary decrees for political, military, or financial services to cite them all; some well-preserved ones include *IG* ii² 1, 8, 19, 31, 103, 106, 109, 110, 127, 174, 222 (=Lambert 3.8), 233 (=Lambert 3.72), 237+Add. (=Lambert 3.5), 238 (=Lambert 3.32), 336+Add. (=Lambert 3.7), 350, 385, 448, 450, and 553.

34. Xen. *Mem.* 3.6.2–13. See also Arist. *AP* 43.4, where it is stated that one of the standing items for consideration at each principal Assembly meeting (*ekklesia kuria*), right alongside defense of territory, is the city's grain supply. Arist. *Rhet.* 1359b–1360a also includes the food supply among the standard concerns of governing assemblies.

35. Garnsey 1988: 107–19. See also Gernet [1909] 1979; Jardé 1925; Gallant 1991; Sallares 1991; Oliver 1995; and Whitby 1998 for other estimates.

36. See [Xen.] *AP* (*Old Oligarch*) 2.2–3 and *IG* i³ 61 (concerning Methone) and 62 (concerning Aphytis). See also app. 3, R4 and R5.

37. Xen. *Mem.* 3.6.12; Isager and Hansen 1975: 43; Kroll 1976: 329–41; Hopper 1979: 179; Kroll 1993: 8.

38. See Stroud 1998: 31–37 for an overview of the importance of these islands for Athens' grain supply.

39. Ar. *Ekk.* 718–25; Xen. *Poroi* 4.28. See also Kroll 1993: 8.

40. *IG* ii² 1604. See Ashton 1977: 1–11 and Gabrielsen 1994: 127.

41. See Dem. 24.135 and Davies 1971: 277–81 for the relationship between Kallistratos and Agyrrhios. Garnsey (1988: 147) and Stroud (1998: 119) believe that the law was a response to these threats to Athens' revenues and grain supply.

42. See Stroud 1998 for the *editio princeps* of this law, which exists on a stele that was found in the Athenian Agora in 1987. See also Dem. 22.15, from 355, which refers to a grain shortage that took place at some time prior to the speech.

43. [Dem.] 49.49 attests to the existence of the *syntaxeis* in 373. See Theopompos *FGrHist* 115 F 98 for the characterization of *styntaxeis* as *phoros* by another name. Cargill (1981: 146–60) examines the cleruchies of the late

360s at length. Androtion served as governor and oversaw a garrison in Arkesine on Amorgos in 358/7–357/6 (*IG* XII (7) 5; Tod 2.152; Harding no. 68).

44. *IG* ii² 1611.3–9. See also Gabrielsen 1994: 127.

45. Ehrenberg 1969: 149; Hornblower 1983: 170–72.

46. See Cawkwell 1963: 47–67 for a thorough treatment of the career of Euboulos, emphasizing his implementation of the program of Isokrates and Xenophon (63–65). Whitehead (1977: 128–29), however, cautions against overemphasizing the point.

47. Finley 1985: 60, 160–62, following Hasebroek 1933: 102, but questioned now by Reed 2003: 52.

48. See Dion. Halik. *Ep. ad Amm.* 1.4 for the date of Dem. 20.

49. The traditional view of this episode is that Athens distributed some of the grain to its citizenry at no charge and then sold the surplus for fifteen talents. Bresson (2000: 209–10), however, argues persuasively that Athens sold the entire amount of Leukon's gift of grain to its citizens at a price reduced from the going rate, which was inflated on account of the shortage.

50. Henry 1996: 105–19, especially 106. See also Hedrick 1999: 387–439 (identifying similar types of motivation clauses for inscribing decrees, which Hedrick calls "formulae of disclosure") and, in general, Whitehead 1983.

51. See also Hakkarainen 1997: 15–19 and Lambert 2006: 116–17.

52. Arist. *AP* 52.2, 59.5; Cohen 1973; Isager and Hansen 1975: 84–87; Rhodes 1981: 582–83, 664–66; Garnsey 1988: 139.

53. Dem. 18.73–78; Philoch. *FGrHist* 328 F 161–62; Theopompos *FGrHist* 115 F 292.

54. There has been some debate concerning the nature of Lykourgos' office and the date of its inception. Markianos (1969: 325–31) and Mitchel (1973: 190) believe that Lykourgos' term began in 338. However, Davies (*APF* 9251, p. 351)—after a suggestion by Lewis—and, more recently, Faraguna (1992: 197–205) hold that the office began in 336 and that Lykourgos controlled it until 324. Sealey (1993: 209–10) doubts whether there ever was an office *ho epi ten dioikesin* and suggests that Lykourgos may have controlled Athenian finances though several different offices over a twelve-year period. See [Plut.] *Ten Orat.* 841b, 852b and Diod. 16.88.1. Concerning the revenues raised by Lykourgos, see [Plut.] *Ten. Orat.* 842f, 852b. Dem. 10.37 says that revenues had dropped to 130 talents after the Social War.

55. See Mitchel 1973: 196–97; Humphreys 1985: 204, 212–13; and Faraguna 1992: 381–96 for Lykourgos' encouragement of voluntary contributions.

56. For commercial lawsuits, see speeches 32–38 and 56 of the Demosthenic corpus. Lykourgos also proposed *IG* ii² 337 in 333/2, which granted *enktesis* in response to a request from Kitian *emporoi* resident in the Peiraieus who wished to build a temple to Aphrodite (see app. 3, R11). See also Burke 1985: 251–64 concerning Lykourgos' trade policy.

57. See Mitchel 1973: 190–214; Will 1983: 79–93; Humphreys 1985: 205–9; Faraguna 1992: 245–85; Tracy 1995: 10–13; and Habicht 1997: 16–18, 22–29 for surveys of Lykourgos' accomplishments, many of which are described in the decree of Stratokles in honor of Lykourgos that is preserved in [Plut.] *Ten Orat.* 852 and in fragments in *IG* ii² 457+513.

58. Garnsey (1988), Oliver (1995), and Lambert (2006, 2007) each stress the negative impact of the Battle of Chaironeia on the Athenian grain supply.

59. [Dem.] 34.38–39. See also Schweigert 1940: 341 concerning several documents (IG ii² 1623.276–85; [Plut.] Ten Orat. 844a; IG ii² 414a=Lambert 1.21) that attest to an Athenian naval expedition in 335/4 to deal with pirates at this time as well.

60. See Diod. 17.62.6–17.63.4 and Plut. Dem. 24.1 concerning the revolt of Agis; see [Dem.] 34.38–39, and Dem.(?) 56.9–10 concerning the grain shortage in Athens.

61. For the epidosis, see nos. 24 and 27; [Dem.] 34.38–39; IG ii² 1628.358–452, 1629.859–975; Kuenzi 1923: 29; Migeotte 1983: 146–48; Garnsey 1988: 155–56; and Migeotte 1992: 20–21, no. 8. Concerning the colony, see IG ii² 1629.163–232.

62. Diod. 20.35–46; Plut. Demetr. 8–10; Diod. 18.74.3; Strabo 9.

63. Plut. Demetr. 10.1–3; Diod. 20.46.4. See also IG ii² 1492.97–99, 119–21.

64. See Oliver 1995: 197–279, 310–17 (the latter pages in tabular form with notes), which collects the evidence for honorary decrees involving the Athenian grain supply between 307 and 229 B.C.E.

65. Other possible but unlikely cases of honors for professional traders after 319 and down to 280 include either citizens or foreigners who contributed to a sitonia (IG ii² 479/480 and 670; Walbank 1980: 251–55, no. 1 [R10]) or those for whom little is known on account of the poor preservation of their decrees (IG ii² 651 and 655).

66. For decrees honoring foreign potentates, see IG ii² 657, 650, 653, 654, and 655 (agent of a foreign potentate). For those honoring citizens, see IG ii² 682; Shear 1978=SEG 28.60; Meritt 1936b: 201–5 [EM 12825] (sitones); and IG ii² 744 (sitonai).

67. Veyne 1976: 76, 81; Veyne 1990: 1, 10, 16, 42–44, 83.

68. See Davies 1984: 306–7; de Ste Croix 1981: 300–315; and Rhodes with Lewis 2003: 52 for the persistence of democracy in the Greek cities of the Hellenistic period.

69. Hakkarainen 1997: 25. See also Billows 2003: 196–97, 211–13, in which Billows argues that Classical Athens provided a model for cities of the Hellenistic period by honoring its benefactors as a means not only to obtain revenue and grain but also to make manifest the shared interests of the masses and the elite within cities and the citizens and kings without, thereby maintaining harmony between these groups.

70. For the breakdown of the ideal of the exclusive polis in the Hellenistic period, see Davies 1984: 309; F. Walbank 1981: 141–58; McKechnie 1989: 3–5; Green 1990: 80, 163, 388; and Shipley and Hansen 2006: 61–62.

71. F. Walbank 1981: 64–65; Shipley and Hansen 2006: 62 and n. 61 for bibliography.

Chapter Four

1. Hasebroek 1933: 4. For a recent critique of this narrow view, see Morley 2007: xiii, 8.

2. For foodstuffs, see nos. 7, 9, 11, 12, 14–27, 29–31, and 33–34; for timber, nos. 4 and 6.

3. Gernet [1909] 1979: 364–75; Hasebroek 1933: 103; Burke 1992, passim.

4. Burke 1992: 199–226. See also Hakkarainen 1997: 1–32 for another argument that stresses revenue as the goal of Athenian trade policy.

5. Nos. 6 (407/6), 9 (389/8), 22 (333–324), 23 (335/4, 331/0, or 326/5), and 27 (325/4 for a gift in 328/7).

6. Nos. 13 (ca. 340), 20 (ca. 334/3–321), and 31 (ca. 321–318).

7. Dem. 4.34; [Dem.] 7 passim; [Dem.] 12.13. See also Gernet [1909] 1979: 357–59; Ormerod 1924: 115; Mitchell 1957: 310; and Heichelheim 1958: 92 on Athens' increasingly futile struggle to rid the Aegean of pirates as the fourth century progressed.

8. No. 13. See also Schweigert 1940: 341 concerning several documents (*IG* ii² 1623.276–85; [Plut.] *Ten Oral.* 844a; and *IG* ii² 414a=Lambert 1.21) that attest to an Athenian naval expedition in 335/4 to deal with pirates.

9. Nos. 20 and 31. See *IG* ii² 1629.217–32 concerning an Athenian naval expedition to deal with pirates in 325/4.

10. [Arist.] *Oik.* 1352b19; [Dem.] 42.20; [Dem.] 34.39. See Isager and Hansen 1975: 200–202 and Garnsey 1988: 154 for the date of these references.

11. Isager and Hansen1975: 200. Böckh (1857: 130) uses a similar method to determine the price of grain and obtains similar results.

12. Gernet [1909] 1979: 307; Isager and Hansen 1975: 23–25.

13. Nos. 15 (ca. 337), 21 (333/2), 24 (330/29–328/7), and 33 (before 320/19).

14. Polanyi 1957: 87; Finley 1965: 26–27, 33; Finley 1985: 22, 177–78; Tandy 1997: 122–25. Polanyi (1957: 87; 1968: 312–18) and Lowry (1979: 68–69) believe that Greek cities as a rule fixed the price of grain. Although this was often true with regard to the *retail* price of grain (Arist. *AP* 52.3), rarely did cities fix the *wholesale* price of grain, which is completely unattested for Athens in the Classical period. See Larsen 1960: 216–18 and Humphreys 1969: 186–87 against Polanyi. Loomis' study of wages in Classical Athens shows, contrary to Finley 1985: 23 and n. 19, that wages were set in accordance with the supply and demand for labor, thus indicating that there was a market organization for wages (i.e., the price of labor) (Loomis 1998: 253–54, 258). Reger (2003: 339–41) has also argued in favor of the existence of price-setting markets. See also app. 3, no. 33 for my arguments against Bresson's hypothesis (Bresson 2000: 183–210) that Athens set a recommended, though not obligatory, wholesale price on grain. Steinhauer (1994: 51–68) and Bresson (2000: 151–82) have published editions of the text of a decree concerning the *agoranomoi* in the Peiraieus, in which the price of fish is set; however, the decree dates to 35/4 B.C.E. and is therefore well beyond the chronological the scope of this study.

15. Other examples that attest to the connection between supply and price in ancient Greece include Lys. 22.14–15 and [Dem.] 17.28, 50.6.

16. Humphreys (1969: 185–87, 186 n. 69; 1970: 9, 13–14, 25) acknowledges the existence of "peripheral" (local and isolated) price-making markets and market exchanges in Classical Greece. Tandy (1997: 117–27) recognizes an even wider array of market types in ancient Greece.

17. Orations 32, 34, 35, and 56. See also Xen. *Oik.* 20.27–28. See Reed 2003: 6–14 concerning the typical activities of traders in carrying out their profession.

18. See And. 1.137–38; Dem. 4.34, 8.25; [Dem.] 12.5, 17.19–20, 33.4, 34.8, 35.11, 50.21, and 13; Isokr. 17.36; Lykourgos *Against Leokrates* 14–15, 18; and [Arist.]. *Oik.* 1346b29.

19. For the typically high interest rates associated with maritime investments, see Xen. *Poroi* 3.9–10; [Dem.] 34.23, 25 (for 30 percent interest on a maritime loan); and [Dem.] 50.17 (for a maritime loan at 12.5 percent, the lowest that we know of). See also Cohen 1992: 44, 52–58.

20. Finley 1985: 22–23, 144, 177–78. See also Millett 1983 and Millett 1991: 15–18, 35, 71–73, 282 n. 15.

21. See Love 1991: 35–55 for a survey of Weber's views on capitalism in antiquity.

22. Finley 1985: 23; Millett 1991: 15–18, 35, 71, 282 n. 15. See also Cohen 1992b, which criticizes Millett's use of the terms *noncapitalist* and *precapitalist*.

23. Nos. 25 (after ca. 330), 16 (ca. 337–330), 17 (ca. 337–325), 18 (ca. 337–320), 19 (ca. 337–320?), and 31 (ca. 321–318).

24. See Isager and Hansen 1975: 55, 200–206; Camp 1982: 9–17; Garnsey 1988: 14, 154–64; and pp. 65–66, for the dates of grain shortages in Athens.

25. See app. 3, nos. 7, 9, 12, 26, and 34 for details and references concerning the brief review that follows.

26. Finley 1985: 162; Hasebroek 1933: 114. See also Hopper 1979: 88, stating that Athens alone benefited from its relations with the Bosporan kings. According to Hopper, Athens gave back only "honorary distinction and not . . . material advantage." Thus, Hopper concluded that the relationship between Athens and Leukon "was not one embodying reciprocal advantages."

27. See Engen 2005, however, for some notable exceptions that indicate that Athens may have had productive interests in trade as well.

Chapter Five

Portions of this chapter have appeared in another form in Engen 2001: 179–202.

1. Hasebroek 1933: 22, 42, 101. Note that Finley (1985: 144) departs from Hasebroek on the subject of the ethnicity of *metics*; Finley acknowledges that most of them were probably Greeks, but he thinks that the point is irrelevant.

2. For arguments in support of the model, see Erxleben 1974 and Millett 1983 and 1991. For arguments against, see Isager and Hansen 1975: 66–67, 72–73; M. V. Hansen 1984; and Cohen 1992: 134–35, 140–41, 152–53.

3. See Reed 2003: 15–26 for an indication of the volume of Athenian trade.

4. Whitehead 1977: 29 and n. 10; Gauthier 1985: 146.

5. For the *metics,* see nos. 4, 5, 23–25, and 27; for the *xenoi,* nos. 6, 7, 9, 11–13, 20, 22, 26 (a naturalized citizen and his *xenoi* sons), 29, 30, and 34.

6. For Greeks, see nos. 1, 4–6, 8, 13, 15, 17–24, 27, and 30; for non-Greeks, nos. 7, 9, 11, 12, 25, 26, 28, and 34.

7. Hasebroek 1933: 22, 42, 101. Note, however, that Finley (1985: 144) departs from Hasebroek on this point, deeming the ethnicity of *metics* to be irrelevant.

8. Isager and Hansen 1975: 33, 69; Garlan 1988: 46–47.

9. For trade routes in the Aegean during the Classical period, see Gernet [1909] 1979: 302–26; Michell 1957: 242–47; Isager and Hansen 1975: 60–62, 214–24; Hopper 1979: 52–60; and Garnsey 1988: 151–54.

10. See also app. 3, Introduction. I follow Reed (2003: 6–14, 34–42, 93) in my criteria for the division of professional traders into the categories of poor, moderately wealthy, and wealthy.

11. See Tandy 2006: 147–49 for a critique of Reed's categories.

12. For common traders, see nos. 8, 10, 17–19, 25, and 31; for moderately wealthy traders, nos. 1–3; for wealthy traders, nos. 15, 16, 21, 23, 24, 27, 32, and 33.

13. Nos. 6, 7, 9, 11, 12, 22, 26, 30, and 34.

14. Nos. 4, 5, 13, 14, 20, 28, and 29.

15. See [Dem.] 33.23; Cohen 1973; and Reed 2003: 89–92.

16. See, e.g., Stroud 1998 (48–50, 109–16) on the law of 374/3 concerning the 8⅓ percent tax in grain from the islands. Lines 10–14 indicate that Athens contracted with private parties to ship the grain from the islands to Athens.

17. Hasebroek 1933: 114; Finley 1985: 162.

Chapter Six

1. Henry 1983, 1996; Whitehead 1983, 1993.

2. *IG* i³ 17 (451/0 or 418/7), 29 (ca. 450), 203 (450–430), 164 (440–425), 43 (ca. 435–427, entirely restored), 162 (435–420), 228 (435–415), 158 (ca. 430), 92 (430–416/5), 167 (430–415), 121 (430–425), 65 (ca. 427/6), 81 (421/0), 114 (425–405), 73 (ca. 424–410), 227 (424–398), 177 (420–405), 96 (412/1), 97 (412/11), 113 (410, naturalized), 102 (410/09), 103 (410/09, naturalized), 101 (ca. 410–407), 108 (ca. 410–407), 109 (410– 407), 106 (410–405), 119 (408/7), 110 (408/7), and 123 (407/6). *IG* i³ 30 (ca. 450, entirely restored) and 62 (428/7 or ca. 426) might concern trade in addition to political and military matters, but see app. 3, R2 and R5, respectively.

3. *IG* ii² 1155 (339/8) includes a Council decree in honor of a tribal taxiarch (see V-T B6). *SEG* 28.52=Traill 1978: 274–77, no. 5=Lambert 1.4 (dated ca. 333 by Traill, ca. 340–325 by Lambert) is a decree of the Council that honors a treasurer of the prytany of Leontis (see V-T B10).

4. *IG* i³ 125 (405/4), 127 (decree 1, 405/4, naturalized), 127 (decree 2, 403/2, naturalization reaffirmed), 127 (decree 3, 403/2), *IG* ii² 145 (decree 1, 402–401), 145 (decree 2, 364/3 or 359/8), 2 (403/2), 7 (403/2), 8 (little after 403/2), 86 (beginning of 4th cent.), 13 (399/8), 17 (394/3, naturalized), 19 (394/3, naturalized, entirely restored), 20+Add. (394/3, naturalization reaffirmed, entirely restored), 27 (ca. 394–387), 26 (394–387), 82 (390–378), 51 (before 387/6), 52 (be-

fore 387/6, entirely restored), 55 (before 387/6, entirely restored), 31 (386/5), and 80 (380–370, entirely restored); *SEG* 32.50 (379/8, entirely restored); *IG* ii² 39 (379/8), 60 (378/7)79 (379–377, entirely restored), 72 (378/7), 76 (378/7?), and 96 (375/4); Meritt 1944: 229–31, no. 3 (ca. 375–350 or 357/6, naturalized); *SIG*³ 158 (369/8); *IG* ii² 103 (369/8), 105 (368/7), 106 (368/7), 107 (368/7), 141 (364?), 110 (363/2), and 117 (361/0, entirely restored); Schweigert 1939: 12–17, no. 4 (357/6, entirely restored); *IG* ii² 127 (356/5, entirely restored), 131 (355/4), 133 (355/4), 134 (354/3), 187 (before 353/2, entirely restored), 138 (353/2), 172 (353/2), 176 (353/2), 191 (353/2, entirely restored), 258+617 (350–340), 206=Lambert 3.23 (349/8), 276=Lambert 3.77 (ca. 340–320), 253(a) (before 336/5), 278 (before 336/5, entirely restored), 290=Lambert 3.15 (before 336/5), 324 (before 336/5, entirely restored), 222=Lambert 3.8 (ca. 334, naturalized), 336+Add.=Lambert 3.7 (334/3, naturalized), 348=Lambert 3.78 (337–323, entirely restored), 660[1]=Lambert 3.110 (ca. 350–300?), 448 (323/2, naturalized), and 450 (314/3, naturalized).

5. See also Adkins 1960: 253, 337, 339, 351 n. 7, 353 n. 14; Dover 1974: 41–45; and Ober 1989: 13.

6. Nos. 14 (entirely restored), 15, 29, 30, and 31 (entirely restored). See Dover 1974: 296–99 on the usage and meaning of the word *chresimos*.

7. *IG* ii² 145, the second decree for Philokles, which dates between 364/3 and 359/8, contains the word *chresimos*, heavily but plausibly restored (V-T A90, p. 64 and n. 196). *IG* i³ 106, dated to 409/8, contains an unlikely restoration of *chresimos* (V-T A32). *SIG*³ 158, from 363/2, also contains a heavily and implausibly restored *chresimos* (V-T A84).

8. *IG* ii² 145 (368–353, 364/3 or 359/8, herald of the Council and the People; see n. 7), 234=Lambert 3.71 (340/39, unknown services, listed as a foreigner in V-T 76 [A119]), 277+428 (after 336/5, unknown services, listed as a foreigner in V-T 103 [A171]), 399+Add.=Lambert 3.56 (328/7?, political/financial), and 374 (after 319/8, dated to ca. 307–302 in Osborne D50, entirely restored, naturalized, doctor, financial). For trade, see, in the present study, nos. 15 (ca. 337), 14 (ca. 340–300), 29 (ca. 322/1–320/19, naturalized), 30 (ca. 321–319), and 31 (ca. 321–318, entirely restored),

9. *IG* ii² 330=445=Lambert 1.3 (336/5 or 335/4, councilors and secretary), 354+*SEG* 18.14=Lambert 1.11 (328/7, priest), 477 (305/4, ambassadors), and 641 (299/8, ambassador).

10. [Xen.] *AP* 1.1, generally believed to have been written between the 440s and 420s. See also Isokr. 3.16.

11. *IG* i³ 113 (ca. 410) and 125 (405/4).

12. The word *arete* first appears in *IG* ii² 107 (368/7); see also n. a for table 6.1. *Philotimia* and its cognates first appear sometime after 352/1 in decrees dated simply to "before 336/5" in *IG*, including *IG* ii² 273 (mostly restored, V-T A131) and 277+428 (mostly restored, V-T A133); see also n. b for table 6.1.

13. Hakkarainen 1997: 13–22. See also Burke 1992: 199–226.

14. See Isager and Hansen 1975: 169 for the date. At the same time, *chresimos* still retained its traditional associations with usefulness in political and military matters. See Dem. 18.311, 19.281–82.

15. *IG* i³ 127, decree 3, which honors Poses of Samos in 403/2, contains doubtful restorations of the word *arete* (Whitehead 1993: 49; V-T A46).

16. For *arete* ascribed to native Athenian citizens, see *IG* ii² 223A=Lambert 1.1 (343/2, Council member), 330+445=Lambert 1.3 (336/5, Council secretary, entirely restored), 338=Lambert 1.15 (333/2, overseer of fountains), 410=Lambert 1.10 (ca. 340–330, priests), 415=Lambert 1.5 (340–325, *anagrapheus*), and 487 (304/3, overseer of writing down the laws); *SEG* 28.52=Trail 1978: 274–77; and, in the present study, no. 5=Lambert 1.4 (ca. 340–325, tribal treasurer and *prytaneis*). For *arete* ascribed to foreigners, see *IG* ii² 107 (368/7), 127 (356/5), 233=Lambert 3.72 (340/39, entirely restored), 237+Add.=Lambert 3.5 (338/7, naturalized), 273 (352/1–337/6, entirely restored), 431=Lambert 3.157 (ca. 350–300?, entirely restored), 347=Lambert 3.40 (332/1), 356+Add.=Lambert 3.103 (327/6), 660(1)=Lambert 3.110 (ca. 350–300?), 364 (ca. 324/3, entirely restored), 448 (323/2, naturalized), 456 (307/6), 492 (303/2, naturalized), and 495 (303/2) and *SEG* 3.83 (365–335?), 35.75=Schwenk no. 72 (324/3), and 16.59=Broneer 1933: 402f., no. 19 (dated 307–302/1 in Osborne D66, naturalized). For trade, see, in the present study, nos. 12 (347/6), 25 (after ca. 330), and 28 (323/2). *IG* ii² 277+428 (before 336/5) contains an entirely and doubtfully restored reference to *arete* (V-T A133). Dem. 18.118 quotes an honorary decree for Demosthenes in which he is praised for his *arete* for services as overseer of fortifications. This may well be the case, but see n. 25 below concerning the doubtful precision of the wording of the decrees quoted by Demosthenes in this speech.

17. Whitehead (1993: 43, 45, 60) notes that praise for a citizen's *arete* was reserved early on in Athenian democracy for those who died heroically on behalf of the city and, therefore, posed no threat to the democracy.

18. See Ober 1989: 11, 249 and Whitehead 1993: 57–61.

19. Adkins 1960: 235; Dover 1974: 67, 164; Whitehead 1993: 46, 57–62; V-T 247–54, 265–67, 270–74.

20. See Hakkarainen 1997: 21. For other officeholders honored, see *IG* ii² 215=Lambert 1.18 (346/5) and 338=Lambert 1.15 (333/2). See also Dem. 18.114–15, 118; Demosthenes cites Athenian citizens, including himself, who were honored for contributing their own funds to carry out their duties as public officials.

21. For *eunoia*, see nos. 12 (347/6), 15 (ca. 337), 17 (ca. 337–325), 18 (ca. 337–320), 20 (ca. 334/3–321), 21 (333/2, entirely restored), 25 (after ca. 330), 27 (325/4), 28 (323/2), and 29 (322/1–320/19, entirely restored); for *eunous*, nos. 14 (ca. 340–300, entirely restored), 18 (ca. 337–320, entirely restored), 21 (333/2, entirely restored), 28 (323/2, entirely restored), 30 (321–219, entirely restored), and 31 (ca. 321–318).

22. *IG* i³ 113 (ca. 410, *eunoia*, naturalized) and 125 (405/4, *eunoia*); *SEG* 21.246 (359/8?, *eunoia*); *IG* ii² 42 (378/7, *eunous*), 127 (356/5, *eunoia*, entirely restored), 169+472 (before 353/2, *eunoia*), and 196 (before 353/2, *eunoia*). V-T A54 questions Wilhelm's (*AM* 39 [1914]: 291) restoration of the word *eunoia* in *IG* ii² 20+Add. (394/3).

23. Schwenk no. 9=Schweigert 1938: 292–94, no. 19=Lambert 1.2.

24. Meritt 1936b: 201–5=EM 12825 (305/4, *eunous*, entirely restored); *IG* ii²

487 (304/3, *eunoia*, entirely restored), 641 (299/8, *eunoia*), 649 (294/3, *eunoia*), and 661 (283/2, *eunous*).

25. Herman (1987: 85) believes that Timo— (name incomplete), the honorand of *IG* ii² 655, from either in 289/8 (*IG*) or 285/4 (Herman 1987: 85; Habicht 1979: 52), who is praised for his *eunoia*, was an Athenian citizen, but there is insufficient evidence to be certain. Dem.18.84 quotes an honorary decree from the 330s that attributes *eunoia* to Demosthenes for various services, some of which may have been performed as a private citizen. But this testimony is unreliable, since the inscription of the decree is not extant, and the speech may not have recorded its precise wording: Dem. 18.54–55 says the decree praises Demosthenes' *andragathia*; Dem. 18.118 says it praises his *kalokagathia*; Aischin. 3.49 says the decree praises Demosthenes' *andragathia*.

26. *IG* ii² 223A (343/2) is the earliest securely dated case. *IG* ii² 273 and 277+428 contain the word *philotimia* or its cognates (much restored) and are dated simply to before 336/5 (and, therefore, after 352/1) on stylistic grounds by Kirchner. Three other decrees are similarly dated in the corpus, but Lambert has revised their dates: *IG* ii² 257+300=Lambert 3.123 (ca. 350–340; see Lambert 2007: 122 n. 101), 269=Lambert 3.152 (ca. 350–300), and 285+414d= Lambert 3.26 (ca. 345–320, entirely restored). *IG* ii² 183 is assigned a date "before 353/2" in the corpus, but the word *philotimomenoi* is entirely and implausibly restored; see n. b for table 6.1.

27. For *philotimia* used for native citizens, see *IG* ii² 223A=Lambert 1.1 (343/2, Council member), 1155=Lambert 1.27 (339/8, taxiarch), 330+445=Lambert 1.3 (336/5 and 335/4, Council secretary), 1156+Add.=Lambert 1.28 (334/3, ephebes), 338=Lambert 1.15 (333/2, overseer of fountain), 410=Lambert 1.10 (ca. 340–330, priests), 487 (304/3, *anagrapheus*), 488 (304/3, officials in charge of sacrifices), 500 (302/1, taxiarchs), 509 (after 307, officials), and 514=*SEG* 21.336 (end of 4th cent., Council members); *SEG* 35.64=Schwenk no. 9=Lambert 1.2 (337/6?, secretary) and 28.52=Trail 1978: no. 5=Lambert 1.4 (ca. 340–325, treasurer and *prytaneis*); Schwenk nos. 41=*IG* VII 4253=Lambert 1.16 (332/1, *nomothetes*), 50=*IG* VII 4254=Lambert 1.17 (329/8, overseer of Amphiaraia), and 56=Lambert 1.6 (328/7, Council members); and Pritchett 1940: 104–11, no. 20 (302/1, taxiarchs). For *philotimia* used for foreigners, see *IG* ii² 273 (352/1–337/6, mostly restored, V-T A131), 277+428 (352/1–337/6, mostly restored, V-T A133), 257+300=Lambert 3.123 (ca. 350–340; see Lambert 2007: 122 n. 101), 269=Lambert 3.152 (ca. 350–300), 285+414d=Lambert 3.26 (ca. 345–320, entirely restored), 543=Lambert 3.73 no. 13 (ca. 340), 423=Lambert 3.76=no. 14 (ca. 340–300), 304+604=*SEG* 18.11 (337/6, V-T A125), 425=Lambert 3.45 (ca. 330–322/1?), 348=Lambert 3.78 (337–323, entirely restored), 360=Lambert 3.43=nos. 24 and 27 (330/29–328/7 and 325/4), 369=Lambert 3.106 (323/2, naturalized), 242+373=*SEG* 40.74=Lambert 3.34 (337/6 and 322/1, later naturalized by *IG* ii² 374), 398a+438=no. 29 (ca. 322/1–320/19, naturalized), 392+586 (321/0–319/8, naturalized), 394 (321/0–319/8, naturalized), 421 (before 318/7), 551 (309/8), 555 (307/6–304/3), 169+472 (306/5), 554 (ca. 306/5), 479 (305/4, entirely restored), 483 (304/3), 491 (303/2), 505 (302/1), 577 (end of 4th cent., naturalized), and 580 (end of 4th cent.); Schweigert 1940: 332f., no. 39=no. 18 (ca. 337–320); and *SEG* 16.59=Broneer 1933: 402f., no. 19 (dated 307–302/1 in Osborne D66,

naturalized). For *philotimia* used for men whose legal status is uncertain, see *IG* ii² 515 (end of 4th cent.), 517 (end of 4th cent.), 539 (before 303/2), 543 (before 303/2), 574 (end of 4th cent.), and 609 (4th cent.). *IG* ii² 183 is a doubtful case; see n. b above for table 6.1. *IG* ii² 379 contains the word *philotimia* and is dated in the corpus to 321/0 or 318/19, but Tracy (1997: 168) argues for a date of ca. 290. *IG* ii² 336+Add.=Lambert 3.7 (334/3 and 333/2) contains the word *philotimia*, but it is entirely and doubtfully restored (V-T A142).

28. Whitehead 1983 has demonstrated such an Athenian practice through an analysis of the wording of 140 honorary decrees containing *philotimia* and its cognates dating from ca. 350 to 250 B.C.E.

Chapter Seven

1. It is well known that *proxenia* may refer either to an institution or to the status of being a *proxenos* (which can be conferred in an honorary decree). It is less well known, however, that, similarly, *euergesia* may refer not only to a benefaction but also to the status of being a benefactor (*euergetes*). See, e.g., *IG* ii² 29.2–3 and 16, 133.1, 286+625.3–4, and 406.3. See Henry 1983: 116 and Whitehead 1993: 55.

2. Hopper 1979: 57, 88; Gauthier 1985: 157–62. Hagemajer Allen (2003: 234–35) states of Gauthier's view, "By implication, the Athenians skillfully exploited the *philotimia* of non-Greek dynasts in order to secure for themselves tangible benefits at a minimal cost."

3. Herman 1987: 86, 121; Hagemajer Allen 2003: 234–39.

4. See Henry 1983: 1–11 for a general discussion of commendations in honorary decrees.

5. Nos. 4, 6, 11–13, 15, 17–19, 21, 24, 25, 27, 28, 30, 31, and 33.

6. Nos. 1, 3, 10, 14, 20, 23, and 29.

7. See the indexes to *IG* i³ and ii² for decrees containing forms of the word *epaineo*, and see chapter 1 of Henry 1983 for the numerous examples of Athenian commendations by formal decree. One can now also run a computer search of the database of inscriptions, including *IG* i³ and ii² available online through Packard Humanities Institute, at http://epigraphy.packhum .org/inscriptions/.

8. *IG* i³ 17 (451/0 or 418/7), 43 (ca. 435–427), 156 (ca. 440–425), 158 (ca. 430), 159 (ca. 430), 62 (428/7), 73 (ca. 424–410), 162 (ca. 440–415), 80 (421/0), 228 (ca. 435–415, reinscribed in 385/4), 167 (ca. 430–415), 91 (ca. 416/5), 92 (ca. 416/5), 96 (412/11), 97 (412/11), 101 (410/09), 102 (410/09), and 103 (410/9).

9. Southern Italy had been a possible supplier of ships timber for Athens before the Sicilian Expedition. See Meiggs 1982: 122–25, 127–28.

10. On the date of And. 2, *On His Return*, see Blass 1887–93: 1.278.

11. *IG* ii² 143+ (371, *diatetai*), 118 (361/0, colonists of Potidaia), 223A–C=Lambert 1.1 (343/2, Council members), 1155=Lambert 1.27 (339/8, taxiarchs), 243=Lambert 1.20 (337/6, unknown), 272+274=Lambert 3.52 (352/1?, cleruchs of Sestos), 330+445=Lambert 1.3 (336/5 and 335/4, Council officials), 1156+Add.=Lambert 1.28 (334/3, ephebes), 338=Lambert 1.15 (333/2, overseer

of fountains), 410=Lambert 1.10 (ca. 340–330, priests), 415=Lambert 1.5 (ca. 340–325, *anagrapheus*), 354+*SEG* 18.14=Lambert 1.11 (328/7, priest), 433=Lambert 1.26 (325–304, *nomothetai* or *thesmothetai*), 478 (305/4, ephebes), 500 (302/1, taxiarchs), 641 (299/8, ambassador), 649 (294/3, general, *agonothetes*), and 656 (284/3, Council members); Knoepfler 1986: 71ff.= Leonardos 1923: 36ff., no. 123 (369/8, priest of Amphiaraion); Schwenk no. 9=*SEG* 35.64=Lambert 1.2 (337/6?, secretary); *SEG* 28.52=Trail 1978: 274ff., no. 5=Lambert 1.4 (ca. 340–325, treasurer and *prytaneis*); Schwenk nos. 41=*IG* VII 4253=Lambert 1.16 (332/1, *nomothetes*), 50=*IG* VII 4254=Lambert 1.17 (329/8, overseers of festival of the Amphiaraia), and 56=Lambert 1.6 (328/7, Council members). *IG* ii² 657, which dates to 283/2, commends Philippides the poet both for his service as an *agonothetes* in 288/7 and for having, as a private citizen, procured grain for Athens from Lysimachos.

12. See Henry 1983: 116–62 for a study of the formulae used in Athenian decrees that granted *proxenia* and *euergesia*. Henry concludes (116 n. 4) that *proxenia* should be categorized as an honor rather than as a privilege. Although I have classified *proxenia* as an honor as well, subsequent discussion will show that it entailed significant practical benefits, too.

13. See pp. 37, 47. See also Wallace 1970: 189 n. 2; Walbank 1978: 2–9; Marek 1984: 1–4; and Herman 1987: 132–35. See Gauthier 1972: 17–61 and Gschnitzer 1973: cols. 629–730 for detailed studies of the nature and development of *proxenia*.

14. *LSJ*[9,] s.v. προξενος; Wallace 1970: 190; Gschnitzer 1973: col. 632; Walbank 1978: 4.

15. See Wallace 1970: 189–94 for the date of the earliest official proxenies.

16. Walbank 1978: 3–5; Henry 1983: 116 n. 2.

17. Henry 1983: 116 n. 4. See Marek 1984: 1–4 and Gauthier 1985: 131–47.

18. Wallace 1970: 189 n. 2, 190. See also Wilhelm 1942: 30–35; Marek 1984: 4, 333–81; and Gauthier 1985: 134–47 (contra Schwahn 1931: 97–118; Schäfer 1932: 18–44; Klaffenbach 1966: 80–86; and Gschnitzer 1973: cols. 629–730).

19. Marek (1984: 359–61; 1985: 67–78) reviews the scholarship on this issue. See in particular Ziebarth 1932–33: 244–45 and Wilhelm 1942: 51.

20. See Walbank 1978: 2–3 concerning the growth of *proxenia* from Archaic to Classical times. Concerning *proxenia* and intercity trading relations, see Wallace 1970: 189; Rostovtzeff 1941: 245, 1375 n. 74; and Shear 1978: 30.

21. Ziebarth 1932–33: 245. Walbank (1978: 74–75, 78, 81, 474 [nos. 2, 3, 6, 9, and 91]) and Burke (1992: 206–8 and notes) make this same assumption.

22. See in particular the objections in Marek 1984: 359–61 and 1985: 67–78.

23. Nos. 1, 2, 4, 6, 8, 10, 17, 25, 27, 28, and 32.

24. Nos. 13, 15, 14, 21, 23, 18, 20, 19, 30, and 31. Although the inscription that contains no. 13 is badly damaged and filled with lacunae, it is unlikely that the decree granted *proxenia* and *euergesia*, since the honorands appear to have been the entire citizenry of an allied city of Athens. The main portion of *IG* ii² 416(b), which is the testimonium for no. 20, was associated with *IG* ii² 416(a) by Wilhelm and was published together with it by Kirchner in *IG* ii² Only 416(a), however, refers to a grant of the title of *proxenos*. Since it is certain

now that the two fragments are not from the same inscription, there is no way of knowing whether the honorand of 416(b) received the title of *proxenos*. See Walbank 1977: 157 n. 31 and Tracy 1995: 123 and n. 4.

25. Nos. 3, 5, 7, 9, 11, 12, 16, 22, 26, 29, 33, and 34.

26. For simple importations, see nos. 17 and 25; for gifts of imported goods, nos. 6 and 27; for miscellaneous or unknown services, nos. 1, 2, 4, 10, 28, and 32.

27. For Greeks, see nos. 1, 4, 6, 8, 22, and 29; for non-Greeks, nos. 25 and 28; for unknown ethnicity, nos. 2, 10, and 32. For *metics*, see nos. 4, 25, and 27; for a *xenos*, no. 6; for an unknown *metic* or *xenos*, nos. 1, 2, 8, 10, 17, 28, and 32. For common professional traders, see nos. 8, 10, 17, and 25; for moderately wealthy professional traders, nos. 1 and 2; for wealthy professional traders, nos. 27 and 32. For a foreign potentate, see no. 6. For unknown socioeconomic status, see nos. 4 and 28.

28. Whitehead 1977: 29 and n. 10. Even Wilhelm (1942: 59–60) admitted this. See also Clerc 1893: 218–20 and Busolt 1920: 320. Scholars such as Gerhardt ([1933] 1935: 76–77) had previously rejected the possibility of *metics* being appointed *proxenoi*.

29. For this view, see Wilhelm 1942: 11–86. See also Gauthier 1985: 131–34 for a critique.

30. Walbank nos. 29 (431/0), 30 (431/0), 39 (428/7), 47 (424/3, reinscribed in 399/8), and 65 (416/5, possibly reinscribed in ca. 400). Five other instances of Athenian grants of *proxenia* and *euergesia* before 415 that were likely, but not certainly, for political or military services are Walbank nos. 40, 44, 48, 49, and 55. Wallace (1970: 194) believes that all the earliest grants of *proxenia* throughout Greece were motivated by political or military interests.

31. Walbank 1978: 366, after Wilhelm 1898: 44. But both the date of the decree and the precise nature of the honorand's services are far from certain.

32. Walbank nos. 1 (before 480/79), 2 (before 481/0), 3 (before 480), 6 (before 460), 9 (ca. 460–440), 16 (449/8), and 55 (420). To this list of proxenies granted to "men actively involved in maritime trade," Burke (1992: 207 and n. 34) adds Walbank nos. 17 (445), 27 (ca. 435–420), and 30 (431/0). But his identifications are even more speculative than those of Walbank. Both scholars assume that if the ethnic of a *proxenos* corresponds to a place situated along a trade route, Athens must have granted the title of *proxenos* in order to fulfill its trading interests. But this is far from certain (see app. 3, R16). In addition, although Walbank no. 16 (449/8) involves trade in some way, it cannot be identified as a decree that grants *proxenia*.

33. Nos. 1, 2, 4, and 6. Note, however, that the trade-related services of the honorands of nos. 4 and 6, who provided Athens with oar spars and ships timber, served Athenian political and military interests as well. Walbank also identifies no. 91 of his catalog as having been for trade-related services during this period, and Burke (1992: 207 and n. 34) so identifies Walbank no. 85. I have not included these identifications in this book, on account of their highly speculative nature. See app. 3, R16.

34. Walbank nos. 73 (412/11) and 86 (408/7). In the remaining nine instances in which Athens granted *proxenia* and *euergesia* during this period

(Walbank nos. 70–72, 74, 76–77, 84, 87, and 89), it is impossible to identify the services of the honorands with any certainty.

35. *IG* ii² 76 (before 378/7), 110 (363/2), 149 (before 355/4), 29 (387/6), 17 (394/3), 22 (390/89), 19 (394/3), 106 (368/7), 111 (363/2), and 141 (ca. 364). *IG* ii² 141 grants *proxenia* to Straton, king of Sidon, for his political services. This grant is distinct from the privileges, which do not include *proxenia* and *euergesia*, granted in a rider to the decree to Sidonian merchants resident in the Peiraieus (see app. 3, R8).

36. Nos. 10 (ca. 350–325?), 17 (ca. 337–325), 25 (after ca. 330), 27 (325/4), 28 (323/2), and 32 (before 320/19).

37. *IG* ii² 130 (355/4, helped battle against Philip II for Methone), 133 (355/4, guided military expedition), 187 (before 353/2, generals mentioned), 149=Lambert 3.24 (348?, allied envoys), 235=Lambert 3.29 (340/39?, helped generals during Philip II's siege of Byzantion), 238=Lambert 3.32 (338/7, probably for aid at Chaironeia), 240=Lambert 3.33 (337/6, helped ambassadors to Phillip II), 278 (352/1–337/6, mention of allies), 284+Add.=Lambert 3.19 (ca. 350–340, ransomed Athenians from pirates), 351+624=Lambert 3.42 (330/29, monetary contributions for war and public works), 564+*SEG* 18.18=Lambert 3.46 (ca. 329–322, envoys), and 466 (307/6, ambassadors of Tenos).

38. For medicine, see *IG* ii² 242+373=Lambert 3.34 (337/6 and 322/1); for religion, *IG* ii² 365=Lambert 3.107 (323/2). For poetry/theater, see *IG* ii² 347=Lambert 3.40 (332/1) and Schwenk no. 39=Lambert 3.39 (332/1).

39. *IG* ii² 136 (354/3), 161 (before 353/2), 162 (before 353/2), 172 (before 353/2), 176 (before 353/2), 182 (before 353/2), 183 (before 353/2), 269 (352/1–337/6), 324 (352/1–337/6), 252 (mid 4th cent.), 267=Lambert 3.17 (mid 4th cent.), 288=Lambert 3.16 (mid 4th cent.), 290=Lambert 3.15 (mid 4th cent.), 406=Lambert 3.18 (ca. 350), 205+Add.=Lambert 3.14 (351/0?), Lambert 3.20 (ca. 350–335?), 579=Lambert 3.22 (ca. 350–300?), 581=Lambert 3.21 (ca. 350–300?), 285+414d=Lambert 3.26 (ca. 345–320), 357=Lambert 3.27 (ca. 345–320?), 206=Lambert 3.23 (349/8), 248 (before 343/2), 416a=Lambert 3.31 (ca. 340?), 231=Lambert 3.30 (340/39), 426=Lambert 3.35 (ca. 337–324), 339+Add.=Lambert 3.36 and 38 (ca. 337–324 and 333/2), 344=Lambert 3.41 (332/1), 368=Lambert 3.13 (332/1 and 323/2), 425=Lambert 3.45 (ca. 330–322/1), 422=Lambert 3.47 (after ca. 329), 184=Lambert 3.48 (ca. 325?), 419=Lambert 3.49 (ca. 325–300), and 308+371=Lambert 3.51 (322/1); *SEG* 21.348=*Agora* 16.145=Lambert 3.25 (ca. 345–320) and 21.340=*Agora* 16.66=Lambert 3.28 (ca. 340–320?).

40. Wallace 1970: 189–208; Gauthier 1972: 23–24; Herman 1987: 61, 80.

41. Marek 1984: 333–81; 1985: 76–77.

42. Wilhelm 1942: 36–37; Henry 1983: 116 n. 4; Gauthier 1985: 19–23.

43. See Henry 1983: 22–38 for a survey of the formulae used for awards of gold crowns in Athenian honorary decrees.

44. Nos. 7, 9, 11, 12, 13, 15, 21, 24, 25, 27, 28, 30, and 31. With regard to the restoration of a gold crown to the text of no. 15, see app. 3.

45. Nos. 1, 2, 4, 5, 10, 14, 16, 18–20, 22, 23, 29, and 32–34.

46. Nos. 3, 6, 8, 17, and 26.

47. See Sealey 1993: 100 for the date of Dem. 51. Dem. 22, *Against Androtion,* is an attack on Androtion's proposal that the Council, of which he was a member, should receive "the customary" crown, even though it had not built

the required number of triremes in 359/8 or 356/5 (see Gabrielsen 1994: 134 for the dates).

48. *IG* ii² 223=Lambert 1.1 (343/2, Council members), 330+445=Lambert 1.3 (336/5 and 335/4, Council members), 338=Lambert 1.15 (333/2, overseer of fountains), 410=Lambert 1.10 (ca. 340–330, priests), 415=Lambert 1.5 (ca. 340–325, *anagrapheus*), 354=Lambert 1.11 (328/7, priest), 433=Lambert 1.26 (ca. 325–304, *nomothetai* or *thesmothetai*), 488 (304/3, officials), and 500 (302/1, taxiarchs); Schwenk no. 9=Lambert 1.2 (337/6?, Council secretary); *IG* ii² VII 4253=Schwenk no. 41=Lambert 1.16 (332/1) *nomothetes* of Amphiaraos; Schwenk no. 56=Lambert 1.6 (328/7, Council members).

49. See above concerning Philippides' honors. A possible earlier case concerns Demosthenes in 338/7 (18.84). But it is uncertain whether he was honored for services performed as a private citizen or a public official. See p. 332, n. 29.

50. See pp. 44–45 concerning *choregoi*. Examples of grants of olive crowns to Athenian ambassadors include *IG* ii² 207=no. 11 (349/8?, ambassador), 1155=Lambert 1.27 (339/8, taxiarchs), and 487 (304/3, *anagrapheus*).

51. *IG* i³ 102+Add. (410/09; the material of the crown is restored in text but is likely in light of the cost, which is given in drachmas, the precise amount of which is restored as one thousand) and 125 (405/4; the material of the crown is not stated in the extant text); *IG* ii² 1C (403/2; the text states that one thousand drachmas was granted for the purpose of making a crown, but the material is not stated) and 20+Add. (393/2; the material of the crown is restored in text as gold, though Wilhelm restores it as olive in the addendum).

52. See Garnsey 1988: 147–48 concerning food shortages in Athens after the Peloponnesian War.

53. Henry (1983: 22, 24–25) argues that the phrase ἀπὸ-δραχμῶν that normally accompanies grants of gold crowns down to the end of the fourth century refers to the total cost of the crown, which would include the value of its weight in gold as well as costs associated with its manufacture. This assumption is supported by *IG* ii² 1 (403/2), in which one thousand drachmas is granted for the purpose of making a crown for the honorand.

54. Dem. 10.37–38. See Sealey 1993: 232–33 for the date.

55. See also Theopompos *FGrHist* 115 F 166 for the figure of four hundred talents in 346. See Michell 1957: 390 and Cawkwell 1963: 61–62 for the dates.

56. Michell (1957: 363), following Böckh (1857: 154–550, estimates the cost to be six thousand drachmas. Trevett (1992: 24 n. 10) estimates the cost of a trireme as five thousand drachmas on average, based on the fine of five thousand drachmas that Athens imposed on trierarchs responsible for losing their ships (see *IG* ii² 1629.569–77). Gabrielsen (1994: 139–45) believes that it is futile to try to calculate the "standard cost" of the hull of a trireme, noting that the costs for materials, such as timber, pitch, and ropes, would have fluctuated greatly over the course of the fifth and fourth centuries.

57. See Tod 2.167 (p. 196); Henry 1983: 36–37, 45–46 n. 6; and Tuplin 1982: 121–22.

58. Leukon and Eumelos also received gold crowns in this manner. It is

uncertain, however, whether Satyros I received only one gold crown or one every four years as his successors did. See app. 3, nos. 7, 9, 12, 26, and 34 concerning the honors awarded to each Bosporan king.

59. Other than those for trade-related services, there are only three extant honorary decrees that mention the source of funds for crowns. See Henry 1983: 36–38.

60. Böckh 1857: 245–48 lists the traditional sources of revenue and uses of the Stratiotic Fund. Hansen 1991: 260–261 notes among the Stratiotic Fund's sources of revenue the bids for the contract to collect the customs duty (*pentekoste*); the treasurer of the Stratiotic Fund as well as the treasurer of the Theoric Fund and the *poletai* presided over the auction of these tax-farming contracts (see Arist. *AP* 47.2). See also Brun 1983: 170 on the tendency toward improvisation in Athenian finances.

61. Burke does not discuss grants of gold crowns for trade-related services in his 1992 study, the thesis of which is that the Athenian state became increasingly interested in maritime trade in the fourth century in order to obtain revenue.

62. This figure is based on the building accounts from Eleusis in 329/8, *IG* ii^2 1672, in which skilled workers (carpenters, sawyers, plasterers, etc.) earned between one and one-fourth and two and one-half drachmas per day. A workweek of 5 days for 52 weeks amounts to 260 days of work, which, multiplied by 2 drachmas per day, equals 520 drachmas. See also Loomis 1998: 111.

63. According to Millett (1983: 36 and n. 2; 1991: 189), maritime loans ranged from one thousand to forty-five hundred drachmas, with a median value of three thousand drachmas.

64. On honorary bronze statues in general, see Henry 1983: 294–300; Dow 1963: 77–92; Welsh 1904–5: 32– 49; and Osborne 1981a: 166–68.

65. See *IG* ii^2 653 and *SEG* 25.112 for the placement of statues. See *IG* ii^2 450, 654, and 983 concerning equestrian statues.

66. See Osborne 1981c: 172–74 for the association of *IG* ii^2 513, which contains the grant of a bronze statue, with *IG* ii^2 457, which names Lykourgos as the honorand.

67. On the Prytaneion, including *testimonia* for invitations to the Prytaneion down to the end of the fourth century, see Miller 1978: 4–11, 136–61. See also Osborne 1981a: 153–70.

68. Concerning the food served and the staff who worked in the Prytaneion, see Miller 1978: 11–13, 20–21.

69. Osborne 1981a: 156. See also Pollux 9.40.

70. Osborne 1981a: 156–58. Dem. 19.234 states that inviting ambassadors to the Prytaneion was "the legal custom."

71. Osborne 1981a: 155, followed by Henry 1983: 285 n. 50.

72. *IG* i^3 63 (ca. 426); *IG* ii^2 141 (ca. 364) and 418 (after 330); nos. 8, 12, and 17 in the present study. See app. 3, R6 and R8, respectively, concerning the first two decrees.

73. *IG* i^3 63 (ca. 426); *IG* ii^2 141 (ca. 364), 418 (after 330); no. 12 in the present study.

74. Ar. *Plout.* 1191–93; Lys. 22 passim, 28.2 and 11, 19.11; Xen. *Hell.*

4.8.25–30, in which a naval expedition led by Thrasyboulos in 390 was compelled to plunder for money. See also pp. 57–58.

75. Böckh 1857: 773–84; Hasebroek 1933: 25; Andreades 1933: 385–86; Cawkwell 1963: 64; Gauthier 1976: 226–27; Finley 1985: 163–64.

76. Marchant 1968: 201; Austin and Vidal-Naquet 1977: 364; Schütrumpf 1982: 87. In his commentary, Gauthier (1976: 84–85) has nothing to say about the translation of this passage.

77. No. 17 (ca. 337–325); *IG* ii^2 456 (307/6), 466 (307/6), 567 (end of 4th cent.). Dem. 18.28 and Aischin. 2.55 state that Athens regularly provided seats for foreign ambassadors when their visits coincided with important Athenian festivals.

78. For fragmentary extant inscriptions (final lines lost, where grants of *thea* appear in the four extant examples), see nos. 1, 3, 6, 10, 11, 13–15, 18–21, 23, 25, 29–31, and 33. For fragmentary *testimonia*, see nos. 2, 5, 7, 9, 16, 22, 26, 32, and 34. The sufficiently well-preserved inscriptions (final lines extant) are nos. 4, 8, 12, 24, 27, and 28.

79. Dem. 18.28, 13.10; Böckh 1857: 300–310; Pickard-Cambridge 1968: 265–66.

80. Pickard-Cambridge 1968: 58–59, 263.

81. Nos. 1, 3, 4, 7–9, 12, 17, 25, 27, 28, and 31.

82. Nos. 10, 11, 13–15, 18–21, 23, 29, 30, and 33.

83. See, e.g., *IG* i^3 156. See also Henry 1983: 12 n. 1.

84. See Jones [1957a] 1986: 102, 154 n. 33, followed by Henry 1982: 111–12 and Hansen 1991: 158.

85. Hansen 1991: 149; Hagemajer Allen 2003: 225.

86. Hagemajer Allen 2003: 224; Lambert 2006: 116.

87. See Adcock and Mosley 1975: 223. Dem. 20.37 argues that it is shameful to abrogate the decree that honors the Bosporan kings (*IG* ii^2 212=no. 12) while the stele on which it is inscribed still stands.

88. Stelai inscribed with honorary decrees for trade-related services and placed on the Acropolis include nos. 1, 3, 4, 6 (restored), 8 (restored), 17, 24/27, and 28. The stele bearing the text of no. 12 was found in the Peiraieus. Dem. 20.36 refers to this stele as well as two others, which were set up at Athenian expense in the Bosporos and at Hieron on the Asiatic side of the entrance to the Thracian Bosporos. See Liddel 2003: 79–93 for the placement of stelai bearing Athenian state decrees in general.

89. Hagemajer Allen 2003: 228. Concerning reliefs on inscribed stelai in general, see Lawton 1995.

90. Inscribed decrees most likely honoring political or military services before 414 include *IG* i^3 23(a, b) (ca. 447), 55 (ca. 431), 65 (ca. 427/6), 73(a, b) (424/3), 162 (440–415), and 80 (421/0). See the commentaries for these inscriptions in *IG* i^3 and Walbank 1978. Such decrees dated to ca. 414–412 include *IG* i^3 96 (412/11), 97 (412/11), 101 (410/09), 102 (410/09), and 118 (408/7).

Chapter Eight

1. Hasebroek 1933: 128 (only within areas of Athenian control); Michell 1957: 227 (only for the protection of Athenian citizens abroad); MacDowell

1978: 78 (only for the protection of privileged foreigners against assaults from Athenian citizens abroad). Hopper (1979: 59) makes no qualifications.

2. No. 3 is the first explicit grant of *asylia* for trade-related services. No. 1, which dates to ca. 414–412, does not explicitly grant *asylia* but rather grants similar privileges.

3. Hasebroek 1933: 126; Hopper 1979: 59.

4. IG ii² 1623.276–85; IG ii² 414a=Lambert 1.21; [Plut.] *Ten Orat.* 844a.

5. See Michell 1957: 227 for the extremely modernist view that grants of *asylia* were intended to provide protection for "nationals abroad."

6. See Henry 1983: 241–45 for the formulae used in Athenian decrees granting *ateleia*.

7. See, e.g., IG i³ 106 and IG ii² 211. See also IG ii² 141, which, although it does not use the standard formula ἀτέλεια τοῦ μετοικίου, clearly grants the privilege of exemption from the metoikion with the phrase μὴ ἐξεῖναι αὐτὸς μετοίκιον πράττεσθαι in lines 33---34.

8. MacDonald (1981: 142–44) argues that the one-hundredth tax was a harbor tax.

9. According to Dem. 20.18 and 30–41, both the trierarchy and the *eisphora* were never exempt; however, IG ii² 141, from 364, grants an exemption to Sidonian traders resident in Athens from the *eisphora*. See also chap. 5, Socioeconomic Status concerning the nature of the *ateleia* granted to the Bosporan kings, and see app. 3, R8, for more on IG ii² 141, including its date.

10. Dem. 20.18 and 29 (Harmodios and Aristogeiton, end of 6th cent.), 67–70 (Konon), 75 (Chabrias), 84 (Iphikrates and Timotheos), 55 (Corinthian exiles). For political or military services, see IG i³ 40 (446/5), 61 (ca. 428–424), 73 (ca. 424–410), 227 (ca. 424/3), 106 (409/8), 107 (ca. 409), and 125 (405/4, Epikerdes; see Dem. 20.41–46) and IG ii² 33 (ca. 385), 37+Add. (after 383/2), 109 (363/2), 211=Lambert 3.61 (mid 4th cent.?), 237+Add.=Lambert 3.5 (338/7), and 545 (318/7). For unknown services, see IG i³ 24 (ca. 450), 164, (ca. 440–425), 159 (ca. 430), and 91 (416/5) and IG ii² 53 (before 387/6), 61 (before 378/7), 180 (before 353/2), 195 (before 353/2), and 265 (352/1–337/6). For examples of political exiles, see IG i³ 73 and 106 and IG ii² 33, 37+Add., 109, 237+Add.=Lambert 3.5, and 545.

11. Only one grant of *ateleia* or its equivalent before 410 had any connection with trade (IG i³ 61, in the 420s [R4]), but it was not an honorary decree for trade-related services and was not designed to fulfill Athens' interests in trade (see app. 3).

12. Hasebroek (1933: 116, 146) believes that the grain supply was Athens' chief interest in granting *ateleia*. Burke (1992: 199–226) argues that the need for revenue was the chief motivation for Athenian interest in maritime trade in the fourth century, but he does not discuss Athenian grants of *ateleia*.

13. Pecirka 1966: v. See Pecirka for a thorough study of the epigraphic evidence for Athenian decrees granting *enktesis,* and see Henry 1983: 204–40 for a study of the formulae employed in such decrees. See Finley 1985: 48 for the close association between landownership and citizenship in ancient Greek *poleis*.

14. Burke (1992: 209 n. 41) includes IG ii² 206=Lambert 3.23, 279, and 285+414d=Lambert 3.26 as further examples of Athenian grants of *enktesis* for

services relating to trade, but I do not share his confidence in the assumption that since the home cities of the honorands lay on known trade routes, the honorands must have been traders.

15. Pecirka 1966: 152–56 (charts). For likely *metics*, see *IG* i^3 102 and *IG* ii^2 351+624=Lambert 3.42, 360=no. 27, and 242+373=Lambert 3.34 (although Pecirka will only allow that the honorand of this decree lived in Athens, which does not necessarily mean that he was officially a *metic*). For likely *xenoi*, see *IG* ii^2 83, 53, 206=Lambert 3.23, 265, 279, and 343=no. 28.

16. For likely *metics*, see *IG* i^3 102 and 81 (*isoteleia* [equal tax burden as citizens] as well); *IG* ii^2 1283 (temple), 287 (*isoteleia*, military service with citizens as well), 342+=no. 25, 337=R11, 351+624=Lambert 3.42, 360=no. 27, 242+373=Lambert 3.34, and 551=Lambert 3.101 (*isoteleia*); and Broneer 1933: 396–97, no. 16 (military service with citizens). For likely *xenoi*, see *IG* ii^2 83, 53, 206=Lambert 3.23, 265, 279, and 466 (ambassadors).

17. Pecirka (1966: 122–30, 152) dates the grant of *enktesis* mentioned in *IG* ii^2 1283 to shortly before 429/8. For political or military services, see *IG* i^3 81 (421/0, likely political or military), 102 (410/09), 106 (409/8), and 107 (ca. 409) and *IG* ii^2 8 (a little after 403/2) and 130 (355/4, likely political or military). For unknown services, see *IG* ii^2 1283 (before 429/8, see above), 53 (before 387/6), 80 (before 378/7), 83 (before 378/7), 86 (before 378/7), 132 (355/4), and 180 (before 353/2).

18. *IG* ii^2 279 (likely). For unknown services, see *IG* ii^2 162(b)+(c), 265, 285+414d=Lambert 3.26, 287, 289, 308+371=Lambert 3.51, and 425=Lambert 3.45 (though a date after 350 is more likely; Lambert [2006: 134 n. 80] dates it to ca. 330–322/1).

19. For political and military services, see *IG* ii^2 237+Add.=Lambert 3.5 (political exiles), 545 (political exiles), and 466 (diplomatic). For other services, see nos. 25, 17, 27, and 28 and *IG* ii^2 337=R11, 242+373=Lambert 3.34, and 551=Lambert 3.101. For political, military, and other services, see *IG* ii^2 351+624=Lambert 3.42. For unknown services, see *IG* ii^2 206=Lambert 3.23, 425=Lambert 3.45 (likely ca. 330–322/1; see n. 18), 184=Lambert 3.48, 426=Lambert 3.35, 396, and 422=Lambert 3.47; Pritchett 1946: 159–60; and Broneer 1933: 396–97.

20. Burke (1992: 209 and n. 41) also argues for such a development, albeit (as in his analysis of grants of *proxenia*) with the addition of some questionable identifications of grants of *enktesis* for trade-related services.

21. Xen. *Poroi* 3.3, 12–13; Gernet [1955] 1964: 173–200; Michell 1957: 350; Cawkwell 1963: 64 and n. 95; Gauthier 1976: 225–26 (though only a remote connection for the speedy trials); Austin and Vidal-Naquet 1977: 367 n. 13; Whitehead 1977: 128; Garland 1987: 43.

22. Herzog (1914: 480), Cawkwell (1963: 64 and n. 95), Bodei (1970: 5758, n. 42, and p. 67), and Burke (1992: 209) all believe that Athens put Xenophon's suggestion concerning grants of *enktesis* into effect. Those who disagree include Pecirka (1967: 25), Gauthier (1976: 223–25), Austin and Vidal-Naquet (1977: 362), and Whitehead (1977: 128–29).

23. See Finley 1952: 77; Pecirka 1967: 25; Austin and Vidal-Naquet 1977: 95–96; Whitehead 1977: 70; Finley 1985: 48; and Manville 1990: 5, 8–9.

24. Finley 1952: 77–78; Pecirka 1967: 24; Austin and Vidal-Naquet 1977: 100.

25. For political or military services, see *IG* ii² 218=Lambert 3.64 (346/5), 237+Add.=Lambert 1.5 (338/7), 505 (302/1), and 545 (after 318/7). For political and military services and contributions for public works, see *IG* ii² 351+624=Lambert 3.42 (330/29). For trade-related, services, see nos. 23 (335/4, 331/0, or 326/5) and 27 (325/4). For unknown services, see *IG* ii² 287 (before 336/5), 516 (end of 4th cent.), and 660(1)=Lambert 3.110 (ca. 350– 300), and see Broneer 1933: 396–97 (ca. 350–300). *IG* ii² 37 may have granted the privilege of serving in the Athenian army and paying the *eisphora* together with the Athenians as early as 383. But the decree has been heavily restored, and I follow Whitehead 1977 and Henry 1983 in omitting it from my analysis.

26. See Henry 1983: 249. *IG* ii² 237+Add.=Lambert 3.5 is the only case in which Athens granted one of these privileges without the other, namely, paying the *eisphora* together with the Athenians.

27. Xen. *Poroi* 2.2; Whitehead 1977: 82–83, 104 n. 105 for bibliography.

28. See Xen. *Poroi* 2.5 and *Hipparchikos* 9.3–7 concerning the cavalry. Concerning the navy, see Thuc. 3.16.1; Xen. *Hell.* 1.6.24; M-L 23 (the "Themistokles Decree"); and Gabrielsen 1994: 108–9.

29. Böckh (1857: 691 cites) Hypereides in Pollux 8.144. See also Isokr. 17.21 and Harpokration, s.v. ἐπιγραφεῖς.

30. Whitehead 1977: 128; see Xen. *Poroi* 3.4.

31. See Plato *Laws* 744C. See also Whitehead 1977: 131 and Saunders 1972: 119–33.

32. Billheimer (1917: 28–29, 62) and Osborne (1983: 141–45) show that Athens granted citizenship almost exclusively in return for benefactions to the state.

33. Nos. 5 (Phanosthenes of Andros, ca. 410), 7 (Satyros and sons, Leukon, Gorgippos, and Metrodoros, ca. 395– 389/8), 9 (Leukon [reaffirmation] and sons, Spartokos, Pairisades, and Apollonios, 389/8), 11 (Orontes, 349/8?), 12 (Spartokos and Pairisades [reaffirmation], 347/6), 16 (Chairephilos and sons, Pheidon, Pamphilos, and Pheidippos, ca. 337–330), 22 (Harpalos, 333–324), 29 (−phanes, ca. 322/1–320/19), and 34 (Eumelos, 310/09). See Osborne 1983: 211–16.

34. See Davies 1971: 566 and Osborne 1983: 75–76.

35. See Osborne 1983: 211–16, Checklist nos. 2, 4, 5, 7, 8, 10, 11, 13–25, 27, 29–31, 33–36, 39–41, 44–49, 51–80, 83, 84, 87–89, 96–100, 103–10, 112, 113, 115, 116, 126–31, 135, 143, 144, 147–52, 154, 155, and 157, for a total of 107 cases. For unknown services (not counted), see Checklist nos. 12, 37, 90–94, 101, 111, 114, 132–34, 136–42, 145, 146, and 153. For possible grants of citizenship, abortive grants, and grants not put into effect (not counted), see Checklist nos. 1, 9, 26, 32, 42, 43, 50, 81, 82, 85, 86, 121–23, and 125. For Chairephilos and sons (not counted), see Checklist nos. 117–20. See Osborne 1983: 188–89 concerning grants of citizenship to honorands who had not yet performed any services for Athens. Athens hoped that such honorands, who usually held powerful positions, would provide services at some time in the future in return for the honor that Athens had bestowed on them.

36. Ibid., 200–202, 211–16, Checklist nos. 3, 38, 95, 124, and 156.

37. Ibid., 211, Checklist no. 6.

38. Of Osborne's 140 cases of naturalization in Athens down to 307/6 (not

counting possible grants, aborted grants, and grants not put into effect), 22 surely involve non-Greeks or block grants that included non-Greeks (Checklist nos. 5, 17, 29, 44–47, 55, 61–64, 71–74, 78, 79, 83, 84, 98, and 99). I assume that former slaves were non-Greeks, since this was true of the vast majority in Athens. Such was certainly the case for Phormion and his sons (nos. 71–73); on many occasions, Phormion was taunted by Apollodoros for being a bought barbarian slave ([Dem.] 45.30, 71, 73, 81). See also Garlan 1988: 46–53 concerning the ethnicity of slaves in Athens.

39. Osborne (1983: 186) states that "clearly only persons of wealth were likely to qualify" for grants of citizenship, since *andragathia* presupposed wealth in most circumstances. The socioeconomic statuses of the honorands of no. 29 is unknown.

40. Osborne 1983: 211–15, Checklist nos. 6, 13 (Phanosthenes), 46, 47, 71–73, 126, and 127. There are two other occasions on which it is certain that *metics* received citizenship (nos. 17 and 29), but these were block grants, which probably included both *metics* and non-*metics*. Seven cases exist in which the honorands may have been *metics*, but it is not certain (nos. 3, 30, 117–20 [Chairephilos and his sons], and 156).

41. [Dem.] 45.85, 59.2. Davies (*APF* 11672 IV) and Trevett (1992: 21–24 n. 9) believe that Pasion received his grant of citizenship for these services, even if they do not agree on the date. Since *metics* were normally barred from holding trierarchies (see p. 45; Dem. 20.18, 20; Thomsen 1964: 96–104; Whitehead 1977: 81; Clark 1990: 65–66; and Gabrielsen 1994: 61, 240 n. 25), it is likely that Pasion did not actually serve as trierarch, even though he provided ships and equipped and manned them.

42. Osborne 1983: 211, Checklist nos. 2, 3 (Polygnotos), and 4–8.

43. Ibid., 211–14. For political and military services exclusively, see Checklist nos. 10–11, 14–25, 27, 29–31, 39–41, 44, 45, 48, 49, 55–70, 75–80, 83, and 84. For unknown services, see Checklist nos. 12 and 37. For poetry, see Checklist no. 38. For other services, see Checklist nos. 13, 33–36, 46, 47, 51–54, and 71–74.

44. Ibid., 214–16. For political and military services exclusively, see Checklist nos. 87–89, 98–100, 103–10, 112, 113, 115, 116, 129, 131, 135, 143, 144, 148–51, 154, and 157. For unknown services, see Checklist nos. 90–94, 101, 111, 114, 132–34, 136–42, 145, 146, and 153. For poets and artists, see Checklist nos. 95, 124, and 156. For other services, see Checklist nos. 96, 97, 117–20, 126–28, 130, 147, 152, and 155.

45. Ibid., 211–16. For bankers between 414/3 and 355/4, see Checklist nos. 46, 47, and 71–73. For trade-related services between 414/3 and 355/4, see Checklist nos. 13, 33–36, 51–54, and 74. For bankers and others who made monetary contributions between 355/4 and 307/6, see Checklist nos. 126, 127, and 147. For trade-related services between 355/4 and 307/6, see Checklist nos. 96, 97, 117–20, 128, 130, 152, and 155.

46. Burke (1992: 210–12) believes that there was a much more radical change in the Athenian practice of granting citizenship for services relating to trade and revenues during the late fourth century. However, he bases his conclusion on overly broad criteria for identifying trade- and revenue-related services, which I have called into question previously (see chap. 7, *Proxenia* and *Euergesia*).

47. Concerning the ancient Greek preference for restricting access to citizenship, see Hansen 1991: 94–95 and Arist. *Pol.* 1278a26–34, 1319b 6–18. See also chap. 3

48. Austin and Vidal-Naquet 1977: 94; Manville 1990: 8–12; Hansen 1991: 97–100.

49. Manville 1990: 5–7. See also Mossé 1979: 241–49; Gauthier 1981: 167–79; Sinclair 1988: 23–25; and Boegehold and Scafuro 1994: 1–20.

50. Knorringa 1926: 102–13, 120–23; Austin and Vidal-Naquet 1977: 95–98; Finley 1985: 48, 95, 97.

51. Plato *Laws* 736C–741E; Arist. *Pol.* 1326a–b.

52. Isokr. 8.50; Dem. 23.126, 196, 200; [Dem.] 13.24. See also Billheimer 1917: 91.

53. Plato *Laws* 705A; Arist. *Pol.* 1258b, 1277b33–1278b5.

54. See, e.g., Osborne 1983: 211–16, Checklist nos. 8, 100, 110, and 112. See also Billheimer 1917: 100.

55. Concerning the honorific value of Athenian grants of citizenship, see Dem. 23.126, 118–19; Billheimer 1917: 98–100; Osborne 1981b: 5; Osborne 1983: 188; and Hansen 1991: 94. Hagemajer Allen (2003: 237) goes a bit too far in downplaying the honorific aspects of Athenian grants of citizenship to its benefactors.

56. Osborne (1983: 139–40) points out that despite the fact that naturalized citizens had all the rights of native citizens, except holding the archonship and priesthoods ([Dem.] 59.92, 104, 106; see also Osborne 1983: 173–76), they could encounter prejudice like that reported by Apollodoros in [Dem.] 45.78 and 50 passim. But see the same speech (45.71ff.) for Apollodoros' own bigotry toward the recently naturalized Phormion.

57. Jordan 1969: 183–207; 1975: 240–67.

58. Jameson 1963: 389–92; Morrison and Williams 1968: 257; Garlan 1972: 15–28; Ruschenbusch 1979: 106– 10; Morrison 1984: 48–59; Garlan 1988: 164–67; Gabrielsen 1994: 106, 248 n. 2.

59. Hasebroek 1933: 114. Finley (1985: 162) also expresses doubts that the interaction between Athens and the Bosporos was a "commercial agreement" ever "formalized by treaty."

Appendix Three

1. See pp. 109–10 for my justification for using these categories.

2. Walbank 282–84, no. 50. Mattingly (1990: 115) places this decree before 422/1, based on the name of the secretary Theaios, the same name that appears as the secretary of *IG* i³ 79, which was passed in the archonship of Alkaios of 422/1. But Develin (1989: 194) questions whether Theaios (partially restored by Walbank in *IG* i³ 174) is indeed the secretary of *IG* i³ 174.

3. Despite listing Lykon as a *naukleros*, Reed (2003: 125, no. 47) does not categorize Lykon as moderately wealthy.

4. Meiggs 1988: 249, no. 80; Walbank 390–92, no. 75. Develin (1989: 191–92) suggests a date of 415/4, but not with any certainty. See V-T 30 n. 84.

5. As in the case of Lykon, Reed (2003: 125, no. 48) does not categorize Pythophanes as moderately wealthy, despite his status as a *naukleros*.

6. Plato *Ion* 541c–d; Athenaios 506a; Xen. *Hell.* 1.5.18; And. 1.149. See also Raubitschek 1938: col. 1786; Walbank 321; MacDonald 1981: 141; and Osborne 1983: 32–33.

7. Mattingly 1966: 200–201; Walbank 323–24.

8. MacDonald 1981: 141–46. Meritt (1945: 129–32) proposed the same dates on purely epigraphic grounds.

9. See Henry 1983: 116–42 (for numerous cases of joint grants of *proxenia* and *euergesia*) and 140–41 (for the only two exceptions to this rule).

10. Meritt 1936a; Meiggs 1988: 278–79, no. 91; McGregor in *IG* i^3; Walbank 467–68, no. 90.

11. Contrary to Bresson 2000: 136.

12. See And. 2.11 and Meiggs 1982: 123 and 126 (for royal control of timber in Macedon) and 128 (for a discussion of Archelaos' services for Athens).

13. See Bresson 2000: 133–38 for a discussion on the methods by which Greek cities could determine the origins and destinations of exports and imports.

14. See Tuplin 1982: 124–26 for the following argument.

15. Diod. 14.93. See Beloch 1923: 91–92 (389–387); Werner 1955: 415–16, 430 (389/8); Burstein 1978: 428 n. 3 (389/8); Tuplin 1982: 125–26 (early 380s); Osborne 1983: 41–42 (389–387); and Hind 1994: 495 (389/8).

16. Johnson 1914: 419; Dinsmoor 1932: 158–59.

17. Johnson 1914: 417–23. See also Henry 1982: 105–7, contra Dinsmoor. Walbank (1990: 438–39, no. 5) argues for a date of ca. 387/6.

18. In his review of Bresson 2000, Harris (2001: 10) misunderstands Bresson's argument to say that Leukon sold grain to Athens at a reduced price and that Athens then sold it to its people at a slight markup.

19. For the date, see above and n. 14. For Leukon's citizenship, see Osborne 1983: 43, T21.

20. Henry (1983: 116–28, 130–40) and Walbank (1990: 442, no. 11) discuss the word order in detail.

21. Diod. 15.90–91; Parke 1935–37: 376; Osborne 1971a: 310–17; Osborne 1982: 65–72; Lambert 2006: 127.

22. Parke 1935–37: 368, 372; Osborne 1971a: 297, 299; Gauthier 1972: 82–83, 168–69; Osborne 1982: 74–75; Lambert 2006: 126.

23. Billheimer 1917: 48; Parke 1935–37: 367–78.

24. Osborne 1971a: 297–321; Osborne 1981b: 51–54, D12; Osborne 1982: 61–80, D12; Lambert 3.2.

25. See pp. 61–62 and 133–34. See also Lambert 2007: 102 n. 10, 104 n. 26.

26. Other possible restorations for line 14 include ἐν τ[ῶι πρόσθεν χρό-νωι or τ[[ῶι πολέμωι . . .]. See Lambert 2007: 104 n. 26.

27. Kuenzi ([1923] 1979: 41) suggests 352/1–337/6, but Migeotte (1983: 145) argues against it. Garnsey (1988: 151) places the decree in the late 340s or early 330s, but without explanation.

28. [Dem.] 34.37. See also Lyk. *Leokr.* 26–27 and Dem. 35.50, 56.6 and 11.

29. *APF* 15187, p. 566, followed by Osborne 1983: 75–76.

30. For the wealth of Chairephilos' sons, see Antiphanes 26 Edmonds and *IG* ii² 417, 1152. Davies (*APF* 15187, p. 566) and Osborne (1983: 75–76, T75) also believe that Chairephilos made monetary contributions to Athens.

31. For the grain shortage of 338/7, see Dem. 18.248; Lyk. *Leokr.* 18; and Plut. *Mor.* 851a. See also Garnsey 1988: 150, 154. Lambert (2006: 132 n. 68) also employs this dating criteria.

32. Camp 1974: 324; Reed 2003: 127, no. 55.

33. Tracy 1995: 123 nn. 4–5, 127–28. See Walbank 1990: 444 for another opinion.

34. Kirchner in *IG* ii²; Isager and Hansen 1975: 202 n. 16; Tracy 1995: 33–34.

35. *IG* ii² 1623.276–85; *IG* ii² 414(a); [Plut.] *Ten Orat.* 844a. Schweigert (1940: 339–41) has attempted to reconstruct the circumstances surrounding these documents concerning Diotimos.

36. [Dem.] 34.39; Garnsey 1988: 154; Isager and Hansen 1975: 201–2.

37. Oliver 1995: 201–3 and n. 16. See also Wilhelm 1942: 65–72, 103–4. *IG* ii² 479 and 480 are two separate inscriptions that record parts of the same text, overlapping each other briefly.

38. Billheimer (1917: 52–53), Hamilton (1973: 132–33), Osborne (1983: 79, T82), Kingsley (1986: 168), and Green (1991: 415, 461–62) all believe that the reference is historical.

39. Tod 2.196; Oliverio 1933: 33–35; Laronde 1987: 30–36; Garnsey 1988: 157–59; Marasco 1992: 12–37; Brun 1993: 190 n. 31, 192; Bresson 2000: 135.

40. Tod 2.196; Laronde 1987: 33; Brun 1993: 185 n. 5, 195–96 and n. 68; Bresson 2000: 135–38.

41. Finley (1985: 170) believes that the grain was given as a gift, free of charge, and cites the gift of grain to Athens by the Egyptian king Psammetichos in 445 as an example (Plut. *Per.* 37; Philoch. *FGrHist* 328 F 119). Harris (2001: 7) is also skeptical of Bresson's thesis.

42. Even Brun (1993: 195–96) does not doubt Alexander's influence.

43. Wilhelm in *IG* ii² (324/3); Meritt 1941: 48–49 (326/5); Meritt 1961: 88–89 (331/0); Meritt 1964: 213–17 (331/0); Isager and Hansen 1975: 202 n. 17 (331/0); Burstein 1976: 72 n. 39 (335/4); Schwenk no. 67 (326/5); Tracy 1995: 31 (326/5); Lambert no. 84 (331/0). For an examination of the arguments for and against these proposed years, see Schwenk no. 67 and Lambert 3.84.

44. Meritt 1941: 48–49; Isager and Hansen 1975: 202; Burstein 1976: 72; Schwenk 331–33.

45. Schweigert 1939: 33–34; Meritt 1941: 48–49; Schwenk no. 67; Lambert 3.84.

46. *PA* 11950; Dem. 9.72; Plut. *Phok.* 9.5 and *Dem.* 23.4; [Plut.] *Ten Orat.* 841e, 844f; Arr. *Anab.* 1.10.4; Suda, s.v. "Antipater." This Polyeuktos is not to be confused with Polyeuktos, son of Timokrates, of Krioa (*PA* 11946), ally of Androtion and proposer of the rider to *IG* ii² 212 (no. 12).

47. [Arist.] *Oik.* 2.1352b 19; Dem. 42.20; [Dem.] 34.39. See also Isager and Hansen 1975: 200–202 and Garnsey 1988: 154 for the dates of these references.

48. Clerc 1893: 219–20; Pecirka 1966: 72; Whitehead 1977: 29; Hopper 1979: 112; Marek 1984: 360.

49. EM 13412 was initially edited by Stroud 1971: 181, no. 29.

50. Clear cases in which Athens granted *enktesis* to nonresidents include *IG* ii² 53 and 265 (in which the honorands were also given the right to trials under the jurisdiction of the *polemarch*, a privilege that already applied to metics) and *IG* ii² 466 (in which the honorands were foreign ambassadors on a diplomatic mission to Athens). See Pecirka 1966: 28, 46, 79.

51. Dittmar (1890: 66, 122), Wilamowitz (*IG* ii² 342), and Marek (1984: 360) have also concluded that the honorands were *metics*; but Reed (2003: 126–27, nos. 51–52) follows Walbank. Oliver (1995: 315 n. 3) states that the honorands "may have been metics," but Pecirka (1966: 63) is uncertain. See also *IG* ii² 360 (nos. 24 and 27 of this study), which grants both *proxenia* and *enktesis* and dates to 330/29–325/4.

52. Pecirka 1966: 62 n. 2. Isager and Hansen (1975: 203) state that this decree is from the year 322 but provide no explanation other than to cite *SEG* 24.104, which in turn reports only Pecirka's readings. Oliver (1995: 307, 315 n. 3) rejects Isager and Hansen's date but does not provide an explanation for his own date of "330s/320s."

53. Walbank 1985: 107–11; 1989: 404 n. 38. Tracy (1995: 138 n. 1) believes that *IG* ii² 418 cannot be contemporary with *IG* ii² 342.

54. The following arguments largely follow Burstein 1978: 428–36. See also Worthington 1992: 205–7.

55. The manuscripts of Deinarchos 1.43 read "Berisaden" (Βηρισάδην), but state that he and his sons are "the tyrants of Pontos." Thus, the person in question is surely Pairisades I. See Worthington 1992: 205.

56. Recipients of grants of bronze statues with *sitesis* or *proedria* include Iphikrates (Dem. 23.130, 136), Diphilos (Dein. 1.43), Demades (Dein 1.101), Asander of Macedon (*IG* ii² 450), and Lykourgos (*IG* ii² 457+513). Recipients of grants of bronze statues without *sitesis* or *proedria* include Konon (Dem. 20.70), Euagoras (Isokr. 9.57; *IG* ii² 20+Stroud 1979, contra Wilhelm's restoration in the addendum), Chabrias (Dem. 20.75–86; Aischin. 3.243), and Timotheos (Dem. 20.84; Aischin. 3.243). See also Henry 1983: 294–95, 306 n. 26, despite the assertion of Osborne (1981a: 167) that a law was passed ca. 330 requiring that grants of bronze statues always be accompanied by *sitesis* and *proedria*.

57. See Isager and Hansen 1975: 169 for the date of [Dem.] 34.

58. See Garnsey 1988: 155–56 concerning the *epidosis* of 328/7.

59. For a full discussion, see Schwenk 1985: 425, no. 84. Lambert (2006: 135 n. 91) finds Schweigert's restoration "attractive."

60. Erxleben 1974: 495; Hopper 1979: 115; Isager and Hansen 1975: 207 and n. 55; Casson 1954: 169 and n. 6.

61. Marek (1984: 360) believes that Apollonides was a *metic*, but Pecirka (1966: 67) and Velissaropoulos (1980: 97) have doubts. See nos. 24 and 25 and n. 50 above concerning the uselessness of *enktesis* and *proxenia* for determining an honorand's residence.

62. Walbank 1987a: 10–12. More recently, Walbank (1990: 444, no. 17) has associated *IG* ii² 398(a)+438 with yet another fragment, *IG* ii² 612. The latter adds little to our understanding of the decree. Osborne included *IG* ii² 438 as D40 in his study of citizenship decrees; see Osborne 1981b: 106–7 and Osborne 1982: 111.

63. Kirchner in *IG* ii^2 398; Osborne 1982: 101, D36; Walbank 1987a: 11.

64. See Diod. 18.15.9; A. C. Johnson in the *apparatus criticus* of *IG* ii^2 398; Ferguson 1911: 17 n. 1; Billheimer 1917: 54; Walbank 1987a: 11.

65. Tracy 1995: 33, 134. See also Habicht 1973: 373.

66. See the restorations and commentary of Wilhelm 1906: 215–18; Scullion 2001: 116–17; Henry 2001: 106–8; and Scullion 2002: 81–84.

67. Walbank 1987b: 165–66; Walbank 1990: 444–45, no. 18.

68. Bresson (2000: 185) states that Wilhelm's restoration is "tout à fait à juste titre pour ce qui est de la restitution."

69. There is some dispute whether speech 56, *Against Dionysodoros*, was actually composed by Demosthenes. Schäfer iii^2 (307–14), Blass (1887–93: 3.582–88), Isager and Hansen (1975: 138 and n. 1), and Carey and Reid (1985: 203–4) all believe that the speech is inauthentic, but Bers (2003: 93) and Usher (1999: 256–57) believe that the speech is authentic.

70. See And. 2.11, where Andokides uses a word derived from καθίστημι to mean "normal" price in the sense of "at cost."

71. See Bresson 2000: 196 for a collection of the evidence. Isager and Hansen (1975: 200 n. 3) argue on the basis of [Dem.] 34.39 that the normal price of wheat was probably somewhere between five and six drachmas per *medimnos*.

72. See Bresson 2000: 185–87 for a discussion of and references to the evidence concerning official price-fixing in Ptolemaic Egypt (in which the prices are referred to as ἐστηκυίας) and a sale of grain at "the established price" by the general Epichares to the demesmen of Rhamnous.

73. For the dates of Eumelos' reign, see Werner 1955: 416–18, 430. Osborne (1983: 43, T84) includes Eumelos in his catalog of those who were naturalized by Athens.

74. The corpus gives "c. 417–413?" as the date for the decree. Meritt dates the decree to "before 432" and identifies it with the alliance between Athens and Macedon mentioned in Thuc. 1.57 (Meritt, Wade-Gery, and McGregor 1939–53: 3.313 n. 61). Others have argued for dating the decree to 423/2, connecting it to another rapprochement between Athens and Macedon within the context of the campaigns of Brasidas and Kleon concerning Amphipolis and the Chalkidike mentioned by Thuc. 4.132.1 (for discussion and bibliography, see Hammond and Griffith 1979: 134–35 and Meiggs 1972: 196–97, 428–30). Hammond provides more compelling arguments that the decree dates to ca. 415 (Hammond and Griffith 1979: 134–36).

75. Diod. 15.79.1; Isokr. *Philip* 53; Plut. *Philopoimen* 14.1–2.

76. Brashinsky (1967: 119–21), Osborne (1981: 80–85, D25; 1982: 95, D25), Schwenk (no. 85, pp. 426–32), and Tracy (1995: 122 and n. 1) have all accepted Schweigert's association of the fragments, though Osborne alters the arrangement of the fragments, and Tracy has doubts about a few of the smaller fragments.

77. Oliver (1995: 309, G12) also includes this decree in his catalog of honorary decrees concerning the grain supply of Athens.

78. Henry 1996: 105, 117; Tracy 1995: 34.

References

Adcock, Frank, and Derek J. Mosley. 1975. *Diplomacy in Ancient Greece*. London: Thames and Hudson.

Adkins, Arthur W. H. 1960. *Merit and Responsibility: A Study in Greek Values*. Chicago: University of Chicago Press.

Adkins, Arthur W. H. 1972. *Moral Values and Political Behaviour in Ancient Greece*. London: Chatto and Windus.

Amemiya, Takeshi. 2007. *Economy and Economics of Ancient Greece*. London and New York: Routledge.

Andreades, Andreas M. 1933. *A History of Greek Public Finance*. Trans. Carroll N. Brown. Rev. ed. Vol. 1. Cambridge, MA: Harvard University Press.

Andreau, Jean. 1995. "Vingt ans d'après *L'économie antique* de Moses I. Finley." *Annales: Histoire, Sciences Sociales* 50: 947–60. Citations in the text refer to "Twenty Years after Moses I. Finley's *The Ancient Economy*." Trans. A. Nevill. In Scheidel and von Reden 2002: 33–49.

Andreau, Jean, P. Briant, and R. Descat, eds. 1997. *Économie antique: Prix et formation des prix dans les économies antiques*. Saint Bertrand de Comminges: Musée archéologique départemental.

Andreau, Jean, and R. Etienne. 1984. "Vingt ans de recherches sur l'archaisme et la modernité des sociétés antiques." *REA* 86: 55–83.

Archibald, Zofia H. 2001. "Setting the Scene." In Archibald et al. 2001: 1–9.

Archibald, Zofia H., John K. Davies, Vincent Gabrielsen, and Graham J. Oliver, eds. 2001. *Hellenistic Economies*. London: Routledge.

Ashton, N. G. 1977. "The Naumachia near Amorgos in 322 B.C." *BSA* 72: 1–11.

Austin, M. M. 1988. "Greek Trade, Industry, and Labor." In *Civilization of the Ancient Mediterranean: Greece and Rome*, ed. Michael Grant and Rachel Kitzinger, 2.723–51. New York: Scribners.

Austin, M. M. 1994. "Society and Economy." In *CAH*[2] 6.527–64.

Austin, M. M., and Pierre Vidal-Naquet. 1977. *Economic and Social History of Ancient Greece: An Introduction*. Berkeley: University of California Press.

Beloch, Julius K. 1899. "Die Grossindustrie im Altertum." *Zeitschrift für Sozialwissenschaft* 2: 18–26.

Beloch, Julius K. 1902. "Zur griechischen Wirtschaftsgeschichte." *Zeitschrift für Sozialwissenschaft* 5: 95–103, 169–79.

Beloch, Julius K. 1923. *Griechische Geschichte*. Vol. 3, pt. 2. Berlin and Leipzig: Walter de Gruyter.

Bers, Victor, trans. 2003. *Demosthenes: Speeches 50–59*. Austin: University of Texas Press.

Berthold, Richard M. 1984. *Rhodes in the Hellenistic Age.* Ithaca, NY: Cornell University Press.

Billheimer, Albert. 1917. "Naturalization in Athenian Law and Practice." PhD diss., Princeton University.

Billows, Richard. 2003. "Cities." In Erskine 2003: 196–215.

Blass, Friedrich. 1887–93. *Die attische Beredsamkeit.* 2nd ed. Vols. 1–3. Leipzig: Teubner.

Block, Fred, and Peter Evans. 2005. "The State and the Economy." In Smelser and Swedberg 2005a: 505–26.

Bloedow, Emund F. 1973. *Alcibiades Reexamined.* Wiesbaden: Franz Steiner Verlag.

Bloedow, Emund F. 1975. "Corn Supply and Athenian Imperialism." *L'antiquité classique* 44: 20–29.

Boardman, J. 1980. *The Greeks Overseas.* London: Thames and Hudson.

Böckh, August. 1817. *Die Staatshaushaltung der Athener.* Realschulbuchhandlung.

Böckh, August. 1857. *The Public Economy of the Athenians.* Trans. Anthony Lamb. 2nd ed. Boston: Little, Brown.

Böckh, August. 1886. *Die Staatshaushaltung der Athener.* 3rd ed. Berlin: Walter de Gruyter.

Boegehold, Alan L., and Adele C. Scafuro, eds. 1994. *Athenian Identity and Civic Ideology.* Baltimore: Johns Hopkins University Press.

Brashinsky, J. B. 1968. *Athen und die Gebiete an der nördlichen Schwarzmeerküste zwischen dem 6. und 2. Jahrhundert v. u. Z.* Abstract. *BCO* 13: 102–8.

Brashinsky, J. B. 1971. "Epigraphical Evidence on Athens's Relations with the North Pontic Greek States." In *Acta of the Fifth International Congress of Greek and Latin Epigraphy, Cambridge, [18th to 23rd September], 1967,* 119–23. Oxford: Blackwell.

Bresson, Alain. 1987. "Aristote et le commerce exterieur." *REA* 89: 217–38.

Bresson, Alain. 2000. *La cité marchande.* Bordeaux: Ausonius.

Broneer, Oscar. 1933. "Excavations on the North Slope of the Acropolis." *Hesperia* 2: 329–417.

Brun, Patrice. 1983. *Eisphora, syntaxis, stratiotika: Recherches sur les finances militaires d'Athènes au IVe siècle av. J.-C.* Paris: Les Belles Lettres.

Brun, Patrice. 1993. "La stèle des céréales de Cyrène et le commerce du grain en Egée au IV° s. av. J.C." *ZPE* 99: 185–96.

Brun, Patrice. 2000. *L'orateur Démade: Essai d'histoire et d'historiographie.* Bordeaux: Ausonius.

Bücher, Karl. 1912. *Industrial Evolution.* Trans. S. M. Wickett. 3rd ed. New York: H. Holt.

Bugh, Glenn R., ed. 2006. *The Cambridge Companion to the Hellenistic World.* Cambridge: Cambridge University Press.

Burke, Edmund M. 1984. "Eubulus, Olynthus, and Euboea." *TAPA* 114: 111–20.

Burke, Edmund M. 1985. "Lycurgan Finances." *GRBS* 26: 251–64.

Burke, Edmund M. 1992. "The Economy of Athens in the Classical Era: Some Adjustments to the Primitivist Model." *TAPA* 122: 199–226.

Burke, Edmund M. 1998. "The Looting of the Estate of the Elder Demosthenes." *C&M* 49: 45–65.

Burstein, Stanley M. 1976. *Outpost of Hellenism: The Emergence of Heraclea on the Black Sea*. Berkeley: University of California Press.

Burstein, Stanley M. 1978. "*IG* ii² 653, Demosthenes, and Athenian Relations with Bosporus in the Fourth Century B.C." *Historia* 27: 428–36.

Burstein, Stanley M. 1985. *The Hellenistic Age from the Battle of Ipsos to the Death of Kleopatra VII*. Cambridge: Cambridge University Press.

Burstein, Stanley M. 1993. "The Origin of the Athenian Privileges at Bosporus: A Reconsideration." *AHB* 7:81–83.

Busolt, Georg. 1920. *Griechische Staatskunde*. Vol. 1. Munich: C. H. Beck.

Buttrey, Theodore V. 1979. "The Athenian Currency Law of 375/4 B.C." In *Greek Numismatics and Archaeology: Essays in Honor of Margaret Thompson*, ed. Otto Mørkholm and Nancy Waggoner, 33–45. Wetteren: Numismatique Romaine.

Buttrey, Theodore V. 1981. "More on the Athenian Coinage Law of 375/4 B.C." *NAC* 10: 71–94.

Calhoun, George. 1926. *The Business Life of Ancient Athens*. Chicago: University of Chicago Press.

Camp, John McK. 1974. "Proxenia for Sopatros of Akragas." *Hesperia* 43: 314–24.

Camp, John McK. 1982. "Drought and Famine in the 4th Century B.C." In *Studies in Athenian Architecture, Sculpture, and Topography: Presented to Homer A. Thompson. Hesperia* Suppl. 20: 9–17.

Carey, Christopher, and R. A. Reid, eds. 1985. *Demosthenes: Selected Private Speeches*. Cambridge: Cambridge University Press.

Cartledge, Paul A. 1983. "'Trade and Politics' Revisited: Archaic Greece." In Garnsey, Hopkins, and Whittaker 1983: 1–15.

Cartledge, Paul A. 1998. "The Economy (Economies) of Ancient Greece." *Dialogos* 5:4–24.

Cartledge, Paul A., Edward E. Cohen, and Lin Foxhall, eds. 2002. *Money, Labour, and Land: Approaches to the Economies of Ancient Greece*. London: Routledge.

Cartledge, Paul A., and F. D. Harvey, eds. 1985. *Crux: Essays Presented to G. E. M. de Ste. Croix on His Seventy-Fifth Birthday*. Exeter and London: Imprint Academic and Duckworth.

Cartledge, Paul A., Paul Millett, and S. Todd, eds. 1990. *Nomos: Essays in Athenian Law, Politics, and Society*. Cambridge: Cambridge University Press.

Casson, Lionel. 1954. "The Grain Trade of the Hellenistic World." *TAPA* 85: 168–87.

Casson, Lionel. 1984. *Ancient Trade and Society*. Detroit: Wayne State University Press.

Casson, Lionel. 1991. *The Ancient Mariners*. 2nd ed. Princeton, NJ: Princeton University Press.

Cawkwell, George L. 1962. "Demosthenes and the Stratiotic Fund." *Mnemosyne* 15: 377–83.

Cawkwell, George L. 1963. "Eubulus." *JHS* 83: 47–67.

Christesen, Paul. 2003. "Economic Rationalism in Fourth-Century BCE Athens." *G&R* 50: 31–56.

Clark, M. 1990. "The Date of *IG* II² 1604." *BSA* 85: 47–67.

Clerc, Michel. 1893. *Les métèques athéniens.* Paris: Thorin et fils.

Cohen, Edward E. 1973. *Ancient Athenian Maritime Courts.* Princeton, NJ: Princeton University Press.

Cohen, Edward E. 1989. "Athenian Finance: Maritime and Landed Yields." *CA* 8 no. 2: 207–23.

Cohen, Edward E. 1990a. "Commercial Lending by Athenian Banks: Cliometric Fallacies and Forensic Methodology." *CP* 85: 177–90.

Cohen, Edward E. 1990b. "A Study in Contrast: 'Maritime Loans' and 'Landed Loans' at Athens." In Nenci and Thür 1990: 57–79.

Cohen, Edward E. 1992a. *Athenian Economy and Society: A Banking Perspective.* Princeton, NJ: Princeton University Press.

Cohen, Edward E. 1992b. Review of Millett 1991. *BMCR,* http://bmcr.bryn mawr.edu/1992/03.04.10.html.

Crosby, Mary. 1950. "The Leases of the Laurion Mines." *Hesperia* 19: 189–312.

Culasso-Gastaldi, Enrica. 2004. *Le prossenie ateniesi del IV secolo a.C. gli honorati asiatici.* Alessandria: Edizioni dell'Orso.

Davidson, James. 1998. *Courtesans and Fishcakes: The Consuming Passions of Classical Athens.* New York: St. Martin's.

Davies, John K. 1967. "Demosthenes on Liturgies: A Note." *JHS* 87: 33–40.

Davies, John K. 1971. *Athenian Propertied Families, 600–300 B.C.* Oxford: Oxford University Press.

Davies, John K. 1981. *Wealth and the Power of Wealth in Classical Athens.* New York: Arno.

Davies, John K. 1984. "Cultural, Social, and Economic Features of the Hellenistic World." In *CAH²* 7.1.257–320.

Davies, John K. 1992. "Society and Economy." In *CAH²* 5.287–305.

Davies, John K. 1998. "Ancient Economies: Models and Muddles." In Parkins and Smith 1998: 225–56.

Davies, John K. 2001a. "Hellenistic Economies in the Post-Finley Era." In Archibald et al. 2001: 11–62.

Davies, John K. 2001b. "Rebuilding a Temple: The Economic Effects of Piety." In Mattingly and Salmon 2001: 209–29.

Davies, John K. 2001c. "Temples, Credit, and the Circulation of Money." In Meadows and Shipton 2001: 117–28.

Davies, John K. 2006. "Hellenistic Economies." In Bugh 2006: 73–92.

De Falco, Vittorio. 1954. *Demade oratore: Testimonianze e frammenti.* 2nd ed. Naples: Libraria Scientifica Editrice.

Descat, Raymond. 1987. "L'économie d'une cité grecque au IVe siècle avant J.-C.: L'example Athénien." *REA* 89: 239–52.

Deuxieme conference internationale d'histoire economique, Aix-en-Provence 1962. Vol. 1, *Trade and Politics in the Ancient World,* ed. anon. Paris: Mouton, 1965.

Develin, Robert. 1989. *Athenian Officials, 684–321 B.C.* Cambridge: Cambridge University Press.

Diller, Aubrey. 1937. *Race Mixture among the Greeks before Alexander*. Urbana: University of Illinois Press.

DiMaggio, Paul. 1994. "Culture and Economy." In Smelser and Swedberg 1994a: 27–57.

Dinsmoor, William B. 1932. "The Burning of the Opisthodomos at Athens." *AJA* 36: 143–72.

Dittenberger, Wilhelm. 1903–5. *Orientis Graeci inscriptiones selectae*. Vols. 1–2. Leipzig: S. Hirzel.

Dittenberger, Wilhelm. 1915–24. *Sylloge inscriptionum Graecarum*. 3rd ed. Vols. 1–4. Leipzig: S. Hirzel.

Dittmar, A. M. 1890. *De Athensiensium more exteros coronis publice ornandi quaestiones epigraphicae*. Leipziger Studien 13. Leipzig.

Dodds, E. R. 1960. *The Greeks and the Irrational*. Berkeley: University of California Press.

Donlan, Walter. 1980. *The Aristocratic Ideal in Ancient Greece*. Lawrence, KS: Coronado.

Dornbusch, Rudiger, and Stanley Fischer. 1990. *Macroeconomics*. 5th ed. New York: McGraw-Hill.

Dover, Kenneth J. 1974. *Greek Popular Morality in the Time of Plato and Aristotle*. Oxford: Oxford University Press.

Dow, Sterling. 1963. "The Athenian Honors for Aristonikos of Karystos, 'Alexander's ΣΦΑΙΡΙΣΤΗΣ.'" *HSCP* 67: 77–92.

Duncan, Colin A. M., and David W. Tandy, eds. 1994. *From Political Economy to Anthropology*. Montreal: Black Rose.

Eadie, John W., and Josiah Ober, eds. 1985. *The Craft of the Ancient Historian: Essays in Honor of Chester G. Starr*. Lanham, MD: University Press of America.

Edmonds, John M. 1957–61. *Fragments of Attic Comedy*. Vols. 1–3. Leiden: Brill.

Ehrenberg, Victor. 1962. *The People of Aristophanes: A Sociology of Old Attic Comedy*. 3rd rev. ed. New York: Schocken.

Ehrenberg, Victor. 1969. *The Greek State*. Oxford: Oxford University Press.

Engen, Darel T. 2001. "Trade, Traders, and the Economy of Athens in the Fourth Century B.C.E." In Tandy 2001: 179–202.

Engen, Darel T. 2004. "Seeing the Forest and the Trees of the Ancient Economy." *AHB* 18: 150–65.

Engen, Darel T. 2005. "'Ancient Greenbacks': Athenian Owls, the Law of Nikophon, and the Greek Economy." *Historia* 54: 359–81.

Erb, Otto. 1939. *Wirtschaft und Gesellschaft im Denken der hellenischen Antike*. Berlin.

Erskine, Andrew, ed. 2003. *A Companion to the Hellenistic World*. Oxford: Blackwell.

Erxleben, Eberhard. 1974. "Die Rolle der Bevölkerungsklassen im Ausenhandel Athens im 4. Jahrhundert v. u. Z." In Welskopf 1974: 460–520.

Erxleben, Eberhard. 1975. "Das Verhältnis des Handels zum Produktionsaufkommen in Attica im 5. und 4. Jahrhundert v. u. Z." *Klio* 57: 365–98.

Faraguna, Michele. 1992. *Atene nell' età di Alessandro: Problemi politici, economici, finanziari*. Rome: Academia nazionale dei Lincei.

Ferguson, John. 1989. *Morals and Values in Ancient Greece*. London: Bristol Classical Press.

Figueira, Thomas J. 1984. "Karl Polanyi and Ancient Greek Trade: The Port of Trade." *AW* 10: 15–30.

Figueira, Thomas J. 1986. "*Sitopolai* and *Sitophylakes* in Lysias' 'Against the Grain Dealers': Governmental Intervention in the Athenian Economy." *Phoenix* 40: 149–71.

Finkelstein [Finley], Moses I. 1935. "Ἔμπορος, Ναύκληρος, and Κάπηλος: A Prolegomena to the Study of Athenian Trade." *CP* 30: 320–36.

Finley, Moses I. 1952. *Studies in Land and Credit in Ancient Athens, 500–200 B.C.: The Horos-Inscriptions.* New Brunswick, NJ: Rutgers University Press.

Finley, Moses I. 1965. "Classical Greece." In *Deuxieme conference internationale d'histoire economique, Aix-en-Provence 1962.* Vol. 1, *Trade and Politics in the Ancient World,* ed. anon. Paris: Mouton.

Finley, Moses I. 1970. "Aristotle and Economic Analysis." *Past and Present* 47: 3–25.

Finley, Moses I. 1978. *The World of Odysseus.* 2nd ed. Harmondsworth: Penguin.

Finley, Moses I., ed. 1979. *The Bücher-Meyer Controversy.* New York: Arno.

Finley, Moses I. 1981. *Economy and Society in Ancient Greece.* Ed. Brent D. Shaw and Richard P. Saller. London: Chatto and Windus.

Finley, Moses I. 1985. *The Ancient Economy.* 2nd ed. Berkeley: University of California Press.

Finley, Moses I. 1999. *The Ancient Economy.* Updated ed. Berkeley: University of California Press.

Fornara, Charles W. 1983. *Archaic Times to the End of the Peloponnesian War.* 2nd ed. Cambridge: Cambridge University Press.

Foxhall, Lin. 1990. "Olive Cultivation within Greek and Roman Agriculture: The Ancient Economy Revisited." PhD diss., University of Liverpool.

Foxhall, Lin, and H. A. Forbes. 1982. "Σιτομετρεία: The Role of Grain as a Staple Food in Classical Antiquity." *Chiron* 12: 41–90.

Francotte, Henri. 1910a. "Le pain à bon marché et le pain gratuit dans les cités grecques." In Francotte 1910b: 291– 312.

Francotte, Henri. 1910b. *Melanges de droit public grec.* Liege: H. Vaillant-Carmanne.

Francotte, Henri. 1916. "Industrie und Handel." *RE* 9: cols. 1381–1439.

French, Alfred. 1964. *The Growth of the Athenian Economy.* London: Routledge and Kegan Paul.

French, Alfred. 1991. "Economic Conditions in Fourth-Century Athens." *G&R* 38: 24–40.

Frösén, Jaako, ed. 1997. *Early Hellenistic Athens: Symptoms of a Change.* Papers and Monographs of the Finnish Institute at Athens, vol. 6. Helsinki.

Gabrielsen, Vincent. 1986. "ΦΑΝΕΡΑ and ΑΦΑΝΗΣ ΟΥΣΙΑ in Classical Athens." *C&M* 37: 99–114.

Gabrielsen, Vincent. 1994. *Financing the Athenian Fleet: Public Taxation and Social Relations.* Baltimore: Johns Hopkins University Press.

Gajdukevic, Victor F. 1971. *Das Bosporanische Reich.* Berlin: Akademie Verlag.

Gallant, Thomas W. 1991. *Risk and Survival in Ancient Greece.* Stanford, CA: Stanford University Press.

Gallo, Luigi. 1984. *Alimentazione e demogràfia nella Grècia antiqua.* Salerno: P. Laveglia.

Garlan, Yvon. 1972. "Quelques travaux récents sur les esclaves grecs en temps de guerre." *Colloque Besançon:* 15– 28.

Garlan, Yvon. 1988. *Slavery in Ancient Greece.* Trans. Janet Lloyd. Rev. ed. Ithaca, NY: Cornell University Press.

Garnsey, Peter. 1985. "Grain for Athens." In Cartledge and Harvey 1985: 62– 75.

Garnsey, Peter. 1988. *Famine and Food Supply in the Graeco-Roman World.* Cambridge: Cambridge University Press.

Garnsey, Peter. 1998. *Cities, Peasants, and Food in Classical Antiquity: Essays in Social and Economic History.* Ed. Walter Scheidel. Cambridge: University of Cambridge Press.

Garnsey, Peter, Keith Hopkins, and C. R. Whittaker, eds. 1983. *Trade in the Ancient Economy.* Berkeley: University of California Press.

Garnsey, Peter, and C. R. Whittaker, eds. 1983. *Trade and Famine in Classical Antiquity.* Cambridge: Cambridge Philological Society.

Gauthier, Philippe. 1972. *Symbola: Les étrangers et la justice dans les cités grecques.* Nancy: L'Université de Nancy.

Gauthier, Philippe. 1976. *Un commentaire historique des Poroi de Xénophon.* Geneva and Paris: Librairie Droz.

Gauthier, Philippe. 1981a. "De Lysias à Aristote (*Ath. pol.* 51,4): Le commerce du grain à Athènes et les fonctions des sitophylaques." *RHDF* 59: 5–28.

Gauthier, Philippe. 1981b. "La citoyenneté en Grèce et à Rome: Participation et intégration," *Ktema* 6: 167–79.

Gauthier, Philippe. 1985. *Les cités grecques et leurs bienfaiteurs.* BCH Suppl. 12. Athens and Paris: Ecole française d'Athènes.

Gerhardt, Paul. [1933] 1935. *Die attische Metoikie im vierten Jahrhundert.* Königsberg: Graph. Kunstanst.

Gernet, Louis. [1909] 1979. *L'approvisionement d'Athènes en blé au Ve et au IVe siècle.* New York: Arno.

Gernet, Louis. [1955] 1964. *Droit et société dans la Grèce ancienne.* Paris: Sirey.

Giglioni Bodei, Gabriella. 1970. *Xenophontis De Vectigalibus.* Florence: La Nuova Italia.

Glotz, Gustav. 1926. *Ancient Greece at Work.* Trans. M. R. Dobie. New York: Alfred A. Knopf.

Golden, Mark. 2000. "Demosthenes and the Social Historian." In Worthington 2000: 159–80.

Gomme, Arnold W. 1937a. *Essays in Greek History and Literature.* Oxford: Oxford University Press.

Gomme, Arnold W. 1937b. "Traders and Manufacturers in Greece." In Gomme 1937a: 42–66.

Granovetter, Mark. 1985. "Economic Action and Social Structure: The Problem of Embeddedness." *American Journal of Sociology* 91, no. 3: 481–510.

Granovetter, Mark. 1993. "The Nature of Economic Relationships." In Swedberg 1993: 3–41.

Granovetter, Mark, and Richard Swedberg, eds. 1992a. "Introduction." In Granovetter and Swedberg 1992b: 1–26.

Granovetter, Mark, and Richard Swedberg, eds. 1992b. *The Sociology of Economic Life.* Boulder, CO: Westview.

Green, Peter. 1990. *Alexander to Actium: The Historical Evolution of the Hellenistic Age*. Berkeley: University of California Press.

Green, Peter. 1991. *Alexander of Macedon, 356–323 B.C.: A Historical Biography*. Berkeley: University of California Press.

Gschnitzer, Fritz. 1973. "Proxenie." *RE Suppl.* 13: cols. 629–730.

Habicht, Christian. 1973. "Literarische und epigraphische Überlieferung zur Geschichte Alexanders und seine ersten Nachfolger." *Vestigia* 17: 367–77.

Habicht, Christian. 1997. *Athens from Alexander to Antony*. Trans. Deborah Lucas Schneider. Cambridge, MA: Harvard University Press.

Hagemajer Allen, Katarzina. 2003. "Intercultural Exchanges in Fourth-Century Attic Decrees." *CA* 22, no. 2: 199–246.

Hakkarainen, Mika. 1997. "Private Wealth in the Athenian Public Sphere during the Late Classical and the Early Hellenistic Period." In Frösén 1997: 1–32.

Hall, Jonathan M. 2007. *A History of the Archaic Greek World, ca. 1200–479 BCE*. Oxford: Blackwell.

Halstead, Paul. 1987. "Traditional and Ancient Rural Economies: Plus ça change?" *JHS* 107: 77–87.

Hamilton, J. R. 1973. *Alexander the Great*. Pittsburgh: University of Pittsburgh Press.

Hammond, N. G. L., and G. T. Griffith. 1979. *A History of Macedonia*. Vol. 2, *550–336 B.C.* Oxford: Clarendon.

Hansen, Marianne.V. 1984. "Athenian Maritime Trade in the 4th Century B.C.: Operation and Finance." *C&M* 35: 71–92.

Hansen, Mogens H. 1976. *Apagoge, Endeixis, and Ephegesis against Kakourgoi, Atimoi, and Pheugontes: A Study in the Athenian Administration of Justice in the Fourth Century B.C.* Odense: Odense University Press.

Hansen, Mogens H. 1983. "*Rhetores* and *Strategoi* in Fourth-Century Athens." *GRBS* 24: 151–80.

Hansen, Mogens H. 1988. *Three Studies in Athenian Demography*. Copenhagen: Det Kongelige videnskabernes selskab: Comissioner Munksgaard.

Hansen, Mogens H. 1991. *The Athenian Democracy in the Age of Demosthenes*. Oxford: Oxford University Press.

Hanson, Victor D. 1995. *The Other Greeks*. New York: Free Press.

Harding, Phillip. 1974. "Androtion's View of Solon's *Seisachtheia*." *Phoenix* 28: 282–89.

Harding, Phillip. 1976. "Androtion's Political Career." *Historia* 25: 186–200.

Harding, Phillip. 1978. "O Androtion, You Fool!" *AJAH* 3: 179–83.

Harding, Phillip. 1985. *From the End of the Peloponnesian War to the Battle of Ipsus*. Cambridge: Cambridge University Press.

Harding, Phillip. 1994. *Androtion and the Atthis*. Oxford: Clarendon.

Hargreaves Heap, Shaun. 1989. *Rationality in Economics*. New York: Blackwell.

Harris, Edward M. 1995. *Aeschines and Athenian Politics*. Oxford: Oxford University Press.

Harris, Edward M. 2001. Review of Bresson 2000. *BMCR* 2001.09.40, http://bmcr.brynmawr.edu/2001/2001-09-40.html.

Harris, William V. 1989. *Ancient Literacy*. Cambridge, MA: Harvard University Press.

Harrison, Alick R. W. 1968–71. *The Law of Athens*. Vols. 1–2. Oxford: Oxford University Press.

Hasebroek, Johannes. 1923. "Die Betriebsformen des griechischen Handels im IV. Jahrh." *Hermes* 58: 393–425.

Hasebroek, Johannes. [1928] 1933. *Staat und Handel im allen Griechenland.* Tubingen: J. C. B. Mohr (P. Siebeck). Citations in the text refer to *Trade and Politics in Ancient Greece.* Trans. L. M. Fraser and D. C. MacGregor. London: G. Bell and Sons.

Hedrick, Charles W. 1999. "Democracy and the Athenian Epigraphical Habit." *Hesperia* 68: 387–439.

Heichelheim, Fritz M. 1935. "Sitos." *RE Suppl.* 6: cols. 819–92.

Heichelheim, Fritz M. 1958. *An Ancient Economic History*. Trans. J. Stevens. 2nd ed. Vol. 1. Leiden: A. W. Sitjhoff.

Henry, Alan S. 1982. "Polis/acropolis, Paymasters, and the Ten Talent Fund." *Chiron* 12: 91–118.

Henry, Alan S. 1983. *Honours and Privileges in Athenian Decrees.* Hildesheim: Georg Olms.

Henry, Alan S. 1996. "The Hortatory Intention in Athenian State Decrees." *ZPE* 112: 105–19.

Henry, Alan S. 2001. "Adolf Wilhelm and IG II2 401." *ZPE* 137: 106–8.

Herman, Gabriel. 1987. *Ritualised Friendship and the Greek City.* Cambridge: Cambridge University Press.

Herzog, R. 1914. "Zu Xenophons Poroi." In *Festgabe Hugo Blümner,* 469–80. Zurich: Buchdrukerei Berichthaus.

Hind, John. 1994. "The Bosporan Kingdom." In *CAH²* 6.476–511.

Hodkinson, Stephen. 1988. "Animal Husbandry in the Greek Polis." In Whittaker 1988: 35–74.

Hodkinson, Stephen. 1992. "Imperialist Democracy and Market-Oriented Pastoral Production in Classical Athens." *Anthropozoologica* 16: 53–60.

Hommel, H. 1932. "Metoikoi." *RE* 15: cols. 1413–58.

Horden, Peregrine, and Nicholas Purcell. 2000. *The Corrupting Sea: A Study of Mediterranean History.* Oxford: Blackwell.

Hopper, Robert J. 1953. "The Attic Silver Mines in the Fourth Century B.C." *BSA* 48: 200–254.

Hopper, Robert J. 1979. *Trade and Industry in Classical Greece.* London: Thames and Hudson.

Hornblower, Simon. 1982. *Mausolus.* Oxford: Oxford University Press.

Hornblower, Simon. 1983. *The Greek World, 479–323 B.C.* New York: Routledge.

Hume, David. 1970. *Writings on Economics.* Ed. Eugene Rotwein. Madison: University of Wisconsin Press.

Humphreys, S. C. 1969. "History, Economics, and Anthropology: The Work of Karl Polanyi." *History and Theory* 8: 165–212.

Humphreys, S. C. 1970. "Economy and Society in Classical Athens." *ANSP* 39: 1–26.

Humphreys, S. C. 1971. "The Work of Louis Gernet." *History and Theory* 10: 172–96.

Humphreys, S. C. 1978. *Anthropology and the Greeks.* London: Routledge and Kegan Paul.

Humphreys, S. C. 1985. "Lycurgus of Butadae: An Athenian Aristocrat." In Eadie and Ober 1985: 199–252.

Isager, Signe, and Mogens H. Hansen. 1975. *Aspects of Athenian Society in the Fourth Century B.C.* Trans. Judith Hsiang Rosenmeir. Odense: Odense University Press.

Jacoby, Felix. 1923–58. *Die Fragmente der griechischen Historiker.* Vols. 1–15. Berlin and Leiden: Weidmann and Brill.

Jacoby, Felix. 1949. *Atthis.* Oxford: Oxford University Press.

Jacoby, Felix. 1954a. *Die Fragmente der griechischen Historiker.* Vol. 3b, Suppl. 1. Leiden: Brill.

Jacoby, Felix. 1954b. *Die Fragmente der griechischen Historiker.* Vol. 3b, Suppl. 2. Leiden: Brill.

Jameson, Michael H. 1963. "The Provisions for Mobilization in the Decree of Themistokles." *Historia* 12: 385–404.

Jameson, Michael H., Curtis N. Runnels, and Tjeerd H. van Andel. 1994. *A Greek Countryside: The Southern Argolid from Prehistory to the Present Day.* Palo Alto, CA: Stanford University Press.

Jardé, Auguste F. V. 1925. *Les céreales dans l'antiquité grecque.* Paris: E. de Boccard.

Johnson, Allan C. 1914. "Notes on Attic Inscriptions." *CP* 9: 417–41.

Jones, A. H. M. [1957a] 1986. *Athenian Democracy.* Baltimore: Johns Hopkins University Press.

Jones, A. H. M. [1957b] 1986. "The Athens of Demosthenes." In Jones [1957] 1986a: 23–38.

Jordan, Borimir. 1969. "The Meaning of the Technical Term *Hyperesia* in Naval Contexts of the Fifth and Fourth Centuries B.C." *CSCA* 2: 183–207.

Jordan, Borimir. 1975. *The Athenian Navy in the Classical Period.* Berkeley: University of California Press.

Kahrstedt, Ulrich. [1934] 1969. *Staatsgebiet und Staatsangehörige in Athen.* Darmstadt: Scientia Verlag Aalen.

Karageorghis, Vassos. 1969a. *The Ancient Civilization of Cyprus.* Geneva: Nagel.

Karageorghis, Vassos. 1969b. *Salamis in Cyprus: Homeric, Hellenistic, and Roman.* London: Thames and Hudson.

Karageorghis, Vassos. 1982. *Cyprus from the Stone Age to the Romans.* London: Thames and Hudson.

Katayama, Y. 1970. "The Social Significance of Liturgies from the Viewpoint of the Participation of Metics." [In Japanese with an English summary.] *JCS* 18: 40–51.

Kim, Henry S. 2001. "Archaic Coinage as Evidence for the Use of Money." In Meadows and Shipton 2001: 7–21.

Kingsley, Bonnie M. 1986. "Harpalos in the Megarid (333–331 B.C.) and the Grain Shipments from Cyrene." *ZPE* 66: 165–87.

Kinzl, Konrad H., ed. 2006. *A Companion to the Classical Greek World.* Oxford: Blackwell.

Kirchner, Johannes. [1901–3] 1981. *Prosopographia Attica.* Vols. 1–2. Chicago: Ares.

Klaffenbach, Günther. 1966. *Griechische Epigraphik.* 2nd ed. Göttingen: Vandenhoeck and Ruprecht.

Knoepfler, Denis. 1986. "Une inscription attique à reconsidérer: le décret de Pandios sur l'Amphiaraion." *Chiron* 16: 71–98.

Knorringa, Heiman. 1926. *Emporos.* Amsterdam: H. J. Paris.

Kroll, John H. 1976. "Aristophanes' *ponera chalkia*: A Reply." *GRBS* 17: 329–41.

Kroll, John H. 1993. *The Athenian Agora.* Vol. 26, *The Greek Coins.* Princeton, NJ: American School of Classical Studies at Athens.

Kuenzi, Adolphe. [1923] 1979. Ἐπίδοσις. New York: Arno.

Kurke, Leslie. 1991. *The Traffic in Praise: Pindar and the Poetics of Social Economy.* Ithaca, NY: Cornell University Press.

Kurke, Leslie. 1999. *Coins, Bodies, Games, and Gold: The Politics of Meaning in Archaic Greece.* Princeton, NJ: Princeton University Press.

Kurke, Leslie. 2002. "Money and Mythic History: The Contestation of Transactional Orders in the Fifth Century B.C." In Scheidel and von Reden 2002: 87–113.

Lambert, Stephen D. 2001. "Fragmente athenischer Ehrendekrete aus der Zeit des Iamischen Krieges (zu *Ag.* XVI 94 und *IG* II² 292)." *ZPE* 36: 65–70.

Lambert, Stephen D. 2002. "Fish, Low Fares, and *IG* II² 283." *ZPE* 140: 73–79.

Lambert, Stephen D. 2004. "Athenian State Laws and Decrees, 352/1–322/1: I. Decrees Honouring Athenians." *ZPE* 150: 85–120.

Lambert, Stephen D. 2006. "Athenian State Laws and Decrees, 352/1–322/1: III. Decrees Honouring Foreigners; A. Citizenship, Proxeny, and Euergesy." *ZPE* 158: 115–58.

Lambert, Stephen D. 2007. "Athenian State Laws and Decrees, 352/1–322/1: III. Decrees Honouring Foreigners; B. Other Awards." *ZPE* 159: 101–54.

Laronde, André. 1987. *Cyrène et la Libye hellénistique: Libykai Historiai de l'époque républicaine au principat d'Auguste.* Paris: Editions du Centre de la Recherche Scientifique.

Lawall, Mark. 1998. "Ceramics and Positivism Revisited: Greek Transport Amphoras and History." In Parkins and Smith 1998: 75–101.

Lawton, Carol L. 1995. *Attic Document Reliefs: Art and Politics in Ancient Athens.* Oxford: Oxford University Press.

Leonardos, V. 1923. "Amphiareion." *AE* 123: 36–42.

Lewis, David M. 1954. "Notes on Attic Inscriptions." *BSA* 49: 17–50.

Lewis, David M. 1955. "Notes on Attic Inscriptions." *BSA* 50: 1–36.

Lewis, David M. 1959. "Attic Manumissions." *Hesperia* 28: 208–38.

Lewis, Napthali. 1960. "*Leitourgia* and Related Terms." *GRBS* 3: 175–84.

Liddel, Peter. 2003. "The Places of Publication of Athenian State Decrees from the 5th Century BC to the 3rd Century AD." *ZPE* 143: 79–93.

Loomis, William T. 1998. *Wages, Welfare Costs, and Inflation in Classical Athens.* Ann Arbor: University of Michigan Press.

Loraux, Nicole. 1981. *L'invention d'Athènes: Histoire de l'oraison funèbre dans la "cité classique."* Paris: Ecole des Hautes Etudes en Sciences et Sociales.

Love, John R. 1991. *Antiquity and Capitalism.* New York: Routledge.

Lowry, S. T. 1979. "Recent Literature on Ancient Greek Economic Thought." *Journal of Economic Literature* 17: 65–86.

MacDonald, Brian R. 1981. "The Phanosthenes Decree: Taxes and Timber in Late Fifth-Century Athens." *Hesperia* 50: 141–46.

MacDowell, Douglas M. 2004. *Demosthenes: Speeches 27–38*. Austin: University of Texas Press.

Malouchou, Georgia E. 2000–2003. "Duo timetika psephismata apo ten Akropole." *Horos* 14–16: 55–59.

Manville, Phillip B. 1990. *The Origins of Citizenship in Ancient Athens*. Princeton, NJ: Princeton University Press.

Marasco, Gabriele. 1988. *Economia, commerci e politica nel Mediterraneo fra il III e II secola a.C.* Florence: Dipartimento di Storia, Università degli studi di Firenze.

Marasco, Gabriele. 1992. *Economia e storia*. Viterbo: Università degli studi della Tuscia.

Marchant, E. C. 1969. *Xenophontis Opera Omnia*. Vol. 5. Oxford Classical Tests. Oxford: Clarendon.

Marek, Christian. 1984. *Die Proxenie*. Frankfurt: Peter Lang.

Marek, Christian. 1985. "Handel und Proxenie." *Münstersche Beiträge zur antiken Handelsgeschichte* 4, no. 1: 67–78.

Markianos, S. 1969. "A Note on the Administration of Lycurgus." *GRBS* 10: 325–91.

Markle, M. M. 1985. "Jury Pay and Assembly Pay at Athens." In Cartledge and Harvey 1985: 265–97.

Mattingly, David J., and John Salmon, eds. 2001. *Economies beyond Agriculture in the Classical World*. New York: Routledge.

Mattingly, H. B. 1966. "Periclean Imperialism." In *Ancient Society and Institutions: Studies Presented to Victor Ehrenberg on His 75th Birthday*, ed. Ernst Badian, 193–233. Oxford: Oxford University Press.

Mattingly, H. B. 1990. "Some Fifth-Century Attic Epigraphic Hands." *ZPE* 83: 110–22.

Mauss, Marcel. [1923–24] 1967. "Essai sur le don, forme primitive de l'échange." *Année sociologique:* 30–186. Citations in the text refer to *The Gift: Forms and Functions of Exchange in Archaic Societies*. Trans. Ian Cunnison. New York: Norton.

McCarty, Marilu H. 2001. *The Nobel Laureates*. New York: McGraw-Hill.

McKechnie, Paul. 1989. *Outsiders in the Greek Cities in the Fourth Century BC*. New York: Routledge.

Meadows, Andrew, and Kirsty Shipton. 2001. *Money and Its Uses in the Ancient Greek World*. Oxford: Oxford University Press.

Meiggs, Russell. 1972. *The Athenian Empire*. Oxford: Clarendon.

Meiggs, Russell. 1982. *Trees and Timber in the Ancient Mediterranean World*. Oxford: Oxford University Press.

Meiggs, Russell, and David M. Lewis. 1988. *A Selection of Greek Historical Inscriptions to the End of the Fifth Century B.C.* Rev. ed. Oxford: Oxford University Press.

Meijer, Fik, and Onno van Nijf. 1992. *Trade, Transport, and Society in the Ancient World*. New York: Routledge.

Meikle, Scott. 1979. "Aristotle and the Political Economy of the Polis." *JHS* 99: 57–73.

Meikle, Scott. 1991. "Aristotle on Equality and Market Exchange." *JHS* 111: 192–96.

Meritt, Benjamin D. 1936a. "Greek Inscriptions." In *Classical Studies Presented to Edward Capps*. Princeton, NJ: Princeton University Press: 249.

Meritt, Benjamin D. 1936b. "The Seventh Metonic Cycle." *Hesperia* 5: 201–5.

Meritt, Benjamin D. 1941. "Greek Inscriptions." *Hesperia* 10: 38–64.

Meritt, Benjamin D. 1944. "Greek Inscriptions." *Hesperia* 13: 210–65.

Meritt, Benjamin D. 1945. "Attic Inscriptions of the Fifth Century." *Hesperia* 14: 129–32.

Meritt, Benjamin D. 1961. *The Athenian Year*. Berkeley: University of California Press.

Meritt, Benjamin D. 1964. "Athenian Calendar Problems." *TAPA* 95: 200–260.

Meritt, Benjamin D., H. T. Wade-Gery, and Malcom F. McGregor. 1939–53. *The Athenian Tribute Lists*. Vols. 1–4. Cambridge, MA: Harvard University Press.

Meyer, Eduard. 1924. "Die Wirtschaftliche Entwicklung des Altertums." In *Kleine Schriften*, ed. Eduard Meyer, 81–168. Halle: M. Niemeyer.

Michell, Humfrey. 1957. *The Economics of Ancient Greece*. 2nd ed. Cambridge: W. Heffer and Sons.

Migeotte, Léopold. 1982. "Epigraphie et littérature grecques: L'exemple des souscriptions publiques." *CEA* 14: 47–51.

Migeotte, Léopold. 1983. "Souscriptions athéniennes de la période classique." *Historia* 32: 129–48.

Migeotte, Léopold. 1992. *Les souscriptions publiques dans les cités grecques*. Geneva: Librarie Droz.

Migeotte, Léopold. 1997. "Le controle de prix dans les cités grecques." In Andreau, Briant, and Descat 1997: 33–52.

Miller, Molly. 1968. "Solon's Timetable: From the Paralysis of the Previous Government to the *Apodemia*." *Arethusa* 1: 62–81.

Miller, Stephen G. 1978. *The Prytaneion*. Berkeley: University of California Press.

Millett, Paul. 1983. "Maritime Loans and the Structure of Credit in Fourth-Century Athens." In Garnsey, Hopkins, and Whittaker 1983: 36–52.

Millett, Paul. 1990. "Sale, Credit, and Exchange in Athenian Law and Society." In Cartledge, Millett, and Todd 1990: 167–94.

Millett, Paul. 1991. *Lending and Borrowing in Ancient Athens*. Cambridge: Cambridge University Press.

Mirhady, David C. 2000. "Demosthenes as Advocate: The Private Speeches." In Worthington 2000: 181–204.

Mitchel, Fordyce W. 1962. "Demades of Paeania and *IG*, II² 1493, 1494, 1495." *TAPA* 93: 213–29.

Mitchel, Fordyce W. 1966. "*IG*, II² 1493: Corrigenda." *AJA* 70: 66.

Mitchel, Fordyce W. 1970. *Lykourgan Athens, 338–322*. Cincinnati: University of Cincinnati Press.

Monceaux, Paul. 1886. *Les proxénies grecques*. Paris: Thorin et fils.

Montgomery, Hugo. 1986. "'Merchants Fond of Corn': Citizens and Foreigners in the Athenian Grain Trade." *SO* 61: 43–61.

Morley, Neville. 2007. *Trade in Classical Antiquity*. Cambridge: Cambridge University Press.

Morris, Ian. 1994a. "The Athenian Economy Twenty Years after *The Ancient Economy*." *CP* 89: 351–66.

Morris, Ian. 1994b. "The Community against the Market in Classical Athens." In Duncan and Tandy 1994: 52–79.

Morris, Ian. 1999. Foreword to *The Ancient Economy*, by Moses I. Finley. Updated ed. Berkeley: University of California Press.

Morris, Ian, and J. G. Manning. 2005. "The Economic Sociology of the Ancient Mediterranean World." In Smelser and Swedberg 2005a: 131–59.

Morrison, J. S. 1984. "*Hyperesia* in Naval Contexts in the Fifth and Fourth Centuries B.C." *JHS* 104: 48–59.

Morrison, J. S., and Roderick T. Williams. 1968. *Greek Oared Ships, 900–323 B.C.* Cambridge.

Moscati Castelnuovo, L. 1980. "La carriera politica dell 'Attidografo Androzione.'" *ACME* 33: 251–78.

Mossé, Claude. 1962. *La fin de la démocratie athénienne: Aspects sociaux et politiques du déclin de la Cité grecque au IVe siècle avant J.-C.* Paris: Presses universitaires de France.

Mossé, Claude. 1973. *Athens in Decline, 404–86 B.C.* Trans. Jean Stewart. London and Boston: Routledge and Kegan Paul.

Mossé, Claude. 1979. "Citoyens actifs et citoyens 'passifs' dans les cités grecques." *REA* 81: 241–49.

Mossé, Claude. 1983. "The 'World of the *Emporium*' in the Private Speeches of Demosthenes." In Garnsey, Hopkins, and Whittaker 1983: 53–63.

Moysey, R. A. 1976. "The Date of the Strato of Sidon Decree (*IG* ii^2 141)." *AJAH* 1: 182–89.

Murray, Oswyn. 1993. *Early Greece.* 2nd ed. Cambridge, MA: Harvard University Press.

Nenci, Giuseppe, and Gerhard Thür. 1990. *Symposion 1988: Vorträge zur griechischen und hellenistischen Rechtgeschichte.* Cologne: Böhlau.

Nippel, Wilfried. 1987. "Finley and Weber: Some Comments and Theses." *Opus* 6: 43–50.

Noonan, Thomas S. 1973. "The Grain Trade of the Northern Black Sea in Antiquity." *AJP* 94: 231–42.

North, Douglass C. 1990. *Institutions, Institutional Change, and Economic Performance.* Cambridge: Cambridge University Press.

Ober, Josiah. 1989. *Mass and Elite in Democratic Athens.* Princeton, NJ: Princeton University Press.

Ober, Josiah. 1996. *The Athenian Revolution.* Princeton, NJ: Princeton University Press.

Oikonomides, A. N. 1956. "Δημάδου το παιανέως ψηφίσματα καὶ ἐπιγραφικαὶ περὶ το βίου." *Platon* 8: 105–29.

Oikonomides, A. N. 1981. "The Athenian Orator Polyeuctos." *AW* 22: 3–8.

Oikonomides, A. N. 1986. "The Epigraphical Tradition of the Decree of Stratokles Honoring 'Post Mortem' the Orator Lykourgos, *IG*, II^2, 457 and *IG*, II^2, 513." *AW* 14: 51–54.

Oliver, Graham J. 1995. "The Athenian State under Threat: Politics and Food Supply, 307 to 229 B.C." PhD diss., Oxford University.

Oliver, Graham J. 2001. "Regions and Micro-Regions: Grain for Rhamnous." In Archibald et al. 2001: 137–56.

Oliver, Graham J. 2006. "The Economic Realities." In Kinzl 2006: 281–310.

Oliver, Graham J. 2007. *War, Food, and Politics in Early Hellenistic Athens.* Oxford: Oxford University Press, 2007.

Oliverio, Gaspare. 1933. *Cirenaica 2.1: La stela dei nuovi commandamenti e dei cereali.* Bergamo: Instituto italiano d'arti grafiche.

Ormerod, Henry A. 1924. *Piracy in the Ancient World.* Liverpool: University Press of Liverpool.

Osborne, M. J. 1971a. "Athens and Orontes." *BSA* 66: 297–321.

Osborne, M. J. 1971b. "Notes on Attic Inscriptions." *BSA* 66: 323–32.

Osborne, M. J. 1972. "Attic Citizenship Decrees: A Note." *BSA* 67: 129–58.

Osborne, M. J. 1981a. "Entertainment in the Prytaneion at Athens." *ZPE* 41: 153–70.

Osborne, M. J. 1981b. *Naturalization in Athens.* Vol. 1. Brussels: AWLSK.

Osborne, M. J. 1982. *Naturalization in Athens.* Vol. 2. Brussels: AWLSK.

Osborne, M. J. 1983. *Naturalization in Athens.* Vol. 3. Brussels: AWLSK.

Osborne, Robin. 1996. "Pots, Trade, and the Archaic Greek Economy." *Antiquity* 70: 31–44.

Osborne, Robin. 2001. Review of Archibold et al. 2001. *BMCR,* http://bmcr .brynmawr.edu/2001/2001-03-24.html.

Parke, H. W. 1935–37. "On Inscriptiones Graecae, II² 207 (= I.G. II, 108)." *Proceedings of the Royal Irish Academy* 43: 367–78.

Parkins, Helen. 1998. "Time for Change? Shaping the Future of the Ancient Economy." In Parkins and Smith 1998: 1–15.

Parkins, Helen, and Christopher Smith. 1998. *Trade, Traders, and the Ancient City.* London: Routledge.

Parsons, Talcott, and Neil J. Smelser. 1956. *Economy and Society.* Glencoe, IL: Free Press.

Pauly, August F. von, and Georg Wissowa. 1894–1980. *Paulys Real-Encyclopädie der classischen Altertumswissenschaft.* Vols. 1–83. Stuttgart: J. B. Metzler.

Pauly, August F. von, and Georg Wissowa. 1903–78. *Paulys Real-Encyclopädie der classischen Altertumswissenschaft, Supplement.* Vols. 1–15. Stuttgart: J. B. Metzler.

Pearson, Harry W. 1957. "The Secular Debate on Economic Primitivism." In Polanyi, Arensberg, and Pearson 1957: 3–11.

Pecirka, Jan. 1966. *The Formula for the Grant of Enktesis in Attic Inscriptions.* Prague: Universita Karlova.

Pecirka, Jan. 1976. "The Crisis of the Athenian Polis in the Fourth Century B.C." *Eirene* 14: 5–29.

Peppas-Delmousou, Dina. 1965. "Epigraphical Notes," *AJA* 69: 151–53.

Perlman, S. 1958. "A Note on the Political Implications of Proxenia in the Fourth Century B.C." *CQ* 52: 185–91.

Pickard-Cambridge, Arthur. 1968. *The Dramatic Festivals of Athens.* 2nd ed. Oxford: Oxford University Press.

Pittakys, Kyriakos S. 1835. *L'ancienne Athènes.* Athens: E. Antoniades.

Placido, D. 1980. "La Ley Atica de 375/4 a. C. y la Politica Ateniense." *Memorias de Historia Antigua* 4: 27–41.

Pleket, Harry W. 1979. Review of *Aspects of Athenian Society in the Fourth Century B.C.,* by Signe Isager and Mogens H. Hansen. *Mnemosyne* 32: 445–48.

Polanyi, Karl. 1944. *The Great Transformation.* New York: Farrar and Winehart.

Polanyi, Karl. 1957a. "Aristotle Discovers the Economy." In Polanyi, Arensberg, and Pearson 1957: 64–94.

Polanyi, Karl. 1957b. "The Economy as Instituted Process." In Polanyi, Arensberg, and Pearson 1957: 242–70.

Polanyi, Karl. [1963] 1968. "Ports of Trade in Early Societies." *JEH* 23: 30–45. Reprinted in Polanyi 1968: 238–60.

Polanyi, Karl. 1968. *Primitive, Archaic, and Modern Economies: Essays of Karl Polanyi.* Ed. George Dalton. Garden City, NY: Anchor.

Polanyi, Karl, Conrad M. Arensberg, and Harry W. Pearson, eds. 1957. *Trade and Market in the Early Empires.* Glencoe, IL: Free Press.

Pope, H. 1935. *Non-Athenians in Attic Inscriptions.* New York: Cosmos Greek-American Printing.

Pritchett, W. Kendrick. 1940. "Greek Inscriptions." *Hesperia* 9: 104–11.

Pritchett, W. Kendrick. 1941. "Greek Inscriptions." *Hesperia* 10: 262–83.

Pritchett, W. Kendrick. 1946. "Greek Inscriptions." *Hesperia* 15: 138–65.

Pritchett, W. Kendrick. 1953. "The Attic Stelai, Part I." *Hesperia* 22: 225–99.

Pritchett, W. Kendrick, and Anne Pippin. 1956. "The Attic Stelai, Part II." *Hesperia* 25: 178–328.

Rangabe, Alexandros R. 1855. *Antiquités Helléniques.* Vol. 2. Athens: Typographie et lithographie royales.

Rathbone, Dominic. 1991. *Economic Rationalism and Rural Society in 3rd Century BC Egypt.* Cambridge: Cambridge University Press.

Raubitschek, Anthony. 1938. "Phanosthenes." *RE* 19: col. 1786.

Raubitschek, Anthony. 1949. *Dedications from the Athenian Akropolis.* Cambridge, MA: Archaeology Institute of America.

Reden, Sitta von. 1995. *Exchange in Ancient Greece.* London: Duckworth.

Reden, Sitta von. 1997. "Money, Law, and Exchange." *JHS* 117: 154–76.

Reden, Sitta von. 2001. "The Politics of Monetization in Third-Century B.C. Egypt." In Meadows and Shipton 2001: 65–76.

Reed, Charles M. 2003. *Maritime Traders in the Ancient Greek World.* Cambridge: Cambridge University Press.

Reger, Gary. 1993. "The Purchase of Grain on Independent Delos." *ClAnt* 12: 300–334.

Reger, Gary. 1997. "The Price Histories of Some Imported Goods on Independent Delos." In Andreau, Briant, and Descat 1997: 53–72. Reprinted in Scheidel and von Reden 2002: 133–54.

Reger, Gary. 2003. "The Economy." In Erskine 2003: 331–53.

Reinhold, Meyer. 1946. "Historian of the Classical World: Critique of Rostovtzeff." *Science and Society* 10: 361–91.

Rhodes, Peter J. 1981. *A Commentary on the Aristotelian Athenaion Politeia.* Oxford: Clarendon.

Rhodes, Peter J., with David M. Lewis. 1997. *The Decrees of the Greek States.* Oxford: Clarendon.

Rhodes, Peter J., and Robin Osborne, eds. 2003. *Greek Historical Inscriptions, 404–323 BC.* Oxford: Oxford University Press.

Rihll, T. E. 2001. "Making Money in Classical Athens." In Mattingly and Salmon 2001: 115–42.

Rostovtzeff, Michael. 1941. *The Social and Economic History of the Hellenistic World*. Vol. 1. Oxford: Oxford University Press.

Ruschenbusch, Eberhard. 1979. "Zur Besatzung athenischen Trieren." *Historia* 28: 106–10.

Sabloff, Jeremy A., and Clifford C. Lamberg-Karlovsky. 1975. *Ancient Civilization and Trade*. Albuquerque: University of New Mexico Press.

Sahlins, Marshall D. 1972. *Stone Age Economics*. Chicago: Aldine Atherton.

Sahlins, Marshall D. 1976. *Culture and Practical Reason*. Chicago: University of Chicago Press.

Sallares, Robert. 1991. *The Ecology of the Ancient Greek World*. London: Duckworth.

Salmon, John. 2001. "Temples the Measures of Men: Public Building in the Greek Economy." In Mattingly and Salmon 2001: 195–208.

Samuel, Alan E. 1983. *From Athens to Alexandria: Hellenism and Social Goals in Ptolemaic Egypt*. Studia Hellenistica 26. Lovain.

Saunders, T. J. 1972. "Notes on the Laws of Plato." *BICS* Suppl. 28.

Schäfer, Arnold D. 1885–87. *Demosthenes und Seine Zeit*. 1st ed. Leipzig: Teubner.

Schäfer, Hans. 1932. *Staatsform und Politik*. Leipzig: Dietrich.

Scheidel, Walter, and Sitta von Reden, eds. 2002. *The Ancient Economy*. New York: Routledge.

Schenkl, H. 1880. "De metoecis atticis." *WS* 2: 161–225.

Schütrumpf, Eckart. 1982. *Xenophon Vorschläge zur Beschaffung von Geldmitteln oder über die Staatseinkünfte*. Darmstadt: Wissenschaftliche Buchgesellshaft.

Schwahn, W. 1931. "Das Bügerrecht der sympolitischen Bundesstaaten." *Hermes* 66: 97–118.

Schweigert, Eugene. 1938. "Inscriptions from the North Slope of the Acropolis." *Hesperia* 7: 264–310.

Schweigert, Eugene. 1939. "Greek Inscriptions." *Hesperia* 8: 1–90.

Schweigert, Eugene. 1940. "Greek Inscriptions." *Hesperia* 9: 309–57.

Schwenk, Cynthia J. 1985. *Athens in the Age of Alexander: The Dated Laws and Decrees of "the Lykourgan Era," 338–322 B.C.* Chicago: Ares.

Scullion, Scott. 2001. "Three Notes on Inscriptions." *ZPE* 134: 116–20.

Scullion, Scott. 2002. "A Reply to Henry on IG II² 401." *ZPE* 140: 81–84.

Seager, Robin. 1966. "Lysias against the Corndealers." *Historia* 15: 172–84.

Seager, Robin. 1967. "Thrasybulus, Conon, and Athenian Imperialism, 396–386 B.C." *JHS* 87: 95–115.

Seager, Robin. 1982. Review of *L'invention d'Athènes: Histoire de l'oraison funèbre dans la "cité classique,"* by Nicole Loraux. *JHS* 102: 267–68.

Sealey, Raphael. 1955. "Athens after the Social War." *JHS* 75: 74–81. Reprinted in Sealey 1967: 164–82.

Sealey, Raphael. 1956. "Callistratos of Aphidna and His Contemporaries." *Historia* 5: 178–208. Reprinted in Sealey 1967: 133–63.

Sealey, Raphael. 1967. *Essays in Greek Politics*. New York: Manylands.

Sealey, Raphael. 1993. *Demosthenes and His Time: A Study in Defeat*. New York: Oxford University Press.

Shear, T.Leslie. 1978. *Kallias of Sphettos and the Revolt of Athens in 286 B.C. Hesperia* Suppl. 17. Princeton, NJ: American School of Classical Studies at Athens.

Shipley, D. Graham J., and Mogens H. Hansen. 2006. "The Polis and Federalism." In Bugh 2006: 52–72.

Shipton, Kirsty. 2001. "Money and the Elite in Classical Athens." In Meadows and Shipton 2001: 129–44.

Silver, Morris. 1995. *Economic Structures of Antiquity.* Greenwood.

Simon, Herbert A. 1957. *Models of Man.* New York: John Wiley and Sons.

Simon, Herbert A., Massimo Egidi, Robin Marris, and Ricardo Viale, eds. 1992. *Economics, Bounded Rationality, and the Cognitive Revolution.* Brookfield, VT: Edward Elgar.

Smelser, Neil J., and Richard Swedberg, eds. 1994a. *The Handbook of Economic Sociology.* Princeton, NJ: Princeton University Press.

Smelser, Neil J., and Richard Swedberg, eds. 1994b. "The Sociological Perspective on the Economy." In Smelser and Swedberg 1994a: 3–26.

Smelser, Neil J., and Richard Swedberg, eds. 2005a. *The Handbook of Economic Sociology.* 2nd ed. Princeton, NJ: Princeton University Press.

Smelser, Neil J., and Richard Swedberg, eds. 2005b. "Introducing Economic Sociology." In Smelser and Swedberg 2005a: 3–25.

Soudek, Josef. 1952. "Aristotle's Theory of Exchange: An Inquiry into the Origin of Economic Analysis." *Proceedings of the American Philosophical Society* 96, no. 1: 45–75.

Ste. Croix, G. E. M. de. 1953. "Demosthenes' TIMHMA and the Athenian Eisphora in the Fourth Century B.C." *C&M* 14: 30–70.

Ste. Croix, G. E. M. de. 1981. *The Class Struggle in the Ancient Greek World.* Ithaca, NY: Cornell University Press.

Steinhauer, G. 1994. "Inscription agoranomique du Pirée." *BCH* 118: 51–68.

Strauss, Barry S. 1986. *Athens after the Peloponnesian War: Class, Faction, and Policy, 404–386 BC.* Ithaca, NY: Cornell University Press.

Stroud, Ronald. 1971. "Inscriptions from the North Slope of the Acropolis, I." *Hesperia* 40: 146–204.

Stroud, Ronald. 1974. "An Athenian Law on Silver Coinage." *Hesperia* 43: 157–88.

Stroud, Ronald. 1979. "Athens Honors King Euagoras of Salamis." *Hesperia* 48: 180–93.

Stroud, Ronald. 1998. *The Athenian Grain-Tax Law of 374/3 B.C. Hesperia* Suppl. 29. Princeton, NJ: American School of Classical Studies at Athens.

Sutherland, C. H. V. 1943. "Corn and Coin: A Note on Greek Commercial Monopolies." *AJP* 64: 129–47.

Swedberg, Richard. 1990. *Economics and Sociology: Redefining Their Boundaries; Conversations with Economists and Sociologists.* Princeton, NJ: Princeton University Press.

Swedberg, Richard, ed. 1993. *Explorations in Economic Sociology.* New York: Russell Sage Foundation.

Swedberg, Richard. 2005. "Markets in Society." In Smelser and Swedberg 2005a: 233–53.

Tandy, David W. 1997. *Warriors into Traders*. Berkeley: University of California Press.

Tandy, David W., ed. 2001. *Prehistory and History: Ethnicity, Class, and Political Economy*. Montreal: Black Rose.

Tandy, David W. 2006. Review of *Maritime Traders in the Ancient Greek World*, by C. M. Reed. *NECJ* 33: 147–49.

Tandy, David W., and Walter C. Neale. 1994. "Karl Polanyi's Distinctive Approach to Social Analysis and the Case of Ancient Greece: Ideas, Criticisms, Consequences." In Duncan and Tandy 1994: 9–33.

Thompson, Wesley E. 1978. "The Athenian Investor." *Rivista di studi classici* 26: 403–423.

Thompson, Wesley E. 1982. "The Athenian Entrepreneur." *L'antiquite classique* 51: 53–85.

Thomsen, Rudi. 1964. *Eisphora*. Copenhagen: Gyldendal.

Thumser, V. 1885. "Untersuchungen über die attischen Metöken." *WS* 7: 45–68.

Tod, Marcus N. [1933–48] 1985. *Greek Historical Inscriptions from the Sixth Century B.C. to the Death of Alexander the Great in 323 B.C.* Vols. 1–2. Chicago: Ares.

Tracy, Stephen V. 1988. "Two Letter Cutters of the Third Century, 286/5–235/4 B.C." *Hesperia* 57: 303–22.

Tracy, Stephen V. 1995. *Athenian Democracy in Transition: Attic Letter-Cutters of 340 to 290 B.C.* Berkeley: University of California Press.

Traill, John S. 1978. "Greek Inscriptions from the Athenian Agora." *Hesperia* 47: 269–331.

Trevett, Jeremy. 1992. *Apollodoros, the Son of Pasion*. Oxford: Oxford University Press.

Tsetskhladze, Gocha R. 1998. "Trade on the Black Sea in the Archaic and Classical Periods: Some Observations." In Parkins and Smith 1998: 52–74.

Tuplin, Chistopher. 1982. "Satyros and Athens: *IG* ii² 212 and Isokrates 17.57." *ZPE* 49: 121–28.

Usher, Stephen. 1999. *Greek Oratory: Tradition and Originality*. Oxford: Oxford University Press.

Veligianni-Terzi, Chryssoula. 1997. *Wertbegriffe in den attischen Ehrendekreten der Klassischen Zeit*. Stuttgart: Franz Steiner Verlag.

Velissaropoulos, Julie. 1980. *Les nauclères grecs*. Geneva: Librarie Droz.

Veyne, Paul. 1976. *Le pain et le cirque*. Paris: Seuil.

Veyne, Paul. 1990. *Bread and Circuses*. Trans. Brian Pearce. Abridged with and introduction by Oswyn Murray. Harmondsworth: Penguin.

Walbank, Michael B. 1976. "Honors for Phanosthenes, Antiochides, and Their Associates." *Hesperia* 45: 289–95.

Walbank, Michael B. 1978. *Athenian Proxenies of the Fifth Century B.C.* Toronto and Sarasota, FL: S. Stevens.

Walbank, Michael B. 1980. "Greek Inscriptions from the Athenian Agora." *Hesperia* 49: 251–57.

Walbank, Michael B. 1982. "Greek Inscriptions from the Athenian Agora." *Hesperia* 51: 41–56.

Walbank, Michael B. 1985. "Athens, Carthage, and Tyre (*IG* ii² 342+)." *ZPE* 59: 107–11.

Walbank, Michael B. 1987a. "Athens Grants Citizenship to a Benefactor: *IG* ii² 398a + 438." *AHB* 1: 10–12.

Walbank, Michael B. 1987b. "IG ii², 407 and SEG xxxii, 94: Honours for a Milesian Grain-Dealer." *ZPE* 67: 165–66.

Walbank, Michael B. 1989. "Two Attic Masons of the Late 4th Century B.C." *BSA* 84: 395–405.

Walbank, Michael B. 1990. "Notes on Attic Decrees." *BSA* 85: 435–47.

Walbank, Michael B. 2002. "Notes on Attic Decrees." *ZPE* 139: 61–65.

Wallace, M. B. 1970. "Early Greek *Proxenoi.*" *Phoenix* 24: 189–208.

Weber, Max. [1896] 1976. "Die sozialen Gründe des Untergangs der antiken Kultur." *Die Wahrheit* 63: 57–96. Citations in the text refer to *The Agrarian Sociology of Ancient Civilizations*. Trans. R. I. Frank . London: NLB.

Weber, Max. [1904–5] 1958. "Die protestantische Ethik und der Geist des Kapitalismus." *Archiv für Sozialwissenschaft und Sozialpolitik* 20: 1–54; 21: 1–110. Citations in the text refer to *The Protestant Ethic and the Spirit of Capitalism*. Trans. Talcott Parsons. New York: Scribners.

Weber, Max. [1909] 1976. "Agrarverhältnisse im Altertum." *Handwörterbuch der Staatwissenschaften* 3, no. 1: 52–188. Citations in the text refer to *The Agrarian Sociology of Ancient Civilizations*. Trans. R. I. Frank. London: NLB.

Weber, Max. [1921] 1958. "Die Stadt." *Archiv für Sozialwissenschaft und Sozialpolitik* 47: 621–772. Citations in the text refer to *The City*. Trans. Don Martindale and Gertrud Neuwirth. New York: Free Press.

Weber, Max. [1921] 1978. *Wirtschaft und Gesellschaft.* 4th ed. Tübingen: J. C. B. Mohr (Paul Siebeck). Citations in the text refer to *Economy and Society*. Ed. Guenther Roth and Claus Wittich. Trans. Ephraim Fischoff et al. 5th ed. New York: Bedminster, 1968.

Weber, Max. 1999. *Essays in Economic Sociology.* Ed. Richard Swedberg. Princeton, NJ: Princeton University Press.

Welsh, M. K. 1904–5. "Honorary Statues in Ancient Greece." *BSA* 11: 32–49.

Welskopf, Elisabeth C., ed. 1974. *Hellenische Poleis: Krise-Wandlung-Wirkung.* Vol. 1. Berlin: Akademie Verlag.

Werner, Robert. 1955. "Die Dynastie der Spartokiden." *Historia* 4: 412–44.

West, William C. 1995. "The Decrees of Demosthenes' *Against Leptines.*" *ZPE* 107: 237–47.

Whitby, Michael. 1998. "The Grain Trade of Athens in the Fourth Century BC." In Parkins and Smith 1998: 102–28.

Whitehead, David. 1977. *The Ideology of the Athenian Metic.* Cambridge: Cambridge University Press.

Whitehead, David. 1983. "Competitive Outlay and Community Profit: *Philotimia* in Democratic Athens." *C&M* 34: 55–74.

Whitehead, David. 1993. "Cardinal Virtues: The Language of Public Approbation in Democratic Athens." *C&M* 44: 37–75.

Whittaker, C. R., ed. 1988. *Pastoral Economies in Classical Antiquity.* Cambridge: Cambridge University Press.

Wilamowitz-Moellendorff, Ulrich von. 1887. "Demotika der attischen Metoeken." *Hermes* 22: 107–28, 211–59.

Wilhelm, Adolf. 1898. "Zur Bronzeinschrift aus Olympia." *JOAI* 1: Beiblatt 195–98.

Wilhelm, Adolf. 1906. *Urkunden dramatischer Aufführungen in Athen*. Vienna: Alfred Hölder.

Wilhelm, Adolf. 1925. *Attische Urkunden*. Pt. 3. Vienna: Hölder-Pichler-Tempsky.

Wilhelm, Adolf. 1942. *Attische Urkunden*. Pt. 5. Vienna: Hölder-Pichler-Tempsky.

Will, Edouard. 1954. "Trois quarts de siècle de recherches sur l'économie grecque antique." *Annales* 9: 7–22.

Will, Wolfgang. 1983. *Athen und Alexander: Untersuchungen zur Geschichte der Stadt von 338 bis 322 v. Chr.* Munich: C. H. Beck.

Williams, J. M. 1989. "Demades' Last Years, 323/2–319/8 B.C.: A 'Revisionist' Interpretation." *AW* 19: 19–30.

Wilson, Peter. 2000. *The Athenian Institution of the Khoregia*. Cambridge: Cambridge University Press.

Woodhead, A. G., ed. 1997. *The Athenian Agora*. Vol. 16, *Inscriptions: The Decrees*. Princeton, NJ: Princeton University Press.

Woodward, A. M. 1956. "Notes on Some Attic Decrees (continued)." *BSA* 51: 1–8.

Worthington, Ian. 1992. *A Historical Commentary on Dinarchus: Rhetoric and Conspiracy in Later Fourth-Century Athens*. Ann Arbor: University of Michigan Press.

Worthington, Ian. 1994a. "The Harpalus Affair and the Greek Response to the Macedonian Hegemony." In Worthington 1994b: 307–30.

Worthington, Ian, ed. 1994b. *Ventures into Greek History*. Oxford: Clarendon.

Worthington, Ian, ed. 2000. *Demosthenes: Statesman and Orator*. London: Routledge.

Worthington, Ian, Craig R. Cooper, and Edward M. Harris, trans. 2001. *Dinarchus, Hyperides, and Lycurgus*. Austin: University of Texas Press.

Wrong, Dennis. 1961. "The Oversocialized Conception of Man in Modern Sociology." *American Sociological Review* 26: 183–93.

Ziebarth, Erich. 1929. *Beiträge zur Geschichte des Seeraubs und Seehandels im alten Griechenland*. Hamburg: Friederichsen, de Gruyter.

Ziebarth, Erich. 1932–33. "Neue Beiträge zum griechischen Seehandel." *Klio* 26: 231–47.

Index of Greek Words

379

Index of Passages Cited

General Index

315, 319–20; honorary language, 119, 134; honors, 140, 175–79

Stratiotic (Military) Fund. *See* Fund, Stratiotic (Military)

Straton (king of Sidon), 188, 321–22, 344 n. 35

substantivism, substantivist, 5, 7, 10, 23, 26–27, 29, 40, 70, 75, 79, 106–7, 118, 213, 215, 217

Successors of Alexander, 6, 66, 69, 166. *See also* Diadochs

supply, supplier, 54–56, 67, 92–93, 101–2, 114

supply and demand, 21–24, 93, 315, 335 n. 14

Swedberg, R., 29–30, 36

Tandy, D., 41–42

tax: Athenian Empire, 56–57; commentaries, 281, 288; Finley model, 7, 22, 25, 75; honors, 161–62, 164, 168; law of Agyrrhios, 58–59, 80; liturgies, 44–45; privileges, 188–89, 195, 198–99, 201–2, 209, 216–17, 219; trade policy, 6, 64, 77–78; Xenophon and revenue generation, 4, 77. *See also* eisphora; liturgy

tax, harbor, 94, 188, 281, 284

tax, import/export, 64, 94, 99–100; commentaries, 281, 284–85, 288, 290, 308

tax exemption. *See* exemption, tax

thea, 174–75. *See also* proedria; theater seats, reserved

theater seats, reserved, 4, 49, 255; honors, 140, 165, 173–75, 180–81; commentaries, 296, 308. *See also* proedria; thea

theorikon, 175, 208

theory, 25, 215

theory, Classical economic, 7–8, 15, 23, 28–29, 31–32

theory, economic, 5, 10

timber, 239; acquisition during Athenian Empire, 55–57; commentaries, 281–83, 318, 320; honors, 143–44, 151; privileges, 185, 189–

90, 216–17; shipbuilding, 43, 55–56, 77, 122, 144; trade policy, 56–57, 67, 76

timé, 4, 38, 41, 52, 202, 215. *See also* esteem; reputation

trade, administered, 23–24, 27

trade, gift, 99, 103, 135, 213; quantitative estimate, 83–84; substantivism, 23–24

trade, maritime, 33, 57

trade, market, 40, 97, 99, 104, 213; definition of trade, 27, 103; substantivism, 23–24; trade policy, 68–69

trade, retail, 4, 327 n. 2. *See also* kapelike

trade interest. *See* interest, trade

trade policy. *See* policy, trade

trader. See *emporos; naukleros*

trader, common (professional), 18, 32, 60, 68–69, 109–13, 117–18; commentaries, 277, 285, 287, 296–98, 306–7, 313–14; honorary language, 127, 129, 132–33, 137, 139; honors, 141, 145, 149, 155, 157, 159, 163–64, 174; privileges, 193, 220

trader, moderately wealthy (professional), 109–13, 117, 164, 277–80

trader, wealthy (professional), 18, 32, 109, 111–13, 118; commentaries, 277, 292–95, 299–300, 303–5, 309–10, 314–15; honorary language, 132, 137; honors, 145, 149, 157, 163; privileges, 187, 190, 193, 198, 218

trade route, 63, 87, 108, 148–49

trade/trader, overseas, 33, 43, 64, 89; market economy for grain, 93, 101, 106, 214, 221, 295

trade/trading needs, 14, 57, 71

trade/trading venture, 91–92, 94–95, 109, 111, 113

transport, transportation, 69, 80, 94, 103, 117

treasury, 59, 63, 65

treasury, military, 59. *See also* Fund, Stratiotic